Best Places to Stay in California

The Best Places to Stay Series

Best Places to Stay in America's Cities
Kenneth Hale-Wehmann, Editor

Best Places to Stay in Asia
Jerome E. Klein

Best Places to Stay in California
Anne E. Wright

Best Places to Stay in the Caribbean
Bill Jamison and Cheryl Alters Jamison

Best Places to Stay in Florida
Christine Davidson

Best Places to Stay in Hawaii
Kimberly Grant

Best Places to Stay in Mexico
Bill Jamison and Cheryl Alters Jamison

Best Places to Stay in the Mid-Atlantic States
Dana Nadel Foley

Best Places to Stay in the Midwest
John Monaghan

Best Places to Stay in New England
Christina Tree and Kimberly Grant

Best Places to Stay in the Pacific Northwest
Marilyn McFarlane

Best Places to Stay in the Rockies
Roger Cox

Best Places to Stay in the South
Carol Timblin

Best Places to Stay in the Southwest
Anne E. Wright

Best Places to Stay in California

Anne E. Wright

Bruce Shaw, Editorial Director

Sixth Edition

HOUGHTON MIFFLIN COMPANY
BOSTON • NEW YORK

Visit our Web site:
www.hmco.com/trade.

Sixth Edition

ISSN: 1048-5422
ISBN: 0-618-00532-3

Printed in the United States of America

Maps by Charles Bahne
Design by Robert Overholtzer

This book was prepared in conjunction with Harvard Common Press.

QUM 10 9 8 7 6 5 4 3 2 1

*For my family and friends, may they enjoy California
as much as I have.*

— A. E. W.

For my family and friends, may they enjoy California as much as I have.

— A. E. W.

Contents

Introduction   ix

California   1
  Bay Area   3
  Central Coast   111
  Desert Country   213
  Northern California   241
  Sierra Country   315
  Southern California   381
  Wine Country   467

What's What
  Bicycling   537
  Boating   537
  Business Services   538
  Croquet   538
  Fine Dining   539
  Golf   539
  Historic Hotels   540
  Horseback Riding   540
  Kitchen/Cooking Facilities   541
  Pets Allowed with Permission   541
  Restaurant Open to the Public   542
  Tennis   544
  Wheelchair Access   545

Recommended Reading   547
Index   549
Best Places Report   553

Introduction

Places to stay in California are as diverse as the state. They range from rustic cabins in the woods to luxurious city hotels, with an astounding variety in between. You can lodge at a luxurious resort, a homey bed-and-breakfast inn, a Victorian mansion, or a romantic retreat in the county. You'll find the best of them all here in this book.

The sixth edition of *Best Places to Stay in California* is divided by region and, within the region, by the city or town where each hotel or inn is located. There are new listings, a few deletions, and numerous changes. These are the result of months of personally investigating hundreds of inns. Again, the best were selected. That does not mean they're the most elegant or expensive. What we look for are comfortable accommodations, cleanliness, a commitment to hospitality, an interesting setting, and personality. These criteria apply to every lodging in the book.

In addition to entries divided by location, the hotels and inns are also listed under the categories that help you decide if this is the type of place you're looking for. The book also has brief descriptions of each region, maps, and a recommended reading list.

The Appendix is a handy reference to help you select your preferences in sports, dining, business services, and other interests. It indicates which inns are accessible to wheelchairs and which have cooking facilities.

The inns are not rated, as each has its own merits, and your choice depends upon the type of place you want. If it's in this book you can assume it is among the best of its kind. **None of the inns paid to be included.**

You may not agree with all the choices. Some fine places were excluded, not as a reflection on their quality, but by necessity (the inn may be changing ownership, for example, with its future in doubt). You won't find many chain hotels in the book because, with a few outstanding exceptions, they differ very little among locales.

Your comments are welcome. If you know of a special place that is not described here, or if you've had an unsatisfactory experience at an inn listed, please let us know. Your suggestions will help with future editions and allow us to provide you and other travelers with accurate information. Send your comments to:

> Chris Paddock
> *Best Places to Stay in California*
> The Harvard Common Press
> 535 Albany Street
> Boston, Massachusetts 02118

Rates

Please note that all the rates given applied at press time and are subject to change without notice. Unless otherwise noted, the rates cited are for one night. "Single" is the cost for one person, "double" the cost for two. Be sure to ask about discount packages, corporate and family rates, and off-season and midweek discounts. These are frequently offered, and you may save a substantial amount.

Meals

Breakfasts are described as Full, Continental, or Expanded Continental. A full breakfast connotes a hot entree; a Continental meal is a light repast, usually coffee or tea, rolls, and fruit; expanded Continental falls between the two, often including cereal, yogurt, or an assortment of cheeses.

Children

By law, California hotels may not refuse to accept children. However, young children aren't appropriate at some lodgings. Bringing a lively three-year-old to a quiet, antique-filled romantic hideaway can be a frustrating experience for everyone. Common sense is your best guide. Some of the larger hotels welcome children, even providing toys and special menus, and many allow children to occupy the same room as their parents at no charge.

Booking a Room

If you explain your needs clearly when you make a room reservation (do you prefer a private bath, a view, quiet surroundings, a firm bed?), they are likely to be met. If you are not satisfied, request a change. Every hotel has less desirable rooms, but you should never have to accept a room you don't like.

The information in this guidebook is as current and accurate as possible, but changes inevitably occur. We recommend asking about rates and policies before you check in. We also strongly urge making reservations ahead. But if you haven't made reservations, try anyway! Innkeepers are delighted to fill rooms that are suddenly empty because of cancellations.

Best Places to Stay in California is the most comprehensive compilation of outstanding lodgings in the state. We hope you enjoy reading and using it as much as we've enjoyed the research and writing. Happy travels!

Bed and Breakfasts

These small inns offer homey accommodation and breakfast is included in the room rate.

Intimate City Stops

This category reviews small hotels and bed-and-breakfast inns that combine sophisticated urban amenities with personal style and attention to detail. They may have as few as four rooms; none has more than 200.

Grand City Hotels

Famous historic landmarks and hotels of contemporary opulence are included in this category.

Country Inns and B&Bs

When you're looking for a peaceful retreat from city noise and bustle, a country inn is the ideal choice. Those described here are not all in rural areas, but each has a distinct country inn atmosphere and offers a chance to enjoy a change of pace.

Family Favorites

If you've wondered where to find a vacation spot for the whole family, possibly offering complete programs for children, these inns, lodges, and ranches are your answer. They fit other categories, too, but they have perfected the art of providing fun for every age, and their rates often favor families.

Inns by the Sea

Resorts, condominiums, lodges, private homes, and old-fashioned beach hotels are the inns described here. Most are right on the shore, with views of the broad Pacific, while some are a few blocks inland in seaside towns. Each has a setting that focuses on the ocean.

On a Budget

These inns are included not only for their unusually low rates, but for other appealing qualities such as an outstanding view, a quaint atmosphere, or a prime location.

Resorts

Resorts offer a wide variety of recreational activities and tend to be more of a destination rather than a stopover.

Romantic Hideaways

No matter what your romantic preferences, you'll find a special place among these choices. They all offer privacy and an enchanting atmosphere.

Spas

When you're ready for a vacation that combines health, fitness, good food, companionship and pampering in a tranquil atmosphere, these are the places to try.

California

Dunsmuir

Northern
California

Wine Country

Mendocino

Healdsburg

South Lake Tahoe

Bodega
Bay

Sacramento

Sierra Country

Napa

Inverness

San Francisco

Oakland

San Jose

Yosemite

Bay Area

Santa Cruz

Central
Coast

Death
Valley

Desert
Country

Santa Barbara

Big Bear
Lake

Los Angeles

Palm Springs

Southern Calif.

Borrego
Springs

San Diego

Bay Area

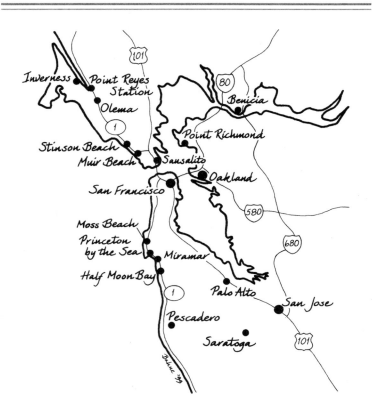

Benicia
The Union Hotel, 10
Half Moon Bay
Cypress Inn on Miramar Beach, 12
Half Moon Bay Lodge, 13
Old Thyme Inn, 15
Inverness
Blackthorne Inn, 17
Holly Tree Inn, 19
Ten Inverness Way Bed and Breakfast, 21
Moss Beach
Seal Cove Inn, 23
Muir Beach
The Pelican Inn, 25
Oakland
The Claremont Resort and Spa, 26
Dockside Boat & Bed, 28
Olema
Point Reyes Seashore Lodge, 29
Roundstone Farm, 31
Palo Alto
Garden Court Hotel, 33
Pescadero
Pigeon Point Lighthouse Hostel, 34
Point Reyes Station
Carriage House Bed and Breakfast, 36
Gray's Retreat, 38
Jasmine Cottage, 39
Point Richmond
East Brother Light Station, 40
Princeton-by-the-Sea
The Pillar Point Inn, 41
San Francisco
The Archbishop's Mansion, 43
Campton Place, 45
Casa Arguello, 47
The Clift, 48
The Fairmont Hotel, 50
Galleria Park Hotel, 52
Golden Gate Hotel, 53

San Francisco *(continued)*
Harbor Court Hotel, 55
Hotel Griffon, 56
Hotel Juliana, 58
Hotel Monaco, 59
Hotel Nikko, 61
Hotel Rex, 63
Hotel Triton, 64
Hotel Vintage Court, 66
The Huntington Hotel, 67
Inn at the Opera, 69
The Inn at Union Square, 70
The Majestic, 71
Mandarin Oriental, 73
The Mansions, 75
The Mark Hopkins Intercontinental, 77
The Maxwell Hotel, 79
The Pan Pacific Hotel, 80
Petite Auberge, 82
Prescott Hotel, 83
The Queen Anne Hotel, 85
The Ritz-Carlton San Francisco, 86
Sheehan Hotel, 88
Sheraton Palace Hotel, 89
The Sherman House, 91
Victorian Inn on the Park, 94
The Villa Florence Hotel, 95
The Westin St. Francis, 96
The White Swan Inn, 98
San Jose
Hotel De Anza, 100
Saratoga
The Inn at Saratoga, 101
Sausalito
Casa Madrona Hotel, 103
Hotel Sausalito, 105
The Inn Above Tide, 106
Stinson Beach
Casa del Mar, 108

Best Bed-and-Breakfasts

Half Moon Bay
Old Thyme Inn, 15
Inverness
Blackthorne Inn, 17
Holly Tree Inn, 19
Ten Inverness Way Bed and Breakfast, 21
Olema
Roundstone Farm, 31

Best Country Inns

Muir Beach
The Pelican Inn, 25
Olema
Point Reyes Seashore Lodge, 29
Saratoga
The Inn at Saratoga, 101

Best Family Favorites

Point Reyes Station
Carriage House Bed and Breakfast, 36
Gray's Retreat, 38

Best Grand City Hotels

San Francisco
The Clift, 48
The Fairmont Hotel, 50
Hotel Monaco, 59
Hotel Nikko, 61
The Huntington Hotel, 67
Mandarin Oriental, 73
The Mark Hopkins Intercontinental, 77
The Pan Pacific Hotel, 80
The Ritz-Carlton San Francisco, 86
Sheraton Palace Hotel, 89
The Westin St. Francis, 96

Best Inns by the Sea

Half Moon Bay
Cypress Inn on Miramar Beach, 12
Half Moon Bay Lodge, 13
Moss Beach
Seal Cove Inn, 23
Oakland
Dockside Boat & Bed, 28
Point Richmond
East Brother Light Station, 40
Princeton-by-the-Sea
The Pillar Point Inn, 41
Sausalito
The Inn Above Tide, 106
Stinson Beach
Casa del Mar, 108

Best Intimate City Stops

Benicia
The Union Hotel, 10
Palo Alto
Garden Court Hotel, 33
San Francisco
The Archbishop's Mansion, 43
Campton Place, 45
Galleria Park Hotel, 52
Harbor Court Hotel, 55
Hotel Griffon, 56
Hotel Juliana, 58
Hotel Rex, 63
Hotel Triton, 64
Hotel Vintage Court, 66
Inn at the Opera, 69
The Inn at Union Square, 70
The Majestic, 71
The Mansions, 75
The Maxwell Hotel, 79
Petite Auberge, 82
The Queen Anne Hotel, 85
Victorian Inn on the Park, 94

The Villa Florence Hotel, 95
The White Swan Inn, 98
San Jose
Hotel De Anza, 100
Sausalito
Hotel Sausalito, 105

Best on a Budget

Pescadero
Pigeon Point Lighthouse Hostel, 34
San Francisco
Casa Arguello, 47
Golden Gate Hotel, 53
Sheehan Hotel, 88

Best Resorts

Oakland
The Claremont Resort and Spa, 26

Best Romantic Hideaways

Point Reyes Station
Jasmine Cottage, 39
Sausalito
Casa Madrona Hotel, 103

San Francisco, an elegant gem of verve and grace, is everybody's favorite city. Despite earthquakes, fires, and ceaseless change, it remains a place of beauty, from the buttercup-strewn meadows of Golden Gate Park to the chic shops on Nob Hill. The hotels and restaurants in San Francisco are, appropriately, among the best in the world.

It is not only San Francisco's striking location on the bay that brings tourists by the droves each year, but the city has so much to offer the visitor that it deserves its reputation as one of the top destinations in the country. What better pleasure than to ride the clanking cable cars over the hilly thoroughfares, zigzag down curving Lombard Street, or dine in the Italian cafés of North Beach or the chic bistros of SOMA and Russian Hill. You can get a bird's-eye view of the city and bay from the top of Coit Tower, and then there are the neighborhoods to explore, such as exclusive Nob Hill and Pacific Heights, the 1960s revolutionary enclave of Haight Ashbury, or bustling Chinatown. In Golden Gate Park there are acres of gardens to enjoy, including the Botanical Gardens, the Conservatory of Flowers, and the famed Japanese Tea Garden. The park also includes the M. H. de Young Museum, Asian Art Museum, and California Academy of Sciences, with its natural history museum, planetarium, and small aquarium to visit when misty weather drives one indoors. Shops abound at Pier 39, the Embarcadero, and in Ghirardelli and Union Squares; and the abandoned prison on the island of Alcatraz has its own spooky allure. The San Francisco Museum of Modern Art in the revitalized SOMA (for South of Market Street) district is further evidence of the city's ongoing appeal.

Yet with all there is to see in San Francisco, the Bay Area has a far wider reach than Marin County and the communities immediately fronting San Francisco Bay. In this context, it extends north as far as the Point Reyes area along the coast, and down the peninsula to San Jose and Saratoga. Immediately north of San Francisco are the waterfront boutiques of **Sausalito;** farther north, in the hilly ranch country close to the ocean and Tomales Bay, lies Point Reyes National Seashore, bordered by charming, unpretentious villages — **Inverness, Point Reyes Station,** and **Olema**.

East Bay visitors like to amble by the marina at Jack London's Waterfront in **Oakland,** and taste the fresh seafood offered in waterfront restaurants. Boaters, joggers, and bicyclists enjoy Lake Merritt, the country's largest saltwater lake within a city.

Up in **Benicia** an art colony has formed, and glass-blowing studios sell works of fine quality. The town, which was California's capital from 1853 to 1854, has antiques shops and 19th-century architecture. Not far from here is the famous Marine World Africa USA, which has more than a thousand animals. If you travel west on the peninsula south of San Francisco, you'll come to the charming seaside towns of **Princeton-by-the-Sea** and **Half Moon Bay.** Surrounded by farmland, Half Moon Bay calls itself the pumpkin capital of the world and holds a popular Pumpkin Festival in October. Princeton Harbor offers charter fishing and whale-watching cruises.

Inland from the coast, the Santa Clara Valley — nicknamed the Silicon Valley for its electronic technology industry — has California's third largest city, **San Jose.** Its best-known attraction is the Winchester Mystery House, a 160-room mansion built by the eccentric heiress of the Winchester rifle fortune. It is said that she believed she would live as long as she kept building — so the house has ten thousand windows and forty staircases, some leading nowhere.

San Jose also has the Rosicrucian Egyptian Museum, with an impressive collection of ancient artifacts from Egypt and Assyria. The San Jose Historical Museum displays items of more recent vintage: buildings and relics from turn-of-the-century California. The Chinese Cultural Gardens are in Overfelt Botanical Gardens, a 37-acre wildlife sanctuary.

Nearby **Saratoga** is known for its fine cuisine; **Palo Alto**, the home of Stanford University, has a collegiate air.

Benicia

The Union Hotel

401 First Street
Benicia, CA 94510
707-746-0100
800-544-2278
Fax: 707-746-6458

> A historic hotel in a quaint town on the bay

Owners: Matt Mathieson and Bruce Indorato. **Accommodations:** 12 rooms (all with private bath). **Rates:** $119–$179 single or double. **Included:** Continental breakfast. **Added:** 9% tax. **Payment:** Major credit cards. **Children:** Welcome. **Pets:** Not allowed. **Smoking:** Allowed.

➤ **Benicia served as a U.S. Army arsenal and fort in the mid-19th century, and was the first state capital. Here, in an adobe saloon, the discovery of gold was announced to the world. California's first public school was also in Benicia.**

It's a pleasant hostelry today, without a tinge of scandal, but the historic Union Hotel has a risqué past. It was established in 1882 as a 20-room bordello, back when Benicia was a bustling port town on the edge of the Carquinez Strait. You can still see the peephole in one of the doors — just about the only piece left of the original building. The trim, three-story hotel was restored in 1981, and redecorated in 1999. Each guest room has a French theme, but all are decorated individually. Although they are furnished with antiques, the rooms have modern features like TVs, VCRs, telephones, CD players, air conditioning, and whirlpool tubs.

The rooms bear names rather than numbers. Provence and Left Bank have a French country look. Metropolitan, named for the Paris Metro, is art deco. Boudoir Bardot has Bridget Bardot memorabilia, and Monte Carlo is an homage to Grace Kelly and Monaco. In Burgundy, vintage wine labels paper one wall, wine barrels accent another, and the headboard has a carved cluster of grapes. Versailles, in golds and burgundies, is fit for a king. It has a marble entryway, Louis XIV–style furniture, two fountains, floor to ceiling mirrors, and a picture window overlooking the water.

The Union's noted restaurant is casually elegant and is on the hotel's main floor. The management takes pride in the fact that everything it serves is fresh. The menu, which the owners describe as Continental and California eclectic, offers daily specials and changes seasonally. A hand-carved mahogany back bar dominates the lounge.

Historic photographs line the hotel's elevator and hallways. In keeping with this step into the past are the antiques shops and historic buildings along Benicia's First Street. Victorian and false-front western architecture dates from the 1850s to the early 1900s. Today the quiet little town on the bay, a 45-minute drive northeast of San Francisco, honors its heritage and thrives on old-fashioned celebrations such as a Fourth of July parade and picnic. The Peddlers Fair in August is the largest antiques and handicrafts fair in northern California.

Half Moon Bay

Cypress Inn on Miramar Beach

407 Mirada Road
Half Moon Bay, CA 94019
650-726-6002
800-83-BEACH
Fax: 650-712-0380
lodging@cypressinn.com
www.cypressinn.com

Seaside inn with a festive atmosphere

Innkeepers: Suzie Lankes and Dan Floyd. **Accommodations:** 12 rooms (all with private bath). **Rates:** $185–$295 single or double, $20 additional person. **Included:** Full breakfast and wine, hors d'oeuvres, and dessert. **Added:** 10% tax. **Payment:** Major credit cards. **Children:** A maximum of 2 people allowed per room. **Pets:** Not allowed. **Smoking:** Not allowed.

➤ **Rooms have ocean views in this light and breezy contemporary inn on a quiet frontage road two miles north of Half Moon Bay. Step out the door and you're facing a five-mile stretch of sandy beach with public access.**

The Cypress Inn's exterior, in quiet sand and teal, gives no hint of the riot of color within. From the yellow parlor to the vividly painted guest rooms, the atmosphere is as bright as an artist's palette. Each room is a different color; they all have a fireplace, wicker furniture, a deck or balcony, featherbed, crisp white linens, a fluffy comforter and pillow, a clock radio, telephone, television, and a tiled bath. They're decorated with carved wooden animals from Mexico — colorful folk art that fits in perfectly with the inn's cheery style.

The rooms have names from nature: La Estrella (Star), El Viento (Wind), and El Mar (Sea) are examples. La Luna (Moon), a ground-floor room with a balcony, has a pine platform bed and Mexican leather chairs. You can hear the waves crash from La Lluvia (Rain) on the second floor, and Las Nubes (Clouds) is a third-floor penthouse in white with an oversize whirlpool tub and a panoramic view.

Guests staying in an adjacent building called the Beach House climb stairs past an aquarium mural to guest rooms named for area beaches (Dunes, Moss, Venice, and Naples). Rooms here are more luxurious than those in the main inn — most have whirlpool tubs for two, and all have fireplaces. Moss Beach is a breath of fresh air in seafoam green and beige tones. A beach scene with pelicans and pampas grass is painted on one wall, and attractive seashell and sealife print fabrics and starfish-shaped brass drawer knobs help to complete the beachy theme. Dunes Beach is the grandest suite, with a terrific view, large deck, and an in-room spa in front of the fireplace.

Breakfast — served in your room or in the dining area under a folk art statue of the tree of life or the vibrant oil painting that the innkeepers affectionately call "the party animals" — is outstanding. In addition to a granola-yogurt-berry parfait, you'll have juice, fresh croissants, and an entrée such as peaches-and-cream French toast or an omelette with tomatoes. Consult the inn's information-packed notebook for nearby attractions and restaurant recommendations. One deservedly popular and festive spot is Pasta Moon, which serves wonderful pasta and cheesecake.

The Cypress Inn has a conference room for use by small groups. There's also an in-house masseuse who can provide massages upon request.

Half Moon Bay Lodge

2400 Cabrillo Highway
Half Moon Bay, CA 94019
650-726-9000
800-368-2468
Fax: 650-726-7951
Rez@halfmoonbaylodge.com
www.woodsidehotels.com

**A comfortable inn
overlooking a golf course**

General manager: Kevin B. Lanigan. **Accommodations:** 80 rooms. **Rates:** $160–$220. **Included:** Continental breakfast. **Added:** 10% tax. **Payment:** Major credit cards. **Children:** Under age 12 free in room with parent. **Pets:** Not allowed. **Smoking:** Not allowed.

➤ **Guests can pick up the morning newspaper from the front desk and help themselves to a Continental breakfast, which is available all day.**

Attractive guest rooms, a capable staff, and a good location make the Half Moon Bay Lodge an appealing lodging option if you're looking to stay near the coast between San Francisco and Santa

Cruz. The long, two-story, yellow stucco buildings with red tile roofs have a Spanish flavor. Tile walkways lead to guest rooms on both sides of the lobby, and wisteria vines climb the walls and railings.

Guest rooms are spacious and comfortable with deep green carpeting and fluffy floral comforters. Wicker chairs pull up to writing desks with green banker's lamps, and glass lamps on bedside tables are filled with seashells as a reminder that you are not far from the ocean. Premium rooms have wood-burning fireplaces and a baker's rack with potted plants and a small library. The tile baths also have live plants, fine toiletries are displayed in a wicker seashell, and even the washcloth is fanned in the shape of a shell. All rooms have coffee makers (coffee is supplied), terry robes, hair dryers, irons and ironing boards, TVs in armoires, stocked refrigerators, and honor bars with reasonably priced snacks.

Rooms in the newer wing have patios that have a view of the lodge's garden. Rooms in the oldest wing (which dates back only as far as the 1970s) have balconies overlooking the adjacent Half Moon Bay Golf Links, designed by Arnold Palmer (golf packages are available). The lodge has an outdoor lap pool, a dry sauna, a spa encased in a gazebo, and a small workout room with a stationary bicycle, stair climber, treadmill, and weight machine.

Old Thyme Inn

779 Main Street
Half Moon Bay, CA 94019
650-726-1616
Fax: 650-726-6394
innkeeper@oldthymeinn.com
www.oldthymeinn.com

> **A bed-and-breakfast in a
> seaside village**

Innkeepers: Rick and Kathy Ellis. **Accommodations:** 7 rooms (all with private bath). **Rates:** $100–$255 single or double, $25 additional person. **Included:** Full breakfast. **Added:** 10% tax. **Payment:** Major credit cards. **Children:** Over age 10 welcome; additional $25 if third person in room. **Pets:** Not allowed. **Smoking:** Allowed outdoors only.

> ➤ **This may be the pumpkin capital of the world. Every October thousands of people drive 30 miles south from the Bay Area to buy their jack-o-lanterns.**

An English herb garden gives this charming bed-and-breakfast inn its name. More than eighty varieties of herbs grow in the garden, spicing the air with their scents and providing dash to breakfast dishes. The Queen Anne home is a comfortable, relaxing place to visit. The hosts offer afternoon wines, restaurant recommendations, information on the sights of Half Moon Bay, and directions to the nine state beaches nearby, the tide pools at the Fitzgerald Marine Reserve, art galleries, and nearby pumpkin patches.

Old Thyme Inn was built in 1897 and restored as a bed-and-breakfast ninety years later. The guest rooms have antique furnishings, original artwork (Kathy is an artist), TV/VCRs, and queen beds with featherbeds and down comforters. Several rooms contain fireplaces and whirlpool tubs. Rosemary, on the main floor, is furnished with a Louis XV–style antique bed, Oriental carpet, and lace curtains. Behind a stained glass window is a blue and white bath with a two-person whirlpool. Thyme, also on the main floor, has a Louis XVI–style bed, a gas fireplace, bay windows, and a double whirlpool in the bathroom. An oak mirrored armoire holds padded hangers for clothing. Guests staying in Thyme are entitled to have breakfast served in their room if they so desire.

On the second floor, Mint's bay windows look out to the front of the house and the street. Decorated in cool colors, the room has a gas fireplace. Two armchairs covered with floral tapestry fabric face the four-poster bed, and there's a clawfoot tub in the bath. In sunny Oregano, windows draped with lace sheers overlook the garden. Chamomile has a brass bed, and lace curtains shield a clawfoot tub that sits in the skylit alcove. Lavender, one of the smaller rooms, is the only one with a detached bath.

The Garden Room offers secluded, quiet, romantic lodgings in a separate building behind the herb garden. Its carved four-poster pine and oak bed is canopied. There is also a fireplace, a refrigerator with complimentary beverages, and a double whirlpool under a skylight. Guests in this room may have breakfast in bed or, if they're feeling sociable, they can join the other guests at a single table in the dining room.

Breakfast includes the inn's own blend of coffee, juice, a selection of teas, fresh seasonal fruit, a homebaked bread (maybe Kathy's rosemary-lemon or coconut-banana crumb cake), and a main dish such as basil featherbed eggs or orange-pecan French toast. For other meals there are a number of restaurants within easy walking distance, including Chateau des Fleurs for French cuisine, Spanishtown for Mexican, 2 Fools for American, and the local favorite, Pasta Moon.

Inverness

Blackthorne Inn

P.O. Box 712
266 Vallejo Avenue
Inverness, CA 94937
415-663-8621
Fax: 415-663-8635
www.blackthorneinn.com

A whimsical, handbuilt home near Tomales Bay

Innkeeper: Susan Wigert. **Accommodations:** 5 rooms (all with private baths). **Rates:** $175-$250 double; $25 less for single during the week. **Included:** Full breakfast. **Minimum stay:** 2 nights weekends. **Payment:** Major credit cards. **Children:** Not appropriate; a maximum of 2 people is allowed per guest room. **Pets:** Not allowed. **Smoking:** Not allowed indoors.

➤ **From the inn's many decks you can hear the babbling of a nearby brook and birds chirping as they flit from tree to tree overhead.**

North of San Francisco, in the wooded hills of the quiet town of Inverness, the Blackthorne Inn offers a unique retreat. It's been called a carpenter's fantasy and an architectural extravaganza — well-deserved labels for a four-story rambling home that resembles an oversize treehouse. It used to be a one-room cabin surrounded by fir, bay, and oak trees. Then Susan and Bill Wigert decided to add a deck. Their plans expanded, local carpenters and woodworkers became involved, and the project got out of control, says Susan. Now it's a delightfully quirky construction with towers, alcoves, nooks, balconies, skylights, and a spiral staircase winding to the top. A 3,500-square-foot deck, complete with fire pole to the ground, circles the house on the second level. The towering trees that surround the house are almost prehistoric in size and scale. One such tree, a 180-foot Douglas fir that was near death when the original home was expanded, was used in the inn's construction.

Stones from eight counties were collected for the inn's big fireplace in the living room on the main floor. Local artisans did the stonework, built fir plank walls, and put in rustic beams that came from San Francisco wharves. In this inviting room are books, games, and a stereo. Alcoves with windows that look into the forest are ideal for curling up with a book and nibbling the brownies and cookies that are set out in the afternoons. There's also a wet bar with tea and coffee, and a refrigerator for guests' use. Breakfast is served here buffet style in the morning. Some choices are fresh fruit, baked apples, orange juice, granola and other cereals, quiche, and pastries.

The spiral staircase winds up to two guest rooms on the third level and one on the top. Under a gable, Lupine has a queen-size bed dressed in a coverlet that resembles an impressionist painter's garden. Eyelet lace curtains at the windows let natural light filter in as soon as the sun is up. There's no tub in the attached bath, but most guests in this room just walk out the suite's back door and climb the stairs to the hot tub under the trees (a flashlight, robes, and extra towels are provided). The Overlook room next door is a light, airy room with a peacock chair and stained glass windows in artful thistle, poppy, and iris designs. Its bath is down the hall. Overlook also has two balconies, one with a view of the treetops and the other above the inn's central living room.

Eagle's Nest is the most enchanting (and the most expensive) space. An octagonal room at the top of the staircase, it's enclosed by glass to give you a fine view of the California buckeye trees and starry sky. Outside, a ladder will take you to a private deck at the uppermost level, where you truly feel as if you're sitting atop the world. Cross a walkway and bridge from your private entrance and you reach another deck, this one with a hot tub and bath. The drawback to Eagle's Nest (if you don't mind all the climbing) is that you must go outside to the bathroom. However, it's a big favorite with those looking for a truly special romantic spot.

The inn's other two rooms are on the lowest level and can be rented out together if desired. Forest View and Hideaway are spacious suites, each with a private entrance and sitting room. Both are nicely furnished with wicker and pastels, and they share a bath with a shower. Forest View has an open feel and a pleasant outdoor deck. In Hideaway there's a round table for two in a bay window looking out to a deck and the trees beyond. The advantage of these rooms is their proximity to the parking area, with few stairs to negotiate.

The atmosphere at the Blackthorne is quiet (there are purposely no televisions or telephones in the rooms), relaxed, and casual, befitting Inverness's homey style. The innkeepers enjoy their guests and are happy to sit down for a chat or to discuss the merits of local beaches and restaurants (they recommend Manka's for a memorable meal and Perry's Deli for sandwiches and picnic supplies). You'll want to explore Point Reyes for its outstanding scenery, flowery meadows, steep headlands, and ocean views.

Holly Tree Inn

3 Silverhills Road
Inverness Park
Mailing address:
Box 642
Point Reyes Station, CA 94956
415-663-1554
800-286-4655
Fax: 415-663-8566
www.hollytree.com

A wooded retreat near Point Reyes National Seashore

Innkeepers: Diane and Tom Balogh. **Accommodations:** 4 rooms and 3 cottages (all with private bath). **Rates:** Rooms, $120–$155, cottages $175–$250. **Included:** Full breakfast. **Added:** 10% tax. **Minimum stay:** 2 nights on weekends. **Payment:** Major credit cards. **Children:** $15 additional per day. **Pets:** Not allowed. **Smoking:** Not allowed indoors.

➤ **The nearest beach is Limintaur, a 15-minute drive; you can walk for miles on its firm sand. The waters of Tomales Bay are warm enough for swimming in summer. In the winter, watch for gray whales from the lighthouse at the tip of Point Reyes. The entire peninsula is a bird-watcher's delight in all seasons.**

An abundance of holly trees give this bed-and-breakfast inn its name. Surrounded by lawns and flowers, it stands on 19 hilly, wooded acres outside Inverness and next to Point Reyes National Seashore, just north of San Francisco.

Holly Tree Inn is a dwelling of quiet comfort, a place for reflection. The heart of the inn is its spacious living room, where overstuffed chairs and sofas face a copper-hooded brick fireplace. Soft music plays and a fire glows on foggy days, a perfect setting for sipping a cup of tea, reading, or visiting.

Each of the guest rooms has its own character. Holly Room features a pencil post king-size bed with a down comforter. A private balcony overlooks the front lawn, creek, and garden of daisies and golden lilies. Mary's Garden, the smallest room, is off the kitchen but has soundproof walls and a private entrance, a loveseat, and a fireplace. Its long windows overlook the rose garden. Ivy, decorated in pale green, has a spool bed and ruffled curtains. Laurel's corner windows, hung with white Priscilla curtains, overlook the crab apple tree in the side garden. This spacious blue and white room has a sitting area with a wing chair and a four-poster king-size bed.

Cottage in the Woods is a few yards up the driveway from the main house. Built in 1987, it is simple, light, and airy; a wonderfully inviting retreat. Bare wood floors are of warm, polished pine, and walls have a wash of pink-toned white. It is furnished with pearwood antiques from Austria — note the carved pear baskets on the headboards and armoire. There are a toaster oven and refrigerator in the kitchenette. There's a sitting room with a woodstove and a clawfoot tub in the bathroom, where you'll catch a whiff of bayberry and lemon verbena from the soaps on the counter. Making the room picture-perfect is the greenhouse window by the tub, framing a view of the fern-covered hill just outside.

Two additional cottages located off the main property — Sea Star Cottage, situated on its own pier over the tidal waters of Tomales Bay, and Vision Cottage, discreetly tucked away among the pines — are ideal for those seeking total privacy. Sea Star accommodates two adults and has a queen-size four-poster bed, a living room with a wood-burning stove, and a fully equipped kitchen. Vision Cottage, named for its view of Mount Vision, is a good option for families as it has two bedrooms as well as a full kitchen. A 1.3-mile-long trail leads from Vision Cottage to the swimming beaches in Tomales Bay State Park. Both cottages have their own private hot tubs.

For cottage guests, breakfast is placed in refrigerators the night before; other guests eat in the inn's dining room by the brick fireplace. Orange juice, fruit, homemade scones, chile egg puffs, and French toast are among the dishes served. After breakfast, guests can relax in the inn's hot tub or visit nearby attractions.

Point Reyes National Seashore has some of the most spectacular scenery and is one of the great hiking areas of the California coast. The inn is a mile from the visitors' center, the starting point for trails that wind to the sea over the woodlands and grassy meadows, often gold with California poppies. The most popular trail is Bear Valley, a 4.1-mile hike to Arch Rock.

Ten Inverness Way Bed and Breakfast

P.O. Box 63
10 Inverness Way
Inverness, CA 94937
415-669-1648
Fax: 415-669-7403
inn@teninvernessway.com
www.teninvernessway.com

A turn-of-the-century redwood home on Point Reyes Peninsula

Innkeeper: Teri Mowery. **Accommodations:** 4 rooms, 1 suite (all with private bath). **Rates:** $145–$180. **Added:** 10% tax. **Included:** Full breakfast; afternoon cookies and tea. **Minimum stay:** 2 nights weekends, 3 nights on holiday weekends. **Payment:** MasterCard, Visa, personal checks. **Children:** Age 12 and over welcome in suite; additional $15. **Pets:** Not allowed. **Smoking:** Not allowed indoors.

➤ **Recommended on the Point Reyes Peninsula are Hearts Desire Beach in Tomales Bay State Park for swimming and picnics, walking at Abbott's Lagoon on a foggy day, whale-watching from Chimney Rock, and hiking Tomales Point Trail, where you may see Tule elk.**

Inverness, a quiet village on Tomales Bay, was formed a century ago as a resort development by James McMillan Shafter, who hoped to recoup his railway investment losses. The town and its streets were given Scottish names such as Hawthornden Way, Dundee Way, and Cameron Street, based on his family's Scottish background. When the fog hangs over the tops of grassy hills around Tomales Bay, Inverness truly does resemble its Scottish namesake, yet Shafter's promotion was not successful in its day. However, today the town is a popular tourist destination due to the area's natural beauty.

The redwood shingle home that is now Ten Inverness Way was built in 1904. In 1980 it was converted into an inn filled with antiques and handmade quilts. There's a lovely English country garden of nasturtiums, iris, penstemon, foxglove, wisteria, honeysuckle, poppies, lilies, roses, and geraniums, under fruit trees, with benches and Adirondack chairs where you can sit and watch the hummingbirds. Paths wind around to the back of the house and the enclosed hot tub (robes are provided).

The Garden suite, entered through a private entrance from the garden at ground level, is decorated in greens and lavenders. With a full kitchen (coffee beans are supplied so you can make your own cup whenever you want), sitting area, sofa bed, and a queen-size bed in an alcove with a handpainted wildflower mural, it's perfect for families. As a suite guest, you may have breakfast in your room or in the private garden.

In the main part of the house, unusual box windows allow plenty of light. In the big living room, a fire burns on cool evenings. There's a phone here and a sideboard where hot teas are always available, and guests can enjoy the guitar, puzzles, and games. The morning meal is also served here. Breakfasts are garnished with edible flowers from the inn's garden and may include crepes filled with Inverness blackberries or the inn's specialty — portabello mushroom and bleu cheese quiche — and plenty of strong coffee.

The living room and adjacent library are upstairs from the inn's entrance. The remaining four guest rooms are a flight above that. Each room has something special — a skylight over the bed, an old wicker table, a bright patchwork quilt, or a daybed piled with pillows. Room 2, at the top of the stairs, with its wainscoting, balloon shades, and comfy chairs, is a favorite for its view of the bay from the high bed. Room 1, in pale yellows and blues, has a window seat you can actually sleep on.

The innkeepers maintain a basket with such items as aspirin, dental floss, a hair dryer, heating pad, and Band-Aids. Other thoughtful touches are the assortment of books in each room, good reading lamps, and numerous hooks, hangers, and pegs.

You can keep very busy on the Point Reyes Peninsula. The innkeepers will give you pages of ideas, along with a trailhead guide for hiking in the area.

Moss Beach

Seal Cove Inn

221 Cypress Avenue
Moss Beach, CA 94038
650-728-7325
Fax: 650-728-4116
sealcove@coastside.net
www.sealcoveinn.com

> **An English country manor
> on the California coast**

Innkeepers: Karen and Rick Herbert. **Accommodations:** 10 rooms. **Rates:** $190–$270 single or double, additional person $30. **Included:** Full breakfast and afternoon hors d'oeuvres. **Added:** 10% tax. **Payment:** Major credit cards. **Children:** Welcome in garden-level rooms. **Pets:** Not allowed. **Smoking:** Not allowed.

➤ **After years of critiquing bed and breakfasts for guidebooks, Karen knew exactly what she wanted when she designed her own inn with her husband, Rick. Together they have created a lodging that incorporates the best components of a first-rate inn — a great location, tasteful decor, good food, and warm and gracious service.**

As you travel up the landscaped driveway to the Seal Cove Inn's sand-colored stucco manor home, you'll feel as if you've been instantly transported to the English countryside. If it weren't for the windblown cypress trees and the faint roar of the ocean in the distance, you might really begin to believe that you had in fact somehow been magically transplanted to merry olde England. Inside the inviting gabled home, the British ambience continues in the room decor as well as in the old world hospitality you'll be treated to during your stay.

Sheffield, Ascot, and Tartan are the guest rooms with English themes. Sheffield, on the first floor, is a light room with pale yellow walls. The bed is covered in yellow chintz and extra pillows, and there's a lovely watercolor of the inn over the fireplace. Sliding glass doors open out to a wonderful cottage garden abloom with sunflowers, shasta daisies, scabiosa, cosmos, status, and evening primrose. Upstairs, as one might guess, the Tartan room is dressed in plaids, while Ascot has a duvet in a jockey-and-horse print.

Other guest rooms include the Carl Larrson room — a tribute to the revered children's illustrator — with framed prints of his work and a Scandinavian decor; the Rote Rose room in pastels with botanical prints; and the Sampler room, where cross-stitch samplers adorn the walls. Rooms have reproduction grandfather clocks, fireplaces, telephones, fresh flowers, and patios, either adjoining or overlooking the colorful garden. Baths are modern and light with pedestal sinks, heated towel warmers, and hair dryers. Coffee and the daily paper arrive at your door in the morning, and in the evening your bed is turned down for your nightly repose.

The innkeepers' attention to detail is evident throughout the inn. In the upstairs hallway there are his and hers reading nooks, each with a small reading library. One (his) has chairs with an equestrian print — the other (hers) is outfitted with chairs with floral cushions. The wide, central staircase was designed with large windows so you can take in the view of nearby hills as you descend.

Afternoon hors d'oeuvres are set out on the dining room table, and in the mornings a full breakfast of fresh fruit, juice, and a hot entrée such as grand marnier French toast, strawberry waffles, eggs Benedict, or an egg soufflé, is served. A Continental breakfast can be delivered to your room if you prefer to dine in private.

The Seal Cove's one-acre property backs up to the Fitzgerald Marine Reserve — one of the best tide pool areas on the coast. The helpful innkeepers are happy to steer you in the direction of pleasant hikes in the parkland or recommend good restaurants in nearby Princeton-by-the-Sea and Half Moon Bay.

Muir Beach

The Pelican Inn

10 Pacific Way
Muir Beach, CA 94965-9729
415-383-6000
Fax: 415-383-3424
innkeeper@pelicaninn.com
www.pelicaninn.com

A touch of old England on the California coast

Innkeeper: Katrinka McKay. **Accommodations:** 7 rooms (all with private bath). **Rates:** $173–$209 single or double. **Included:** Full English breakfast. **Payment:** MasterCard, Visa. **Children:** Welcome ($27 for rollaway bed). **Pets:** Not allowed. **Smoking:** Not allowed.

➤ **In 1579, when Sir Francis Drake beached the *Pelican* (later renamed the *Golden Hind*) here on the Marin coast a few miles north of the Golden Gate Bridge, there were no country inns offering a warm bed, a mug of ale, and a game of darts. He might have enjoyed this one in Muir Beach, but this bit of Britain arrived four hundred years late.**

The Pelican nestles among pine and alder trees in the hills a short distance from the ocean (there is no water view). The Tudor-style half-timbered inn, surrounded by lawns and flowers, looks like a manor house from Elizabethan England though it was built in 1979. Inside it's even more British.

The restaurant and pub are on the ground floor. Leaded glass windows, heavy beams, worn Oriental carpets on brick flooring, and a menu that offers Beef Wellington, Yorkshire pudding, bangers and mash, and cottage pie would have made Sir Francis feel right at home. Benches against dark wood walls, tall candles on trencher tables, and a crackling fire in the fireplace create a cozy atmosphere on the foggiest of nights. Open to the public for other meals, the dining room serves guests only for a breakfast of toast, marmalade, English sausage, and eggs. There's also a sitting area — the Snug — for guests' use, with a decor that continues the English-country theme.

The guest rooms have low doors with wrought-iron hardware. Room 1 features a half-tester with a white eyelet quilt, lined tapestry curtains, an upholstered couch, and an old chest so battered it could have been left behind by the crew of the *Pelican*. Room 5 is smaller, its mullioned windows overlooking a balcony. One bedpost is an aged beam into which honeymooning guests often carve their initials; the obliging innkeeper will provide a knife if you ask. Room 2 is the smallest and, though cozy, it has plenty of room for two. Here you ascend a stepladder to the high bed and fall asleep to the scent of jasmine, which climbs to the roof outside your window. Handsome Room 6 looks out over the inn's front lawn to the Marin headlands beyond. Horses clip-clopping down the street only add to the rural ambiance.

The staff's hospitality, the inn's charm, and the proximity to Muir Woods and Muir Beach make rooms at the Pelican in great demand. You'll need reservations far in advance, especially for summer weekends. Spring and fall weekdays are more peaceful — and every bit as beautiful.

Oakland

The Claremont Resort and Spa

4 Tunnel Road
Oakland, CA 94705
510-843-3000
800-551-7266
Fax: 510-843-6239
reservations@claremontresort.com
www.claremontresort.com

A contemporary spa resort in a convenient East Bay location

General manager: Ted Axe. **Accommodations:** 262 rooms and 17 suites. **Rates:** $190–$400 single or double; suites $350–$850. **Added:** 11% tax. **Payment:** Major credit cards. **Children:** Under age 18 free in room with parent. **Pets:** Not allowed. **Smoking:** Nonsmoking rooms available.

➤ **Highly recommended for dining are Chez Panisse, as good as its stratospheric reputation, and Santa Fe Bar and Grill, where the chef performs magic with the mesquite grill. Citron and Bay Wolf are also notable eateries.**

Across the bay from San Francisco, the Claremont has been a hilltop landmark in the Oakland-Berkeley hills since 1915. The original castlelike home on the site, built by a farmer from Kansas who struck it rich in the gold mines, burned to the ground in 1901. A sprawling, many-gabled resort hotel was erected in its place, opening in time for the 1915 Panama-Pacific Exposition. It has undergone several refurbishments, including a $40 million overhaul started in 1988. Today the Claremont reigns over 22 landscaped acres and a lofty view of San Francisco Bay, its bridges, and the glimmering skyline.

The location is a plus. It's convenient to the city yet offers resort facilities. The Claremont boasts ten tennis courts, an Olympic-size pool and an exercise pool, saunas, whirlpools, and a luxurious, European-style health spa. It offers a full program of spa treatments, personal training, and wellness services. Both spa cuisine and traditional fare are featured on the menu of the poolside café.

Jordan's is the resort's showcase restaurant, specializing in seafood. The wine collection is extensive and highly rated, and the restaurant is noted for its lavish Sunday brunch. The Terrace Bar offers entertainment and dancing Tuesday through Saturday, and there are gift and florist shops, car rentals, and easy parking.

The guest rooms at the front of the hotel overlook the city and bay; the back rooms look toward the Berkeley hills and eucalyptus groves. The colors and designs are different in all the rooms, and every six months another block is refurbished. Suite 606 (with adjoining 605) is the Tower Suite, featuring long, low windows with great views of the bay and city skyline. The secluded suite is reached by a short flight of stairs. More stairs lead to a private balcony in the tower itself, at the top of the hotel. Suite 409 has the widest picture window in the hotel. The view is spectacular. There's a wet bar and, under a skylight in the bath, a tub big enough for two. In 1997, a North wing was added to the hotel with forty new guest rooms, many with whirlpool tubs, and all with extras such as VCRs, CD players, and refrigerators.

The Claremont offers several weekend packages (some include spa services) and an array of activities. Downtown San Francisco is only twenty minutes away, and other attractions lie close at hand. The East Bay regional park system, with walking and bridle trails, lakes, forests, and panoramic viewpoints, is just out the back door. The campus of the University of California is a few minutes' drive away. Oakland and Berkeley have excellent restaurants and shopping and interesting historic districts to explore. If you're a walker, pick up a guide to walks in the area and you'll find dozens of byways through gardens and residential neighborhoods.

Dockside Boat & Bed

77 Jack London Square
Oakland, CA 94607
510-444-5858
800-436-2574
Fax: 510-444-0420
boatandbed@aol.com
www.boatandbed.com

A bed-and-breakfast afloat in the bay

Proprietors: Rob and Mollie Harris (Jack London Square location); Mac McDaniel (Pier 39 location). **Accommodations:** Approximately 14 yachts. **Rates:** $115–$325 single or double, $25–$100 additional person. **Included:** Continental breakfast. **Payment:** Major credit cards. **Children:** $25 additional. **Pets:** Not allowed. **Smoking:** Not allowed indoors.

➤ **From the deck of a sailboat or motor yacht, you can watch the sunset over the San Francisco skyline while you listen to the gulls' cries and water lapping against the hull of the boat.**

Hundreds of yachts and sailboats bob at the marina off Jack London Square in Oakland, in Long Beach, and at Pier 39 in San Francisco. Dockside Boat & Bed makes a few of them available to guests looking for unusual lodgings. The vessels Dockside handles range from thirty-three feet to sixty-eight feet long. All are equipped with showers, television, coffeemakers, stereos, refrigeration, and microwaves. Some have VCRs and complete entertainment centers.

Arnie's Ark is a 35-foot boat with narrow gangways, a snug salon, a small modern bathroom, and a queen-size bed in the master stateroom. The boat is available for charter trips at a rate of $35 per person per hour, and three hours is the suggested minimum time to get a good, exhilarating sail on the bay. *The Voyager*, a 46-foot motor sailer, is a good option for families because it has three staterooms and sleeps up to six people.

Dockside also rents out several yachts at Pier 39 in San Francisco. The 51-foot *Athena* is docked at the Pier 39 location, and with three staterooms, it is available for overnight accommodations as well as private cruises.

Breakfast — orange juice, baked goods, and a basket of fresh fruit — is brought to your boat in the morning along with the local paper. Dockside can also arrange for catered candlelight dinners on board some of the yachts by prior arrangement. Concierge services such as limousines, gourmet picnic baskets, floral bouquets, and massages can also be arranged.

Most guests board their yacht-for-a-day looking for relaxation in a romantic setting, but there are other diversions nearby. Jack London Square, a gangplank walk away from boats at the Oakland dock, has about a dozen restaurants and shops, including the largest Barnes & Noble bookstore in northern California. The U.S.S. *Potomac*, formerly used by President Franklin D. Roosevelt, is docked at the marina and can be toured by the public. Ferry service connects Oakland with San Francisco.

Overnight guests staying in Dockside's San Francisco boats will find themselves adjacent to Pier 39, popular with tourists because of its many shops and restaurants. Fisherman's Wharf and the Hyde Street Maritime Museum are nearby. Dockside also offers three boats for overnight stays at Rainbow Harbor in Long Beach.

Point Reyes Seashore Lodge

P.O. Box 39
10021 Coastal Highway 1
Olema, CA 94950
415-663-9000
800-404-5634 in California
Fax: 415-663-9030
prsl@worldnet.att.net
www.pointreyesseashore.com

A country lodge by a magnificent park

Innkeepers: Greg and Susan Cockcroft. **Accommodations:** 18 rooms, 3 suites, 2 cottages. **Rates:** $95–$295, $25 additional person. **Included:** Continental breakfast. **Added:** 10% tax. **Payment:** Major credit cards. **Children:** Under age 12, $5 additional per day; over age 12, $25 additional per day. **Pets:** Not allowed. **Smoking:** Not allowed.

➤   **Everyone at the inn offers a friendly welcome and is happy to tell you about outstanding beaches and viewpoints in the neighboring park. They'll make reservations at restaurants, arrange for horseback rides or bicycle rentals, tell you about the park's naturalist activities, and help you find shops with special handicrafts.**

The entire Point Reyes National Seashore, 65,000 acres of scenic parkland, abuts the backyard of this attractive luxury lodge. It stands on an acre of landscaped grounds in Olema, 35 miles north of San Francisco. Though the three-story cedar inn resembles a turn-of-the-century country lodge, it was built and opened in 1988. The lodge combines the elegance and comfort of a hotel with the personal warmth of a bed-and-breakfast.

You enter to an open lobby of light, natural wood and bright lighting. Directly above, up a few steps, is a cozy library with books, games, and walls adorned with pleasing watercolors by Nell Melcher, an artist who, until recently, resided in Stinson Beach. A few steps down from the lobby is the fireplace room, where a buffet breakfast of fruit, muffins, and croissants is served. You may take a tray to your room, if you prefer, or breakfast can be brought to you.

Off to the side is a game room with pool table. Walls are hung with old photographs of the area, reflecting the owners' interest in local history. There are four guest rooms on this lower floor, each with a private entrance from the flagstone terrace. A lawn slopes west, down to Olema Creek, where willows and eucalyptus grow. A bridge across the creek leads to a path to Bear Valley Visitor Center, the park headquarters and starting point for numerous hiking trails.

Other guest rooms are located on two floors in the main lodge and in wings on either side. They all have direct-dial phones, digital clocks, down comforters, and contemporary colors of mauve, green, blue, and aqua. The quality is excellent, and the mixture of rough woods with European fixtures, shoji screens, and modern brass is a refreshing change from standard hotel rooms.

Some rooms have a fireplace, whirlpool tub, and magnificent views of the pastoral surroundings and Mount Wittenberg. An unusual feature of the rooms is the sliding screen in an arched opening between sitting room and bathroom; from the tub you can see the trees in the park. The three suites have wet bars, refrigerators, and bedroom lofts with featherbeds.

Birds are the theme of the Audubon Suite. An Audubon egret print hangs above the sofa bed and Roger Tory Peterson's book on the famed ornithologist lies on the fireplace mantel. White walls extend up to a high ceiling and loft. A balcony overlooks the grounds and park.

The Garcia Suite is named for the original owner of the land grant on the hotel's site and contains artifacts that were found in his barn. The Sir Francis Drake Suite has books on the early sea voyager, a globe, and a painting of Drake's ship, *The Golden Hinde*. Sir Francis Drake landed on these shores in 1579 and named the area Nova Albion (New England), perhaps because the pale cliffs that rise steeply above the beach reminded him of the coast of Dover.

On one side of the lodge is a croquet lawn, and nearby there's an arbor shading a picnic table and outdoor barbecue. Beyond that is Casa Olema, a cottage with its own living room, dining area, full kitchen, private patio, and hot tub.

Roundstone Farm

9940 Sir Francis Drake Blvd.
Olema, CA 94950
415-663-1020
800-881-9874
Fax: 415-663-8056
www.roundstonefarm.com

A ten-acre farm with a view near Point Reyes National Seashore

Innkeeper: Frank Borodic. **Accommodations:** 5 rooms (all with private bath). **Rates:** $135–$150. **Included:** Full breakfast. **Added:** 10% tax. **Minimum stay:** 2 nights on weekends. **Payment:** Major credit cards. **Children:** Discouraged; 2-person maximum per room. **Pets:** Not allowed. **Smoking:** Not allowed indoors.

➤ **Point Reyes National Seashore is an immense seaside park north of San Francisco Bay. Within its boundaries — Tomales Bay and Sir Francis Drake Boulevard on the east and the Pacific Ocean on the west — are miles of hiking trails, sand dunes, rolling moors, forests of oak and pine, and far-reaching views of the sea.**

Roundstone Farm occupies ten acres of hilly ranchland above Olema, a village on the Point Reyes Peninsula. From the deck of the cedar board-and-batten farmhouse you can see Mount Wittenberg and Mount Vision, Inverness Ridge, Olema Valley, and Tomales Bay.

The solar home was built in 1987 specifically as a bed-and-breakfast and is a comfortable haven for visitors. Each soundproof guest room is on a different level. The furnishings and color schemes vary, but all have fireplaces, thick carpeting, and goose down comforters. Bay, in gray and pale pinks, has a metal bed; Ridge has a handsome floral quilt; and Meadow, overlooking the meadow, is decorated in soft peach and white tones.

Fresh flowers or plants lend color to the understated decor. The quality is first rate, with bathroom fixtures from Copenhagen, Swiss linens, and armoires from England and Denmark providing Old World charm and workmanship. Wooden headboards, patterned after ranch gates, were made by a local craftsperson.

The large, sunny living room has a 16-foot ceiling, with skylights in the pitched roof and sliding doors along one glass wall that open to a deck and a magnificent view. Guests enjoy reading by the fire, playing board games, listening to CDs, and admiring the broad expanse of forest, meadow, and ranchland. From here you can see the farm's pond, where waterfowl and red-winged blackbirds nest; binoculars are provided for a closer view.

A few steps up from the living room is the dining area. Early morning coffee is on the sideboard. Later a substantial breakfast is served at one seating — although guests are welcome to take their meal out onto the patio in nice weather if they would like. The repast usually consists of juice, fresh fruit, and a dish such as quiche, frittata, or apple puff pancakes with sausage. The meal is always hearty, to prepare you for a day of hiking, bicycling, and exploring the Point Reyes National Seashore. Tea and coffee are available all day.

The farm was named after the village of Roundstone in the Connemara district of western Ireland, where Connemara ponies first lived in the wild. The innkeepers have raised Connemara ponies and Arabian horses for years. There are several on the property now, and guests are welcome to visit them.

Many guests enjoy relaxing in the inn's outdoor spa, which offers a view of the valley. For those wishing to explore the area, the Bear Valley Visitor Center, headquarters for the Point Reyes National Seashore, is just a few minutes away. It has extensive displays of natural and historic highlights of the park. From here, trails lead over ridges and cliffs to protected beaches. There are several good restaurants a short distance from Roundstone Farm. Visitors give the Olema Inn, which is just down the road, high praise for its light, pleasant atmosphere and excellent food.

Palo Alto

Garden Court Hotel

520 Cowper Street
Palo Alto, CA 94301
650-322-9000
800-824-9028
Fax: 650-324-3609
hotel@gardencourt.com
www.gardencourt.com

**A small hotel with a
Mediterranean atmosphere**

General manager: James Kirk. **Accommodations:** 62 rooms and suites. Rooms $260–$305 single or double, $15 additional person; suites $330–$505; weekend rates are available. **Added:** 8.5% tax. **Payment:** Major credit cards. **Children:** Free in room with parent. **Pets:** Not allowed. **Smoking:** Nonsmoking rooms available.

➤ **When you arrive, you're greeted by the parking valet and the fragrance of freshly baked bread wafting from Il Fornaio, a handsome ground-floor restaurant serving fine Italian food.**

In cozy little Palo Alto, on the peninsula twenty minutes south of the San Francisco airport, the Garden Court nestles snugly in the heart of the downtown district. The four-story Mediterranean-style building, of ochre stucco with dark green wrought iron trim and curving archways, has a casual, inviting look.

The hotel's residential ambience is apparent in the small second-floor lobby, where soft chairs and a couch face a fireplace, a big bowl of apples sits on a table, and a windowed alcove has benches filled with pillows. Off to one side are the check-in counter and concierge desk. The staff here is patient and helpful, ready to decipher a foreign accent or lend an umbrella.

Each of the spacious pastel rooms has a small balcony with just enough room for two chairs and a trellised, potted vine. Palo Alto is quiet at night, but to ensure peace, request an inside room above the courtyard. You'll look down upon an array of colorful flowers and the restaurant terrace. All rooms have two-line phones, high-speed Internet access, fax and copy machines, mini-bars, fresh flowers, and four-poster beds. Some include fireplaces and whirlpool tubs. The newspaper of your choice is delivered to the door in the morning, and complimentary shoeshine service is offered.

The Garden Court, which has banquet and meeting rooms that accommodate up to 250, caters to business travelers, visitors to Stanford University, and those looking for a relaxing getaway. It has an exercise room but no swimming pool. This hotel concentrates only on fine-quality accommodations. In addition to the hotel's restaurant, several cafés in the district are open for breakfast — a good excuse for a stroll into the Palo Alto lifestyle.

On a larger scale, the Stanford Shopping Center is a short distance away, along with more typical roadside development.

Pescadero

Pigeon Point Lighthouse Hostel

210 Pigeon Point Road
Pescadero, CA 94060
650-879-0633
www.norcalhostels.org

**An inexpensive place to
stay in a spectacular setting**

Managed by: Hostelling International. **Accommodations:** 52 beds. **Rates:** $14 per person for American Youth Hostel members; $17 nonmembers, $12 additional for private room. Linen rental: $1 per person. **Maximum stay:** 3 nights. **Payment:** MasterCard, Visa, and personal checks. **Children:** Half price in room with parent. **Pets:** Not allowed. **Smoking:** Allowed outside only.

➤ **At Año Nuevo State Reserve, six miles south of Pigeon Point, you can see elephant seals. This is the only mainland breeding colony of the 3,500-pound mammals.**

Between San Francisco and Monterey Bay, where the rocky shore curves into the sea, the lighthouse at Pigeon Point stands at the edge of a steep, rugged cliff on scenic Highway 1. Below it, breakers crash and foam against the rocks, and seals bob in the surf. It's a dramatic location for a lodging. American Youth Hostels owns and operates this and other hostels in California, which are open to all ages.

The accommodations are next to the lighthouse, in four low white bungalows surrounded by geraniums and ice plant. Each building has a carpeted living room, kitchen, two bathrooms, a couple's bedroom, and dorm rooms with six bunk beds each. Furnishings are basic: plain pine beds with covered mattresses, lamps, closets, and carpeting. Baths have showers and you can bring your own food to cook in the somewhat worn kitchen. The view from the window over the sink is a knockout, placing this hostel far above the simple category of low-cost lodging.

At the edge of the bluff is the former Fog Signal Building, now a recreation and meeting room with table tennis, couches, and a woodstove. Here you'll find brochures on area attractions and other hostels. There's also an outdoor hot tub that can be rented in the evening. A boardwalk and steps extend over the cliff to a fenced viewpoint where you gain a closer look at the Pacific panorama.

When you stay at a hostel, you're assigned an easy cleanup chore (vacuuming, dusting, etc.), and you bring your own bedding, linen, and food. (Linen rental is available for an additional charge.) Alcohol is not allowed. The hostel is closed during the day, from 9:30 A.M. to 4:30 P.M., check-in is after 4:30 in the afternoon.

This is open coastal country and there are no facilities or shops nearby, though in Pescadero, five miles north and two miles inland, there are gift and clothing stores, a gas station, and a restaurant that serves lunch. Just down the road from the hostel you can buy fresh artichokes that were picked in nearby fields.

Pigeon Point Lighthouse, 115 feet tall, has been guiding mariners since 1872. It's open for tours on Sundays, May through August. (A small donation is requested.) Watch for migrating whales and explore tide pools along the coast, or you can drive six miles inland to Butano State Park, where you may hike through redwood forests.

Point Reyes Station

Carriage House Bed and Breakfast

325 Mesa Road
P.O. Box 1239
Point Reyes Station, CA 94956
415-663-8627
800- 613-8351
Fax: 415-663-8431
felicity@nbn.com
www.carriagehousebb.com

> **A family-friendly bed-and-breakfast in Point Reyes**

Innkeeper: Felicity Kirsch. **Accommodations:** 1 room, 2 suites (all with private bath). **Rates:** $125–$160 single or double, $20 for each additional person; discounts for midweek and long-term stays available. **Included:** Continental breakfast. **Added:** 10% tax. **Payment:** MasterCard, Visa. **Children:** Welcome; additional $20 for third person in room. **Pets:** Not allowed. **Smoking:** Allowed outside only.

➤ **The Carriage House is just a short drive from nearby restaurants and galleries. It's 15 minutes from the ocean and 20 minutes from Point Reyes' famed lighthouse.**

The Point Reyes area, with its wealth of hiking, biking, horseback riding, and beachcombing opportunities, is a marvelous place to spend a family vacation. Yet with many bed-and-breakfasts discouraging children, and others too formal to make them feel comfortable, an inn such as the Carriage House is a welcome find for families traveling together.

The mood is relaxed and casual at the Carriage House, run by affable innkeeper Felicity Kirsch. In 1991 she opened her bed-and-breakfast in a 1920s carriage house behind her private home, with an additional guest room located on the second floor of the main residence. Reached by its own outdoor staircase, that room is called Sunrise. It's a high-ceilinged room with a brass bed, curly maple antique dresser, and a TV/VCR.

The Garden Suite, on the ground floor of the carriage house, is ideal for families (or anyone desiring a lot of space) with a full kitchen and separate living room and bedrooms. The living room is good-sized and is furnished with a wood-burning stove, TV/VCR, tape deck/CD player, as well as a daybed and pull-out queen-size sofa that will accommodate additional persons. Sliding glass doors from both the bedroom and living room open out to a big backyard liberally shaded by a giant cypress tree.

Upstairs, the Sunset Suite also has a large living room with a daybed, a separate bedroom, a full kitchen with an eat-in breakfast nook, and a full bath. All the rooms are comfortable and are decorated in a manner that makes you feel right at home — not as though you're visiting a museum. Cribs are available upon request, and the innkeeper can also help arrange child care.

Felicity stocks each refrigerator with fresh juice, seasonal fruits, yogurts, and pastries from a local bakery so guests can fix their breakfasts at their leisure. There are coffee grinders with fresh beans in each room, and firewood is provided for the wood-burning stoves.

The ample grounds provide one of the best features of the inn. In addition to the large backyard behind the carriage house, there's a smaller, more sheltered yard in front of the duplex, and the innkeeper's own backyard is also open to guests. In short, there is plenty of space for young ones to expend their energy, and the yards are protected enough that you'll feel at ease letting them do so. If more sedentary activities appeal to you, there's a wooden swing and a hammock to relax in.

Gray's Retreat

P.O. Box 56
Point Reyes Station, CA 94956
415-663-1166
Fax: 415-663-1343

> **A country home for a couple or a family**

Innkeeper: Karen Gray. **Accommodations:** 1 cottage. **Rates:** $185 per night for 2; $15 additional person; $1,100 per week. **Added:** 10% tax. **Payment:** Master-Card, Visa, personal checks. **Children:** $15 charge for each child over double occupancy. **Pets:** Allowed by arrangement, $20 charge. **Smoking:** Not allowed.

➤ **The town of Point Reyes Station is within walking distance and is home to the Tomales Bay Food Company, a delicatessen that makes gourmet take-out meals using locally made products. Another recommended dining spot is Tony's, on the water in Marshall.**

If you're bringing the family to Point Reyes Peninsula for a few days of rest, bird-watching, hiking, and enjoying the scenic beauty, Gray's Retreat is an excellent lodging choice.

Set in an open pasture and sheltered by a cypress windbreak, the rough cedar home overlooks Inverness Peninsula. Built as a guest house for the owner's parents, it has an occupied apartment on the upper floor and an apartment on the ground level where overnight visitors stay. Furnished with wicker and assorted wooden chests and chairs, the living room is bright and homey. Sunlight streams through western windows onto honey-colored walls and big bouquets of flowers. Beyond the living room is a full kitchen, and beyond that a dining area that opens to an enclosed patio.

Gray's Retreat accommodates six, with a trundle bed, a sofa bed, and a queen-size four-poster. Cribs, high chairs, and laundry facilities are available. Other helpful features for those traveling with children are soundproof walls, fenced front and back patios, shelves with games and a children's nature library (including the innkeeper's own book *The Family Guide to Point Reyes*), as well as a jogger stroller and a playground across the road. Young guests particularly enjoy meeting the two donkeys who graze in the adjoining pasture.

Jasmine Cottage

P.O. Box 56
Point Reyes Station, CA 94956
415-663-1166
Fax: 415-663-1343

A romantic cottage in the country

Innkeeper: Karen Gray. **Accommodations:** 1 cottage. **Rates:** $145 single or double; $15 additional person; $900 per week. **Included:** Full make-your-own breakfast. **Added:** 10% tax. **Payment:** MasterCard, Visa, personal checks. **Children:** $15 charge each child over double occupancy. **Pets:** Welcome with permission, $15 charge. **Smoking:** Not allowed indoors.

➤ **One of Jasmine Cottage's greatest assets is its innkeeper, Karen Gray. If you want seclusion, she'll leave you to your own devices; if you want sightseeing ideas, she's very knowledgeable. Having written a guide to Point Reyes, she is thoroughly familiar with the area and what it has to offer.**

Set apart from the innkeeper's home by private flower gardens, Jasmine Cottage is for the exclusive use of one group of guests, from one to four people. There are two cabinet beds in the light-drenched sitting room and a queen-size bed in an alcove that the innkeeper says some guests refer to as the love nest.

A crib, high chair, and jogger stroller can be provided if desired. The refrigerator in the fully equipped kitchen contains breakfast makings: coffee, jam, granola, milk, fruit, cheese, and eggs from the chickens that live in the yard. Flowered quilts, posters of native flora, fresh flowers, and Karen Gray's fabric art complete the gardenlike ambience, enhanced by the sweet fragrance of jasmine and views of fruit trees, geraniums, and roses.

The shed outside is well stocked with wood for the fireplace. Linens and housekeeping supplies are provided, and a Weber barbecue stands at the ready, should you wish to grill freshly caught fish from local waters. The cottage's shelves are full of books about local wildlife, including Karen's own family guide to the Point Reyes area. There's also an album full of information on local points of interest. There is no telephone or television to intrude upon the tranquil scene, but if you can't live without TV during your visit, cable TV can be provided if you request it in advance.

Outside the gate is a brick patio with a hot tub and a view across rolling pastureland to Inverness Ridge. In the cottage you'll find a picnic basket, complete with dishes and a Thermos bottle, ready to pack with a lunch and take into the park or to the seashore; but Jasmine's setting is so irresistible you may get no farther than the picnic table on your own patio.

Point Richmond

East Brother Light Station

117 Park Place
Point Richmond, CA 94801
510-233-2385 or 510-812-1207
Fax: 510-291-2243
ebls@ricochet.com
www.ebls.org

> **A cozy lighthouse on an island**

Managers: Ann Selover and Gary Herdlicka. **Accommodations:** 5 rooms. **Rates:** $290–$390. **Included:** Breakfast and dinner; transportation from harbor. **Payment:** Major credit cards. **Children:** Under 18 allowed by special arrangement only. **Pets:** Not allowed. **Smoking:** Not allowed indoors. **Open:** Thursday, Friday, Saturday, Sunday.

➤   To get to East Brother, a one-acre island in San Pablo Bay, you take an exhilarating, 15-minute boat ride from Point San Pablo Yacht Harbor. Once on the island, you're surrounded by peace and quiet. This is a place to visit when you want to do nothing but watch the cormorants and seagulls.

When his grandfather was the lighthouse keeper, between 1914 and 1921, Walter Fanning used to come to the tiny island to visit. Today, East Brother Light Station looks just as Walter remembers it — a trim and tidy, well-kept lighthouse of the Victorian era, with carved railings and gingerbread. Volunteers (Walter among them) worked long hours to restore and maintain the lighthouse, which was built in 1873 and automated in 1969. It's owned by the U.S. Coast Guard and is on the National Register of Historic Places.

There are two rooms on the ground floor, each with a brass bed and period furnishings, and a cozy parlor that guests share. The best views are upstairs. The Marin Room faces west toward the Marin County hills and Mount Tamalpais. It's romantic in rose and pink, with lace-edged pillows on the brass bed. The San Francisco

Room, in blue and white, has a view of the bay and the city beyond San Pablo Bridge. There's a parlor upstairs, too, which has a woodstove and a nautical theme.

The enthusiastic managers enjoy showing the lighthouse and preparing hearty meals, which are served in the dining room at a single table for eight. Wine and apéritifs are included. They sell T-shirts and a few gift items in the office that was once Walter Fanning's grandmother's parlor.

Princeton-by-the-Sea

The Pillar Point Inn

380 Capistrano Road
Princeton-by-the-Sea, CA
Mailing address:
P.O. Box 388
El Granada, CA 94018
650-728-7377
800-400-8281
Fax: 650-728-8345
www.pillarpointinn.com

A New England–style inn on the harbor

Manager: Marny Shuster. **Accommodations:** 11 rooms (all with private bath). **Rates:** $155–$195 single or double, $22 additional person. **Included:** Full breakfast. **Added:** 10% tax. **Payment:** Major credit cards. **Children:** $22 additional if third person in room. **Pets:** Not allowed. **Smoking:** Not allowed.

➤   **The inn has menus for the few nearby restaurants. Across the street is Barbara's Fish Trap, a casual spot by the water. Moss Beach Distillery is a dinner house, and Shore Bird is a favorite for brunch before going whale-watching.**

Halfway between San Francisco and Santa Cruz, facing the only harbor for seventy-five miles, Pillar Point Inn provides a touch of Cape Cod on the West Coast. The solidly built gray hotel trimmed in white and nautical blue sits behind a white picket fence, its curved and gabled windows looking toward the boats bobbing a few yards away.

Princeton-by-the-Sea is an idyllic setting for relaxing, boating, and fishing. An unpretentious little town with a livelihood that comes from the sea, it has a waterfront busy with boat building and repairs, charters, fishing, pleasure boats, and whale-watching excursions. There are a few shops, galleries, and restaurants, but this working port has nothing like the tourist activity of its neighbor, Half Moon Bay. It does have a romantic inn offering warm hospitality and luxurious accommodations, however.

In the small living room, guests can enjoy the sherry, fresh fruit, and cookies that have been set out; relax on loveseats by the double-sided fireplace; and peruse the shelves of books and movies. You can watch old-time favorites such as Robin Hood, Abbott & Costello, and even Hopalong Cassidy on your own video player — there is one in every room.

The rooms also have European-style featherbeds, radios, fireplaces, telephones, and refrigerators hidden in antique-looking cabinets. Baths have pedestal sinks, tub/shower combinations, wicker towel stands, and heat lamps. Two rooms have king beds, the rest have queens, and ten have views of the water. The white and blue color schemes complement the seaside setting, and themes from local history provide a different decor in each room.

El Granada, a second-floor room that faces the road and harbor, holds photographic reminders of 1909, when a developer tried to turn the region into a major resort. Nobody was interested in buying, but many took the offer of a free lunch and a train ride to and from the beach. El Granada has a brass and white iron bed and a white rocker by the high, arched window. A writing table stands in one corner and a tiled gas fireplace with raised hearth in another. Sounds of traffic and restaurant noise from across the street fade in the late evening, as the village settles down, until finally all you hear is the moan of the buoy in the harbor.

Café curtains hang in the windows of the Lighthouse Room on the first floor. There's also a cushioned window seat, a wicker armchair, and a photograph of a lighthouse hangs on the wall above the fireplace. The Whaling Room, also called the Hideaway, is extra large, very quiet, and has a view of the mountains and a partial harbor view.

From the dining room, where breakfast is served on pine tables, you can see the morning fog cling to the headlands. Pastries, fruit blintzes, homemade granola, and a hot entrée such as quiche are typical of the breakfast fare.

San Francisco

The Archbishop's Mansion

1000 Fulton Street
San Francisco, CA 94117
415-563-7872
800-543-5820
Fax: 415-885-3193
abm@jdvhospitality.com
www.sftrips.com

| A romantic, historic home on Alamo Square |

Owners: Jonathan Shannon and Jeffrey Ross. **Manager:** Sondra Lender. **Accommodations:** 15 rooms (all with private bath). **Rates:** $159–$419 single or double, $20 additional each person. **Included:** Continental breakfast and evening wine and cheese service. **Added:** 14% tax. **Minimum stay:** 2 nights on weekends. **Payment:** Major credit cards. **Children:** $20 additional if third person in room. **Pets:** Not allowed. **Smoking:** Not allowed.

➤ **The owners have been careful to encourage a lively, friendly ambience. "I've been in historic inns where you're afraid to sit on the sofa," says Jonathan Shannon. "Antiques are wonderful, but I want people to be comfortable. I like to see them in jeans and shorts, being casual."**

If you want lodgings in San Francisco that remind you of home, don't stay at this inn unless you live in an opera set. The opulence of The Archbishop's Mansion is best enjoyed by those who revel in the lavish, the lush, and the extravagant — all carried off with great taste and a sense of humor.

The inn is across the street from Alamo Square, a hillside park eight blocks from Golden Gate Park and six blocks from the Civic

Center, Davies Symphony Hall, the Opera House, and the Museum of Modern Art. The Alamo Square area, its streets lined with lovely Victorian houses, has been designated a City Historic District, thanks in large part to the efforts of Jeffrey Ross and Jonathan Shannon. They have also worked to preserve other parts of the city. In 1980 they began the painstaking task of restoring their time-battered mansion.

The three-story home, built in 1904 as a residence for Archbishop Patrick Riordan, was based on Second Empire French styling, so the new owners gathered furnishings from around the world to reflect that period. When they were through, they had created a belle époque French château and, because it is so grand (and so close to the Opera House), they named the rooms after romantic 19th-century operas.

Because the owners are former set designers, the rooms, all with impressive antiques or reproductions, are furnished with comfort and flair. La Bohème has a partial canopy above a bed that is as elaborate as the tent of a fabled sheik. Romeo and Juliet is another elegant room, with soft pastels, floral patterns, a crown canopy bed, and a Jacuzzi tub for two. Cosi Fan Tutti is a suite with antique lace, gilded molding, and French doors separating the bed and sitting areas.

Don Giovanni, once the archbishop's own private bedroom suite, is expansive with a wonderful four-poster bed graced with carved cherubs and a lace coverlet. There's a fireplace (one of eleven in the inn) and, in the bath, a seven-headed shower the archbishop specifically asked to have installed. Oriental vases, a crystal chandelier, leather sofas, and a second fireplace compose the decor in the suite's spacious living room. Carmen is another suite with two fireplaces — one in its bedroom and one in its large, carpeted bath, which also has an antique clawfoot tub.

La Tosca, with a fireplace, was once the archbishop's private dining room. There are cherub lamps at the bedside and Oriental rugs on the floors, as well as a lovely marble-topped washstand in the bath. La Traviata, on the main floor, features a sitting room with a glazed tile fireplace, head-high wainscoting, and a gilded chandelier hanging from a high, coffered ceiling. In the white tiled bathroom are robes, a shower, a pedestal sink, and a lighted makeup mirror.

The main hall is another example of the owners' sense of atmosphere. It has a gilt-framed mirror from Abraham Lincoln's home in Illinois and columns of polished redwood and mahogany. At one end is a grand piano that once belonged to Noel Coward. It's playable, but also computerized, so you may hear a tune without a player at its keyboard. Above the wide staircase is a large stained glass dome.

Newspapers are delivered to the guest rooms each day. Morning coffee and wine in the evening are offered in the front parlor. Breakfast, brought to your room on a silver tray, includes juice, croissants, and granola with tea or coffee. You may have breakfast in the formal dining room if you prefer.

The inn's staff, which is competent if not overly warm, will make restaurant reservations and help with tour ideas. Parking is available in a tiny area beside the house, but it's less than convenient, as cars must stack up and then be moved. Additional on-street parking in front of the mansion is sometimes available.

Campton Place

340 Stockton Street
San Francisco, CA 94108
415-781-5555
800-235-4300
Fax: 415-955-5536
reserve@campton.com
www.camptonplace.com

> **A small central hotel known for its high quality**

General manager: Paul Zuest. **Accommodations:** 110 rooms. **Rates:** Rooms $275–$400, suites $520–$2,100. **Added:** 14% tax. **Payment:** Major credit cards. **Children:** Under 17 free in existing bedding. **Pets:** Dogs and cats allowed for an additional $30. **Smoking:** Nonsmoking rooms available.

➤ **In a pastel setting of peach and apricot walls, white Wedgwood china, and Swiss linens, diners feast on foods presented as works of art in Campton Place's restaurant.**

Campton Place is a jewel. Around the corner from Union Square, in busy downtown San Francisco, it offers extraordinary luxury, superb service, and a fine restaurant.

When you arrive, uniformed doormen usher you into a marble lobby with a theme both French and Oriental. Carved Buddhas, antique jars, and a 16th-century Japanese sumi screen accent the graceful curves of French furniture. An antique Swedish chandelier hangs above a glass table supported by four swans. Off the lobby is a sunken lounge, divided from the dining room by a curving sweep of glass etched with a swan, the hotel's emblem.

Since the restaurant opened in 1983, it has consistently received rave reviews for complex flavors in an outstanding cuisine. Both California and European wines are available.

Service throughout the hotel is cheerful, personal, and efficient. There are no VIP floors or differing levels of attention. A valet will unpack your luggage and, when you leave, repack it in tissue paper. The concierge will assist you with tours, or, if you prefer, set up your entire visit. Other routine services include a choice among four complimentary morning newspapers, overnight shoeshine, immediate pressing, same-day laundry and dry-cleaning (if you spot your jacket during lunch, it will be cleaned and returned to you before the bill for your meal arrives), twice-daily housekeeping, and a full concierge service. Valet parking is available.

The guest rooms, decorated in soothing pale gold, peach, and tan tones, have a residential ambiance. Furnishings are both contemporary and traditional, with attractive Oriental print fabrics. There are oversize beds with comforters, Henredon armoires housing remote control television sets, Louis XVI writing tables, mini-bars, and limited-edition art on the pastel walls. Double-glazed windows keep street noise at a distance, but they open if you prefer the city's sea breezes to air conditioning. Marble baths with brass fixtures contain vanities, scales, night-lights, phones, hair dryers, and terry-cloth robes. Luxurious French milled soaps and a supply of cotton balls are among the toiletries provided.

The hotel is actually two buildings, one of seventeen stories and the other, eight stories. On the lower rooftop is a garden with potted petunias and citrus trees and a view of Union Square. This is a pleasant little oasis for enjoying the morning sun.

Campton Place used to be the Drake-Wiltshire Hotel, dating from the early 1900s. Changed and remodeled several times, it lapsed into decline until 1981, when Ayala International acquired and rebuilt the property, turning it into the fine, charming hotel it is today.

Casa Arguello

225 Arguello Boulevard
San Francisco, CA 94118
415-752-9482
Fax: 415-681-1400
103221.3126@compuserve.com

> **A classic San Francisco home in a city neighborhood**

Innkeepers: Emma Baires, Marina McKenzie, and Pete McKenzie. **Accommodations:** 5 rooms (3 with private bath). **Rates:** $66–$135. **Included:** Expanded Continental breakfast. **Added:** 14% tax. **Minimum stay:** 2 nights. **Payment:** Major credit cards. **Children:** Over age 7 welcome. **Pets:** Not allowed. **Smoking:** Not allowed.

➤ **An international clientele comes to Casa Arguello, so you're likely to meet people from all over the world — especially from Switzerland, Germany, and England.**

As you walk and drive the hilly streets of San Francisco, you pass hundreds of stucco rowhouses, each with a bay window and, usually, a trim box of geraniums in front. Casa Arguello is one of them, located in a neighborhood of similar homes, apartments, and shops. Clement Street restaurants and the boutiques on Sacramento are nearby; Golden Gate Park is five blocks away. The beautiful Temple Emmanuel is across the street.

This bed-and-breakfast is larger than it seems from the outside, extending back to a courtyard and up some stairs. Owning such an inn was Emma Baires's childhood dream when her father had a hotel in El Salvador. Emma and her daughter opened their B&B in 1978.

As in many similar homes, the main floor is up a flight of stairs from the entrance. The walls are white, hung with prints of San Francisco scenes, and in the living room are floral couches, rosy carpeting, and arched windows. Antique and contemporary furnishings have been tastefully combined. Coved ceilings and the original wall sconces and moldings date the building to the 1920s.

All the guest rooms have cable TV. Room 1 is a small, sunny, corner room with a western view. It shares a bath with Room 2, which has a king-size brass bed. Room 3, looking toward Lincoln and Golden Gate parks, has a king-size bed in white iron. Room 4 is spacious enough to include three armchairs and a refrigerator. Sheer curtains topped by floral swags lend soft color and style to this airy room, which has a view of the University of San Francisco campus. The large Master Suite has a walk-in closet, two twins and one king bed topped with pretty floral spreads, and a private bath.

Breakfast is served family-style in the dining room. Fresh fruit, juice, a choice of cereals, muffins, croissants, scones, and coffee and tea are the usual offerings. The breakfast table is a fine place to meet and talk with other guests and trade sightseeing ideas and restaurant discoveries.

The Clift

495 Geary Street
San Francisco, CA 94102
415-775-4700
800-65-CLIFT
Fax: 415-441-4621

**A top-quality historic hotel
near Union Square**

General manager: Sileshi Mengiste. **Accommodations:** 326 rooms and suites. **Rates:** $255–$305 single or double, suites $360–$1,500. **Added:** 14% tax. **Payment:** Major credit cards. **Children:** Age 12 and under free in room with parent. **Pets:** Dogs and cats allowed, additional $40. **Smoking:** Nonsmoking rooms available.

The 1915 Clift has always been a luxury hotel of dignity that attracted the celebrated and the elite. But it didn't keep up with the times, and by the early 1970s the grand old place seemed a relic of a bygone era. After a multimillion-dollar renovation, the Clift surpassed its initial luster and was on its way to becoming the jewel it is today. Its sense of history and elegance remained, while its facilities were modernized.

From the buff brick exterior and snazzy glass and brass entry, you step into a wood-paneled lobby. Not imposing or grand, it's a gracious, welcoming place where businesspeople with briefcases and kids with lollipops are equally at home.

One of the main attractions of the Clift, and of San Francisco, is the Redwood Room. Built in 1934, it is an art deco masterpiece that shouldn't be missed, whether you stay at the hotel or not. The walls of the lounge, reaching twenty-two feet to a ceiling of pressed metal, are paneled in aged redwood, taken from toppled giants that had lain in northern California streambeds and gullies for years. The heartwood from these ancient tree trunks, when polished, takes on a deep patina of bronze and topaz. Frosted glass sconces and pyramid chandeliers continue the art deco motif. The most striking element of the room, other than the redwood itself, is the mural above the 75-foot bar, a stylized forest scene of inlaid woods. In the restaurant diners enjoy fine California-French cuisine featuring regional foods and a California-dominated wine list.

The guest rooms in the 16-story hotel are spacious and luxurious with large windows. Request a room on one of the higher floors to avoid traffic noise. They all have numerous amenities: mini-bars, two-line phones with modem access, remote control TV, hair dryers in marble bathrooms, and tiny booklights for bedtime reading. A Petite Suite has a sitting room with Henredon furniture, window drapes in sophisticated gray and white stripes accented with peach, pearly gray walls, and windows that view Nob Hill on one side and Twin Peaks on the other. Theatre Suites have two baths so that several people trying to make a curtain can get ready at the same time.

A typical corner Deluxe Suite has plush rose carpeting, a wet bar in the living room, a CD player, a VCR, a glass coffee table, and a dining table for six, lighted from above by a teardrop chandelier. There are potted palms, original artwork, soft robes, an array of toiletries in a white ceramic basket, and a dressing room bigger than many San Francisco apartments.

At press time, the Clift had come under the management of Ian Schrager, a hotelier with a number of properties on each coast. Changes were planned for the hotel, but as specifics were not given, it was impossible to predict which features of the hotel would be affected. As Schrager is also responsible for the ultra-hip Mondrian Hotel in Los Angeles, it should be interesting to see how his management will influence a historic property such as the Clift.

Several function rooms provide space for meetings, receptions, and parties of 8 to 250. Many a bride and groom have chosen to be married at the Clift before slipping upstairs to celebrate with champagne for two in a sybaritic honeymoon retreat.

The hotel is within walking distance of the shops near Union Square, fine restaurants, Theater Row, museums, and art galleries; and it's a cable-car ride away from other San Francisco attractions.

The Fairmont Hotel

950 Mason Street
San Francisco, CA 94106
415-772-5000
800-527-4727
Fax: 415-837-0587
www.fairmont.com

**A Nob Hill classic
overlooking the city and
bay**

General manager: Mark Huntley. **Accommodations:** 540 rooms and 60 suites. **Rates:** $189–$389 single or double, $30 additional person, suites $500–$8,000. **Added:** 14% tax. **Payment:** Major credit cards. **Children:** Age 16 and under stay free. **Pets:** Dogs under 20 pounds allowed. **Smoking:** Nonsmoking rooms available.

➤ **Guests were entertained in the darkly rich Venetian Room from 1947 until 1989, when Tony Bennett sang "I Left My Heart in San Francisco" for the last time in that room and the supper club closed. Now it's used for private banquets.**

Opulence on the grand scale in a historic building at the top of one of the world's great cities — that's the Fairmont. When it opened in 1907 (after a delay caused by the 1906 earthquake and fire), the community was impressed by its resemblance to a European royal palace. It's still impressing locals and visitors alike with its ornate facade, magnificent lobby, fine accommodations, and panoramic views of the city and San Francisco Bay.

The Fairmont, long known for its luxury and upper-income clientele, was used as the location of the television series *Hotel*. Television and film celebrities show up regularly, both as guests and performers.

The Fairmont has several restaurants. Off the lobby, the plush Squire features seafood and an extensive wine list. Masons is downstairs, as is Bella Voce, where you'll hear operatic arias as you dine on pizza, pasta, and seafood. From Chinese food in the Polynesian-style Tonga to chocolate sundaes in Sweet Corner, you can find just about anything your taste buds yearn for in this hotel. The Fairmont Crown, reached by a glass-enclosed elevator, is noted for its stunning views as well as its lavish buffets. The New Orleans room, adjacent to the lobby, has live entertainment Tuesday through Saturday.

If it's people-watching you want, just sit on one of the red velvet sofas in the lobby for a while. Fascinating crowds come and go between the massive marble Corinthian columns that soar to a gilt-detailed ceiling. Adjacent to the grand lobby are galleries selling Oriental art.

Ten of the hotel's suites overlook the rooftop garden and terrace, a green oasis of palm trees and flowers. There is no pool, but a fitness center with weight machines, sauna, whirlpool, steam room, and massage service is available.

The guest rooms feature simple, elegant furnishings. Down pillows, 200-count cotton sheets, a TV with video games and movies on command, electric shoe buffers, and daily maid and turndown service are some of their luxuries. To assist the corporate traveler, multiline modem phones and fax machines are in each room. Voice mail and a business center are available.

The rooms in the main building vary, but in general they are larger and have more spacious baths and closets than those in the adjoining 23-story tower. The architecture of the tower, which went up in 1963, is outlandishly inappropriate to the imposing original building, but there's no denying the beauty of its views. Some suites feature balconies that overlook the garden or downtown to the financial district. Corner suites have separate living rooms and a total of four telephones.

The suites vary in decor. You may see a classical Roman theme, with off-white colors and low tables made to resemble temple columns, or a more traditional look with dark woods and antique reproductions. Members of the Fairmont's frequent guest club, the President's Club, can be upgraded to a suite and have complimentary fitness center privileges for only $25 more than a standard room.

For the ultimate in luxury, reserve the penthouse, probably the most expensive hotel suite in the nation. The eighth-floor, eight-room, duplex suite, reached by a private elevator, rents for $8,000 a night, which includes an around-the-clock butler, maid, and private limousine to and from the airport. Ten can be seated for a meal in the suite's dining room, the living room has a grand piano, and there's also a full kitchen and a private workout room with fitness equipment. At press time the Fairmont was undergoing a major renovation, so the hotel may have a slightly different look during your visit.

Galleria Park Hotel

191 Sutter Street
San Francisco, CA 94104
415-781-3060
800-792-9639
Fax: 415-433-4409
reservations@galleriapark.com
www.galleriapark.com

> **A stylish hotel in the heart of the city**

General manager: Mark Schwass. **Accommodations:** 177 rooms and suites. **Rates:** $175–$225 single or double, suites $359–$529; weekend and corporate rates available. **Added:** 14% tax. **Payment:** Major credit cards. **Children:** Under 16 free in room with parent. **Pets:** Not allowed. **Smoking:** Nonsmoking rooms available.

➤ **The Galleria Park offers a variety of packages with special rates.**

Urbane and sophisticated, the eight-story Galleria Park is one block from the financial district and two blocks from Union Square and Chinatown. One of the Kimpton Group's boutique hotels, it offers incentives designed for the business traveler. There are conference and reception rooms, a full array of support equipment for meetings, and a catering service. A full-time program coordinator will handle arrangements with professional care. Parlor suites are suitable for small and informal meetings.

The hotel offers same-day laundry and valet service and a parking garage. Runners appreciate the track on the rooftop terrace, as well as the workout equipment in the fitness center. Each room has large soundproof windows, well-lighted writing desks, cable television with movies on command and Nintendo, digital clock radios, and direct-dial two-line telephones with long cords, voice mail, and data ports.

Guest rooms are decorated in rose and teal tones. Baths tend to be on the small side, but are clean and have hair dryers. The room configurations vary, because a restoration in 1988 worked within the existing spaces. The Galleria Park is an extensive remake of the Sutter Hotel, which was built on the site in 1911. The seven park studios are large rooms with sitting areas. There are seven hospitality suites, plus the popular two-bedroom Grand Suite, with a fireplace and a whirlpool tub.

A typical hospitality suite has a sitting room with a large TV (making it a good gathering place for a small group wanting to watch a ball game together) and, in a few, a white brick fireplace on a raised hearth. In the bedroom are a king-size bed and a small television. The suites' comfortable furniture and assortment of potted plants and flowers create the ambience of a city apartment. As in most Kimpton hotel suites, the space is in the sitting area.

Each evening hotel guests are invited to sip wines under the lobby's frosted glass skylight while listening to music provided by a jazz duo. Perry's Downtown, which is just off the lobby, is a casual eatery and sports bar. For a quick meal try Café Briazz, at the hotel's doorstep, or Jamba Juice, for fruit smoothies.

The hotel is next to Crocker Galleria, three levels of shops and restaurants under a vaulted glass dome. Two rooftop parks in the shopping center have benches and greenery, pleasant sites for a picnic lunch or a rest.

Golden Gate Hotel

775 Bush Street
San Francisco, CA 94108
415-392-3702
800-835-1118
Fax: 415-392-6202
ggatehotel@aol.com
www.goldengatehotel.com

A European-style hotel at bargain prices

Innkeepers: John and Renate Kenaston. **Accommodations:** 25 rooms (some with shared bath). **Rates:** $72–$125 single or double. **Added:** 14% tax. **Included:**

Continental breakfast and afternoon tea. **Payment:** Major credit cards. **Children:** Welcome. **Pets:** Not allowed. **Smoking:** Not allowed.

➤ **Golden Gate Hotel is not a luxury establishment, but it offers excellent quality for the price. It's a good San Francisco find.**

In the heart of downtown San Francisco, just north of Union Square, this hotel is more than a terrific bargain. It has several extras you wouldn't expect at these prices. The narrow yellow Edwardian building was built in 1913 and has been carefully maintained by the Kenastons, who manage it with warmth and enthusiasm. Half their guests are experienced travelers from abroad, and many are return visitors.

Bright geraniums bloom at bay windows in front, where a glass awning marks the marble entrance. In the little parlor with windows overlooking the rush of Bush Street traffic, coffee (the city's strongest, Renate claims), tea, and croissants are served in the mornings. Afternoon tea and cookies are also offered by the fireplace. It's a relaxing spot to read, chat, and listen to classical music.

An old-fashioned birdcage elevator, operated by the original drums and relays, connects four floors of guest rooms. The more expensive rooms have private baths; the others have washbasins and share bathrooms nearby. All the rooms have television and phones, and some have bay windows that overlook a tree-filled courtyard. Renate sees that every room has fresh flowers. Some accommodations are quite small, but they are clean, have a European charm, and are nicely furnished with antique armoires, floral wallpaper, and wicker pieces. Some have brass beds.

The friendly, multilingual (German, French, and Spanish) hosts are delighted to help with sightseeing tours. The hotel is within walking distance of the city's great shops, many of its best restaurants, and Chinatown. The cable car stops at the corner and follows Powell Street to Fisherman's Wharf and North Beach.

Guests can park at the garage across the street, where the fee for 24 hours with in-and-out privileges is $12.

Harbor Court Hotel

165 Steuart Street
San Francisco, CA 94105
415-882-1300
800-346-0555
Fax: 415-882-1313
www.harborcourthotel.com

| A bay-view hotel with top-quality fitness facilities |

Manager: Lisa Kershner. **Accommodations:** 130 rooms, 1 penthouse suite. **Rates:** $235–$325. **Added:** 14% tax. **Payment:** Major credit cards. **Children:** Rooms accommodate 2 people. **Pets:** Not allowed. **Smoking:** Nonsmoking rooms available.

➤ **Menu offerings at the popular Harry Denton's restaurant are as basic as Yankee pot roast with mashed potatoes and as imaginative as grilled filet mignon with cracked peppercorns and warm new potato salad, seasonal vegetables, and a cognac sauce.**

At last the Embarcadero freeway is gone and the view toward East Bay is open again. The Harbor Court Hotel is a prime viewing spot, as half of its guest rooms overlook the bay. The eight-story hotel was built in 1907 and was once a YMCA. The Harbor Court, which opened as a European-style hotel in 1991, one of the Kimpton Group hotels, now adjoins a renovated YMCA. Guests may use all the Y facilities — an Olympic-size pool, weight room, racquetball courts, basketball court, exercise machines, steam room, sauna, and rooftop running track.

Another bonus, especially for business travelers, is the Harbor Court's location: close to the financial district as well as to Embarcadero Center. The hotel provides limo service twice each morning to the financial district. The hotel also has a business center with fax, photocopying, and typing services; same day valet service; and complimentary coffee, tea, fruit, and evening wine in the lobby.

Nautical prints adorn the walls of the guest rooms, which are on the top four floors. Comfortably elegant bay-view rooms, decorated in shades of olive, are small but adequate — it's the panoramic view that makes them so popular. Half-canopy beds with matching European shams are elevated so that guests can lie in bed and still see the view. Space-savers include under-the-bed storage drawers, built-in ironing boards hidden behind mirrors, and wardrobes that hold closet space, TVs, and honor bars. Wide mirrors add an illusion of expanse. Interior rooms, which view a flowery courtyard, are larger. Baths in all rooms are modern, and in-room extras include hair dryers, voice mail, computer hook-ups, and Nintendo.

For relaxation, the Harbor Court has a sizable lobby lounge with sofas and chairs in intimate groupings in front of a fire that blazes in the hearth behind a frosted glass screen. For fine dining and entertainment, Harry Denton's, adjoining the lobby, is considered a hot spot in the Bay Area. A festive restaurant with a beautiful mahogany bar, rich wood columns, and red velvet booths, Harry Denton's is open for breakfast, lunch, and dinner seven days a week. It has live music nightly (generally jazz and rhythm and blues), with dancing on Thursday, Friday, and Saturday nights.

Hotel Griffon

155 Steuart Street
San Francisco, CA 94105
415-495-2100
800-321-2201
Fax: 415-495-3522
reservations@hotelgriffon.com
www.hotelgriffon.com

A sophisticated waterfront hotel with a Bay Bridge view

General manager: Linda Turnidge. **Accommodations:** 62 rooms and suites. **Rates:** $230–$285 single or double, suites $395–$435. **Included:** Continental breakfast. **Added:** 14% tax. **Payment:** Major credit cards. **Children:** Welcome (cribs available). **Pets:** Not allowed. **Smoking:** Nonsmoking rooms available.

➤ **The hotel is close to the BART system and the Bay Bridge and is a few steps from Embarcadero Center, cable car stops, and ferry service.**

With the dismantling of the Embarcadero Freeway, the view from the back of this small hotel near the waterfront has improved dramatically. Now you can see boats scudding across the water and the Bay Bridge stretching to the East Bay (six guest rooms and two suites have views of the Bay Bridge). The front of the hotel faces San Francisco's busy financial district.

As you enter the hotel, which was built in 1906 but was refurbished and opened as the Griffon in 1989, you notice its namesake, a papier-mâché griffon standing beside the fireplace in the small lobby. Hotel guests partake of a complimentary Continental breakfast here between 6:00 A.M. and 9:00 A.M. Marble floors and plush loveseats in front of a fireplace invite you to make yourself at home.

Divided from the lobby by an etched glass partition is the Red Herring Restaurant and Bait Bar. With a waterfront view, raw bar, and nautical décor, seafood naturally gets top billing; however, game and fowl spit-roasted on a wood-fired rotisserie are also on the menu. Dungeness crab chops — Chef James Ormsby's signature crab cakes shaped like pork chops with a crab claw serving as the bone — are a specialty.

Upstairs, the fresh, light rooms have mahogany, cherry, or rosewood headboards — custom carved with the Griffon motif — and marble baths. Lots of style went into appointing these rooms. Exposed brick behind the beds contrasts with the creamy alabaster-toned walls, 12-foot high ceilings, mahogany writing desks, original artwork, and inviting window seats. In keeping with the European flavor, vanities with sinks are located in the bedroom, separate from the bathroom. Among the items in the stocked mini-bars are bottles of Sonoma Valley chardonnay with the hotel's own label. All rooms have robes, coffeemakers, clock radios, and CD players. Suites on the fifth floor, which was built during the 1989 renovation, have private terraces, comfortable sitting areas with pull-out sofabeds, wet bars, large closets, and oversize bathtubs. Two deluxe suites have bay views and TVs with surround sound.

An alternative to the big central hotels, the Griffon has become a favorite with business travelers and tourists for its atmosphere, service, and convenient location. Business travelers especially appreciate the dual-line telephones in the guest rooms, which have voice mail and data ports for fax machines and PCs. All guests have complimentary use of the fitness facilities at the YMCA a couple of doors away. Parking is available, with 24-hour in-and-out privileges. Morning Towncar service throughout downtown is offered free of charge.

Hotel Juliana

590 Bush Street
San Francisco, CA 94108
415-392-2540
800-328-3880
Fax: 415-391-8447
www.julianahotel.com

A small urban hotel with European charm

Manager: Jeri Riggs. **Accommodations:** 107 rooms and suites. **Rates:** $149–$199 single or double, suites $179–$249. **Added:** 14% tax. **Payment:** Major credit cards. **Children:** Under age 12 free in room with parent. **Pets:** Not allowed. **Smoking:** Nonsmoking rooms available.

➤ **With guest rooms named for famous San Francisco women, corporate packages designed to cater to women travelers, and soothing decor, Hotel Juliana is an especially hospitable lodging for women traveling on their own.**

During the past decade or so, a number of affordable little first-class hotels have opened in San Francisco, filling a niche between small economy and big luxury hotels. Bill Kimpton, founder of Kimpton Group, has opened a number of these hostelries since 1981; one of them is the charming Juliana.

The nine-story beige brick building with burgundy and blue trim is on a busy corner on the Nob Hill side of Union Square. Built in 1903, it has been completely renovated and boasts modern comforts.

The strains of taped viola music play in the lobby, which is handsome in rusts and blacks. Soft chairs and couches covered with Egyptian print fabrics are grouped near the pink marble fireplace. Against one wall is a table with always-hot coffee, tea, and a tray of fresh fruit. Complimentary wines are served every evening. On the walls in the lobby and throughout the hotel hang artwork provided by local galleries. The rotating collection showcases contemporary pieces that are available for purchase.

Classical music plays softly in the background as you enter your guest room. Attractively decorated in sunny yellows, corals, and greens with flowered drapes and bedspreads coordinated with striped bedskirts, walls and chairs, the atmosphere is that of a nicely furnished private apartment with a French flair, befitting this traditionally French area of San Francisco. The Juliana is next to Notre Dame de Victoire, where Mass is still spoken in French. All the rooms have direct-dial telephones with voice mail and data ports, fax machines, built-in ironing boards, well-lighted desks, coffee makers, honor bars, televisions with in-room movies, and large baths with hair dryers and makeup mirrors. Complimentary limousine service is provided to the financial district in the mornings. These and other services, such as same-day laundry and valet service, put the Juliana in the category of the city's better hotels, while its budget-minded aspects (room service is available only part of the day; the bellman doubles as concierge) keep it affordable.

Hotel Monaco

501 Geary Street
San Francisco, CA 94102
415-292-0100
800-214-4220
Fax: 415-292-0111
sales@hotelmonaco.com
www.hotelmonaco.com

**A posh hotel with
imaginative interiors**

General manager: Nanci Sherman. **Accommodations:** 201 rooms and suites. **Rates:** $219–$279 single or double, suites $299–$479. **Included:** Evening wine hour. **Added:** 14% tax. **Payment:** Major credit cards. **Children:** Free in room with parent. **Pets:** Allowed in cages. **Smoking:** Nonsmoking rooms available.

➤ **Built as the American Beaux Arts building in 1910, in 1995 it was gutted, earthquake reinforced, and completely renovated before reopening as the sumptuous Hotel Monaco.**

When the Hotel Monaco opened its doors in 1995, it quickly became one of the most talked about hotels in San Francisco. In a city filled with wonderful hotels, that is saying a lot. The largest and most luxurious of the Kimpton Group hotels, it was designed to be the jewel in the Kimpton crown. With a style uniquely its own, the Monaco is all of that and more.

On your first visit to the hotel you'll probably pay little attention to the amicable staff members that greet you with a smile as your eyes are likely to wander to the grand hall beyond the entrance. Like a medieval castle brought up to date with end-of-the-millennium tastes and sensibilities — and a touch of whimsy — it's a feast for the eyes. The massive French inglenook fireplace at the far end is befitting of a chateau's great hall, and hot air balloons appear to drift lazily overhead amidst puffy white clouds. An angel rises to the heavens over a marble staircase that leads to meeting rooms.

Down a hallway there's a salon — much smaller in scale but no less interesting. Corinthian columns painted gold reinforce the fireplace's mantel. On either side are paintings of Eden, while benchlike sofas covered in velvet and a surrealist painting of the earth complete the fantasy.

Guest rooms and suites are decorated with the same imaginative flair — no boring white walls here, just a daring blend of colors, patterns, and textures that work surprisingly well together. In a typical room the bed is dressed with a pretty yellow paisley coverlet and broadly striped bedskirts in gray and ivory that match the padded fabric headboards and striped button-backed chairs. A band of red, black, and yellow pinstriped fabric is rolled at one end and tied with ribbons to form a partial canopy over the bed, and an Oriental armoire hides a television equipped with Nintendo. Even the ice bucket, metal with cutout stars, has a sense of style.

The beds in canopy queen rooms are fully draped to form romantic and cozy nests. Extra pillows on the bed line the wall to create the effect of a sofa, and there's a plump round ottoman for resting tired feet. A two-room luxury suite has a salmon-colored velveteen sofa in the living room, fleur de lis patterned drapes in red and gold at the window and behind the bed, and a bath with a two-person Jacuzzi, separate shower, and telephone. Double-paned windows, fax machines, bathrobes, stocked bars, two-line phones with data ports, and hair dryers are standard in all of the rooms.

A wine hour, complimentary for guests, takes place in the lobby each night. Morning coffee and the daily paper are also complimentary, as is use of the hotel's fitness center, which is equipped with free weights, stretching mats, stair climbers, stationary bicycles, treadmills, and videos for aerobic workouts. The center also has a personal trainer on staff, a steam room, sauna, men's and women's locker rooms, and a nice spa by an etched glass mural. Massage therapists are on duty each evening in case you need a massage at the end of a long day.

Adjacent to the Monaco's lobby is the Grand Café — another striking space with a look that harks back to the '20s and '30s. Bronze sculptures enhance the entrance to the café, with its sturdy columns, high molded ceilings, walls bearing Moulin Rouge murals, and terrazzo tile floors. Although the room is large and open, the tables are set for intimacy and the lighting is soft. Polenta soufflé with wild mushroom ragout and cambozola fondue, sweetbread fricassee with mixed vegetables and truffle sauce, and chicken breast stuffed with wild mushrooms and haystack potatoes are examples of the California-French bistro cuisine created by Executive Chef Denis Soriano.

Hotel Nikko

222 Mason Street
San Francisco, CA 94102
415-394-1111
800-NIKKO US
Fax: 415-421-0455
resdept@hotelnikkosf.com
www.nikkohotels.com

A touch of Japan near Union Square

Deputy general manager: John Hutar. **Accommodations:** 510 rooms and 22 suites. **Rates:** Start at $250 single and $275 double; suites $475 and up. **Added:** 14% tax. **Payment:** Major credit cards. **Children:** Under age 18 free in room with parent. **Pets:** Seeing Eye dogs allowed. **Smoking:** Nonsmoking rooms available.

➤ **The Nikko's restaurant, Anzu, serves prime cuts of beef as well as Japanese dishes. However, sushi lovers needn't leave their rooms to dine if they don't want to, as the hand-rolled delicacy is available on the hotel's room service menu as well.**

In angular simplicity, the Nikko rises 300 feet above Mason and O'Farrell streets, two blocks from Union Square and four blocks from the Moscone Center. The hotel's sleek, modern look has been modified in recent years with warm jewel tones and sheer curtains in the marble lobby. Cascading water, recessed lighting, and elegant floral arrangements create a soothing effect and a welcoming atmosphere.

Prosperous-looking business travelers, many of them Japanese, patronize the Nikko, which Japan Air Lines opened in 1987. Business and leisure travelers alike receive the best of care, from a computerized key system for security to a fitness center where you can relax under a shiatsu massage. You never have to stand three-deep waiting for an elevator at the Nikko. Swift Mitsubishi elevators whisk you to your floor at 700 feet per minute. The ride is said to be so smooth that a nickel placed on end will remain standing throughout the trip.

The guest rooms and suites, serene in neutral shades and earth tones, are furnished in a contemporary style. Conveniences include two-line speaker phones with data ports, voice mail, coffee makers, hair dryers, irons and ironing boards, a stocked refrigerator that automatically charges your bill when an item is dispensed, a switch by the king-size bed that turns on all room lights, and speedy in-room television checkout. Many rooms have CD players with a supply of CDs featuring local musicians. Rooms on the Nikko floors are slightly larger and have extras such as bathrobes and silk drapes. Guests staying on the Nikko floors are also entitled to a complimentary Continental breakfast and afternoon snacks in the Nikko lounge.

For a rare treat, book one of the Nikko's two Japanese suites. With tatami rooms, silk futons, western baths with huge soaking tubs as well as a traditional Japanese bath, and even the accoutrements to perform a Japanese tea ceremony, the suites are truly special.

Business travelers may prefer one of the four business suites on the sixth floor; they have meeting rooms and the latest audiovisual equipment. Other conference rooms are available — the Nikko offers 18,000 square feet of meeting space. It also has a business center providing fax, FedEx, translation, photocopying, and other office services, including computers that have word processing software in Japanese.

On the fifth floor there's a health facility with an inviting swimming pool under a glass-enclosed atrium, a whirlpool tub, tanning machine, saunas (one is a Kamaburoa Japanese dry sauna), massage service, exercise equipment, and two Ofuros — soaking tubs in the Japanese tradition. The center is attractive and useful — just bring your tennis shoes; everything else is provided, even swimsuits. The shiatsu massage is a refreshing way to unwind af-

ter a business meeting or a day's sightseeing. Outside on the rooftop there's a sunning area with lounge chairs and a Japanese garden.

To lure vacationers, the Nikko offers special weekend packages
that include deluxe accommodations, use of the fitness center, and
free valet parking.

Hotel Rex

562 Sutter Street
San Francisco, CA 94102
415-433-4434
800-433-4434
Fax: 415-433-3695
www.citysearch.com/sfo/hotelrex

**This hotel caters to a
literary crowd**

General manager: Veronica Saba. **Accommodations:** 92 rooms and 2 suites.
Rates: Rooms start at $165, suites start at $575. **Included:** Evening wine service. **Added:** 14% tax. **Payment:** Major credit cards. **Children:** Under 12 free in
room with parent. **Pets:** Not allowed. **Smoking:** Nonsmoking rooms available.

➤ **The Joie de Vivre hotel group, which operates the Rex, is known for
its creative and sometimes eclectic hostelries throughout the city. The
group is headed by visionary Chip Conley.**

An antiquarian bookstore fittingly fronts the Hotel Rex, which is
two blocks from Union Square. Chip Conley and his innovative
Joie de Vivre hotel group purchased the former Orchard Hotel,
renovated it, and reopened it under its new name in 1996. With a
literary theme, the hotel was modeled after New York's Algonquin
hotel and named after Beat poet Kenneth Rexroth, whose quotes
line the hallway walls.

Bookcases filled with leatherbound volumes separate the registration desk from a salon where readings and literary roundtables
are held. Bookshelves also adorn the walls on either side of the bar
at the far end of the room, and even the fireplace is filled with
books. There are café tables near the bar where you can order
breakfast, telephone tables with rotary dial phones, and easy chairs
if you wish to linger in a bookish milieu.

A small elevator — papered with the San Francisco Social Register of years gone by — will transport you to the upper floors where
the guest rooms are located. The rooms are stylish with rich wood
reproduction furnishings, green and tan checked bedspreads with

matching curtains, and colorful ceramic lamps with sheepskin shades painted in a design reminiscent of the Bloomsbury period. There's also a writing desk in case you're inspired by the literary surroundings to create a work of your own. Amenities include robes, irons and ironing boards, makeup mirrors, hair dryers, cable television and in-room movies, CD players, and modern touchtone telephones with voice mail, call-waiting, and data ports. King executive suites also have a sofa and a coffee table. Some rooms look out to trees in the backyards of neighboring buildings.

In the evening there's a complimentary wine hour, and the daily paper is also free of charge. Room service is available. The Hotel is centrally located, putting it within walking distance of Union Square, the theater district, Nob Hill, Chinatown, and the financial district.

Hotel Triton

342 Grant Avenue
San Francisco, CA 94108
415-394-0500
800-433-6611
Fax: 415-394-0555
www.hoteltriton.com

> **A sophisticated small hotel with a sense of fun**

General manager: David von Winckler. **Accommodations:** 140 rooms. **Rates:** $179–$219 single or double, suites $299. **Included:** Complimentary morning coffee and wine in the afternoon. **Added:** 14% tax. **Payment:** Major credit cards. **Children:** Free in room with parent. **Pets:** Cats and small dogs allowed for an additional $50. **Smoking:** Nonsmoking rooms available.

➤ **Lined with black-and-white photographs of actors and rock stars, even hallways are distinctive at the Triton. On the mezzanine level the artwork changes every three months, and there's a meeting room called the Creative Zone with an adjacent patio. Meals are casual at Café de la Presse, also on the premises.**

Whimsical designs and bright colors in deep hues set the tone for the Triton's mood. It's playful, creative, and sophisticated, but guests' needs for comfort and efficiency come first.

The hotel, which opened in 1991 as one of the Kimpton Group's small hotels, is conveniently located across from the gate to Chinatown and close to Union Square and the financial district. Entering guests first notice the dramatic, curving columns in vivid gold, teal, and purple, and the gold chairs with undulating backs. The walls are painted with a dreamlike mythological mural, while sea-grass-green stars stud the royal blue carpet. Soft couches are arranged in conversation nests; one by the fireplace is built into a purple wall and surrounded by painted flames.

Guest rooms are equally interesting. The smallest, called Zen-dens, were designed to maximize limited space and appeal particularly to the business traveler. The full-size bed, fitted into a corner and used as a couch during the day, is covered with a handsome striped spread. There are cleverly angled drawers, mirrors to visually enlarge the space, and theater-style curtains at the windows. Other rooms are larger and more traditionally furnished, though they too have unusual elements, such as curved fixtures and walls painted with big blue and yellow diamonds or pastel swirls. Among the services and features are honor bars with reasonably priced items, first-run movies on command, Nintendo, and individual climate control. For the ecologically minded, the Triton has an eco-floor where the linens are made from organically grown cotton, garbage is recycled, the water is filtered, natural soaps and shampoos are dispensed from reusable containers, and baths are outfitted with low-flow plumbing fixtures.

For a hotel room that you won't soon forget, splurge and rent one of the Triton's designer suites. The Jerry Garcia suite, dedicated to the late rocker, is decorated with colorful fabrics Garcia designed (if you've seen his ties and scarves you'll know the look). The featherbed, covered in a Garcia-print silk comforter, is so plump it resembles an over-puffed soufflé, and the bath has a lively silk shower curtain. In the Wyland suite on the eco-floor, Wyland's marine art adorns the walls, the coffee table is a dolphin sculpture topped with glass, and live fish swim in a nearby tank. Yet another suite is dedicated to the musician Carlos Santana. The newest theme suite is the "Rent" suite, which was created by the Broadway hit show's stage designer. The suites have coffeemakers, stereos with CD players, and, adding to the whimsy, each has a rubber duckie in the bath.

Hotel Vintage Court

650 Bush Street
San Francisco, CA 94108
415-392-4666
800-654-1100
Fax: 415-433-4065
www.vintagecourt.com

A boutique hotel with one of the city's best restaurants

Manager: Jeff Martella. **Accommodations:** 106 rooms, 1 suite. **Rates:** $119–$169 single or double, suite $275. **Added:** 14% tax. **Payment:** Major credit cards. **Children:** Under age 16 free in room with parent. **Pets:** Not allowed. **Smoking:** Nonsmoking rooms available.

➤ **At Masa's, etched mirrors reflect tables set with crisp burgundy and white linens, Christofle silver, and fresh flowers, all under a coved ceiling with moldings of polished oak. The lighting is subdued and the music soft.**

A restful environment, reasonable rates, and one of the city's best French restaurants draw increasing numbers of travelers to this attractive downtown hostelry. The Vintage Court is a part of the collection of boutique hotels that have provided a new lodging option in San Francisco in recent years. Bill Kimpton, with his highly successful Kimpton Group hotels, is a leading figure in the move to renovate old buildings and turn them into distinctive, stylish hotels with rooms at comparatively low prices.

The Vintage Court opened in 1983, built in an eight-story hotel originally constructed in 1913. Its wine theme is evident each evening, when complimentary Napa Valley wines are served in the lobby living room near the marble fireplace while classical music plays in the background.

Guest rooms, which are spacious for an older hotel, are attractively decorated with contemporary furnishings, rose motif comforters, coordinating drapes, and complementing striped bedskirts and padded fabric headboards. Cabinets house stocked refrigerators and additional comforts, many geared to the business traveler, include writing tables with good lighting, direct-dial phones, and digital clock radios. Some rooms have bay windows with window seats, and there are comfortable sitting areas on each floor for guests seeking even more room to lounge. A single corner suite on the eighth floor has a separate living room with a sleeper sofa and wood-burning fireplace, a bath with Jacuzzi tub and brass fixtures, an original 1913 stained glass skylight, and views of the city skyline.

Complimentary morning transport to the financial district is provided, and coffee and tea are available around the clock in the lobby. Same-day laundry service and express check-out are also available. In the mornings, guests help themselves to a complimentary French Continental breakfast, with more substantial breakfast items available at a nominal charge.

The hotel's restaurant, Masa's is mentioned in tones of hushed reverence by San Francisco gastronomes. Exquisite food is served in the small, flawless restaurant. Chef Julian Serrano, from Spain, follows the tradition established by the late Masataka Kobayashi, the restaurant's founder. Serrano combines fresh ingredients with classic sauces to create dishes that are works of art. The prix fixe menu changes regularly but entrées such as grilled Maine lobster with herbed butter and shrimp quenelles, or Sonoma milk-fed spring lamb with tomato confit and cumin potatoes are examples of the restaurant's choice cuisine. The wine list, with more than five hundred fine French and California selections, is extraordinary. Desserts include a silky lemon charlotte with raspberry sauce, feather-light puff pastries, thick wedges of chocolate with hazelnuts, and fruity mango sorbet in a praline cone.

Predictably, reservations at Masa's can be difficult to come by — Tuesday or Wednesday nights are your best chances of getting a table in the dining room, which seats one hundred. If you can't get into Masa's, you can order room service from a variety of restaurants offering everything from Indian to Italian, Mexican to Japanese.

The Huntington Hotel

1075 California Street
San Francisco, CA 94108
415-474-5400
800-652-1539 in California
800-227-4683 in U.S.
Fax: 415-474-6227
reservations@huntingtonhotel.com
www.huntingtonhotel.com

| **A Nob Hill hotel of elegance and luxury** |

General manager: Gail Isono. **Accommodations:** 100 rooms and 38 suites. **Rates:** $250–$420 single or double, suites $450–$1,000. **Added:** 14% tax. **Pay-**

ment: Major credit cards. **Children:** Under age 4 free in room with parent. **Pets:** Not allowed. **Smoking:** Nonsmoking rooms available.

➤   **Understated elegance, unobtrusive service, and assurance of privacy make this San Francisco landmark a romantic retreat and a favorite with a demanding clientele that includes many famous names.**

This dignified, 12-story, red brick hotel at the top of Nob Hill thrives on tradition and a reputation for excellence. It has been owned by the same family almost since the day it opened in 1924 as an apartment building. John Cope, president of the ownership company, is the great-grandson of the developer who bought the property the year it was built. Many on the staff have been with the Huntington for years. Whether you're a repeat guest or a newcomer, you are greeted by name, and the concierge always calls to be sure you're comfortably settled in.

Off the gracious lobby is the hotel's dining room, the Big Four. It's named for the early San Francisco railroad tycoons Collis P. Huntington, Leland Stanford, Charles Crocker, and Mark Hopkins, and it displays a collection of railroad memorabilia. The masculine room has dark woods, etched mirrors, and reflective walls. The menu, under the skilled direction of Gloria Ciccarone-Nehls, offers innovative American and Continental dishes, with seafood and wild game specials. The chef's spectacular chocolate creations give new meaning to dessert. Wines are California and French vintages. A pianist performs nightly in the Big Four's lounge.

The guest rooms and suites are all larger than average, a legacy from their former years as residential apartments. Each was individually decorated by Anthony Hail, Lee Radziwill, Elizabeth Bernhardt, and Charles Gruwell using differing color schemes and furnishings that include a generous smattering of antiques and original art. Suites have refrigerators and wet bars and some contain kitchenettes. Every room has large windows that open to gorgeous views of San Francisco Bay, the city, or Huntington Park and stately Grace Cathedral. Accouterments include fluffy down cushions, hair dryers, plush bath towels, and linen hand towels. Business travelers will appreciate the fact that there are special TI phone lines in each room for fast Internet access; most rooms also have fax machines.

Twice-daily housekeeping, overnight laundry service, valet parking, and your choice among three daily newspapers are some of the services provided by the Huntington. One block away is the Club One fitness center; guests are welcome.

The hotel has several handsome meeting rooms suitable for board meetings and receptions. The concierge is on duty all day and will arrange for tours, theater and restaurant bookings, secretarial services, and babysitters. On weekdays a Cadillac limousine will take you to the financial district and Union Square at no charge, and the cable car stops at the hotel's front door.

Inn at the Opera

333 Fulton Street
San Francisco, CA 94102
415-863-8400
800-325-2708
Fax: 415-861-0821
www.shellvacationsonline.com

A small, elegant hotel close to the Civic Center

General manager: Carl Bober. **Accommodations:** 30 rooms and 18 suites. **Rates:** $145 single, $160 double, $15 additional person, suites $225. **Added:** 14% tax. **Included:** Continental breakfast. **Payment:** Major credit cards. **Children:** Under age 12 free in room with parent. **Pets:** Not allowed. **Smoking:** Nonsmoking rooms available.

➤ **A pianist plays every night in Ovation. The restaurant's menu, which changes regularly, features California cuisine and wines. Ovation is one of the city's few restaurants offering after-theater dinner.**

Although San Francisco's Civic Center has long been the cultural and governmental focus for the city — with the Opera House, Davies Music Hall, San Francisco Ballet School, Civic Auditorium, Museum of Modern Art, and City Hall grouped closely together — the area lacked a first-class hotel. With the restoration of the seven-story Inn at the Opera, it gained a gem. Originally called the Alden, the hotel was built in 1927 to house visiting opera performers. Over time it fell into disrepair and was eventually purchased in 1983; after a multimillion-dollar renovation it reopened in 1985, again hosting internationally acclaimed singers and conductors as well as patrons and tourists.

Entering the inn is like stepping into the parlor of a gracious private home. Classical music flows around French armchairs in silk and damask, past tall, mullioned windows, potted palms, and porcelain jardinières painted with curling dragons. At the end of a short hallway lined with Paul Renouard sketches of Paris Opera

Ballet dancers is the focal point of the hotel: Ovation. This intimate lounge and restaurant is rich in texture and color. Its dark woods, muted jewel tones, subdued lighting, green velvet sofas, and exotic fabric wall coverings patterned with jungle birds create a sensuous, elegant mood.

You may choose to have breakfast delivered to your room or eat in the restaurant, where fresh flowers grace tables with white linens. The buffet includes fresh fruit, yogurt, cereals, muffins, quiche, and a cheese tray.

There's only one elevator, but it takes you swiftly to guest rooms in the boutique hotel. Accommodations include six junior suites, six one-bedroom suites, and six two-bedroom/two-bath suites. All rooms and suites have half-canopy queen-size beds, microwave ovens, ceiling fans, stocked mini-bars, and oversize baths. They're furnished with dark mahogany and color schemes of blue, green, and peach that exude a soft and welcoming warmth. The least expensive and smallest are Standard rooms; Superiors are larger, but all have the same amenities. At evening turndown each night you'll find cookies in your room.

You may park on the street, but it's not recommended in this urban neighborhood. Valet parking is available for $22 per day.

The Inn at Union Square

440 Post Street
San Francisco, CA 94102
415-397-3510
800-288-4346
Fax: 415-989-0529
inn@unionsquare.com
www.unionsquare.com

A small urban hotel of comfort and style

Manager: Brooks Bayly. **Accommodations:** 30 rooms. **Rates:** $200–$250 single or double, suites $220–$350. **Added:** 14% tax. **Included:** Continental breakfast; gratuities; evening wine and hors d'oeuvres. **Payment:** Major credit cards. **Children:** Additional $20 per night if third person in room. **Pets:** Not allowed. **Smoking:** Not allowed.

➤ **If you like European charm and attention to detail combined with the atmosphere of old San Francisco, the Inn at Union Square is an excellent choice.**

In the heart of downtown San Francisco, half a block from Union Square, this little urban retreat is a delight. Behind the green and white awning that extends over the sidewalk is a narrow lobby, made to appear larger by the trompe l'oeil wallpaper resembling open windows and shelves of books. A lovely floral display stands behind the front desk.

Intimate in size and tone, each floor of seven rooms has its own sitting area with a fireplace where morning muffins, fresh juices, and fruit are served (or breakfast will be brought to your room if you prefer). In the evening, wine and hors d'oeuvres are provided. All this is complimentary, along with a daily paper and use of a nearby health club.

The rooms are attractively furnished with light wood furniture, canopy beds, and sophisticated striped fabrics. Ultra-soft sheets, downy pillows, wide windows that open, fresh flowers, a desk — these are the ingredients of a small and worthy hotel. Bathrooms are not immense marble affairs; they are simple with tiled floors, granite countertops, hair dryers, night-lights, and mirrored walls.

The larger rooms have sitting areas; one has a fireplace. There are two-room suites with fold-out love seats, a large two-room suite with a living room, and a penthouse suite with a king-size canopy bed, whirlpool bath, sauna, fireplace, and wet bar.

The Majestic

1500 Sutter Street
San Francisco, CA 94109
415-441-1100
800-869-8966
Fax: 415-673-7331
hotelmaj@pacbell.net
www.expedia.msn.com

A lovely restored landmark, the essence of old San Francisco

General manager: Richard Dunkelberger. **Accommodations:** 48 rooms and 9 suites. **Rates:** $145–$225 single or double, $15 additional person, suites $425. **Added:** 14% tax. **Payment:** Major credit cards. **Children:** Welcome (no charge for use of a crib). **Pets:** Well-behaved pets allowed with prior approval from the general manager. **Smoking:** Nonsmoking rooms available.

➤ **The Café Majestic — actually a full-scale dining room with a pleasantly French ambience — is noted for its combination of California cuisine with Asian influences.**

San Francisco's turn-of-the-century golden era is brought to life at the Majestic, a beautifully restored five-story Edwardian structure. It's outside the bustling downtown area, about ten blocks from Union Square and only a couple of blocks from the city's Japantown.

Entering the glass-paned double doors of the hotel takes you even farther from the modern rush and city noise. Wide stairs of green marble lead to a carpeted lobby where a chandelier with torch globes gives a warm glow to the antiques-filled room. It's a gracious space where a fire burns in the fireplace and Oriental vases hold handsome floral arrangements. Fringed lampshades and cushions, velvet couches, lace-curtained windows, soft music, and glass-fronted bookcases add atmosphere.

To the left of the lobby are the Café Majestic and bar. Metal chairs with caned backs pull up to tables dressed with crisp linens in the airy dining room. There's a piano soloist during Sunday brunch, and guests staying on weekends are greeted with a smile and a story by the ever-colorful Tom McEntee — every guest knows him by the time they leave. The adjoining bar is a clubby spot with a nineteenth-century mahogany bar from France and a collection of framed butterflies on the walls.

The elevator, painted in gold with charming fairy-tale mice, leads to the upper hallways, with textured walls, and to the guest rooms. (With only 57 rooms in the entire hotel, the central stairs may be just as convenient for those staying on the lower floors.) Four-poster canopy or two-poster bonnet beds, boudoir chairs, and velvet or plush couches are typical of the comfortably elegant decor. It's easy to imagine yourself in an old San Francisco residence — an updated one, however, with TVs, clock radios, and direct-dial telephones. Deluxe rooms and suites have extras such as fireplaces and refrigerators. Deluxe rooms also have clawfoot tubs. The suites offer the greatest amount of luxury, with a spacious living room, separate bedroom, two closets, a tray for reading or eating in bed, terry robes, and roomy tubs, marble vanities, and two sinks in the baths.

If you'd like to step into a long-gone era, you'll enjoy the Majestic's charm. Soak in the clawfoot tub or sit at your desk in the bay window overlooking the trees and strollers on Sutter Street, and you might be a guest visiting in 1902, when the hotel was built. It has received state recognition for historic and architectural preservation.

Services at the hotel are provided by a capable and friendly staff and include valet parking, complimentary limousine service to the financial district and Union Square, afternoon sherry in the library,

and nightly turndown service — which includes Ghirardelli chocolates, printed homilies, and special tea bags for refreshing tired
eyes. The concierge will arrange for restaurant reservations and
wine country tours. During the off-season (November through
March) the Majestic offers packages at lower rates.

Mandarin Oriental

222 Sansome Street
San Francisco, CA 94104
415-276-9888
800-622-0404
Fax: 415-433-0289
www.mandarin-oriental.com

**A service-oriented hotel
with grand city views**

General manager: Wolfgang K. Hultner. **Accommodations:** 158 rooms and
suites. **Rates:** $395–$550 single or double; suites $900–$1,800. **Added:** 14% tax.
Payment: Major credit cards. **Children:** $45 additional for children over 12;
maximum 3 persons per room. **Pets:** Small pets allowed, additional $25 per
day. **Smoking:** Nonsmoking rooms available.

➤ **Services at the Mandarin Oriental include a fully equipped business
center, guest privileges at a nearby health club, and meeting rooms.**

Located in the heart of the financial district, the Mandarin Oriental
continually gets high marks for its service and its award-winning
restaurant. Opened in the mid-1980s as the prestigious Mandarin
Oriental Group's first U.S. hotel, the Mandarin Oriental San Francisco has only enhanced the chain's stateside reputation.

Guests register in the hotel's sleek, modern, marble lobby. Guest
rooms are located on the top ten floors (floors 38-48) of the First
Interstate Center — the third tallest building in the city. Glass-
enclosed sky bridges lead from elevators to guest rooms, and although many may be tempted to stop and take in the incredible
views of the city and the Golden Gate Bridge beyond, there is no
need as views from the rooms are equally spectacular.

Rooms are spacious and attractive in creamy yellow, beige, and
rosy brick tones. Comforters with complementing shams are striking — Oriental scenes appear to be etched on an ivory background.
With rose-colored marble, a separate tub and oversize shower, the
baths are luxurious. They feature a scale, clock, makeup mirror,
hair dryer, English toiletries, Oriental silk slippers, an emergency

flashlight, terry robes, and in the eastern tradition, a lightweight cotton robe is also provided. Room amenities include two-line phones with PC/modem hookups, writing desks, a clothesbrush, and a built-in luggage bench — a welcome change from the more precarious fold-up luggage racks often found in hotels.

Junior suites, called Mandarin Kings, have 100 more square feet of space than standard rooms, and their sitting area with a sofa and easy chair is partially separated from the sleeping area. Best of all, their roomy tubs are set below large windows strategically placed to take full advantage of the view. For a real splurge, the Oriental Suite has two bedrooms, a living room with a dining area, a Jacuzzi bath, and a 2,000-square-foot private terrace.

In keeping with the chain's eastern emphasis on service, thoughtful provisions have been made with the guest in mind. Doorbells at each room lend an air of distinction, while twice-daily housekeeping service keeps the rooms looking fresh. As part of nightly turndown, cookies at the bedside provide a comforting touch, while the room service kitchen, located just one floor below the guest rooms, ensures that meals are still oven-warm when they arrive.

Silk's is the hotel's top-rated restaurant. The cuisine is billed as Californian with Asian influences. The Mandarin Lounge, adjacent to the lobby, serves Continental breakfast in the morning, appetizers and desserts from 3:00 P.M. to 8:00 P.M., and evening cocktails.

The Mansions

2220 Sacramento Street
San Francisco, CA 94115
415-929-9444
800-826-9398
Fax: 415-567-9391
www.themansions.com

> **A pair of mansions featuring luxurious style and a sense of fun**

Owner: Robert C. Pritikin. **Accommodations:** 21 rooms. **Rates:** rooms $187–$368. **Included:** Full breakfast. **Added:** 14% tax. **Payment:** Major credit cards. **Children:** Welcome. **Pets:** Allowed. **Smoking:** Not allowed indoors.

➤ **With all its trappings, this hotel has a lighthearted atmosphere. Even the ghost seems to have a good time.**

Two long-time San Francisco hotels, side by side in a neighborhood of apartments, homes, and a medical center, form an unlikely lodging combination. The Mansion Hotel, a twin-towered Queen Anne structure, is known for its sense of fun and eclectic mixture of whimsy and Victoriana. The grand home was built in 1887 by a senator from Utah, Charles Chambers, who earned a fortune in silver mines and moved to San Francisco. It's a historic landmark now, filled with museum-quality art and antiques. Next door, the Hermitage House is a serene urban refuge. Connected by a hallway, they are The Mansions.

Robert Pritikin is a hotelier of boundless energy and many interests. He writes books *(Christ Was an Ad Man)*, collects sculpture (he has a major Benjamin Bufano collection — the large monk sculpture in front of the hotel is a Bufano), keeps a macaw in the hotel parlor, and plays the musical saw. A couple of his very original hotel's features are a hauntress named Claudia who plays the piano and a billiards room with a wall-size mural of mythological creatures such as dragons and unicorns. There are also caged white doves, life-size fabric dolls of Bill Clinton and George Bush on the stairwell landing (the hotel is a polling place on election days), Oriental antiques in the hallways, priceless Joseph Turner and Joshua Reynolds paintings, and rare political memorabilia that includes Nixon's letter of resignation and Ford's subsequent letter pardoning him.

Prix fixe dinners are served nightly in the dining room, where one of the world's largest examples of stained glass can be found. The colorful mural, first created for a villa in Spain, is nine feet high and stretches the length of the room.

Accommodations, divided among three floors, are sumptuous, with four-poster beds, potted palms, and elaborately trimmed wardrobes. They all have piped-in classical music, fresh flowers, candy, velvet quilts, and red carpets. The Lillie Coit Room, once a third-floor hideaway, has been combined with the de Young Room to form a small suite with windows that look out on the Golden Gate Bridge and Mount Tamalpais.

Named for a San Francisco socialite, the Crocker Room, on the second floor, is semicircular in shape as it is in a turret at the front of the home. Lace curtains hang at the tall windows, a large mirror is framed in gold leaf, there's a brass queen-size bed, mirrored armoire, antique sideboard, and the sofa is draped with a fringed, fuzzy, leopard print blanket.

Breakfast is served in a side dining room. Fresh coffee ground in an antique grinder, cereal, fruit, crumpets, eggs, English sausage, and potatoes are on the wide-ranging menu.

The west wing (formerly Hermitage House) has a different flavor. On the first floor there's a living room with sofas, a grand piano, a table set for chess, and cherublike pigs floating in a sky of puffy clouds on the ceiling above. Upstairs, tasteful prints and fabrics grace most rooms with a French country decor. High coffered ceilings, mullioned windows, antiques, and flowers give this side of the hotel a European flavor. Most suites have fireplaces. This building also houses the Bufano Conference Center, the hotel's meeting space.

The Mark Hopkins Intercontinental

999 California Street
Number One Nob Hill
San Francisco, CA 94108
415-392-3434
800-327-0200
Fax: 415-421-3302
www.interconti.com

A 1920s landmark on the crest of Nob Hill

General manager: Sandor Stangl. **Accommodations:** 360 rooms, 30 suites. **Rates:** $230–$350 single, $260–$380 double, suites $475–$1,430. **Added:** 14% tax. **Payment:** Major credit cards. **Children:** Under age 19 free in room with parent. **Pets:** Not allowed. **Smoking:** Nonsmoking rooms available.

➤ **The Top of the Mark is obligatory on every San Francisco tourist's must-see list. As a result, the rooftop lounge is crammed every night with imbibers trying to catch a glimpse of the breathtaking views. Afternoon tea is served here during the week.**

In the devastating earthquake and fire of 1906, the fabulous Mark Hopkins mansion at the top of Nob Hill burned to the ground. The more modest structure that followed was moved in 1925 by a mining engineer, George D. Smith, who then began building the luxury hotel that stands today.

The 19-story Mark Hopkins, a combination of French château and Spanish Renaissance architecture, has been a world-famed city landmark since it opened in 1926 and was proclaimed "perfect, flawless." Ownership has changed several times (in early 1989 it was acquired by a Japanese firm), but its traditional style and quality of service remain. A major renovation updated the tired lobby, restaurant, and all the guest rooms and suites, so the hotel is again a place of grandeur, with marble floors and Persian carpets in the light-filled lobby. Off the bustling lobby is the Nob Hill Terrace, where cocktails and light meals are served under a Tiffany-style skylight.

Because the hotel comprises a central tower and two wings, every room has a view of San Francisco Bay and the city skyline. Even the lowest rooms, on the second floor, overlook machinery-screening flower boxes to the city below. The public spaces are grand and gilded, befitting a hotel of such prestige.

In the hotel restaurant, the chef prepares creative contemporary cuisine. Among his specialties are sautéed escalope of foie gras with lentils, apple purée and olive oil and roast loin of lamb in a fresh herb coulis. The herbs come from what is probably the most expensive herb garden in the world: a little plot of land the hotel owns on nearby Mason Street, valued at $4,000 a square foot. The wine list includes labels from thirty-four out of forty-one wine-producing states.

The guest rooms have been redone in neoclassic style, with color schemes of gray or khaki and gold. The quilted chintz bedspreads, thick carpeting, and damask wall coverings were all designed for the hotel. The nightstands have tortuma tops made with crushed South American gourds in black resin. Televisions and mini-bars are encased in cherrywood armoires.

The best of the preferred accommodations are the corner terrace suites. Each features an enclosed solarium with a close-up of the hotel's elaborate architectural ornamentation and the spectacular panorama beyond. Each suite has three phones, a desk, and a white marble bath with pedestal sink, hair dryer, oversize towels, robes, and assorted toiletries.

The presence of groups (the hotel has a conference capacity of 750) can at times detract from the hotel's appeal to the leisure traveler, but the concierge will handle most individual requests. An additional level of service, Guest Relations, provides for special needs — interpreters, VIPs, and group assistance.

The Maxwell Hotel

386 Geary Street
San Francisco, California 94102
415-986-2000
888-SF-4-MAXX
Fax: 415-397-2447
www.maxwellhotel.com

> **A hotel with art deco flair in the heart of the city's shopping district**

General manager: Ingrid Summerfield. **Accommodations:** 151 rooms and 2 suites. **Rates:** $119–$215. **Added:** 14% tax. **Payment:** Major credit cards. **Children:** Free in room with parent. **Pets:** Not allowed. **Smoking:** Nonsmoking rooms available.

➤ **The Joie de Vivre hotel group — to which the Maxwell belongs — produces useful flyers called *Finding the Joy of Life in San Francisco*. They offer guests insiders' suggestions on everything from restaurants to art galleries to romantic excursions throughout the city.**

A statue of a tired shopper, complete with shopping bags, sits at the entrance to the Maxwell Hotel. The hotel was conceived by Joie de Vivre hotelier Chip Conley as a lodging that would cater to visitors who came to the Union Square area for the theater or to go shopping. In fact, the Maxwell has what no other Joie de Vivre hotel has — "The Shopologist" — a newsletter geared to the serious shopper. But the Maxwell is really a hotel for anyone who likes stylized decor and a convenient location.

The hotel, formerly known as the Raphael, was originally constructed in 1908. Joie de Vivre hotels purchased the property in the mid-1990s, renovated it, imbued it with its own unique character — a trait that all Joie de Vivre hotels have in common — and launched it with its new look and name in 1996.

The Maxwell's personality is immediately evident as you enter the lobby. The registration desk is draped in red velvet, sofas are covered in red, black, and olive velveteen, and railings have art deco designs. Across the hall in Max's on the Square, an eatery specializing in New York–style fare, booths are upholstered with palm fabrics and the deep burgundy ceilings are painted with art deco motifs. Toulouse Lautrec and Edward Hopper prints line the hallways, and even the elevator has an attitude, with walls padded in red velvet and dotted with leopard-print buttons.

Upstairs the guest rooms are equally distinctive, featuring paisley bedspreads, red and gold curtains with velvet tie backs, green carpeting, textured wall coverings, and reproduction furniture. Standard rooms are on the small side but have in-room movies, air conditioning, writing desks, irons and ironing boards, and two telephones (one in the bath) with voice mail and data ports. Robes can be requested.

Corner rooms are a popular choice. They have canopy beds, windows on two sides, and larger baths. Deluxe king rooms have make up vanities in the room with sinks. Junior suites have double or queen-size sleeper sofas in their living rooms. The Grand Terrace Penthouse has a bedroom with a king-size bed, living/dining room with a stereo system, kitchenette, two full baths, and a rooftop terrace overlooking downtown.

The Maxwell's multilingual staff provides concierge and business services. The daily newspaper is complimentary, and guests have privileges at a fitness center several blocks away.

The Pan Pacific Hotel

500 Post Street
San Francisco, CA 94102
415-771-8600
800-533-6465
Fax: 415-398-0267
www.panpac.com

A contemporary hotel of cool elegance

Managing director: Volker Ulrich. **Accommodations:** 311 rooms, 19 suites. **Rates:** $300–$400 single or double, $25 each additional person, suites $390–$1,700. **Added:** 14% tax. **Payment:** Major credit cards. **Children:** Free in room with parent. **Pets:** Small pets allowed by arrangement; additional $25 charge. **Smoking:** 13 nonsmoking floors.

➤ **The hotel is noted for its impeccable service, a continuation of the tradition established by the Portman Hotel when it opened in 1987.**

The Pan Pacific rises 21 stories above the corner of Post and Mason streets, a block west of Union Square. Famed for its elegant, contemporary style, the hotel was designed by architect John Portman, who is known for introducing the open atrium to large convention hotels. This is a smaller, more opulent version of the Portman trademark.

In the porte-cochere you are met by a white-gloved attendant who welcomes you effusively and whisks your car away. Inside, on the third-floor lobby level, a 17-story glass and brass atrium soars above a dazzling array of lights and the focal point of the lobby area — a wonderful Elbert Weinberg fountain sculpture of women dancing called Joie de Danse. Sitting areas atop Oriental carpets on either side of the sculpture provide intimate gathering spots in the otherwise vast atrium.

Nearby the Pacific restaurant offers French-accented California cuisine. Representing the French side of things, the pastry chef once worked for Prince Ranier. Fittingly, Chocolate Napoleon is one of his specialties. Mustard roasted rabbit and filet of salmon with Niçoise-style salad are just some of the main courses offered. Room service also features dishes from the restaurant's menu.

The floor below the entry level has an executive conference center, the only one like it in downtown San Francisco, containing four conference suites and a dining room. There's a large ballroom on the second floor.

Each room has a personal valet call button that summons a valet to unpack luggage, press clothing, shine shoes, draw a bath, or bring fresh ice. The valet can even bring exercise equipment if you want to work out in the privacy of your own room. The guest rooms include sixteen Pacific Suites and three specialty suites: The Penthouse, The Olympic, and The California. The Penthouse occupies 3,000 square feet on the 21st floor. It has two bedrooms with canopy beds, two baths (and a huge whirlpool tub), powder room, living room with working fireplace, dining room, study, access to an open-air terrace, valet's room, and pantry.

Standard guest rooms, which have a contemporary Oriental look, are decorated in gray on gray with accents of pale mauve, reminders of the sea fog that swirls through this coastal city's streets. Lavish Portuguese marble in the baths mirror the colors of the bedroom. Rooms have two TVs (one in the bath), phones with voice mail, Neutrogena toiletries, makeup mirrors, hair dryers, and terry robes.

There is an on-site fitness facility with cardiovascular and weight-training equipment, or you can arrange to use a larger health club nearby. The check-out system is flexible, and the hotel will provide in-city transportation in a Rolls-Royce. Other hotel services include nightly turndown and a foreign currency exchange.

Petite Auberge

863 Bush Street
San Francisco, CA 94108
415-928-6000
800-365-3004
Fax: 415-775-5717

| **A small city hotel with country charm** |

Manager: Brian Larsen. **Accommodations:** 25 rooms, 1 suite. **Rates:** $125–$165 single or double, $15 additional person, suite $245. **Included:** Full breakfast and afternoon tea. **Added:** 14% tax. **Payment:** Major credit cards. **Children:** Under age 2 free in room with parent. **Pets:** Not allowed. **Smoking:** Not allowed.

➤ **The inn has a quiet breakfast area where guests have their juice, cereals, egg dish, croissants, and coffee at round tables, viewing a little garden full of well-tended shrubs and delicate ferns.**

A French country inn in the heart of San Francisco, between Nob Hill and Union Square, Petite Auberge offers the best of both romantic worlds. It has flower-filled window boxes on every floor, and French and American flags fly over a green awning.

Inside the narrow five-story hotel, light and breezy pastels, floral fabrics, comfortable antiques, and French landscapes set the tone. The registration desk is just inside the front beveled glass doors, but the gathering place for guests is below stairs, where couches are pulled up to the fireplace, daily newspapers lie on the tables, and afternoon tea is served.

The guest rooms line pale cream halls with paneled wainscoting. The rooms on the first floor tend to be dark; those above are more attractive. They vary in size and are decorated individually, but all carry through the French country theme with striped and flowered wallpapers, pastel comforters, muslin curtains, handmade pillows, and fresh flowers and fruit. Most have gas fireplaces.

Every room has a teddy bear, one of the signature touches in all Four Sisters Inns. The company, which owns a collection of inns, was begun by Roger and Sally Post in Pacific Grove, when they opened their own 19th-century home to guests. The Posts' four daughters helped make it a family venture and gave the innkeeping company its name. The sisters are still involved in the operation of the inns. Sally Post, who decorates with flair, worked with other designers to create inns modeled on those in Europe. Each inn has bits of whimsy. At Petite Auberge they include an antique carousel horse by the front door, floppy-eared ceramic rabbits, and the ubiquitous bears, which may be purchased.

The staff at Petite Auberge is helpful in arranging for dinner reservations or tickets to the symphony or other events. Valet parking is available.

If you're looking for flowery charm, downtown convenience, and warm hospitality, this little inn is an excellent choice.

Prescott Hotel

545 Post Street
San Francisco, CA 94102
415-563-0303
800-283-7322
Fax: 415-563-6831
www.prescotthotel.com

A sophisticated hotel with an urban mood

Manager: Jim McPatlian. **Accommodations:** 166 rooms, including 34 suites. **Rates:** $195–$245 single or double, suites $245–$1,200. **Added:** 14% tax. **Payment:** Major credit cards. **Children:** Welcome. **Pets:** Not allowed. **Smoking:** Nonsmoking rooms available.

➤ **When the hotel opened in 1990, its restaurant, Postrio, earned immediate raves. Lavish bouquets, Robert Rauschenberg paintings, and hand-blown light fixtures hung with copper spirals create a bright and whimsical setting for the outstanding California cuisine.**

Here's another boutique hotel with the winning Kimpton Group combination: small but attractive rooms, reasonable rates, a well-trained and responsive staff, and a top-quality restaurant. Curved copper awnings mark the entrance to the hotel, which is close to Union Square. Inside you'll find a quiet sitting area with couches and wingback chairs in the lobby and curving staircases leading to the mezzanine meeting rooms and guest rooms above.

The smartly appointed rooms, more elaborate than the other Kimpton hotels, have hair dryers, robes, and Neutrogena toiletries in the modern, well-lighted baths. Some baths have Japanese soaking tubs, others have Jacuzzis. CD players, fax machines, and two-line phones in all the rooms appeal to frequent business travelers. The compact suites, with sleeper sofas in their living rooms, make efficient use of the space and are more like urban apartments than hotel lodgings.

On the Club Level (the fourth through seventh floors), guests have private check-in as well as their own concierge and a lounge where appetizers — catered by the Prescott's restaurant, Postrio — are served in the evenings along with cocktails. A complimentary buffet breakfast that includes items such as pecan muffins, pancakes, omelettes, coffee, and Mexican quiche is also provided, along with the morning papers.

The Mendocino Penthouse is the Prescott's premier accommodation. With hardwood floors, a grand piano, a dining table that seats ten, a fireplace in the bedroom, a top-of-the-line stereo system in the living room, and a private deck with a Jacuzzi, it's like having your very own pied-à-terre in the city.

Room service at the Prescott is handled by Postrio. While pizza is a specialty, you won't go wrong ordering anything on the menu. If you prefer to dine in the restaurant rather than your room, be sure to reserve a dinner table when you make your room reservation — Postrio is usually booked weeks in advance, though a few tables are held for hotel guests.

For all hotel guests, there's complimentary coffee and tea in the mornings, and a wine and cheese reception in the afternoons by the large brick fireplace around the corner from the lobby. On Sunday evenings storytellers are featured.

The Queen Anne Hotel

1590 Sutter Street
San Francisco, California 94109
415-441-2828
800-227-3970
Fax: 415-775-5212
www.queenanne.com

A pleasant Victorian hotel near Japantown

General manager: Brad Seymore. **Accommodations:** 48 rooms and suites. **Rates:** $120–$175 single or double, additional person $10, suites $185–$395. **Included:** Continental breakfast and afternoon refreshments. **Added:** 14% tax. **Payment:** Major credit cards. **Children:** Age 12 and under free in room with parent. **Pets:** Not allowed. **Smoking:** Allowed in certain areas.

➤ **The Queen Anne fortunately managed to escape the devastating fire that ripped through the city after the 1906 earthquake. The fire was finally contained just three blocks from the property.**

It's hard to miss the handsome Queen Anne Hotel standing on a quiet corner of Sutter and Octavia streets. The structure, painted brightly in salmon, rose, white, and green — with flowering window boxes at street level — is both eye-catching and inviting. Inside the front door a friendly staff member welcomes you to this amiable small hotel.

The Queen Anne was built as a girl's school in 1890. Over the years it has housed everything from an exclusive gentlemen's club to a lodge for women run by the Episcopal diocese. Eventually the Queen Anne fell into disrepair and was boarded shut until it was renovated and opened as a 49-room hotel in 1981. The current owners, the Gokel family, assumed ownership in 1994.

The Queen Anne's parlor was originally a gymnasium. Now it's filled with elegant antiques. There are Victorian sofas trimmed in gold or carved with red velvet cushions. Red sateen drapes with gold tassels hang in the windows over lace sheers. An ornately carved sideboard holds a silver tea service, and a golden cherub graces the fireplace. Beyond is a smaller, slightly less formal sitting room, while a 19th-century potbelly stove, a safe dating to the women's lodge days, and an unusual wooden and stained glass phone booth — once a confessional — stand in the lobby.

You can take the panelled elevator to your room. (The elevator is outfitted with a velvet bench if you need to rest legs weary from negotiating San Francisco's hills.) Or you can climb the handsome central staircase, which is English oak on the first level and Spanish cedar on the upper levels. The wide hallways, which contain antiques including a bishop's throne and a Victorian pulpit, are bordered by original inlaid parquet floors. Mismatched doorknobs are representative of the various stages of the hotel's evolution.

The guest rooms, on the three upper floors, vary in size and shape. Decorated in wines, teals, and whites with English and American antiques and few wall adornments — they are less elaborate than the hotel's public spaces. They are equipped with brass and frosted glass reading lamps, telephones (one is in the bath), televisions, and hair dryers. Eight rooms have fireplaces.

A Continental breakfast is served each morning, and tea and sherry are offered in the evenings. The daily newspaper is complimentary, as is limousine service within the downtown area on weekday mornings. The restaurants of Japantown and Fillmore street are just a few blocks away.

The Ritz-Carlton San Francisco

600 Stockton Street
San Francisco, CA 94108
415-296-7465
800-241-3333
Fax: 415-291-0147
www.ritzcarlton.com

A luxury hotel in a historic building

General manager: Edward Mady. **Accommodations:** 292 rooms, 44 suites. **Rates:** Rooms start at $309, suites start at $450. **Added:** 14% tax. **Payment:** All major cards. **Children:** Free in room with parent. **Pets:** Not allowed. **Smoking:** Not allowed.

➤ **The hotel bustles with activity, as many functions take place at the Ritz, but the halls, padded in gray damask, are quiet.**

One of the city's best examples of neoclassical architecture is part of the Ritz-Carlton group of luxury hotels. Built in 1909 for the Metropolitan Life Insurance Company, the stately structure on Nob Hill was restored and reopened in 1991. Like the other Ritz-Carlton hotels, it offers sumptuous accommodations in a conservative setting. The staff dresses in navy or black, however, this being San Francisco, there's a lighthearted quality that keeps pretension at bay. Heavy, dark woods have been kept to a minimum.

Oriental rugs are spread on marble floors in the lobby, and crystal chandeliers are elegant but not ostentatious. The walls are adorned with museum-quality 18th- and 19th-century paintings, while a grandfather clock and china cupboard add a residential flavor. Across from the main entrance, afternoon tea is served in the lobby lounge — a Ritz-Carlton tradition.

One of the most appealing places in the imposing hotel is its sunny outdoor Terrace restaurant, with its fountain and umbrella tables. Roasted Tuscan baby chicken with braised Swiss chard and orzo, and grilled veal chops with eggplant fennel gratin, soft polenta, and sweet pepper compote are examples of the restaurant's contemporary Mediterranean cuisine. You may also dine in the more formal yet intimate and elegant Dining Room, where French-inspired dishes such as filet of beef with pancetta oysters are served and the wine list is lengthy.

Guest rooms are handsomely decorated in classic residential style, with rich wood furniture, botanical or hunt prints on the walls, and dashes of color. The marble bathrooms are lovely, down to the orchids on the counter and white eyelet shower curtains, though you may notice minor flaws such as no shelf in the oversize shower and only a single hook on the door. Amenities include bathrobes, irons and ironing boards, hair dryers, makeup mirrors, European toiletries, and scales.

Rooms and suites on the eighth and ninth floors are designated the Ritz-Carlton Club. Guests have the use of a concierge, a private lounge with a subdued atmosphere, and complimentary snacks and cocktails. All rooms have numerous useful features: remote control TVs (VCRs and a video library are available), stocked honor bars, clock radios, safes. Some have bay views, but if you prefer a quiet room, follow the example of frequent San Francisco visitors and request one on the courtyard side.

Services by the multilingual staff include twice-daily maid service, valet parking, a 24-hour concierge, child care, and newspaper delivery. Swimwear is available in the fitness center, where you'll find a swimming pool, whirlpool, sauna, and weight machines.

Sheehan Hotel

620 Sutter Street
San Francisco, CA 94102
415-775-6500
800-848-1529
Fax: 415-775-3271
sheehot@aol.com
www.sheehanhotel.com

> **A comfortable budget hotel
> in a great location**

Manager: Don Hayden. **Accommodations:** 65 rooms (several with shared bath). **Rates:** $109–$119 single, $129–$149 double, $20 additional person. **Included:** Continental breakfast. **Added:** 14% tax. **Payment:** Major credit cards. **Children:** Under 12 free in room with parent. **Pets:** Not allowed, with the exception of guide dogs. **Smoking:** Nonsmoking rooms available.

➤   **If you'd rather spend your money on San Francisco's wonderful restaurants than on fancy digs, this is a good choice. The location — just two blocks from Union Square — and the price are unbeatable.**

It's unusual to find clean, quiet lodgings for two in an excellent downtown San Francisco district for under $150 a night — especially when it includes breakfast. Not only are the Sheehan's room rates are a relative bargain, the staff is friendly, the hotel has a swimming pool, workout facilities, and a café where you can buy snacks, caffé latte, beer, wine, espresso, cappucino, and afternoon tea.

Admittedly, the amenities are basic. Most rooms are simple, with carpeting, a dresser, a closet, and, usually, a washbasin. All have remote cable TV, hair dryers, direct-dial phones, and clock radios. A few rooms are as well appointed as those in any good hotel. All the shared bathrooms are well maintained and clean and have several showers.

If you're traveling alone and want to spend the minimum, the least expensive room is decent, if small. The most expensive accommodations are larger and have a private bath. Breakfast is usually juice, coffee or tea, and homemade scones, muffins, or brown soda bread. Cereal and hot breakfasts are available upon request, for an additional fee.

The swimming pool, the largest hotel pool in the city, dates from the days when this was a YWCA, a favored lodging for many young women in San Francisco. The new owners remodeled the building in 1988.

In the large, open lobby you'll hear a dozen languages spoken as world travelers come and go. At one side of the lobby is a box office that sells tickets to the Lorraine Hansberry Theater next door. Parking is available in a garage across the street for $18 per day.

There's nothing luxurious about the Sheehan, but the Ferdon brothers, while planning to keep their hotel in the budget range, have more improvements under way.

Sheraton Palace Hotel

2 New Montgomery Street
San Francisco, CA 94105
415-512-1111
800-325-3589
Fax: 415-543-0671
www.luxurycollection.com

> **A glamorous old hotel near the convention center**

General manager: Hans Altenhoff. **Accommodations:** 552 rooms, including 78 suites. **Rates:** Rates start at $350. **Added:** 14% tax. **Payment:** Major credit cards. **Children:** Under age 18 free in room with parent. **Pets:** Not allowed (though actress Sarah Bernhardt brought her pet tiger and parrot in 1887). **Smoking:** Nonsmoking rooms available.

➤ **Take a trip back to the Gilded Age in the Sheraton's palatial Garden Court. It's a beloved lunch, tea, and Sunday brunch spot for San Franciscans who remember the old days, as well as for awed newcomers.**

With names such as Winston Churchill, Franklin D. Roosevelt, Warren G. Harding (who died in the hotel's Presidential Suite while still in office in 1923), and Nikita Khrushchev appearing on the roster over the years, the Palace Hotel's guest list reads like a who's who of the twentieth century and with good reason. After a 27-month, $150 million restoration that returned the historic hotel to its former glory, the Palace opened again in April of 1991. The original Palace Hotel was built on the site in 1875 as the first hotel west of the Mississippi; it was designed to be the most luxurious lodging in the world at that time. The hotel's sturdy construction survived the 1906 earthquake, but guest Enrico Caruso's nerves didn't — running from his room in only a towel, he promised never to visit San Francisco again. The Palace, however, did not survive the subsequent fire that swept through the city immediately following the massive earthquake, so the hotel was rebuilt; it is the 1909 structure that remains today.

The glamour has returned to the aptly named Palace with the 1991 renovation, and the exquisite Garden Court is its centerpiece. the setting for many a grand banquet over the years (Woodrow Wilson gave two luncheons here in 1919 in celebration of the signing of the Treaty of Versailles), the Garden Court now serves classically inspired American cuisine, but it's the room's sheer beauty and grandeur that diners remember long after their meal. A magnificent leaded glass dome (over 80,000 pieces of glass were used) covers the famous restaurant, where ten chandeliers sparkle above the potted palms and marble columns. Linen-covered tables are set with purple irises complementing deep royal carpeting and adding to the overall lavish ambience.

Other public spaces in the Palace are also appealing, if not on such a grand scale as the Garden Court. A large mural of the Pied Piper of Hamelin by Maxfield Parrish hangs over the polished wood bar in the pub named for the painting. The painting was especially commissioned to commemorate the hotel's 1909 reopening and is currently valued at over two million dollars. From the Pied Piper Bar diners walk through a wine display to Maxfield's restaurant, named for the renowned artist. Maxfield's, a San Francisco-style grill, is a handsome eatery with green leather-backed chairs and booths and a lovely stained glass ceiling and tiled mosaic floor that were discovered in the 1991 restoration. Maxfield's features steaks, seafood, and pasta. Kyo-Ya, the Palace's third restaurant, is attractively appointed in the Japanese tradition and serves award-winning sushi and Japanese cuisine at both lunch and dinner.

Acres of marble, high ceilings, polished wood reproduction furniture, and numerous amenities characterize the classically elegant guest rooms and suites. Although some of the rooms are on the small side, there are hair dryers and magnifying mirrors in the marble and brass baths, irons and ironing boards, safes, refrigerators, movies, robes, and hookups for personal computers. Overnight valet service, nightly turndown, and 24-hour room service are offered. Business travelers like the telephones with custom message, conference call, voice mail, and call waiting features.

Recent additions to the hotel include a conference area and business center, a health spa, and a sunny, skylighted swimming pool pleasantly surrounded by striped chaises and glass tables. The hotel's location is convenient for both business and pleasure. It's adjacent to the financial district and within walking distance of Moscone Center and the Embarcadero Center. Theaters and shops are nearby.

The Sherman House

2160 Green Street
San Francisco, CA 94123
415-563-3600
800-424-5777
Fax: 415-563-1882
tshrez@mhotelgroup.com
www.theshermanhouse.com

An elegant mansion offering distinctive service and fine views of the bay

Owner: Manou Mobedshahi. **Accommodations:** 8 rooms, 6 suites. **Rates:** $360–$445 single or double, suites $675–$850. **Added:** 14% tax. **Payment:** Major credit cards. **Children:** Free in room with parent. **Pets:** Not allowed. **Smoking:** Not allowed.

➤ **In the Music Room, where finches trill in a birdcage that is a miniature of Château Chenonceau in France, it's easy to imagine Paderewski playing the grand piano in the corner, as he did in years past.**

This intimate, exclusive hostelry in one of the city's most fashionable districts is an 1876 French-Italianate mansion. Once the home of Leander Sherman, founder of the Sherman Clay Music Company, it is now a princely enclave catering to a discriminating clientele. The rich and famous find it a haven, as do those looking for service far above the ordinary. Manou Mobedshahi, an Iranian economist turned San Francisco entrepreneur, bought the historic landmark in 1981 and with his wife, an art preservationist, carefully restored the house and its formal gardens.

The gallery above the Music Room provides a pleasant sitting area, with cushioned seats at five bay windows, a fireplace, and French provincial armchairs and sofa.

The guest rooms are in the main house and former carriage house. One of the suites has its own garden with a deck and arbor. Furnishings in all rooms are antique or custom-made. Hand-loomed carpets, Coromandel screens, Belgian tapestries, marble fireplaces, brass fixtures, crystal chandeliers, and original art fill the interiors, planned by the late great designer William Gaylord. Most rooms adhere to a French Second Empire theme, popular in Leander Sherman's day, with a few in a Biedermeier or Jacobean motif. All have a sense of solidity and permanence.

Some rooms have sweeping views of the bay, Golden Gate Bridge, and Alcatraz. The Garden Suite, set among the multilevel lawns and cobblestone pathways, is the largest and has the most contemporary decor. It has a spacious living room with a free-standing fireplace, lattice walls, slate floors, and wide windows overlooking shrubs and flowers, a gazebo, and a pond. Hollow-core rattan wraps the four-poster bed. The suites upstairs in the carriage house are equally light and bright. The top-floor suite features a sunken living room with French doors to a balcony overlooking the bay.

In the main house, the Biedermeier Suite, with its window seat invitingly set with plump pillows in a bay window offering glorious views of the Golden Gate Bridge, is a personal favorite. If you can tear your eyes away from the view, you'll find a cozy suite tastefully appointed in cranberries and golds with fringed velvet chairs, round ottomans, reading lamps, botanical prints, and a queen-size canopy bed draped in tapestry fabric. The Pacific Heights room, so named because it faces the fashionable neighborhood, has high ceilings, yellow-washed walls, and a marble fireplace. Heavy drapes separate the bedroom from the parlor, where an antique trunk doubles as a coffee table, and the tan leather sofa matches the bed's headboard. Amenities in all of the rooms include down comforters, dimmer light switches, thick fabric shades to keep out early daylight, and elegant black marble baths with a second telephone and plush white towels and robes.

Three meals a day are served in the intimate dining room, which is open to guests only. French cuisine with California accents is served. Custom meals can be designed for guests and served in the privacy of their suites for special occasions and, because of the inn's distinctive service and ambience, many guests do make the Sherman House their lodging of choice for important personal anniversaries.

Needless to say, the service and attention to detail at this hotel are impeccable. Whatever your special needs may be, the able staff at the Sherman House is more than willing to oblige. This is a lodging of polish, privilege, and ease.

Victorian Inn on the Park

301 Lyon Street
San Francisco, CA 94117
415-931-1830
800-435-1967
Fax: 415-931-1830
vicinn@aol.com
www.citysearch.com/sfo/victorianinn

A Queen Anne mansion overlooking Golden Gate Park

Innkeepers: Lisa and William Benau. **Accommodations:** 12 rooms and suites (all with private bath). **Rates:** $130–$350. **Included:** Expanded Continental breakfast. **Added:** 14% tax. **Minimum stay:** 2 nights on weekends. **Payment:** Major credit cards. **Children:** Welcome, additional $20 if third person in room. **Pets:** Not allowed. **Smoking:** Not allowed.

➤ **A cozy fire burns in the parlor's white tiled fireplace on foggy afternoons, and a game table with a backgammon set stands by the curved windows. A tapestry-covered fainting couch, baskets of flowers, fringed lamps, and a red settee make the parlor a place of comfort and charm.**

Directly across the street from the Panhandle of Golden Gate Park, in an area of noble Victorian homes, the hospitable Benaus welcome guests to this Queen Anne mansion. It was built in 1897 for Thomas Jefferson Clunie, a prominent lawyer and legislator, who piled on the gingerbread and fretwork and added an open belvedere tower. Only two homes in the city still boast such towers.

After the Clunies were gone, the green brick house underwent a steady stream of changes, going from a private residence to a haven for '60s flower children and rock bands to a rebirthing center. In the early 1980s, Shirley and Paul Weber took over and began a handsome restoration. Shirley's daughter and son-in-law now run the inn with casual, good-humored style.

Marble steps lead to a front door with stained glass side panels and a foyer beautifully paneled in mahogany. Up the carpeted stairs, past 19th-century opera posters, you come to six guest rooms on the second floor and four on the floor above. Each bedroom has special characteristics — a brass bed, a freestanding mirror, a fireplace, a sunken tub. Each has a phone, a decanter of sherry, and an honor basket filled with snacks. Television and a fax machine are available upon request.

Clunie, on the second floor, has a wine-colored velvet coverlet and complementing pillows, fringed lamps, and a fireplace. The Briar Rose has an antique bed and a Victorian bath complete with a marble washbasin, pull-chain toilet, and clawfoot tub.

On the top floor, the Belvedere has French doors that open onto the belvedere porch overlooking the bay and eucalyptus trees of the Panhandle. In this pleasant little room you can lie in the bathtub and watch flames flicker in the marble fireplace, their reflections dancing in stained glass. It connects with another room (Golden Hideaway) next door to form a suite, if desired. Victorian replica wallpaper with an iris motif covers the walls in Iris, and there's a queen brass bed.

The rooms on the garden level, below the main floor, face the sidewalk and passersby through curved, lace-curtained windows. One large room, which has a brass bed and a working fireplace of ceramic tile, combines both antique and contemporary furnishings.

The inn's location is ideal for jogging — it's both flat and scenic. You can run without interruption through the Panhandle and Golden Gate Park, all the way to the ocean. After your morning jog, you'll be served a breakfast of scones, croissants, and freshly baked poppyseed or strawberry bread, along with juice and platters of fresh fruits and cheeses, in the bay-windowed dining room. It all comes with full pots of coffee or tea and the morning paper.

The innkeepers know the local restaurants and will steer you in the right direction for sightseeing, dining, and recreation. Limited parking is available. Two bus lines run within one or two blocks, leading downtown or to the Marina district, near the Golden Gate Bridge.

The Villa Florence Hotel

225 Powell Street
San Francisco, CA 94102
415-397-7700
800-243-5700
Fax: 415-397-1006
www.villaflorence.com

| **A boutique hotel with an Italian flavor** |

General manager: Sharon Tripp. **Accommodations:** 183 rooms, including 36 suites. **Rates:** $135–$250. **Added:** 14% tax. **Payment:** Major credit cards. **Children:** Under age 17 free in room with parent; $15 additional if rollaway is needed. **Pets:** Not allowed. **Smoking:** Nonsmoking rooms available.

➤ **Highlights in Kuleto's are the pastas, innovative salads, grilled fish and meats, and the excellent antipasto bar. A specialty is chicken breast stuffed with herbed ricotta in a roasted pepper butter sauce.**

The Villa Florence is one of the city's distinctive small hotels, offering stylish lodgings in a historic building to cost-conscious travelers. Bill Kimpton helped lead the way for these boutique hotels when he saw a niche to be filled and began renovating a few of San Francisco's rundown but usable structures.

Formerly the Manx Hotel, built in 1916, the Villa Florence was remodeled with an Italian Renaissance theme and opened as one of the Kimpton Group hotels in 1986. In the busy lobby are a marble fireplace and a gauzy mural depicting 16th-century Florence. Indirect lighting on the marble columns highlights ceiling detail.

Separated from the lobby by etched glass walls is Kuleto's Restaurant, which is known for its Italian food with a California perspective. Baked goods and desserts such as pumpkin tarts and rich chocolate decadence on raspberry sauce are made daily on the premises. The restaurant's ambience combines an aura of old San Francisco with Italian vitality. Dark wood, warm lighting, and strings of peppers, herbs, sausages and garlic hanging above the bar add to the atmosphere. Ficus trees grow to the ceiling under three stained glass skylights in the light and airy dining section.

Guest rooms, which include junior and deluxe suites, have an upscale look, with fine fabrics, wooden blinds, and painted headboards. All include honor bars, concealed televisions, coffee makers, hair dryers, robes, direct-dial phones with long cords, and soundproof walls and windows. Desk space is on the skimpy side

— adequate for writing postcards. Some bathrooms are very small. Much roomier are those in the junior suites; these suites also have sitting areas, though not divided rooms. The deluxe suites have two rooms.

The hotel offers morning and evening room service, complimentary limousine service to the financial district, and same-day laundry and valet service. There are three meeting rooms and a full range of audiovisual equipment. Room keys are coded for security.

Villa Florence is just south of Union Square on the main cable car line, not a poor location but highly touristed, with many trinket shops and hordes of people.

The Westin St. Francis

335 Powell Street
San Francisco, CA 94012
415-397-7000
800-WESTIN-1
Fax: 415-774-0124
www.westin.com

A historic hotel on Union Square

Managing Director: Mike Cassidy. **Accommodations:** 1,192 rooms and suites. **Rates:** $219–$379 single or double; suites $450–$2,550. **Added:** 14% tax. **Payment:** Major credit cards. **Children:** Under age 18 free in room with parent. **Pets:** Small, well-trained dogs allowed. **Smoking:** Nonsmoking rooms available.

➤ **The St. Francis has the cleanest coins in town. The hotel possesses a money-laundering machine that was brought to the hotel in the late 1930s**

by a general manager in order to keep dirty coins from soiling ladies' white gloves.

The St. Francis has been a landmark on Union Square since it first opened in 1904. The interior had to be redone following the fire that swept through the city immediately after the great earthquake of 1906. The hotel reopened in 1907, along with a third wing that was added during the renovation. In 1913 a fourth wing was built onto what is now considered the historic section of the hotel, and a 32-story tower was constructed behind the main hotel in the early 1970s, bringing the total number of rooms to 1,192 — making the St. Francis one of the largest hotels in the city.

The St. Francis certainly has its share of history. Every President since Taft has visited the hotel, as have dignitaries such as Queen Elizabeth, two Japanese emperors, and King Juan Carlos of Spain. It is said that a strike by the hotel's waitstaff may have swayed the 1916 presidential election, and President Gerald Ford successfully evaded a second assassination attempt while leaving the hotel.

Because of the hotel's size and location, its lobby is almost always buzzing with activity. Here the walls have hand-painted murals, and chandeliers dripping with crystal beads hang from the high ceilings, while an ornately carved rosewood grandfather clock, which has been holding court in the lobby since the hotel's reopening in 1907, stands as a reminder of an earlier era. Mirrored columns shield sofas arranged in intimate groups to provide a quiet respite from the bustle beyond.

Down the hall, the Compass Rose is grand with marble columns topped with gold leaf, carved wooden ceilings and Oriental screens. Evocative of a slower time, it is the spot to linger over champagne and caviar. This spectacular room also serves lunch (try the Nordic toast — smoked salmon on crispy toast with honey Dijon sauce accompanied by Sonoma greens). Afternoon tea is served daily, followed by an evening tasting menu.

Other dining choices at the hotel include the St. Francis Café, where you can get everything from pasta to prime rib for dinner, and homemade pastries and muffins are the specialty at breakfast. Dewey's has all-you-can-eat lunch buffets, a sports bar, and a good beer selection.

Guest rooms in the main section of the hotel have sleigh beds, writing desks, armoires, end tables, and small crystal chandeliers. The small baths have marble vanities and Caswell and Massey toiletries. Glass elevators, with views of the city and bay, transport guests to their rooms in the tower. In teals, beiges, and salmons, with satiny fabrics, the tower rooms have an Oriental flavor. They have marble-topped honor bars and their baths, which are larger than those in the main building, have extra amenities such as hair dryers, safes, irons and ironing boards.

With the Westin Kids Club the youngest members of your family will be treated like special guests, with their own room registration card, a sports bottle with free refills, maps of the hotel and San Francisco, coloring books, and crayons. In-room refreshment centers are stocked with kid favorites, and the restaurants and room service have special children's menus. The hotel's fitness room is small but adequate for light workouts. More extensive facilities are available at a nearby health club.

With almost 1,200 rooms the hotel naturally caters to groups, and there is a business center with secretarial services on the property. Other services include a concierge, valet parking, an on-site florist, foreign currency exchange, a barber and beauty salon, and menus in Braille.

Although the St. Francis tends to be group-oriented, there is still much to draw the leisure traveler. The hotel's Union Square location means that Macy's, Neiman Marcus, Saks Fifth Avenue, Tiffany's, and Nordstrom's, among others, are just steps away, as is the cable car line. The kid-friendly programs offered by the hotel also make it an appealing choice for families.

The White Swan Inn

845 Bush Street
San Francisco, CA 94108
415-775-1755
800-999-9570
Fax: 415-775-5717
www.foursisters.com

| **An English garden theme in a small city hotel** |

Innkeeper: Brian Larsen. **Accommodations:** 23 rooms, 3 suites. **Rates:** $145–$165, single or double; suites $195–$250. **Included:** Full breakfast and afternoon refreshments. **Added:** 14% tax. **Payment:** Major credit cards. **Children:** Over age 5; additional $15 if third person in room. **Pets:** Not allowed. **Smoking:** Not allowed.

Once this four-story hotel with a marble facade and bay windows was the Hotel Louise, built after the great earthquake of 1906. Renovated in 1986, it now provides a tranquil downtown retreat from the busy city. This is one of the more expensive of the Four Sisters inns and has the most amenities.

Beveled glass doors open to a large reception area with granite floors, an antique carousel horse, English art, and the Four Sisters' signature teddy bears. Downstairs is the guests' lounge, where breakfast and a full afternoon tea, with scones, cheeses, fondues, and other hearty snacks are served. In the parlor and library are inviting chairs before the granite fireplace, shelves full of books, and a standing world globe — a peaceful setting with a manor house motif.

There's a terrace outside the dining room shaded by an avocado tree. From there, a passageway leads to a small patio with a few tables and chairs, potted plants, and a barbecue. The White Swan has a conference room that can accommodate up to thirty people. The hotel will also do catering upon request.

The guest rooms all have wet bars, a television, fireplaces, and phones. Four-poster beds, floral wallpapers, antique reproductions, and books in the rooms lend a residential ambience. The baths are modern, with basins set in granite counters, but contain some original tiles. The Ashleigh Suite, the hotel's largest, has a fireplace in the bedroom as well as in the living room. A needlepoint bench sits at the foot of the canopy bed, which is draped in floral fabric. In the living room, the tapestry print sofa pulls out to a bed, and the window seat looks out onto Bush Street.

Valet parking is available, and the front desk provides concierge services, booking restaurant tables and tickets to events. A few of the hotel's special services are one-day laundry and pressing, complimentary cookies and fruit all day, business equipment, and complimentary wine and roses in every guest room. On Thursday evenings the White Swan holds wine tastings.

San Jose

Hotel De Anza

233 W. Santa Clara Street
San Jose, CA 95113
408-286-1000
800-843-3700
Fax: 408-286-2087
getinfo@hoteldeanza.com
www.hoteldeanza.com

> **An updated historic hotel in Silicon Valley**

General manager: Lori Kohler. **Accommodations:** 94 rooms, 6 suites. **Rates:** $175–$299 single or double, $20 additional person (special packages available), penthouse suite $1,350. **Added:** 10% tax. **Payment:** Major credit cards. **Children:** Under age 18 free with parent. **Pets:** Not allowed. **Smoking:** Allowed on one floor only.

➤ **Business is the mainstay on weekdays, but romance takes over on weekends at the De Anza. With the Remember the Romance package you'll receive champagne, a red rose, dinner for two at La Pastaia, chocolates, a night in a standard room or suite, and a generous breakfast.**

Originally opened in the 1930s, this art deco landmark fell into decay. Restored and reopened in 1990, the De Anza again offers fine accommodations with a sophisticated flavor. This architectural classic, a few blocks from the Convention Center, the Center for the Performing Arts, and the Civic Arena, is a part of San Jose's revitalized downtown area.

You won't find resort amenities here — there's no pool, the health club is tiny and seldom used, and the views are mainly of freeways and buildings. But the distinctive character and in-room conveniences make up for any deficiencies. In keeping with its Silicon Valley location, state-of-the-art technology is provided. Each room has two TVs, a VCR (movies are complimentary), three phones, a two-line desk phone with fax and computer capabilities, and voice mail message service.

Meeting more leisurely needs are honor bars, ice machines on every floor, terrycloth robes, turndown service, and an unusual offering called Raid Our Pantry. Your room key opens a fully stocked bar on the second floor where you can help yourself to drinks and snacks (salads, fruits, deli sandwiches) at any time. Most of the rooms are unusually large for a city hotel and have king-size beds. In a small suite you'll find a foyer with wet bar, a cozy sitting area with puffy cushions on the couch, and a green granite and tiled bath with a whirlpool tub. Most elaborate is the penthouse suite, an apartment with two rooftop patios. Furnished in an Egyptian theme, it has a black tiled fireplace, a glass-topped bar, and a luxurious bathroom.

Off the lobby on the main floor are La Pastaia, a restaurant noted for its Italian food, and The Hedley Club lounge. The lounge, named for an architect who was influential in South Bay building design, is an inviting spot to enjoy cocktails and listen to opera on Sundays. The Hedley Club's painted ceiling is one of the few pieces remaining from the original hotel.

The De Anza has several meeting rooms and an enclosed outdoor patio, The Patio Court Terrace.

Saratoga

The Inn at Saratoga

20645 Fourth Street
Saratoga, CA 95070
408-867-5020
800-543-5020 in California
800-338-5020 in U.S.
Fax: 408-741-0981
info@innatsaratoga.com
www.innatsaratoga.com

An inn of contemporary comfort in the Santa Cruz Mountains

Manager: Jack Hickling. **Accommodations:** 39 rooms, 7 suites. **Rates:** $185–$275 single or double, suites $445–$485. **Added:** 10% tax. **Included:** Continental breakfast. **Payment:** Major credit cards. **Children:** Under 12 free in room with parent. **Pets:** Not allowed. **Smoking:** Not allowed.

➤ **In this shady spot you feel miles from anything remotely resembling a city. Yet you're just a few steps from Saratoga's main street, Big Basin Way, which is lined with excellent restaurants, chic boutiques, and galleries.**

Saratoga is a special place. A hidden village tucked away among the redwoods on a hillside south of San Jose, Santa Clara, and Silicon Valley, Saratoga offers a retreat from high tech, an escape from high rise.

This historic resort area in the Santa Cruz Mountains first began to lure visitors in the 1860s because the waters of its hot springs were said to be as therapeutic as those in Saratoga, New York. For nearly fifty years the springs (long since abandoned) attracted city-weary Bay Area residents for a few days of relaxation and rejuvenation.

Today, Saratoga has become a fashionable dining spot, with an array of award-winning restaurants, and it's a good base for exploring some of California's most interesting wineries. Outdoor enthusiasts enjoy Big Basin Redwoods State Park and its miles of hiking trails. Via Montalvo and Hakone Gardens invite visitors to stroll their manicured pathways.

When the Inn at Saratoga opened on the site of the old Toll Gate in 1987, it fit in well with this relaxing environment. Intended as a retreat for the executives of Silicon Valley, the inn offers quiet, privacy, proximity to fine dining, and rooms appointed to meet the needs of business travelers.

Nestled in a glen overlooking Saratoga Creek, the inn is surrounded by elm, sycamore, and eucalyptus trees and colorful gardens, giving it a sense of seclusion. All the guest rooms are spacious, with separate sitting areas, balconies, and views of Saratoga Creek and the gardens. The appointments include two phones, robes, double sinks, hair dryers, cable television, and honor bars.

The suites serve as midweek meeting sites for businesspeople as well as romantic weekend retreats. These elegant two- and three-room arrangements have separate living rooms with a wet bar, refrigerator, and a television with VCR. The bathrooms are large, with double whirlpool baths and — a nice touch — European towel warmers. Two suites are named for the actresses Olivia de Havilland and Joan Fontaine, sisters who grew up in Saratoga. These suites include formal dining rooms that can accommodate up to six people for private dining.

The Inn at Saratoga places a premium on personal service. A light breakfast is served in the lobby. Tea, complimentary wine, and hors d'oeuvres are set out every evening. The newspaper is delivered to your room and the inn offers nightly turndown service. Secretarial and valet service are available.

Like Saratoga itself, this inn offers a touch of tranquillity in a stressful world.

Sausalito

Casa Madrona Hotel

801 Bridgeway
Sausalito, CA 94965
415-332-0502
800-567-9524
Fax: 415-332-2537
www.casamadrona.com

> **A romantic inn with a bay view**

Proprietor: John Mays. **Accommodations:** 34 rooms (all with private bath). **Rates:** $188–$340 single or double. **Included:** Breakfast and afternoon wine and cheese. **Added:** 10% tax. **Minimum stay:** 2 nights on weekends during low seasons and 3 nights on weekends May through October. **Payment:** Major credit cards. **Children:** Under age 2 free in room with parent. **Pets:** Not allowed. **Smoking:** Not allowed.

➤ **During the day you can watch the boats come and go over the moody bay waters; at night the lights of the city sparkle against the horizon or are diffused by drifting fog.**

Few inns are as romantic in atmosphere and style as the lovely Casa Madrona. Terraced on a hillside above the chic town of Sausalito, just across the Golden Gate Bridge from San Francisco, the hotel offers comfortable accommodations, excellent food, and superb views. Every room has a view — sometimes breathtaking — of the harbor, San Francisco Bay, and the city, or the bridge and headlands. Brick paths and stairs separate the rooms (there are elevators, too), winding up the hill to a Victorian mansion, the oldest building in Sausalito.

Built in 1885 by William Barrett, a wealthy San Franciscan, the Italianate villa later became a boarding house, an inn, a '50s crash pad, and a fine country inn and restaurant. In the late 1970s, the now-historic landmark was purchased by John Mays, a lawyer with a vision. He renovated and expanded on the property, creating an exceptional hotel.

The retreats range from a Parisian artist's loft, complete with easel, paints, and brushes, to a tribute to Hollywood, which has a harbor view from the elevated canopy bed, epic movie prints, a neon flamingo, and classic films. Kathmandu is a regal room of paisley fabrics, huge cushions, and alcoves. It has a fireplace, a deck, and tub for two. A 19th-century English merchant would feel at home in Lord Ashley's Lookout, where he could keep an eye on the ships in the harbor from sunny bay windows in this oak-and-brass-filled room.

In the gardenlike Renoir Room an inviting window seat set with pillows is ideal for gazing at the sails in the bay below. Summer House, with wicker furniture, white oak walls, a high bed, and an array of books, is reminiscent of a New England vacation home. Ascot suite has an English tone and separate sitting room. Casa Cabana is southwestern in style with a crown canopy bed and marble fireplace. Salon Nouveau is fittingly art nouveau in decoration, and 1000 Cranes has a contemporary Oriental look.

The cottages are: Calico Cottage, cozy with a rocking chair by the fireplace; English Gate House, which has two bedrooms and a sun porch; and La Tonnelle, a little hideaway with a panoramic view. It has a tiled tub for two and a garden deck.

Rooms in the main house have period decor, with brass beds, flowered quilts, greenery, and wicker furniture. Perhaps most romantic is the soft blue Belle Vista Suite, two rooms divided by a partition. It has a tub for two near a window overlooking Angel Island and the San Francisco skyline.

In Mikayla, the hillside restaurant, you may eat indoors or on a deck with retractable glass walls and roof. A buffet breakfast of fruit, cheese, scones, and juice is served here. Dinner specialties are roasted Colorado lamb with toasted cumin oil, and grilled hamachi with bok choy, daikon sprouts, and barbecued cabbage cakes.

Casa Madrona also has a private Jacuzzi available to guests by reservation.

At press time, plans were under way to double the size of the hotel, so there may be an even greater variety of accommodations to choose from during your visit.

Hotel Sausalito

16 El Portal (at Bridgeway)
Sausalito, California 94965
415-332-0700
888-442-0700
Fax: 415-332-8788
hotelsaus@aol.com
www.hotelsausalito.com

| **A European-style hostelry in the heart of Sausalito** |

General manager: William Purdie. **Accommodations:** 14 rooms and 2 suites. **Rates:** $135–$270. **Included:** Continental breakfast. **Added:** 10% tax. **Payment:** Major credit cards. **Minimum stay:** 2 nights on weekends. **Children:** Free in room with parent. **Pets:** Not allowed. **Smoking:** Not allowed.

➤ **The ferry to San Francisco is just a few hundred yards from the hotel's front door. It's a scenic way to visit the city by the bay.**

When you see the words "Hotel Sausalito" impressed high up on the grand, mission revival–style building on a prominent corner in Sausalito, you immediately envision a large lobby bustling with people and activity. The hotel, built in 1915, does have a varied past. There are rumors it was once a bordello, and during the age of gangsters Baby Face Nelson was reputedly a frequent guest. Yet today the Hotel Sausalito is quite different. It's an intimate property with only sixteen guest rooms, perfectly suited for travelers seeking quiet luxury.

And there are no cavernous common rooms — no hustle or bustle. In fact, the lobby is quite diminutive, it's barely more than an entryway. But you'll be warmly greeted — possibly by a staff member with a foreign accent as the owner is originally from Glasgow. Scotsman William Purdie and his partners gave the hotel, which had been closed for a number of years, a facelift and opened it in its latest incarnation in 1996.

The tiny lobby is the only part of the hotel that remains on the first story. The rest of the ground floor is now filled with shops and restaurants that are completely separate from the lodgings. The guest rooms, off mustard-colored hallways lined with fine art reproductions, are on the second floor.

The light and airy rooms are handsome in soft pastels with iron beds, plentiful pillows, fine linens, large mirrors, armoires, and furniture painted to match the individual room's color scheme.

The air conditioning in each room is operated by remote control, as is the cable television, and telephones have voice mail and data ports. (Fax machines can be supplied upon request.) In the baths, glass mosaics frame the mirrors and skylights illuminate tiled showers.

Corner rooms have bay windows with puffy drawstring curtains. One room in a turret can connect with an adjoining room to form a suite. Another room overlooks a city park with a fountain and palm trees. Still another looks to Sausalito's marina and the headlands in the distance. A few rooms at the back of the hotel offer peeks of San Francisco (albeit over air conditioning units of the building next door).

If you wish to sit outside and read the morning paper, which is complimentary, there's a sun deck with a fountain, potted plants, and tables with fanciful wrought iron chairs. Guests are also given vouchers for coffee and pastries at a café on the street level.

The Inn Above Tide

30 El Portal
Sausalito, California 94965
415-332-9535
800-893-8433
Fax: 415-332-6714
inntide@ix.netcom.com
www.innabovetide.citysearch.com

A contemporary inn on the bay

General manager: Mark Davis Flaherty. **Accommodations:** 30 rooms and suites. **Rates:** $195–$265 single or double, additional person $15, suites $310–$485. **Included:** Continental breakfast and sunset wine and cheese reception. **Added:** 10% tax. **Minimum stay:** 2 nights on weekends and holidays. **Payment:** Major credit cards. **Children:** $15 for a rollaway bed. **Pets:** Not allowed. **Smoking:** Allowed in designated areas only.

➤ **The sun and sea flood this shingled, three-story property that was built as an apartment building in the 1960s but was converted to an inn in 1995.**

The Inn Above Tide could not be more aptly named — the waters of San Francisco bay gently lap below guest room balconies. Appropriately this is an inn that plays on its waterfront location fully — blue, white, and pale green room decor reflects and emphasizes the shimmering water and sky that lie just beyond each guest room's floor-to-ceiling windows. Fish motif bedspreads and fabric-covered headboards only add to the maritime mood.

Rooms at the inn are comfortable and contemporary with blond wood furnishings, overstuffed chairs, and binoculars for enjoying the view. Almost all of them have private terraces with wooden chairs for relaxing and glass panels that shield the wind but retain the view. Those rooms that don't have balconies have more floor space. About two thirds of the rooms have fireplaces, and baths have either Jacuzzis or oversized sunken tubs. All rooms have two-line phones with data ports, hair dryers, and makeup mirrors.

Vista Suite, with a king-size canopy bed, a sitting area in front of a rounded fireplace, and a wet bar, is the inn's largest. On a corner of the building, it looks out to Angel Island, Alcatraz, the Bay Bridge, and, of course, San Francisco.

On the second floor there's a shared common deck that gets afternoon sun. In good weather, a wine and cheese hour, featuring Napa and Sonoma vintages, is served here — otherwise the reception moves indoors to the drawing room overlooking the bay.

A Continental breakfast is delivered to your room each morning, along with the daily paper. Room service is available from a number of local restaurants, and although you'd be hard-pressed to find an eatery that has a better view than the one from your own balcony, many Sausalito restaurants are within easy walking distance.

Stinson Beach

Casa del Mar

P.O. Box 238
37 Belvedere Avenue
Stinson Beach, CA 94970
415-868-2124
800-552-2124
Fax: 415-868-2305
inn@stinsonbeach.com
www.stinsonbeach.com

> **A hillside villa near the shore**

Innkeeper: Rick Klein. **Accommodations:** 6 rooms (all with private bath). **Rates:** $140-$280. **Included:** Full breakfast. **Added:** 10% tax. **Minimum stay:** 2 nights on weekends. **Payment:** Major credit cards. **Children:** Age 6 and older welcome. Additional $20 if third person in the room. **Pets:** Not allowed. **Smoking:** Not allowed.

➤ **Meandering the rocky paths of Casa del Mar's extraordinary garden, with the sound of the surf in the background, is a special pleasure. Herbs and wisteria scent the air, while jacarandas, palm trees, cacti, and Oriental statues lend exotic appeal.**

Like a Mediterranean villa, this peach stucco home with a red tile roof rises above a blue sea and masses of flowers in a terraced garden. This hillside, though, is on the Pacific shore, in a village north of San Francisco. It's a 35-minute drive from the Golden Gate Bridge to Stinson Beach, which lies at the foot of Tamalpais State Park.

Casa del Mar is a block inland from the beach. Wooded trails extend from the back door up Mount Tamalpais, through meadows of wildflowers to wide ocean views. Rick Klein moved to the area in the mid-1980s, planning to settle down after a checkered background as a restaurateur, fisherman, treasure hunter, builder, and attorney. Gardening was to become his next passion, along with rebuilding the house he purchased and turning it into a bed-and-breakfast. His efforts have created an inn that is a work of art and a lovely sanctuary.

Light streams through many windows in the open, white interior, where Rick's collection of works by Marin County artists is displayed. Guests share two breakfast tables in the informal, sun-splashed dining area, getting acquainted as they feast on fresh fruit, granola, yogurt, pastries, and a main dish. The guest rooms, varied in size, are named for the hand-painted ceramic designs in the showers: Shell, Passion Flower, Hummingbird, and Heron. Each has a queen-size bed covered with a duvet, fine cotton linens, and a private balcony with a view of the woods or ocean.

The penthouse on the third floor contains an additional single bed. Decorated in blue and white, this skylighted room has a big bathroom with a two-person tub. The Garden Room, below the kitchen, has its own entrance and patio.

The softspoken, hospitable innkeeper has numerous suggestions for things to do during your visit. You're close to Point Reyes National Seashore, the giant redwoods in Muir Woods, and Audubon Canyon Ranch, where in spring you can watch herons nesting in the treetops. Stinson Beach has three miles of white sand to stroll.

Central Coast

Davenport
Soquel
Capitola
Gilroy
Santa Cruz
Aptos
Pacific Grove
Monterey
Pebble
Beach
Carmel Valley
Carmel
Big Sur
1
101
Cambria
Shell Beach
Arroyo Grande
Los Alamos
Ballard
Solvang
Montecito
Goleta
101
Ojai
Santa Barbara

Aptos
Apple Lane Inn, 118
Bayview Hotel, 120
Mangels House, 122
Arroyo Grande
Crystal Rose Inn, 124
Ballard
The Ballard Inn, 126
Big Sur
Deetjen's Big Sur Inn, 128
Post Ranch Inn, 130
Ventana Inn and Spa, 131
Cambria
Olallieberry Inn, 133
The Squibb House, 135
Capitola
Inn at Depot Hill, 137
Carmel
Cobblestone Inn, 139
Cypress Inn, 141
Happy Landing Inn, 143
Highlands Inn, 144
La Playa Hotel, 146
Mission Ranch, 148
Sundial Lodge, 149
Vagabond's House Inn, 151
Carmel Valley
Carmel Valley Ranch, 152
John Gardiner's Tennis Ranch, 154
Quail Lodge Resort and Golf Club, 156
Stonepine, 157
Davenport
Davenport Bed & Breakfast Inn, 159
Gilroy
Country Rose Inn Bed and Breakfast, 162
Goleta
Circle Bar B Guest Ranch, 163

Los Alamos
Union Hotel, 165
Victorian Mansion, 167
Montecito
Montecito Inn, 169
San Ysidro Ranch, 170
Monterey
The Jabberwock, 172
Monterey Plaza Hotel, 174
Old Monterey Inn, 176
Spindrift Inn, 178
Ojai
Ojai Valley Inn and Spa, 180
Pacific Grove
The Centrella, 182
Gatehouse Inn, 184
The Green Gables Inn, 185
The Martine Inn, 187
Seven Gables Inn, 189
Pebble Beach
The Inn at Spanish Bay, 191
The Lodge at Pebble Beach, 193
Santa Barbara
Four Seasons Biltmore, 195
The Glenborough Inn, 197
The Old Yacht Club Inn, 198
Secret Garden Inn and Cottages, 200
Simpson House Inn, 202
Villa Rosa, 204
Santa Cruz
The Babbling Brook Inn, 206
Shell Beach
The Cliffs at Shell Beach, 208
Solvang
The Alisal Guest Ranch, 209
Soquel
The Blue Spruce Inn, 211

Best Bed-and-Breakfasts

Aptos
Apple Lane Inn, 118
Mangels House, 122
Arroyo Grande
Crystal Rose Inn, 124
Cambria
Olallieberry Inn, 133
The Squibb House, 135
Davenport
Davenport Bed & Breakfast Inn, 159
Gilroy
Country Rose Inn Bed and Breakfast, 162
Monterey
The Jabberwock, 172
Pacific Grove
The Centrella, 182
Gatehouse Inn, 184
Santa Barbara
The Glenborough Inn, 197
Soquel
The Blue Spruce Inn, 211

Best Country Inns

Ballard
The Ballard Inn, 126
Los Alamos
Union Hotel, 165
Montecito
San Ysidro Ranch, 170

Best Family Favorites

Goleta
Circle Bar B Guest Ranch, 163

Best Inns by the Sea

Big Sur
Deetjen's Big Sur Inn, 128
Post Ranch Inn, 130
Ventana Inn and Spa, 131
Carmel
Highlands Inn, 144
Mission Ranch, 148
Monterey
Monterey Plaza Hotel, 174
Spindrift Inn, 178
Pacific Grove
The Green Gables Inn, 185
Seven Gables Inn, 189
Santa Barbara
Four Seasons Biltmore, 195
The Old Yacht Club Inn, 198
Shell Beach
The Cliffs at Shell Beach, 208

Best Intimate City Stops

Aptos
Bayview Hotel, 120
Carmel
Cobblestone Inn, 139
Cypress Inn, 141
La Playa Hotel, 146
Sundial Lodge, 149
Montecito
Montecito Inn, 169
Santa Barbara
Villa Rosa, 204

Best Resorts

Carmel Valley
Carmel Valley Ranch, 152
John Gardiner's Tennis Ranch, 154
Quail Lodge Resort and Golf Club, 156

Ojai
   Ojai Valley Inn and Spa, 180
Pebble Beach
   The Inn at Spanish Bay, 191
   The Lodge at Pebble Beach, 193
Solvang
   The Alisal Guest Ranch, 209

Best Romantic Hideaways

Capitola
   Inn at Depot Hill, 137
Carmel
   Happy Landing Inn, 143
   Vagabond's House Inn, 151
Los Alamos
   Victorian Mansion, 167
Monterey
   Old Monterey Inn, 176
Pacific Grove
   The Martine Inn, 187
Santa Barbara
   Secret Garden Inn and Cottages, 200

From **Santa Cruz** to **Santa Barbara,** the California coastline is a constant and changing panorama of ocean vistas. With the spectacular, 90-mile exception of Big Sur, the shore is less rugged here than in the northern part of the state. Numerous public parks along the way make broad sandy beaches and gentle waves easily accessible. Around the long crescent of Monterey Bay is some of the world's most celebrated scenery — wind-twisted cypress trees, hidden coves, and inviting towns with sophisticated shops and restaurants. World-class golf courses, grand estates, and a pine forest cover the southern peninsula to the resort town of **Carmel**.

South of quaint Carmel and the resorts and pastoral landscape of **Carmel Valley,** past the wooded bluffs of Point Lobos State Reserve, is **Big Sur.** Here Highway 1 winds through the western slopes of the Santa Lucia Mountains as they tilt toward the Pacific. Streams rush down ravines, tawny cliffs drop steeply to the sea, and spindrift plumes above waves that rush to break against jagged rocks far below. Under the glare of the sun, a silvery sea glints, occasionally turning a brilliant green in the eddies of a shallow cove.

The mountains move inland as you near San Simeon and **Cambria,** and the crumpled ridges soften to grassy rolling hills, green in winter and seared dry in summer. On a hill above San Simeon is the Hearst Castle, a state historic monument open to the public. The palatial estate is filled with fabulous antiques and art treasures.

Development crowds the shoreline as you continue south to **Shell Beach** and **Arroyo Grande,** then fades to miles of ranches and vineyards as the main highway travels inland toward the Santa Ynez valley.

The city of **Santa Barbara** lies beside the sea and climbs the steep slopes of the Santa Ynez Mountains, which form a dramatic backdrop to one of California's loveliest communities. The white walls of the city's Spanish Mission-style architecture gleam in the ever-present sun, palm trees wave in gentle breezes, and a civilized attitude prevails. Every visitor plans to tour the beautifully restored mission. Fewer see the county courthouse, but it's well worth a visit for its outstanding architecture, colorful tiles, and artwork reminiscent of old California.

Inland from Santa Barbara, near the Topatopa Mountains and Los Padres National Forest, are vineyards, sprawling horse ranches, and the small town of **Ojai**.

Aptos

Apple Lane Inn

6265 Soquel Drive
Aptos, CA 95003
831-475-6868
800-649-8988
Fax: 831-464-5790
ali@cruzio.com
www.applelaneinn.com

A 19th-century farmhouse
close to Santa Cruz

Innkeepers: Douglas and Diane Groom. **Accommodations:** 5 rooms. **Rates:** $90–$180 single or double, $25 additional person. **Included:** Full breakfast. **Added:** 10% tax. **Payment:** Major credit cards. **Children:** Welcome by arrangement; $25 additional if third person in room. **Pets:** Allowed by prior arrangement; additional $25. **Smoking:** Not allowed indoors.

➤ **After driving up the hillside lane from the highway, you park under the grape arbor and walk a brick path bordered by jade plants and rosemary to the front porch. Inside, the present day recedes; you've entered the Victorian era.**

Three acres of fields and gardens surround this Victorian farmhouse just south of Santa Cruz. The house was built in the 1870s, and though it's now close to a busy town and you can hear traffic in the distance, it retains the sense of seclusion and quiet you'd expect from a country home of decades past.

The Grooms are fourth-generation Californians, and their interest in preserving both their family's and their state's heritage is in evidence throughout their home. In the front parlor, velvet ties hold back the drapes, a player piano stands against the wall, a red settee faces the fireplace, a baby dress once worn by Diane's mother is framed over the mantel, and family photos adorn a nearby wall. Shelves filled with books on art and local history reach to the ceiling. A mantel clock chimes the hour. A bay window overlooks the garden, wisteria vines, and gazebo, where deer regularly pass at dusk.

The guest rooms are furnished with antiques, many of them Groom family heirlooms, and Diane makes sure there are at least a dozen fresh roses in each room. In Blossom, the gorgeous Chinese rug belonged to an ancestor of Diane's who was the first geology professor at Stanford — the rug originally lay on his office floor there. The 18th-century French canopy bed has a ring-patterned quilt, and the flowery bathroom is as big as the bedroom. It has a wicker lounge, a rocker, and a pink clawfoot tub with hand shower.

Uncle Chester's Room contains a heavy Spanish mahogany four-poster bed that has been in Douglas's family for more than 260 years. The silk-screened wallpaper with shell motifs and 22-carat gold leafing is handmade by Bradbury and Bradbury. The ornate pressed-tin ceiling is also handmade. The Pineapple Room is dominated by a four-poster pineapple bed and features a pineapple motif.

The attic suite, called Orchard, is kept light and airy by its vaulted ceilings. In the living room the wicker sofa is topped with lovely floral cushions and there's a writing desk under the eaves. A queen-size bed with mother-of-pearl inlay matches the washbasin that belonged to Diane's great-grandmother.

The inn's wine cellar has been turned into spacious guest room with a wine theme. There are wooden wine casks at the base of the stairs, wine bottles in racks, and a stained glass window depicts a wine press. Somewhat dark because it is in the basement, the suite does have extras such as a refrigerator, stereo, television, and coffee maker. With a queen as well as a twin bed and a round dining table for four, this is where families stay.

On the second-floor landing there's a sitting area with a telephone, modem, fax machine, a television, and a little refrigerator full of juices. Morning coffee is set out here for early risers to take back to their rooms. Breakfast, served in the dining room, includes fresh fruit, a pitcher of juice, homemade granola, Diane's blue-ribbon baked goods, and a hot dish with eggs from the inn's own chickens.

The inn is a quiet and relaxing place to stay. Santa Cruz is not far away, but if want a diversion closer to home, you can gather eggs from the Grooms' pedigree chickens; feed Rio, their horse; milk their cows, Bonnie and Skippy; or take a ride in the buggy.

Bayview Hotel

8041 Soquel Drive
Aptos, CA 95003
831-688-8654
800-422-9843
Fax: 831-688-5128
lodging@bayviewhotel.com
www.bayviewhotel.com

> **A historic hotel in the
> village center**

Innkeepers: Suzie Lankes and Dan Floyd. **Accommodations:** 11 Rooms and suites. **Rates:** $90–$160 single or double, $20 additional person. **Included:** Full breakfast. **Added:** 10% tax. **Payment:** Major credit cards. **Children:** Welcome. **Pets:** Not allowed. **Smoking:** Allowed outside only.

➤ **It is said that Jose Arano received the property on which he built the Bayview from his father-in-law, Don Rafael Castro, as payoff for Castro's high tab at Arano's grocery store.**

Just inland from the coast south of Santa Cruz, Aptos is a small town that grew up in the late 19th century around the lumber industry. For the century since, the white clapboard Bayview Hotel has been part of the town's history. Built in 1878 by Jose Arano, the eleven-room hotel is listed on the National Register of Historic Places. Unlike other historic hotels that have served as schools or hospitals at various times, the Bayview has always been a hostelry. Today it is owned by Suzie Lankes and Dan Floyd, who also run the charming Inn at Depot Hill in neighboring Capitola.

The Bayview's lobby is informal, as is the neighboring breakfast room, where a gourmet meal is served in the mornings. Guest rooms are located on the second and third floors of the hotel. They are furnished with antiques and have private baths, featherbeds, extra pillows, clock radios with alarms, bathrobes, and direct-dial telephones.

Some of the rooms are named for people who played a role in the Bayview's history — Arano for the first owner, Amelia for Arano's daughter who ran the hotel for many years, and Sprekels for the prominent family that helped settle Aptos. Arano, on the second floor, has wingback chairs and a queen-size bed that's original to the hotel. Amelia, at the front of the building, is a small, sunny room with ivory balloon shades, a wicker rocker, and white iron bed topped with a floral coverlet and Battenburg lace pillow shams.

Sprekels is more masculine. Loma Prieta, pleasant in blue and white, has a cozy rocker and two queen-size beds. Redwood is a two-room suite; there's an Eastlake bed with a matching dresser in the bedroom, and a sofa bed and television in the living room.

The third floor was gutted and renovated after the 1989 Loma Prieta earthquake, so rooms there have larger and more modern baths. They also have hand-painted designs such as ivy and floral bouquets adorning their walls. Seacliff and Rio Del Mar are deluxe rooms with fireplaces, TV/VCRs, and giant tubs for two set in marble tile. Vintage photographs of the area line the hallway walls, and both the second and third floors have a table set with sherry and fruit, as well as a bookcase holding a reading library for guests to enjoy.

The original porches of the Bayview were enclosed in the 1940s and now house a restaurant serving California cuisine for lunch and dinner five days a week. Called the White Magnolia for the massive tree that fronts the hotel, it offers special sandwiches such as achiote lamb tenderloin on focaccia at lunchtime. For dinner, entrées range from pastas and vegetarian dishes to pork loin and broiled halibut.

Mangels House

P.O. Box 302
570 Aptos Creek Road
Aptos, CA 95001
831-688-7982
800-320-7401
mangels@cruzio.com
www.innaccess.com/mangels

A large country home by a forested park

Innkeeper: Jacqueline Fisher. **Accommodations:** 6 rooms (all with private bath). **Rates:** $125–$165 single or double, $20 additional person. **Included:** Full breakfast. **Added:** 10% tax. **Minimum stay:** 2 nights when Saturday is included. **Payment:** Major credit cards accepted, check or cash preferred. **Children:** Over age 10 welcome; $20 additional if third person in room. **Pets:** Allowed outside. **Smoking:** Not allowed indoors.

➤ **Once the canyons and ridges were covered with redwoods, but by 1923 the last stand of old-growth forest was gone. When the loggers left Aptos Canyon, the forest gradually began to heal. That process continues today as new redwoods grow and wildlife returns. There are thirty miles of hiking and biking trails in this peaceful refuge.**

Aptos is a small community just south of Santa Cruz, in the northern curve of Monterey Bay. It was here, in the woods along Aptos Creek, that Claus Mangels built his vacation home in the 1880s. Mangels and his brother-in-law, Claus Spreckels, founded the sugar beet industry in California. The home in Aptos stayed in the family until 1979, when the Fishers purchased the country estate and turned it into a bed-and-breakfast.

The two-story white frame house bears some resemblance to an imposing antebellum mansion, but it's comfortably rather than lavishly furnished. This is a large, airy country home with verandas, four acres of lawns and gardens, and two creeks nearby. English antiques and contemporary decor are combined to pleasing effect. In the immense living room a rough marble fireplace stands eight feet wide and reaches from floor to ceiling, with high windows beside it. Books fill the built-in shelves and there's a grand piano at one end of the room.

The dining room has a long table where breakfast is served if the house is full, but if only a few guests are present, they eat in the kitchen. Juice, scones, muffins, persimmon bread, fruit, and an egg entrée are a few of the dishes Jackie likes to serve her guests. Coffee is always set out early on an antique oak sideboard on the upstairs landing.

The large upstairs guest rooms have views of the orchards, the garden, or the wooded canyon. The smallest is the cozy Mediterranean room, decorated in bright red, blue, and green prints. Nicholas's Room, named for the Fishers' son, is exotic with African artifacts, mementos of Nicholas's two years in Zaire. The Mauve Room, with a daybed, sleeps three people. It has a marble fireplace, stencils on the pink walls, and tall windows.

In the Guest Room, you can raise one of the floor-to-ceiling windows to get to the balcony overlooking the English garden. This room has a cheery country look, with a wicker couch, white lattice headboard, and fresh roses on the table.

Mangels House is on a quiet road on the edge of the Forest of Nisene Marks State Park, 9,600 acres of wooded wilderness. The park was donated to the state by the Marks family in memory of their mother in 1963.

Arroyo Grande

Crystal Rose Inn

789 Valley Road
Arroyo Grande, CA 93420
805-481-1854
800-ROSE-INN
Fax: 805-481-9541
stay@callamer.com
www.centralcoast.com/crystalroseinn

> An ornate pink home a mile
> from the sea

Innkeeper: Bonnie Royster. **Accommodations:** 8 rooms (all with private bath). **Rates:** $95–$185 single or double, $35 additional person. **Included:** Full breakfast, afternoon tea, and evening hors d'oeuvres. **Added:** 6% tax. **Minimum stay:** 2 nights on holiday weekends. **Payment:** Major credit cards. **Children:** Under age 16 not appropriate; additional $35 if third person in room. **Pets:** Not allowed. **Smoking:** Allowed outside only.

➤ **There are more than forty wineries in San Luis Obispo County, many of them open for tours and tastings. Lopez Lake, the valley's water source, is ten miles inland; it's a popular site for water sports.**

Rose is the theme of this inn on the coast halfway between San Francisco and Los Angeles. The four-story home is painted in four shades of pink, each guest room is named for a type of rose, and the garden is full of roses that are picked to adorn every room.

The ornate house, built in 1885 as a homestead for a walnut farm, is surrounded by farmland with a sprinkling of houses here and there. Development is encroaching, but for now the fields of green beans, lettuce, and celery provide a rural context. The ocean is a mile away, as the crow flies. You can see the sand dunes from the upper floors of the Crystal Rose.

The inn also has a successful restaurant called the Hunt Club. In the garden-level eatery, pink and white linens grace the tables, and windows overlook the gazebo and rose arbor. In the afternoons high tea is served in the tearoom. Scones topped with homemade rose petal jam made from roses on the property is the specialty. Later there are hors d'oeuvres and wine.

Breakfast is served in the tearoom, your guest room, or in the garden. The menu varies but there is always a fresh fruit plate, pastry basket, coffee, tea, and juice. Guests then choose an entrée, which may be the inn's own granola, a vegetable and sausage strata, or wild rose pancakes with applesauce and country bacon.

At the front of the mansion is a parlor with a fireplace, a pump organ, and a bay window. Another sitting room, a favorite of guests, features a square grand piano and table with an ongoing jigsaw puzzle.

The guest rooms are furnished with a combination of antiques and period reproductions. Each is named for a rose, with decor and a color scheme that are representative of its namesake. In Intrigue, the queen-size brass bed is covered with a plum velvet bedspread. The spacious Queen Elizabeth Tower Suite has a separate sitting area, the Tiffany Suite overlooks the gardens, and the Honor Suite is decorated in white lace. Peace, located in the garden cottage, is cozy and has its own private deck.

For recreation the inn has an exercise room, bicycles, croquet, badminton, darts, bocce ball, and horseshoes. For a romantic bike ride there's even a tandem bicycle handy. Massages are available by appointment.

Ballard

The Ballard Inn

2436 Baseline
Ballard, CA 93463
805-688-7770
800-638-BINN
Fax: 805-688-9560
kelly@ballardinn.com
www.ballardinn.com

A peaceful retreat in a
frontier village

Owners: Steve Hyslop and Larry Stone. **Manager:** Kelly Robinson. **Accommodations:** 15 rooms. **Rates:** $170–$250 single or double, $50 additional person. **Included:** Full breakfast, wine, and hors d'oeuvres. **Added:** 11% tax plus 10% service charge. **Minimum stay:** 2 nights on weekends. **Payment:** Major credit cards. **Children:** Charged as an additional person if third person in room. **Pets:** Not allowed. **Smoking:** Not allowed.

➤ **If you really want to get in the spirit of the place, go to the antique trunk in the corner of the Stagecoach Room and pull out a hat with trailing boa, a coonskin cap, or a shawl and imagine yourself just stepping off the stage.**

Some forty miles north of Santa Barbara, in the scenic Santa Ynez Valley, is a village with a frontier history. It's the valley's oldest town, with a quaint church and an 1883 red schoolhouse still in operation.

On the main road, behind a white picket fence bordered with roses, is the Ballard, the image of a genteel country inn. From a long porch with white rocking chairs, double doors lead to a foyer with a vaulted white ceiling and a three-sided green marble fireplace. On the right is the dining room where a sumptuous breakfast is served. Omelettes, French toast with sautéed bananas and cinnamon, muffins, and fruit are a few of the morning offerings. At night the dining room becomes Café Chardonnay, serving creative wine-country cuisine such as filet mignon topped with blue cheese and a cabernet sauce and marinated grilled leg of lamb with a red wine and garlic demiglace.

The Vintner's Room is on the other side of the lobby. Here a carved cabinet holds games and puzzles, local wines are on display, and hors d'oeuvres and wines are set out in the evening. In keeping with the wine theme are the burgundy wallpaper in a trellis pattern, an oak bar with legs carved in grapevines, and displays of wine labels.

Sofas by the fireplace and a case of books and antiques make the living room an inviting place to relax and contemplate the portrait of William Ballard. The bearded patriarch built and operated a stagecoach stop here for the two-day run from San Luis Obispo to Santa Barbara. His adobe home has been preserved and is still in use.

The Stagecoach Room, dark with black leather chairs and a braided rug on a polished floor, is done in the colors of the original stage: burgundy, black, and gold. A painting of the Ballard Stage Station and coach hangs on the wall, along with coach lanterns and photographs of other valley coaches.

All the rooms, named for places and people important in Ballard's history, have phone jacks, air conditioning, and soundproof walls. Oak bathroom cabinets are stocked with wine soap, wine hand lotion, and champagne shampoo.

Western Room is a tribute to the cowboys who worked the cattle ranches. It has a log cabin quilt, old-fashioned rockers, a fireplace, and a collection of western hats. Davy Brown's Room, in honor of a rugged frontiersman who rode with the Texas Rangers, also has a rustic charm. It has a fireplace made of native stone, a wagon-wheel quilt, and American antiques.

Quite different is the Valley Room, commemorating five little valley towns. There is a Belgian armoire and matching dresser and a friendship quilt made by local quilters. Jarado's Room takes its theme from a Chumash Indian who helped construct the Ballard Station. It contains the red, white, and black designs of Chumash cave paintings. Pine furniture and arrowheads add to the atmosphere.

Cynthia's Room recalls a pioneer who came west to marry her sweetheart, William Ballard, on his deathbed. Ballard's last wish was that she marry his friend George Lewis, which she did. The room holds a portrait of the youthful widow; the handmade quilt on the bed is, appropriately, in a double wedding ring pattern.

When you wish to explore the picturesque countryside, with its highly regarded wineries and thoroughbred horse ranches, the innkeepers can help you plan your route. To the south is Solvang, a tourist-oriented village in quaint Danish style. Los Olivos, north of Ballard, has numerous art galleries.

Big Sur

Deetjen's Big Sur Inn

Highway 1
Big Sur, CA 93920
831-667-2377
Fax: 831-667-0466

A rustic group of cabins among the trees

Manager: Laura Moran. **Accommodations:** 20 rooms (15 with private bath). **Rates:** $90–$180 single or double, $11 additional person. **Payment:** MasterCard and Visa accepted. **Children:** Under age 12 not appropriate. **Pets:** Not allowed. **Smoking:** Not allowed.

➤   **Big Sur is an 80-mile stretch of wild coastline that runs from Carmel south to San Simeon. Rugged cliffs and wooded ridges rise steeply from the shore, and every curve of the snaking road presents another astounding view of green coves, blue ocean flecked with white, and rocky headlands and beaches.**

In the early 1930s, when the coastal highway was a dirt road, Helmuth Deetjen, a Norwegian immigrant, built a homestead by the road in Castro Canyon. He and his wife, Helen, welcomed overnight guests. They gradually added more simple frame buildings until the home became the Big Sur Inn.

There is no real town of Big Sur, though there is a post office, but you feel a sense of community in the group of homes and shops that extends for six miles along the highway. Its heart is the Big Sur Inn, where locals and tourists alike come for coffee, meals, and conversation.

The restaurant is in Helmuth Deetjen's original house. With windows that look out to wisteria vines, low-beamed ceilings, low lighting, and dark walls, the restaurant has several rooms and rustic charm. Woodstoves help to ease the chill of an early morning or a cool evening, and excellent breakfasts and dinners are served. The morning menu offers pancakes, oatmeal, eggs Benedict, French toast, and other dishes at reasonable prices. Dinner, by reservation, is served by candlelight with classical music in the background. Roasted New Zealand rack of lamb with a honey-mustard pecan crust, filet mignon with sautéed shiitake and oyster mushrooms, and fresh herb-marinated, oak-grilled chicken breast topped with virgin olive oil, caper sauce, and herb salsa served with a grilled risotto cake are some of the tempting dishes you may find on the ever-changing menu.

The guest rooms are back among the trees in various buildings lining a dirt path that extends above the canyon creek. No two rooms are alike, but in general, with unpainted plank walls and rough-hewn doors, they are dark and rustic but comfortable and clean. Amenities are few and simple, such as wind-up alarm clocks and doors that can only be locked from the inside (none of the rooms has keys). Despite the rustic environment, the beds are firm and cozy under down comforters. In Grampa's, across from the restaurant, an old radio rests on the big desk and an antique pump organ stands against a wall. In Château Fiasco, behind the restaurant, you feel as if you're in a treehouse. It has a writing desk, private porch, and a small but modern bath with a shower. There's a wood-burning stove and a handsome coverlet on the bed in Antique Apartment, and the adjoining room, called the Hostelry, has a twin bed topped with a teddy bear.

Not all the rooms have a backwoods atmosphere. Faraway, perched at the edge of the canyon, has an all redwood interior, a small porch, and a private, fenced area with ferns and fuchsias. Chalet, a personal favorite, is brighter than many of the rooms because of its white walls and plentiful windows. The front room, which looks out to towering redwoods and a running stream below, has a queen-size bed and an attractive antique vanity. In the adjoining room, two twin beds with French country print coverlets, a stuffed bunny on the pillow, and framed illustrations from children's books on the wall will take you back to your childhood.

Post Ranch Inn

Highway One
P.O. Box 219
Big Sur, CA 93920
831-667-2200
800-527-2200
Fax: 831-667-2824
www.postranchinn.com

> **A unique contemporary inn above the Pacific**

Manager: Larry Callahan. **Accommodations:** 30 suites, 1 house. **Rates:** $395–$695 single or double, $50 additional person, Post House $700. **Included:** Expanded Continental breakfast. **Added:** 10.5% tax. **Minimum:** 2 nights on weekends. **Payment:** Major credit cards; no personal checks. **Children:** Discouraged; charged as an additional person if third person in room. **Pets:** Not allowed. **Smoking:** Not allowed.

➤   In building this resort, only one tree came down, an example of a concern for the environment that is apparent at every turn. Some call the construction politically correct; more astute observers note that this commitment to protecting the land is more than merely political.

Tucked against a cliff 1,200 feet above the spectacular Big Sur coast, this is the resort that critics have raved about since it opened in 1992. Imaginative and whimsical, yet filled with the practical comforts travelers appreciate, Post Ranch deserves all its accolades. Great care was lavished on the planning and construction, and it shows in almost every detail.

Five of the redwood guest units are Ocean Houses. Overlooking the Pacific, they have sod roofs covered with grass and wildflowers. Others, as round as giant tree trunks, are Coast Houses and Mountain Houses. The seven Tree Houses stand on stilts, designed to protect the roots of the surrounding redwood trees. When these houses are wreathed in the mists that often move along the coast, they seem to float in the branches. One building, the Butterfly House, has six units and is shaped like a butterfly with its wings outstretched.

Inside, the rooms have character and style, as well as the usual luxury hotel features: coffeemakers, mini-bars, phones, music systems, fireplaces, and Jacuzzi tubs. The floors are of slate and the angled and curved walls of natural wood. The decor is spare, with nothing to detract from the dramatic views. Quiet and privacy are paramount.

Also on the 98-acre property, once part of a 1,600-acre cattle ranch, are groves of madrone and oak trees, trails, grassy meadows, and a fish pond.

Guests are invited to enjoy the panorama from the outdoor basking pool, swim in the lap pool, get a massage or tarot card reading, select a book from the little library, and, especially, dine in the exquisite Sierra Mar restaurant. Perched at the edge of a cliff, it looks out over the riveting ocean view. Raised sections allow every table to have a view. A buffet breakfast is set out here (or breakfast will be brought to your room if you prefer). Sierra Mar also serves lunch and memorable dinners.

Chef Craig Foerster incorporates international influences in his regional fare. His fresh and creative cuisine features simple but interesting dishes on a fixed price menu that changes regularly. The restaurant's organic garden provides much of the produce. The broad wine list offers more than 3,000 selections.

Ventana Inn and Spa

Highway 1
Big Sur, CA 93920
831-667-2331, 831-624-4812
800-628-6500
Fax: 831-667-2419
www.ventanainn.com

A contemporary inn with a grand view and a quiet location

General manager: Sal Abaunza. **Accommodations:** 59 rooms and suites, 3 houses. **Rates:** $340 single or double, $50 additional person; suites $850–$1,050. **Included:** Expanded Continental breakfast and wine and cheese buffet.

Added: 10.5% tax. **Minimum stay:** 2 nights on weekends. **Payment:** Major credit cards. **Children:** Discouraged. **Pets:** Not allowed. **Smoking:** Not allowed.

➤ **This is country lodging at its best, offering relaxation and tranquillity in a setting of stunning beauty. There are no tennis courts or golf courses within miles; Ventana is a place to relax, unwind, go for walks, go for a swim, get a massage or facial, take a sauna, and read in the sun or by the fire.**

A thousand feet above the sea, where the Santa Lucia Mountains rise in steep folds and ridges along the dramatic Big Sur coast, Ventana's weathered cedar buildings blend with their environment of rocky canyons, meadows, and redwood groves.

The inn, built in 1975, is 150 miles south of San Francisco. Monterey Peninsula Airport, 35 miles north, has rental cars. Contemporary buildings, latticed against the sun, are dispersed among groves of redwood, oak, and bay laurel. In the main lodge is an airy glass and cedar lobby with a large stone fireplace. Every afternoon complimentary wines and cheeses are presented, and breakfast — with pastries made on the premises — is served here or delivered to your room.

The guest rooms are decorated tastefully in Swedish country style, all light woods and wide windows. Most of them have wood-burning fireplaces and hot tubs, or dining alcoves with wet bars and refrigerators. All the rooms are furnished with wicker and rush chairs, natural wood paneling, hand-painted headboards with complementing handmade quilts, fine pastel linens, honor bars, and televisions with VCRs. The large tiled baths have separate vanities, coffeemakers, hair dryers, and make-up mirrors. Every room has a private balcony or patio with an ocean or mountain view. The rooms in the Pacific House have window seats and canopy beds set with fluffy pillows.

A library and a lounge, which serves as another breakfast room, are near the second swimming pool and a Japanese hot tub complex. With a casual European attitude toward sunbathing, nudity is allowed in some areas and swimwear is optional in the coed hot tub.

Cielo, Ventana's dining room, a delightful walk up lighted paths from the inn, is noted for its cuisine. Chef Jerauld Regester calls his culinary creations "rustic with robust flavors." The menu features fresh local fish, herbs and vegetables grown on the grounds, wild mushrooms and berries, and breads from the inn's own bakery. There's an extensive wine list of California and imported labels.

The food may be exceptional, but the setting is incomparable. The 50-mile view of the misty Big Sur coast from above is breathtaking, worthy of hours of admiration from the restaurant windows or from the broad, flowery terrace where lunch and cocktails are served.

Ventana, which means window in Spanish, offers many vistas of mountains, sea, and sky, and given its peace and serenity, it can also be a window to renewed inner perspectives. If you are more concerned with exterior perspectives, you can treat your body to pampering services at the inn's spa.

Cambria

Olallieberry Inn

2476 Main Street
Cambria, CA 93428
805-927-3222
888-927-3222
Fax: 805-927-0202
ollieinn@olallieberry.com
www.olallieberry.com

> **A congenial bed-and-breakfast on the edge of Cambria**

Innkeepers: Peter and Carol Ann Irsfeld. **Accommodations:** 9 rooms (all with private bath). **Rates:** $90–$185. **Included:** Full breakfast and afternoon hors d'oeuvres. **Added:** 9% tax. **Payment:** Major credit cards. **Children:** Not appropriate for small children. **Pets:** Not allowed. **Smoking:** Allowed outside only.

➤ **Take some time to enjoy the inn's gardens. Artichokes, colorful red and green Swiss chard, rosemary, marjoram, thyme, lettuce, and mint are just a few of the plants found in the bountiful herb garden. The adjoining**

Secret Garden has a central fountain and a white wrought-iron bench, inviting visitors to linger.

This pleasant beige clapboard house with white and plum trim sits on the edge of the coastal town of Cambria. Built in 1873, when the town was in its infancy, the home is a registered historic landmark. The giant redwood that towers over the front yard garden was planted in 1885.

Just inside the front door there's a formal Victorian parlor with a handsome china display case. Yet despite the formal first impression, the mood is casual at this homey inn. You'll be welcomed by one of the convivial innkeepers and be taught a fetching trick by Niki, their friendly black cocker spaniel.

Beyond the front parlor there's the considerably less formal gathering room with blue and white checked country fabrics and a long Pennsylvania farmhouse table (made from barn siding), where breakfast is served. Guests are welcome to use the refrigerator, stereo, telephone, and books located in an adjoining alcove. French doors lead from the gathering room out to a back porch where you can watch a game of croquet on the back lawn or wander down to Santa Rosa Creek, bordering the property.

Three guest rooms are on the first floor. San Simeon has a tub for two, a fireplace, petit rose wallpaper, and a king-size bed with embroidered pillows, a rose print coverlet, and matching curtains. Cambria, with a fireplace and sunken tub, is the most popular room for honeymooners. Wheelchair accessible, it has a queen-size iron bed draped in pink taffeta and a mirrored armoire. Of all the guest rooms, Santa Rosa has the most Victorian decor.

There are three additional guest rooms upstairs. Olallieberry, under slanted ceilings, is a riot of violet with a lavender velvet fainting couch and a violet motif coverlet atop the queen-size bed. Olallieberry's clawfoot tub for two is well known among repeat guests. Harmony Room, in lace, has a hall bath; and in Room at the Top you can enjoy the wicker furnishings, a gas fireplace, and a Nancy Drew mystery (there's a complete set), while curled up in the window seat overlooking the garden.

In 1996, the Irsfelds turned their former residence, which was adjacent to the back of the inn, into three additional guest rooms. These rooms have antique furnishings, fireplaces, and modern baths.

In keeping with Peter and Carol Ann's emphasis on hospitality, they provide ample meals. In the morning, crêpes filled with almond custard, fresh strawberries, kiwi, and banana; eggs baked in a hash brown potato crust topped with cheddar and salsa; or stuffed

French toast are served. Freshly baked muffins, granola, yogurt, seasonal fruit, freshly squeezed juice, and gourmet coffees and teas are also offered. Afternoon hors d'oeuvres may be goat cheese and roasted garlic served with freshly baked focaccia or a black olive, roasted garlic, and rosemary pizza garnished with herbs from the garden. If you're still hungry, Cambria's shops and restaurants are nearby.

The Squibb House

4063 Burton Drive
Cambria, CA 93428
805-927-9600
Fax: 805-927-9606
www.cambria-online.com/TheSquibbHouseandShopNextDoor/

> **A beautifully restored Victorian in the heart of Cambria**

Owner: Bruce Black. **Accommodations:** 5 rooms (all with private bath; outhouse available upon request). **Rates:** $95–$155. **Included:** Continental breakfast. **Added:** 9% tax. **Payment:** MasterCard and Visa. **Children:** Not appropriate. **Pets:** Not allowed. **Smoking:** Not allowed.

➤ **Because of its in-town location, the Squibb House is convenient to many shops and restaurants. Cambria Beach is about a mile from the inn, and the incredible Hearst Castle is less than ten miles away.**

Guests are not the only ones to pause in front of this cheerful yellow Gothic-style Victorian home in downtown Cambria. On one of the main streets in the shopping district, tourists are often seen stopping to enjoy its gingerbread trim and colorful garden abloom with hollyhocks, nasturtiums, snapdragons, daisies, pansies, and geraniums.

The home was built in 1877 and named for the Squibb family, who were former owners. Over the years the Squibb House was occupied by many of Cambria's most active citizens, until Bruce Black took over ownership in the early 1990s, saving the splendid structure from an uncertain fate. A master craftsman, Bruce restored the home with loving care and furnished the bed-and-breakfast with many pieces he built himself.

Throughout, the inn has a crisp, clean look. There are two bedrooms on the first floor and three on the second. The Village Room looks out to charming Burton Street, lined with shops and restaurants. Gray-washed furniture, wicker chairs, a wooden washstand, a floral wreath, and a queen-size bed topped with a patchwork quilt give the room a fresh country flavor.

In the Gothic Room there is a lovely pine wardrobe with matching bedside tables and a gas-lit stove. On the ground floor, the Garden Room has its own entrance, and the bed's headboard matches the gingerbread scrollwork on the private porch. Telephones are not provided but are available upon request.

Breakfast, which consists of fresh pastries from a neighboring bakery and fruit, is served in the formal parlor downstairs, or in bed if you prefer. In the afternoon, coffee, tea, fruit, cheese, and a sweet treat are offered to guests. Off-street parking is available behind the inn.

Capitola

Inn at Depot Hill

250 Monterey Avenue
Capitola, CA 95010
831-462-3376
800-572-2632
Fax: 831-462-3697
lodging@innatdepothill.com
www.innatdepothill.com

An opulent hillside inn near the sea

Innkeepers: Suzie Lankes and Dan Floyd. **Accommodations:** 12 suites (all with private bath). **Rates:** $195–$275 single or double. **Included:** Full breakfast, afternoon wine and hors d'oeuvres, and evening dessert. **Minimum stay:** 2 nights on weekends when Saturday is included. **Payment:** Major credit cards. **Children:** Maximum 2 persons per room. **Pets:** Not allowed. **Smoking:** Not allowed indoors.

➤ **The inn holds a few reminders of turn-of-the-century rail travel. The original columns and ticket windows are here, and the dining room, once the ticket office, is decorated with a rack of old-fashioned baggage and a trompe l'oeil scene that creates the illusion of countryside seen from a train window.**

Sumptuous and sophisticated, the Inn at Depot Hill is one of the best-run and most romantic lodgings on the coast. It's come a long way from its origins as a 1901 train depot on a hill above Capitola, a charming seaside village south of Santa Cruz. The depot lobby is now a parlor with polished floors, a two-sided fireplace, a baby grand piano, a circular settee, and built-in bookshelves.

Beyond is a lovely brick patio adorned with flowers and highlighted by a lily pool. Off to one side is a hot tub for those guests who don't have a private spa in their room.

Each suite at this first-rate inn has been painstakingly furnished and decorated to evoke the mood of a train destination. The Paris Room is an elegant study in black and white. It has fabric-covered walls, a double fireplace, French doors that lead to a patio, and a bath in black and white marble. Sissinghurst is like a garden room in a traditional English country inn, with a canopy bed and a raised fireplace.

Delft is exquisite in blue and white. A personal favorite, it's romantic with a cozy window seat, a fireplace surrounded with Dutch tiles, a chaise, and a canopy bed draped in Battenburg lace. It has a private patio with a hot tub that you fill yourself so you know the water is fresh.

The Orient Express, also referred to as the Library suite, is another favorite. You step into a small den with leather armchairs, a table set for a game of chess, and bookshelves that are stocked with books that guests are invited to peruse. From there, steps lead down to a bedroom, elegant in rose and yellow, with a queen bed set in front of the fireplace and topped with a white matelasse spread and fringed pillows. From the bedroom, another staircase leads up to a twin bed cozily tucked away behind coral velvet drapes reminiscent of the luxurious pullman cars of yore. Guests staying in this room share it with a handpainted mouse — see if you can spot it.

Stratford-on-Avon is cozy with a window seat and trellis wallpaper. The smallest room, it has an English country look. Portofino has the frescoed walls of an Italian villa; and Cote d'Azur, once the depot's baggage room, has a Mediterranean theme with tiled floors, whitewashed columns, and an iron bed draped in chintz.

Capitola Beach, in tans and ivories, with a metal four-poster bed, is more casual and contemporary than some of the other rooms. The Railroad Baron's Room is masculine with custom-made fabric walls, red velveteen chairs, thick draperies, a domed ceiling, and a deep soaking tub under a skylight.

Three rooms are located in two separate buildings behind the main inn. Valencia, in bright yellows and blues, and Costa del Sol have Spanish themes. Kyoto is the most exotic, with shoji screens, a pine platform bed, bamboo tea tray, and a Japanese soaking tub with a dragon faucet. From the suite's front door you can step into your own Japanese garden.

Each room has a feather bed, television with VCR, a stereo system, phones with modem and fax capability, a marble bath with a two-person shower, and such luxuries as crystal wine glasses, extra pillows, a hair dryer, makeup mirror, clothes steamer, mini-TV in each bath, Egyptian cotton towels, robes, fresh roses, and embroidered Belgian linens. Some rooms have private brick patios with hot tubs and separate entrances.

Breakfast is served in the dining room, on the terrace, or in your own room. Entrées such as frittatas make up the international menu, and Depot Hill eggs is the inn's specialty dish. For other meals, there are almost twenty restaurants within walking distance. The inn provides afternoon tea or wine, after-dinner dessert, and off-street parking.

Carmel

Cobblestone Inn

Junipero between 7th and 8th
P.O. Box 3185
Carmel, CA 93921
831-625-5222
800-833-8836
Fax: 831-625-0478
www.foursisters.com

An inn with English charm in the heart of Carmel

Owners: Roger and Sally Post. **Innkeeper:** Sharon Carey. **Accommodations:** 24 rooms. **Rates:** $105–$150 single or double, suites $190–$240. **Included:** Full breakfast and afternoon refreshments. **Added:** 10% tax. **Payment:** Major credit cards. **Children:** Additional $15 if third person in room. **Pets:** Not allowed. **Smoking:** Not allowed.

➤ **The Cobblestone offers services often found only at luxury hotels, such as twice-daily housekeeping and a morning newspaper.**

It could be said that the Cobblestone Inn is Carmel to the core, as the rocks that make up its stone exterior and stony interior fireplaces all came from the Carmel River. On the edge of the downtown shopping district, the inn is perfectly situated for exploring the charming seaside town.

A carousel horse in the lobby alerts well-traveled guests that they are checking into a Four Sisters Inn. For those not familiar with the well-run inn group owned by Roger and Sally Post, they are about to be treated to the quality service and accommodations common to all Four Sisters Inns. Teddy bears in the comfortable main living room are another trademark of the respected inn group.

The horseshoe shaped inn wraps around a central slate courtyard and parking lot. Guests dine on breakfasts of muesli, home-baked breads, fresh fruit, cereal, and a hot entrée on the brick patio. When the weather does not permit patio dining, however, breakfast is served in the dining room — or you can request breakfast in bed if you prefer. In the afternoons guests gather for tea or wine, and later retire to their rooms with homemade cookies in hand.

Each room in the two-story inn is individually decorated. Some have canopy beds, others have pine furnishings and dried floral arrangements. Mauve carpeting, floral wallpaper, and a cobblestone fireplace are common to each, and all rooms have an English country flavor. Although the rooms vary in size, all have telephones, televisions, private baths, terry robes, and small refrigerators stocked with cold drinks. Suites have sitting areas and wet bars.

The shops and restaurants of Carmel are in easy walking distance from the inn. For those wishing to venture farther, the inn has bicycles that guests can use to explore the area's glorious coastal terrain.

Cypress Inn

P.O. Box Y
Lincoln & 7th
Carmel, CA 93921
831-624-3871
800-443-7443
Fax: 831-624-8216
info@cypressinn.com
www.cypress-inn.com

> **A small hotel with a light, bright atmosphere**

General manager: Hollace Thompson. **Accommodations:** 34 rooms. **Rates:** $125–$350 single or double, $20 additional person, off-season rates available. **Included:** Continental breakfast. **Added:** 10% tax. **Minimum stay:** 2 nights on weekends. **Payment:** Major credit cards. **Children:** Welcome (no cribs or rollaways available). **Pets:** Allowed with permission; $20 per night for first pet, $10 per night for each additional pet. **Smoking:** Nonsmoking rooms available.

➤ **This is one of the few hotels where pets are welcome, thanks to the influence of animal lover and part owner Doris Day. You will often see pampered pets being paraded through the lobby by adoring owners, and there's a photo album of pet guests in the living room.**

In the heart of quaint Carmel-by-the-Sea on the Monterey Peninsula, the Cypress first captures your eye with its white Moorish Mediterranean facade and red Spanish tile roof. When the hotel opened in 1929, it was hailed as a landmark for its classic exterior and stately interior. That charm has been restored, and it is again a fine and quiet place to stay, gracious in its tasteful simplicity. With the updated accommodations are hints of the hotel's origins in ceramic tiles, arched windows, oak flooring, and a few antiques.

The Cypress abuts the sidewalk on Lincoln Street (there's no number — Carmel doesn't allow street addresses), facing the

Church of the Wayfarer and its garden across the street. A few brick steps lead to the reception area. On the right is a sitting room, warm with comfy sofas, a fire blazing in the large fireplace, and a beamed ceiling. Tall windows face the street on one side; on the other are three sets of double glass doors leading to a serene courtyard with blooming fuchsia and morning sun. Garden furniture is placed among the shrubs and topiary ivy, and an outdoor fireplace blazes on cool evenings.

Guest rooms, on two floors, are cheerful, decorated in peaches and ivories. They look out to the garden courtyard, the flowering alley, or to town. Each room has fresh fruit and flowers, sherry, a telephone, a television, and a tiled bath. Different configurations are available: some have two twin beds, others have a double or a king, and some include fireplaces.

Six specialty rooms are noted for their size and amenities — sitting areas, wet bars, balconies, and ocean views. One has a pleasant terrace with blooming bougainvillea and geraniums and an ocean view. Another has a fireplace and a Jacuzzi. The Tower Suite has a bedroom upstairs surrounded by arched windows with ocean views and a living room and bath downstairs. Room 219 is reached by climbing a flight of stairs from the courtyard. It has comfy seating in front of its fireplace, and French doors open onto a small balcony.

The daily paper is delivered to each guest room in the morning, and treats for canine guests are available at the front desk. The concierge and staff are uniformly obliging about providing information on nearby attractions and restaurants. Menus are available to help you choose a spot for dinner. Breakfast is served in the courtyard, in your room, or in the library bar, where Doris Day movie posters grace the walls.

Happy Landing Inn

P.O. Box 2619
Monte Verde between 5th and 6th
Carmel, CA 93921
831-624-7917

A quaint, relaxing inn with a garden setting

Innkeepers: Robert Ballard and Richard Stewart. **Accommodations:** 5 rooms and 2 suites. **Rates:** $90–$175. **Included:** Expanded Continental breakfast. **Added:** 10% tax. **Minimum stay:** 2 nights on weekends. **Payment:** MasterCard, Visa. **Children:** Age 12 and over welcome. **Pets:** Not allowed. **Smoking:** Non-smoking rooms available.

➤ **Although it is a few blocks from the sea and you can glimpse the water from some windows, Happy Landing is not the place to go for panoramic views of the Pacific. "We get glimpses, not ocean views," says Robert Ballard. "Carmel is really an urban forest, full of trees."**

The focus of this pretty inn is its central garden. If you like ponds and fountains, lush vines, garden gnomes, and pots overflowing with geraniums and fuchsias, you will love this spot. It's a beautiful retreat where you can sit under a white trellis with hanging plants or watch the goldfish dart among the water lilies.

Most of the guest rooms are in three pink, one-story buildings that form a U around the garden; their private entrances are blue doors under curved arches, each painted with birds and vines — quintessentially quaint Carmel. On the fourth side of the garden, the street side, is the main building with the office and common room. Here guests may relax, read, or have tea and cookies.

The rooms are furnished individually with antiques and modern comforts such as hair dryers and thick pink towels. There are brass beds, balloon shades or cottage curtains, iron latches on the built-in drawers, casement windows, and fresh flowers.

Room 1, in yellows, has a queen-size brass bed and a Mexican tiled fireplace. Room 7 is pretty and feminine and has charming animal lithographs on the walls. Room 4 is a suite with a fireplace and sofa bed in the living room, a king-size bed in the bedroom, and a lovely hand-painted sink and floral wallpaper in the cheerful bath. Gorgeous foxgloves grow just outside the door of Room 3. Also a suite, it has a hand-painted floral design on its ceiling, wicker furnishings, and stained glass windows in the bath.

When you're ready for breakfast, you part the curtains or raise the shades — that's the signal for the innkeeper to bring your tray. You'll have fruit, fresh orange juice, muffins or scones, and quiche or strata for breakfast.

Happy Landing has menus for nearby restaurants. Among those recommended are Flying Fish for good seafood and a casual atmosphere, and Piatti's for flavorful Italian cookery.

Highlands Inn

P.O. Box 1700
Carmel, CA 93921
831-624-3801
800-682-4811
Fax: 831-626-1574
www.hyatt.com

> **A contemporary resort with an ocean view**

General manager: Ulrich Samietz. **Accommodations:** 142 rooms and suites. **Rates:** $155–$875. **Added:** 10.5% tax. **Payment:** Major credit cards. **Children:**

Under age 18 free in room with parents. **Pets:** By prior arrangement only. **Smoking:** Not allowed.

➤ **Although the views of the Monterey pines and the ocean are striking, there is no immediate access to the shore. The action is at the resort itself. There are three whirlpool tubs, a swimming pool, board games, a video library, and dancing to the music of a jazz combo in the lounge. Mountain bikes are available and tennis, golf, and horseback riding are nearby.**

Terraced against the hillside above the rocky, rugged cliffs south of Carmel, this contemporary inn of stone and wood offers grand views, fine food, and luxurious accommodations. Completely transformed in the 1980s from a humbler lodging, the main building now has a skylighted promenade, bleached oak floors, a big lobby with a beamed ceiling and two granite fireplaces, and a snazzy restaurant, Pacific's Edge. It's a curious blend of formal (jackets and ties are requested in the restaurant) and casual (the friendly parking valets wear shorts), of natural beauty and corporate sleekness.

In the lounge, wide windows overlook spectacular vistas of sea and sky, and entertainment is offered in the evenings. Around the corner is the two-tiered restaurant, known for its outstanding thirty-one-page wine list, regional cuisine, and fresh seafood. You can eat more casually on the terrace at the California Market, a combined deli, tavern, and boutique.

The Highlands's guest rooms are scattered among twenty-two buildings and the main lodge. They're all furnished in a contemporary style, and amenities include binoculars for looking at the view, televisions with built-in VCRs, bathrobes, coffeemakers, and refrigerators. Most rooms have fireplaces and kitchens. Some are equipped with CD players and spa baths. Sizes and views vary; you can get a single room or a two-bedroom townhouse, a view of the road or a panoramic ocean view. Generally, the higher up the hill you go, the better the room. Some of the rooms close to the pool are good choices, too.

La Playa Hotel

P.O. Box 900
Camino Real & 8th
Carmel, CA 93921
831-624-6476
800-582-8900
Fax: 831-624-7966

A Mediterranean hotel with ocean views

Owner: Newton A. Cope, Sr. **General manager:** Tom Glidden. **Accommodations:** 75 rooms and 5 cottages. **Rates:** $140–$255 single or double, $15 additional person; suites and cottages $255–$550. **Added:** 10% tax. **Payment:** Major credit cards. **Children:** Under age 12 free in room with parents. **Pets:** Not allowed. **Smoking:** Nonsmoking rooms available.

➤ **"Our concierges are human encyclopedias," the desk clerk declares proudly, citing a few of the requests they fill with ease, from getting postage stamps or a recipe to assisting you with golf reservations.**

Two blocks from Carmel's beach is a hotel that is a lovely find. La Playa has a classic Mediterranean look, with pink walls, red tiled roofs, and terraced gardens. In the gardens are a heated swimming pool, a fountain, a filigreed black iron gazebo, and a brick patio. There are hundreds of colorful flowers and beds of pungent herbs, many used in the kitchen.

The hotel grew from a rockwork mansion built in 1904 by artist Chris Jorgensen for his bride, a daughter of San Francisco's Ghirardelli family. Later, the property was turned into a hotel and in 1983 sold to the Cope family and completely restored. Newton Cope is a historian who concentrates on turn-of-the-century California and the Old West. Photographs and memorabilia from his collections hang on the walls of La Playa's public spaces.

Parts of the original mansion still exist, mainly the rockwork at the entrance of the L-shaped building and the curving staircase that leads up from the lobby.

The hotel's restaurant, the Terrace Grill, is open for three meals a day and Sunday brunch. California cuisine, using local seafood and produce, is served in this room above the gardens. The wine list includes California and French labels, and several rare old ports and sherries. If you wish to eat outdoors while you watch the sunset, the terrace is a romantic spot.

About a third of the guest rooms have ocean views, three are beside the pool, and nine have private, walled patios. Those without an ocean view overlook the fragrant garden, the patio, or residential Carmel. The hotel's mermaid motif is seen in unexpected places — embroidered on the towels and carved into the driftwood-like headboards. The decor includes light wood furnishings, terra cotta walls, and louvered shutters. The views, especially from the upstairs rooms that face west, are stunning.

In a separate building on Camino Real, the executive suite is a good choice for entertaining a group. It has a meeting room, a kitchen, a living room with a gas fireplace, and an angled glass wall that opens to broad patios. There's a large bedroom with solid carved furniture, a vaulted beam ceiling, and two closets.

La Playa's five cottages are a block away from the hotel, toward the beach. Tucked away amid their own gardens, they are much more private than the hotel rooms, yet cottage guests are welcome to use the swimming pool and all of the other facilities at the hotel. Room service delivery is available to the cottages during the day. You can hear the ocean's roar from the one-bedroom Skyway Cottage, and the sunny yellow shingled Moongate Cottage also has one bedroom. Loghaven, named for its log exterior, is the largest. A good choice for a family, it contains three bedrooms, two and a half baths, and a full kitchen, living room, and dining room. Four cottages have kitchens.

Mission Ranch

26270 Dolores Street
Carmel, California 93923
831-624-6436
800-538-8221
Fax: 831-626-4163

> **A pleasant getaway behind
> Carmel's Mission**

General manager: John Purcell. **Accommodations:** 31 rooms. **Rates:** $95–$275 single or double, $15 additional person. **Included:** Continental breakfast. **Added:** 10.5 % tax. **Payment:** Major credit cards. **Children:** Welcome; additional $15 per child. **Pets:** Not allowed. **Smoking:** Not allowed.

> ➤ **Two giant eucalyptus trees stand on either side of the driveway at the entrance to Mission Ranch. The 22-acre ranch is set in a valley overlooking pastures dotted with grazing sheep and horses.**

Innkeeper is not a title that first springs to mind when you mention the name Clint Eastwood. Yet the award-winning actor/director and former mayor is the owner of this appealing 31-room inn on the edge of Carmel.

In the 1850s the ranch was one of California's first dairies. In the mid-1980s a developer wanted to build condominiums on the property, so Eastwood stepped in and purchased the ranch in order to save the historic buildings. Today the 19th-century dairy buildings still stand on the property — the creamery is now the restaurant, while the 1852 bunkhouse and 1850 farmhouse accommodate overnight guests.

The cheerful Farmhouse is one of the first structures you see as you enter the ranch. Roses and petunias line the walkway that leads to the front door, lace curtains hang in the windows, and flowers spill over the railing from the second-story porch. Inside, six guest rooms share a common living room with a fireplace, and the house can be rented out as a single unit.

Brilliant bougainvillea frames the entryway to the honeymoon cottage next door. It has a living room with a brick fireplace, wet bar, and small dining table. There's a Jacuzzi tub in the bath, and out back, a private yard.

Beyond the ranch office, Hayloft has an iron stove, sofa, and king bed under slanted ceilings; the bed is topped with a patchwork quilt. Across the walk, the Meadowview triplexes, which were built in 1992, house deluxe guest rooms with fireplaces, Jacuzzi tubs, and outdoor decks. Guests staying in the newer rooms have views across wetlands to a white sandy beach, the blue of the ocean, and Point Lobos in the distance.

The restaurant, which serves traditional favorites such as prime rib, filet mignon, and pork tenderloin for dinner, and burgers and sandwiches at lunchtime, has a similar view. An Officer's club during WWII, the restaurant still provides entertainment in the form of a piano bar. For more active recreation, the ranch has a putting green, fitness center, and six outdoor tennis courts.

Sundial Lodge

P.O. Box J
Monte Verde and 7th Avenue
Carmel, CA 93921
831-624-8578
Fax: 831-626-1018
sundial@netpipe.com
www.sundiallodge.com

> **A small hotel surrounding a flower-filled courtyard**

Manager: Robbin Abouhala. **Accommodations:** 19 rooms. **Rates:** $145–$275. **Included:** Continental breakfast. **Minimum stay:** 2 nights on weekends. **Added:** 10% tax. **Payment:** Major credit cards; no personal checks. **Children:** Over age

5 welcome; additional $25 if third person in room. **Pets:** Not allowed. **Smoking:** Not allowed.

➤   **Despite its heavily congested tourist traffic in summer, Carmel-by-the-Sea retains its charm. The shops are a delight, the restaurants are excellent, and the beaches are inviting.**

Two hours south of San Francisco, the little town of Carmel lies on a long, gradual slope between Highway 1 and the Pacific. Sundial Lodge is on Monte Verde Street, a few blocks above the beach. The two-story building with gray shutters and a blue awning has tidy boxes of privet in front. Red and pink impatiens tumble from window boxes, and bright yellow marigolds bloom against the wall.

The flowery entrance hints at what you'll see as you step through a jasmine-covered trellis to a central brick courtyard. It's a bower of pansies, begonias, ferns, impatiens, marigolds, and bougainvillea, with an old-fashioned rusty metal sundial in the center. Peeking from among the flowers and ivy are Chinese animal sculptures. White chairs and glass-topped tables are set about the two-level terrace; in warm weather, you might enjoy breakfast here.

The guest rooms surround the courtyard and have garden or ocean views over the rooftops. They all have cable television, refrigerators, terry robes, and direct-dial phones. Ten rooms include kitchens, useful for preparing light snacks. Silverware and dishes are provided; ask at the office for pots and pans. A breakfast of juice, toast, freshly baked breads and muffins, and coffee or tea is served in the small lobby, where paintings of the inn's gardens and awards from the local garden club adorn the walls.

The rooms, in French country or Victorian styles, are attractively decorated and have Italian marble in the baths. Room 17, on the ground level, has a garden view and a four-poster bed with a canopy. An armoire serves as the closet and a curtained alcove holds an extra bed. In the trim little kitchen there's a fold-down ironing board and a table for two.

Room 28 has an ocean view through the trees. Decorated in light blues and ivories, it has a brass king-size bed set against long windows, a loveseat covered in satin damask, a small kitchen, and a twin bed in an adjoining room perfect for a child. Windows run almost the entire length of one wall in Room 26, which is furnished with country antiques. It has a walk-in closet, king-size bed, writing desk, and armchair.

Sundial Lodge has no off-street parking, but you can easily find long-term parking on the street within the blocks surrounding the inn. Many restaurants are within walking distance, such as Café

Napoli, an intimate Italian bistro a couple of blocks away. Chez Felix, for fine French cuisine, is just outside the inn's front door.

Vagabond's House Inn

P.O. Box 2747
4th & Dolores
Carmel, CA 93921
831-624-7738
800-262-1262
Fax: 831-626-1243

> **A quiet inn surrounding a courtyard garden**

Innkeeper: Dennis LeVett. **Accommodations:** 11 rooms (all with private bath). **Rates:** $95–$165 single or double, $20 additional person. **Included:** Continental breakfast. **Added:** 10% tax. **Minimum stay:** 2 nights on weekends. **Payment:** Major credit cards. **Children:** Over age 12 welcome; $20 additional if third person in room. **Pets:** Allowed with permission; $20 additional per night. **Smoking:** Allowed in courtyard only.

➤ **Vagabond's House is a five-minute drive from Carmel's beautiful mission, which dates from 1793 and is one of only two basilicas in the western United States. The annual Carmel Bach Festival is held at the mission during the summer.**

This cluster of half-timbered, shingled cottages blends perfectly with the quaint ambience of Carmel-by-the-Sea, as the village of Carmel is often called. The main building, which was a private home in the 1940s, and the one- and two-story guest accommodations face a flagstone courtyard with a waterfall. An immense old oak tree grows in the center of the courtyard, which is lush with color and greenery: camellias, rhododendrons, and trailing vines fill every nook; ferns grow against the oak tree and fuchsias hang from its branches. On December nights, the tree twinkles with hundreds of tiny lights. The effect is magical.

Vagabond's House was named for a poem written by Don Blandings in 1928, in which the poet, who stayed at the inn in years past, describes his dream house. Several copies of a book of Blanding's poetry are on display in the parlor, where you may also see the owner's intriguing collections of British lead soldiers and Big Little Books.

All the guest rooms have fireplaces with wood supplied, and most have kitchens. Those rooms without full kitchens have small refrigerators. Some of the guest rooms have individual themes, such as a nautical decor and an English hunt motif. Others are decorated in a comfortable residential style, with flowered comforters, easy chairs, and balloon shades. They have roomy closets, luggage racks, full baths with tubs and showers (or shower only), and good reading lamps. Some have white wicker furnishings and beds with a partial canopy. Breakfast (breads, fresh fruit, orange juice, a hot beverage, and an egg dish) is delivered to your room within minutes after you call the office.

Treasure-filled shops, art and antiques galleries, and restaurants are within a short walk of the inn, and a long curve of surf-lapped sandy beach lies at the bottom of the hill.

Carmel Valley

Carmel Valley Ranch

One Old Ranch Road
Carmel, CA 93923
831-625-9500
800-4-CARMEL
Fax: 831-624-2858
www.grandbay.com

A hillside golf resort with grand valley views

General manager: Martin Nicholson. **Accommodations:** 144 suites. **Rates:** Start at $295, single or double; $20 additional person; luxury suites start at $950. **Added:** 10.5% tax. **Payment:** Major credit cards. **Children:** Under age 17 free in room with parents. **Pets:** Allowed for an additional $75. **Smoking:** Non-smoking rooms available.

➤   **The 18-hole golf course, designed by Pete Dye, is known for its chal-lenges and beauty. Five fairways climb the mountainside, offering wide views of the valley floor. Three manmade lakes, the Carmel River, and nu-merous sand and grass bunkers provide opportunities to test all levels of skill.**

Carmel Valley Ranch is six miles east of Carmel on the Monterey Peninsula. The only resort in the area with a private, guarded gate, it is sequestered on 1,700 hilly acres above the valley.

Once admitted, you drive up a hillside, past fairways and greens, to the main lodge and 23 buildings of suites clustered among the oak trees. You immediately notice the striking display of color: hundreds of flowers — geraniums, dahlias, roses, irises, day lilies, rhododendrons, petunias, and zinnias — surround the contempo-rary ranch-style lodge, maintained by the chief gardener and artist Doris Ewing. Her creative skills are also evident in the resort's flo-ral arrangements.

The lobby and lounge have gray-stained redwood walls and a blend of antiques and early California furnishings. Floor-to-ceiling windows overlook the golf course on one side and a terrace and free-form swimming pool on the other. Tucked against one corner of the terrace is a whirlpool spa, one of six on the property.

The Oaks, the resort's intimate, formal dining room (jackets are suggested for men) is decorated with artwork by Doris Ewing, and features coastal ranch cuisine. There's a varied wine list, and a pi-anist plays light jazz on Friday and Saturday evenings. The kitchen will also pack a picnic basket if you request it.

Some suites are near the lodge; the rest are above it, in buildings with sweeping views of the valley. The commodious suites are tastefully furnished and comfortably elegant with sofas, easy chairs, and two-poster beds in tapestry and tweed fabrics. Standard features include a stocked wet bar, two TVs (VCRs are available), three two-line phones, robes, and wood-burning fireplaces. Half of the suites have two fireplaces, and twelve suites have a private hot tub out on the deck. Cookies are left at turndown, and coffee, tea, and cocoa are in every room.

Each of the one- and two-bedroom accommodations has a large deck with a view of the oak groves, golf course, gardens, or valley. A luxury master suite has a dining room often used for business hospitality or executive conferences. There are granite fireplaces in both bedroom and living room, a pink granite bar between the din-ing room and kitchen, and a deck on two sides jutting into the tops of oak trees.

Country club facilities are open to resort guests. The Club Grill is down the hill from the main lodge and overlooks the front nine holes of the golf course. Poolside dining is also available. In addition, the resort has one grass, two clay, and ten hard-surface tennis courts, along with a pro shop and instructors who will arrange matches, lessons, special events, and tournaments. Horseback riding is also available on the property.

For a luxurious golf or tennis vacation in a serene setting, Carmel Valley Ranch is an excellent choice. The service and staff are excellent, and the security of a guarded entrance is important to many guests, who like knowing that the only visitors who wander around uninvited are the deer that come to nibble the begonias hanging from oak tree branches by the front door.

John Gardiner's Tennis Ranch

114 Carmel Valley Road
P.O. Box 228
Carmel Valley, California 93924
831-659-2207
800-453-6225
Fax: 831-659-2492
www.jgtr.com

**An exclusive tennis resort
in the country**

Owner: John Gardiner. **Accommodations:** 14 houses and cottages. **Rates:** $325–$350 single, $425–$450 per couple. **Included:** All meals, taxes, and gratuities. Tennis packages start at $825 per person, double, for a two-day stay. Two-, three-, and five-day packages are available. **Payment:** Major credit cards. **Children:** With the exception of the Youth Tennis Camp in the summer, the resort is geared to adults. **Pets:** Not allowed. **Smoking:** Not allowed.

➤   **The giant stuffed animals that you see throughout the clubhouse —
the camel in the living room, the rabbits in the breakfast room — were
handmade by Mrs. Gardiner.**

The sign pointing to John Gardiner's Tennis Ranch from the main road is so small you'd certainly miss it if you weren't specifically looking for it. Ranch management no doubt wants to keep it that way for John Gardiner's, which celebrated its fortieth anniversary in 1997, is an exclusive resort where serious tennis players (some of them celebrities) go to improve their game in a secluded environment. Set in a valley on 25 acres, well back from the main road, the resort does offer plenty of privacy as well as personalized tennis instruction from the six pros on staff.

There are fourteen championship tennis courts on the property — one per guest room — as well as two specialized teaching courts. Instructional aids include closed circuit television and a computerized ball machine. Four instruction sessions are scheduled each day with breaks for energy-replenishing refreshments, a two-and-a-half-hour siesta at midday for lunch, a massage, a dip in the pool, or, if you prefer, a little bit of rest and relaxation.

Tennis whites should be worn on the courts and are allowed in the clubhouse until 7:00 P.M. Then the attire becomes more formal — a coat and tie for men, cocktail wear for women — as guests gather in front of the fire in the clubhouse's living room for hors d'oeuvres and cocktails. This is followed by a gourmet meal served by candlelight on white linens under crystal chandeliers in the adjoining dining room. The menu changes nightly, but the repast might include a seafood appetizer, followed by filet mignon or lamb, and then tiramisu or chocolate gateau. Homemade popovers and dessert soufflés are house specialties.

Breakfast is served in the sunny breakfast room, while lunch — weather permitting — is served outdoors on a brick patio filled with flowering marigolds, zinnias, and bougainvillea. The color-splashed patio is just one example of the beautiful garden oases that highlight the property. With flowerbeds near the tennis courts and several gazebos surrounded by blooms, handsome botanical displays seem to be everywhere you look.

Lodging is either in houses, which have full kitchens, or cottages, which do not. All units have wood-burning fireplaces and are individually decorated. Forest Hills house has two bedrooms, each with its own patio. There's a large tennis-themed painting over the sofa in the living room and a commodious hot tub on an outside deck. The bright baths have high ceilings, two closets, bathrobes, a vanity with two sinks, and a mirror lit by theatrical bulbs.

If your unit doesn't have its own hot tub, you can treat your tennis elbow in the two communal spas located on either side of the main swimming pool. In an adjacent building there are saunas and a massage room. Alternative recreation is available in Carmel, less than 15 miles away, where you can browse through the quaint seaside town's numerous galleries and boutiques.

Quail Lodge Resort and Golf Club

8205 Valley Greens Drive
Carmel, CA 93923
831-624-2888
888-828-8787
Fax: 831-624-3726
qul@peninsula.com
www.quail-lodge-resort.com

A well-known resort on a golf course

General manager: Michael Hoffmann. **Accommodations:** 100 rooms and villas. **Rates:** $295–$345 single or double, $25 additional person; suites $395–$550. **Added:** 10.5% tax. **Payment:** Major credit cards. **Children:** Under age 12 free in room with parents. **Pets:** Allowed with permission. **Smoking:** Nonsmoking rooms available.

➤   **Candlelit and romantic, with natural wood, rose upholstery, and white linens, the two-level dining room overlooks Mallard Lake and its lighted fountain. A pianist plays in the small bar five nights a week.**

A few miles east of Highway 1, off Carmel Valley Road two hours south of San Francisco, this resort stands in the middle of an 850-acre tract of land that includes a nature preserve and a championship golf course. Ten small lakes, the habitat of wildlife and waterfowl, dot the grounds, and the 18-hole course sprawls across the valley floor.

You drive down a road lined with pepper trees to a scattering of buildings behind winding paths. Inside the main lodge, there's a two-story atrium with dark beams and skylights above the mezzanine. Around the corner are the Covey restaurant and a cocktail lounge. In the plant-filled sunroom, a few steps down from the lounge, the glass walls offer views of the lake and lush grounds. Breakfast is served at the Covey restaurant, and lunch is available at the Club, a casual restaurant overlooking the driving range just across the Carmel River.

The guest rooms are beside walks with trellises that bloom with trumpet vines. Fragrant blossoms scent the air as you walk or ride in a golf cart to your room. Every room has either a patio or a balcony. All have phones and television, and VCRs can be requested. A typical room will have two queen-size beds, a dressing area, and a tiled bath with a lighted makeup mirror, hair dryer, coffeemaker, and separate vanities. A pants press and a complimentary fruit plate are also provided, but the rooms are not air-conditioned.

The light cottage suite has a sitting room-bedroom combination with a wet bar, gas fireplace, and vaulted ceiling with track lighting and skylights. The windows overlook the curving lakeshore, and from the patio you see ducks swimming on the lake and the arching bridge under graceful trees.

All the rooms have stereo systems, but the California suite has a VCR as well. A pocket door leads to a bath in deep red tile with a tub and shower. On the private deck, behind vine-covered walls, is a wooden hot tub. The suite has a living room, which can be rented separately if you wish to host a meeting.

Most of the guests at Quail Lodge are repeat visitors. Among the recreational diversions are four tennis courts, two swimming pools, and guest privileges on the golf course. The generally well-heeled patrons make occasional use of the helicopter landing next to the country club's driving range.

Stonepine

150 East Carmel Valley Road
Carmel Valley, CA 93924
831-659-2245
Fax: 831-659-5160
www.stonepinecalifornia.com

An exclusive inn in the country

General manager: Gordon Hentschel. **Accommodations:** 14 suites. **Rates:** $295–$1,500 single or double, $50 additional person. **Included:** Expanded Continental breakfast. **Minimum stay:** 2 nights on weekends, 3 nights on holidays. **Added:** 10.5% tax. **Payment:** Major credit cards. **Children:** Welcome in Paddock House and Briar Rose Cottage, age 12 and older in main château. **Pets:** Not allowed. **Smoking:** Not allowed.

➤ **Enter through the triple-arched porch and you're greeted by a gracious staff member who will invite you to have cognac in the living room after dinner or perhaps attend the performance of a string ensemble on a summer afternoon.**

This luxurious retreat began in the 1930s as a thoroughbred racing farm in the hills east of Carmel. Called the Double H Ranch by its owners, Helen and Henry Potter Russell of the Crocker banking family, it covered 7,000 acres of the valley. No effort was spared in creating the perfect estate, from the Mediterranean main house to the carefully designed gardens and orchards.

By 1983, when it was purchased by Noel and Gordon Hentschel, the property had dwindled to 330 acres. Its new owners renamed the place after the Italian pines that Helen Russell had planted as saplings and began an extensive restoration that would turn the estate into an opulent inn and equestrian retreat.

Eight suites make up Château Noel, a pink French country mansion with a tower, black ironwork, and red tiled roof. The château is at the end of a mile-long road that winds up a hill, past meadows and trees, and over a creek to a circular gravel drive punctuated with oak trees and low stone walls.

The living room is furnished in a combination of contemporary and traditional styles. Its seven-foot carved limestone fireplace is from 19th-century Italy; the French tapestries above it date from the 1700s. The theme is light and restful, and the mood tranquil.

French doors lead to a loggia with stone arches supported by carved columns from ancient Rome. Tall stone pines edge the sheltered lawn and garden beside it. Flowering shrubs scent the air, and vines and gnarled olive trees cast leafy shadows over the chairs and tables, where breakfast may be served. Around the corner, below walls cascading with white wisteria and purple bougainvillea, is the pool level, reached by descending broad stairs.

Indoors, in the dark, elegant dining room, guests who choose to dine here sit at a single table set with fine china, crystal, and sterling silver. The oak paneling is from 19th-century France — a wedding gift to Helen Russell from her family. The same burnished paneling is in the library, a comfortable nook for reading, chess, and conversation by the marble fireplace.

The only lodging on the main floor is the Don Quixote Suite, which has a king-size bed with partial canopy, a sitting room with a fireplace, two baths (one has a Jacuzzi), and a lovely walled garden. You'll find a fresh floral arrangement and a welcoming bottle of wine upon arrival, and since the suite is set off on its own, it offers more privacy than some of the second-floor suites.

Up timeworn stairs are the other suites, all lavishly appointed with antiques, down comforters, and luxurious baths. Each room has cable television and a VCR, fresh flowers, lounging robes, and shelves of books. Several have fireplaces laid with wood and ready to light.

Wedgwood, in blue, has a king-size bed and Wedgwood china on display. The big bathroom contains a two-person whirlpool tub. Chanel is a favorite of many guests, with its soft gray satins, a fireplace, antiques, and a whirlpool tub. The bedroom has two double beds. Taittinger is the largest and most expensive suite. A chilled bottle of Taittinger champagne awaits your arrival, and a champagne satin decor sets the tone. There are two bathrooms (one with a whirlpool tub and bidet) and dressing rooms.

Four more suites are down the hill in the Paddock House, an old-fashioned green and white country ranch house with a large veranda and lawn. If you bring young children, this is where you'll stay. Guests in the informal but well-furnished house can use its kitchen and dining room. A third building is Briar Rose Cottage, which has two suites, a kitchen, a fireplace, and a garden with a gazebo.

The Gate House, at the entrance to the estate, once belonged to Joan Baez. Now it offers another lodging option for guests at Stonepine. With high ceilings, attractive furnishings, its own private guesthouse, swimming pool, and tennis court, it's a good option for those seeking secluded luxury. It's rented out by the week.

Horseback riding lessons and trail rides are offered at the equestrian center. Stonepine also has a soccer field, an archery range, a four-hole golf course, a croquet lawn, tennis courts, and a horseshoe pitch. There's also an exercise room, and mountain bikes are available.

Davenport

Davenport Bed & Breakfast Inn

31 Davenport Avenue
P.O. Box J
Davenport, CA 95017
831-425-1818
800-870-1817 in California
Fax: 831-423-1160
inn@swanton.com
www.swanton.com/BnB

A seaside inn with artistic flair

Innkeepers: Bruce and Marcia McDougal. **Accommodations:** 12 rooms (all with private bath). **Rates:** $78–$140 single or double, $15 additional person. **Included:** Full breakfast and complimentary drink. **Added:** 10% tax. **Payment:** Major credit cards. **Children:** Allowed in some rooms; over age 5 charged as an additional person. **Pets:** Not allowed. **Smoking:** Not allowed.

➤ **Within walking distance are several studios and showrooms where local craftspeople display their works. The historic St. Vincent de Paul Church and the restored jail are interesting photographic subjects.**

The seaside community of Davenport, halfway between San Francisco and Carmel on Highway 1, was an active port at the turn of the century. When a cement plant went up in 1906, the town grew to include blacksmith shops, a general store, and half a dozen hotels.

Over time, Davenport gradually declined, but in recent years new homes and businesses have sprung up. On the site of the former Cash Store, which burned down in 1953, Bruce and Marcia McDougal built the New Davenport Cash Store and opened it in 1978 as a pottery gallery, restaurant, and lodging. Next to the two-story brick structure is the area's oldest remaining building, which has served as a public bath, bar, restaurant, dance hall, and private home. The McDougals renovated this cottage and opened it to guests.

They brought a background of hospitality to their venture, for they had fed and housed hundreds of people at Big Creek Pottery, their studio and school. The present gallery, on the ground floor of the inn, has become a center for folk art, textiles, pottery, and jewelry from around the world.

Across the room is the rustic restaurant, with brick walls hung with masks and carvings. Here you may sit at wooden tables on mismatched chairs or benches — there are even a few church pews — and dine on inventive pasta and seafood dishes such as grilled filet of salmon served with salmon ravioli and a warm ginger and scallion vinaigrette sauce. Hotel guests order from a special breakfast menu in the restaurant on weekdays; on weekends, breakfast is served in the cottage. In the evenings, inn guests are welcome to a complimentary cocktail from the bar.

Above the Cash Store and Restaurant are eight guest rooms with a sheltered balcony that stretches around two sides of the building, overlooking the highway and, beyond it, a bluff above the ocean. Wide doors open to rooms furnished with antiques and ethnic art from the McDougals' extensive collection. Some rooms have televisions; all have telephones and armoires or pegs rather than closets.

An art nouveau lamp with a stained glass shade stands on the bedside table in China Ladder; and there's a darling little antique rolltop desk. Pigeon Point is small, cool, and blue, decorated with a New England flavor. Whale Watcher has a sleigh bed and handsome, mirrored dressing table. Ano Nuevo is Spanish in tone with an iron bed topped with a woven bedspread from South America. Captain Davenport's Retreat, on the corner, is the largest room. It has a sitting area with four double doors opening to the balcony, peacock wicker chairs, and the best ocean view of all of the guest rooms.

If you're willing to sacrifice the view for quiet (Highway 1 can be noisy, though it's usually peaceful at night), request one of the four rooms in the cottage around the corner. It has a common area decorated with Indian wall hangings where guests may relax, read, and visit. There are games, a sideboard with coffee, tea, mugs, and plates for breakfast, and a small kitchen. As one visitor wrote in the guest book, "All the comforts of home — or the home you'd like to have — and yet you're on a holiday."

The decor in the cottage is light and bright, with country furnishings. Grandma's Room, small and serene, has a white iron bed and eyelet curtains at a high window. It faces east to a small garden and patio. The other three — Nellie's Sewing Room, The Guest Room, and Mike's Room — are also furnished in white wicker and have cotton print quilts on white iron beds.

Across the highway there's a secluded beach to stroll, and from the ocean cliffs you may see migrating gray whales spouting just offshore.

Gilroy

Country Rose Inn Bed and Breakfast

P.O. Box 2500
Gilroy, CA 95021-2500
408-842-0441
Fax: 408-842-6646
www.bbonline.com/ca/countryrose/

> **A serene home in garlic-growing country**

Innkeeper: Rose Hernandez. **Accommodations:** 5 rooms (all with private bath). **Rates:** $129–$199, $30 additional person. **Included:** Full breakfast. **Added:** 8% tax. **Minimum stay:** 2 nights on summer weekends. **Payment:** Major credit cards. **Children:** Not appropriate; charged as an additional person if third person in room. **Pets:** Not allowed. **Smoking:** Not allowed.

➤ **Rose, a former teacher, is a conscientious hostess. She will offer information on accessible attractions such as San Juan Bautista and Pinnacles National Monument and recommend good restaurants in the area.**

Roses dominate this charming inn, from the flowers in the rooms to the innkeeper's name. Carefully tended gardens and shade trees grow by the white Dutch Colonial home, which was built in the 1920s on a chicken ranch. The chickens are gone, but the sense of rural tranquillity remains on these five acres surrounded by farmland. Gilroy, the garlic capital of the world, is a few miles away, and San Jose is a 30-minute drive.

The simply furnished parlor has a brick fireplace and a baby grand piano. The dining rooms have a view of the front veranda and rosebed. Also on the main floor is the Garden Room, originally the living room. It reflects Rose Hernandez's interests and family, with its carved antique bed and trunk and a photograph of her parents.

The upstairs rooms have views of the big valley oaks and, in the distance, the Gabilan Hills. Imperial Rose is secluded behind two doors; Sterling Rose is a corner room with a window seat and a view of the magnolia tree and its bird's nests. Usually the magnolia blooms in time for Rose's annual Valentine tea.

Double Delight has a window seat and a walk-in closet. Rambling Rose is a large suite with French doors between the sleeping and sitting areas. Its balcony extends to the branches of a 300-year-old oak tree.

Goleta

Circle Bar B Guest Ranch

1800 Refugio Road
Goleta, CA 93117
805-968-1113
circleb@silcom.com
www.circlebab.com

| **A family ranch for relaxing and horseback riding** |

General manager: Pat Brown. **Accommodations:** 14 rooms (all with private bath). **Rates:** $186–$225 double, $60–$75 additional person. **Included:** All meals. **Added:** 9% tax. **Minimum stay:** 2 nights on weekends, 3 nights on holidays. **Payment:** MasterCard, Visa. **Children:** Under age 5 free in room with parents. **Pets:** Not allowed. **Smoking:** Allowed outside only.

➤ **On nearly 1,000 acres of hilly, coastal countryside, the ranch offers great scenery and good food and lodging, but for many guests its major appeal is horseback riding. Experienced wranglers take riders of all levels of ability on daily rides. They'll give individual instruction, too.**

The Circle Bar B, twenty miles north of Santa Barbara, combines a country atmosphere with contemporary comforts. Tucked in a wooded canyon in the Santa Ynez Mountains, the ranch has stables, a chicken coop, and assorted animals, including peacocks that wander the grounds and peer from the branches of the walnut trees. The atmosphere is down-home casual, befitting a place that opened sixty years ago as a children's camp.

Rooms have western decor with down comforters on the beds and free-standing fireplaces. Five are small, attached rooms; the rest are in separate cabins. All are set against a hillside of olive trees and reached by brick paths bordered by large jade plants. Cabins resemble spacious hotel rooms. Two-bedroom cabins are useful for families. The kids' favorites, though, are the two cabins with pull-down stairs that lead to lofts with double beds. Linens are changed daily, and full cleaning is provided on alternate days.

The ranch, begun by the Brown family in the 1930s, is still a family operation. Pat Brown runs the stables and Jim, his father, handles maintenance and the Friday and Saturday night cookouts. Weekend barbecue buffets feature country-style ribs, steak, chicken, baked beans, three kinds of salad, garlic bread, and carrot cake. Afterward, those who've come for the dinner theater mosey down to the Old Barn to watch a Circle Bar B production. The theater, which has been operating since the early 1970s, presents comedies, mysteries, and musicals that are usually (though not always) suitable for the whole family.

Meals are eaten at common tables in the dining room of the main ranch house or under the grape arbor. Breakfast is hearty country fare — fruit, eggs from ranch chickens, pancakes, potatoes, and strong coffee. After breakfast you may want to take a picnic lunch on a hike to the swimming hole beneath a waterfall or a trail ride to a scenic vista above the coast. The ranch is three and a half miles inland from Refugio State Beach. When you return, you can wash off the trail dust with a dip in the pool, play croquet or table tennis, soak in the hot tub, or get a massage. The living room — also the lobby, office, and game room — has books, games, a television, VCR, and a selection of videos.

Los Alamos

Union Hotel

P.O. Box 616
362 Bell Street
Los Alamos, CA 93440
805-344-2744
800-230-2744
Fax: 805-344-3125

Owner: Christine M. Williams. **Accommodations:** 13 rooms (5 with private bath). **Rates:** $100–$180 single or double. **Included:** Full breakfast. **Payment:** Major credit cards. **Children:** Not appropriate. **Pets:** Not allowed. **Smoking:** Allowed in designated areas only.

➤ **Each room has a reminder of the past: a pot-bellied stove, an antique trunk, a candelabra. The hotel even has a secret passage.**

It took the wood from twelve old barns to restore the original appearance of the Union Hotel. That was just a part of the work that was done to turn it into a restored version of a 19th-century lodging. Along with the potted palms and Victorian furniture in the lobby are a fireplace mantel taken from a Pasadena mansion, a clawfoot copper bathtub topped with beveled glass, a pair of 200-year-old Egyptian burial urns, and a *Gone with the Wind* lamp.

Saloon doors swing open to a 150-year-old mahogany bar. Headlights from a 1914 Oldsmobile hang on the side wall, along with washboards, saws, boots, well-used tools, horseshoes, and a moose head. There's a jukebox and an upright piano, and the ceiling was once the wall of the oldest store in town.

The dining room has chandeliers made from gas lights and an oak dining set that once graced a Mississippi plantation home. Here, dinner is served in the evenings. The menu includes filet mignon, scallops, and chicken. (Dinner reservations are required because of the many special events going on at the hotel.)

The first Union Hotel was built in 1880 as a stagecoach stop. It went up in flames in 1886, and was rebuilt of eighteen-inch-thick adobe and renamed the Los Alamos. When the late Dick Langdon found a picture of the hotel as it was in 1884, he determined to restore it. So the old barns were dismantled to create the dark facade it has today. After Langdon's death, Christine Williams purchased the hotel in 1997 (as well as the Victorian Mansion next door), and continues to emphasize the preservation of the property as well as keep up with the ongoing restoration of the hotel's antiques.

The hotel stands behind an old-fashioned boardwalk on the main street of tiny Los Alamos, fourteen miles from Solvang, a Danish-style village. Inside, you can while away an evening in the large, skylighted parlor upstairs. It has an 1880 Brunswick pool table, game tables, and shelves filled with books. The guest rooms, which surround the parlor, contain antique furniture, sleigh beds, handmade quilts, ceiling fans, pedestal sinks, and authentic Victorian wallpapers. The rooms with private baths have clawfoot tubs.

In this quiet place your sleep will be undisturbed. Come morning, the scent of freshly brewed coffee will lure you downstairs to breakfast. As you linger over bacon and eggs, you can chat with other guests and plan the day. Art galleries are beginning to spring up in town, and there are more than thirty-five wineries within a fifteen-minute drive. There are also numerous events at the hotel, such as stagecoach murder mysteries, historic hotel tours with special guest Abraham Lincoln in attendance, and Victorian tea parties, for which the participants dress in vintage clothing stored in hotel trunks, play parlor games, try their hand at croquet, and attempt to find their way out of a maze.

You may want to take a ride in a 1918 White touring car, originally used in Yellowstone National Park and now parked in front of the hotel. And you can take a tour of the Mansion, the amazing Victorian house next door run by the same owner (see Victorian Mansion, on the following page). Lounging on the brick terrace by the swimming pool and soaking in the hot tub, which sits under a heart-shaped trellis in a gazebo entwined with night-blooming jasmine, or getting lost in the backyard maze, are also favorite pastimes.

Victorian Mansion

P.O. Box 616
Los Alamos, CA 93440
805-344-2744
800-230-2744
Fax: 805-344-3125

> **A one-of-a-kind hotel with fantasy-themed rooms**

Owner: Christine M. Williams. **Accommodations:** 6 rooms. **Rates:** $200–$250. **Included:** Full breakfast. **Payment:** Major credit cards. **Children:** Not appropriate. **Pets:** Not allowed. **Smoking:** Allowed in designated areas only.

➤ **The whole house is an illusion. It lets you step into another world for a day. The place could be hopelessly hokey, but because of the exceptional quality of the workmanship, the clever ideas, and the playful approach, it's highly successful.**

From the outside, this Victorian with gingerbread trim looks like a quaint and perfectly preserved example of a 19th-century home. Step inside and you enter a unique world that is far from anything even remotely Victorian. It bears no resemblance to the rest of southern California, either, or the little agricultural town of Los Alamos. Each room is a fantasy, a dream brought to life by the late Dick Langdon's fertile imagination and the two hundred artisans who turned his ideas into reality. The immortalization of some of the artisans' faces crafted into the inn's hallway wall should be some hint of the tremendous creativity to come.

For starters, there's the '50s Drive-In Room. Enter the padded black leather door and you see a yellow 1956 Cadillac convertible. That's the bed, facing a screen where a movie from the '50s will be shown later. The rear of another Cadillac forms a magazine table, and the trunk of yet another holds a black porcelain washbasin. In the room is a sunken tub operated by remote control. A neon sign reads SNACK BAR. There are no visible windows — here or in any of the rooms. The walls are meticulously painted with scenes of the Hollywood hills and Mickey and Minnie Mouse dancing to a jukebox.

That's just the beginning. In the Roman Room you sleep in a silver *Ben Hur* chariot that holds a queen-size bed. You're surrounded by paintings of arbors, arches, busts, ruins, and Rome burning in the distance. The bathroom, behind a bookcase, has ancient battle scenes hand-painted on the tiles. Wide marble stairs lead to sunken Roman tub. A remote control operates the lights, television, fireplace, and the tub.

The Egyptian Room, behind a stone door, is a sheik's oasis with a canopy bed on a platform, a fabric ceiling, Oriental carpets, and a tiled fireplace. A low table, set with teapots from Arabia, is surrounded by plush cushions. Pull the beard of a life-size King Tut and the mummy pulls away from the wall to reveal a bathroom with an Egyptian motif. There's also a hidden balcony.

If you've ever wanted to be a swashbuckling buccaneer, Pirate is the room for you. Shaped like the interior of a Spanish galleon, it has a bed tucked into a corner, an open treasure chest full of sparkling booty, a low table set on a 700-pound cannon, and a stone fireplace carved with dragons. Ships' lanterns sway from the ceiling, mocking the movement of the ocean, and best of all is the small leaded glass window, with scenes of battling ships behind it. Open the window and you hear the sounds of creaking masts and a stormy sea. A map covers a door that slides open to reveal a tiled bathroom where painted parrots watch pirates at work. The sink is made of a rum cask and Blackbeard hides in the shower.

The French Room was the creator's idea of an 18th-century Parisian artist's studio. It includes a spiral staircase leading to a curtained bed, an alcove with a view of the French countryside, a tiny French fireplace, and a fainting couch. The walls are painted with views of Paris, and on the high-pitched ceiling a hot air balloon appears to be floating in the sky. Over the deep, two-person soaking tub there's a mural of Marie Antoinette's cottage, and Toulouse Lautrec would have been pleased with the tiled shower.

Picture a Gypsy encampment in the forest and you have the Gypsy Room. Portières hang over the bed, which appears to be a Gypsy wagon, embellished with carved mythological horses. Every season in the woodland is painted on the walls, from the blossoms of spring to the snow-clad trees of winter. There's a stone fireplace and a sunken pool. At the touch of a button, a hidden TV swings out; another button operates the hot tub.

Guests are offered local Santa Barbara County wine on arrival, and they can dine at the Union Hotel, where the menu offers steak, seafood, and pasta entrées. More unusual items, such as armadillo eggs and buffalo burgers, are often on the menu.

Montecito

Montecito Inn

1295 Coast Village Road
Santa Barbara, CA 93108
805-969-7854
800-843-2017
Fax: 805-969-0623
info@montecitoinn.com
www.montecitoinn.com

A cheerful hotel in the heart of Montecito

General manager: Linda Spann. **Accommodations:** 50 rooms and 10 suites. **Rates:** $185–$225 single or double; suites $265–$625. **Included:** Continental breakfast. **Added:** 10% tax. **Minimum stay:** 2 nights on weekends; 3 nights on holidays. **Payment:** Major credit cards. **Children:** Under age 17 free in room with parents; $15 for rollaway beds. **Pets:** Not allowed. **Smoking:** Nonsmoking rooms available.

➤ **Montecito's shops and restaurants are just a few steps from the inn, but many guests are drawn by the fabulous smells emanating from the lively Montecito Café, adjacent to the lobby, and decide to dine close to home. Seafood dishes are highlighted at this popular café.**

The Montecito Inn, located on Montecito's main street, has been welcoming guests since 1928. The three-story Mediterranean-style hotel, with its earthquake-resistant red tile roof, whitewashed exterior walls, and overflowing flower boxes, was funded by Charlie Chaplin (among others), and Chaplin's image can still be seen throughout the hotel. A Chaplin figure stands by the elevator, there are Chaplin movie posters behind the front desk and in the hallways, and the hotel maintains a Chaplin film library.

However, you don't need to be a Chaplin aficionado to enjoy a stay at the Montecito. Rooms, which range in size from small rooms with queen-size beds to luxury suites with living rooms, are attractive, with French Provincial furnishings. All rooms have cable television and alarm clock radios. King rooms and suites have added amenities such as refrigerators and VCRs. Seven luxury suites have fireplaces and baths with Jacuzzis. The split-level Tower Suite was Charlie's favorite and is often requested by honeymooners today.

The hotel has a small fitness room and an outdoor swimming pool and spa surrounded by potted bougainvillea. Beautiful wooden game tables are laid out for checkers in a downstairs hallway, and bicycles are available on loan. The friendly and helpful front desk staff can steer you in the direction of additional recreation, as both the beach and downtown Santa Barbara are nearby. In the morning Continental breakfast is served in the lobby, and hot coffee is always available.

San Ysidro Ranch

900 San Ysidro Lane
Montecito, CA 93108
805-969-5046
800-368-6788
Fax: 805-565-1995
ressyr@west.net
www.sanysidroranch.com

An exclusive cottage resort in the coastal hills

General manager: Janis Clapoff. **Accommodations:** 38 cottages. **Rates:** $395–$3,500 for 2 to 4 people. **Minimum stay:** 2 nights on weekends, 3–4 nights on holidays. **Added:** 7.75% tax. **Payment:** Major credit cards. **Children:** Welcome. **Pets:** Allowed; $75 additional. **Smoking:** Discouraged.

➤ **A part of San Ysidro's history is an 1825 adobe building, once the home of a pioneer family. Another is a former citrus fruit packing house that is now Stonehouse, an award-winning restaurant.**

This cottage resort in the hills above the sea has been like a second home to famous names and discerning travelers since it opened in 1893. Somerset Maugham, Sinclair Lewis, and John Galsworthy stayed in bungalows and wrote; Laurence Olivier and Vivien Leigh were married in the garden. John Huston stayed for three months, writing the screenplay for *The African Queen*; John F. and Jacqueline Kennedy honeymooned here, and celebrities from Jean Harlow to Julia Child have lauded the breathtaking views.

Once these 500 acres just south of Santa Barbara served as a way station for Franciscan friars. The property was later a cattle ranch and citrus tree farm. Now it's a resort that attempts to preserve San Ysidro's traditional calm, beauty, and history while providing contemporary luxury. A friendly staff insures a comfortable, casual feeling throughout the resort.

The single-story white cottages with peaked roofs are spread across the hillside under stately palms, eucalyptus, oak, and sycamore trees. Most of the cottages contain one, two, or three units; one has eight. They all have views of the distant sea or wooded foothills of the Santa Ynez mountains.

Each room is decorated differently and with traditional good taste. All the rooms have fireplaces or wood-burning stoves, wet bars, coffeemakers, hair dryers, makeup mirrors, down comforters, and terrycloth robes. Several feature private outdoor Jacuzzis. Canyon Cottage, surrounding an oak-shaded terrace, has some of the smallest rooms and best views. Behind it is Lilac, highest on the hill and closest to the tennis courts and heated swimming pool. Lilac 2, with high vaulted ceilings and a country French interior, has a king-size bed set back in an alcove and an outdoor hot tub on a large deck. Geranium is one of the original cottages. It's been refurbished with a country flavor in white and natural wood and has an outdoor Jacuzzi under flowering vines. The Sycamore cottages, with gleaming hardwood floors and four-poster beds, are located on the creekside. With its own private swimming pool, Eucalyptus is the resort's most deluxe accommodation.

The Stonehouse is the Ranch's fine-dining restaurant, and there is a stunning view from the terrace. Ancho pepper and honey glazed lamb shank with herbed cornmeal johnnycake and fire-roasted peppers and onions is an example of the restaurant's Mexican- and southwestern-influenced American cuisine. Downstairs in the basement is the cozy Plow and Angel Bistro.

Most admired are San Ysidro's grounds. Scarlet-blooming bottle-brush trees, brilliant lantana, Natal plum, and roses grow in profusion around lawns and paths. Vines cover a trellis in the wedding garden — a gorgeous garden terrace with a spectacular mountain backdrop. The air is fragrant with honeysuckle, jasmine, and orange blossoms, and birds can be heard singing from atop stately trees. Tidy herb and vegetable gardens keep the Stonehouse kitchen well stocked.

The Hacienda Lounge is in the main building, next to the registration office. Here you'll find a stone fireplace and a pool table, and chess and backgammon are set up for play. There's also an exercise room and a children's playground. Groups and small conferences are welcome at the ranch. Catering, audiovisual, and meeting materials are available.

Monterey

The Jabberwock

598 Laine
Monterey, CA 93940
831-372-4777
888-428-7253
Fax: 831-655-2946
www.jabberwockinn.com

A well-located bed-and-breakfast with warm hospitality

Innkeepers: John and Joan Kiliany. **Accommodations:** 7 rooms (5 with private bath). **Rates:** $110–$230 single or double. **Included:** Full breakfast and afternoon refreshments. **Added:** 10% tax. **Minimum stay:** 2 nights on weekends, 3 nights on some holidays. **Payment:** MasterCard, Visa. **Children:** Older children welcome; additional $25 if third person in room. **Pets:** Not allowed. **Smoking:** Outdoors only.

➤ **Some recommended restaurants in Monterey are Domenico's, on the wharf, for its view and bouillabaisse; the Sardine Factory on Cannery Row for seafood; and the Old Bath House, known for its Continental menu.**

"'Twas brillig, and the slithy toves did gyre and gimble in the wabe." So begins "Jabberwocky," Lewis Carroll's poem in *Through the Looking Glass.* The Kiliany's decided that it provided the perfect theme for their bed-and-breakfast, so every room has a Jabberwocky name, and bits of Lewis Carroll whimsy are found throughout the house. Be assured, however, that it's not overdone; the decor is charming but never precious.

The pleasant home, on a residential corner away from seaside tourist traffic, was built in 1911. Used as a convent for years, it was converted to a bed and breakfast in 1982. The Kilianys, former residents of San Mateo, just South of San Francisco, wanted a change and purchased the inn in 1996.

On the nicely landscaped grounds are lovely gardens of impatiens, fuchsia, geraniums, gaillardia, and roses. There are ponds, waterfalls, a sundial, flower boxes bursting with pansies, and red gravel paths traversing green lawns as well as a brick parking lot.

Inside you'll find early morning coffee on the dining room table, and dishes with such names as snarkleberry flumpsious and razzleberry flabjous are served later by the fireplace in the dining room or on the sun porch. Sherry and hors d'oeuvres are served on the sun porch at 5:00 P.M. Bedtime cookies and milk are the final treats of the day. Soft drinks and juices are always available in the refrigerator (called the Tum Tum Tree) on the upper stair landing, and you may store your own snacks and wine there.

The comfortable living room is available for relaxing, reading, listening to the stereo and tape deck, and looking through local menus and other guests' restaurant critiques. Beyond is the cheerful sun room, filled with plants, overlooking the side gardens.

The Toves, the only guest room on the main floor, has an eight-foot carved walnut Victorian bed, a private bath with a clawfoot tub and shower, a little patio, and a white rabbit–sized closet. High on the third floor are two garret rooms, the Mimsey and the Wabe, which share a bathroom and sitting room with an ocean view. Mimsey is a hideaway overlooking the bay and town, and binoculars are provided for looking at the view. A crisp eyelet lace coverlet tops the lovely queen-size bed. Peach-toned Wabe gets afternoon sun and has an Austrian carved bed.

The other rooms are on the second floor. Each is furnished distinctively and includes thoughtful accents such as fresh flowers, sachets, bathrobes, and fruit liqueurs. You may feel that you, like Alice, have stumbled through the looking glass when you see the card on your bedside table. It must be held to a mirror to be read.

Brillig, Mome Rath, and Borogrove all have fireplaces. Brillig's antique rolled oak bed with crocheted afghan gives it an old-fashioned country atmosphere. Mome Rath, with a Jacuzzi, is dramatic and the most masculine of all the rooms. Borogrove is the largest and best room, running the width of the house and overlooking Monterey Bay and the garden through three walls of windows. It has a white brick fireplace, a king-size bed, and a bath with a shower.

The innkeepers go out of their way to assure that you have a good time in their home and in Monterey. They'll give you lists of sightseeing suggestions, sell admission tickets to the aquarium so that you won't have to wait in line, and provide you with dozens of restaurant recommendations.

Monterey Plaza Hotel

400 Cannery Row
Monterey, CA 93940
408-646-1700
800-334-3999 in California
800-631-1339 in U.S.
Fax: 408-646-5937
reservations@montereyplazahotel.com
www.woodsidehotels.com

An elegant hotel above the bay

General manager: John Narigi. **Accommodations:** 291 rooms and suites. **Rates:** $135–$340 single or double; $365–$2,400 suites. **Added:** 10% tax. **Minimum stay:** 2 nights on weekends. **Payment:** Major credit cards. **Children:** Under age 17 free in room with parents. **Pets:** Not allowed. **Smoking:** Not allowed.

➤ **The hotel is not merely close to the ocean, it's virtually on it. Waves crash, the surf splashes, and sea lions bark right below your balcony and beside the terrace where lunch and dinner are served.**

This is the snazziest hotel of size in Monterey, so grand and sophisticated it seems slightly out of place on Cannery Row, where rustic remnants of John Steinbeck's colorful stories still cling. Fish processing was the main activity here until the bay was fished out and the sardine canneries deserted. Now they house art galleries, shops, and restaurants, and tourism brings in new life.

Like a transplant from San Francisco, 120 miles north, the Monterey Plaza boasts uniformed valets who greet you in the porte-cochere, take your car, and open the doors to a marble lobby. The exterior resembles Spanish Colonial buildings, but inside, all is Mediterranean luxury. Custom carpets, gleaming Italian marble floors, sweeping staircases, and dramatic flower arrangements create an elegant mood.

Directly across the lobby is a wall of windows framing the water and mainland mountains across from this western hook of the bay. Downstairs, the Duck Club restaurant has an even closer proximity to the kelp-covered surf. The open kitchen turns out wood-roasted specialties such as duck, beef, and seafood, as well as fresh pasta dishes. Schooner's, with a nautical theme, offers more casual dining with light bistro cuisine. On the fifth floor there is a fitness center and spa. Over thirty spa treatments are available.

Some guest rooms are in another building across Cannery Row, but since the main attraction here is the stunning view, the oceanside rooms are far superior. The best are the "02" rooms on the corners. The rooms and suites have deep green carpeting, light-colored walls, floral bedspreads, honor bars, brass lamps, ceiling fans, round tables, leather chairs, irons and ironing boards, a desk, and television with in-room movies. Baths have coffee makers, hair dryers, robes, laundry baskets for used towels, and separate vanities with makeup mirrors.

A deluxe suite with a view offers a spacious, light-filled sitting area and two balconies from which you can watch the pelicans, seagulls, kayakers, fishing boats, and sailboats. As you sniff the salt air, watch the sea otters cracking oyster shells, and listen to the sea lions beg for sardines at Fisherman's Wharf, you'll know this is unmistakably Monterey Bay.

Old Monterey Inn

500 Martin Street
Monterey, CA 93940
831-375-8284
800-350-2344
Fax: 831-375-6730
omi@oldmontereyinn.com
www.oldmontereyinn.com

> **A tranquil bed-and-breakfast in a luxurious setting**

Innkeepers: Ann and Gene Swett. **Accommodations:** 8 rooms, 1 cottage, 1 suite. **Rates:** $200–$350 single or double. **Included:** Full breakfast and afternoon refreshments. **Added:** 10% tax. **Minimum stay:** 2 nights on weekends. **Payment:** MasterCard, Visa. **Children:** Not appropriate. **Pets:** Not allowed. **Smoking:** Not allowed.

➤ **For years the big, half-timbered house was the Swetts' family home, where they raised six children. In 1977 it opened to guests and now is one of the gems of the Monterey Peninsula, a thoroughly charming, peaceful retreat set on more than an acre of lovely grounds and gardens.**

Tucked away on a side street in a residential district of Monterey is Old Monterey Inn, a world removed from the crowds of Cannery Row.

Brick paths wind past birdbaths under oak trees, ferns, a trickling fountain, blooming begonias, and drought-resistant succulents. Outside the dining room window, baskets of impatiens hang from the branches of an immense oak tree. Around the corner are painted carts from Costa Rica and other pieces of folk art collected during the Swetts' travels. The fragrant and colorful English rose garden is Gene's labor of love.

In the large common room, tea and cookies are set out in the afternoon. They're replaced by wine and hors d'oeuvres in the evening, when the gracious hosts encourage mingling and getting acquainted. This is a good time to check through an assortment of local restaurant menus and consult with other visitors or ask the Swetts for a recommendation.

On the other side of the foyer is the dining room, which still has the original metal fireplace built in 1929, and a stucco ceiling with hand-painted designs. A gourmand's breakfast is served here at one 9 A.M. seating. The dishes are different every day. You may feast on California quiche with chiles and pimentos, poached pears, crêpes, or Belgian waffles with Gene's special syrups. Takahashi china, painted with delicate birds and flowers, graces the table, which is also decorated with flowers from the garden.

The romantic rooms have no TV or phone to interrupt the mood. The beds are puffy with down comforters and pillows, and handcrafted natural woods and family antiques furnish the rooms. Most rooms have featherbeds, wood-burning fireplaces, skylights, and stained glass windows.

The most spacious is the Ashford Suite, once the master bedroom. The sitting area has a tiled fireplace, an antique pine daybed, and bay windows overlooking the gardens. In the bedroom is a king-size bed and more windows above the flowers.

Appropriately named, the Library Room boasts walls of books and a stone fireplace. It also has a private sun deck. Third-floor hideaways are Dovecote, with a built-in loveseat by the hearth, and Rookery, sunny with a skylight and wicker chairs.

Some rooms are in a cottage with private entrances behind the house. Shuttered windows, wicker furniture, and colors of white and green complement the inn's English country garden theme. The most secluded is wisteria-vined Garden Cottage, a suite with three skylights for stargazing, a private patio, and bay windows. Soft yellows and greens and a bed with a partial canopy of antique lace add to the romantic mood. Off-street parking is available.

Spindrift Inn

652 Cannery Row
Monterey, CA 93940
831-646-8900
800-841-1879
Fax: 831-646-5342

A romantic retreat on the bay

General manager: Randy Venard. **Accommodations:** 42 rooms. **Rates:** $199–$525 per room. **Included:** Continental breakfast and afternoon wine and cheese reception. **Added:** 10% tax. **Minimum stay:** 2 nights on some weekends. **Payment:** Major credit cards. **Children:** Welcome. **Pets:** Not allowed. **Smoking:** Not allowed.

➤ **There's an additional romantic retreat in the rooftop garden. Flower boxes and lounges behind a white railing provide a relaxing place to enjoy the sun and Monterey's blue sea and sky.**

The Spindrift Inn stands between Cannery Row and the Pacific; aloof from the souvenir shops, its focus is the rumbling sea. The hotel's history is as storied as its Cannery Row locale, and the building once housed everything from a Chinese hotel in the 1920s and 1930s to a bordello. It was abandoned until the mid-1970s, when an impressive restoration was begun. The hotel reopened as the Spindrift in 1984, and today the elegant four-story hotel possesses residential charm in a turn-of-the-century environment. Fine reproductions of period furniture are enhanced by Italian and French influences.

Valet parking takes care of your car, and you step into an atrium lobby with a skylight above. Just past it is an intimate, carpeted sitting area where wine and cheese are served in the afternoons; it has soft chairs and a couch facing a fireplace. The concierge desk is nearby, where you can obtain information about sightseeing, restaurants, and tickets to peninsula attractions from a helpful member of the staff.

Upstairs, the guest rooms are romantic and inviting, with walls in soft peach, hardwood floors topped by Chinese carpets, wood-burning fireplaces, feather mattresses, down comforters, and marble baths with brass fixtures, bath salts, and botanical toiletries. Many have king-size beds with full or partial canopies.

Plush terrycloth robes, nightly turndown service with Swiss chocolates, and breakfast on a silver tray in your room are a few of the special touches. A television and a mini-bar stocked with soft drinks are in the armoire. Room service is provided by a local Italian restaurant.

Your room is likely to have a cushioned window seat piled with pillows, an ideal spot for contemplating the bay in sun and fog and watching for whales, sea lions, and the endlessly fascinating sea otters (oceanside rooms have binoculars). The corner rooms are the largest and have the best views, but no room lacks for space.

Ojai

Ojai Valley Inn and Spa

Country Club Road
Ojai, CA 93023
805-646-5511
800-422-OJAI
Fax: 805-646-7969
www.ojairesort.com

A golf resort in a tranquil valley

General manager: Thad Hyland. **Accommodations:** 206 rooms and suites. **Rates:** $230–$310 single or double, suites $375–$2,000. **Payment:** Major credit cards. **Children:** Free in room with parents. **Pets:** Allowed in certain rooms. **Smoking:** Nonsmoking rooms available.

➤ **The finish materials used in the inn's renovation are of indigenous materials, with a strong influence of Southwest Indian art. Rose and lavender touches are in the shades of the valley's remarkable pink moment, when sunset hues bathe the mountains in color.**

In 1923 the wealthy glass manufacturer Edward Drummond Libbey began turning a long-held dream into reality: building a private club in the idyllic Ojai Valley. Libbey commissioned Pasadena architect Wallace Neff to design a classic resort that would harmonize with the tranquil valley's oak and orange groves and the encircling mountains. The result was an enduring example of southern California architecture — a low, rambling adobe hacienda with a red tile roof and a flagstone terrace.

Over the years the inn and country club expanded, changed hands several times, and had a $35 million renovation. Now, spread over the property's 220 hilly acres, it offers modern luxury accommodations, four dining areas and a bar, and many kinds of recreation.

An 18-hole golf course plays 6,235 yards across green hills edged with oak trees. There are eight hard-surface tennis courts, four of them lighted; clinics and private lessons are available. Two swimming pools are appealing on summer days that may reach 100 degrees in Ojai, some fourteen miles inland from the ocean. Bikes can be rented for touring the countryside, and the inn grounds are connected to a bicycle path and equestrian trail. There's also a year-round Jacuzzi and a putting green, while a steam room, sauna, and exercise equipment are located at the fitness center. Children will see pygmy goats, bunnies, and Tiffany the pot-bellied pig at the ranch's petting farm.

Breezeways, arcades, and the arbored terrace freshen and cool the air during the day. In the evening, fireplaces in some rooms and in the lounge ward off the chill. The original lobby is now the lounge, where a ceiling of heavy, rough beams and white walls give it a southwestern flavor. It's a relaxing place for conversation, a game of chess, or snacking from the cookie tray. The new lobby is open and light, with a beamed ceiling three stories high, a wrought-iron chandelier, and palms in terra cotta pots.

Vista, the main dining room, emphasizes light, healthy fare, with a special focus on fish of the central California coast and wines from small nearby vineyards. The menu includes dishes such as seared ahi tuna and crispy roast duck in an orange chipolte sauce with red wild rice. In the formal restaurant, the light bamboo decor is cheerful and jackets are recommended.

The Oak Grill & Terrace, serving steaks, chicken, salads, sandwiches, and Sunday brunch, is more casual. The restaurant has a Mexican look and good views, but the Terrace, offering al fresco dining under live oaks, provides the best mealtime views of Ojai's pastoral valley, golf course, and mountains.

The larger-than-average guest rooms have sofa beds and private patios or balconies with golf course or mountain views. Amenities include two separate vanities, scales, night-lights, irons and ironing boards, robes, coffeemakers, mini-bars, and televisions in armoires. New suites have two working fireplaces.

One section's four connecting rooms make it a good choice for several couples traveling together. If you're looking for the romance of the past, the oldest rooms, which are smaller and cozier, are the most appealing. Arched ceilings over the halls, solid doors, four-poster beds, and baths in tiles of the period give these rooms character.

The Honeymoon Suite, in the old section, has just one room but is popular for its view and its private terrace. A cottage, with a parlor and two bedrooms — each with a king-size bed — is a good choice for a family.

Ojai is often called California's Shangri-La because the 1937 movie *Lost Horizon* was filmed there. The spectacular view of the rocky massif that was the backdrop for the film can be seen from the terraces of the ballroom in the Topa Center, which accommodates groups and meetings.

Pacific Grove

The Centrella

612 Central Avenue
Pacific Grove, CA 93950
408-372-3372
800-233-3372
Fax: 408-372-2036
concierge@innsbythesea.com
www.centrellainn.com

> **A hotel with comfort and character on the Monterey Peninsula**

Manager: Mark Arellano. **Accommodations:** 21 rooms and suites (all with private bath) and 5 cottages. **Rates:** $109–$209 single or double, $15 additional person, cottages $189–$229. **Included:** Buffet breakfast and afternoon refreshments. **Added:** 10% tax. **Minimum stay:** 2 nights on weekends. **Payment:** Major credit cards. **Children:** Welcome in cottages, $15 additional if third person in room. **Pets:** Not allowed. **Smoking:** Not allowed.

➤ **Take the historic walk through old Monterey, play golf on some of the world's best courses, or go to the Monarch Natural Preserve to marvel at the thousands of butterflies that return every year.**

Once a boarding house, this attractively restored inn on the Monterey Peninsula, a two-hour drive south of San Francisco, adds personal, homey touches to its hotel amenities. In the reception area and parlor, bright flames burn in the fireplace, and trays of afternoon cookies, sherry, and hors d'oeuvres sit on an old oak table. There's also a player piano. Against a wall, a framed stitchery is in progress. It's a design of the hotel and any guest so moved may add a few stitches to it; eventually it will join a similar picture on the corridor wall.

Up the open, skylighted staircase are the guest rooms; each door bears a brass number on fabric of the same colors as the room. Furnished with antiques, down comforters, and armoires, they have starched lace curtains at the windows, baths with showers or tubs with hand-held showers, and Neutrogena toiletries. Preferred rooms are those overlooking the lovely gardens abloom with camellias and gardenias. These are the most quiet, away from the street.

Room 24 is a two-room suite with a white iron bed and clawfoot tub. Room 17 is smaller. It has a white wicker chair, its iron bed is topped with a floral comforter, and its bath has a shower with a built-in bench. There's a sofa and a wet bar as you enter the Anna Beighle Suite on the third floor. Under slanted ceilings, its king bed is dressed in white lace, and a writing desk illuminated by a banker's green glass and brass lamp stands at the window.

On the ground floor is the Garden Room, which has its own entrance from a side porch. Popular with honeymooners because of the large Jacuzzi tub in its white tiled bath, the room is a pleasant retreat. The metal bed is draped in gauze and invitingly topped with lots of pillows, a pretty patchwork quilt, and a cozy comforter. There's a plump easy chair with a footrest in one corner, a Franklin stove in another, and a table for two overlooks a garden of ferns.

The cottages are reached by brick paths that wind through the courtyard gardens of calla lilies, palm trees, and Norfolk pines. Their rooms are furnished with a mixture of antiques and modern pieces. Each has a fireplace, wet bar, television, and phone.

A buffet breakfast of fresh fruit, juice, pastries, eggs, yogurt, and granola is presented in the parlor. Sometimes the old-fashioned waffle iron is put to use and you'll have crisp, buttery waffles to enjoy at an alcove table by the garden.

The Centrella is close to many of the Monterey Peninsula's attractions. You can stroll two blocks to Lover's Point for a view of the bay or drive to Monterey to meet sea creatures face to face in the highly acclaimed aquarium.

Gatehouse Inn

225 Central Avenue
Pacific Grove, CA 93950
831-649-8436
800-753-1881
Fax: 831-648-8044
www.sueandlewinns.com

| A historic home within walking distance of Monterey Bay |

Manager: Lois DeFord. **Accommodations:** 9 rooms (all with private bath). **Rates:** $110–$165 single or double, $15 additional person. **Included:** Full breakfast. **Added:** 10% tax. **Minimum stay:** 2 nights on weekends. **Payment:** Major credit cards. **Children:** Over age 5 welcome, $15 additional. **Pets:** Not allowed. **Smoking:** Not allowed indoors.

➤ **In the kitchen of the main house, coffee, tea, cookies, and fruit are always available. The informal buffet breakfast may be taken to your room or eaten in the dining room or parlor, and some guests choose the table in the kitchen.**

The Gatehouse has an interesting history. It was built in 1884 by a state senator, Benjamin Langford, as a seaside retreat for his family. In those days, Pacific Grove was a religious meeting ground surrounded by a white picket fence. If the senator came home late and the gates were locked, he had to hunt up the keys and then return them. One night in 1885, tired of this ordeal, he chopped the gate down; it was never rebuilt.

There's no barrier now to this lovely old home on a residential corner. Guests are welcomed into the parlor, which retains the atmosphere of a Victorian summer house with its antique furniture, pale green walls, and stained glass windows. Several of the rooms have views of Monterey Bay, which is a short walk down the hill from the inn. The Langford Room, which has a stove and a sitting area, has the best water view. The small Sun Room, cheery in white and green, is flooded with morning sun through its two walls of windows. On the ground floor are the Steinbeck Room and Italian Room. Each has its own entrance and latticed patio.

Behind the main house, in a separate building, are the Cannery Row and Wicker rooms. Cannery Row has a king-size bed topped with floral pillows, a woodstove, and a clawfoot tub. Wicker has a Victorian garden theme, with a white lattice fence on the wall and exuberant flower displays.

The only drawback to this charming inn is the noise. In the main house you're likely to hear traffic from the busy street, early morning street cleaners, the clatter of dishes, and footsteps. If you're a light sleeper, the rooms in the back building are preferable.

The Green Gables Inn

104 Fifth Street
Pacific Grove, CA 93950
831-375-2095
800-722-1774
Fax: 831-375-5437
www.foursisters.com

| A restored Victorian with contemporary comfort |

Owners: Roger and Sally Post. **Innkeeper:** Tamara Kirkland. **Accommodations:** 11 rooms (6 with private bath). **Rates:** $110–$240 single or double, $15 additional person. **Included:** Full breakfast and afternoon tea and hors d'oeuvres. **Added:** 10% tax. **Payment:** Major credit cards. **Children:** Welcome in Carriage House; charged as an additional person if third person in room. **Pets:** Not allowed. **Smoking:** Not allowed.

➤ **Pacific Grove is a fine place to relax, walk, and enjoy the sea views
and tide pools. At Natural Bridges State Beach you may see thousands of
wintering Monarch butterflies in the Monarch Natural Preserve.**

This half-timbered Queen Anne mansion, built in 1888, stands on
a corner across the street from beautiful Monterey Bay. The home
has been in the Post family since 1974. Roger and Sally Post are the
founders of the Four Sisters Inns, a group of attractive and well-
managed lodgings.

Soft music plays as you enter the Green Gables, and rainbows
dance against the wall from the stained glass window in the front
door. Flowered carpeting, pale yellow walls, and carved molding
details create a warm setting in the living room. Here guests sit by
the white fireplace and play chess or retire to the alcove window to
browse through restaurant menus. There are numerous reading
lamps but, oddly, no books or magazines.

Through the double doors is the dining room, where a buffet
breakfast is set out. After helping yourself to juice, fruits, cereal, a
hot egg dish, muffins, and coffee, you may sit at the main table
under a crystal chandelier or at a table by the window overlooking
the sea.

The five upstairs rooms are furnished with antiques, soft quilts,
and ruffled curtains. They all feature typical Four Sisters Inns decor: coordinated fabrics and wallpapers, fresh flowers, lavish greenery, and the occasional teddy bear, ceramic rabbit, or stuffed goose.
Most of the rooms have ocean views and six have fireplaces.

Chapel Room is reminiscent of a chapel on a private estate, with
its mullioned windows, heavy woodwork, beamed ceiling, and
straight-back benches. The room is full of cupboards and nooks,
and the bed is a hand-carved antique topped with a white cotton
spread, lacy pillows, and a teddy bear. Floral wallpaper with a rose
motif and matching curtains add a feminine touch.

A ladder takes you up to a loft with a window seat lookout in the
Gable Room. The Lacey Suite can accommodate four people. It has
a sitting room with a fireplace and an antique tub in the bath. Balcony Room, which has the best ocean view from its sun room, accommodates three and shares a bath. In back, behind the main
house and a tiny garden, is the Carriage House, with five rooms on
three levels. All have fireplaces, king- or queen-size beds, television, and private entrances.

The staff at Green Gables seeks to please and enjoys supplying
the extras that make a stay memorable. Holiday celebrations,
birthday and honeymoon specials, and arranging reservations at

golf courses, concerts, theatrical events, and restaurants are among the services they provide.

The Martine Inn

P.O. Box 232
255 Ocean View Boulevard
Pacific Grove, CA 93950
831-373-3388
800-852-5588
Fax: 831-373-3896
www.martineinn.com

A castlelike home
overlooking the sea

Innkeeper: Don Martine. **Accommodations:** 20 rooms and 3 suites (all with private bath). **Rates:** $155–$300 single or double, $35 additional person; suites $250–$300. **Included:** Full breakfast and afternoon wine and hors d'oeuvres. **Added:** 10% tax. **Minimum stay:** 2 nights on weekends, 3 nights on holidays. **Payment:** Major credit cards. **Children:** $35 additional if third person in room. **Pets:** Not allowed. **Smoking:** Allowed in fireplace rooms only.

➤ **The innkeeper's goal is "to recreate the experience you would have had a century ago if you'd been a personal guest of the Parkes."**

Like a little Mediterranean castle, this rose-colored stucco mansion stands on a cliff above Monterey Bay. The first thing you notice when you enter the parlor is the irresistible view; from the picture window you see a panorama of surf and rocks, sea and sky. You may catch glimpses of the sea otters, seals, and whales that frequent these waters.

The next eye-catcher is the gleam of silver from the innkeepers' collection of ornate teapots, trays, vases, and other museum-quality pieces. Don Martine has myriad interests, as a quick glance around his home reveals. His antique collection fills the common rooms and guest rooms.

The home was built in 1899 and purchased in 1901 by Laura and James Parke, of Parke-Davis Pharmaceuticals. Many dignitaries were entertained here over the years, and some major remodeling took place. Eventually the cupola and dormers were removed and the house was converted from a Victorian to a Mediterranean style. Don Martine and his parents bought it in 1972.

Later, Don fully renovated the mansion, adding modern plumbing and heating but replacing the fixtures, wall coverings, colors, and furniture with authentic turn-of-the-century pieces. Some are particularly outstanding: a mahogany suite from the 1893 Chicago World's Fair, an Eastlake suite from the estate of C. K. McClatchy (it's in the McClatchy Room), Edith Head's bedroom suite, and an 1860 Chippendale Revival four-poster bed with a canopy and side curtains.

The four-poster is in the original master bedroom, the Parke Room, now the most expensive and most popular room at the inn. It has a spectacular bay view, a white brick fireplace, a ceiling-high armoire with a beveled mirror, and bathroom doors that open to an iron railing.

The Early American Room has a rope bed of solid burled walnut, dated 1800. In the Art Deco Room the walls are trimmed with an art deco pattern, and there's a massive art deco armoire. In the Pineapple Room, the dresser, mirror, and four-poster bed all have carved pineapples and the color scheme is pineapple as well. The Edith Head Room has a clawfoot tub and fireplace, and you can see the ocean as you lie in the costume designer's former bed.

Behind the main house, on the other side of a courtyard with a dragon fountain, is the Carriage House, which has six rooms. The Captain's Room is furnished with a carved, inlaid American bedroom set, a rare standing mirror from 1840, peacock wallpaper, and a view through double doors to the breezeway and courtyard. All rooms have refrigerators and fresh fruit. The only television is in the inn's conference room.

Guests gravitate to the courtyard, bright with potted flowers, to see the marble bar with stained glass windows and the Coinola player piano. There's a pool table behind the bar and a whirlpool tub around the corner. Many guests also ask to see Don's collection of classic cars.

Intriguing collectibles are only part of what makes the Martine Inn superior. The service and hospitality are exceptional, drawing visitors back again and again.

The innkeeper also offers hors d'oeuvres with wine and sparkling cider, and champagne in a silver ice bucket will be brought to your room upon request. Breakfast, which is served on Sheffield china with sterling silver and crystal, is different every day. Fresh orange juice, muffins, quiche, eggs with artichoke sauce, and fruit in a spicy sauce are a few of the dishes.

A page of suggestions of things to see and do on the Monterey Peninsula is given to each guest, and the innkeeper will arrange for tours and restaurant reservations. The inn also handles conferences, seminars, and weddings.

Seven Gables Inn

555 Ocean View Boulevard
Pacific Grove, CA 93950
831-372-4341
www.7gables-grandview.com

**A Victorian mansion
overlooking Monterey Bay**

Innkeepers: Susan, Ed, and John Flatley. **Accommodations:** 14 rooms (all with private bath). **Rates:** $155–$350 single or double. **Included:** Full breakfast and afternoon tea. **Added:** 10% tax. **Payment:** MasterCard, Visa. **Children:** Not appropriate. **Pets:** Not allowed. **Smoking:** Not allowed.

➤ **Anyone at the inn will make golf reservations for you, recommend restaurants and entertainment, and tell you about nearby attractions such as Cannery Row, the Monterey Bay Aquarium, and Lover's Point Beach, a sheltered stretch of white sand that's just a 2-minute walk from the inn.**

When this showy, yellow and white Victorian was built in 1886, it was one of a series of mansions fronting Monterey Bay. Few are left today, but the panorama of sea and surf and rocky bluffs remains much the same. Lucie Chase, a wealthy widow and civic leader, owned Seven Gables at the turn of the century; she added the sun porches and gables that give the home such distinctive style.

The Flatley family, who restored the old home and opened it as a bed-and-breakfast in 1982, maintain it with loving care. It's a gingerbread delight on the outside and a treasure chest within, full of the fine antiques the Flatleys have collected. Chinese carpets, ornate chandeliers, marble pedestals, gilded tables, and armoires mingle in tastefully furnished rooms.

A leaded glass front door leads you into a parlor where a beaded crystal chandelier hangs from the ceiling, an inlaid table stands in the center of the room, a velveteen fainting couch sits in a corner, cloisonné vases hold potted palms, and a lavish Victorian sofa is covered in pink damask. A mirror with a gilded frame reaches to the ceiling in the adjoining dining room, where a vase filled with fresh flowers rests on the table. Tea is served here in the afternoon, and in the morning guests get acquainted over a generous breakfast.

A stained glass window divides the dining room from a sun room filled with statuary, Oriental rugs, fringed lamps, and plenty of armchairs. With a wall of lace-curtained windows, the sun room has a view of the bay and the coastal mountains to the north.

The guest rooms are divided among four buildings: the main house, a guest house, and two cottages, one a separate unit and the other with rooms on two levels. All are furnished with antiques and a romantic but not fussy decor.

The Gable Room is tucked under a high gable in the main house. With windows on four sides, it has views from the village streets to the horizon of sea and sky. The room is at the top of narrow, steep steps and has a low ceiling and slanted walls — cozy, but not a good choice for tall visitors.

Fairlawn, a ground-floor room, is also attached to the main house. It has a private entrance from the garden and you can hear the trickling from the nearby stream that runs through the property. Since it is situated at the front of the house, it has a direct view of the ocean, which is just across the street. With a crown canopy bed draped in lace and a great view, it's a pleasant room even if it's the inn's smallest.

The guest house in back, off the flowery courtyard, has four rooms, all with refrigerators. There's a pay phone in the hall and a television in a sunroom. The Cypress Room, one of the most expensive and most elaborate, is in a corner with wide windows and a window seat, a gilded couch, fabric walls, and Oriental pillows.

Spacious Ocean Mist has inlaid wood antiques, stained glass, and a bay window; Mayfair views the brick courtyard and cottage and catches a glimpse of the sea. Baskets of candies and fruit are provided in every room.

Despite all the gilt and marble elegance, you won't feel surrounded by formality at Seven Gables. The Flatley family is eager to see that you're comfortable. "We want to keep things homey," they say.

The Flatleys have opened up another, less formal inn in the Edwardian home next door. Called the Grand View Inn, it has ten guest rooms and was built by the town's first woman mayor. You may want to inquire into whether the Grand View has space available if the Seven Gables is already booked (which it so often is due to its popularity).

Pebble Beach

The Inn at Spanish Bay

2700 Seventeen Mile Drive
Pebble Beach, CA 93953
831-647-7500
800-654-9300
Fax: 831-644-7960
www.pebblebeach.com

> **A seaside resort with a world-class golf course**

General manager: Gary Davis. **Accommodations:** 269 rooms and suites. **Rates:** $350–$475 single or double, $25 additional person; suites $675–$2,165. **Added:** 10.5% tax and $18.50 per night gratuity. **Payment:** Major credit cards. **Children:** Under age 18 free in room with parents. **Pets:** Not allowed. **Smoking:** Not allowed.

➤ **Monterey Peninsula, 120 miles south of San Francisco, boasts some of the world's most spectacular coastal scenery. Winding above its rugged headlands, the renowned Seventeen Mile Drive is contained entirely within the Del Monte Forest Preserve, which covers some 5,300 acres.**

The Inn at Spanish Bay and its 18-hole, par-72 golf course opened in late 1987, at the northern end of the sand dunes of Spanish Bay. The low-profile, red-roofed buildings of the complex blend with the setting, their walls the color of the dunes around them. Accommodations, located in two wings off the central lobby area, are spacious and well-appointed, with blond woods, gas fireplaces, wall-to-wall carpeting, and small decks or balconies that overlook the forest, golf course, or ocean.

Stocked refrigerators, televisions, large baths with deep soaking tubs, terrycloth robes, and assorted toiletries (including sewing kits and clothes steamers) are among the amenities. Abstract paintings and landscapes add a dash of color to the off-white and neutral tones of the rooms.

The resort has eight tennis courts, two with lights for night play, as well as a swimming pool and spa, but the main attraction is the golf course. The Links at Spanish Bay was modeled after the demanding seaside courses of Scotland and Ireland, with the game played close to the ground to avoid the wind. Fescue grasses, native to Scotland, provide a hard, fast surface. There's even a kilted bagpiper who plays at dusk as he strides across the fairway.

Several meeting rooms and a ballroom big enough to hold a banquet for four hundred give the resort a conference orientation. When a group is on the site, the lobby is often filled with name-tagged crowds, all enjoying the country club atmosphere. Past the large, busy lobby is a lounge where appetizers and cocktails are served in the evenings by the stone fireplace; musicians play there nightly. Just outside is the Grill, open in summer. Roy's Spanish Bay is two-level dining room offering Euro-Asian cuisine in a light, bright, casual atmosphere. More intimate, elegant, and dressy than Roy's is the Bay Club, featuring a Mediterranean menu and a fine wine list.

One of Spanish Bay's greatest attractions — after its location and golf course — is its service and attention to detail. A concierge and thirteen assistants are on hand to help you register, escort you to your room, and deal with special needs, such as finding a dentist, making tour reservations, or dressing up as elves for your group's Christmas party.

A gratuity is charged each day. Room service is available 24 hours a day. You'll receive twice-daily housekeeping and a morning newspaper. Convenient racks are available to store your golf clubs, and you may have one-hour shoe shines and pressing and same-day dry cleaning. A complimentary airport shuttle from Monterey is provided. If you don't want to head in to Carmel for shopping, there are several shops off the breezeway by the main entrance.

The Lodge at Pebble Beach

P.O. Box 1128
Seventeen Mile Drive
Pebble Beach, CA 93953
831-624-3811
800-654-9300 in California
Fax: 831-644-7960
www.pebblebeach.com

**A classic golf resort
overlooking the Pacific**

Manager: David Oliver. **Accommodations:** 151 rooms, 10 suites. **Rates:** $400–$1,250, $25 additional person, suites $1,000–$1,925. **Added:** 10.5% tax and a $15 gratuity per night. **Payment:** Major credit cards. **Children:** Under age 18 free in room with parents. **Pets:** Small pets allowed with permission. **Smoking:** Not allowed.

➤ **The Pebble Beach Golf Links is often called the premier golf course in the world open to the public; you'll need a reservation far in advance to play. The site of many tournaments, it is both challenging and beautiful, perched at the edge of a seaside cliff.**

Since 1919, the Lodge at Pebble Beach has catered to travelers seeking luxurious accommodations in one of nature's most spellbinding and magnificent settings. Some 120 miles south of San Francisco, in the heart of the Del Monte Forest Preserve along the rocky coast, the sprawling resort stands on a bluff, under towering pines and gnarled cypress trees. Between the main lodge and the sea lies hallowed ground to golfers: the famed Pebble Beach fairways.

Until 1977 the hotel was known as Del Monte Lodge, after Charles Crocker's original resort; then the name was changed, but the superior hospitality and accommodations remained. Eleven guest rooms are in the original lodge. The rest are in rambling, low-rise buildings laced throughout the six acres of grounds and golf links.

Each room has its own patio or balcony with a view of the gardens, fairways, or the surf-pounded shore. The traditional, residential furnishings feature natural fabrics and light woods. There are fireplaces ready to light, stocked bars, televisions, and gracious accents such as fresh flowers and original art. The one- and two-bedroom suites are lavishly decorated and have grand views of the golf course and sea. Most in demand are the 18th-fairway suites, with their marble fireplaces and unobstructed, spectacular ocean vistas.

A $15-per-night gratuity is added to all room rates. This is intended, say staff members, to cover housekeeping, baggage handling, shuttle transportation, and airport pickup. So tipping in these areas is not expected.

If you're unable to get a reservation at the famed main course, guests do receive preferential tee times at the resort group's other golf courses: Spyglass Hill, the Links at Spanish Bay, and Del Monte Golf Course. If you prefer other sports, the lodge has some options. There are 12 tennis courts and games and lessons can be arranged. You may swim in a pool above the surf, hike or jog the trails in the Del Monte Forest, play polo or soccer, bicycle, sail, or fish. Horseback riding on 34 miles of scenic trails is offered; the Pebble Beach Equestrian Center is considered one of the finest on the West Coast.

There is no good beach at the resort. For strolling on the sand, go next door to Stillwater Cove. Four restaurants give you a choice of cuisine. In the glass-walled Stillwater Bar and Grill, the menu favors seafood. The Tap Room is an informal spot for sandwiches and pub specials while you check the display of golfing memorabilia and photographs.

Club XIX overlooks the golf course and the sea. During the day it's an al fresco café serving sandwiches and salads at outdoor tables hedged by cascading flowers; at night you dress up and dine by candlelight on contemporary French cuisine. The Gallery, above an arcade of a dozen shops across from the main lodge, is a bar and grill serving breakfast and lunch. It accommodates early birds eager to head for the first tee.

The Terrace Lounge is the place for cocktails, conversation, and gazing through wide windows at the seascape framed by cypress trees. A pianist plays during the day, and jazz artists or guest combos perform evenings and weekends. In this calm room, with its glass chandelier, two fireplaces, and soft couches in neutral colors, there's a sense of stability and tradition — an atmosphere that permeates the resort. It's too sporty for elegance, but the Lodge at Pebble Beach has been catering to elite crowds for some time and it clearly intends to maintain the quality it takes to continue doing so.

At press time, Pebble Beach Resorts had just opened 24 European-style accommodations at Casa Palermo adjacent to the lodge, as well as the Spa at Pebble Beach, offering a variety of health and beauty treatments, massages, and therapeutic baths. You may wish to inquire about the availability of these facilities when you make your reservations.

Santa Barbara

Four Seasons Biltmore

1260 Channel Drive
Santa Barbara, CA 93108
805-969-2261
800-332-3442
Fax: 805-565-8323
www.fourseasons.com

A Mediterranean style hotel with Pacific views

General manager: John Indrieri. **Accommodations:** 217 rooms and suites. **Rates:** $795–$2,000 double and suites, $35 additional person. **Added:** 10% tax. **Payment:** Major credit cards. **Children:** Under 18 free in room with parents. **Pets:** Well-behaved pets allowed with permission. **Smoking:** Nonsmoking rooms available.

➤ **The Four Seasons Biltmore combines California style, Mediterranean ambience, and a superb location on the southern edge of Santa Barbara with verve and a sense of history. This is a resort for the discriminating traveler who expects fine service in beautiful surroundings.**

Directly facing the Pacific Ocean and backed by the Santa Ynez Mountains, the Four Seasons Biltmore has a magnificent location. The accommodations live up to the setting. Elegance, serenity, and luxury come to mind when touring the 19 acres of landscaped gardens and white buildings with red tile roofs. The restored hotel dates from 1927, when the Bowman Biltmore chain planned it as the chain's crown jewel. The romantic structure has thick walls, Moorish arches, Portuguese tiles, and little balconies above intimate patios. Recent renovations left the richly designed tile work, carved lamps, and high entry ceiling, but the dark woods were lightened and a more open mood created.

Walkways edged with impatiens and fuchsia lead to guest rooms in two-story buildings tucked among the shrubs and palm trees of the lovely grounds that keep a crew of gardeners busy. Each room has a view of the ocean, the mountains, the lush gardens, or a pool. Many have balconies or private patios, fireplaces, vaulted ceilings, and oak ceiling fans. Walk-in closets and louvered shutters add to the sense of spaciousness. Botanical prints and tapestry fabric create an attractive look, while comforts include terry robes, hair dryers, safes, makeup mirrors, TVs with VCRs, bath phones, and two sinks — one in the bath and one in a separate vanity in the dressing area.

In junglelike gardens, there are cottages that vary in size. The larger units have two executive suites. Each cottage has a parlor with a fireplace, decorative chairs, and soft couches. The most luxurious is the Odell Suite, with four baths, three bedrooms, three fireplaces, and a parlor furnished with antiques.

On the property are an 18-hole putting green, a croquet field, three lighted tennis courts, and a small health club where fitness equipment and massages are available. A swimming pool shimmers under tall palms and an immense fig tree. The concierge staff can arrange for sport fishing, sailing, horseback riding, polo, scenic tours, and golfing.

The service at the Biltmore, as at all Four Seasons hotels, is far above average. The staff is well trained in the art of pampering guests — even the youngest ones. During the summer and on winter weekends, children can participate in Kids For All Seasons, a free program of activities.

La Marina is the Biltmore's formal dining room. Its high, arched windows look toward the front lawn and across the road to the sea. California cuisine is served in a candlelit setting, with fresh flowers and Wedgwood china.

You may also dine under the stars in The Patio, where the roof rolls back to reveal the sky. The café has an informal garden atmosphere, complete with tropical blooms, rattan furniture, and pink linens. Special ethnic buffets are sometimes offered, otherwise the menu leans toward California cuisine, gourmet pizzas, pastas, and veal and lamb chops. In La Sala Lounge, a cozy library with a fireplace, English tea is served. At sunset guests spill out onto the terrace for cocktails, and later there is nightly entertainment.

Several meeting and banquet rooms make the hotel popular with groups, but even large numbers of people don't disturb the serene ambience.

Across the road, on the beach side, is the Coral Casino Beach and Cabana Club, which is open to hotel guests. It has a private beach, cabanas, and a 50-meter pool so close to the sea wall that, at high tide, swimmers may be splashed with sea spray.

The Glenborough Inn

1327 Bath Street
Santa Barbara, CA 93101
805-966-0589
800-962-0589
Fax: 805-564-8610
info@glenboroughinn.com
www.glenboroughinn.com

Friendly innkeepers make this lodging a good choice while visiting Santa Barbara

Innkeepers: Michael Diaz and Steve Ryan. **Accommodations:** 14 rooms in 4 homes. **Rates:** $100–$460 single or double, $30 per additional person per night. **Included:** Full breakfast. **Added:** 10% tax. **Minimum stay:** 2 nights on weekends and most holidays. **Children:** Welcome in 2 suites; $30 additional. **Pets:** Not allowed. **Smoking:** Allowed outdoors only.

➤ **A selection of menus from area restaurants can be browsed through in the living room of the Main House. The downtown shopping district is just a few blocks from the inn.**

The Glenborough Inn consists of not one but four separate buildings on a residential street near downtown Santa Barbara. Fourteen guest rooms are distributed among the Main House, a two-story Craftsman bungalow that was built in 1906; the White House, also dating from 1906; a gray 1885 Victorian cottage bordered by a lovely side garden; and a vacation rental home called La Casa Cottage that was built in the late 1920s.

The Main House serves as the focal point for guest activities. It is here that guests gather each afternoon between five and six o'clock for a social hour with wine and hors d'oeuvres while classical music plays in the background. There's a central guest refrigerator, and a tea caddy and home-baked cookies are always available. In the quiet yard, the outdoor hot tub can be used by all guests on a sign-up basis. (Spa towels and robes are provided in each of the guest rooms.)

There are five guest rooms in the Main House, four upstairs and the deluxe Nouveau Suite with its own private garden and hot tub downstairs. Upstairs, Garden, as one might expect, overlooks the garden and has a white iron bed. Aurelia's Fancy features Norman Rockwell prints, slanted ceilings, and a fireplace. French Rose is romantic with inlaid furnishings, valentines, a fireplace, and a Jacuzzi tub.

In the Victorian Cottage, the Grand Suite has a canopy bed, while the decor in the nautically themed Captain's Quarters includes an antique cloth map. In the White House, the two-room Upper Chambers suite is where families stay. One room has a mirrored wardrobe and big walk-in closet, the other is cheerful, with lace curtains and a wicker sofa topped with chintz cushions. The bath is Victorian — complete with a pull-chain toilet and clawfoot tub.

The private La Casa Cottage, which can sleep up to six people, is rented out as a single unit. Its living room has a fireplace and a TV/VCR. There's also a kitchen and dining room.

Breakfast is delivered to each room in a picnic basket in the morning. Frittatas, blintzes, or stuffed French toast accompanied by scones and fruit smoothies are typical, and accommodations are also made for those with dietary restrictions. In fact, it is the innkeepers' sincere desire to make their guests feel welcome that sets this bed-and-breakfast apart from other establishments.

The Old Yacht Club Inn

431 Corona Del Mar Drive
Santa Barbara, CA 93103
805-962-1277
800-676-1676 in U.S.
800-549-1676 in California
Fax: 805-962-3989
info@oldyachtclubinn.com
www.oldyachtclubinn.com

A bed-and-breakfast inn close to the beach

Innkeepers: Nancy Donaldson and Sandy Hunt. **Accommodations:** 12 rooms (all with private bath). **Rates:** $105–$185 single, $110–$190 double, $30 additional person. **Included:** Full breakfast. **Added:** 10% tax. **Minimum stay:** 2

nights on weekends. **Payment:** Major credit cards. **Children:** Additional $30 if third person in room. **Pets:** Not allowed. **Smoking:** Not allowed indoors.

➤ **After one of Nancy's superb dinners, you may wish to visit on into the night with other guests — this is a get-acquainted sort of place — or stroll to the beach to see the waves in the moonlight.**

Once upon a time this really was a yacht club. It had been built as a private home in 1912, but served as the boaters' headquarters when the first clubhouse was swept out to sea. Then it was moved inland a few yards and in 1980 opened as an inn.

The capable owners are friends who met as school administrators in Los Angeles and were eager to try something different. They bought and restored the clubhouse, filled it with turn-of-the-century furnishings, and invited visitors to Santa Barbara to stay. It was the city's first bed-and-breakfast and is still the only one close to the beach.

The casual, friendly warmth of the inn is evident from the moment you walk in the door and are welcomed by one of the partners — and perhaps by the tiny poodle with the big name, Bella Mia Barbone. The front room of the stucco Craftsman home feels lived-in and homey. Dozens of guidebooks and travel books fill the bookshelves, fresh flowers grace the tables, and a ceramic cat rests on the hearth of the white brick fireplace. Notes from grateful visitors spill from an album on the piano.

On the other side of the room, tables are set for breakfast or for Nancy's famous Saturday night dinners. Coffee is on the sideboard by 6:30 A.M., followed by breakfast served course by course. Orange juice, fruit with flavored yogurt, muffins, a Spanish omelette, and sour cream coffeecake are part of a typical meal.

Dinners, presented three Saturdays a month, are usually booked far in advance. They start with champagne by the fire and move on to a fixed menu that might include mushroom soup, salmon in a raspberry beurre blanc sauce, and asparagus wrapped in phyllo topped with a cheese sauce. A tempting dessert such as strawberry cream pie and coffee follow. Several wines are available. Popular demand brought about a collection of Nancy's favorite recipes called *The Old Yacht Club Inn Cookbook.*

Captain's Corner, the only main floor room, has a king bed that can be made into two twins if requested, and a private deck. Upstairs, where the walls hold pictures of yachts and sailing vessels, are four rooms. Castellammare is light, done in lace and shades of rose. It has a two-person whirlpool tub and French doors that open to a balcony. Portofino is cool in blue and has a built-in window seat and dresser and a bath with shower.

The other part of the inn is next door: Hitchcock House, stucco with a red tile roof and a broad deck (made by the talented Nancy) in back. Grapevines climb over the lattice fence and a lemon tree lends bright color to the deck, a pleasant place for lounging.

Hitchcock's seven rooms all have separate entrances, three have whirlpool tubs, and several bear names of the innkeepers' family members. There's a childhood portrait of Nancy in the Gallaher Room as well as a picture of her ninety-something-year-old mother in younger years. The comforter, pillows, and curtains all complement one another in light shades of blue, pink, and green, and the bath has a whirlpool tub. The Belle Caruso Suite has a king-size bed and a separate living room on a sun porch with a wicker daybed. A pastel floral comforter tops the four-poster king-size bed in the Channel Islands suite, and there's a whirlpool tub in the bathroom. The suite also has its own living room. Julia Metelmann is furnished in an eclectic assortment of antiques. A narrow armoire, a black and gold dresser, and a red and black Chinese dragon carpet are a few of the interesting collectibles.

Every guest room has a phone, but there's no radio or television (though one will be provided in Hitchcock House upon request). This is a place to sip sherry by the fire, relax on the flowery front porch, or chat with the innkeepers, who know a great deal about Santa Barbara and are happy to lend a beach chair or a bicycle and send you in the right direction.

Secret Garden Inn and Cottages

1908 Bath Street
Santa Barbara, CA 93101
805-687-2300
800-676-1622
Fax: 805-687-4576
garden@secretgarden.com
www.secretgarden.com

A romantic bed-and-breakfast in central Santa Barbara

Innkeepers: Jack Greenwald. **Accommodations:** 11 rooms (all with private bath). **Rates:** $120–$220 single or double, $20 additional person; weekday discounts November to mid-May. **Included:** Full breakfast, afternoon wine and cheese, and evening refreshments. **Added:** 10% tax. **Minimum stay:** 2 nights on weekends and holidays. **Payment:** Major credit cards. **Children:** Welcome in certain rooms; under 6 are free; over 6 are an additional $20 if third person in room. **Pets:** Not allowed. **Smoking:** Not allowed indoors.

➤ **The innkeeper places morning newspapers on the dining room window seat (guarded by Quincy, the quilted bear), offers wine or hot spiced cider and hors d'oeuvres in the afternoon, and lends you one of the inn's bicycles for your Santa Barbara excursion if you request it.**

All the rooms and cottages at the Secret Garden Inn have a pleasant country charm and offer comfortable lodging close to the center of Santa Barbara. Especially appealing and romantic is Wood Thrush Cottage, a quaint and private little brown home behind the main house. Wood Thrush has two sitting rooms and a bedroom furnished in French country style. It has a refrigerator, a small bath with a clawfoot tub and shower, and a daybed that allows the cottage to hold a third person. Outside, oleander grows by the front porch and around the lawn, where lounges await sunbathers.

The main house, a one-story family home with big oak and fragrant pittosporum trees in front, has two cheery rooms, Meadowlark and Bobwhite. The other guest rooms are in several cottages in back. Cardinal, a pretty suite with a deck overlooking the garden, has English decor in hunter green and cardinal red. Mockingbird, in pale yellows, has a chintz coverlet and a country atmosphere. Nightingale has a fireplace and canopy bed. Whippoorwill and Hummingbird are in a cottage tucked away in back under eugenia and orange trees, and Hummingbird has a hot tub on its very private patio. Still farther back, off-street parking is provided.

The innkeeper serves breakfast specialties of popovers and muffins in the dining room of the main house or outdoors under the avocado tree. Breakfast includes a baked entrée such as quiche or an egg casserole, a bread basket, and fruit.

If you like Victorian decor and the luxury of Jacuzzi tubs, the owners of the Secret Garden also operate another inn in Santa Barbara. Called the Cheshire Cat, the well-run, tastefully furnished inn is about four blocks from the downtown business district.

Simpson House Inn

121 East Arrellaga Street
Santa Barbara, CA 93101
805-963-7067
800-676-1280
Fax: 805-564-4811
reservations@simpsonhouseinn.com
www.SimpsonHouseInn.com

> **A historic mansion near the heart of Santa Barbara**

Owners: Glyn and Linda Davies. **Manager:** Dixie Budke. **Accommodations:** 14 rooms (all with private bath). **Rates:** $195–$450 single or double. **Included:** Full breakfast, hors d'oeuvres, and local wines. **Added:** 10% tax. **Minimum stay:** 2 nights on weekends, 3 nights on holidays. **Payment:** Major credit cards. **Children:** Allowed in appropriate rooms, $40 additional if third person in room. **Pets:** Not allowed. **Smoking:** Allowed on patio only.

➤   **The innkeepers suggest visiting Santa Barbara in fall or winter, when the skies are usually clear and sunny, restaurants and shops are uncrowded, and the calendar is full of cultural events.**

This extraordinary inn is one of the loveliest places to stay in Santa Barbara. Though it's very close to the downtown area, it stands secluded behind wrought-iron gates and high hedges on nearly an acre of lawn under majestic oak, pittosporum, and magnolia trees.

The grand Eastlake-style Victorian, built in 1874, came perilously close to demolition to make way for condominiums or office units, but it was saved by Glyn and Linda Davies. Their extensive renovation brought the home back to its original splendor, with some updated comforts, and earned it a Structure of Merit award for its architecture and period setting. Now a historic landmark, the house was built for Mary and Margaret Simpson, the daughters of Scottish immigrants Robert and Julia Simpson, and it remained in the family until 1921. By then, Santa Barbara had been a winter resort favored by the wealthy for decades.

Today guests are welcomed into a Victorian parlor with rose velvet sofas and chairs, Oriental rugs, and bookshelves holding volumes of Shakespeare as well as guidebooks. An art book stands open on an easel at one of the windows. A lavish Mediterranean hors d'oeuvre buffet is set out on the table in the adjoining dining room, where there's a chintz-covered chaise and potted orchids. Soft music plays in the background.

The guest rooms, several named in honor of the Simpson family, have down comforters under lace coverlets, antique furniture, and fresh orchids. In the main house, the largest room is the Robert and Julia Simpson Room, which has an antique queen-size bed, clawfoot tub, and French doors to a deck above the rose garden. The Parlor Room has an ornamental gas fireplace, shelves full of books, an iron and brass queen-size bed covered in lace, fringed lamps, a lovely Oriental vase, and two easy chairs set in a bay window covered with rose damask fabric. Even the small but sunny bath has a Victorian flavor, with the same Victorian replica wallpaper, an inlaid wooden toilet seat cover, and an old-fashioned sewing machine table serving as a base for the marble-topped washbasin with brass fixtures. Smaller and cozier are the Sun Room, light with white wicker and a private sun deck, and Katherine McCormick, in deep red and blue, with a queen-size spool bed.

Behind the main house are four Old Barn rooms and three cottages. The 1874 barn was dismantled and rebuilt with the original wood on the interior. It now houses Weathervane, Hayloft, Tack Room, and Carriage Room. The decor in Weathervane — Oriental rugs atop antique pine floors, a king-size bed, wood-burning fireplace, a tapestry-covered chaise, a damask loveseat, pine furnishings including a blanket chest, a television, VCR, stereo system, and skylighted Italian marble bath — is typical of the spacious barn rooms. The most expensive rooms are the cottages, furnished with understated elegance. They have fireplaces, Jacuzzi tubs, and private gates that open to an intimate fountain patio.

Breakfast can be delivered to your room if you request it, or it's served on the verandah overlooking the garden, or in the dining room if the weather prohibits outdoor dining. The meal generally includes fresh fruit and juices, an array of cereals, yogurt, and a main dish such as apple-baked French toast, huevos Santa Barbara, or scones with savory eggs. After breakfast you may wish to enjoy the inn's lovely gardens, where stone walkways wind past beds of lavender, lilies, roses, impatiens, and snapdragons. Benches are provided for relaxing and listening to the sounds of the birds or water splashing in a nearby fountain.

Although this distinguished inn has a stately quality, it offers a warm welcome from the affable owners, who know how to make you feel at home. They've put vast amounts of time and energy into restoring the old place but managed to do so without losing their sense of humor. And your comfort always comes first. If you want to chat, one of the Davieses or a member of their staff is available; if you prefer to be left alone with the complimentary morning and evening newspapers provided, you will be. The inn-keepers know Santa Barbara, too, and will tell you about restaurants, shopping, scenic drives, and attractions not to be missed. All guests receive a free pass to the Santa Barbara trolley in addition to complimentary use of the inn's bicycles. Day use of a local athletic club is also available for an additional fee.

Villa Rosa

15 Chapala Street
Santa Barbara, CA 93101
805-966-0851
Fax: 805-962-7159

> **A small, cozy inn within walking distance of the beach**

General manager: Annie Puetz. **Accommodations:** 18 rooms. **Rates:** $110–$230 single or double; winter weekday discounts. **Included:** Continental breakfast and afternoon refreshments. **Minimum stay:** 2 nights on weekends. **Added:** 10% tax. **Payment:** Major credit cards. **Children:** Over age 14 welcome. **Pets:** Not allowed. **Smoking:** Not allowed.

➤ **In the heart of beautiful Santa Barbara, just 84 steps from the sea (somebody counted), Villa Rosa welcomes guests to a Spanish Colonial Revival inn of style and warmth.**

Built in 1931, this two-story hotel was renovated in 1981 and de-signed to offer the amenities of a larger resort with the intimacy of a small inn. A few of those amenities are breakfast in the lounge or in your room, the *Los Angeles Times* delivered to your door, com-plimentary wine and hors d'oeuvres in the afternoon, port and sherry in the evening, same-day dry cleaning, and turndown serv-ice with roses on your pillow. The staff pays careful attention to guests' needs. Whether you request an iron, an aspirin, or a Band-

Aid, the desk clerk will get it for you and ask if you need anything more.

The inn is decorated in southwestern style, with earth and clay colors and rough-hewn beams in the lobby. Here tables are covered with magazines, daily newspapers, and menus from local restaurants. A fire crackles on cool evenings on the tiled hearth. Double doors lead from the lobby and lounge to a pretty courtyard with a small swimming pool and a whirlpool under pepper, banana, and palm trees.

The guest rooms have different configurations but similar decor. They are done in colors of muted putty, blues, and rose; accessories are minimal, but their texture and tone are warm. Heavy, weathered pine from New Mexico, weavings on the walls, and rawhide chairs continue the desert-country theme, as do the beehive fireplaces in four rooms. Four of the rooms have partially equipped kitchens and a small dining area tucked back in a semicircular alcove. Two have oval tubs under a window that looks out to a small garden.

The views vary, from glimpses of the ocean to mountains or the courtyard and gardens. Room 18 offers views of both ocean and pool, a sitting area, a kitchen, and a fireplace.

The inn's courtyard conference room is available to groups (up to twenty people) and there is a full range of audiovisual equipment.

Santa Cruz

The Babbling Brook Inn

1025 Laurel Street
Santa Cruz, CA 95060
831-427-2437
800-866-1131
Fax: 831-427-2457
lodging@babblingbrook.com
www.babblingbrookinn.com

A romantic inn set in a landscaped garden

Innkeepers: Dan Floyd and Suzie Lankes. **Accommodations:** 17 rooms (all with private bath). **Rates:** $145–$195 single or double, $20 additional person. **Included:** Full breakfast, afternoon wine and cheese, and cookies. **Added:** 10% tax. **Minimum stay:** 2 nights on weekends if Saturday included. **Payment:** Major credit cards. **Children:** $20 additional if third person in room. **Pets:** Not allowed. **Smoking:** Allowed on outside private decks only.

➤ **Below the deck, brick paths wind through the garden. Water cascades down the rocky cliff, and calla lilies bloom by the edge of the stream. Benches and a fanciful white iron gazebo provide resting spots to contemplate this beautifully kept refuge, which is often used for weddings.**

This garden retreat sits on an acre of flowers, pines, fruit trees, giant ferns, ivy, redwoods, and waterfalls in the shadow of a cliff by, Laurel Creek. The creek, which runs from spring-fed lakes on a hill by the university, is churned through an old-fashioned wooden water wheel before meandering through the garden, under bridges, and past guest room windows.

The innkeepers bring a wealth of experience in the travel and hospitality industry to their inn. Although its logs and shingles give it a rustic appearance, the accommodations are pure luxury. The original inn was built in 1909 on the foundation of an 1870s tannery and 1790s grist mill. It became a restaurant in 1942 and, in 1981, the first bed-and-breakfast in Santa Cruz.

Now it offers lodging in rooms with a French country theme, most named for impressionist painters and decorated in the colors they used. Rooms, in shingled cottages throughout the grounds, have cable TV, phones, and a fireplace, and most have a private deck and outside entrance; several feature deep soaking jet bathtubs.

Toulouse Lautrec, with one of the whirlpool tubs, is in a little cottage on the way up the hill to the main inn. Flooded with light from the five-sided window alcove, it is a sunny room and has a balcony overlooking the stream. Monet, in a remote corner of the property and shielded from view, is in Delft blue and white, with a beamed ceiling and private deck across from the waterfall and footbridge. Degas is decorated with the artist's favorite subject, dancers. Secluded Cézanne is wheelchair-accessible. It has a corner fireplace and private deck above the brook.

Two of the largest rooms are Tennyson and Artist's Retreat. Attached to the main inn, they have fireplaces and CD players and are decorated in shades of salmon and seafoam green. The bed is set back in an alcove in Tennyson, and there's a jet tub in the bath. Artist's Retreat, which looks out over the property, has a hot tub on its deck. Inside, a combination bookcase and headboard with a writing desk built-in to the back separates the sleeping area from the bright bath where there's a two-sink vanity and oversized shower.

From the kitchen come wondrous smells and tastes — an elaborate buffet breakfast with dishes that change daily is prepared here. Fresh fruit, granola, yogurt, muffins, croissants, and a hot entrée are always served. You may have breakfast in your room, in the garden, or in the dining area at round tables under a glass roof.

Tea, coffee, and cookies are available all day, and wine and sherry are offered in the evenings. Guests enjoy sipping their wine on the Babbling Brook's wide deck, listening to the trickling fountains and rushing brook. Redwood trees grow through the deck, and pots of impatiens and cyclamen stand in the nooks and corners. The innkeepers have menus of nearby restaurants and can provide recommendations. A few favorites are the Bittersweet Bistro, Theo's, Casablanca, and Shadowbrook.

Shell Beach

The Cliffs at Shell Beach

2757 Shell Beach Road
Shell Beach, CA 93449
805-773-5000
800-826-7827 in California
800-826-5838 in U.S.
Fax: 805-773-0764

A light, breezy, oceanside resort

General manager: Joseph Violi. **Accommodations:** 165 rooms and 27 suites. **Rates:** $145–$375. **Payment:** Major credit cards. **Children:** Under age 12 free ($10 for rollaway bed). **Pets:** Not allowed. **Smoking:** Nonsmoking rooms available.

➤ **The list of things to see and do in this area is a long one. You can rent horses, fish from the Pismo Beach pier or ask the concierge about a charter boat, tour Hearst Castle (55 miles north), go skin diving, watch the sea otters at play, dig clams, and taste regional wines.**

Shell Beach is just north of Pismo Beach, the only shore's-edge town on Highway 101 between Santa Barbara and San Francisco. The view from the Cliffs, a white and blue five-story resort on a bluff, is of the wide beach and rolling surf.

The Cliffs mixes luxury and the informality of a beach resort with ease. You're greeted at the door by a bellman in a gray and burgundy uniform; then you enter an open, light lobby with white walls and high windows. Across the way is a terrace with white umbrella tables, next to the dramatic restaurant with a tropical theme. Birds of paradise are etched on glass partitions; tall palms grow beside anthuriums and other exotic plants. There's also a cocktail lounge with music for dancing nightly. On the other side of the terrace is the pool and spa, on an island surrounded by a waterfall. Beyond it is a lawn and paths at the edge of the bluff.

The guest rooms are furnished in traditional style, some with English reproductions and others in imitation French Provincial. The suites have white marble baths, balconies with views of the sea, and Jacuzzi tubs.

The Cliffs has complimentary valet parking, a fitness center, gift shop, beauty salon, meeting rooms, catering, room service — all the features of a modern resort, plus a stunning location and a helpful staff.

Solvang

The Alisal Guest Ranch

1054 Alisal Road
Solvang, CA 93463
805-688-6411
800-4-ALISAL
Fax: 805-688-2510
sales@alisal.com
www.alisal.com

A country retreat in the Santa Ynez Valley

General manager: David Lautensack. **Accommodations:** 73 rooms. **Rates:** Studio: $315 single, $355 double, $70 additional person; suites $380–$435. **Included:** Breakfast and dinner. **Added:** 10% tax and 12% gratuity. **Minimum stay:** 2 nights. **Payment:** Major credit cards. **Children:** Under age 2 free, age 3–5, $45 per day; over 6, $70 per day. **Pets:** Not allowed. **Smoking:** Not allowed in public spaces.

➤ **If you wish to explore, you have many options in this valley of majestic oaks, vineyards, horse ranches, grassy meadows, and little towns. Visit quaint Solvang, tour and taste at nearby wineries, browse the art galleries of Los Olivos, or step into the Old West in Santa Ynez. Guided tours of the area are available.**

Some visitors come to this extraordinary, 10,000-acre retreat just for the horses. Experienced wranglers take guests out on daily trail rides, winding through the meadows, loping along ridgetops, and ambling beside a 96-acre manmade lake where fish leap and deer graze on the shore. It's far from the urban world most guests have left behind.

The Alisal, about a three-hour drive from Los Angeles, is in the hills of the Santa Ynez Valley near Solvang, a town modeled after a Danish village. The resort has been open to guests since 1946, after a long history of cattle ranching. In addition to horseback riding, it offers golf on two 18-hole championship courses, seven tennis courts and a pro shop, swimming in a freeform heated pool, boating, and fishing. Recreational activities are included as part of a Round-up Vacation package during certain times of the year, otherwise there's an additional charge on weekends for golf, tennis, and horseback riding.

Breakfast and dinner are included in the room rate and are served in the Ranch Room or Sycamore Room. You can choose the buffet or order off the menu at breakfast, and there's a five-item menu at dinner. Imported and domestic wines, some with Santa Ynez labels, are available.

Musicians perform in the Oak Room Lounge, where a fire crackles on cool evenings. Leathery furnishings and western accessories add to the casual, welcoming ambience.

The guest rooms are in single-story cottages under the sycamore trees (alisal means "grove of sycamores" in Spanish). Rooms are furnished in Old West ranch style, with rough-paneled walls, oak beds and tables, wood-burning fireplaces, and Western art. Executive suites sleep up to five people and have a patio with an outside fireplace. There are no phones or televisions in the rooms, but several are available for guests' use elsewhere on the ranch.

The real interest at Alisal lies in the outdoor activities and beautiful surroundings. Horseshoes, croquet, shuffleboard, badminton, and volleyball are a few sports to enjoy on the wide green lawns. The Ranch Golf Course, lush and secluded, is reserved for ranch guests. The River Course is open to ranch guests and the public alike. If tennis is your game, the resident tennis pro will provide lessons or set you up for a tournament. You can jog a half-mile course, play pool or table tennis in the recreation room, soak in a bubbling hot water spa, or relax poolside in a lounge chair. Occasionally the ranch offers breakfast haywagon rides, arts and crafts are available year-round, and special children's programs are offered during the summer and on holidays.

Soquel

The Blue Spruce Inn

2815 South Main Street
Soquel, CA 95073
831-464-1137
800-559-1137 (in California)
Fax: 831-475-0608
innkeeper@bluespruce.com
www.bluespruce.com

> **A homey bed-and-breakfast
> south of Santa Cruz**

Innkeepers: Patricia and Tom O'Brien. **Accommodations:** 6 rooms (all with private bath). **Rates:** $85–$175 single or double, $25 additional person. **Included:** Full breakfast. **Added:** 10% tax. **Minimum stay:** 2 nights on weekends. **Payment:** Major credit cards. **Children:** Over age 12 allowed, $25 additional if third person in room. **Pets:** Not allowed. **Smoking:** Not allowed indoors.

➤ **Fifteen restaurants are within walking distance of the inn. Theo's is known for its fine French cuisine and the casual Star of Siam for flavorful Thai meals and swift service.**

Each room in this pleasant bed-and-breakfast is named for its own work of art, painted by a local artist. The theme is an indication of the owners' love of art and the care that has gone into the selection of colors, fabrics, and furnishings at the Blue Spruce.

The 120-year-old home stands behind a white picket fence and a blue spruce in a community just south of Santa Cruz. It's a short distance from the beaches of Capitola and Santa Cruz. The O'Briens purchased the home in 1990 and renovated it in addition to working at their regular jobs — Pat as a school principal, Tom in the mental health profession.

If you're new to B&B lodgings, the Blue Spruce is a good choice because of the options available. You may prefer to have breakfast with other guests in the dining area, eat at a table for two by the fireplace, or take breakfast to your own room or patio. If you wish to sit in silence behind the morning newspaper, that's all right too. Breakfast always includes juice, fruit, and an entrée such as baked ham strata or enchiladas, and Pat has collected the most popular recipes in a cookbook.

All rooms have telephones and bathrobes. There are three rooms in the main house, and each has a private entrance except for Two Hearts. The least expensive room, it's romantic in red and white with a heart motif. Seascape has a gas fireplace, wicker armchair, white iron and brass bed, antique washbasin, whirlpool tub, and a small brick patio with wisteria vines. Bloomin' Farm boasts a whirlpool.

In back of the main house, by the little pond and flower garden, is the Carriage House, the largest room. It has a gas fireplace, a king-size bed dressed in white, a whirlpool in the corner, and a shower with a stained glass mural.

Somewhat removed from the others, Summer Afternoon offers the most privacy in an airy nest. It has a small sitting area with a bay window seat and a gas fireplace. Around the corner the bed is topped with a botanical print comforter and stuffed sheep. The tiled bath has two tiny sinks. Outside, enclosed in the private garden area, is a clawfoot tub for bathing under the stars.

Gazebo is charming, with a picket fence headboard behind the feather bed. Lavish Waverly fabrics, boudoir chairs, a gas fireplace, a TV/VCR behind shutters, and a small desk furnish this room.

Just outside the door, on the deck by the garden, is a hot tub that all guests may use, a relaxing end to a day of exploring the beach or the many local antiques shops and sampling the area's notable restaurants.

Desert Country

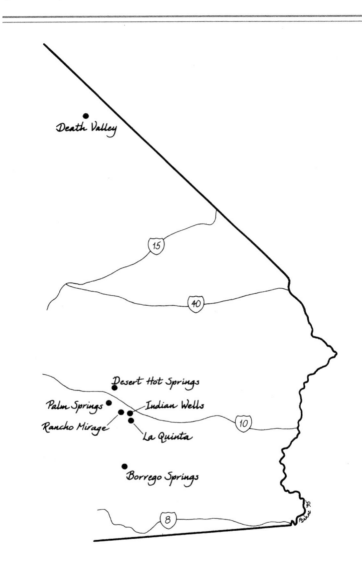

Borrego Springs
La Casa del Zorro Desert Resort, 218
Death Valley
Furnace Creek Inn, 220
Desert Hot Springs
Travellers Repose, 222
Indian Wells
Renaissance Esmeralda Resort, 223
La Quinta
La Quinta Resort and Club, 225
Palm Springs
Ingleside Inn, 228
Korakia Pensione, 230
La Mancha Resort Village, 232
L'Horizon, 234
Villa Royale, 235
Rancho Mirage
The Ritz-Carlton Rancho Mirage, 236
The Westin Mission Hills Resort, 238

Best Bed-and-Breakfasts

Desert Hot Springs
Travellers Repose, 222
Palm Springs
Korakia Pensione, 230
L'Horizon, 234

Resorts

Borrego Springs
La Casa del Zorro Desert Resort, 218
Death Valley
Furnace Creek Inn, 220
Indian Wells
Renaissance Esmeralda Resort, 223
La Quinta
La Quinta Resort and Club, 225
Rancho Mirage
The Ritz-Carlton Rancho Mirage, 236
The Westin Mission Hills Resort, 238

Romantic Hideaways

Palm Springs
Ingleside Inn, 228
La Mancha Resort Village, 232
Villa Royale, 235

The deserts of California range from the dry expanses of Death Valley National Monument to the rugged mountains and green golf courses of the **Palm Springs** area.

Death Valley lies in the northeastern Mojave Desert, where great canyons, salt flats, ancient lake beds, and cliffs washed in a multitude of colors draw thousands of tourists yearly. This seemingly desolate land shelters a surprising amount of life — snakes and desert animals, bighorn sheep, a few burros, and, in protected pools, the desert pupfish.

The valley has resorts, campgrounds, swimming pools, a ghost town, a borax museum that records the old mining days, and a grand mansion. Scotty's Castle is a Mediterranean-style structure with three towers and 25 rooms filled with artwork and fine furniture, including a grand piano and a pipe organ. Once the home of a sometime miner and teller of tall tales, it's now open for tours.

Far to the south of the great desert lies the Coachella Valley, where Mount San Jacinto rises a steep 10,000 feet from the sandy sea-level floor, a backdrop to Palm Springs. The valley sits atop a huge underground lake, and so the popular resort oasis uses water lavishly. There are more than 10,000 swimming pools and 85 golf courses in the region — and there's even a pool with waves big enough for surfing.

Lodgings in the valley, from simple motels to opulent and expensive resorts, are spread through seven adjoining cities; among them are Palm Springs, **Desert Hot Springs**, **La Quinta**, and **Rancho Mirage**. They're famous for their lush golf courses, boutiques, and celebrity homes; but the region has many lesser-known attractions. In the Palm Springs Desert Museum you can view outstanding art and natural science collections; at the Living Desert you'll see desert animals and plants. The 1,200-acre park has hundreds of cactus varieties as well as gila monsters, foxes, and antelope.

Beyond the fountains and green lawns of Palm Springs, the desert has its own haunting, quiet beauty, with rocky outcroppings and cliffs in a multitude of hues and cacti that blossom bright with color in the spring. In nearby Joshua Tree National Monument you can see cacti, underground springs, palm trees, yucca plants, wildlife, and the spring-blooming Joshua tree among the granite monoliths. One of the best ways to see it is by touring with Desert Adventures. The company's knowledgeable guides will tell you about the botany, wildlife, geology, and history of the fascinating park.

In stark contrast to the rocky gorges and open desert in much of the valley are the Indian Canyons, a series of canyons with palm trees and streams. Some of the canyons are listed on the National Register of Historic Places, as the Agua Caliente Cahuilla Indians had complex communities here.

For a panoramic view of the valley, ride the Palm Springs Aerial Tramway up San Jacinto Mountain. The cable cars climb through five climatic zones, from the desert floor to the cool mountaintop, in 15 minutes.

California's largest state park is another desert landscape and geological wonder, Anza-Borrego Desert State Park. Known for its diversity, with rocky canyons, dry lake beds, palm groves, and year-round springs, it's a favorite in the spring when the wildflowers turn the desert to fields of color. The park is close to the quiet, pleasant town of **Borrego Springs**.

Borrego Springs

La Casa del Zorro Desert Resort

3845 Yaqui Pass Road
Borrego Springs, CA 92004
760-767-5323
800-824-1884
Fax: 760-767-5963
www.lacasadelzorro.com

> **A luxury hideaway in the Anza-Borrego Desert**

General manager: Jim McCullough. **Accommodations:** 77 rooms. **Rates:** $75–$875. **Added:** 9% tax. **Payment:** Major credit cards. **Children:** Welcome; $10 for rollaway. **Pets:** On a limited basis; $50 additional. **Smoking:** Nonsmoking rooms available.

➤ **An unusual and delightful feature at La Casa del Zorro is its evening treat: instead of a mint on your pillow, you're given a booklet of short stories just right for bedtime reading.**

Clear air and the silence of the desert surround this pleasant resort, spread over 32 acres of landscaped grounds. La Casa del Zorro is close to Anza-Borrego Desert State Park, California's largest state park, with 600,000 acres of canyons, palm groves, wildflowers, and rugged backcountry. The first structure, built in 1937, was an adobe ranch house that expanded over the decades into La Casa del Zorro; some of the original walls and beams remain as part of the lobby and lounge.

On the grounds, sprinkled with lawns, palm trees, and a fountain, are three night-lit swimming pools and spas, tennis courts, an

Olympic-size lap pool, and a putting green. The rose garden and gazebo provide a pretty setting for parties and weddings. Guests can attend aerobics classes, rent bicycles, dance to live music, rent movies, shop in a boutique, hike nearby trails, play volleyball and table tennis, and dine on steaks, seafood, and pastas in the Butterfield Dining Room. They can also have more casual meals in the Fox Den Lounge, surrounded by playful fox murals. As this is the type of resort that appeals to families as well as couples, parents will be happy to know that childcare can be arranged, and the staff is warm and friendly.

Despite all the activity, the atmosphere is serene at La Casa del Zorro, with casitas spread over the property. Standard rooms and suites are located in two-story stucco buildings with red tile roofs. Guest rooms have a crisp southwestern look. Cheerful in blues and tans, they have lightly washed or blue-stained wood furnishings and high ceilings. All rooms are supplied with coffee and coffeemakers, and a morning paper is delivered to your door.

Standard suites are attractively decorated and have a separate living room and shuttered windows. A deluxe suite features a fireplace edged with colorful tiles, artwork and books in lighted niches, a wet bar, and a private patio. Most spacious are the adobe casitas, set off on their own and surrounded by a native desert landscape. One-bedroom casitas have outdoor hot tubs, and the three-bedroom casita has a large tiled patio and private swimming pool.

Death Valley

Furnace Creek Inn

P.O. Box 187
Death Valley, CA 92328
760-786-2345
800-236-7916
Fax: 760-786-2423
www.furnacecreekresort.com

| A resort oasis in the desert |

Manager: Toni Doyle Jepson. **Accommodations:** 66 rooms. **Rates:** $230–$290 single or double, $325–$340 suite. **Added:** 9% tax. **Payment:** Major credit cards. **Children:** Under age 18 free in room with parents; $15 for rollaway or crib. **Pets:** Not allowed. **Smoking:** Nonsmoking rooms available.

➤ **Most visitors take excursions to Death Valley landmarks. You can go on your own or with a guide who will explain the geology and history of Artist's Palette, Zabriskie Point, Dante's View, the jagged salt crystals of Devil's Golf Course, and Badwater, the lowest spot in the United States. Along the way you'll see wild burros, sand dunes, dry lakebeds, and wide craters.**

Death Valley is the hottest, driest place in the world. Ground temperatures higher than 200 degrees Fahrenheit have been recorded here in summer. The landscape is stark, almost surreal in its contorted shapes, stretches of salty floor, brilliantly colored rocks, and high mountains.

In the midst of this desert on the Nevada border, 300 miles northeast of Los Angeles, Furnace Creek shimmers like a green mirage. Underground springs feed a garden of tropical flowers and palm trees, a swimming pool, and an 18-hole golf course. The rambling stone inn looks like a Spanish villa among the palms, with its red tile roof and Moorish arches.

Furnace Creek Inn was built in the late 1920s in response to public interest in Death Valley. Visitors were eager to see the strange and desolate beauty of a desert 200 feet below sea level. It had long been known for its rich mineral deposits, especially borax, which was brought out by the famous 20-mule team wagons. The Pacific Coast Borax Company built the resort and promoted it as a train destination, in connection with the company's own railroads.

Today the yellow, Spanish-style inn commands the desert valley from its hillside perch, and guest rooms have modern amenities such as air conditioning, television, refrigerators, irons, ironing boards, and ceiling fans. Some rooms also have whirlpool tubs. The three categories of rooms — Deluxe, Desert, and Garden View — are furnished in a contemporary style. In desert tones of sand, salmon, and aqua, they have brass beds, floral comforters, and views of the desert or gardens. In the evening, from your room or patio, you can hear the coyotes howl.

Jackets are suggested in the dining room, which specializes in California cuisine. From the inn, paths wind down the hillside through green lawns and a palm oasis to a spring-fed swimming pool. In addition to the 18-hole golf course, other recreational facilities include four tennis courts, shuffleboard, croquet, and horseback riding. There's no charge for tennis; a round of golf costs $30 for registered guests.

Manmade attractions are as unique as the landscape. Marta Becket's Amargosa Opera House, up a remote canyon, is a remarkable one-woman show. The artist and dancer from New York has been performing for 20 years in the theater she restored in a former ghost town. Scotty's Castle is a Mediterranean-style structure with three towers and 25 rooms filled with artwork, fine furniture, and china. Once the home of a sometime miner and teller of tall tales, it's now open to the public and well worth a tour.

Desert Hot Springs

Travellers Repose

P.O. Box 655
66920 First Street
Desert Hot Springs, California 92240
760-329-9584

| A charming bed-and-
breakfast in the desert |

Innkeeper: Marian Relkoff. **Accommodations:** 3 rooms. **Rates:** $70–$90 double, 10% less for single. **Included:** Expanded Continental breakfast. **Added:** 10% tax. **Payment:** Cash, personal checks, or travelers checks. **Children:** Over age 12 welcome. **Pets:** Not allowed. **Smoking:** Not allowed indoors. **Open:** September through June.

➤   **For unusual views of the desert, take a covered wagon tour or a jeep ride with a Desert Adventures naturalist into the canyons or Joshua Tree National Monument.**

About 12 miles from the resorts of Palm Springs, Desert Hot Springs is a small, quiet community. On a slope above town stands the Victorian-style Travellers Repose. It's unusual to find a Victorian home in the desert, and this one — gray, with dark blue and white trim — is not really of Victorian vintage; it was built in 1985 by Marian and Sam Relkoff as a bed-and-breakfast. Sam, formerly a contractor in Los Angeles, made much of the wood furniture and incorporated details in the building's structure such as heart cutouts in the gingerbread trim. (Ask Marian about the heart-shaped shadow that appears on the front walkway after dark that the Relkoffs did not discover until the home was completely built.) Obvious care went into the construction of the home, and it is immaculately maintained by Marian.

In front, by the white picket fence and vine-covered trellis, masses of flowers grow. There's a garden in back, too, by the swimming pool and spa. Just inside the front door there's a comfy parlor where guests can play board games or relax with a book. Breakfast, usually fruit, homemade granola, and home-baked rolls such as scones, cinnamon rolls, or muffins, is sometimes served on the patio by the pool. Marian also provides afternoon refreshments.

The guest rooms are spotless and attractive, and each is individually furnished in a country style. Buttons & Bows, on the main floor, is romantic in lavender and lace. It has antique oak furniture, a mirrored armoire, an iron and brass queen bed, and a velvet hat, beaded bag, and old pair of shoes hang on a wooden rack in the corner. You can see San Jacinto Peak from the bay window. The private bath has a wooden water closet and brass fixtures.

Upstairs, the Pine Room is handsome in mint greens and also has views of the peak. There is a cannonball bed and Sam made the dresser and armoire of honey pine. Hearts are everywhere in the cheerful Heart Room across the hall, and Marian quilted the heart-patterned quilt.

An added plus to staying at Travellers Repose is the price. For as little as $70 (plus tax), two people can enjoy pleasant accommodations, breakfast, afternoon tea, the use of a pool (which is not heated), spa, and the hospitality of the kindly innkeeper — a true bargain in the often expensive Palm Springs area.

Indian Wells

Renaissance Esmeralda Resort

44-440 Indian Wells Lane
Indian Wells, CA 92210
760-773-4444
800-552-4FUN
Fax: 760-346-9308
www.renaissancehotels.com

A golfer's paradise in the desert

General manager: Dennis Wagner. **Accommodations:** 560 rooms and suites. **Rates:** $150–$400 single or double; suites $380–$2,500; $25 per additional adult. **Added:** 9.25% tax. **Payment:** Major credit cards. **Children:** Under 18 free in room with parents; $15 charge for rollaway. **Pets:** Not allowed. **Smoking:** Non-smoking rooms available.

➤ **Las Estrellas Bar is dark and comfortably elegant, with sofas and rounded easy chairs placed in cozy groupings. Just outside the lounge's windows the moat cascades into a long pool.**

About 20 minutes from Palm Springs, Indian Wells is a quiet community with date-bearing palm groves and some of the best golf courses in the area. As available land became more and more scarce in Palm Springs, a long-time winter destination, developments and resorts began to spring up all along the valley, and the Renaissance Esmeralda Resort, which opened in 1989 just off Highway 111 in Indian Wells, is one such resort.

Lanky palm trees line the driveway that leads from the highway to the resort. Like a fortress, the six-story peach-colored stucco hotel with contrasting green-tinged oxidized copper balcony railings, is surrounded by a moat. Inside an impressive curved double staircase made from anagre (a rare African wood) winds down one flight to the polished marble base of the atrium lobby. Strains of music from a ghostly pianist at the grand player piano fill the air, and restaurants border both sides of the lofty hall. At the far end, opposite the staircase, doors open out to the pool area.

Guests check in at a registration counter down a hallway on the entry level. Rooms surround the central atrium or are located in outlying wings. Decorated in pleasant pastels and contemporary furnishings, they have balconies that offer pool, golf course, or mountain views. Two-poster beds are painted in pale yellows, Impressionist prints adorn the walls, and TVs are hidden in armoires (in-room movies are complimentary). Other amenities include stocked refreshment centers, bathrobes, and irons and ironing boards. Baths have marble vanities, a small television, phone, hair dryer, and Bath & Bodyworks toiletries.

Corner rooms, with large windows on two sides, are sunny and cheerful. They are more spacious than standard rooms so they also include a sofa, easy chair, and two closets. For those needing even more space, spa and one-bedroom executive suites are also available.

Active guests will find there is plenty to do at the resort. Beyond the lobby is an extensive pool complex with a waterfall pavilion, gazebo bar, and sandy beach. There's a fitness center with a professional masseuse on staff, two outdoor spas, steam rooms, and a sauna. Two of the resort's seven tennis courts are lighted for nighttime play. For golf lovers there are two 18-hole championship golf courses designed by Ted Robinson.

Sirocco's Mediterranean cuisine, such as basil lemon linguini with clams, shrimp, scallops, white wine, and tomatoes or broiled tenderloin of beef with roasted garlic and thyme butter and smoked mushroom sauce gets high marks from diners in the valley. Charisma is more casual and has a contemporary Californian slant, although its southwestern buffet on Saturday night is quite popular.

La Quinta

La Quinta Resort and Club

P.O. Box 69
49-499 Eisenhower Drive
La Quinta, CA 92253
760-564-4111
800-598-3828
Fax: 760-564-5718

> **A village-style resort known for its privacy and recreation**

General manager: Eric Affeldt. **Accommodations:** 720 rooms and suites. **Rates:** $129–$550 single or double; suites $350–$4,000. **Added:** 11% tax. **Payment:** Major credit cards. **Children:** Under 18 free in room with parents. **Pets:** Small pets allowed with permission and a $100 nonrefundable deposit. **Smoking:** Nonsmoking rooms available.

➤ **Water cascades in tiers to a fountain near the hotel entrance, and the sweet scent of grapefruit blossoms wafts on the air.**

In 1926, a Spanish hacienda-style hotel was built in the California desert, 20 miles from the sleepy village of Palm Springs. From that day to this, La Quinta has been known for its hospitality and distinctive style. During the '30s it was a haven for Hollywood stars such as Greta Garbo, Charlie Chaplin, Errol Flynn, Bette Davis, and Clark Gable. In 1932, Frank Capra first visited La Quinta; his stay inspired the creation of *It Happened One Night,* which won an Academy Award. Capra returned to the hotel later to write eight additional scripts.

Since then, the resort has expanded into a 45-acre compound of rooms and suites, 35 swimming pools, and 48 spas. Yet, because of its careful design, there's no sense of overcrowding. Rather, you feel as though it's fiesta time in a village where shops, meeting rooms, and restaurants surround a colorful tiled plaza.

You reach the hotel by a cypress-lined drive and enter a small lobby with tile floors, white walls, and Spanish wrought-iron accents. In the adjacent Santa Rosa Lounge, Mexican art objects — bright papier mâché fruits, Guerrero coconut masks, a tin-framed mirror — add to the Old California atmosphere. Here guests gather before dinner or read the morning paper on overstuffed chairs and sofas. Afternoon tea is also available.

A champagne brunch is offered on the hotel's original patio from October to May. Montañas is the place to go for fine dining. Pancetta-wrapped chicken breast and tiger shrimp ravioli with sea scallops are examples of the restaurant's Mediterranean cuisine. Morgan's, named for Walter Morgan, the founder of La Quinta, is a casual 1920s American café with black and white checked tile floors, wood paneling, and an open kitchen. At the entrance to the restaurant there are photos of Frank Capra; outside tables provide additional dining. The Adobe Grill offers elegant presentations of dishes such as grilled breast of duck with a tamarind chile sauce or Mexican molés. With talavera tile, leather-backed chairs, and jumbo margaritas, the mood is definitely Old Mexico.

One thing you can't help but notice at La Quinta is the landscaping. The grounds are beautifully maintained all year long and the plants in the flowerbeds are continually rotated, providing maximum color in every season. So pleasant are the surroundings that Ginger Rogers held her wedding here in front of a courtyard waterfall.

One- and two-story bungalows, called casitas, are scattered over the property, many behind whitewashed walls espaliered with red-blooming bougainvillea, and some date from the 1920s, when the hotel first opened. Each casita has from three to eight units. For the best views of the Santa Rosa Mountains, request a second-floor room.

A typical Double Deluxe room has two beds and a simple decor. The mood is cool, with white walls and white louvered shutters at the windows. The room has a television, a writing table, and a refrigerator. The large baths have double sinks and assorted toiletries that include sewing kits, loofahs, and sachets.

The suites are larger and offer more amenities. Many have private wraparound patios with whirlpools. Wet bars are stocked with liquors and snacks, soft drinks and complimentary boxes of dates

— this is date growing country — and baths have Crabtree and Evelyn toiletries. In one suite, louvered double doors divide the sitting room from a white and blue bedroom with a two-poster bed. A second TV is tucked into a niche beside a fireplace that passes through the wall to the bathroom. Firewood is provided in another niche. The Eisenhower Villa has a southwestern look, with a large living room with a long dining table, a spacious bedroom with its own fireplace, and a kitchenette.

Yellow ribbons are placed on the doors of returning guests, and many come back to La Quinta year after year, but all guests get the same care. There's a private outdoor cubicle that has been available for massages in the sun since the 1930s. Twice-daily maid service and same-day laundry and dry cleaning are provided. The resort has nightly entertainment, several gift shops on the central plaza (including a wine shop with a wine-tasting bar), and all kinds of meeting and conference space, including a 17,000-square-foot ballroom, but its main focus is tennis and golf.

There are 30 tennis courts; guests play free of charge. Clinics are offered regularly and include video analysis, programmable ball machines, and unlimited open play. Packages are available for both tennis and golf players. Between the resort and PGA West, four championship golf courses are available to La Quinta guests. The 18-hole Dunes course, adjacent to the resort, is especially demanding, with water on eight holes, rolling hills, and scrubby desert to skirt. Shuttle service is provided to the PGA West course.

La Quinta also has a spa with more than 30 treatment rooms. There's a sanctuary courtyard, a 4,000-square-foot fitness center, and a number of inhalation rooms. Hot rock massages and celestial showers are two of Spa La Quinta's signature treatments.

Luckily for families, La Quinta has not overlooked the needs of its youngest guests. The resort has a year-round children's camp where children can play on computers or participate in organized activities. On Saturday nights during the summer and on holidays throughout the year (weather permitting), "drive-in" movies are shown: kids screen family-friendly flicks while floating on inner tubes in a resort swimming pool.

Palm Springs

Ingleside Inn

200 West Ramon Road
Palm Springs, CA 92264
760-325-0046
800-772-6655
Fax: 760-325-0710
ingleside@earthlink.net
www.inglesideinn.com

A secluded inn frequented by movie stars

Owner: Melvyn Haber. **Accommodations:** 18 rooms and 12 suites. **Rates:** $125–$265 single or double in season; suites $265–$425. **Included:** Continental breakfast. **Added:** 10% tax. **Payment:** Major credit cards. **Children:** Not appropriate, additional $20. **Smoking:** Nonsmoking rooms available.

➤ **Among the pictures on the lobby wall is one of June Allyson's 1976 wedding that took place at the inn along with her quote "Everyone should be married at the Ingleside Inn at least once in their lifetime."**

There's an air of exclusivity as you turn into the curved driveway of the Ingleside Inn. The parking lot is filled with fancy cars, and if you arrive at night, the trees sparkle with lights — perhaps representing the hundreds of movie stars who have frequented the inn over the years. The list of celebrities that have visited the Ingleside is several pages long, and some Hollywood types have been known to fly into town just for a meal at Melvyn's, the inn's well-known restaurant.

A local historic site, the Ingleside was originally built in the 1920s as a private home for the Birge family, owners of the Pierce Arrow Automobile Company. Later it was purchased by Ruth Hardy, the city's first councilwoman, and turned into an inn. In recent years the Ingleside has been in the hands of nightclub owner Melvyn Haber.

Set back from the road, on 2-1/2 tree-shaded acres almost at the foot of San Jacinto Mountain, the inn feels removed and secluded even though it is only a few blocks from the center of Palm Springs. It is this sense of privacy that no doubt appeals to beleaguered celebrities in search of some peace and quiet.

The inn's front porch, set with cushioned rattan chairs, a porch swing, and hummingbird feeders, is all but obscured by thick vines. Inside the lobby is an unusual mix of antiques. A romantic 100-year-old Belgian tapestry hangs above a sideboard that was once used as a vestment chest by priests in the 15th century. An intricately carved cherry screen with willow pattern china insets stands behind the concierge desk, and Oriental rugs and plush velvet sofas sit atop parquet floors. In one corner there's a unique iron light fixture in the shape of the sun topped by a cross that came from a church.

Two marble columns outside the lobby frame a courtyard with a cherub fountain. Here there is also a wonderful sculpture of Selene, the Goddess of the Moon. Some guest rooms are reached via this courtyard, while others are located in villas sprinkled over the grounds. One room accessed off the main building's front porch is called the Library. It has Queen Anne furnishings, a brass bed, and wood-burning fireplace. Other suites in the main building include the Lily Pons Room (named in honor of the diva who was a regular guest at the inn for many years), with Louis XV furniture, and the Princess Room, which is romantic with a half-canopy bed, white tile floors, and two loveseats in front of a fireplace.

Villa 2 is attractive and comfortable in cool blues and greens. It has stars on the ceiling, a fireplace, writing desk, and colorful prints evocative of the Riviera. Villas 7 and 8 can be rented together to create the Royal Suite, a large two-bedroom suite accommodating four people. The living room is formal, with Oriental chests and chairs covered in pink damask. The bedroom in Villa 8 has a lovely hand-painted dressing screen that's over 350 years old, and both villas have sunken tubs. All guest rooms have steam baths with whirlpool tubs, refrigerators stocked with complimentary refreshments, coffee makers, makeup mirrors, alarm clock radios, telephones, TVs, air conditioning, and English toiletries. In the morning, a Continental breakfast is brought to your guest room along with the morning paper,

Most guests spend at least some time lounging around the pool or soaking in the outdoor Jacuzzi. There's also shuffleboard, darts, croquet, and Ping-Pong; and a gazebo is tucked back in a corner of the lawn beyond the swimming pool. The shops and restaurants of downtown Palm Springs are within easy walking distance, although many guests choose to dine at Melvyn's, located next to the main building.

Mirrors, gold and black shimmering fabrics, and silver-plated chargers add more than a touch of glitz to Melvyn's main dining room and bar area, while diners in the adjoining glass-enclosed "patio," with its white wrought-iron chairs and lattice-covered ceiling, will find themselves in a more gardenlike setting overlooking a fountain and ornamental pool. Veal Ingleside (veal medallions served with avocado and a mousseline sauce along with fettuccine) is the restaurant's signature dish, while other entrées include salmon Grand Marnier and steak au poivre. Of course caviar is on the appetizer menu, and the champagne Sunday brunch is extremely popular. Jackets are recommended for dinner, and jeans are discouraged.

Korakia Pensione

257 S. Patencio Road
Palm Springs, CA 92262
760-864-6411
Fax: 760-864-4147

| A Mediterranean villa built in the 1920s |

Proprietor: Douglas Smith. **Accommodations:** 20 rooms. **Rates:** $119–$425. **Included:** Continental breakfast. **Added:** 10% tax. **Payment:** No credit cards. **Children:** Welcome on weekdays; additional $38. **Pets:** Not allowed. **Smoking:** Not allowed in rooms.

➤ **The white, uncluttered rooms feature antiques, worn Oriental rugs, period lamps, leatherbound books, and artifacts from Mediterranean countries.**

In 1924 the Scottish artist Gordon Coutts constructed a villa in the then-remote desert area adjacent to the village of Palm Springs. The architecture was reminiscent of Morocco, where the artist had spent some time, and a radical departure from the Spanish Colonial style favored in southern California.

Over the years, cultural leaders and dignitaries visited the castle-like home (Sir Winston Churchill painted in the upstairs studio), but after Gordon Coutts' death the villa deteriorated. In 1989, Douglas Smith, an architectural preservationist, purchased the building and began its restoration. Bougainvillea against the whitewashed walls give the inn an exotic look, and the atmosphere and furnishings throughout reflect the five years that Doug spent living in Greece.

A fanciful wooden entryway from Afghanistan leads from the parking lot to the inn, which stands behind an oleander hedge. In the lobby, fabulous carved chests and Mediterranean music immediately set the tone. Beyond the lobby, you can see a courtyard with a small swimming pool, chaises, large pottery urns, and a stone wall with a spouting waterfall. Each guest room is different, but each feels as if it has been transported from somewhere along the Mediterranean coast. All have kitchens or refrigerators, fresh flowers, crisply ironed sheets, and individual charm. The rooms do not have phones or TVs, though those are available upon request.

Climb tiled steps to the Artist Studio, where Churchill painted. It is a big, open space with slanted windows and a telescope so you can better admire the view of Mount San Jacinto and garner artistic inspiration. There's a Moorish trunk in the living room, and the bedroom has a feather bed. The Library, where literary discussions and chamber music concerts were held in decades past, has a beamed ceiling, a gas fireplace, French doors leading to a shaded patio, a queen-size handmade poster bed, and, of course, shelves full of books.

The Lower Guest House is a spacious suite with a living room, bedroom, kitchen, bath, and simply furnished dining room. There's a fireplace, a black futon sofa, and tapestry-backed chairs in the living room, and cement tile floors help keep the rooms cool in hot weather. The Adobe Room, once the villa's master bedroom, is the smallest and is different from the rest, with ochre adobe walls. In Garden Suite B in an adjacent building, there is little decoration on the walls, but furnishings such as the fantastic Middle Eastern sideboard that was originally designed to be carried on the back of a camel create enough visual interest on their own. Eight guest rooms are located in Doug's former residence across the street. It was built in the 1930s and is referred to as the Mediterranean Villa.

A Continental breakfast of fresh fruit and pastries is served in your room or on the flagstone terrace beside the antique Moorish fountain, where doves coo in antique birdcages under the fruit trees. A communal kitchen is available for preparing light fare. Service can be nonchalant at the inn, so if a highly attentive staff is important to you, you might feel more comfortable seeking lodgings elsewhere.

La Mancha Resort Village

P.O. Box 1606
444 Avenida Caballeros
Palm Springs, CA 92263
760-323-1773
800-255-1773
Fax: 760-323-5928
info@la-mancha.com
www.la-mancha.com

**A cluster of luxurious villas
in central Palm Springs**

Owner: Ken Irwin. **Accommodations:** 65 rooms and villas. **Rates:** $165–$1,150, $25 additional person. **Added:** 10% tax. **Payment:** Major credit cards. **Children:** Free in room with parents. **Pets:** Not allowed. **Smoking:** Nonsmoking rooms available.

➤ **La Mancha has its own fleet of ten white Chrysler LeBaron convertibles (named for each of Ken Irwin's ten children), which can be rented by guests at quite reasonable rates. Bicycles are also available for jaunting about town.**

One of the most extravagant, secluded, charming getaways in California is right in the middle of Palm Springs. Tucked behind walls and electronic security gates, La Mancha stands on twenty lushly landscaped acres, a Mediterranean-style village of stucco buildings with red tile roofs. Once inside the secured compound the rest of the world seems far removed, even though the center of Palm Springs is just steps away.

The private villas range in size from one bedroom and one bath to three bedrooms with three baths. Some are one-story casitas, others loft villas with two levels. Every imaginable luxury is provided, depending upon the lodging you choose. Traditional hotel-style guest rooms, mini-suites, or sections of the three-bedroom villas are also available.

The most expensive are the four private tennis villas. Each boasts a tennis court, a walled courtyard patio, a private swimming pool, a therapy pool and bath, an outdoor wet bar with icemaker, a split-level living and dining room with a fireplace, an equipped kitchen, laundry facilities, and a state-of-the-art video and sound system.

The luxury estate villas have the same features without the tennis courts. They all resemble fine private homes in a well-to-do neighborhood, but even when the complex is full there's no sense of crowding. Some have their own security entrances and garages — favorites with celebrities who wish anonymity. Each is individually decorated, many have big-screen TVs, and all lodgings have VCRs — rentals are available from La Mancha's video library.

In addition to the private pools or spas (or both) in 47 villas, La Mancha has a centrally located free-form pool with a waterfall and stream that is convenient for guests in the few rooms that don't have their own pool. On a raised deck beside it are yellow tent cabanas and a thatch-roofed bar. There are five tennis courts (one is grass), two croquet courts (one is regulation size for tournaments), a golf green for chipping and putting, and facilities for small meetings. For workouts, there is a small fitness center over the lobby with exercise equipment and a sauna.

You may dine on a terrace near the pool or in La Mancha's tiny restaurant called the Don Quixote Room. It is only open to La Mancha guests so it has just seven tables — although a wall of mirrors makes the room appear twice as large as it really is. Continental favorites dominate the menu, which changes nightly.

Four stained glass windows depicting scenes from *Don Quixote* hang in the dining room, further clues to the owner's interest in Cervantes' hero. Ken Irwin has long been fascinated by the legendary figure and his own "impossible dream" is the resort he and his late wife made a reality.

La Mancha specializes in superb service that goes beyond daily maid service and cheese and fruit baskets. With advance notice you can request a private dinner in your villa that the chef will prepare for you in your own kitchen. If you want a violin serenade of your favorite song, you have only to ask. Or you may ride in a limousine, compliments of La Mancha, when you're in the mood for a Palm Springs shopping foray. Babysitting service is available, and there's a masseuse on call. Airport pickup is complimentary.

In short La Mancha is an extraordinary hideaway. It's the place to go when you tire of those incessant autograph hunters — or when you simply want total privacy in a romantic dream.

L'Horizon

1050 East Palm Canyon Drive
Palm Springs, CA 92264
760-323-1858
800-377-7855
Fax: 760-327-2933

> **A tranquil inn for sunshine and relaxation**

Manager: Nickie McLaughlin. **Accommodations:** 22 rooms and 1 2-bedroom house. **Rates:** $115–$255 single or double (rates vary according to season), $650 for a house which sleeps up to 6. **Added:** 10% tax. **Included:** Continental breakfast. **Payment:** Major credit cards. **Children:** Not appropriate. **Pets:** Not allowed. **Smoking:** Allowed outside only. **Open:** October-July 4th weekend.

➤ **Built in the 1950s and remodeled in the late 1980s, the rooms surround a swimming pool, Jacuzzi, and barbecue area with lounge chairs and umbrella tables. There's a fine view of San Jacinto Mountain.**

This quiet enclave in the desert city of Palm Springs has a crisp clean look to its lodgings and grounds. Behind walls covered with scarlet bougainvillea, two and a half acres of lawns, tall palm trees, and spicy-scented pepper trees provide the setting for seven low-lying buildings and a two-bedroom home, which can accommodate up to six people, with a private swimming pool.

Each lodging building has three guest rooms and a kitchen. Generally the guest rooms are rented out separately, but groups can rent out an entire unit if they choose. The cheerful, sunny rooms, have interesting configurations. Decorated in light white and pastels, they are tastefully furnished in a contemporary style and have tall, shuttered windows and private patios. In the bathroom, a glass door leads to an atrium fragrant with the scent of orange blossoms. Breakfast is brought to your door with a morning newspaper. The staff will bring lunch from a nearby eatery, and several restaurants are within walking distance.

L'Horizon lends bicycles and will make reservations for golf, tennis, and horseback riding. The inn also has a library and facilities for croquet and horseshoes. Desert Adventures offers noteworthy, highly recommended tours to Indian Canyon and Joshua Tree National Monument.

Villa Royale

1620 Indian Trail
Palm Springs, CA 92264
760-327-2314
800-245-2314
Fax: 760-322-3794
info@villaroyale.com
www.villaroyale.com

**A friendly inn with an
international theme**

Innkeeper: Greg Purdy. **Accommodations:** 20 rooms and 11 suites. **Rates:** $105–$325. **Included:** Continental breakfast. **Added:** 10% tax. **Payment:** Major credit cards. **Children:** Not appropriate. **Pets:** Not allowed. **Smoking:** Non-smoking rooms available.

➤ **You may borrow bicycles, purchase a picnic lunch from the inn's restaurant, or join a tour of the boutiques and shopping centers on Palm Canyon Drive.**

This European-style country inn is a gem hidden among the flashier baubles around it. Behind its stucco walls and iron gates, Villa Royale holds many surprises. First is the series of interior tree-shaded courtyards, each bright with cascading bougainvillea and pots of flowers. There are two swimming pools — one in the main courtyard, where a light breakfast is served. You reach the other, smaller pool by following brick pathways that amble past fountains and vine-covered trellises to another courtyard. The atmosphere at Villa Royale is low-key and friendly. Most guests spend at least part of their time here relaxing and reading by the pools.

The Mediterranean-style compound covers 3-1/2 acres. Each guest room has a different country theme: Morocco, France, Portugal, Germany, Italy, England, and Greece to name a few. The Spain Room has Spanish ceramic tile edging the curved brick hearth of the fireplace and dark, carved furniture. Decorative plates hang over an arch to the full kitchen, and double doors open to a courtyard with a fountain.

The Monte Carlo Suite has red tile floors, a bleached-beam ceiling, and a fireplace. Its private patio faces a garden of roses and palm trees and, at night, the soft glow of filigreed Moroccan lamps hanging in the rubber trees. In another suite, a Grecian urn, blue tiled bath, and travel posters of the sun-splashed Mediterranean countryside let you know you're in a room dedicated to Greece.

Compared to recent developments in luxury hotels, amenities are basic: simple soaps, no hair dryers, few writing tables, no stationery. Television sets are hidden under tablecloths. But the charm of the place more than outweighs any such flaws; indeed, many guests view them as attributes. Even the smallest room, which has a Dutch theme, is appealing with slate floors, a brass bed, and Dutch doors. It's a bargain to boot (although it's too small for comfort if you're planning a lengthy stay).

In keeping with the international theme, the Europa Restaurant features Continental cuisine, an antique bar that came from a Parisian restaurant, and pottery from various European countries adorns its walls. Cozy and attractive, with brick floors and floral fabric tablecloths, the Europa is known as one of the best dining spots in Palm Springs. Examples of the excellent entrées are roasted duck with caramelized orange and sweet and sour cabbage, and veal scallops sauteed with capers, lemon demi-glaze, and fresh thyme. California and European wines are available.

Rancho Mirage

The Ritz-Carlton Rancho Mirage

68-900 Frank Sinatra Drive
Rancho Mirage, CA 92270
760-321-8282
800-241-3333
Fax: 760-321-6928

| A traditional luxury hotel above the desert

General manager: Lenny Zilz. **Accommodations:** 219 rooms and 21 suites. **Rates:** $240–$395 single or double; suites $425–$1,000; reduced rates available in summer. **Added:** 10% tax and $10 per night resort fee per room. **Payment:** Major credit cards. **Children:** Under 17 free in room with parents. **Pets:** Not allowed. **Smoking:** Not allowed.

➤ **Some of the sky views are glorious. Ask for a west-facing room and you may see both color-streaked skies at sunset and pastel reflections against Mount San Jacinto at sunrise.**

Above the desert valley and village of Rancho Mirage, on a 650-foot-high plateau south of Palm Springs, the beige toned buildings of the Ritz-Carlton stand like great boulders against a rocky land-scape. It's a stark setting, here in the rugged foothills of the Santa Rosa Mountains. At the entrance to the hotel a bronze bighorn sheep sculpture stands at attention in deference to the wildlife that shares the surrounding terrain.

Inside, the contrast is astounding — you enter a world of Euro-pean antiques, marble floors, crystal chandeliers, heavy drapes, and museum-quality oil paintings on paneled walls. In the lobby, fine Meissen china is on display in a Dutch rococo walnut breakfront, there's also a handsome Regency sideboard in mahogany, an an-tique map of California (circa 1666) hangs on one wall, and a lovely Persian rug lies on the marble floor before the registration desk. At the far end of the long chandeliered hallway leading from the lobby is a scene that appears surreal in this context but is in fact a picture window framing a view of the desert and mountains beyond a ter-race with white canvas umbrellas.

All hotels with the Ritz-Carlton name specialize in a strong tra-dition of luxury along with an emphasis on personal service. Ran-cho Mirage is no exception. Ignoring the desert surrounding it, the resort is all damask drapes, dark woods, and formal furniture.

The accommodations feature custom crown moldings, writing tables, balconies or patios, and marble baths with telephones. Plush terrycloth robes (or lightweight cotton robes in summertime) and Scottish Fine shampoos are among the amenities. The decor, in muted silver, tan and gold, reflects the hills outside while dam-ask fabrics set the tone of understated luxury. Television sets are tucked into antique reproduction highboys; stocked honor bars hide behind false drawers. Rooms have balconies overlooking the grounds, the pool, or the mountains.

Standard rooms have two doubles or one king bed. Executive suites have a separate living room; Presidential suites have a spa-cious living room with a baby grand piano and a dining room. The Club Floor has its own concierge and a lounge where breakfast, lunch, tea, afternoon appetizers, cold beverages, beer, cordials, and desserts are served complimentary to Club Floor guests only.

The resort has a fitness center with workout equipment, steam and sauna rooms, and massage (a personal trainer can be provided upon request). The center is near the outdoor pool, which is in a grassy plateau above the Coachella Valley. Across the road are ten tennis courts, a pro shop, and an outdoor basketball court. There's a small pitch-and-putt course at the resort (you can borrow clubs from the fitness center) and several nearby golf courses are open to guests (—the closest is Rancho Mirage Country Club). For families traveling with children, the hotel runs a "Ritz Kids" activity program.

The hotel restaurants vary in terms of decor and cuisine. For fine cuisine, diners reserve a table at the Dining Room. In the 75-seat room, elegant with damask walls, light blue velvet chairs, and silver candle holders, Continental and American dishes such as roasted pink snapper served with warm couscous salad and sundried tomato tapenade are beautifully presented.

There are two more casual cafés. The Café, open for all three meals daily, serves soups, salads, pastas, and grilled pizzas at lunch and has a menu that ranges from mahi mahi to jerked New York steak in the evening. Mirada, right on the edge of the hillside, has outdoor dining and serves sandwiches and tropical drinks; poolside snacks are served all day. In the afternoon, tea is served in the lobby lounge. The bar has the rich wood paneling and hunt scenes often found in a gentlemen's club.

The friendly service in this atmosphere of refined gentility is pure West Coast. The bellman who carries your luggage may linger to lean on the balcony railing and chat about the desert sunset and life in Palm Springs. The desk clerk may grab your arm and point out an unusual sight he thinks you shouldn't miss: the bighorn sheep that wander in every day from the mountains to graze on the lawn or the roadrunners that also roam the property. This may be the Ritz, but it's still California.

The Westin Mission Hills Resort

71333 Dinah Shore Drive
Rancho Mirage, CA 92270
760-328-5955
800-WESTIN-1
Fax: 760-770-2199
ranch@westin.com
www.westin.com

> **Recreational activities abound at this extensive resort**

General manager: Ed Wetzhammer. **Accommodations:** 512 rooms and suites. **Rates:** $420–$460 single or double in high season; rates start at $99 in summer; suites $560–$1,200. **Added:** 10% tax and $9 per day resort fee per room. **Payment:** Major credit cards. **Children:** Free in room with parents. **Pets:** Not allowed. **Smoking:** Nonsmoking rooms available.

➤   **Landscaping at the resort will make you forget you're in the desert. Everywhere you look there is the deep green of the lush golf course fairways or the manicured lawns bordered by colorful annuals that lead to the guest pavilions. Lagoons wind between buildings, and sculptures add an artistic touch to the already pleasing grounds.**

An island of green grass with rows of flowerbeds, palms, and citrus trees, accentuated by a granite pyramidal fountain stands like an oasis in the desert at the entrance to the Westin Mission Hills Resort. Beyond it the pink Moorish structure of the main building is striking with its multiple arches, wings, and courtyards. Upon reaching the entrance a valet will whisk away your car, and you'll pass through a dramatic colonnade to the lobby. Outside the lobby is a rock waterfall with a 60-foot waterslide on the reverse side spilling into a small pool that adjoins the much larger, meandering Las Brisas swimming pool. All of this is just a hint of what the resort has to offer.

The resort originally opened in 1987 with 200 rooms. Westin Hotels took over the property in 1989 and closed the hotel while they added convention space, a golf course, and more than 300 additional guest rooms. The resort reopened in August of 1991. Now in addition to the impressive main building there are 16 separate pavilions housing about 30 guest rooms each, 75,000 square feet of meeting space, a 20-acre resort park (with a paved jogging and bike path), seven lighted tennis courts, and three swimming pools spread over 360 acres. There's also a fitness center, sand volleyball court, croquet, shuffleboard, and two 18-hole golf courses — one designed by Pete Dye the other by legendary Gary Player.

The two-story guest pavilions are grouped around courtyards with small gardens. Rooms in shades of mauve, taupe, and blue, have contemporary and light wood furnishings and modern art prints on the walls. In some rooms the bed is placed at an angle to create a more interesting look. Rooms have either a king or two queen beds, balconies or patios, alarm-clock radios, remote control televisions with in-room movies, stocked refreshment centers, two direct-dial telephones with computer capability and voice mail, safes, and baths with double vanities, hair dryers, and coffeemakers.

Resort suites have a separate living room with a marble dining table and chaise lounge and a separate tub and shower in the bath. Chairman suites are the most deluxe with two bedrooms, 2-1/2 baths, a fireplace, baby grand piano, a whirlpool, and three private patios. A $9 per day resort fee covers phone charges, daily newspaper delivery, in-room coffee, and use of the fitness center.

The resort's restaurant, Bella Vista, serves both Californian and Southwestern favorites, and light meals are also available at each of the swimming pools as well as in the Lobby Lounge.

Although there is plenty to do at the resort, many guests steal time away from the golf course or swimming pool to visit the attractions of nearby Palm Springs or shop at the chic boutiques on El Paseo — Palm Desert's version of Rodeo Drive — about fifteen minutes from the resort. The hotel's excellent concierge can help you with sightseeing arrangements. For arrivals and departures, the Palm Springs airport is only seven miles from hotel.

Northern California

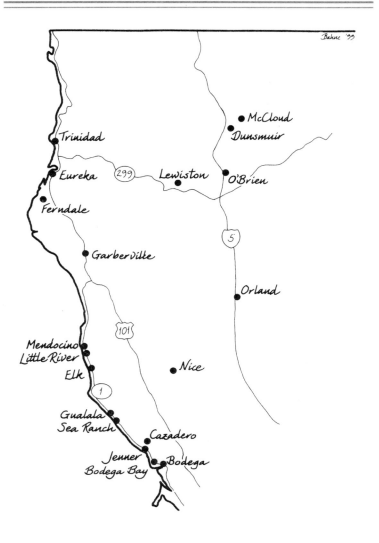

Bodega
Sonoma Coast Villa, 247
Bodega Bay
The Inn at the Tides, 249
Cazadero
Timberhill Ranch, 251
Dunsmuir
Railroad Park Resort, 253
Elk
Elk Cove Inn, 254
Greenwood Pier Inn, 256
Harbor House, 258
Eureka
Abigail's Elegant Victorian Mansion, 260
Carter House Victorians, 263
Ferndale
The Gingerbread Mansion, 265
Garberville
Benbow Inn, 268
Gualala
The Old Milano Hotel, 270
St. Orres, 272
The Whale Watch Inn, 273
Jenner
Stillwater Cove Ranch, 275
Lewiston
Trinity Alps Resort, 276

Little River
Glendeven, 278
Heritage House, 280
Little River Inn, 282
McCloud
McCloud Guest House, 284
Mendocino
Agate Cove Inn, 286
The Headlands Inn, 288
Hill House Inn, 289
Joshua Grindle Inn, 291
MacCallum House, 293
Mendocino Hotel, 295
Reed Manor, 297
The Stanford Inn by the Sea, 299
The Whitegate Inn, 301
Nice
Featherbed Railroad Company Bed & Breakfast Resort, 303
O'Brien
Holiday Harbor, 305
Orland
The Inn at Shallow Creek Farm, 307
Sea Ranch
The Sea Ranch, 309
Trinidad
The Lost Whale Inn, 311
Trinidad Bay Bed & Breakfast, 312

Intimate City Stops

Eureka
Abigail's Elegant Victorian Mansion, 260
Carter House Victorians, 263

Country Inns

Garberville
Benbow Inn, 268
Little River
Glendeven, 278
McCloud
McCloud Guest House, 284
Nice
Featherbed Railroad Company Bed & Breakfast Resort, 303
Orland
The Inn at Shallow Creek Farm, 307

Family Favorites

Dunsmuir
Railroad Park Resort, 253
Lewiston
Trinity Alps Resort, 276
O'Brien
Holiday Harbor, 305
Trinidad
The Lost Whale Inn, 311

Inns by the Sea

Bodega Bay
The Inn at the Tides, 249
Elk
Elk Cove Inn, 254
Greenwood Pier Inn, 256
Harbor House, 258
Gualala
The Old Milano Hotel, 270

St. Orres, 272
The Whale Watch Inn, 273
Little River
Heritage House, 280
Little River Inn, 282
Mendocino
Agate Cove Inn, 286
The Headlands Inn, 288
Hill House Inn, 289
Joshua Grindle Inn, 291
MacCallum House, 293
The Stanford Inn by the Sea, 299
The Whitegate Inn, 301
Trinidad
Trinidad Bay Bed & Breakfast, 312

On a Budget

Jenner
Stillwater Cove Ranch, 275

Resorts

Sea Ranch
The Sea Ranch, 309

Romantic Hideaways

Bodega
Sonoma Coast Villa, 247
Cazadero
Timberhill Ranch, 251
Ferndale
The Gingerbread Mansion, 265
Mendocino
Reed Manor, 297

For unspoiled, uncrowded wilderness, head for California's far north. The Klamath, Shasta, and Trinity regions are vast stretches of thick forestland, rugged mountains, alpine meadows, rushing rivers, and deep canyons. Towns are few and cities nonexistent.

Mount Shasta, rising 14,162 feet from the valley floor, dominates much of the landscape. South of the dormant volcano is Shasta Lake, fed by rivers and dammed to form an immense reservoir where every sort of freshwater recreation is available.

East of Shasta and I-5 are trout-filled rivers, dark lava beds, and sanctuaries for birds and wildlife. In Lassen Volcanic National Park, deep craters and steaming sulfur vents are reminders of Mount Lassen's explosive past. The southernmost volcano in the Cascade chain, 10,000-foot Lassen last erupted in 1917.

West of I-5 lie the Trinity Alps, where angular peaks reach 8,000 feet above evergreen forests and steep ravines. This is prime fishing and backpacking country.

Still farther west is, finally, the edge of the continent, the end of the American frontier. Here the redwoods grow — the tallest trees in the world. Most of the primeval forests are gone now, cut for lumber, but in Redwood National Park and the state parks along Highway 101, cathedral-like groves are preserved. The largest park is near the little town of **Trinidad**.

Continuing south past **Eureka**, a bay city known for its Victorian architecture, Highway 101 turns inland toward **Garberville** and then hugs the coastline again, offering spectacular scenes of rugged beauty. Ceaseless, wind-driven waves with spindrift pluming crash against craggy cliffs and sea arches; white surf curls against smooth sand. Coves and inlets, lagoons and tide pools wait to be explored. From any bluff along the way you may see gray whales spouting as they migrate between Alaska and the sheltered waters off Baja California.

Small communities such as **Mendocino**, **Little River**, and **Elk**, separated by high cliffs and empty beaches, punctuate the winding ribbon of coastal road from Oregon to San Francisco Bay.

Bodega

Sonoma Coast Villa

16702 Coast Highway One
P.O. Box 236
Bodega, CA 94922-0236
707-876-9818
888-404-2255
Fax: 707-876-9856
reservations@scvilla.com
www.scvilla.com

> **A Mediterranean ambience awaits at this Sonoma coast inn**

Proprietors: Cyrus and Susan Griffin. **Accommodations:** 12 rooms. **Rates:** $255–$295; off-season discounts available. **Included:** Full breakfast. **Added:** 9% tax. **Minimum stay:** 2 nights on weekends. **Payment:** Major credit cards. **Children:** Not encouraged. **Pets:** Not allowed. **Smoking:** Not allowed.

➤ **The inn is just five minutes from the ocean. Other area diversions include golf, enzyme baths, and the wineries of the Russian River and Dry Creek valleys. If you just want to stay at the inn and relax, spa services there include massages, body wraps, facials, and salt scrubs.**

The Sonoma Coast Villa is located off Highway One about three miles from the ocean on a stretch of the coastal route that turns inland for a short while between Tomales and Bodega Bay. With only 12 rooms on 60 acres, the inn is a good option for anyone seeking a peaceful retreat with a bit of luxury thrown in for good measure. Because it stands on such a large parcel of land, the inn compound is set well back from the main road, thus insuring a tranquil and private environment.

A Labrador Retriever sleeping on an Oriental rug at the inn's front entrance immediately sets the tone of comfortable elegance. Beyond the lobby, several pink stucco Mediterranean-style buildings with red tile roofs encompass a pool terrace bordered by slender Italian cypress trees. Nearby is an indoor spa surrounded by marble tile and illuminated from above by a ceiling of skylights.

The inn's six original guest rooms are located in a one-story building that runs along one side of the swimming pool. Nicely furnished, each room is spacious and has its own entrance and fireplace (wood is supplied). Room Two has a king-size bed, built-in sofa/window seat with tapestry print and needlepoint pillows, two easy chairs in front of the fireplace, and a writing table in an alcove. The bath has an oversized shower, marble tiling, and a marble vanity.

In Room Four, natural wood paneling behind the bed serves as the headboard. A small china cupboard stands in a corner, an ivory sofa faces the fireplace, and there are two sinks in the large, sunny bath. The bed is secondary in Room Six, as the living area is emphasized; and Room Three is the smallest — but skylights in the room's high ceiling and a window in the bath add a sense of light and space.

Six new rooms were added in an adjacent building built in 1997. The decor is similar to that of the original six, but the new rooms have Jacuzzi tubs in addition to fireplaces. All rooms have honor bars, stocked refrigerators, coffeemakers, hair dryers, irons and ironing boards, TV/VCRs (guests are welcome to borrow movies from the inn's video library), and a complimentary bottle of wine.

In the morning a hot country breakfast is served in the French country dining room in the main villa. On weekends Mediterranean-influenced prix fixe dinners are served using local meats, seafood, and fresh produce from the inn's own organic garden. Billiard and Ping-Pong tables are set up in the Carriage House when it's not in use by a group, and there's a meadow on the grounds with an adjoining brick patio shaded by corkscrew willows that is a popular spot for wedding receptions.

Bodega Bay

The Inn at the Tides

P.O. Box 640
800 Pacific Coast Highway 1
Bodega Bay, CA 94923
707-875-2751
800-541-7788
Fax: 707-875-2669
iatt@monitor.net
www.innatthetides.com

| **A hilltop resort in a seaside village** |

General manager: Carlo Galazzo. **Accommodations:** 86 rooms. **Rates:** $160–$270 single or double, $20 additional person. **Included:** Continental breakfast. **Added:** 9% tax. **Payment:** Major credit cards. **Children:** Under 12 free in room with a parent. **Pets:** Not allowed. **Smoking:** Nonsmoking rooms available.

➤ **Bird-watching opportunities abound. Great blue herons, pelicans, cormorants, osprey, sandpipers, and scores more have been sighted here. Movie fans may remember that Alfred Hitchcock's *The Birds* was filmed at Bodega Bay.**

This resort on six hilltop acres faces the bay some 60 miles north of San Francisco. It offers visitors to the Sonoma coast a quiet, sophisticated retreat with a host of facilities.

The guest rooms are divided among twelve two-story shingled redwood lodges, every one with a view of the harbor. From your window you can watch the fishing fleet come and go and see the sun set over the Pacific, beyond lawns bordered by hardy native plants and blooming annuals.

Most of the rooms have vaulted ceilings and a few have patios. Rooms feature a television with a movie channel, direct-dial phones, coffeemakers, clock radios, refrigerators, and terrycloth robes in roomy closets. The baths have hair dryers, custom soaps and gels, and — convenient for wet swimsuits — a clothesline that stretches over the tub.

A typical room is furnished with a sturdy oak table and chairs and a gray couch with soft cushions. Half the rooms have blue ceramic tile fireplaces with a basket of wood nearby; more will be brought upon request, at a nominal charge. In this quiet retreat, nighttime sounds fade away until all you hear are the moans of a distant buoy and the crackle of your fire.

A complimentary newspaper will be delivered to your door in the morning. When the mood strikes you can amble down to the Tide Wharf Restaurant for a complimentary Continental breakfast of croissants, muffins, and fruit. A wall of windows offers fine views of the harbor and Bodega Head, and there's a terrace just outside where you can have breakfast in warm weather.

The Bay View restaurant in the main lodge has an à la carte dinner menu that changes weekly and features fresh seafood and local game, fowl, and produce. It also offers a Dinner with the Winemaker series, a chance to meet local winemakers and sample their wines while dining on a five-course meal.

In-room massages are available upon request. Also on the property are a whirlpool spa, a sauna, and an indoor/outdoor heated lap pool protected from sea breezes by glass walls. For more outdoor recreation, you may golf at Bodega Harbour Golf Links, an 18-hole course a mile away, or go whale-watching, horseback riding, charter boat fishing, clamming, or beachcombing.

The annual Fishermen's Festival in April features a decorated boat parade, the blessing of the fleet, arts and crafts shows, food stalls, and races. Crabbing season runs from mid-November through April, and crab feasts are a Bodega Bay specialty. Try them at the Tide Wharf Restaurant's annual Crab Feed, or buy or catch your own and have a feast, accompanied by sourdough bread and chilled Sonoma County wine.

Cazadero

Timberhill Ranch

35755 Hauser Bridge Road
Cazadero, CA 95421
707-847-3258
800-847-3470
Fax: 707-847-3342
timber@mcn.org
www.timberhillranch.com

> **A luxurious ridgetop ranch and cottages**

Owner: Tarran McDaid. **Accommodations:** 15 cottages. **Rates:** $345 single, $395–$415 double. **Included:** Breakfast and dinner. **Added:** 9% bed tax, 7.5% sales tax. **Minimum stay:** 2 nights on weekends, 3 nights on holiday weekends. **Payment:** Major credit cards. **Children:** Charged at 50% of adult rate. **Pets:** Not allowed. **Smoking:** Restricted.

➤   **If you want to tour the surrounding countryside during the day, the kitchen will pack a picnic basket for you. A good place to picnic is Salt Point, a beach park with convoluted lava formations, colorful tide pools, and high bluffs that are good for whale-watching.**

Timberhill is a mile inland from the rugged northern Sonoma coast as the crow flies, two and a half hours from San Francisco. But the road you take to get there twists five miles from the shoreline highway up into the hills.

The luxurious ranch stands on a ridgetop more than a thousand feet above sea level. If you're in need of a soothing haven with no phone, television, or harsh intrusions, the drive is worth it. Add superb meals to the peaceful ambience and pampering Timberhill offers, and you understand why it's in great demand. Hiking trails meander through 80 acres of grassy meadows, towering redwoods, and placid ponds, leading to wide views of Salt Point State Park and Kruse Rhododendron Reserve. The park and reserve cover 6,000 acres of wooded hills and ferny glens, extending to the sea.

Tennis courts are tucked away behind a hill overlooking a wooded canyon. A 40-foot swimming pool surrounded by decking is set below the main lodge, with a whirlpool spa in one corner.

The ranch's restaurant, with high vaulted ceilings and candles and fresh flowers atop tables covered in green tablecloths is an elegant spot where guests dine on the six-course dinners served nightly. The menu changes daily, but there's always a choice of at least five entrées and desserts. Local products are used to prepare the California French cuisine, which features specialties such as roasted quail with red and black currant sauce, Peking duck under a sour cherry sauce, and pan-grilled salmon with fresh papaya chutney. The extensive wine list, which offers more than thirty chardonnays alone, concentrates on Sonoma County wines.

The cedar cottages are scattered over the property, some hidden among the redwoods and others on the edge of a meadow overlooking the duck pond. Handmade quilts grace the beds, tile fireplaces are laid with wood, and traditional furniture stands against rustic walls. Fresh flowers add dashes of color in pottery vases, on the pillows, and even placed carefully atop a stack of fluffy towels in the bathroom.

The innkeepers have added a few unexpected touches such as flashlights for late-night walks, matchbooks and napkins with your name in gilt lettering, and coffeemakers with Timberhill's own blend of coffee.

Privacy is respected in this rarefied atmosphere. The owners are available to answer questions and will show up at your cottage door with a breakfast tray (fruit, muffins, juice, and tea or coffee); otherwise, you're on your own for solitary rambles, tennis, sunning by the pool, or hot-tubbing. The skylighted common room in the main building has soft couches facing a big stone fireplace, a bar area, and jigsaw puzzles in progress, but most guests prefer the seclusion of their own cottage and crackling fire.

Long ago the property was a Pomo Indian encampment; after the redwood forest was logged, it became a working ranch and the site of an alternative school before the present owners took over in 1983. Two couples from the Bay Area decided to build the perfect country retreat with their own hands. With little help they constructed the lodge, the cottages, the pool, barns, and tennis courts. More cottages have been added in recent years, along with a conference room with satellite TV (since there are no televisions in the rooms).

Dunsmuir

Railroad Park Resort

100 Railroad Park Road
Dunsmuir, CA 96025
530-235-4440
800-974-RAIL in California
Fax: 530-255-4470
www.rrpark.com

A group of railroad cars restored as lodgings

Innkeeper: Angie Pelletier. **Accommodations:** 22 cabooses, 1 boxcar, 4 cabins. **Rates:** $70–$85 double occupancy; $8 each additional person in room. **Added:** 8% tax. **Payment:** Major credit cards. **Children:** $8 additional if third person in unit. **Pets:** Allowed with approval; $8 additional. **Smoking:** Nonsmoking units available.

➤ **The innkeepers are proud of their region and resort in the Sacramento River Canyon. They lend mountain bikes and will direct you to hiking trails and their trout pond. Their unusual resort also has sixty campsites and RV sites.**

In the 19th century, the last car on a train was used for storage space and living quarters and, as time went on, it became the personal domain of the conductor. To live the life of such a railroader, visit Railroad Park Resort. It takes a leap of imagination, for these cabooses go nowhere. Each is anchored firmly to its own brief stretch of track just off I-5, south of the little town of Dunsmuir in the mountains of northern California, but children and railroad buffs will enjoy the idea of sleeping in a caboose.

The cabooses bear fresh coats of paint — green, blue, yellow, and, mostly, a familiar railroad red. The Santa Fe, Great Northern, Southern Pacific, and the McCloud River are a few of the rail lines represented, and each has a different interior decor. Some are painted, others paneled in knotty cedar. A typical rectangular room has a brass bed, table and chairs, a dresser, a coffeemaker, telephone, refrigerator, and a TV (with satellite reception). Fluffy blue curtains hang at small windows. The effect is not unlike a mobile home except for the metal braces and pipes, the iron ladders and lofts that are evidence of the car's railroading days. The only other mementos are the photographs on the walls.

The circle of cabooses make a colorful railyard below the craggy peaks, and they surround a free-form swimming pool, wooden deck, and a spa. A stream runs by, winding through the property to a pond. Off to the side are four attached housekeeping cabins that hold four people each.

The resort's office and gift shop are in a faded yellow building that resembles an old-fashioned train depot with a high boardwalk entrance. Near it is the showpiece of the resort, its restaurant. Made from antique dining cars, it's steeped in railroad history. Above the bar is a hand-built scale model of the Cascade, which ran from San Francisco to Portland in the 1930s. Antique hand tools, lamps, and steam gauges make this a railroad buff's delight.

Dinners are served in an equally nostalgic atmosphere, with a view of relics of the steam era. Among them are an 1893 Wells Fargo car, a gear-driven logging engine, and a restored water tower. The menu offers American fare—steak, chicken, pasta, and seafood dominate the dining scene. The restaurant is only open for dinner. For other meals, drive a mile north into Dunsmuir, where there are several good cafés (try Rosie's Ice Cream Parlor for homemade soups and sandwiches).

Outside the Patio Car there's a deck for relaxing with a cocktail and enjoying the fine view of the gray spires of Castle Crags State Park. In the shadow of these steep granite outcroppings, the last Indian battle fought with bows and arrows occurred in 1885.

Elk

Elk Cove Inn

P.O. Box 367
6300 South Highway 1
Elk Cove, CA 95432
707-877-3321
800-275-2967
Fax: 707-877-1808
elkcove@mcn.org
www.elkcoveinn.com

An ocean-view inn and cottages

Innkeeper: Elaine Bryant. **Accommodations:** 10 rooms, 4 suites (all with private bath). **Rates:** $118–$308. **Included:** Full breakfast. **Added:** 10% tax. **Minimum**

stay: 2 or 3 nights on weekends and holidays. **Payment:** Major credit cards. **Children:** Not appropriate, additional $30 if third person in room. **Pets:** Not allowed. **Smoking:** Not allowed indoors.

➤   **Climbing roses, boxes of pink geraniums, and flower beds under the cypress trees give this gabled white inn and its guest cottages a country atmosphere. The inn stands on 1 ½ acres on a cliff above the ocean.**

The main house of this clifftop inn was built in 1883 by the L. E. White Lumber Company as an executive guest house. In 1968 it was reborn as a bed-and-breakfast. At Elk Cove, the energetic innkeeper will greet you with a smile, give you a hearty welcome, and treat you like an honored friend.

The guest rooms are in the main house, an adjacent building, and four cabins that stand at the edge of the cliff. They have fine views of the driftwood-strewn sandy beach, offshore rock formations, and surf. The furnishings include antiques, down comforters, feather beds, coffee makers, and bathrobes. Fresh flowers, potted greenery, hand-embroidered linens, and a welcome basket with fruit, wine, and freshly baked cookies add a personal note, while port, chocolates, and candles, create a romantic ambience. Cards, games, books, and blankets to take to the beach are other thoughtful touches.

The large, bright rooms upstairs in the main house have wainscoting, window seats, and skylights. They share a sitting area and a redwood deck. Cypress Garden, in pinks and greens, has a four-poster canopy bed, floral duvet, a fainting couch, easy chairs, a gas fireplace, and a garden view. Swallow's Nest, on the first floor, is the least expensive. It's sunny and cozy, with an ocean view from its white iron bed.

The rooms in a duplex addition feature large bay windows, high beamed ceilings, skylights, and fireplaces. The windows in the Greenwood Room overlook Greenwood Creek and the beach below. Even the shower stall, its tiles bright with hand-painted folk art, has a long window with a view.

Four American arts-and-crafts-style suites in an oceanfront stone and shingle building that was constructed in 1997 are the newest additions to the inn. With vaulted redwood ceilings, they have king-size beds, whirlpool tubs, balconies, fireplaces, wet bars, microwaves, refrigerators, and, of course, great views. Three have separate living rooms.

A buffet breakfast is served in the oceanfront dining room of the main house. Elaine says that because she's originally from the South, she always cooks more than what people can possibly eat.

The buffet features a variety of seasonal fruits, freshly baked breads, an oatmeal bar with all of the fixings, and an assortment of hot entrées which change on a daily basis. A selection of juices and teas and the inn's own specially blended coffee round out the morning meal.

Guests staying at the inn on a Tuesday or Wednesday evening can opt to sit down to a gourmet meal prepared by a professional chef. You can watch the sun set over the ocean as you dine on the likes of herb-rubbed prime rib with horseradish-garlic flan and parmesan roasted potato wedges, or free-range chicken in a Thai-coconut curry sauce, and then top it off with a sinfully delicious chocolate cake. The meals are tasty, and it's hard to beat the setting.

Many guests enjoy the inn's gazebo or taking a walk down the path that leads to the beach — Asta, the inn's friendly fox terrier, will happily show you the way. Here great blue herons and snowy egrets often visit, and two ravens are such frequent visitors they are virtually pets. For exploring farther afield, the inn is close to a number of Anderson Valley wineries and 15 miles south of the shops and art galleries of Mendocino.

Greenwood Pier Inn

Box 336
5928 South Highway 1
Elk, CA 95432
707-877-9997
Fax: 707-877-3439
gwpier@mcn.org
www.greenwoodpierinn.com

| An artistic inn overlooking the sea |

Innkeeper: Kendrick Petty. **Accommodations:** 7 rooms and 5 suites (all with private bath). **Rates:** $120–$250 single or double, $15 additional person. **Included:** Continental breakfast. **Added:** 10% tax. **Minimum stay:** 2 nights on weekends in most rooms. **Payment:** Major credit cards. **Children:** $15 additional. **Pets:** Allowed in some of the units with prior arrangement; $15 additional. **Smoking:** Not allowed.

➤   **It's a 10-minute walk to the beach from the inn. You can also go sea kayaking or horseback riding and see the giant redwoods in Hendy Woods State Park, 19 miles inland.**

A bower of flowers, an art gallery, a charming café, clifftop views of the Pacific surf—all this and comfortable rooms make up the unique Greenwood Pier Inn. The energetic and talented innkeeper started his venture in 1980 with two cottages. Now there is a complex of lodgings, all connected by paths that wind through extravagant gardens, high above the sea.

The rooms have hand-painted tiles, stained glass by regional artists, leaded glass windows, skylights, and pieces collected by the innkeeper on his world travels. In one corner you might see a huge vase filled with calla lilies four feet high; in another, a pink dressing table painted with flowers.

In Sea Castle North, Sea Castle South, and Cliffhouse Kendrick's seascapes hang on the walls and sliding glass doors open to a deck at the edge of a cliff, overlooking the ocean. A staircase spirals up to a tub for two next to a wide window. Books fill the shelves, and tapes and CDs are provided for the stereo.

The restaurant is open every day for breakfast and lunch, and for dinner as well Thursday through Monday. Breakfast and dinner can be brought to your room on a tray if you wish (dinner is extra; Continental breakfast is included in the room rate). And while you're at the inn, don't miss a trip to Greenwood Pier's intriguing Country Store and Garden Shop.

Harbor House

P.O. Box 369
5600 South Highway 1
Elk, CA 95432
707-877-3203
800-720-7474
Fax: 707-877-3452
harborhs@mcn.org
www.theharborhouseinn.com

> **A seaside home in the grand style**

Innkeepers: Sam and Elle Haynes. **Accommodations:** 10 rooms (all with private bath). **Rates:** $150–$305 single, $195–$350 double, $50 additional person; winter discounts available. **Included:** Breakfast and dinner. **Added:** 10% tax on lodging; 7.25% on dining. **Minimum stay:** 2 nights on weekends. **Payment:** Visa, MasterCard, and personal checks accepted. **Children:** Over 16 welcome. Additional $100 if third person in room. **Pets:** Not allowed. **Smoking:** Not allowed indoors.

➤ **The inn was built in 1916 by the Goodyear Redwood Lumber Company as a residence and a guest house for VIPs. It is a larger version of the Home of Redwood building at the Panama-Pacific International Exposition, held in San Francisco in 1915.**

On a bluff facing a spectacular seascape is Harbor House, one of the finest examples of luxury lodging on the coast. The all-redwood inn stands above Greenwood Landing, once a busy port for lumber schooners.

The beamed ceiling and paneled walls in the living room glow with the rich patina of polish and age. A century-old Persian rug lies under deep cushioned couches grouped around the big fireplace. In one corner is a Steinway console piano; occasionally concerts are held in this room. A niche near the fire holds a phone and shelves of books and games for guests to use.

Beyond is the dining room, where a wall of windows faces the irresistible view. Breakfast here is different every day — fruit juice, homemade pastries and breads, and coffee always accompany main dishes such as eggs Benedict, huevos rancheros, pancakes, and quiche. Eggs come from the inn's own chickens. Dinners feature home-grown produce, meats and cheeses from nearby farms, and fresh seafood. California wines are served.

The guest rooms, six of them in the main house, have antique furnishings and fireplaces. Harbor Room, one of the largest, has room for two beds, comfortable chairs, and an English library table. The views of the sea from this attractive, rose-colored room are stunning. Lookout is the smallest and most popular room in the house. It has a deck that is ideal for watching the sun set over the Pacific.

The other rooms are in four red and white cottages on the south side of the inn, under tall cypress trees. Seaview and Oceansong share a deck that juts dramatically over a ravine that descends to a cove. For privacy, the deck is divided by a lattice with an ivy vine. Shorepine and Edgewood have partial ocean views from their decks; Edgewood is closest to the highway and therefore least desirable (however, the busy road quiets at night).

Harbor House offers comfortable accommodations, beauteous surroundings, fine food, and, most important, superb service. Innkeepers Sam and Elle Haynes will point out the path that leads from the lawns and garden down to the cove, introduce you to the attractions of Elk and Mendocino, and join you by the fire for evening conversation and music. Winter is a good time to visit, they say. The weather is often clear, and the coastal storms are thrilling to watch.

Eureka

Abigail's Elegant Victorian Mansion Lodging Accommodations

1406 "C" Street
Eureka, CA 95501
707-444-3144
Fax: 707-442-5594
www.bbhost.com/eureka-California

> **A historic home with warm hospitality**

Innkeepers: Doug and Lily Vieyra. **Accommodations:** 3 rooms (1 with private bath, 2 rooms share 3 baths). **Rates:** $79 single; $85–$185 double; suite $135–$195 (corporate and midweek rates available). **Included:** Full breakfast. **Added:** 10% tax. **Payment:** MasterCard, Visa. **Children:** Over 14 welcome; charged as an adult. **Pets:** Not allowed. **Smoking:** Not allowed.

> ➤   **One of the most ornate and well preserved of Eureka's numerous Victorian homes, the inn is owned by people who delight in sharing its history and beauty with their guests.**

When you're greeted at the door by a smiling "butler" in formal dress who escorts you to an elegant parlor and then to a finely furnished guest room, you know you're in an unusual bed and breakfast. Doug Vieyra is the tuxedoed greeter. Full of enthusiasm, he and Lily will show you around the parlors, the library, the sitting room and garden, suggesting a game of croquet or a ride in the inn's "horseless carriage."

The house was built in 1888 for William Clark, a successful businessman and Eureka's mayor. Now the home is on the National Register of Historic Places and is a California State Historic Site. It's considered a prime example of Queen Anne—influenced Eastlake Victorian architecture.

Authenticity was very important to the innkeepers when it came to furnishing their bed-and-breakfast. Lily made most of the drapes in the home from Victorian fabrics or from fine reproduction fabrics of Victorian prints. Wall coverings are reproductions of William Morris patterns, and some of the home's original carpeting is still intact and in remarkably good condition. Molded plaster ceiling medallions are colorfully painted as they would have been at the turn of the century to protect the ceilings from the emissions of the gas light fixtures. All the rooms contain period furnishings and the walls are adorned with old family portraits.

Straw boaters, men's bowlers, and other antique hats hanging on a wonderfully carved hat rack at the entrance immediately set the nostalgic tone. Then there are the parlors. One has a velvet fainting couch set with embroidered silk pillows. On a table nearby there's a *Ladies' Home Journal* from 1890, and a *Saturday Evening Post* dated 1905. The fine china displayed in a sideboard has been in Lily's family since the 1800s. Another parlor has a pink and green tiled fireplace with intricate walnut fretwork and an old-fashioned gramophone set to play one of the inn's collection of vintage 78-rpm records. One parlor has an open game of Scrabble awaiting players and a chess set in a window alcove, while the most informal sitting room is where guests gather in front of a wood-burning stove to watch classic movies on the TV/VCR or listen to music.

Guest rooms are located on the second floor, and each room has a queen-size bed, a desk, and a sitting area. Some have views of Humboldt Bay and the Samoa Peninsula. A fringed drape divides the bed from the sitting area in the Van Gogh suite, where books of the artist's works can be perused while sitting on tapestry-upholstered chairs lighted by beaded lamps. The bedroom set and lacy black dress hanging on the wall belonged to Lily's mother.

Lillie Langtry, a celebrated 19th-century actress, once stayed in the home, so the room she slept in is now named for her. It is highlighted by a dark oak four-poster bed and a Palladian window that overlooks Humboldt Bay. A lace umbrella and decorative fans add a feminine touch. French Country furnishings create a warm, bright atmosphere in The Governor's Room. It has a private bath, queen bed, and a fine view. A daybed, easy chair, and writing desk make the small connecting room a perfect reading or writing nook, or sleeping quarters for a third person.

All rooms have bedside tables equipped with reading lamps. Of the three shared bathrooms, one is upstairs and two are on the main floor. Robes are provided for the trip down the hall and for visiting the Finnish sauna.

The day begins in the formal dining room with breakfast at a single table set with placecards and red and white china on a lace cloth. Served by Lily wearing authentic Victorian clothing, the heart-healthy Continental breakfast buffet typically includes a variety of fruits, cereals, pastries, and liquid refreshments.

For other meals Doug and Lily are happy to provide dining suggestions. One of their favorite restaurants, The Sea Grill, is certainly worth a visit for its outstanding salad bar and fresh seafood dishes. Ask the Vieyras what there is to see and do in the area, and you'll be given a list that could keep you busy for days. Stroll through the shops, galleries, and restaurants of Old Town, see Eureka's architectural treasures, cruise on the bay, or take a deep-sea fishing charter. Don't miss the astonishing Carson Mansion, probably the most-photographed Victorian creation in California.

Doug and Lily have an array of books and magazines, lend tandem bicycles, and hold occasional musical events. In the afternoon they often serve ice cream sodas while guests play croquet in the side yard. These sociable hosts claim to provide "the lavish hospitality of a bygone era." With good cheer and charm, that's exactly what they do.

If you're looking for a truly private retreat, ask the Vieyras about their secluded Swiss-style chalet set on 300 acres amidst redwoods atop a mountain about 25 miles from Eureka. The hideaway has a full kitchen, fireplace, sun deck, and swimming pond, and fixings for a self-serve breakfast are provided.

Carter House Victorians

301 L Street
Eureka, CA 95501
707-445-8062
800-404-1390
Fax: 707-444-8067
carter52@carterhoose.com
www.carterhoose.com

> **Victorian style,
> contemporary flair, and fine
> cuisine are the highlights of
> this lodging group**

Innkeepers: Mark and Christi Carter. **Accommodations:** 20 rooms and 11 suites. **Rates:** $105–$500. **Included:** Full breakfast; afternoon and evening refreshments. **Added:** 9% tax. **Payment:** Major credit cards. **Children:** Additional $25. **Pets:** Not allowed. **Smoking:** Not allowed.

> ➤ **The handsome redwood Carter House draws travelers who admire the quality of workmanship and Victorian structure, yet appreciate the light, uncluttered interior.**

The port city of Eureka boasts a wide variety of Victorian architecture, including what is probably the finest example in the country, the ornate Carson Mansion.

Another Victorian-style home is the Carter House — but this one was built in the 1980s, not the 1890s. Mark Carter, a long-time admirer of 19th-century design, had restored several houses before he found a book of drawings by Samuel and Joseph C. Newsom, architects of the Carson Mansion and other Eureka buildings. One drawing showed a house that had been built in San Francisco in 1884 and destroyed in the 1906 earthquake. Mark decided to recreate that house in Eureka. He and a crew of three handcrafted the spacious four-story structure, following the Newsom plans in almost every intricate detail.

High, curtainless windows, polished oak floors, white walls, and a collection of abstract art make a pleasing contrast to the rich, dark wainscoting and woodwork. Orchids add delicate color. A basket of apples stands on the sideboard in the front parlor; in the evenings, you'll find cookies and decanters of after-dinner drinks. Wine and hors d'oeuvres are served in the afternoons.

Mark and Christi have furnished the guest rooms with a few well-chosen antiques, fresh flowers, clock radios, robes, and special soaps. The two 2-bedroom suites are good choices for families or couples traveling together. The suite on the second floor is particularly spacious and has a fireplace, numerous windows, and a tiled bathroom with a whirlpool tub and a double- headed shower.

Three more rooms, plus kitchen facilities, are offered in the Bell Cottage, a remodeled turn-of-the-century home a few doors from the inn. The cottage guest rooms have a more contemporary look than those in the Carter House, and they have modern amenities such as TVs, VCRs, CD players, and marble double Jacuzzis. All three rooms share a common living room and fully equipped kitchen.

Guests at the inns register at the Hotel Carter across the street from the Carter House. The hotel has 24 tastefully furnished rooms and romantic suites. Standard rooms are pleasant, with light pine furniture, blanket chests, armoires, and woven rugs.

The luxury suites are more spacious and have extra amenities. The first thing you see when you enter suite 301 is a giant round Jacuzzi below a bay window with town and marina views. French doors separate the living room and bedroom, and the bath has an oversize shower with two showerheads. The suite also has its own CD player, VCR, and refrigerator, and robes are provided.

There are fine restaurants in Eureka, but the best by far is in the Hotel Carter. The light and airy restaurant is superb and has earned a nationwide reputation. Here you'll find dishes based on fresh ingredients, a relaxed atmosphere, an exceptional wine list, and a talented chef. Dinner entrées might include sautéed cervina venison escalopine in a wild mushroom and green peppercorn sauce, or blackened fresh sturgeon served with tomatoes dressed in a balsamic basil marinade. A lighter café menu is also available.

All overnight guests go to the restaurant for breakfast — one of the best breakfasts you'll ever have at an inn. The emphasis on quality is evident in the breads, pears poached in wine sauce, eggs Florentine, pasta, and strawberry cake (and that's just one flower-garnished meal).

The well-tended gardens that supply much of the produce and herbs for the restaurant intrigue guests almost as much as the food. The Carters offer garden tours and a lecture series. The hotel also has a wine shop where you can purchase some of the wines you may have sampled from the restaurant's 21-page wine list while dining.

Ferndale

The Gingerbread Mansion

400 Berding Street
Ferndale, CA 95536
707-786-4000
800-952-4136
Fax: 707-786-4381
www.gingerbread-mansion.com

**A historic home in a
Victorian village**

Innkeeper: Ken Torbert. **Accommodations:** 11 rooms (all with private bath). **Rates:** $120–$140 single, $140–$170 double, $170–$350 suite. **Included:** Full breakfast and afternoon tea. **Added:** 8% tax. **Minimum stay:** 2 nights on summer weekends and holidays. **Payment:** Major credit cards. **Children:** $40 additional. **Pets:** Not allowed. **Smoking:** Not allowed indoors.

➤ **The quiet roads around Ferndale pass acres of green fields and dairy farms that once formed the economic base of the region, which is why the Victorian mansions are called Butterfat Palaces.**

In the far northwestern corner of California, the little town of Ferndale lies steeped in the past. The entire village of restored Victorian buildings is a State Historical Landmark. Its main street is probably the brightest in the West, with facades painted in a rainbow palette of hues that lend welcome color to the often foggy area.

The most striking home in this quiet backwater is the Gingerbread Mansion. The ornate bed-and-breakfast inn is surrounded by English gardens with boxwood-edged paths that wind through archways and tulip beds, past topiary, fountains, and statuary. In the center is a silver reflecting ball on a pedestal.

The mansion, built in 1899, is a showcase of turn-of-the-century elegance. Five parlors are filled with antiques and settees where visitors may sit to browse through travel books and magazines, play games, and enjoy an elaborate tea with petits fours and chocolate-dipped strawberries in the afternoons. A 1,000-piece jigsaw puzzle of the mansion lies partially completed on a separate table, while the third floor parlor has a VCR where guests can view classic films.

Antiques, Egyptian cotton towels, and high quality linens are common to all guest rooms, and several have old-fashioned clawfoot tubs. In fact, the Fountain and Gingerbread suites each have two such tubs for romantic "his and hers" bubble baths. The twin tubs in the luxurious Fountain Suite are side by side, facing a mirrored wall. The bed has a canopy and a bay window looks out on the village and garden. In the Gingerbread Suite, the tubs are in the bedroom on a raised platform surrounded by a Victorian railing.

Each room offers something special. The Rose Suite has two fireplaces and a tub in a flowery bower with mirrors on the walls and ceiling. Strawberry Hill, in peach and green, has a fireplace and lots of windows and light; Garden overlooks a multitude of flowers; and Lilac has a burled maple bed with walnut trim draped in purple, a fainting couch, clawfoot tub, and a lovely stained glass window. Hideaway, one of the newer rooms at the back of the inn, has a country garden atmosphere but is consistent with the mansion's style in its molding detail and carved wood.

On the top floor, the Empire Suite is the newest addition to the inn and the most deluxe. From the marble entryway French doors open into a luxurious and spacious suite that any emperor would approve of. There's a bed draped in black and gold Egyptian cotton and footed by dramatic columns, a clawfoot tub before one of the marble fireplaces, and an Empire sofa in front of the second fireplace. Other features include a Biedermeier-style antique armoire, a reading alcove, a dining area set back in another gable, and a bath with a two-sink vanity, bidet, and sit-in shower with three showerheads and five massage sprays.

One of the outstanding features here is the innkeeper's attention to detail. Nothing a guest could need has been overlooked. You'll find bathrobes in your dresser drawer, hand-dipped chocolates by the bed, and a tray of coffee or tea on the hall sideboard in the morning. Clock radios are discreetly hidden in nightstands, and two rooms have inconspicuous TVs.

Breakfast, served at two tables in the formal dining room, includes fresh juice, homemade granola, local cheeses, various pastries, and a hot entrée such as cheese blintzes or an egg dish individually baked in a ramekin.

Ferndale has shops, art galleries, a repertory theater, and a museum. Yearly events fit the small-town image: an ice cream social in September, a county fair and horse races in August, an Easter egg hunt. There are the Beef Bar-B-Que and the Firemen's Annual Main Street Games, and for something out of the ordinary, the Portuguese Holy Ghost Festival (many of the early settlers were Portuguese). In late May the Great Arcata-to-Ferndale Cross-Country Kinetic Sculpture Race takes place. In wild and crazy contraptions, racers from around the country compete for three days and two nights, ending in a grand finale on Main Street.

Moviemakers felt so strongly that Ferndale was the quintessential small American town that they used it as a backdrop for the movie *Outbreak*. If you watch the film closely enough, you can spot the Gingerbread Mansion's cheerful yellow and salmon exterior briefly in one scene.

Garberville

Benbow Inn

445 Lake Benbow Drive
Garberville, CA 95442
707-923-2124
800-355-3301
Fax: 707-923-2897
www.benbowinn.com

**An old-fashioned
atmosphere with
contemporary touches**

Proprietors: John and Teresa Porter. **Accommodations:** 55 rooms. **Rates:** $99–$315 single or double, $15 additional person. **Added:** 10% tax. **Minimum stay:** 2 nights on some weekends. **Payment:** Major credit cards. **Children:** Welcome; $15 for rollaway. **Pets:** Not allowed. **Smoking:** Not allowed. **Open:** Mid-April through January 2.

➤   **The inn overlooks little Benbow Lake, which is filled only in summer, when the Eel River is dammed. You may swim in the lake, and canoes and paddleboats are available from the Park Service.**

This unusual inn in the north coast redwood country is a National Historic Landmark. The three-story, half-timbered hotel was built in 1926 and welcomed many famous people, including Herbert Hoover and Eleanor Roosevelt, before it gradually fell into disrepair. In recent years the inn has been restored to its original elegance. The Benbow stands just west of (and unfortunately close to) Highway 101, south of Garberville.

Inside the hotel is a lobby and lounge, paneled in dark woods, with an immense stone fireplace at one end. A jester holds court on one side of the fireplace, and a table in the center bears a swan vase filled with fresh flowers. The floors are covered with Oriental rugs and alcoves hold partially completed jigsaw puzzles; every afternoon guests may be found pondering them as they enjoy their tea and scones or mulled wine.

Off the lobby is a bar with an antique fireplace and a tapestry-adorned, half-timbered dining room that offers Continental cuisine. Meals are served on tables set with linens, candles, and fresh flowers. The menu features dishes such as roasted salmon filet, local lamb, and fresh daily specials often made with produce from the inn's own garden. For dessert, don't miss the crème brûlée

In back of the hotel is a large, partially shaded terrace, with several guest rooms beyond it, each with its own patio overlooking the lawn and river. The separate Garden Cottage boasts a four-poster canopy bed on a carpeted platform. Books on the mantel, a grandfather clock, and an Oriental rug fit the mood of rock-solid stability in a room that's big enough to dance in. It also has a whirlpool tub and separate shower in the bath.

The older guest accommodations in the main hotel are on the small side but are tastefully furnished with antiques, four-poster reproduction beds, red velvet chairs, tile baths, irons and ironing boards, sherry, fresh ground coffee and coffeemakers, reading lamps, and a basket of magazines and well-worn paperback mysteries. They're just right for an evening of reading by the crackling fire in the parlor — when you're not working on a puzzle or sipping sherry.

As Teresa, the innkeeper, is also a writer, she tries to incorporate literary themes into inn activities whenever possible. There's a magnetic poetry board on a table near the fireplace in the lobby. In July the Benbow throws a Shakespeare-style poetry contest. In the past, the inn inspired artistic creativity of another sort. While *Bambi* was being made, some of the animators stayed at the inn and sketched background drawings for the movie from area scenes.

Gualala

The Old Milano Hotel

38300 Highway 1
Gualala, CA 95445
707-884-3256
Fax: 707-884-4249
coast@oldmilanohotel.com
www.oldmilanohotel.com

A landmark inn with lush gardens and a panoramic view

Innkeeper: Leslie Linscheid. **Accommodations:** 7 rooms (6 with shared baths), 5 cottages, 1 caboose. **Rates:** $115–$210 single or double. **Included:** Full breakfast. **Added:** 10% tax. **Minimum stay:** 2 nights on weekends. **Payment:** MasterCard and Visa accepted. **Children:** Allowed in cottages, additional $15 if third person in room. **Pets:** Not allowed. **Smoking:** Not allowed indoors.

➤ **When you're ready for the ultimate in relaxation, sign up for a private sunset session in the spa, pick up your towel and flashlight, and amble down the path to the secluded hot tub. As you soak in bliss, you'll be gazing out at craggy Cathedral Rock and a blue-green sea.**

The setting for this historic landmark hotel could not be more splendid — three acres of lawns and gardens bordered by tall cedar trees on the edge of a cliff. In the cove below, waves crash against boulders and slide over smoothly worn pebbles; the sea stretches beyond to a misty horizon.

On this prime property a mile north of Gualala and 100 miles north of San Francisco, the hotel opened in 1905 as the Milano, noted for its Italian food and hospitality. Since 1984 it has been owned by Leslie Linscheid, who continues to offer excellent meals and comfortable accommodations to north coast travelers.

The house is furnished with rich Victorian pieces set against floral wallpapers and red carpeting. Two guest rooms, a parlor, and a dining room occupy the main floor.

The dining room, which is a full restaurant open to the public Tuesday through Sunday, is actually two rooms on either side of the main stairwell. Here, tables set with linens and glowing lanterns are placed around sofas, a piano, and a stone fireplace that dates from the hotel's early days. Fringed lampshades, a candelabra, a gilt-framed mirror, and an old-fashioned cash register add to the period mood. The menu changes seasonally, but a prix fixe dinner might include spice-crusted lamb skewers, grilled pork tenderloin, or Pacific king salmon. Seafood is fresh and local, as are most vegetables and herbs. There's an extensive wine list.

On the other side of the house is the Master Suite, the largest and most expensive room in the main house. It has a sitting room with a separate outside entrance, a bed of carved wood, and, best of all, a superb ocean view. The other rooms all have sea views and individual furnishings — a big armchair by a window, a high armoire, built-in bookshelves, framed musical scores, and a high brass bed are a few examples. Most rooms have double beds (some are soft, so if you prefer a firm mattress, be sure to request it).

Of the five upstairs rooms, Room 3 is the smallest. It has a double bed, a little desk graced with fresh flowers, and a large closet where you'll find towels and a flashlight for night visits to the outdoor spa. This room overlooks the garden, with its huge dahlias and rose-covered trellis. Room 4 has a sleigh bed, a mirrored armoire, and a writing desk in the window that offers a fabulous view of the rock outcroppings and surf below. Room 5 has a velvet loveseat in its window and a handsome antique dresser. The sofa at the end of Room 6's white iron bed looks out to the sea. The shared hall baths have pull-chain toilets and oversize showers.

Outside, behind the circular herb garden and immense fuchsias and under salmon-colored passion flowers is Passion Vine Cottage. This cozy spot has a Jotul woodstove, a double bed, a full kitchen, and a reading loft. There's a shower stall in the tiny bathroom. With their own spas, Iris Cottage and Appletree Cottage are the Old Milano's most expensive lodgings.

The Caboose, or Engine 9, is a railroader's dream, tucked among the cedars for privacy. A warm and rustic nest, it has a woodstove, a small bath, and a refrigerator. There's a deck at one end of the authentic car and an observation cupola on top.

Breakfast is served in the dining room, in your own room, or on the patio. Leslie oversees the preparation of such morning delectables as fresh fruit turnovers, quiche, French toast, and baked eggs. After breakfast you might stroll through the gardens and down to a rocky beach at the foot of the cliff. You're likely to see seals, sea lions, numerous birds, and possibly whales on their annual migrations. Other activities include badminton and croquet. Nearby are tennis, golf, horseback riding, bicycling, hiking, and fishing.

St. Orres

P.O. Box 523
36601 South Highway 1
Gualala, CA 95445
707-884-3303
Fax:707-884-1840
www.saintorres.com

A seaside hotel and
cottages with unusual
architecture

Owners: Rosemary Campiformio and Eric and Ted Black. **Accommodations:** 8 rooms (share 3 baths), 12 cottages. **Rates:** $70–$85 single or double in hotel, $100–$225 in cottages. **Included:** Full breakfast. **Added:** 7.25% tax. **Minimum stay:** 2 nights on weekends. **Payment:** MasterCard, Visa. **Children:** Welcome (rollaways available). **Pets:** Not allowed. **Smoking:** Not allowed.

➤ **Across the road from the inn, at the bottom of grassy cliffs, are coves to explore and the inn's private beach, a bit of sheltered sand where St. Orres Creek joins the Pacific surf.**

You may have heard that there was a Russian settlement on the coast in the late 1800s, so when you first see the St. Orres' onion-domed towers and weathered cedar exterior, you might think it's a remnant of the past. But it's not even a restoration. The inn was built in the mid-1970s by California master carpenters Richard Wasserman and Eric Black.

Their love of fine wood is evident throughout their handsome creation. The doors are of California oak, the redwood walls are paneled in intricate geometric patterns. They used the work of local craftspeople to furnish the inn, from the stained glass windows to the colorful velvet quilts on the beds. The colors and styles look a bit dated now, but the overall effect is still impressive.

One tower holds a spiral staircase that winds up to the guest rooms on the second floor. In the other is a restaurant of renown, where meals are served in an octagonal room with three levels of windows rising to the dome. Guests, dining on a three-course, prix fixe meal that might consist of Sonoma county quail marinated in tequila and garlic or an eggplant terrine, can look across the highway to rugged bluffs above the sea.

The guest rooms in this building share three baths: "his," "hers," and "ours," which boasts an oversize dual shower. The rooms aren't large, but they're designed with care to avoid a cramped feeling.

The cottages are more spacious and modern. Three are off paths that wind up the hillside to the edge of a redwood forest where wild orchids grow. Tree House has an elevated sleeping area, a Franklin stove, and French doors that open onto a sun deck with a wide ocean view. Rose Cottage also has an elevated bed, and Wildflower is a rustic cabin with a sleeping loft.

In the newest area, Creekside, are seven more cottages with polished woods, skylights, and ocean or forest views. They have the use of a hot tub under multi-tiered glass domes, a sauna, and an expansive sun deck edged with flower boxes.

The most dramatic cottage is Pine Haven, which accommodates four. The two-bedroom, two-bath home has three copper domes, a beach stone fireplace, a breakfast nook with an ocean view, a wet bar, and a patio by the old apple tree.

All the cottages have refrigerators and coffeemakers. Breakfast will be delivered in a basket, or you may go to the dining room if you prefer.

St. Orres stands above the highway, outside the village of Gualala, 3 hours north of San Francisco.

The Whale Watch Inn

35100 Highway 1
Gualala, CA 95445
707-884-3667
1-800-WHALE-4-2
Fax: 707-884-4815
whale@mcn.org
www.whale-watch.com

A well-run inn on the Mendocino coast

Owners: Jim and Kazuko Popplewell. **Accommodations:** 18 rooms. **Rates:** $170–$270. **Included:** Full breakfast. **Added:** 10% tax. **Payment:** Major credit cards. **Minimum stay:** 2 nights on weekends; 3 nights on holiday weekends. **Children:** Welcome in the Sea Bounty building, additional $20 if third person in room. **Pets:** Not allowed. **Smoking:** Allowed outside only.

➤ **Amenities such as fireplaces, down comforters, in-room ice makers or small refrigerators, whirlpool tubs, and private decks are among the highlights of the Whale Watch Inn. Telephones and televisions have purposely been omitted from the rooms to heighten the relaxed environment, although you can have a telephone placed if your room if you request it.**

On a bluff overlooking the Pacific, the Whale Watch Inn is perfectly situated for viewing the majestic mammals during their annual migration, February through early May. Yet the inn's pleasant accommodations and prime location on the Mendocino coast — putting it within comfortable driving distance for day trips to Mendocino or the wineries of the Anderson Valley — make it a good choice in any season. It's just off Highway 1, about five miles North of Gualala.

Eighteen guest rooms and suites are located in five buildings that were all built between 1973 and 1985. The Pacific Edge building, one of the newer structures, houses guest registration, a sitting room, and eight guest rooms. The Rose Room on the first floor, as one might guess, is decorated in rose tones. The room's cherry antique reproduction furnishings include a highboy and a four-poster bed. Wingback chairs stand facing the wood-burning fireplace and the balcony looks out to large cypress trees and the ocean below.

Other rooms in Pacific Edge include Reflections, with modern decor and a two-person whirlpool; and the Bath and Country French suites, both with spiral staircases leading up to lofts, fireplaces, and whirlpool tubs for two. Silver Mist, which is above the inn's front entrance, has a whale of a stained glass window above its whirlpool tub. Decorated in soft silvers and pinks, the bed has a rose damask spread and there's a floral chair with a matching loveseat.

Families stay in the condominium-style units of the Sea Bounty building that have their own kitchens. The two suites in Cygnet House, beyond Sea Bounty, can be rented out as a single unit. In Quest, early risers should request the Ocean Sunrise Room, while guests staying in the Crystal Sea Room, on the second floor, have fine views of the coastline.

Two additional guest rooms and the inn's common room are located in Whale Watch, once a private home. The Whale Watch room, which is available to all guests, has windows on three sides and a circular fireplace, and is stocked with games, puzzles, and a library. Coffee and tea are available throughout the day, and guests gather here on Saturday evenings for wine and hors d'oeuvres.

Next door is Cliffside — the inn's least expensive guest room because it's on the small side. But it still has appealing features such as a wood-burning stove and ocean views. Morning Light, also in Whale Watch house, has its own private sauna.

Full breakfasts that include such items as frittatas, crepes, and potato pies are delivered to guest rooms each morning. Guests are given a list of local restaurants, parks, and services upon arrival.

They are also invited to take advantage of the inn's private beach access.

Jenner

Stillwater Cove Ranch

22555 Coast Highway 1
Jenner, CA 95450
707-847-3227

A ranch with inexpensive cottages and an ocean view

Proprietor: Linda Rudy. **Accommodations:** 6 rooms and bunkhouse (all with private baths). **Rates:** $40–$80 single or double; $10 each additional person; bunkhouse $115–$125 for 8. **Added:** 9% tax. **Minimum stay:** 2 nights on weekends. **Payment:** No credit cards. **Children:** Age 3 and over charged as an additional person. **Pets:** Leashed pets allowed with permission in some rooms, $5 additional. **Smoking:** Allowed. **Open:** Year-round except for Christmas week.

➤ **Stillwater Cove is near Fort Ross, the historic site of a 19th-century Russian outpost, and Kruse Rhododendron State Reserve.**

On the scenic north coast, 16 miles north of Jenner, a 150-acre ranch once sprawled across the rolling hills that rise from surf-splashed rocks. Now most of that ranch is parkland and belongs to the state, but 50 acres remain as a destination for coastal travelers. Furnishings are simple, but the views of headlands, the kelp-strewn cove, and the ocean are fantastic. And the rates make it an extraordinary value.

In 1931 Clarinel Ione and Paul Rudy founded a boys' school on the site. They had cows, pigs, horses, a barn, and a dairy, and they boarded fifty boys at a time until 1966, when the school closed. Now the property is owned by the sons and daughter of the Rudys.

There are still a few animals on the ranch, and dozens of peacocks roam the grounds, preening, displaying their colors, and dropping gorgeous feathers.

Four rooms are in an L-shaped building on a knoll under eucalyptus and pine trees. The identical East and West rooms, side by side, face the sea. Each has linoleum floors, two beds, a stone fireplace, a bath with a tub and shower, and a kitchenette. They share a long front porch.

Behind them is King Room, a large room with director's chairs, a small desk, and views of the trees and rocky outcroppings. Next to King is the Science Room, with a soft bed, a daybed, a Berber carpet, and a Swedish fireplace. In recognition of the room's original use, there's a microscope on the table.

Teacher's is a separate cottage with two beds, a fireplace, a bath with a tub and shower, and big windows. Cook's Cottage is for romantics who want a private hideaway removed from the rest of the lodgings. This cozy unit has two beds, a stone fireplace, white wicker chairs, and cottage-style windows. The small bath shows signs of wear but is clean. It has a tub only, and with it a rubber ducky.

The Dairy Barn, at the top of the hill, offers the most basic accommodations. The concrete block building is a large bunkhouse with two shower rooms and a kitchen. Extra cots are available; bring your own bedding. The well-equipped kitchen includes a gas range. A woodstove heats the big, open space; wood is supplied for one night's use. The Dairy Barn is a good choice for groups, as eight people can cook, sleep, and shower for less than $15 per person per night. The inn is popular among divers who come to the area for its excellent diving sites.

A low, native stone building was used as a dorm and dining room during the ranch's days as a boys' school. Now it's available for weddings, seminars, meetings, conferences, and retreats.

Lewiston

Trinity Alps Resort

1750 Trinity Alps Road
Trinity Center, CA 96052
530-286-2205
Fax: 530-286-2205

A family favorite in the wilderness

Owners: Morgan and Margo Langan. **Accommodations:** 40 cabins and 3 apartments. **Rates:** $495–$955 per cabin per week; off-season and group rates available. **Added:** 5% tax. **Minimum stay:** 1 week in June, July, and August; 3 nights in May and September. **Payment:** No credit cards; personal checks accepted. **Children:** Welcome. **Pets:** Allowed with prior arrangement. **Smoking:** Discouraged. **Open:** May 15 through September.

➤ **In the evenings there are talent shows, square dancing, movies, and bingo. Sing-alongs around the campfire, rafting, backpacking, and doing nothing but relaxing are big favorites.**

This family resort has changed very little since it was built in the 1920s. Its rustic cabins stand on 90 acres of forest surrounded by 500,000 acres of magnificent Trinity Alps Wilderness west of Trinity Lake in northern California. High mountain peaks rise above tree-clad slopes, while the wild Stuart Fork flows through the property carrying rainbow and native brown trout.

Trinity Alps Resort is off a steep, winding road north of Weaverville, a village with an eventful logging and railroad history. The Langan family bought the resort in 1987 and quickly learned that their guests wanted nothing changed or "improved." Many had been coming here for years and considered it their place, perfect in all its quaint and woodsy charm. So the cabin doors are creaky and the furniture is worn. One improvement the Langans were forced to make was to replace the original iceboxes in the units with modern refrigerators, as the iceboxes no longer worked properly. Many regular guests miss the iceboxes, but the Langans felt that the modernization was a necessity.

The large, rambling general store is the community gathering place, where you're bound to meet everyone if you sit on the porch a while. You can buy groceries in the store (except for fresh produce and meat), fishing supplies, and locally handcrafted gifts. There's a soda fountain and, toward the back, a recreation room with a pool table and video games (another concession to the modern age). A daily schedule of activities is posted on a bulletin board.

During the summer, the Bear's Breath Bar and Grill serves family dinners that range from prime rib and steak to pasta and daily specials. A reasonably priced children's menu is available. Most visitors prepare their own meals, planning to eat once or twice in the restaurant above the river.

Simple cabins are tucked among the wild lilacs and maple and alder trees along a mile of the Stuart Fork. Each has a sleeping veranda, one or two bedrooms, a bath with a shower, an outdoor barbecue, and an equipped kitchen.

Entering one of these cabins is like stepping sixty years back in time. The screen door slams, and you're in a kitchen with uneven painted floors, a gas stove, a linoleum-covered table, and a wooden counter at the sink. In the bedroom are a double and two single platform beds. A few steps farther is the verandah, overlooking the trees and river. Strung around it is a clothesline, where those seeking privacy can hang sheets. You sleep well on the verandah, for you're surrounded by the world's most peaceful sounds: leaves rustling in the breeze and a rushing, gurgling river below.

The larger one-bedroom cabins sleep six. Some two-bedroom units have two bathrooms and can accommodate ten. Bring your own linens and blankets, or rent them from the office at $20 per bed. No towels are available, so be sure to bring them. A crib will be supplied for $15 per week.

The range of activities includes fishing, swimming, tennis, badminton, volleyball, horseshoes, gold panning, inner-tubing, and basketball. The stable has dependable trail horses. Children under age 8 can enjoy pony rides in front of the general store. Hiking trails along the river lead to limpid pools and waterfalls, and wilderness trailheads are just 2 miles away.

In the height of summer the resort books up quickly, often with families who return year after year, so be sure to make your reservations well in advance if you plan to visit during June, July, or August. In May and September things are quieter, and special sports and fishing weekends are offered. Packages including all horseback riding are also available.

Little River

Glendeven

8205 North Highway 1
Little River, CA 95456
707-937-0083
800-822-4536
Fax: 707-937-6108
innkeeper@glendeven.com
www.glendeven.com

A stylish, artistic country inn

Innkeepers: Sharon and Higgins Williams. **Accommodations:** 10 rooms (all with private bath). **Rates:** $110–$170 single, $160–$190 double, $20 additional person; suites $160–$250. **Included:** Full breakfast and afternoon wine and hors d'oeuvres. **Added:** 10% tax. **Minimum stay:** 2 nights on weekends, 3 nights on some holidays. **Payment:** Major credit cards. **Children:** Not appropriate. **Pets:** Not allowed. **Smoking:** Not allowed indoors.

➤ **The Kelley House Museum in nearby Mendocino has a walking tour map, and the Mendocino Art Center exhibits the work of some of the area's talented artists. There are also several good restaurants in town.**

Little River is a quiet village that scarcely causes a ripple in the twisting coastal road south of Mendocino. But the scenery around it is spectacular: giant redwoods, open fields dotted with wildflowers, rocky beaches, and high cliffs above the Pacific. Here Sharon and Higgins Williams own a charming New England Federalist-style clapboard farmhouse, built in 1867 by one of the area's first settlers. Now called Glendeven, the house is a gracious, comfortable inn on a slope of Monterey cypress and eucalyptus trees, with brick walks, camellias, and pampas grass in the front garden.

Guests are housed in three buildings: the Main Farmhouse, Stevenscroft, and the Carriage House. The Eastlin Suite, on the ground floor of the main house, has a sitting room, French rosewood bed, fireplace, and French doors that open to a brick terrace and a view of the bay. Other farmhouse rooms are smaller but equally charming, furnished with an assortment of antiques and decorated with color and verve. A perennial favorite is the Garret, a floral attic room with dormer windows framing meadow and ocean views. In the bathroom, a floor-to-ceiling window overlooks the front yard's greenery.

Stevenscroft contains four rooms, all with fireplaces. Bayloft, colored in soft, muted tones and accented with redwood, has a cozy bed alcove with skylight above and a wide view from a bay window. On the second floor, Briar Rose is light and airy, with high-vaulted ceilings, French country decor, and a private balcony. With pine paneling and a four-poster bed, Pinewood has a rustic country look. East Farmington, on the ground floor, is wheelchair accessible.

With its own balcony overlooking the garden, the Carriage House suite is the inn's most luxurious accommodation, and affords guests the most privacy. It has a separate living room with a fireplace, love seat, and reading areas. It comes equipped with a refrigerator and microwave. The suite's bedroom has a king-size woven brass bed, and there's a bidet and a shower for two in the bath. All rooms have CD players, robes, hair dryers, and featherbeds.

A hot breakfast is delivered to your room each morning (along with the newspaper on Sunday). There's always a seasonal fruit dish, hot beverage, freshly squeezed juice, homemade bread, and an egg dish (maybe made with feta, nutmeg, spinach, lemon, and cayenne, or with roasted red peppers, corn, and cream and cheddar cheeses). Wine and hors d'oeuvres are served in the evenings.

There's a cooperative art gallery at Glendeven featuring the contemporary sculpture, photographs, ceramics, paintings, and jewelry of ten local artists. The inn is a quarter-mile north of 1,800-acre Van Damme State Park, which extends from deep forest to the coast. Just two miles north of Glendeven is the pretty town of Mendocino, founded by New Englanders who brought their distinctive style of architecture to the California coast more than a century ago.

Heritage House

5200 North Highway 1
Little River, CA 95456
707-937-5885
800-235-5885
Fax: 707-937-0318

> **A romantic inn on a seaside cliff**

Proprietor: Gay and RJ Jones. **General manager:** Candace Prairie. **Accommodations:** 54 rooms and 12 suites. **Rates:** $105–$280 single or double, $20 additional person; $15 weekday discounts February-April and during November. **Added:** 10% tax. **Payment:** MasterCard, Visa. **Children:** Charged as an additional person if over 6. **Pets:** Not allowed. **Smoking:** Allowed in rooms; not allowed in dining rooms or lounge. **Open:** Early February through Thanksgiving as well as Christmas week.

> ➤ **The main activity here is walking the paths and brick steps that wind between cottages and around the cliff while admiring the moody Pacific.**

This romantic inn on the Mendocino coast began with a farmhouse, built in 1877 in the Maine style popular in the area at the time — probably because so many settlers came from Maine. The yellow farmhouse is still there, covered with ivy. Over the years the place became run-down; it was abandoned but then transformed into a top-quality inn in 1949. That year it opened with three rooms in the farmhouse. The inn gradually expanded, and today most of the lodgings are in cottages, with two to eight rooms, spread over 37 acres.

The cottages, tucked unobtrusively into the landscape on a cliff above the sea, were given names associated with early buildings in the area, such as Country Store, Bonnet Shop, Barber Pole, and Ice

Cream Parlor. Two cottages have a more recent history. Same Time and Next Year were a single cottage in 1978 and were used in the film *Same Time Next Year*. The cabin was split in two after the movie, with each half taking half of the movie title.

Furnishings vary from contemporary pieces to four-posters and antiques bought from local families. Many pieces were handcrafted in the community and many more came around the Horn and up the coast by schooner a hundred years ago. The Carousel Suites, built in 1990, are the closest to the ocean and offer terrific ocean views as well as double Jacuzzi tubs, wet bars, dining tables for four, and wood-burning fireplaces (some have two-sided fireplaces). Because the inn is meant to be an escape, there are no telephones or televisions in any of the rooms.

The farmhouse is now used as the reception area, restaurant, and lounge, with three guest rooms upstairs. Meals are served in the dining room under an oval dome painted with fruits and flowers. Upholstered chairs stand at tables set with white linens, candles, and flowers, all reflected in a wall of mirrors. Beyond the main room is a smaller dining area; next to that is a deck with a stunning view of the cypress trees, a rocky headland, and the ocean.

The restaurant serves breakfast during the week, dinner daily, and brunch on the weekends. Breakfast entrées include raisin brioche French toast served with a dried fruit compote and maple syrup, and piperade, poached eggs served with creamy polenta and grilled ham. Brunch features many of the same dishes as breakfast, but with additions such as a baked portobello mushroom sandwich with smoked gouda and red onion, and a roast chicken sandwich with cheddar cheese grits. In the evening, choices range from homemade pasta with Mendocino wild mushrooms and parmigiano reggiano to grilled pork tenderloin accompanied by a cabbage walnut salad and green apple relish.

The lounge in the farmhouse is an addition made from an apple storage house that was dismantled and moved. Apple House is a comfortable place to relax by the huge fireplace, read, play cards, or, if the musical urge strikes, play the square grand piano. With prism chandeliers and rough-hewn walls, the atmosphere in the lounge successfully combines rusticity with elegance. And the view is breathtaking.

If you're looking for more active pursuits, the town of Mendocino, just five miles up the coast, has bicycle and canoe rentals as well as many shops, galleries, and restaurants.

Little River Inn

Little River, CA 95456
707-937-5942
888-INN-LOVE
Fax: 707-937-3944
lri@mcn.org
www.littleriverinn.com

| A resort with an ocean view |

Innkeepers: Mel and Susan McKinney. **Accommodations:** 65 rooms and cottages. **Rates:** $90–$275. **Added:** 10% tax. **Minimum stay:** 2 nights on weekends. **Payment:** Major credit cards. **Children:** Under 18 free in room with parents. **Pets:** Not allowed. **Smoking:** Nonsmoking rooms available.

➤ **The most private and luxurious lodgings are in their own wooded enclave by the sea. They all have private decks with lounge chairs, hot tubs, and good views of the crashing waves. Each unit has a brick fireplace and tiled bath with a whirlpool tub.**

In the mid–19th century pioneers came to Little River from Maine to log the region's redwood forests to build the rowhouses and mansions of San Francisco. One of those pioneers was Silas Coombs who, in 1853, built his family a home that also served as a haven for stagecoach and lumber schooner travelers. Two generations later, Cora Coombs and Ole Hervilla were married, and the homestead was turned into the Little River Inn. The parlors became lobbies and dining rooms, and the conservatory was converted into a bar. Later, cattle pastures and apple orchards were cleared for a golf course. The inn is still owned by the same family.

The main house, white with gables and window boxes and an old-fashioned veranda, is situated on a slope above the busy (and often noisy) highway. Its rooms are furnished in early California style, with antiques and double beds.

The other rooms are in a newer two-story annex, duplex units higher on the hillside near the golf course, and a fourplex across the road on low bluffs above the sea. More than half the rooms have fireplaces. Duplex rooms have light wood furnishings, Berber carpeting, sofas, king beds, wood burning fireplaces, TV/VCRs, refrigerators, coffeemakers and wet bars. There are few pictures on the wall, but the artwork that is there is original. Sliding glass doors open onto private patios with Adirondack chairs facing the ocean. The bright, white tile baths are spacious and have deep whirlpool tubs, a separate shower, and a two-sink vanity.

The rooms in the annex are furnished with oak tables and chairs and sliding glass doors that open to a long, shared balcony. From the fourplex you can see the cove and beach and watch the skin divers bob in the sparkling surf. For sweeping, unrestricted views, request Hilltop Annex, near the 9-hole golf course.

Breakfast, dinner, and a weekend brunch are served in the dining room in the main house — a pleasant spot, with handsome floral watercolors on the walls and large windows designed to show off the garden that covers the hill. The restaurant specializes in seafood and flavorful country dining using fresh local products, and the breads, soups, and desserts are all made on the premises. In the adjacent bar, you can enjoy a drink with an ocean view.

Two lighted tennis courts and the golf course are open to the public as well as to guests, so the inn bustles with activity, especially in the summer. For group meetings there are conference facilities in Abalone Hall. The inn also has a day spa and salon where treatments such as facials, hair styling, and massages are offered by appointment.

McCloud

McCloud Guest House

P.O. Box 1510
606 West Colombero Drive
McCloud, CA 96057
530-964-3160
Fax: 530-964-3202
www.mccloudguesthouse.com

**A comfortable country inn
in rural Northern California**

Owner: Linda Baldwin. **Innkeeper:** Betty Stuart. **Accommodations:** 5 rooms (all with private bath). **Rates:** $103–$119 single or double. **Included:** Full breakfast and evening refreshment. **Added:** 8% tax. **Payment:** MasterCard and Visa. **Children:** Not appropriate. **Pets:** Not allowed. **Smoking:** Allowed outdoors only.

➤ **A full gourmet breakfast is served downstairs in the dining room.**

This gracious country home on the lower slopes of Mount Shasta was built in 1907 as the summer residence of J. H. Queal, president of the McCloud River Lumber Company and employer of most of the townspeople. Queal would leave his Minnesota home in the spring, traveling west in a private railroad car to McCloud, and return to the Midwest in October, for in those days the mill shut down in the fall.

After Queal's death in 1921, the lumber company kept the house for visiting executives and dignitaries. Herbert Hoover stayed here while he was running for president, and many celebrities attended gala parties here. That era too ended, and the house stood idle until 1984, when it was turned into an inn.

Nearly six acres of lawn and cedar and oak trees surround the house and its wide, wraparound verandah. Mount Shasta, 14,126 feet high, looms above — a snow-capped giant amidst a rural landscape. Cherry-stained southern pine panels the interior, richly detailed with coffered ceilings, beveled glass, and built-in cabinets. A massive, two-sided, stone fireplace divides the lobby from the dining room.

Lodgings are upstairs, off of a central parlor. The wall fixtures in the parlor are replicas of those in Queal's railroad car. A gray patterned velvet couch stands by a coffee table full of magazines, and a desk is available for writing. The focus of the room is the antique hand-carved pool table with inlaid wood that is said to have come from the Hearst estate.

The large bedrooms off the parlor are well kept and have air conditioning, antique furniture or reproductions, and private baths. Room 1 has an elegant lace bedspread, two wicker chairs, and a window seat overlooking the front lawn. In the bath a clawfoot tub sits atop hardwood floors. Room 5 is the smallest, with a four-poster spool bed placed at an angle and a shower only in the bath. In pale pastels, Room 2 is especially light and pleasant. It has a brass bed, eyelet-trimmed pillows, a white wicker chair, and a spacious closet. There's a white and yellow clawfoot tub in the bright bathroom.

The inn is in a beautiful part of California. The area lacks crowds, noise, and heavy traffic. Although Siskiyou is the second largest county in the state, it has the lowest population. The Shasta-Cascade wilderness is replete with tall green forests, sparkling lakes and streams, and dancing waterfalls. Here, easily accessible from the inn, are downhill and Nordic skiing, trout fishing, bicycling, golfing, hiking, and swimming.

Mendocino

Agate Cove Inn

P.O. Box 1150
11201 N. Lansing Street
Mendocino, CA 95460
707-937-0551
800-527-3111
Fax: 707-937-0550
agate@mcn.org
www.agatecove.com

> **This inn has one of the best ocean views in Mendocino**

Innkeepers: Dennis and Nancy Freeze. **Accommodations:** 11 rooms. **Rates:** $109–$269. **Included:** Full breakfast. **Added:** 10% tax. **Payment:** Major credit cards. **Children:** Under age 12 discouraged, additional $25 if third person in room. **Pets:** Not allowed. **Smoking:** Not allowed.

➤ **The Agate Cove is run by Dennis and Nancy Freeze, a couple who maintain their bed-and-breakfast with pride and care. The inn, on the outskirts of Mendocino, is not far from the town's galleries and restaurants.**

Because of its popularity as a tourist destination, Mendocino has no shortage of inns, but you'd be hard-pressed to find another bed-and-breakfast in town that has a view to rival the Agate Cove Inn's. Thunderous waves crash resoundingly against the rocky headlands that jut out into the ocean just across the street from the inn. Flowering sweet peas that line the roadway in summer add a splash of color to the already breathtaking view.

The Agate Cove consists of an 1860s farmhouse, where the dining room and three guest rooms are located, and a number of newer slate blue cottages sprinkled about the inn's grounds. In between are lawns enhanced by gardens and set with Adirondack chairs for enjoying the seascape.

The simple decor of the main dining room is not on a par with the attractive guest rooms, but with a wall of windows offering a sensational ocean vista, no one pays attention to the room's interior decoration anyway. Here a breakfast that includes fresh fruit of some kind (maybe baked pears or a fruit plate) and a hot entrée (eggs Benedict, omelettes, French toast, and frittatas to name a few) is cooked on an antique cast iron stove each morning.

Guest rooms are named for gemstones. Although Diamond is attached to the farmhouse, it has its own entrance. It's the least expensive room because it lacks an ocean view and fireplace (all others have views and either a fireplace or wood-burning stove), but it's cheerful with floral wallpaper and a patchwork quilt and eyelet lace pillow shams atop the bed. Sunstone, also part of the main building, has one of the best ocean views of all of the guest rooms.

Cottages, which are set further back from the ocean, offer greater privacy. Emerald, an upstairs suite in one of the cottages, is especially appealing. The white, four-poster, king bed rests in a sunny alcove and has a fluffy down comforter with a lively hydrangea floral print; matching curtains hang in the windows. The TV/VCR is hidden away in an armoire, and the gas fireplace lights at the flick of a switch. Other highlights in Emerald include a cedar-lined closet, a tub for two, and a sofa strategically placed so you can admire the view.

Zircon, a ground-level room with white iron beds, blue and white striped wallpaper, and two easy chairs covered in plaid in front of a gas fireplace, is decorated in Waverly fabrics. (Zircon can be subject to traffic noise as it is located at the far end of the property, near Highway One.) All guest rooms have live orchids or fresh flowers, a decanter of sherry, down comforters, quality toiletries, TV/VCRs, CD players, and use of the inn's video library.

The Headlands Inn

P.O. Box 132
Corner of Howard and Albion
Mendocino, CA 95460
707-937-4431
800-354-4431
Fax: 707-937-0421
www.headlandsinn.com

> **A historic home with views of a coastal town**

Owner: Gail Erickson. **Accommodations:** 6 rooms and 1 cottage (all with private bath). **Rates:** $100–$200 single or double. **Included:** Full breakfast. **Added:** 10% tax. **Minimum stay:** 2 nights on weekends, 3–4 nights on holidays. **Payment:** Major credit cards. **Children:** Over age 12 welcome. **Pets:** Not allowed. **Smoking:** Not allowed.

➤   Guests are welcome to relax by the fireplace in their rooms or enjoy afternoon tea and cookies in the sitting area on the upstairs landing.

This attractive Victorian home was built in 1868 as a small barbershop on Main Street; a second story was added in 1873 to serve as living quarters for the barber and his family. Later it became a restaurant. In 1893 it was moved to its present location, on the corner of Howard and Albion streets, by horses pulling the house over logs used as rollers. From then on it was used as a private home. The Headlands has been a popular bed-and-breakfast inn for several years. Gail Erickson, who has owned it since 1997, made few changes when she took over.

The guest rooms, named for former owners of the historic home, have fireplaces and antique furnishings. Welcoming touches include chocolate mints, feather beds, and down comforters. Bessie Strauss, on the second floor, is a spacious room with pots of greenery, an oversize armoire, and, the most outstanding feature, an ocean view from the bay window. The bed in W. J. Wilson is a four-poster. There's a private deck with an ocean view, pleasant for an alfresco breakfast.

George Switzer, on the third floor, is a many-angled hideaway with window seats at alcove windows. A green velvet chair stands by the fireplace, where a fire is laid and extra wood is at the ready in a brass holder. John Barry, also on the third floor, is named for the home's original owner. It has a cushioned seat in a dormer window and a view across the nasturtium beds and lawn to open fields, part of the town, and the sea. Yet another room is in a separate building, Casper Cottage, just right if you want complete privacy. It has a cannonball four-poster, a sitting area with a small refrigerator, television and VCR, and a large bath complete with bubbles and tub toys.

Breakfast is brought to your room on a tray, along with a *San Francisco Chronicle*. The artistically arranged meal may include baked pears in ginger sauce, Mexican artichoke soufflé, chocolate zucchini bread, and a pitcher of hot coffee, tea, or cocoa.

The inn has an array of menus, brochures, and maps on hand. You'll want to browse in the shops and art galleries, many in historic buildings, and try Mendocino's excellent restaurants, such as Café Beaujolais and The Moose Café.

Hill House Inn

P.O. Box 625
10701 Palette Drive
Mendocino, CA 95460
707-937-0554
800-422-0554 in Northern California
Fax: 707-937-1123
www.hillhouseinn.com

**A New England–style inn
overlooking the Pacific**

General manager: Denise Vicars. **Accommodations:** 40 rooms and 4 suites. **Rates:** $145 single or double; suites $300. **Included:** Continental breakfast. **Added:** 10% tax. **Minimum stay:** 2 nights on weekends. **Payment:** Major credit cards. **Children:** Welcome; rollaway beds $15 additional. **Pets:** Not allowed. **Smoking:** Nonsmoking rooms available.

➤ **The theme is comfortable and casual in Spencer's Lounge, which has a large-screen TV and a sunken fireplace area — just the spot to relax with a warm brandy on a brisk fall evening.**

If you watch *Murder, She Wrote,* this hotel may look familiar. The popular television program, which supposedly takes place in New England, has been filmed here, with Hill House as the backdrop. It fits well with Mendocino, a north coast town built mostly by settlers from Maine.

The gray-green inn trimmed in white stands on a hill behind a white picket fence among neat gardens. With a jaunty whale weathervane on the pitched roof, it has the look of a classic hotel on the New England coast. In fact, the main house was built in 1978 with that architecture in mind. It has been expanded since to include a two-story wing with guest rooms off two courtyards.

In the main house there are two sitting areas, a lounge, a restaurant, and a chapel for meetings and weddings. In the spacious front parlor and lobby, chess is set up for the next group of players. With antiques, lace curtains, and a quiet atmosphere, the mood is of another time and another place. On the walls are photographs of the actors and crew of *Murder, She Wrote,* along with pictures of Mendocino in an earlier day.

Upstairs, diners enjoy sweeping coastal views while lingering over their meals. The atmosphere is romantic, with deep rose walls, crystal, and candlelight. Fresh fish, steak, chicken, and pasta dominate the menu. A number of wines have Mendocino County labels.

About half the guest rooms overlook the ocean. They all have television, direct-dial phones, and baths with tubs and showers and assorted toiletries. A typical room with a view features brass beds with comforters, lace curtains, burgundy or deep green carpeting, and antique reproductions. An armoire holds hanging clothes. Through the windows you see the dark green of cypress trees on grassy bluffs and the Pacific beyond them. The second-story rooms have the best views. The fireplace suites are the most expensive and spacious, with sitting areas in front of the hearth.

Joshua Grindle Inn

P.O. Box 647
44800 Little Lake Road
Mendocino, CA 95460
707-937-4143
800-GRINDLE
stay@joshgrin.com
www.joshgrin.com

| **A 19th-century home with New England charm** |

Innkeepers: Arlene and Jim Moorehead. **Accommodations:** 10 rooms (all with private bath). **Rates:** $110–$205 single or double. **Included:** Full breakfast. **Added:** 10% tax. **Minimum stay:** 2 nights on weekends. **Payment:** MasterCard and Visa. **Children:** Not appropriate; if third person in room, $30 additional charge. **Pets:** Not allowed. **Smoking:** Not allowed.

➤ **You are welcome to play the antique pump organ, enjoy a game of backgammon or chess, relax in an Adirondack chair on the inn's two acres, read by the fire, or chat with the innkeepers about the exceptional attractions of the Mendocino area.**

This quiet, New England–style home sits on a knoll overlooking Mendocino. The two-story white farmhouse was built in 1879 by an early settler who came from Maine to make his fortune in redwood lumber. Joshua Grindle prospered, becoming the town banker and primary owner of the Bank of Commerce, forerunner of the Bank of America. The home he built remained in the Grindle family until 1967. In 1978, the house opened as the first small bed-and-breakfast in Mendocino. The inn and its 2-acre property were purchased in 1989 by the Mooreheads, who came from San Francisco seeking a change.

There are five guest rooms in the main house, some with an ocean view and others with a wood-burning fireplace. Early American antiques in cherrywood and pine fill the rooms. The Grindle is the room Joshua built for himself, above the kitchen for warmth. It's a big, hearty room with a sitting area overlooking the town's distinctive water towers and the bay.

The Library, which was once a dining room, has a four-poster bed, country pine furniture, an old-fashioned typewriter on the floor-to-ceiling bookcase, and a fireplace with hand-painted tiles. Treeview is one of the inn's least expensive rooms. It's a light, airy space with such old-fashioned touches as a cut-paper lampshade and a sled now used to hold magazines. From the window you can see hundred-year-old cypress trees.

Behind the main house stands the redwood Water Tower, of recent vintage but architecturally designed to blend with the old water towers of Mendocino. It has three guest rooms on two floors furnished in antique country pine. An interesting detail is the lack of art on the walls of the second-story room; pictures will not hang flat because the walls slant inward as the tower rises.

Two rooms are in the weathered saltbox cottage. North Cypress contains Early American antiques and a Franklin fireplace; South Cypress has Shaker furniture and a country flavor. The Salem rocker and wing club chair are inviting places to read by the fire as the coastal fog creeps in. There's no sea view from the cottage, but it has a pretty little garden.

In the evenings, the Mooreheads place California cream sherry and fruit on the sideboard in the parlor. Breakfast is taken in the main house at a long, narrow harvest table that dates from the 1830s. The innkeepers serve fresh fruit, a choice of cereals, homemade muffins, and a hot dish such as quiche with a mushroom crust. The Mooreheads have collected the recipes for their most popular breakfast dishes in a cookbook.

MacCallum House

P.O. Box 206
45020 Albion Street
Mendocino, CA 95460
707-937-0289
800-609-0492
Fax: 707-937-3076
machouse@mcn.com
www.maccallumhouse.com

> **A historic Victorian home in a picturesque town**

Proprietors: The Redings. **Accommodations:** 19 rooms (all with private bath). **Rates:** $100–$195 single or double, $15 additional person; midweek winter discounts available. **Included:** Continental breakfast. **Added:** 10% tax. **Minimum stay:** 2 nights on weekends, May through December; 3 nights over holidays. **Payment:** MasterCard, Visa; personal checks preferred. **Children:** Under 10 free in room with parents. **Pets:** Not allowed. **Smoking:** Not allowed.

➤ **MacCallum House is noted for its restaurant, which serves North Coast cuisine showcasing regional wines, seafood, meats, and produce.**

When Daisy MacCallum was married in 1882, her parents, William and Eliza Kelley, gave her a house across the street from their own home as a wedding present. The Kelley house is now a museum of Mendocino and coastal history, and Daisy's home, where she lived until her death in 1953, is a busy and popular inn.

The Redings have put considerable effort into preserving the atmosphere Daisy created in her gracious Victorian home. Active socially and in civic affairs, Daisy entertained often, seeking to promote refinement in this frontier lumber town. She would have approved of the restored garden and the furnishings that were resurrected from the attic. She might have been less approving of the bar — she was a staunch advocate of temperance — but today's visitors appreciate the friendly, casual Grey Whale Bar.

There's a wide range of accommodations. Those in the main house have sleigh or iron and brass beds, floral comforters, country antiques, and windows that get morning sun or have an ocean view. The attic rooms, off a hall papered with the *San Francisco Chronicle* from the 1920s, look over the gardens or Mendocino's rooftops. You must go down a short flight of stairs to the bathroom for one of the attic guest rooms; the other is a two-room suite with its own spa tub.

The other rooms are in the former barn and cottages. One suite with a private entrance has hefty beams from the original barn and redwood slabs for the kitchen and bath counters. There's no view — in fact, the bed is set against a window facing the street — and the room is somewhat dark, but it's roomy and comfortable. From the bed you can watch the fire in the stone fireplace. In the kitchen are a small refrigerator, stove, and beaten copper sink. The bath has a Roman tub, a tile shower, and a small and impractical copper basin.

Other barn accommodations are equally individual. An upstairs suite features a stone fireplace, a burl coffee table, and a similar rough-beamed style but with country antiques and a lighter atmosphere. In the bath are a shower with a skylight and the same pretty but small copper sink.

The units in the Carriage House are furnished with wicker and vintage pieces and have Franklin stoves and private baths. The Green House has two beds — a king and a double — a rustic Franklin fireplace, and a private patio. It is handicapped accessible. The three-story Water Tower offers the best ocean view. The Gazebo, once a child's playhouse, has a double bed with a wicker headboard. There are two tiny windows, each barely a foot square. The outside bathhouse, a few steps away, has a stained glass window in the shower.

MacCallum House is not a hideaway. Crowds come and go, and tourists are forever wandering through the gardens and taking photos of the picturesque home and its weathered picket fence. Also, the inn is done in a curious mixture of new and old that works well only part of the time. Yet, steeped in Mendocino history and reflecting the personality of the strong woman who lived here for most of her adult life, it has a special ambience that draws guests back again and again.

Mendocino Hotel

45080 Main Street
P.O. Box 587
Mendocino, CA 95460
707-937-0511
800-548-0513
Fax: 707-937-0513
www.mendocinohotel.com

| A historic hotel on
| Mendocino's waterfront

General manager: Cynthia Reinhart. **Accommodations:** 51 rooms. **Rates:** $85–$275 single or double; $20 each additional person. **Added:** 10% Tax. **Payment:** Major credit cards. **Children:** Welcome in garden cottages. **Pets:** Not allowed. **Smoking:** Not allowed.

➤ **The hotel reputedly has a resident ghost. The apparition of a woman in Victorian dress is said to haunt the hotel dining room and a number of staff members claim to have encountered the spirit.**

In the late 1800s Mendocino was a busy logging town with some 20,000 residents and a rather active nightlife. In contrast to some of the more colorful establishments, the Mendocino Hotel opened in 1878 as the Temperance House, offering those with "good Christian morals" a respite from the town's seamy saloons and pool halls. Today Mendocino, with only about 1,000 residents, is frequented primarily by artists and tourists, and the Mendocino Hotel has been restored to reflect its Victorian origins.

The hotel's unassuming clapboard exterior does not adequately prepare you for the comfortable elegance that awaits within. The lobby is lovely, with Oriental rugs, Victorian antiques, and lots of sofas and comfy chairs that are perfect for quiet conversation or curling up with a novel. A fire blazes in the fireplace, and some seating groups look out to the ocean across the street. An oval stained glass ceiling sets the tone in the bar, where a piano player entertains in the evenings and light meals are served.

Separated from the lobby by 19th-century stained glass panels from British train stations (Cheltenham, Brighton, Southampton, etc.), the Victorian dining room offers gourmet meals such as fresh seafood poached in a savory fumé with a white chocolate beurre blanc and Muscovy duck accompanied by French lentils and barley; tempting appetizers such as grape leaves filled with homemade lamb sausage and feta cheese dressed with a balsamic vinaigrette and roasted tomatoes stuffed with gorgonzola served with baked garlic and Italian puff bread; and an extensive wine list that emphasizes local vintages. With meals by candlelight the mood is intimate in the dining room, while nearby green tile floors, floral seat cushions, fresh flowers, and a trellis lend a garden atmosphere to the aptly named Garden Room Bar and Café.

There are 26 rooms in the hotel's main building. They vary in size and decor, but all have period furnishings and crisp linens. Some of the interior rooms are quite small and must share hall baths, but each has an in-room washbasin and bathrobes are provided for those rooms without private baths. Suites contain old photographs and memorabilia from some of Mendocino's founding families. Suite 225A on the second floor is especially desirable because of the view from its balcony. There's a queen-size bed and fainting sofa in the bedroom and an easy chair with an ottoman and a powder blue velvet Victorian loveseat in the sunny living room. Rooms in the historic section of the hotel do not have televisions, but all rooms have telephones.

The remaining 25 rooms are situated in garden cottages behind the hotel. Although they tend to be larger than some of the rooms in the main building, the cottages are still decorated with antiques, and some have modern luxury features such as Jacuzzi tubs. The gardens that surround the cottages include plants that date from the 1800s and a latticed gazebo.

Reed Manor

Palette Drive
P.O. Box 127
Mendocino, CA 95460
707-937-5446
Fax: 707-937-5407
mreed@mcn.org
www.reedmanor.com

A luxurious mansion on a hilltop

Innkeepers: Monte and Barbara Reed. **Accommodations:** 5 suites. **Rates:** $175–$450 single or double. **Included:** Continental breakfast. **Added:** 10% tax. **Minimum stay:** 2 nights on weekends. **Payment:** Major credit cards. **Children:** Not appropriate. **Pets:** Not allowed. **Smoking:** Not allowed.

➤ **Next to the inn is a cemetery on a windswept hillside ("We have quiet neighbors," Barbara jokes); it's an interesting place to stroll and read the headstones, which date from 1852.**

Reed Manor, which opened in 1990, sits on the highest hill in Mendocino. Here the former owners of Hill House, the hotel across the road, have created a haven of luxury and intimacy. Behind a brick entrance and courtyard is an imposing house with slate floors, sofas covered with tapestry fabrics, crystal chandeliers, and lighted display cases showing the owners' numerous collections. There are celebrity dolls, wildlife sculptures and plates, paintings, and a remarkable array of model cars. There's even a stained glass window showing a 1955 Chevrolet convertible.

The suites are spacious and tastefully furnished — never fussy or overly ornate. Each has fireplace, TV with VCR, a refrigerator (where a light breakfast is stored), a phone with an answering machine, a coffeemaker, and a private deck or patio. Baths have whirlpool tubs, hair dryers, makeup mirrors, and English herbal toiletries. Two rooms have wet bars.

You will truly feel like the lord of the manor in the luxurious Napoleon Room. Here the Reeds' Napoleon collection is on display, including books, plates, wineglasses, and a chess set. Decorated in soft colors, the room has light wood furnishings including a king-size four-poster bed and a writing desk. When you are not gazing at the stars through the telescope or admiring the grand view of Mendocino and the ocean beyond from your porch, you can soak in the deep whirlpool tub in front of the double-sided fireplace, which can be enjoyed from both the bedroom and the sumptuous bath.

The Morning Glory Room, in ivory, seafoam, and pale pink florals, is on the main floor. Its slate patio also offers views of the village and the sea, and from the room's open-sided tub, you can see the TV and fireplace. Josephine's Garden Room, in French country style, has no view; it faces the gardens and has its own sunny, fenced deck. Imperial Garden is decorated with an Oriental motif. This suite has poppies touched with gilt in the wallpaper; it also has a bamboo mat ceiling and Chinese and Japanese plates and figures. The Majestic Rose is a large two-room suite with a queen-size Murphy bed in the living room.

Nut bread, fruit, juice, and coffee are provided in the rooms. The Reeds have several classic movies such as *Gone With the Wind* to lend, along with the episodes of *Murder, She Wrote* that were filmed in Mendocino. They keep an album of restaurant menus and will make recommendations and reservations.

The Stanford Inn by the Sea

P.O. Box 487
Coast Highway 1 and Comptche-
Ukiah Road
Mendocino, CA 95460
707-937-5615
800-331-8884
Fax: 707-937-0305
stanford@stanfordinn.com
www.stanfordinn.com

> A country inn with ocean views

Innkeepers: Joan and Jeff Stanford. **Accommodations:** 10 rooms and 23 suites. **Rates:** $215–$275 single or double, suites $275–$640, $30 additional person. **Included:** Full breakfast. **Added:** 10% tax. **Minimum stay:** 2 nights on weekends, 3 nights on holiday weekends. **Payment:** Major credit cards. **Children:** Five and over additional $10–$30, depending upon age if third person in room. **Pets:** Allowed with permission; additional $25 per stay. **Smoking:** Not allowed indoors.

➤ **The owners' commitment to the environment is evident in their use of organic products, recycled notepads, and reminder signs for guests to conserve water.**

Where Big River meets Mendocino Bay, Stanford Inn faces the sea from a green hillside. Once this area grew produce for villagers and loggers during the redwood lumber boom. Today, llamas and horses graze under the old apple trees. The stagecoach road is now a hiking trail, and canoeists paddle the river where logs once floated to the mill.

Joan and Jeff Stanford took over a standard two-story motel and turned it into an outstanding hostelry in 1981. They now offer charming accommodations and a wide range of services. The original, long, dark shingle ranch house, is set above pastures and ponds, and has rooms off a loggia with ivy-covered columns. In 1996, two similar buildings were constructed on either side of the ranch house — one containing luxury suites, the other housing the dining room, a homey common living room, small workout room, and lobby.

In the lobby are menus from area restaurants and a gift shop corner. A complimentary breakfast is served in the adjoining dining room near windows that overlook the ocean beyond the inn's barns, gardens, and llamas. Guests can choose a cooked-to-order hot entrée such as blue corn waffles or eggs Florentine off the vegetarian restaurant's menu.

The guest rooms are individually decorated and furnished with country antiques, plants, a decanter of wine, a coffeemaker with a supply of the inn's private blend of organic coffee, and cable television with a VCR (the inn has some 1,200 movies to rent). Most have a refrigerator and fireplace.

The second-floor rooms are the best because of their balcony views. They overlook gardens, a pond with swans and geese, and the bay, ocean, and a corner of Mendocino. To the south, the view is of a sheltered, wooded headland that juts into the sea.

All of the rooms are attractively decorated, but the suites in the new wing are especially appealing. For example, the Monterey Cypress Suite on the second floor has a large living room with original artwork, light pine ceilings, a TV/VCR in an armoire that's handpainted with a fishing scene, an easy chair with accompanying footstool, a cuckoo clock, a refrigerator stocked with juice, spring water, and a split of wine, a sleeper sofa, and a wood-burning fireplace with the fire laid and ready to go. There are chocolates on the mantel, a selection of current magazines on the coffee table, and fresh flowers on the dining table for two. French doors lead to the bedroom that has reproductions that include a writing desk, dresser, and a sleigh bed topped with a down comforter. There's a second television, an alarm clock/radio, and the bath has amenities such as toothpaste and toothbrushes, a makeup mirror, hair dryer, and Aveda skin care products.

Don't miss a tour of the inn's bountiful organic gardens. The raised beds supply produce to area restaurants. The Stanfords also have mountain bikes that their guests can use free of charge, as well as canoes to rent that provide an opportunity to explore the estuary filled with wildlife. Big River flows gently through a narrow canyon, winding between redwoods and firs, passing the habitat of osprey and the great blue heron. Big River is tidal for eight miles, so you can float up on the incoming tide and back as it recedes.

Other activities include swimming in the indoor pool, hiking, fishing, beachcombing, and whale-watching. The best sites for spotting whales are the coastal headlands, Mendocino village headland, or the beach at Fort Bragg, 6 miles north.

The Whitegate Inn

P.O. Box 150
499 Howard Street
Mendocino, CA 95460
707-937-4892
800-531-7282
Fax: 707-937-1131
staff@whitegateinn.com
www.whitegateinn.com

A charming Victorian inn in the heart of Mendocino

Innkeepers: Carol and George Bechtloff. **Accommodations:** 7 rooms. **Rates:** $129–$249 single or double, $30 additional person. **Included:** Full breakfast and afternoon hors d'oeuvres. **Added:** 10% tax. **Minimum stay:** 2 nights on weekends, 3 nights on holiday weekends. **Payment:** Major credit cards. **Children:** Over age 2 charged as an additional person. **Pets:** Not allowed. **Smoking:** Allowed outdoors only.

➤ **A recent addition to this home, built in 1883, is a large stained glass skylight that was installed above the main staircase in the 1970s.**

The Whitegate Inn, named for the white wooden gate that leads to the inn, is certainly aptly named, but the bed-and-breakfast could also easily be called the Garden Gate Inn for the bountiful blooms that encompass the gate and adjoining picket fence. Cornflowers, shasta daisies, English lavender, bachelor's button, foxglove, lilies, roses, hollyhocks, penstemon, and deep purple delphiniums spill forth from every available inch of the front yard — and the colorful display does not end there. In the back of the Victorian home a gazebo is encircled by pots of flowering plants. Below the gazebo, dense flower beds create a gorgeous show of blue, white, and fuschia during the summer months. Even the pump shed is cheerful amidst pansies and blooming window boxes. Quite simply, the Whitegate Inn has one of the prettiest gardens in Mendocino — and that is saying a lot.

Of course, one chooses an inn for its accommodations and service, not just its gardens, and happily the Whitegate delivers in those areas as well. Carol and George Bechtloff bought the Whitegate in 1992 and quickly applied the same thoroughness and eye for detail exhibited in their gardens to the entire operation and decoration of the inn. Collectors for some three decades, the antiques they've acquired over the years can be seen throughout the inn.

Fittingly, Victorian settees and a grandfather clock grace the front parlor. There's a view of the ocean from the bay window, and freshly cut flowers stand atop a carved gargoyle pedestal next to the fireplace. The piano was once owned by none other than Alexander Graham Bell.

A full breakfast is served on fine china with sterling silver place settings under a crystal chandelier in the adjoining dining room. You'll always have fresh fruit of some kind (perhaps in the form of a fruit parfait or fruit salad), freshly baked scones, cinnamon rolls or coffee cake, and a hot entrée such as caramel apple French toast, tomato surprise (a hollowed out tomato baked with egg and parmesan), waffles, or maybe a soufflé. Coffee, tea, and hot chocolate are set out for early risers. In the afternoon, there's wine, cheese, and light hors d'oeuvres, and home-baked chocolate chip cookies can be found in the cookie jar in the hallway.

Rooms in the main house have botanical names. There's Garden Path, with a cranberry glass chandelier and a canopy bed draped in lace netting. Cypress has a carved rosewood Louis XIV bed, a mirrored armoire, bay windows, a fireplace with an oak mantel, and a hand-painted scene on the wall of an open window looking out to a garden. In Violets, violets adorn the patchwork quilt, a hatbox atop an armoire, and china plates on the wall. Hand-painted ivy climbs out of nooks and crannies.

Spring Meadow is cozy, with slanted ceilings, a wood-burning stove, white iron bed with a floral comforter and matching wallpaper, eyelet lace curtains, and a shortened clawfoot tub. Daisy's, also with slanted ceilings, has a hall bath (robes are provided).

Two windows face the ocean in French Rose, which is decorated with a handsome empire bed with a carved pineapple motif and a matching giant armoire. A loveseat stands at the foot of the bed, there's a fireplace, and the fanciful Italian ceramic chandelier with touches of gold and three dimensional flowers is a highlight.

The enchanted cottage, reached by walking through the inn's back garden, is the most private of all the accommodations, with a small porch shaded by fragrant jasmine and potato vines. Inside the cottage is a pretty room in lavenders with a king-size bed, a separate daybed, a fireplace, and a clawfoot tub in the bath. An armoire hides the television. All rooms have cable television, feather beds, and fresh orchids. There's a house telephone in the main hallway and a central refrigerator at the top of the stairs.

While staying at the Whitegate be sure to check out the sweet little powder room under the stairs. It has one of the smallest sinks you're likely to see. And don't be surprised if you're joined in your room by Violet, one of the inn's resident cats, for she loves cozying up to guests. Oliver — the Whitegate's other feline — prefers to spend his time out of doors.

has been strung for afternoon naps.

Nice

Featherbed Railroad Company Bed & Breakfast Resort

P.O. Box 4016
2870 Lake Shore Boulevard
Nice, CA 95464
707-274-4434
800-966-6322
Fax: 707-274-1415
room@featherbedrailroad.com
www.featherbedrailroad.com

A lakeside resort of railroad cars

Innkeepers: Lorraine and Len Bassignani. **Accommodations:** 9 cabooses. **Rates:** $95–$150. **Included:** Full breakfast. **Added:** 9% tax. **Payment:** Major credit cards. **Children:** $10 additional. **Pets:** Not allowed. **Smoking:** Allowed outdoors only.

➤ **The stationary railroad cars are a few yards from Clear Lake, which is popular with water sports enthusiasts. Boat rentals are nearby, and the fishing is good. Clear Lake is noted for its largemouth bass and crappie.**

Railroad buffs and aficionados of the unusual are bound to fall in love with this assemblage of vintage cabooses. They're permanently stationed on five tree-shaded acres in Nice, close to the north shore of Clear Lake. The lakefront property is enhanced by turn-of-the-century street lamps, park benches, and an authentic Old English phone booth.

Effervescent Lorraine and affable Len Bassignani have impeccably restored the cabooses — a labor of love. Before opening in 1989, the couple and their partner-son removed thick layers of grime, soot, and rust that had accumulated on the 25- to 50-year-old cars.

Why cabooses? "We were looking for something different to put our hearts into," explains Lorraine, "and both Len and I have always loved trains. It took several years to locate the cabooses to carry out our dream. This is a family endeavor."

Conductors never had it so good. The interior of each caboose has been decorated around a theme. The romantic Lovers' Caboose has a hand-hewn four-poster feather bed draped with a lace canopy, and a whirlpool tub for two. The Rosebud, painted in ashes of roses, is abloom with roses on the floral bedspread, matching balloon valance curtains, and hand-painted flowers (all done by Lorraine) on the walls. It has a Jacuzzi for two.

Mint Julep, as refreshing as its name, has mint-green walls and white wicker furniture. A cushioned cupola provides a retreat for sipping a cool drink, reading, or conversing. Casey Jones, the only car with a railroad theme, features a red, cream, and navy blue decor, a gleaming brass bed, authentic switchman's lanterns, and vintage railroad prints. Unlike the other cars, this caboose was left largely intact, which you can see in the original brass fittings, exposed pipes, and two padded conductor's chairs in the cupola. Other cars include Wine Country, Mardi Gras, Chocolate Moose, and the Loose Caboose.

Each caboose has a coffee pot, a television, books and games, fresh flowers, and potpourri. Special touches include sewing kits, candies on the pillows, and newspapers delivered to the door. Breakfast is served in the Bassignanis' 100-year-old ranch house. You may choose to eat on the flagstone verandah or by the swimming pool. Breakfast includes juices, fresh fruit, assorted breads and quiches, and coffee and tea.

Lake County is an emerging wine-producing region, and tours of nearby wineries are available. Other attractions include Clear Lake

State Park and Anderson Marsh State Park, a Native American archaeological site and excellent bird-watching area. The Harbor Bar & Grill in Nice is recommended for its good food and interesting decor.

O'Brien

Holiday Harbor

P.O. Box 112
O'Brien, CA 96070
530-238-2383
800-776-2628
Fax: 530-238-2102
www.lakeshasta.com

Cruising houseboats on Lake Shasta

Owners: Stephen and Ann Barry. **Accommodations:** 70 houseboats. **Rates:** $1,310–$3,885 per week in summer, 6–16 people; off-season rates available. **Minimum stay:** 2 nights. **Payment:** Major credit cards. **Children:** Welcome. **Pets:** Allowed with permission. **Smoking:** Allowed.

➤ **Running a houseboat is easy. If you can drive a car, you can handle one of these floating RVs. Moving slowly on pontoons, they never exceed a speed of six or seven knots. At night they tie up along the shore, usually in a protected cove.**

Three rivers and a major creek are the main water sources of Shasta Lake, at the northern end of the Sacramento Valley. The Sacramento flows in from the northwest, the McCloud from the northeast, and Squaw Creek and Pit River join on the east side. A huge dam, with the highest center overflow spillway in the world, forms the sprawling blue lake. It has 370 miles of shoreline, bounded by steep, wooded hills. Majestic Mount Shasta, snow-capped in all but the driest of weather, looms to the north. You'll find virtually every type of freshwater recreation on this immense body of water. A big favorite, especially with families and groups, is houseboating.

Holiday Harbor, tucked against Bailey Cove on the McCloud, is an easily accessible resort, 15 minutes from Redding and a mile off I-5. The Barrys take pride in keeping their houseboats in peak condition. Theirs is one of the few companies offering smaller-sized houseboats suitable for six or eight people. They also have 56-foot boats that can sleep 12.

The boats each have one or two sleeping areas, one or two bathrooms with a tub or shower, an equipped kitchen, and an eating space. All have roof decks. Furnishings are simple — molded plastic chairs, some bunk beds, and benches that pull out to become double beds. Pillows, soap, dishes, and pots and pans are supplied. You bring your own groceries and blankets, linens, or sleeping bags.

"This is glorified camping," cautions Steve Barry, "and most people love it. They come in uptight and stressed out, and by the time they leave they're so relaxed they're practically comatose." The Barrys have owned Holiday Harbor since 1980, when they left a business life in San Francisco. "Now I'm hooked on this," Steve says.

Some houseboaters like simply to cruise on the lake and inlets, enjoying the slow pace and taking a dip now and then. Others fish, swim, visit Lake Shasta Caverns, and hike the numerous trails. Steve recommends the walk to an old iron mine on Bully Hill. For more fun on the water, you can rent anything that floats from Holiday Harbor's "Toy Box": canoes, kayaks, jet skis, sailboards, paddleboats, rowing sculls, ski boats (with water skis), sailboats, and more.

Bring your fishing rod or go to one of the many sporting goods stores around the lake and you can fish for rainbow and brown trout, salmon, smallmouth bass, largemouth bass, crappie, and catfish. To catch the big trophies, fish the lake in cooler months. It gets hot here in summer — 90 to 100 degrees Fahrenheit and more. But temperatures can plummet thirty degrees at night.

Orland

The Inn at Shallow Creek Farm

4712 County Road DD
Orland, CA 95963
530-865-4093
800-865-4093

A relaxing retreat in the country

Proprietors: Kurt and Mary Glaeseman. **Accommodations:** 4 rooms (2 with private bath). **Rates:** $60–$85 single or double, $15 for rollaway. **Included:** Full breakfast. **Added:** 5% tax. **Payment:** MasterCard, Visa. **Children:** Not appropriate. **Pets:** Not allowed. **Smoking:** Not allowed.

➤ **The Glaesemans raise unusual birds such as Polish crested chickens, buff orpingtons, and voiceless Muscovy ducks. One of the farm's most endearing creatures is Rutherford B. Squeak, the pet goose who considers Kurt his best friend.**

Behind a white picket fence, shaded by big walnut trees, this turn-of-the-century ranchhouse offers comfortable lodging and an atmosphere of serenity. On the 3-acre farm west of I-5 and 20 miles from Chico, there are citrus orchards, plums, persimmons, figs, and pomegranates. Squirrels scamper in the trees, roosters crow in the background, and chickens and geese scratch near the barn. Giant black walnut trees in the yard and sinewy ivy vines climbing over the front of the house help to keep things shady and cool in the summer.

Kurt and Mary Glaeseman opened their place to guests in early 1987, after visiting many B&Bs. "We modeled ours after things we liked," Mary says. They have furnished the inn with soft easy chairs, country antiques, books (they're both teachers), and such conveniences as air conditioning and electric baseboard heat.

The common room, with TV, stereo, and a stone fireplace, is for guests' exclusive use; the Glaesemans occupy separate, attached quarters. Next to the common room is the dining room, its glass-paned windows overlooking the front lawn. Breakfast is served here at one table — fresh muffins, juice and fruit from the farm's trees, egg dishes, and homemade breads such as prune oatmeal bread or California polka dot bread with raisins and oranges from Shallow Creek's own orchards. There's a sun porch too, where breakfast is occasionally served.

The Penfield Suite, off the parlor, is the former master bedroom. It has a queen-size bed, white walls and louvered shutters, and its own telephone and bath. The upstairs rooms have the use of a phone on the landing, and they share a bath with a tub and shower. The Heritage Room, in the oldest part of the house, has an old-fashioned flavor, with its morning glory wallpaper, complementing lamps, priscilla curtains, an oak dresser from Kurt's family, and framed vintage valentines that once belonged to his aunt. The Brookdale Room has two twins, a nice antique oak dresser, and a big window overlooking the trees. The four-room caretaker's cottage, across the yard from the ranchhouse, has wicker furnishings, a fully equipped kitchen, a separate living room and bedroom, a wood-burning stove, and an enclosed sun porch.

At this casual, friendly place you can feed the chickens, go for walks, or relax with a book under a fragrant orange tree. You can also explore the little-known northern Sacramento Valley, where the fields turn gold and purple with poppies and lupine. In spring the undulating hills are a brilliant green and dotted with oak trees. You can pick kiwis and boysenberries, visit a pioneer cemetery, go boating and fishing on Black Butte Reservoir, bird-watch at the wildlife refuge, and attend the rodeo at Paskenta. Orland has a few coffee shops, and Chico has a number of good ethnic restaurants.

Sea Ranch

The Sea Ranch

Lodge: P.O. Box 44
Sea Ranch, CA 95497
707-785-2371
Rental Homes: Sea Ranch Escape
P.O. Box 238
Sea Ranch, CA 95497
707-785-2426
800-SEARANCH (for information on all accommodations)
Fax: 707-785-2917
info@searanchlodge.com
www.searanchlodge.com

A resort colony and coastal retreat

Innkeeper: Marianne Harder. **Accommodations:** 20 lodge rooms, 55 rental homes. **Rates:** lodge $150–$250 single or double, $20 additional person; rental homes $200–$620 for 2 nights, plus refundable deposit. **Added:** 9% tax. **Payment:** Major credit cards. **Minimum stay:** 2 nights on weekends in lodge, 2 nights in rental homes; 3- to 4-night minimum on some holiday weekends. **Children:** Over 5 $20 per child if more than two people are occupying the room. **Pets:** Not allowed. **Smoking:** Nonsmoking units available.

➤ **Guests staying in Sea Ranch's rental homes have access to two swimming pools, tennis courts, and sauna, as well as private beaches and miles of trails through forest and meadows. As you walk the headlands, you may see blacktail deer, great blue heron, or even a bobcat or gray fox.**

The Sea Ranch, 29 miles north of Jenner on a wild and lovely stretch of the Sonoma County coast, is a second-home colony and resort on one of the last great Mexican land grants. The location, on 5,000 acres of bluffs and wooded slopes overlooking the Pacific, is outstanding.

The architecture blends unobtrusively into its surroundings. The vertical gray siding and fences are brightened by barrels of flowers, but most of the color here comes from wildflowers and natural vegetation, not from planted gardens.

The lodge's inviting lounge has high rough-hewn walls and wide windows overlooking the bluffs and sea. The dining room, open for three meals a day, serves California cuisine with an emphasis on fresh ingredients and seafood. The menu changes, but coriander-crusted bay salmon or maple-glazed pork tenderloin medallions are examples of the types of offerings you may find during your visit. Breads and desserts are baked on the premises, and the coffee is the ranch's special blend. The view from the picture windows is spectacular.

The guest rooms are in an L-shaped building north of the lodge. Two are family units, with two bedrooms. Several have fireplaces with wood provided, and almost every room has an ocean view. There are no phones or television sets, though there's a TV in the bar and pay phones in the lodge. Carpeted and furnished in the style of a good-quality motel room, the accommodations are comfortable, but not outstanding.

Sea Ranch's privately owned rental homes, which sleep from two to eight people, offer the best variety of accommodations. Several agencies handle the rentals; Sea Ranch Escape carries many of the finest in the choicest locations. Among them are two of the original award-winning condominium units.

Set on bluffs directly above the ocean, in grassy meadows, or under the pines and redwoods east of the highway, the homes are, for the most part, furnished in a tasteful, contemporary style. Your rental might contain a dishwasher, washer and dryer, stereo, video player, pool or Ping-Pong table, or any combination of the above.

You can bring your own bed linens, towels, and kindling for the fireplace, or the rental agency will provide them at extra cost. Sea Ranch Escape has three levels of service: you can bring supplies and do your own cleaning, have the agency make up the beds and clean, or choose to have everything, including the catering of meals, taken care of.

The most expensive rentals are the newest. One is a four- bedroom, three-bath home with a Jacuzzi in the master bath. It has a commanding ocean view from the edge of the bluff and is a five-minute walk from the recreation center and the beach.

On the property is a challenging, top-rated, 9-hole golf course. Nearby are a clubhouse, snack bar, and pro shop. In the main lodge, the Fireside Room serves as a conference room and can accommodate meetings of up to 25 people boardroom style or 35 with theater seating. The room is available to lodge guests when not in use by a conference.

At press time plans were under way to add 80 new rooms and a spa to the resort, so you may wish to inquire about the availability of these new facilities when making your reservations.

Trinidad

The Lost Whale Inn

3452 Patrick's Point Drive
Trinidad, CA 95570
707-677-3425
800-677-7859
Fax: 707-677-0284
lmiller@lostwhaleinn.com
www.lostwhaleinn.com

> **An oceanfront inn ideal for family vacations**

Innkeepers: Susanne Lakin and Lee Miller. **Accommodations:** 8 rooms (all with private bath). **Rates:** $126–$176 single, $136–$186 double; $20 additional adult or child over age 3. **Included:** Full breakfast, afternoon tea, and refreshments. **Added:** 10% tax. **Payment:** Major credit cards. **Children:** Under 3 free. **Pets:** Not allowed. **Smoking:** Not allowed.

➤ **For dinner, try the nearby Larrupin Café, which is famous for its barbecue sauce and excellent cooking.**

Adults and children alike are enchanted by this warm, spacious, Cape Cod–style inn with plank floors and a modern country decor. High on a grassy bluff, it faces the Pacific and you can hear the sea lions that bask on Turtle Rock bark as you drive up.

The blue frame inn was built in 1989 as a bed-and-breakfast. Originally from Los Angeles, Susanne and Lee moved to Trinidad with their daughters ready to try a different way of life. A number of years later and after finding Trinidad to their liking, they purchased four acres of land, built their B&B, and have been welcoming visitors ever since.

Games are laid out on tables in the common room, where comfy blue and white sofas are set on hardwood floors in front of a fire. Here guests have afternoon tea, pastries, and wine. Breakfast is served in a separate dining room on pine tables. A wall of windows brings sunshine and ocean views into the cheerful room, and spinach frittata, raspberry coffeecake, Parmesan potatoes, Dutch babies, and grapefruit, or sour cream pancakes, salmon eggs, currant scones, and fruit salad are typical of the bountiful morning meals.

Guest rooms are soundproofed and practical, but a light decor, fresh flowers, greenery, and books and magazines lend sparkle as well. Two rooms have balconies and skylights and five have stunning ocean views. The Sea Lion Room on the main floor is crisp and airy with high ceilings and skylights. The decor, in seafoam and wedgewood blue, includes charming floral lamps and a diamond-patterned patchwork quilt with matching pillows. In the Egret Room a bird's-eye redwood egret stands in the corner and a batik egret hangs on one wall. The Beluga Room has an upstairs sleeping loft with a queen-size futon and a queen-size iron bed with brass accents downstairs. The Orca Whale Room, with a four-poster pine bed with heart cutouts downstairs, also has a sleeping loft. The Humpback Whale room has a garden view, and a large overhead skylight makes the room sunny and pleasant.

Youngsters love to amuse themselves in the charming playhouse. You can walk a path to a private beach, relax in the hot tub, go deep-sea fishing, explore tide pools, windsurf in fresh water lagoons, and walk in Redwood National Park, the largest redwood forest in the world. It's a 15-minute drive from the inn.

Trinidad Bay Bed & Breakfast

P.O. Box 849
560 Edwards
Trinidad, CA 95570-0849
707-677-0840
Fax: 707-677-9245
www.trinidadbaybnb.com

**A casual home with
panoramic ocean views**

Innkeepers: Corlene and Don Blue. **Accommodations:** 4 rooms (all with private bath). **Rates:** $140–$170 single or double, $30 additional person; special off-season discounts available February to mid-April. **Included:** Full breakfast. **Added:** 8% tax. **Minimum stay:** 2 nights on weekends and holidays. **Payment:** MasterCard, Visa. **Children:** $30 additional if third person in room. **Pets:** Not allowed. **Smoking:** Not allowed. **Open:** February through November.

➤ **In ancient times, Trinidad was Tsurai, a village of the Yurok Indians, active until the early 1900s. Direct descendants of the tribe continue to live and work in the area.**

The most populous state in the union has a number of great vacation spots waiting to be discovered; Trinidad is one of them. This is not palm tree country. Trinidad Bay is on the far north coast,

22 miles above Eureka, just off Highway 101. Fog often drifts in, and the winter storms are wild. Nightlife consists of stargazing on clear nights or curling up with a good book and hot cider by a fire.

If that prospect appeals, and if you like gorgeous scenery, pristine beaches, good fishing, and intriguing history, you may enjoy Trinidad. You're close to wilderness here, with forests of redwood giants lining the highway. Redwood National Park is 20 miles to the north. Between it and I-5 on the east are many mountains and very few roads.

Overlooking Trinidad Bay, with broad views of the coastline and harbor, is a 1949 Cape Cod–style home with accommodations for travelers. When you arrive, Corlene and Don greet you with warmth and show you where to find the cider mix and cookies and the refrigerator for chilling wine. It's clear that they want you to feel welcome in their pleasant home. Hot and cold beverages are available all day.

The guest rooms have a comfortable, casual atmosphere, traditional furnishings, and ocean views. The first-floor room has a fireplace and king-size bed. There's a telescope in the upstairs room so you can watch the boats and whales go by. Both rooms have microwave ovens, and popcorn is provided. If you are in one of the two rooms in the main house, you'll be served a family-style breakfast in the dining area; if you're staying in a room with an outside entrance, breakfast will be brought to your room.

The house sits on a cliff directly above Indian Beach and the bay, facing south down the coast; you can see all the way to Mendocino Cape. Across the street is a little lighthouse, a memorial to those lost at sea. It's a replica of the working lighthouse on Trinidad Head.

Trinidad was named by a Spanish explorer, Don Bruno de Hezeta, in 1775. Landing on Trinity Sunday, he erected a wooden cross, christened the point of land Trinidad, and held the first mass in California's history. The wooden cross remained on the head until 1913, when a granite cross replaced it.

The town became a port supplying gold-rush miners, a lumber town, and, in the 1920s, a whaling station. Lying in the path of the great gray whales' annual migration, it's an excellent place for viewing them. From the headlands, and even from the Blues' front yard, you can see mother whales with their new youngsters heading north from Baja California.

Other activities are beachcombing for agates, kayaking, walking the trails of Trinidad Head, and watching sea lions cavort on the rocks. You can charter a boat at the pier if you want to fish for salmon or cod or go crabbing. An excursion boat offers harbor cruises. At Telonicher Marine Lab you can see aquariums, touch intertidal animals, tour the research lab, and watch slide presentations on marine life.

Sierra Country

Nevada City
Truckee
Olympic Valley
Homewood
Lake Tahoe
Georgetown
South Lake Tahoe
Coloma
Hope Valley
Sacramento
Amador City
Sutter Creek
Jackson
Murphys
Columbia
Jamestown
Coulterville
Yosemite
Mammoth Lakes
Wawona
Crowley Lake
Bishop

80

395

120

5

Amador City
Imperial Hotel, 321
Bishop
Chalfant House, 323
Coloma
The Coloma Country Inn, 325
Columbia
City Hotel, 327
Fallon Hotel, 329
Coulterville
The Hotel Jeffery, 330
Crowley Lake
Rainbow Tarns Bed & Breakfast, 332
Georgetown
American River Inn, 333
Homewood
Rockwood Lodge, 335
Hope Valley
Sorensen's, 337
Jackson
Gate House Inn, 339
The Wedgewood Inn, 341
Jamestown
The National Hotel, 343
Mammoth Lakes
Edelweiss Lodge, 345
Mammoth Mountain Inn, 346
Tamarack Lodge Resort, 348

Murphys
Dunbar House, 1880, 350
Nevada City
Red Castle Historic Lodgings, 352
Olympic Valley
Resort at Squaw Creek, 354
Squaw Valley Lodge, 355
Sacramento
Amber House, 357
The Delta King Hotel, 359
Hartley House, 361
The Sterling Hotel, 363
Vizcaya, 364
South Lake Tahoe
Lakeland Village Resort, 366
Sutter Creek
The Foxes Bed and Breakfast Inn, 367
The Grey Gables Inn, 370
Sutter Creek Inn, 371
Truckee
Northstar at Tahoe, 373
The Truckee Hotel, 375
Wawona
Wawona Hotel, 377
Yosemite
The Ahwahnee, 379

Best Bed-and-Breakfasts

Bishop
Chalfant House, 323
Coloma
The Coloma Country Inn, 325
Columbia
City Hotel, 327
Fallon Hotel, 329
Georgetown
American River Inn, 333
Homewood
Rockwood Lodge, 335
Jackson
Gate House Inn, 339
The Wedgewood Inn, 341
Murphys
Dunbar House, 1880, 350
Nevada City
Red Castle Historic Lodgings, 352
Sutter Creek
The Grey Gables Inn, 370
Sutter Creek Inn, 371

Best Family Favorites

Hope Valley
Sorensen's, 337
Mammoth Lakes
Edelweiss Lodge, 345
South Lake Tahoe
Lakeland Village Resort, 366

Best Intimate City Stops

Amador City
Imperial Hotel, 321
Sacramento
Amber House, 357
The Delta King Hotel, 359
Hartley House, 361

The Sterling Hotel, 363
Vizcaya, 364
Truckee
The Truckee Hotel, 375

Best on a Budget

Coulterville
The Hotel Jeffery, 330

Best Resorts

Mammoth Lakes
Mammoth Mountain Inn, 346
Olympic Valley
Resort at Squaw Creek, 354
Squaw Valley Lodge, 355
Truckee
Northstar at Tahoe, 373

Romantic Hideaways

Sutter Creek
The Foxes Bed and Breakfast Inn, 367

Wilderness Retreats

Crowley Lake
Rainbow Tarns Bed & Breakfast, 332
Mammoth Lakes
Tamarack Lodge Resort, 348
Wawona
Wawona Hotel, 377
Yosemite
The Ahwahnee, 379

The broad Sacramento River delta holds the capital city of **Sacramento**, with its peaceful tree-shaded streets, lovely capitol grounds, art museums, and restored Old Town. Sutter's Fort, a state historic park, replicates the fort built in 1839 by John Sutter on the American and Sacramento rivers.

Not to be missed in Old Sacramento is the California State Railroad Museum, which exhibits restored locomotives, a luxurious private railroad car, and hundreds of items from train history. It's near the waterfront, where old-fashioned paddle wheelers cruise the river.

Sacramento is the gateway to the gold country in the foothills of the Sierra Nevada. Ghosts of the 49ers still linger in former mining communities like **Sutter Creek**, **Jackson**, and **Jamestown**. Some have more than a touch of the old frontier. **Nevada City** has carefully nurtured its heritage by restoring a 19th-century atmosphere. Columbia, a state park, is an authentic recreation of a mid-1800s mining town.

Reach deeper into the High Sierra and you find a lake-dotted wilderness with high cliffs, dancing waterfalls, and immense sequoia trees. The great granite mountains, called a "range of light" by the naturalist John Muir, extend from the Cascades on the north to the desert Tehachapis.

South of dazzlingly blue and clear Lake Tahoe, the largest alpine lake in North America, is California's crown jewel: **Yosemite** National Park. At its heart lies Yosemite Valley. Sculpted by glaciers eons ago, it's an awe-inspiring wonderland of vertical cliffs, massive granite domes, streaming waterfalls, and lush meadows. With three million visitors annually, Yosemite can seem as crowded as a San Francisco suburb. But a few steps away from the campgrounds, 750 miles of trails traverse pristine country where the only sounds you hear belong to the wild.

Tioga Pass Road leads through Yosemite's northern peaks and subalpine meadows and descends sharply to desert country on the east side. The road south then heads toward **Mammoth Lakes** and some of California's best skiing and High Sierra scenery.

In Owens Valley, between the Sierra Nevada and Inyo/White Mountain range, you can go hiking, fishing, bird-watching, horseback riding, and boating. South of **Bishop**, in the Inyo National Forest, you can walk among the earth's oldest living trees: bristlecone pines. The oldest in this awe-inspiring forest of twisted trunks and weathered branches is 4,700 years.

Still farther south lie California's extreme points: Mount Whitney, at 14,494 feet the highest peak in the continental United States, and Badwater in Death Valley, 282 feet below sea level.

Amador City

Imperial Hotel

P.O. Box 195
Amador City, CA 95601
209-267-9172
800-242-5594 in California
Fax: 209-267-9249
www.imperialamador.com

A historic hotel in gold country

Proprietors: Bruce Sherrill and Dale Martin. **Accommodations:** 6 rooms (all with private bath). **Rates:** $75–$105. **Included:** Full breakfast. **Payment:** Major credit cards. **Children:** Welcome; although rooms accommodate a maximum of 2 guests. **Pets:** Not allowed. **Smoking:** Not allowed.

➤ **In the heart of the gold country and once a major mining center, Amador City is known today for its numerous antiques shops and for the excellent restaurant in the Imperial Hotel.**

This brick hotel, which faces busy Highway 49, was first built as a mercantile store and then redone and opened as a hotel in 1879, when Amador was a bustling town. It was made to last — the walls are twelve bricks thick at its base and four bricks thick at the roof. The Imperial closed in 1927; the present owners restored it in 1988, adding bathrooms, air conditioning, a restaurant, and other modern niceties.

The Imperial's restaurant is open daily for dinner and on Sundays for brunch. With exposed brick walls, white tablecloths, candlelight, and large folksy, floral paintings, it has achieved distinction for its fine California cuisine. Asian pasta with pan-seared sea scallops in a sesame-ginger sauce and tossed with red chile linguine, or chicken breast sautéed with artichoke hearts, sun-dried tomatoes, capers, white wine, and lemon juice and served with grilled polenta are typical items, although the menu changes four times a year. Guest breakfast is served in the dining room, on a patio, or in your room. The original hotel bar is opposite the restaurant.

Upstairs, the guest rooms have such old-fashioned features as high ceilings, antique beds, and paddle fans. They have a delightfully whimsical decor, with designs by the talented John Johannsen — the same artist who painted the colorful paintings downstairs in the restaurant. One room, for example, has a corner armoire with ties, socks, and a gown painted as if they're hung over the door. Another has a headboard made from Johannsen's hand-painted murals.

Room 1 is bright, decorated in white with a canopy bed, sofa, and double doors that open out onto a balcony. Room 4 has a well-worn antique writing desk with a brass study lamp and a mirrored armoire. Room 3 is sunny in pastels with wicker furnishings and an iris-patterned quilt. The baths are contemporary, in white and brass, and have hair dryers and towel warmers. As the Imperial is close to the highway, it's best to request a room at the back if you're a light sleeper.

A deck with flowerpots and chairs is at one end of the second-floor hall. Across the front of the hotel there's a balcony accessible to guests. Inside, on the landing, are a desk and phone, shelves of books and games, and a basket of fruit. In back of the hotel there's a quiet garden patio to relax in.

Bishop

Chalfant House

213 Academy Street
Bishop, CA 93514
760-872-1790
Fax: 760-872-9221
chalfantbb@qnet.com
www.thesierraweb.com

> A cozy B&B in a town on
> the east side of the Sierra
> Nevada range

Innkeepers: Fred and Sally Manecke. **Accommodations:** 8 rooms (all with private bath). **Rates:** $50–$65 single, $60–$75 double, $80–$100 suite, $15 additional person. **Included:** Full breakfast and refreshments. **Added:** 9% tax. **Payment:** Major credit cards. **Children:** Over age 8 welcome; $15 additional. **Pets:** Not allowed. **Smoking:** Not allowed.

➤ **Bishop is a small, peaceful town in the Owens Valley of the Eastern Sierra, halfway between Reno and Los Angeles. It provides easy access to mountain trails, lakes, the Mammoth Mountain ski area, and the ancient bristlecone pine forest.**

Chalfant House offers comfortable lodging while you explore the Owens Valley area. The turn-of-the-century inn, built for the publisher of the first newspaper in the valley, is a block from Main Street and within walking distance of shops, restaurants, and a pleasant park. After the Chalfants sold it in the 1920s, the house changed hands numerous times over the years and was everything from a boarding house for "ladies of the night," referred to locally as the "Loose House," to a more respectable lodging called the Academy Hotel for forty years up until it closed in 1983. Soon thereafter the house was left vacant and was virtually in ruin when the Manecke's bought it in 1987 and turned it into the amiable bed and breakfast it is today.

Guest rooms are named for members of the Chalfant family and each is furnished with antiques and handmade quilts; all rooms are air conditioned. Pleasant, named for Mr. Chalfant, has an inlaid oak armoire that came from Belgium, a queen white iron and brass bed, an exposed stone wall in the bath, and a private patio with a grape arbor. In Adeline, named for Pleasant's wife, the tub is draped in lace.

Other guest rooms are named for the Chalfant children. In Agnes there's a patchwork quilt on a bed under a slanted roof; Willie has twin beds and is masculine; and the Blanche suite has a Victorian parlor.

There are two additional suites behind the main house. The upstairs suite has a carved walnut queen-size bed attractively set with a floral comforter and lots of pillows, a sofa bed in the living room, and a kitchen. The Flora Suite, downstairs, decorated in shades of green, pink, and white, has a four-poster bed and a separate sitting room with a fireplace.

The Maneckes have restored the B&B with care and put equal effort into creating a welcoming atmosphere for their guests. They'll greet you with a mug of hot cider in the cool months and a frosty drink in summer, take you to and from the Bishop airport at no charge, provide a sink for cleaning the fish you catch and a freezer to store it in, and invite you to join them for homemade ice cream sundaes in the evening.

Breakfast includes fruit, cinnamon rolls or homemade breads and jams, and a hot dish such as cream cheese French toast with apple cider syrup and turkey sausage or a baked omelette. It is served on fine table linens and china in the dining room, and you can take your coffee to the side terrace or parlor if you like. There's a piano and TV in the parlor, where guests gather to visit with each other and their hospitable hosts.

Coloma

The Coloma Country Inn

P.O. Box 502
345 High Street
Coloma, CA 95613
530-622-6919
info@colomacountryinn.com
www.colomacountryinn.com

> A quiet country home in a
> historic park

Innkeepers: Cindi and Alan Ehrgott. **Accommodations:** 5 rooms (3 with private bath) plus 2 suites in Carriage House. **Rates:** Rooms, $90–$145; suites, $195. **Included:** Full breakfast and afternoon refreshments. **Added:** 10% tax. **Payment:** No credit cards; personal checks accepted. **Children:** Welcome. **Pets:** Not allowed. **Smoking:** Allowed outdoors only.

➤ **Alan Ehrgott is a veteran pilot and offers hot-air balloon flights over the American River Valley. First thing in the morning, balloonists are given coffee and sweet rolls and then a ride over the pine trees, oak-studded hills, and the American River. The flight is followed by champagne and a full breakfast.**

In 1848 gold was discovered in the American River in the foothills of the Sierra Nevada. That event changed the face of the nation, helped the Union win the Civil War, and brought both fortune and disaster to thousands. By 1865 at least $750 million in gold had been mined in California.

It all started here, in the little town of Coloma, when James Marshall pulled a nugget from the tailrace of John Sutter's lumber mill. Richer diggings were soon found elsewhere, and Coloma became the commercial center for nearby mining camps. Saloon keepers prospered mightily from the newfound gold. Hugh Miller, who ran a saloon in Coloma, was able to build himself a fine home in 1852. This home, after several renovations, is now a delightful inn at Marshall Gold Discovery State Historic Park.

Coloma Country Inn has been open as a bed-and-breakfast since 1983. The inn stands behind a white picket fence on 5 acres of beautifully landscaped grounds, with fruit trees, flowers, a gazebo, a heritage rose garden, an old-fashioned well, and a pond where bullfrogs croak among the cattails. The Ehrgotts offer warm hospitality and a touch of New England — plaid wingback chairs, patchwork quilts, hand-dipped candles, charming wall stencils — in the furnishings and decor of their inn. In the parlor there are Shaker boxes, birdhouses, Oriental rugs, and a lace-draped mantel. Pewter mugs adorn the walls of the dining room, where breakfast is served on an heirloom Duncan Phyfe table underneath a pewter chandelier.

In the main house, the Rose Room is bright with a rose motif decor and a private courtyard where roses bloom. Lavender Room is a light, cheerful space in lavender and white, with a white spool bed, lace curtains, stained glass windows, a clawfoot tub, and an apple tree outside a window with a view of the pond. The Blue Room has long, narrow windows hung with lace and framed with flowers. It shares a bathroom with the Garden Room, which is furnished in white wicker and pine. In the Eastlake Room cushioned benches stand on either side of French doors that open out onto a small widow's balcony. The carved Eastlake bed is topped by a chenille spread. Each room has a small sitting area.

A few yards away, behind a lavish country garden and brick courtyard, is the Carriage House, with two enchanting suites. Cottage Suite is a good choice for families, since it has two bedrooms and a kitchenette (not for cooking full meals, but quite adequate for storing snacks). Geranium Suite has a folk country feel and lives up to its name with a garden motif and geranium-patterned fabrics. It also has a kitchen where the red, white, and green color scheme is repeated down to a rooster egg cup set that was given to the inn by a guest who felt it just belonged there (and it does). Outside, grapes and wisteria cover trellises on the large patio.

You may have breakfast in your room, on the patio, or in the main dining room, where French doors open to the grassy slope above the pond. You'll be served juice, fresh fruit, homemade baked goods, and a hot entrée such as scrambled eggs with salsa. In the afternoon, cookies, lemonade, and iced tea are in the kitchen for guests.

The innkeepers have binoculars to lend for bird-watching at the pond, and will arrange for whitewater rafting trips. If you tour the state park, you'll see a replica of Sutter's sawmill, James Marshall's

cabin, tinsmith and blacksmith shops, and other historic structures. Guests can get into the spirit of the period at the Olde Coloma Theater, where melodramas are presented on weekends.

Columbia

City Hotel

P.O. Box 1870
Main Street
Columbia, CA 95310
209-532-1479
800-532-1479
Fax: 209-532-7027
info@cityhotel.com
www.cityhotel.com

**A frontier hotel in an Old
West town**

Manager: Tom Bender. **Accommodations:** 10 rooms. **Rates:** $90–$110 single,
$95–$115 double, $10 additional person. **Included:** Buffet breakfast. **Added:** 8%
tax. **Payment:** Major credit cards. **Children:** Under age 4 are free in room with
parents. **Pets:** Not allowed. **Smoking:** Not allowed. **Open:** All year with the
exception of the first few weeks in January.

➤ **Columbia is the best-preserved gold-rush town in the Mother Lode.
Faithfully restored, it's now a state park where you can experience life as
it was in the 1850s, when this was a boomtown of 15,000 people and 40
saloons. When you walk into town (no cars are allowed) you enter the
mid-19th century.**

Horses clop down the street in Columbia, pulling stagecoaches to
the Wells Fargo office. The blacksmith is in his shop repairing
wagons. Melodramas are performed regularly at the theater. The
barber cuts hair in an 1856 barbershop, and old-fashioned candies
are sold in the sweetshop. And the same hotel that housed successful miners is open for business.

City Hotel is a two-story brick edifice that opened in 1856, fell
into disrepair when the boom faded, and reopened in 1975 as a museum and hotel under state ownership. Now, just as in earlier days,
lace curtains hang at glass-paneled doors and a ticking clock and
heavy safe stand behind a wooden registration counter. The crowd

in the What Cheer Saloon isn't quite as boisterous as in decades past, but the atmosphere is convivial around the cherrywood bar, which was shipped around the Horn from New England.

The frontier inn is well kept and comfortable, and the service attentive. The highly reputed restaurant serves a light French cuisine and has a wine list that includes labels from Amador County, an area noted for its zinfandels. The restaurant and hotel are also a training ground for students in the hospitality management program at nearby Columbia College. Eager and enthusiastic, they assist a professional staff.

Guest rooms are upstairs, two in front (Balcony Rooms), four down the hall, and four off the large parlor (Parlor Rooms). In the Victorian parlor are games, playing cards, and a revolving bookcase of books and magazines. A breakfast of fresh juice, granola, fruits, and breads from the hotel kitchen is set out in the parlor and may be taken to your room.

The rooms are on display when they're not occupied. When you stay here, the chain across the door is unhooked and you're left to spend the night as a traveler of a century ago would have been; in the finest accommodations the gold country had to offer. The rooms are larger than they were originally, when the hotel was strictly for gentlemen and ladies were allowed only in the parlor and dining areas. The addition of running water is another modern nicety. There's a half bath in each room, but showers are down the hall. You're supplied with a basket containing robes, soft slippers, towels, soap, and shampoo.

Oriental rugs, 12-foot ceilings, lace curtains at high windows, and heavy, carved furniture bring back the romance of another era. The two Balcony Rooms have private balconies with wrought-iron railings facing the trees above Main Street.

Room 1, a perennial favorite, is the haunted room. It seems that a wealthy man from the Midwest bought a massive carved bedroom set for his bride and had it shipped to San Francisco. But the newlyweds never slept in the bed, for the bride died of a fever. The grieving husband shut the furniture in a warehouse. Later, after a stint in a museum, it ended up in a Balcony Room here, and occasionally visitors insist that they feel peculiar vibrations.

In Columbia State Historic Park you can have your name stamped on a horseshoe or printed in headlines in a period newspaper, ride in a stagecoach, and pan for gold. You can also buy leather goods and wines, stop by the ice cream parlor, tour the museum, and have lunch or dinner at the best restaurant in town, the City Hotel. Miners who got lucky drank champagne here; you can too.

Fallon Hotel

P.O. Box 1870
11175 Washington Street
Columbia, CA 95310
209-532-1470
800-532-1479
Fax: 209-532-7027
info@cityhotel.com
www.cityhotel.com

> **A Victorian hotel in a gold-rush setting**

Manager: Tom Bender. **Accommodations:** 14 rooms. **Rates:** $50–$110 single, $55–$115 double, $10 additional person; $165 suite **Included:** Buffet breakfast. **Added:** 8% tax. **Payment:** Major credit cards. **Children:** Age 4 and under free in room with parents. **Pets:** Not allowed. **Smoking:** Not allowed. **Open:** Thursdays through Sundays, except Memorial Day through Labor Day, when the hotel is open 7 days a week.

> ➤ **Next to the hotel is a tree-shaded garden with a brick terrace. In the nearby Fallon Theater, the Columbia Actors' Repertory performs year-round.**

In Columbia State Historic Park, where gold rush days have been brought to life, the Fallon Hotel offers lodging just as it did when Columbia was a rip-roaring miners' town in 1857. Owned by the state, the hotel was authentically restored in 1986, using many of the antiques and furnishings discovered in the neglected, dilapidated building.

Now, when you enter the lobby, you're engulfed in the atmosphere of a fine Victorian hotel in the countryside. A green plush loveseat and burgundy velvet couch are set off by an Oriental carpet and dark, carved moldings. When the restoration began, bits of the original wallpaper were found still clinging to the walls, so the noted firm of Bradbury and Bradbury was called in to recreate them. Elaborate, colorful designs cover the 15-foot walls and ceiling.

Upstairs guest rooms contain double or twin beds and half baths. Spacious and modern shared showers with skylights are down the hall. Baskets with soaps, towels, robes, and slippers are provided. At the end of the hall, French doors open to a balcony overlooking the traffic-free street — no cars are permitted in Columbia — and some rooms have private balconies.

The best and largest rooms are toward the front of the hotel, but all are homey and comfortable, with carved or iron bedsteads, rocking chairs, and throw rugs on pine floors. Every morning, juice, coffee, assorted muffins and rolls, and jam are served in the ice cream parlor.

Coulterville

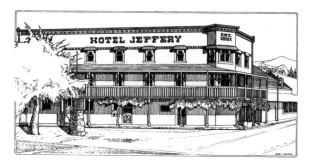

The Hotel Jeffery

P.O. Box 440B
1 Main Street
Coulterville, CA 95311
209-878-3471
800-464-3471
Fax: 209-878-3473
www.yosemitegold.com/jefferyhotel

> **A former stagecoach stop in the Sierra foothills**

Proprietor: Karin Fielding. **Accommodations:** 20 rooms (5 with private bath), 1 suite. **Rates:** $59–$74 single or double, $10 additional person; suites $99–$179 for up to 6 people. **Added:** 10% tax. **Minimum stay:** 2 nights on holiday weekends. **Payment:** Major credit cards. **Children:** Under 12 free in room with parents. **Pets:** Not allowed. **Smoking:** Allowed.

➤ **This former stagecoach stop has a classic saloon with sawdust and peanut shells on the floor, lace at the windows, and a second-story balcony with flags at the railing.**

Travelers looking for the Old West love the Jeffery — it's the real thing, here in the foothills of the Sierras, 31 miles west of Yosemite National Park. The three-story rock and adobe hotel was first built in 1850 as a store and fandango hall for the Mexican community. It burned and was rebuilt three times over the years, but has been owned by the same family since 1851. Karin Fielding, one of the present owners, is a descendant.

There is little luxury at the Jeffery, but plenty of character and charm. In 1903 Theodore Roosevelt stayed in Room 1, one of two rooms with bay windows above the main street of this sleepy little village. Some windows overlook the county park across the street, which has a playground, swimming pool, and tennis courts.

The rooms are of different sizes, and there are a few cracks in the walls from the settling of the building. Pegs or rails with hangers take the place of closets. Big windows, transoms above the doors, and ceiling paddle fans provide air circulation. There are four bathrooms on each floor for the rooms that share baths.

The hotel was redone in 1988 and now has nicely decorated rooms large enough for families. The two most spacious rooms, done in blue and peach, are on the third floor. Like most old hotels, the Jeffery claims a ghost room that a spirit visits on occasion. You wouldn't know it to see the place; on the third floor, it's cheerful in bright red and has twin beds.

There is a meeting/banquet room with 1,600 square feet of space and a nice courtyard in back. The plain and simple restaurant serves lunch and dinner. Magnolia Saloon, with authentic frontier flavor, has pool tables and one of the oldest bars in the West. On display are military memorabilia and a whimsical, life-size scene of old-time poker players.

Coulterville has antique shops to browse and a historical museum that is well worth visiting.

Crowley Lake

Rainbow Tarns Bed & Breakfast

HC 79, Box 1053
Crowley Lake, CA 93546
760-935-4556
888-588-6269
info@rainbowtarns.com
www.rainbowtarns.com

An Old West farm home in the country

Innkeepers: Brock and Diane Thoman. **Accommodations:** 3 rooms (all with private bath). **Rates:** $95–$140 in summer; $75–$120 in winter; midweek discounts available. **Included:** Full breakfast and afternoon refreshments. **Added:** 9% tax. **Minimum stay:** 2 nights on weekends, 3 nights on holidays. **Payment:** No credit cards. **Children:** Over age 12 welcome; additional $20 if third person in room. **Pets:** Not allowed. **Smoking:** Not allowed indoors. **Open:** Late April through October and Thanksgiving through March.

➤ **The restaurant at nearby Convict Lake is the place for dining by candlelight. Tom's Place, down-home and friendly, is where local residents go for good hamburgers and conviviality.**

On the east side of the Sierra range, 18 miles south of Mammoth Lakes, is a tiny community called Tom's Place. You can find it on your road map, but in reality it's little more than a restaurant and bar. About a mile farther, on a dirt road, is Rainbow Tarns, a secluded, quiet, country home owned by Diane and Brock Thoman.

The log and tan brick inn, built in the 1920s against granite boulders, has a rustic quality that is right out of the Old West. A battered wagon wheel leans against the verandah's log posts. The living room, with its log walls and high, vaulted ceilings, has the feeling of a lodge. There's a deer over the stone fireplace, a wagon wheel light fixture, and a table set for a game of chess.

The guest rooms are furnished in country style, with lace curtains and down duvets to warm you on chilly mountain evenings (the elevation is 7,000 feet). Rainbow Room, furnished with pieces from the 1920s and 1930s, has a brass queen-size bed topped by a floral comforter, lamps with stained glass shades on bedside tables, an oversize tile bath with a double Jacuzzi, and a deck. The Gemini Room has the feel of a wilderness lodge, with oak furnishings and strong colors. Artwork depicting mountains and streams adorns the walls. The bath has single spa tub with a view of boulders and a tree-covered hillside. Grandma's Room is decorated with a four-poster bed, antiques, and photos of the innkeepers' grandparents.

This is a homey, casual spot where guests dine on ranch breakfasts served in the country kitchen or outside on the deck. In the afternoons Diane and Brock serve wine and hors d'oeuvres.

From the inn's verandah or chairs on the grass you can watch the trout leap and ducks swim in the ponds. Rainbow Tarns is ideally situated for outdoor recreation — you can go bicycling or horseback riding, hiking on the John Muir Trail, cross-country skiing in open meadows, bathing in hot mineral springs, bird-watching, and star-gazing.

Georgetown

American River Inn

P.O. Box 43
Main at Orleans
Georgetown, CA 95634
530-333-449
800-245-6566 in CA
Fax: 530-333-9253
www.pcweb.net/ari

> **A casual, quiet inn near a former mining camp**

Innkeepers: Will and Maria Collin. **Accommodations:** 20 rooms (11 with private bath), 6 suites. **Rates:** $85–$150. **Included:** Full breakfast. **Added:** 10% tax. **Payment:** Major credit cards. **Children:** Over 7 welcome; additional $15 per child. **Pets:** Small pets allowed by prior arrangement only. **Smoking:** Allowed outdoors only.

➤ **The promise of gold drew prospectors to Georgetown, in the foothills of the Sierra Nevada, in the mid-1800s. The mining camp, then called Growlersburg, was a rich source of the precious stuff. By 1853, an estimated $2 million in gold had been found; one famous nugget weighed in at 126 ounces.**

Georgetown is a quiet backwater between the middle and south forks of the American River, about an hour's drive east of Sacramento. There are few tourist attractions here — just scenic surroundings of mountains, lakes, and streams.

The original American Hotel, built in 1853, was all but lost to flames forty-six years later. Fire was commonplace in those days, often destroying entire towns. One Georgetown blaze raced up Main Street to a cache of miners' dynamite, which exploded and tossed debris for two miles.

Today's American River Inn, a complex covering one square block, is on the same site as its forebear. Three buildings are set among lovely gardens, along with a dove aviary and a swimming pool. The main building, with a verandah and a long balcony, houses fifteen guest rooms.

The comfortable accommodations have a flowery charm and furnishings that include unusual brass beds, patchwork quilts, feather beds, ceiling fans, antique lamps and armoires, and clawfoot tubs. At the end of the upstairs hall, lighted by red glass lamps, a door opens to the front balcony, overlooking the quiet road.

Each room has a different decor, ranging from country calico to Victorian grandeur. There are two suites on the third level, one with a canopy bed and fireplace. The main house also has a gift shop and a parlor with a potbelly woodstove, wingback chairs, and a bar in the corner. Classical music plays in the afternoon while guests enjoy wine and appetizers and thumb through the album of local history. On the walls are historic prints of naval heroes and, of course, a "God Bless America" sampler.

A substantial breakfast is served at small tables in the dining room. Belgian waffles with bananas, spinach quiche, sausage, and ham are some of the dishes prepared, always with muffins, fruit cup, coffee, and tea.

In back of the hotel, down brick steps and past a big magnolia tree, are the fig-shaded pool and the aviary. Next to the patio, the Queen Anne House has five guest rooms, two with private baths. The big living room has a brick fireplace, Oriental carpets, and double doors to the deck. The most romantic of the light and airy rooms is the upstairs suite, with a partially canopied bed, white brick fireplace, and a balcony with a wrought-iron railing.

A third building holds the five Woodside Mine Suites, which have living rooms, wet bars, and one or two bedrooms. Attractively furnished in wicker and brass and decorated with stenciled designs, they have private entrances from the garden and the parking area.

The innkeepers can help you plan sightseeing tours of the gold country and will arrange for whitewater rafting trips or hot air balloon rides over the American River. They'll lend mountain bikes for biking the backroads that wind through masses of purple irises and brilliant yellow daffodils and Scotch broom.

Hiking, fishing, and golf are nearby. The hotel has a putting green and driving range as well as facilities for horseshoes, badminton, table tennis, and croquet. The kitchen will prepare a luxury picnic basket for a day of exploring, at $100 for two people. It includes a bottle of wine, and you may keep the basket and all its accessories for future picnics.

Homewood

Rockwood Lodge

P.O. Box 226
5295 West Lake Boulevard
Homewood, CA 96141-0226
530-525-5273
800-LETAHOE
Fax: 530-525-5949
rockwood@inreach.com
www.rockwoodlodge.com

> **A comfortable bed-and-breakfast near the lake**

Innkeepers: Constance Stevens and Lou Reinkens. **Accommodations:** 4 rooms (all with private bath). **Rates:** $100–$200. **Included:** Continental breakfast and evening refreshments. **Added:** 10% tax. **Minimum stay:** 2 nights on weekends, 3 nights on holidays. **Payment:** No credit cards; personal checks accepted. **Children:** Under 18 not appropriate. **Pets:** Not allowed indoors. **Smoking:** Not allowed indoors.

➤ **There are several excellent restaurants along Tahoe's shores. In the summer you may rent or charter a boat for fishing. Brown and Mackinaw trout inhabit the clear waters of the lake.**

"Skiing down Homewood Run feels as if you're flying right into the lake." Connie Stevens is enthusiastic when she's talking about skiing and Lake Tahoe, two of her favorite subjects. She and her husband, Louis Reinkens, live in an ideal area to enjoy them both. Their bed-and-breakfast is just across the road from the lake and within walking distance of downhill ski slopes.

Homewood is a quiet community on the northwestern shore. Rockwood Lodge was built in 1939, in the old Tahoe style of stone and knotty pine, as a vacation home for a dairyman from Vallejo. Forty-five years later, Connie and Louis left their Bay Area home and bought Rockwood, renovated it, and opened it to guests. Long-time travelers, they know the comforts travelers look for.

There are walk-in closets with thick velour bathrobes, wines and appetizers by the fire or on the patio, cordials in the evenings, sweets by the bed, and books to read. The innkeepers can lend beach towels and chairs in the summer and gloves and scarves in the winter. There are ski and bicycle storage areas, backpacks and walking sticks to borrow, and flashlights for evening walks.

Once inside the lodge — even on August weekends, when Tahoe traffic and crowds reach temper-fraying levels — the atmosphere is one of peace, soft music, and good taste. Wingback chairs and fender benches provide seating comfort in the living room, where a fire on the stone hearth takes away the chill of winter evenings. On the mantel is a miniature of the Tahoe steam train that once ran to the lake.

French doors open to the dining room and breakfast table. Connie and Louis prepare fresh juice, croissants and preserves, quantities of fruit, Dutch babies with blueberries, Belgian waffles, and other delectable items, which they serve here or on the patio.

The guest rooms are named for places around the lake: Zephyr Cove, Emerald Bay, Secret Harbor, and Carnelian Bay. Zephyr Cove, the only room on the third floor, contains a queen-size bed and has a private bathroom. From its windows you look into the green branches of a 100-year-old pine tree. Emerald Bay, on the second floor, has a hall bathroom with a seven-foot-long Roman steeping tub and a double shower. Secret Harbor, overlooking the lake, is the largest room and has extra appeal: a four-poster bed, an 18th-century cobbler's bench, and a bath with a double shower. All the rooms feature feather beds, down comforters, and sitting areas.

Hope Valley

Sorensen's

14255 Highway 88
Hope Valley, CA 96120
530-694-2203
800-423-9949
www.sorensensresort.com

> A group of wilderness
> cabins near Carson Pass

Proprietors: John and Patty Brissenden. **Accommodations:** 30 cabins (all but 2 have private baths). **Rates:** $80–$450. **Added:** 10% tax. **Minimum stay:** 2 nights on weekends, 3–4 nights on some holidays. **Payment:** Major credit cards. **Children:** Welcome. **Pets:** Allowed with prior arrangement (in 4 cabins). **Smoking:** Not allowed.

➤ **The Sorensen family homesteaded here a century ago; in 1902 they built a cluster of cabins, the start of a resort that is still expanding. It now covers 165 acres at an elevation of 7,000 feet.**

South of Lake Tahoe and north of Yosemite, the rugged, mountainous country of the High Sierra has a scenic grandeur that rivals the Alps'. In fact, it's called Alpine County and most of it is public land — a colossal park covering nearly 800 square miles of lakes, meadows, rivers, mighty forests, and high peaks. Just east of Carson Pass, where Kit Carson explored and mapped the territory, are the green meadows of Hope Valley and this homey resort.

Owned by the Brissenden family since 1981, Sorensen's offers a full range of activities for all ages. Favorites are fishing, fly-tying and rod building courses, hiking, river rafting, kayaking, bicycling, soaking at the hot springs, and llama trekking. In winter, the resort is a cross-country ski center with miles of trails in the peaceful valley and Toiyabe National Forest. Ski lessons, equipment rentals, and classes in winter survival skills are available.

All but three of the cabins are clustered in the woods around a central building that houses a country café (serving three hearty meals daily) and a gift shop. Each little building and its steeply pitched roof is outlined with tiny lights, creating a charming village effect at night.

Most of the cabins, which are named for local trees and flowers, have woodstoves (wood is supplied) and kitchens. Breakfast is provided for the three bed and breakfast cabins that do not have cooking facilities.

Piñon, next to the sauna cabin, is one of the coziest, with cedar walls and an old-fashioned tub. Aspen, in 1930s knotty pine, has a homespun style with calico bedspreads. Snowshoe is a classic log cabin furnished with a pole bed, wood-burning stove, a tree slab dining table, and a kitchenette. Waterfir is beloved by romantics looking for a quiet spot. Nestled among the aspen trees, with a creek running by, it has a brass double bed, a kitchen in the same room, a unique shingled shower, and a woodstove with a rock hearth.

The most unusual cabin is Norway House, a replica of a 13th-century, sod-roofed Scandinavian home. The two-story cabin sleeps up to six people and has a full kitchen. In back, there's a deck with benches under the aspen trees. Chapel also has two floors, with a spiral staircase leading to a loft bedroom. The cabin, which originally was part of Santa's Village in Santa Cruz, was reconstructed on the site and remodeled.

This is a great place for children. John Brissenden, a former preschool teacher, has built a cunning log playhouse and stocked a pond with fish for kids under 12. There are puzzles, games, and a playground, as well as special programs like the October Star Watch and the Husky Express sled dog tours. If you're interested in both hiking and history, sign up for the Historical Emigrant Trail Walking Tour. The tour crosses parts of the Mormon-Emigrant Trail and the early Pony Express Route.

For an enchanting winter holiday, come to Sorensen's in December and cut a fragrant Christmas tree. After a day on the snowy mountain, return to the café for hot cinnamon cocoa, mulled wine, or spiced cider and shop for gifts of books, jams and jellies, watercolors, and Native American wall hangings.

Jackson

Gate House Inn

1330 Jackson Gate road
Jackson, CA 95642
209-223-3500
800-841-1072
Fax: 209-223-1299
info@gatehouseinn.com
www.gatehouseinn.com

> **A Victorian in the gold
> country**

Proprietors: Keith and Gail Sweet. **Accommodations:** 4 rooms (all with private bath) and Summerhouse. **Rates:** $100–$150 single, $105–$155 double, $20 additional person. **Included:** Full breakfast. **Added:** 8% tax. **Minimum stay:** 2 nights on weekends and for special events or holidays. **Payment:** Major credit cards. **Children:** Over age 12 welcome. **Pets:** Not allowed. **Smoking:** Not allowed indoors.

➤ **Jackson is close to all the diversions Amador County offers: wineries, golf courses, historic gold-mining towns, and the Indian Grinding Rocks State Historic Park.**

On an acre of sloping land that blooms with a thousand daffodils in spring, this turn-of-the-century Victorian home stands in quiet seclusion in the heart of the gold country. It was built by the son of one of Jackson's earliest settlers, Agostino Chichizola, a merchant and rancher, and today looks much as it did when it was new.

Oriental carpets, crystal chandeliers, antique furnishings, marble fireplaces, and a leaded and stained glass window retain the home's period atmosphere. Elegant royal blue velvet settees and a French rosewood table grace the parlor. The parquet floor in the dining room cost $10,000 to install at the time the home was built — a sizeable sum in those days.

The single guest room on the main floor has a brass bed, a marble-topped sideboard, and, in the bathroom, the home's original lionfoot tub, which is so massive and ornate, it took six men to install it for the home's first owner. Upstairs, the French Room features Louis XIV walnut furniture, while the Master Suite boasts an Italian tile fireplace and a rose velvet sofa that belonged to the Chichizola family. On the rose floral wallpaper (vintage 1948) there are pictures of cherubs, reflecting the inn's angelic theme, and the bed is topped by an ivory eyelet comforter and lacy pillows. It's the only room with a hall bath, just a couple of steps away.

Woodhaven, at the top of a private staircase and under the eaves, has a country atmosphere with pine furnishings, a braided rug, and a white iron bed. The painted chest was used by Gail's grandparents when they immigrated from the Netherlands in 1919. There's a half bath on one side of the room and a clawfoot tub on the other. Lace-curtained windows overlook the lushly flowered garden. Woodhaven has a sitting room and can accommodate two extra adults; the inn has no cribs for young children.

A favorite among returning guests is Summerhouse, a cottage by the back gate and arbor. Built as the caretaker's residence, it has an antique wooden headboard, chintz fabrics, wicker furnishings, air conditioning, and a stove on a brick hearth. There's a whirlpool tub for two in the bathroom.

Next to the garden is a screened area with table tennis. Brick-walled flowerbeds and rosebushes edge a path leading to a secluded swimming pool and a barbecue.

Guests can choose whether to have breakfast in their rooms or in the dining room at a single table set with fresh flowers, china, and candles. The menu varies; among the Gate House specialties are caramelized French toast with pecans and apples, salmon quiche, Belgian waffles, and a fresh fruit and yogurt parfait. Guests have the use of the kitchen refrigerator and can help themselves to complimentary soft drinks and homemade cookies.

The thorough innkeepers try to accommodate their guests' needs and interests, whatever they might be. For history buffs, they've prepared a detailed history of the Chichizola family, who built the home, including a family tree. For nature lovers, the informative guest book in each room has a diagram of the plants in the garden, and each guest is given a helpful packet of area sightseeing information and coupons upon arrival. The Sweets also keep a supply of area restaurant menus on hand and can help you with dining suggestions and dinner reservations.

The Wedgewood Inn

11941 Narcissus Road
Jackson, CA 95642
209-296-4300
800-933-4393 1-800-WEDGEWD
Fax: 209-296-4301
www.wedgewoodinn.com

A gracious country home

Innkeepers: Jeannine and Vic Beltz. **Accommodations:** 5 rooms, 1 suite (all with private bath). **Rates:** $100–$140 single, $120–$160 double, $165–$185 suite. **Included:** Full breakfast and afternoon refreshments. **Added:** 6% tax. **Payment:** Major credit cards. **Children:** Welcome in suite only; $20 additional. **Pets:** Not allowed. **Smoking:** Not allowed indoors.

➤   **With the Wedgewood as your headquarters, you can explore the gold country, shop for antiques, and tour museums. Back at the inn, you can play croquet or horseshoes or relax in the hammock under the oak trees.**

If you had saved all those toys that are now collector's items, along with your parents' and grandparents' heirlooms, you too could furnish a home like the Wedgewood. Items the Beltzes have saved and antiques they've collected fill the rooms of their gracious Victorian replica, a blue frame house in the country, six miles east of Jackson, off Highway 88.

Both Vic and Jeannine have an artistic flair that is evident in the stained glass, needlework, and lace lampshades on display throughout the inn. They're gardeners, too, and have landscaped the grounds in an English country style, with flowerbeds, a rose arbor, a gazebo, and fountains.

Pendulum clocks tick in the quiet parlor, where there's a wood-stove and a baby grand piano. In the dining room beyond, guests gather for breakfast — a memorable meal of several courses by candlelight. Baked apples, spiced pears, quiche, and blueberry–sour cream coffee cake are a few of the dishes served. Afternoon refreshments and early morning coffee are also provided.

The Wedgewood is a comfortable home operated by kindly people with traditional values. They set out Christian books and say grace at breakfast. If this is not to your liking, you may not feel at ease, though the innkeepers handle the issue with tact and do not push their beliefs on guests.

The upstairs guest rooms are spacious and have views of the garden and oak grove or the wooded hills. Their furnishings reflect the innkeeper's interests and strong family ties. Victorian Rose is the most popular, with its rose motif, wood-burning stove, English carved bedroom set, walnut table, loveseat, and tapestry chairs. Its balcony, overlooking the rose arbor, is shared with Wedgewood Cameo. As one might expect, Wedgewood Cameo holds a cameo collection.

In Heritage Oak, the smallest room, there's a four-poster bed, tapestry rocker, and an old-fashioned spinning wheel. Jeannine's wedding dress is on display, and the bath has an antique shaving stand. Country Pine, in green and peach, features an iron scroll bed, carved armoire, a family christening gown, a cradle made by Vic's father, and an antique swift used in the counting of yarn. Up on the third floor is Granny's Attic, named for Jeannine's mother. A light, airy room, it has a four-poster bed, skylight, wood-burning stove, and clawfoot tub draped in peach-colored lace.

The Carriage House, a separate cottage, is a two-room suite with a private patio, old iron stove, a canopy bed, two-person Jacuzzi, and window that looks out to the forest. Jeannine's childhood toys are displayed in a loft over the living room, and oval picture frames preserve old photos of her great-grandparents. The Carriage House is the only guest room with a TV, and it also has its own refrigerator. Other guests are welcome to beverages from the refrigerator in the upstairs hallway in the main house.

If you like vintage automobiles, ask Vic to show you Henry, his 1921 Model-T. Vic is also an amateur gold prospector, and can demonstrate proper gold panning procedure and fill you in on gold-country history.

Jamestown

The National Hotel

P.O. Box 502
77 Main Street
Jamestown, CA 95327
209-984-3446
800-894-3446
Fax: 209-984-5620
info@national-hotel.com
www.national-hotel.com

> A historic hotel in a
> picturesque gold-mining
> town

Proprietor: Stephen Willey. **Accommodations:** 9 rooms (all with private bath). **Rates:** $80–$120 double; midweek discounts available. **Included:** Expanded Continental breakfast. **Added:** 8% tax. **Payment:** Major credit cards. **Children:** Under 10 by prior arrangement only; $15 additional. **Pets:** Allowed by prior arrangement; additional $10. **Smoking:** Allowed on balcony only.

> ➤   **If you've caught gold fever and hanker for a real nugget, you may find one in August during Gold Nugget Days. Clues, sold for a dollar each, lead modern argonauts to nuggets hidden around town.**

Fortunately for those who revel in glimpses of the past, progress has bypassed Jamestown. Because it looks much as it did in the 1870s, the well-preserved gold-mining town has been used as a background for such movies as *High Noon* and *Butch Cassidy and the Sundance Kid,* and for the television series *Little House on the Prairie.*

Some 2-1/2 hours east of San Francisco and just south of Sonora, Jamestown is considered the gateway to the Mother Lode. Tourists love its antiques shops and the classic brick and gingerbread Emporium. One of the most historically significant buildings in

Jamestown is the National Hotel, which has been open continuously since 1859. Today, as in the past, it offers comfortable accommodations, good food, and a convivial atmosphere.

Many a bag of gold dust has changed hands over the redwood bar in the saloon, where guests register. It's a casual, friendly spot, with a bartender who serves concoctions with such names as Gold Rush Margarita and Miner's Punch as well as more usual drinks. The guest rooms, up carpeted stairs, are furnished in country antiques, with handmade quilts and lace curtains. "They're simple, because that's the way they were in the 1800s in the gold country," says the congenial innkeeper.

Stephen Willey has owned the hotel since 1974 and has been instrumental in helping Jamestown turn from slow decay to a revitalized community. He was careful in restoring the National to keep it authentic, except for the plumbing. All the rooms contain washbasins and spotlessly clean private baths.

The doors to rooms that are not occupied are open, so you can peek in and select your favorite. A typical example has a brass bed with a handmade quilt, lace curtains, pegs to hold hanging items, and fresh flowers. Some rooms overlook the courtyard and a century-old grape arbor covered with Virginia creeper vines.

In the downstairs dining room, an expanded Continental breakfast is set out for guests: freshly sliced fruits, coffee, assorted juices, hard-boiled eggs, teas, cereals, fresh sourdough French bread, and homemade muffins. Victorian relics — white kid boots, a doll, long gowns — are on display here. The restaurant's meals are excellent, with a different special daily and more than 80 wines from regional wineries available. Champagne brunch, lunch, and dinner are served. In the summer, you can eat outside under the vine-shaded grape arbor.

Television does not fit the hotel's motif (though it will be provided upon request). Jigsaw puzzles, chess, checkers, and bragging at the bar are activities more in tune with the times. Jamestown also offers other forms of entertainment. You can shop for antiques, see stagecoach robberies enacted, pan for gold, ride a steam train, and, in June, attend the widely acclaimed Dixieland Jazz Festival.

Mammoth Lakes

Edelweiss Lodge

P.O. Box 658
1872 Old Mammoth Road
Mammoth Lakes, CA 93546
760-934-2445
Toll free: 877-2EDELWEISS
edelweiss@qnet.net
www.mammothweb.com/lodging/edelweiss

> **A chalet-style inn with a quiet atmosphere**

Innkeepers: Chris Draper and Diana Wilde-Draper. **Accommodations:** 8 units (all with private bath). **Rates:** $90–$175 (2 to 4 people), $10 additional person. **Added:** 10% tax. **Minimum stay:** 2 nights. **Payment:** MasterCard, Visa. **Children:** Welcome. **Pets:** Allowed with permission only; $25 additional. **Smoking:** Not allowed.

➤ **After a day of skiing in crystal air, under an intense blue sky, you can luxuriate in the cedar and redwood whirlpool spa at Edelweiss. Sign up to reserve a time and you'll have it all to yourself.**

Mammoth Lakes, on the slopes of Mammoth Mountain in the High Sierras, is a resort town that draws vacationers all year. In summer its environs offer great hiking, mountain biking, and fishing. But ski season, from November to July (!), is really special. And Edelweiss is one of the places where skiers like to stay.

Forest green shutters with heart cut-outs and carved porch railings decorate the alpine chalets, which cover three-quarters of an acre south of town. The personable owners, who came from southern California and took over the lodge in 1998, offer clean, roomy, one- and two-bedroom accommodations with equipped kitchens.

Cabin eight has honey-colored walls of knotty pine, a vaulted ceiling with hand-hewn beams, and a spiral staircase leading up to the living room and second bedroom. There's a full bath upstairs and a half bath downstairs. Café curtains hang at the kitchen window, and there are TV sets (with HBO) on both levels. Bedroom suites have oak interiors, a living room with an adjoining eat-in kitchen, and a king-size bed in the bedroom. A few rooms have stone fireplaces, and others feature woodstoves; all have microwaves. Area artists painted the landscapes on the walls.

At Edelweiss you can go cross-country skiing from your door. For downhill skiers, a short drive or shuttle bus ride takes you to Mammoth's 39 chairlifts and groomed slopes of powdery snow.

The lodge offers quiet relaxation under the trees on a pine swing or in Adirondack chairs. There's also a barbecue for guests who wish to cook their meals outside when the weather permits. The Edelweiss is not the place to stay if you're looking for the lights, music, and action some mountain resorts provide.

The innkeepers say, "What we like best about running this place is seeing guests who arrive tired and tense leave a few days later relaxed and happy. Some people never leave their cabin. They just sit and read or look out the window and rest."

Mammoth Mountain Inn

P.O. Box 353
1 Minaret Road
Mammoth Lakes, CA 93546
760-934-2581
800-228-4947
Fax: 760-934-0700

A mountainside resort for all seasons

General manager: Tom Smith. **Accommodations:** 213 rooms. **Rates:** $99–$205, 2–13 people in summer, $110–$425 in winter **Added:** 10% tax. **Payment:** Major credit cards. **Children:** 13 and under free in room with parents. **Pets:** Not allowed. **Smoking:** Nonsmoking rooms available upon request.

➤ **Drive up to Minaret Vista to see sensational views of the 13,000-foot Ritter Range and the Ansel Adams Wilderness. Devil's Postpile National Monument, east of Mammoth, is well worth a visit. This 60-foot wall of symmetrical basalt columns is a geological wonder.**

Mammoth Mountain, in the eastern High Sierra, southeast of Yosemite National Park, is one of the major ski areas in the country, drawing thousands yearly to its 3,500 acres of skiable terrain. On its broad slope, a short drive from the resort village of Mammoth Lakes, stands Mammoth Mountain Inn, the only full-service hotel in the eastern Sierra.

The redwood inn's exterior, with its steeply pitched roof and balconies with flags snapping in the wind, resembles a large mountain chalet. Inside, a stone fireplace rises to the loft lounge, where another fireplace offers warmth on winter evenings. Guests gather in the paneled lounge after a day of skiing Mammoth's powdery runs, or out on the sun deck facing the mountain slopes.

Guest rooms in the main building have either two queen-size beds or a queen and a twin, and portable cribs are available. The furnishings are comfortable and modern, with television, phones, plenty of closet space, and a balcony filled with flowers in summer. Some view the 11,053-foot mountain; others, the parking lot or forest.

In the East/West building are rooms and suites ranging from a studio that accommodates two to a two-bedroom unit with a loft that sleeps thirteen. Once privately owned, the units are now all operated by the inn. Suites have kitchenettes, dining tables, and sitting areas. Ski storage is provided. Preferred for mountain views are corner rooms (515, 516, 617, or 717) and the executive suite, Room 600. The best buy is a studio with a kitchenette. The inn has covered parking available on a first-come first-served basis, laundry facilities, and three whirlpool spas.

The Mountainside Grill is the main restaurant. Recommended are the homemade soups, the teriyaki chicken, and the chef's special dish — broiled jumbo shrimp wrapped in bacon and topped with a jalapeño hollandaise sauce. There's nothing rustic in this mountain retreat. You may sip a good California wine while listening to Chopin in the background. To really get into the Alpine spirit, try the Yodler Restaurant and Bar in an authentic Swiss chalet brought over from Switzerland in 1959. Fittingly, the restaurant serves European dishes such as Wiener schnitzel and knockwurst in beer with sauerkraut, along with more traditional steak, seafood, and pasta.

You may rent skis and buy lift tickets at the ski area's main lodge just across the road from the inn or at the front desk. The slopes are just out the door. Mammoth has 31 lifts, 150 trails, and a 3,100-foot vertical drop. (Skis can be checked at the bellhop stand during ski season, and bikes can be checked during the summer months.) You can also go cross-country skiing, dogsledding, snowmobiling, or bobsledding.

Skiers flock to Mammoth Lakes in winter, but the area is a fine summer destination as well. It has cool mountain air, dozens of clear alpine lakes, miles of backcountry trails, and good fishing. To encourage summer visitors, Mammoth Mountain Inn offers mountain biking, fly-fishing, horseback riding, kayaking, golfing, and hiking excursions, among others. In addition, the inn offers scenic gondola rides to the summit, outdoor barbecues, and a play area for children. Mammoth Lakes is only 35 miles south of the Tioga Pass entrance to Yosemite National Park, so Yosemite tours are also popular when weather permits.

Tamarack Lodge Resort

P.O. Box 69
Mammoth Lakes, CA 93546
760-934-2442
800-237-6879
Fax: 760-934-2281
www.tamaracklodge.com

> **A lakeside wilderness resort in the High Sierra**

Manager: Roy Moyer. **Accommodations:** 10 rooms (5 with private bath) and 1 suite, 26 cabins. **Rates:** $75–$195 in rooms, $80–$360 for 1–11 persons in cabins; rates vary according to size of cabin and season. **Minimum stay:** 2 nights on winter weekends, 3–5 nights summer and holidays. **Payment:** Major credit cards. **Children:** Infants free. **Pets:** Not allowed. **Smoking:** Not allowed indoors.

➤ **The lakes teem with native brown trout, brooks, and native and stocked rainbows, offering some the best fishing in the eastern Sierra. At the lodge they'll give you maps and information on obtaining daypacks, rowboats, and canoes. They will also pack a lunch to take along on your adventure.**

You know you're in wild country when the sign on your cottage wall reads, "Bears dwell here. Do not leave food on your porch or near windows." On the other hand, the restaurant a few steps from your door serves beef Wellington, rack of lamb, eggplant parmigiana, and the latest in colorful pasta dishes.

Tamarack Lodge is located on the shore of the Twin Lakes, the last and lowest of the Mammoth Lakes group. The lakes lie in an immense glacial basin scooped out of the eastern High Sierra.

Here in the woods, just three miles from the resort town of Mammoth Lakes, the lodge was built in 1924 by the Foy family of Los Angeles. (Later the family gained fame through the Bob Hope movie, *The Seven Little Foys.*) It has had a number of owners since then and is now owned by the Mammoth Mountain Ski Resort.

Entering the lodge, you find a knotty pine parlor where kerosene lamps stand on the mantel and skis crisscross above a stone fireplace. Sleds and snowshoes adorn the walls, a desk and phone for guest use are in one corner, and there are bookshelves stacked with games and paperbacks. A log table holds coffee and snacks available for purchase. It's a cozy scene in winter, when skiers come in to a hot lunch and mulled wine and cider by the fire.

The guest rooms line the pine-paneled hall upstairs, one side viewing the forest and cabins and the other overlooking the two lakes and mountain peaks in the background. The decor is simple but comfortable and clean. White curtains hang at the windows, and baskets of dried flowers and pastel watercolors add to the homey atmosphere. Some share well-maintained baths, others have private baths. Top of the Lodge is the two-bedroom suite with great views of the lakes and mountain ridges. It has a living room, a dining area, and a small kitchen.

The housekeeping cabins are clustered around the lodge under pines and aspens on six wooded acres. They all have carpeting, linens, and kitchens, and a few have fireplaces. There is no daily maid service in the cabins, but you can pick up fresh towels at the lodge; weekly cleaning is provided for extended stays.

After a day of skiing or hiking, you may not want to cook. Lakefront Restaurant, at the south end of the lodge, is the only other choice; fortunately, it's excellent. The setting is rustic, but white tablecloths are topped with country floral cloths, and classical music plays in the background. California cuisine and wines are served. Breakfast is also available.

The resort rents ski equipment, offers private and group lessons, and keeps 25 miles of cross-country trails groomed. You can ski right from your door. The variety of terrain and beautiful forest and mountain views provide plenty of winter interest.

In summer, boating, hiking, fishing, and mountain biking are the favorite activities. Miles of trails lead to Mammoth Mountain and its pass and crest, Coldwater Canyon, and spectacular Cascade Canyon. A day's hike to the west takes you to Red's Meadow and Devil's Postpile National Monument.

At press time plans were under way to add fifteen additional cabins and expand the resort's cross-country skiing facilities.

Murphys

Dunbar House, 1880

P.O. Box 1375
271 Jones Street
Murphys, CA 95247
209-728-2897
800-692-6006
Fax: 209-728-1451
dunbarhs@goldrush.com
www.dunbarhouse.com

An inviting B&B in a
historic gold-mining town

Innkeepers: Barbara and Bob Costa. **Accommodations:** 4 rooms (all with private bath). **Rates:** $135–$205. **Included:** Full breakfast and afternoon refreshments. **Added:** 6% tax. **Minimum stay:** 2 nights on weekends. **Payment:** Major credit cards. **Children:** Under 10 not appropriate. **Pets:** Not allowed. **Smoking:** Not allowed.

➤ **Crowds come to Murphys and the surrounding area in fall to see the brilliant foliage against dark green pine trees. Murphys boasts six wineries, tennis courts, a community swimming pool, and three nearby golf courses. It's a short drive from the village to Mercer Caverns, Moaning Caves, and Calaveras Big Trees State Park, where ancient sequoias grow.**

Murphys is a quiet little town now, drowsing in the Sierra sun, but in 1850 it bustled with action as prospectors and miners rushed in, lured by gold. Over a ten-year period, Wells Fargo shipped more than $15 million in gold dust from the Murphys office. Meanwhile, settlers looking for more than quick riches moved in.

In 1880 Willis Dunbar built an Italianate home for his bride, Ellen Roberts of Douglas Flat. A citizen of substance, he was the superintendent of the local water company, a member of the state assembly, and the head of a ranch and a lumber company. Willis and Ellen raised five sons in their big country home.

A century later, the Dunbar home became Calaveras County's first bed-and-breakfast, and in 1987 Barbara and Bob Costa took it over. They welcome guests looking for pleasant, homey accommodations with character and history. This is the sort of place where you sit in wicker chairs on the porch and sip lemonade on summer afternoons while bees hum in the old-fashioned flower garden.

The roomy parlor is decorated in English chintz. Lace and flowers and turn-of-the-century photographs fill the house, but it's not overly fussy and the furnishings aren't all antiques. "This is our home," says Barbara. "We enjoy sharing it and treat guests as new friends."

The hospitable innkeeper likes to serve breakfast by candlelight in the dining room or outside at white wrought-iron tables. You can also have breakfast in your room. Some of Barbara's dishes are crab and cheese delight, peach or cherry turnovers, fresh fruit with Grand Marnier sauce, and a sweet fruit spritzer. She provides appetizers in the afternoon and homemade chocolates in the evening. Each guest receives a complimentary bottle of locally produced wine.

All the guest rooms have stoves, refrigerators, and TVs with VCRs. In the Sequoia Room, on the ground floor, you can watch the birds bathe while you do the same; the clawfoot tub, screened from the bed, stands by a window overlooking the back lawn and birdbath. The bed has a lushly flowered comforter and ruffled pillows; bouquets of dried flowers hang on the wall above. By the door, a pair of high laced boots look as if they've just been left by their owner. Space for hanging clothes is limited. A basket of lemon drops, a painted globe lamp, delicate doilies, and windows overlooking the wraparound porch and white picket fence are touches that give the inn distinction and charm.

The Cedar Room, off the dining area, is a suite with a sitting area, a two-person Jacuzzi, and a sun room overlooking the back lawn and flowers. Champagne is served to guests who stay in the suite. Ponderosa, at the front of the house, is light and sunny in yellow. Sugar Pine is a two-room suite with a private balcony in the trees.

The Costas' love of gardening shows in their landscaped half-acre. Lilac and crape myrtle bloom in the front yard, elm trees line the fence, and baskets of blooms provide color on the verandah.

Nevada City

Red Castle Historic Lodgings

109 Prospect Street
Nevada City, CA 95959
916-265-5135
800-761-4766

An elaborate hillside
mansion overlooking a
gold-country town

Innkeepers: Mary Louise and Conley Weaver. **Accommodations:** 7 rooms (all with private bath). **Rates:** $95–$130 single, $100–$145 double, $110–$150 suite. **Included:** Full breakfast and afternoon tea. **Added:** 10% tax. **Payment:** Master-Card, Visa. **Children:** Young children not appropriate; additional charge for rollaway. **Pets:** Not allowed. **Smoking:** Not allowed indoors.

➤ **This red brick Gothic Revival mansion, dripping with gingerbread, has been a landmark in Nevada City for more than a century. Set high against Prospect Hill, it overlooks the little town that is a living museum of the gold rush era.**

This mansion was built in 1860 for Judge John Williams, his wife, Abigail, and their eleven children — four of their own and the rest taken in as orphans. Some say their nanny, a woman in gray, can still be glimpsed occasionally in the former children's quarters.

Even without a ghost, the Red Castle is full of reminders of the past. It became an inn in 1963, after a major restoration effort. The current owners continue to put careful attention into creating a world far from the late 20th century. Mary Louise has done extensive research and insists on authenticity in the period furnishings. "This is a mixture of what might have been and whimsy," she says.

The Weavers collect Renaissance Revival furniture. In the formal parlor, an Oriental carpet covers the floor and a prism chandelier flickers light on gold walls. A 19th-century burled walnut Jelliff settee, dark wicker armchairs, a pump organ with candle sconces, and vases of peacock feathers set the Victorian tone. Afternoon tea is served, with spiced tea, cakes, pies, and pastries, and sometimes hot cider or lemonade.

Breakfast is a buffet in the main foyer. The five-course meal, artfully prepared by the pastry chef, changes daily. You may help yourself to orange juice or berry flips, homemade breads, poached pears with crème anglaise, quiche, granola, and coffee or tea. You can take your tray to the parlor, your own room, out to the garden, or to the verandah set with white iron tables for two.

Each guest room has its own character. Forest View, a honeymoon favorite, is the only room on the lower floor, one flight down from the entrance. It has a crystal chandelier, complete with dimmer switch inside the lacy folds of the bed's canopy and a private entrance under old and gnarled grapevines. It also has private access to the balcony and garden.

The Rose Room has a pineapple four-poster, a brass and custard glass chandelier above the bed, red velvet curtains, and tall French doors opening out to the wraparound porch. It's a pretty room; the bathroom is small, however. The Garden Room, also on the main level, is big and bright and has a canopy bed and a sitting area. One of its striking features is an antique hall tree of carved walnut.

It's a steep climb to the upstairs rooms, but some guests prefer these for their charm and decor. There are two suites on the third floor, and the entire fourth floor, formerly the judge's study, is now a two-bedroom suite with a sitting room. In this private enclave, nooks under the eaves have quaint arched windows at knee level, and the private verandah has a treetop view of the town.

Gravel paths wind down the hill, under a grove of trees, from the house to the road below. From there it's a few yards to the highway overpass and the main historic part of town. Here you'll find quaint shops, fine restaurants, and gold rush memorabilia in a preserved remnant of the Old West.

Olympic Valley

Resort at Squaw Creek

P.O. Box 3333
400 Squaw Creek Road
Olympic Valley, CA 96146
530-583-6300
800-327-3353
Fax: 530-581-5407
www.squawcreek.com

> **An all-purpose resort in a dramatic mountain setting**

General manager: Ron Vuy. **Accommodations:** 403 rooms and suites. **Rates:** $250–$1,900, rates vary seasonally. **Added:** 10% tax, plus daily service fee. **Payment:** Major credit cards. **Children:** Under age 16 free in room with parents. **Pets:** Not allowed. **Smoking:** Nonsmoking rooms available.

➤ **Although it's surrounded by forest and mountains, the atmosphere here is more suburban country club than wilderness. In addition to a nine-story, glass-faced building with guest rooms, there are the main Plaza Building and a promenade of retail shops. The Plaza holds the fitness center, a 33,000-square-foot conference center, and five restaurants.**

In late 1990, this $100-million resort opened on 626 acres near Lake Tahoe. Year-round outdoor recreation is the main draw of the complex, which has a dramatic setting at the base of Squaw Valley's surrounding peaks.

In winter, skiers come for some of the nation's most challenging slopes. A triple lift links the resort with the Squaw Valley network of 33 lifts covering 4,000 acres of ski slopes. Groomed trails on the meadows and hillsides attract the cross-country skier. There's an ice skating pavilion, and you can take bell-jingling sleigh rides over the snow.

Golfers and tennis players take over in the summer. Squaw Creek has an 18-hole championship golf course designed by Robert Trent Jones, Jr. Its scenic, mountainous terrain includes wetlands, ponds, and a meandering creek. There are also putting greens, a practice range, and a pro shop.

Seven miles of walking and biking paths surround the golf course, while five miles of horseback riding trails continue through the meadows and into the hills. The all-purpose resort has three swimming pools and spas in an aquatic center with a waterfall and a sandy beach, and a fitness center featuring weight training equipment, an aerobics studio, massage rooms, and beauty salon. In the winter there's a locker room for storing skis; in the summer Chuckwagon dinners are held on the Sun Plaza Deck.

The casual Cascades Restaurant, serving regional American foods and elaborate buffets, showcases a stone hearth as an open cooking area. You can eat on the balcony here, overlooking Squaw Peak. Ristorante Montagna specializes in California-Italian cuisine, rotisserie cooking, and fresh-baked breads. Bullwackers Pub has steakhouse food, pool tables, and tabletop shuffleboard. Glissandi offers contemporary California cuisine from a seasonal menu in an elegant setting where diners linger over their meals. For gigantic deli sandwiches and fresh pastries, casual Sweet Potatoes, in the gift shop arcade, is the place to go.

All the guest rooms have views of the valley or the forest. They contain fine-quality contemporary wood furniture and have such amenities as dimmer lights, two TVs (with movies available), polished granite sinks, coffeemakers, robes, wet bars, hair dryers, irons, and ironing boards. Cribs are available upon request, and express video checkout is another convenience. Some suites have gas fireplaces and large bay windows that draw the mountain views right into the room. Two-story penthouses have 1-1/2 baths and a kitchen.

The resort is popular with business groups for its 33,000 square feet of meeting space and up-to-date audiovisual equipment.

Squaw Valley Lodge

P.O. Box 2364
Olympic Valley, CA 96146
530-583-5500
800-922-9970
Fax: 530-583-0326
www.squawvalleylodge.com

A contemporary hotel in a skier's paradise

General manager: Dan Tester. **Accommodations:** 178 rooms. **Rates:** $120–$725 (rates vary by season and number of people). **Added:** 10% tax. **Minimum stay:** 2 nights on weekends in ski season. **Payment:** Major credit cards. **Children:** Welcome. **Pets:** Not allowed. **Smoking:** Nonsmoking rooms available.

➤ **The Squaw Valley beginner's area may be unrivaled in the world because of its location — on top of the mountain instead of the bottom. It's accessible by cable car or gondola, so you don't have to ski down. If you're more adventurous and prefer a wilderness experience on undeveloped slopes, you'll find that vast areas have been left untouched.**

In 1960 the eighth Winter Olympics was held in Squaw Valley, a wide bowl at the foot of Squaw Peak, west of Lake Tahoe. Today you can step out the door of the lodge and ski the expert runs where Olympians raced. The 32 lifts lead to slopes with challenges for every level of skill.

Six mountain peaks, all overlooking Lake Tahoe, hold 4,000 acres of slopes. The highest is Squaw Peak, at 8,900 feet. The lodge itself is at an elevation of 6,200 feet.

Light gray with burgundy trim, the modern lodge is surrounded by pine trees and, in summer, lawns and flowers. The rooms and condominiums overlook a protected terrace and free-form outdoor swimming pool and whirlpool tub. Just off the terra cotta tile terrace is the fitness center, with a well-equipped weight room and three tile whirlpools. Potted palms and windows that view the snowy peaks make this one of the lodge's most attractive features.

The open lobby area has a touch of the Southwest in its decor. Desert colors, rough rocks as lamp bases, leather couches, framed weavings, and Indian paintings are strikingly offset by brightly colored banners.

The rooms are in three buildings connected by covered walkways — an important feature in this snowy terrain. Units are individually owned, but those in Buildings A and B are furnished in Scandinavian style, while those in C have a southwestern decor. They all have pegs, with copper troughs below, for hanging wet clothing. A typical room has a waist-high partition dividing the bed from the sitting area, generous cupboard and drawer space, and a compact kitchenette with a microwave oven, stove, dishwasher, and refrigerator. Skis may be kept in your room or stored near the rental shop. You can have minor tune-ups done at the shop as well.

The Squaw Valley resort area has the facilities you would expect in a major resort. There are restaurants and delis and malls with video stores, a beer garden, a doctor's office, and a ski school. More than 150 instructors staff the ski school, offering a wide variety of programs for all ages and abilities and several specialty clinics. Daycare for children is available. Squaw Valley makes an unusual guarantee: Register (for a nominal fee) as a beginner, intermediate, or expert, and if the wait for lifts at your skill level is longer than ten minutes, you receive a full refund and ski free the rest of the day. Another appealing feature is the first-timer's offer. Beginners are given free lift tickets, ski lessons, and equipment rentals for one day.

When the snows melt and wildflowers spring up in the meadows, the valley offers summer pleasures, such as hiking, bicycling, horseback riding, and fishing in mountain streams. You can swim and play tennis at the lodge.

Between mid-June and October you can take the cable car to the 8,200-foot level for a stunning panorama of the High Sierra and have lunch or Sunday brunch at Alexander's Bar & Grill on the mountaintop. Also at the top are a swimming lagoon and spa, mountain bike rentals, and year-round ice skating.

Sacramento

Amber House

1315 22nd Street
Sacramento, CA 95816
916-444-8085
800-755-6526
Fax: 916-552-6529
innkeeper@amberhouse.com
www.amberhouse.com

A luxurious bed-and-breakfast in a central location

Innkeepers: Mike and Jane Richardson. **Accommodations:** 14 rooms in 3 houses (all with private bath). **Rates:** $129–$149 single, $149–$269 double. **Included:** Full breakfast. **Added:** 12% tax. **Payment:** Major credit cards. **Children:** Well-behaved children welcome. **Pets:** Not allowed. **Smoking:** Not allowed.

➤ **If you're eating out, some good choices are Biba's for Italian food; Celestin's, with a Caribbean menu; and Harlow's, serving innovative California cuisine in a lively, art deco atmosphere.**

Only eight blocks from the State Capitol and the Convention Center, Amber House is popular with business travelers, offering both easy access to the city and a relaxing retreat. It's in a residential neighborhood where elm trees line the streets, shading turn-of-the-century homes.

The inn is actually three houses with very different styles. The main house is a 1905 Craftsman home in rich brown with the original woodwork intact. It has stained glass windows, antique furnishings, a fireplace in the living room, and a cozy little den with books, games, and puzzles. Guests are welcome to play the banjo that rests in the corner, curl up on the window seat with a book, peruse restaurant menus, and sip sherry in the evenings.

This house is called the Poet's Refuge, with each room named for a poet and containing examples of that poet's works. Lord Byron, on the first floor, has a queen-size canopy bed and a Jacuzzi for two in the bath. A rose motif dominates the decor in Longfellow, which has a luxurious bath in rose-colored marble and a Jacuzzi tub under a skylight. Chaucer, in tranquil green, is the smallest room. Emily Dickinson, with windows on three sides, was once a sun porch and is a good choice for sun worshippers. Its queen bed has a sumptuous ivory comforter with complementing shams, and there's also a fireplace and heart-shaped Jacuzzi set beneath skylights.

Next door is Artist's Retreat, a well-restored 1913 white stucco home with a Mediterranean look. The Monet room, with a garden atmosphere, lies behind beveled glass curtained in pastel fabric. For atmosphere, the stained glass window above a large square Jacuzzi can be lighted at night. Degas features ballet prints, a queen-size canopy bed draped in lace, and a double-size Jacuzzi tub. Renoir, a semi-suite in burgundy and gold, also has a Jacuzzi for two.

As lovely as the other rooms in Artist's Retreat are, Van Gogh has to be the favorite. The bedroom is pleasant, with yellow walls, chintz fabrics, and wicker furniture, but it's the bath that makes the room extra special. The solarium bath, with an exterior wall of glass and a glass ceiling overhead, is sun-filled and almost large enough to live in on its own. There's a wicker chaise and a heart-shaped tub for two. Even on a rainy day, it's a cheerful room — and hard to leave.

The third house, called Musician's Manor, was built in 1895. The Colonial Revival home has a garden courtyard, and each guest room here bears the name of a classical composer. Mozart is romantic with a fireplace, heart-shaped Jacuzzi, and French doors leading to a private balcony. Decorated in burgundy and deep forest green, Vivaldi has a Jacuzzi tub, gas log stove, and private balcony. Beethoven has a musical motif and luxurious green marble; while Brahms and Bach have antique bathtubs and soothing color schemes.

The innkeepers understand that visitors' hours vary — business travelers are early risers, while vacationers like to sleep in — so breakfast is served at the hour you request it, anytime from 7 A.M. to checkout, and can be brought to your room if you'd like. That's an example of the determination to meet guests' needs. "We'll accommodate in any way we can to make our guests' experience perfect," say the innkeepers. That includes supplying silver and china if you wish to have dinner delivered to your room by a restaurant. Or you can dine on the verandah, in the dining room, or in the garden courtyard if you prefer.

Other amenities and services the inn provides one might expect to find only at a first-rate hotel. There's nightly turndown service, televisions (all have VCRs and cable) are hidden in armoires, rooms have telephones with voice mail (some rooms even have an extra phone in the bath), clock-radios with cassette players, and baths have English herbal toiletries and robes. All are just further evidence of the quality of this professionally run inn.

The Delta King Hotel

1000 Front Street
Sacramento, CA 95814
916-444-5464
800-825-5464
Fax: 916-444-5314
www.delking.com

An old-fashioned stern-wheeler on the Sacramento River

General manager: Charlie Coyne. **Accommodations:** 43 staterooms, 1 suite. **Rates:** staterooms $109–$164 single or double, suite $400. **Included:** Expanded Continental breakfast. **Added:** 12% tax. **Payment:** Major credit cards. **Children:** Additional $10. **Pets:** Not allowed. **Smoking:** Not allowed.

➤   **Preserved as a 28-acre historic district, Old Sacramento includes the Sacramento History Center, a State Railroad Museum (the largest of its kind), an 1860s railroad station, and shops and restaurants. All are within easy walking distance of the gleaming white *Delta King*.**

If you yearn to return to the days when river travel reigned supreme, step aboard the historic *Delta King,* an authentic 1926 stern-wheel paddle steamer permanently moored along the waterfront of Old Sacramento.

The five-story, 285-foot paddlewheeler was built during the peak of the steam navigation period in the Sacramento Delta. Like its twin, the *Delta Queen* (now on the Mississippi River), the *King* once plied the Sacramento from the capital to San Francisco, offering overnight dinner and entertainment cruises that were especially popular during prohibition because drinking and gambling were allowed. During World War II the *King* served as barracks for the troops tending the submarine nets under the Golden Gate Bridge. Following the war the ship sank twice and fell into disrepair until it was finally restored in 1984. Although the riverboat was originally built for a then-staggering sum of $1 million, the meticulous restoration has cost more than $8 million.

Now in its original condition, the *King* gleams with polished brass fittings and the patina of wooden paneling, window trim, doors, and benches. A carpeted grand staircase sweeping from the Promenade Deck to the Observation Deck is back in place. At the top of the stairs is the mahogany-paneled Delta Lounge, featuring an oyster bar and decorated with stained glass scenes of the Sacramento River of yesteryear. The lower deck lounge, the Paddlewheel Saloon, offers dancing on weekends. The gigantic revolving paddlewheel can be seen through the glass-walled stern.

Even more spacious than the originals, the staterooms are furnished with brass beds and wicker furnishings. Some of the baths have clawfoot tubs and pull-chain toilets. Other features, such as air conditioning and tile showers, have been added. The Captain's Quarters is a posh bilevel suite with a queen-size bed, a wet bar, and a wheelhouse loft with an observation deck.

Morning fruit, juice, granola, yogurt, and pastries are served to overnight guests in the Pilothouse Restaurant. It also serves lunch, dinner, and a highly reputed Sunday brunch. The 43,745-square-foot vessel contains a theater showing musical revues and other productions. Weddings can be performed on board, and an outdoor plank landing is next to the boat for receptions. Valet parking is available.

The last of California's original steam paddlewheelers, the *Delta King* has been placed on the National Register of Historic Ships. It is the only lodging in old Sacramento.

Hartley House

700 22nd Street
Sacramento, CA 95816
916-447-7829
800-831-5806
Fax: 916-447-1820
randy@hartleyhouse.com
www.hartleyhouse.com

A bed-and-breakfast in a gracious Victorian home

Innkeeper: Randy Hartley. **Accommodations:** 5 rooms (all with private bath). **Rates:** $120–$150 single, $135–$180 double. **Included:** Full breakfast. **Added:** 12% tax. **Payment:** Major credit cards. **Children:** Not appropriate. **Pets:** Not allowed. **Smoking:** Not allowed.

➤ **Hartley House offers a Romance Package. It includes fresh flowers, chocolate truffles, and champagne or sparkling cider; you can keep the vase and wineglasses.**

This Colonial revival redwood home is in a residential area but is close to downtown, the capitol, and the Convention Center. Built by the innkeeper's great grandparents in 1906 in what was then Sacramento's first subdivision, the house remained in the family for many years, until a Mrs. Murphy purchased it and ran it as a boarding house. Randy Hartley bought it back from Mrs. Murphy in 1987 and has been operating it as a bed-and-breakfast ever since.

The home's character has been preserved inside and out. The original hitching posts still stand in front of the home, as do the elm trees planted by Randy's grandfather. Inside, the hardwood floors, dark woodwork, leaded and stained glass windows, and brass light fixtures converted from gas are also original. Some of the furniture, such as the English oak sideboard in the dining room, belonged to Randy's grandparents, and other antiques and artworks were carefully selected to match the period decor — although modern comforts have been added throughout the inn to suit today's tastes. Downstairs, the large living room has a four-window bay with a window seat and a fireplace. Couches provide comfortable seating for a game of chess or lounging by the fire on a chilly night.

The rooms have English place names. Brighton, once a sun porch, is the least formal and has a light and sunny aspect with twelve windows in three walls. Dover, the largest room, has an antique curved brass bed and a marble sink and clawfoot tub in the bath. Canterbury, in pale green, has a mirrored armoire that the innkeeper's grandparents had made in London. The other rooms are Southampton and Stratford.

During the week most guests are business travelers who appreciate rooms with private baths, phones, voice mail, cable TV, clock radios, and air conditioning, as well as fax and copy facilities. For a small daily fee, guests can use the health club down the street, and inn guests receive discounts at a number of area restaurants. Massages are available by appointment.

All guests like the lavish breakfasts, which are cooked-to-order entrées from the twenty-item menu such as blueberry pancakes, quiche, blintzes, and Belgian waffles served with fruit, muffins, juice, and house blend coffees in the dining room or outside in the pleasant walled courtyard. Cookies are baked daily, and iced tea is always available in the refrigerator.

The Sterling Hotel

1300 H Street
Sacramento, CA 95814
916-448-1300
800-365-7660
Fax: 916-448-8066
www.sleepingsacramento.com

A small and sophisticated historic hotel

Innkeeper: Bill McFerson. **Accommodations:** 13 rooms, 3 suites. **Rates:** $159–$360. **Included:** Continental breakfast. **Added:** 12% tax. **Payment:** Major credit cards. **Children:** Welcome. **Pets:** Not allowed. **Smoking:** Not allowed.

➤ **Among Sacramento's attractions are the lovely tree-shaded capitol grounds and the oldest public art museum in the west, Crocker Art Museum. Old Sacramento has a railroad museum, a reconstruction of Sutter's Fort, and more than 250 shops and restaurants.**

The Sterling is a small luxury hotel in central Sacramento. Its amenities and convenient downtown location — near the capitol, Convention Center, and county courthouse — make it a favorite of business and government travelers, while its elegance and style draw discriminating vacationers.

The three-story, century-old Victorian structure was renovated in 1987 to remove all vestiges of the apartment building it had been for fifty years. Now it has a gracious facade with a generous porch entry, a lobby with a marble floor, and a lounge where guests enjoy morning coffee. Oriental simplicity is emphasized by Japanese paintings and Chinese rugs. More ornate are the lobby mirror, framed in painted birds and flowers, and the filigreed brass chandelier hanging from the open loft.

There are no ruffles or fringes in this contemporary hotel, but touches of its origins may be seen in the molding detail, lace curtains, and paintings by Old Masters. The spacious guest rooms, on all three floors, have four-poster, canopy, or sleigh beds and Queen Anne–style furniture. The pink marble baths contain pedestal sinks with gleaming brass taps and oversize whirlpool tubs and showers enclosed by brass and glass.

On the hotel's lower level is an exquisite little restaurant, Chanterelle. It seats only forty people in three glass-partitioned rooms of restrained decor enlivened by colorful modern art prints on the walls. The Continental cuisine is expensive but is considered some of the best in Sacramento. Fresh regional ingredients are used with traditional French techniques and California creativity. A specialty is veal with chanterelle mushrooms. There's an excellent champagne brunch on Sundays, and the restaurant provides full room service to the guest rooms until 9 pm.

Next door is the Glass Garden, a conservatory imported from England. The 40-foot-long structure, with a glass roof in three graceful tiers, is used for receptions, parties, dances, and weddings. At press time plans were in the works to add a ballroom and five additional guest rooms.

Vizcaya

2019 21st Street
Sacramento, CA 95818
916-455-5243
800-456-2019
Fax: 916-455-6102

An elegant home with antiques and contemporary comforts

Innkeeper: Bill McFerson. **Accommodations:** 7 rooms, 2 suites (all with private bath). **Rates:** $129–$229. **Included:** Full breakfast. **Added:** 12% tax. **Payment:** Major credit cards. **Children:** Welcome. **Pets:** Not allowed. **Smoking:** Not allowed indoors.

➤ **This bed-and-breakfast inn was once a private mansion owned by Philip Driver, a prominent attorney in the late 1800s. The mansion remained in the Driver family until 1977 and now is owned by the Kanns, who are also part-owners of the luxurious Sterling Hotel.**

Formerly called the Driver Mansion Inn, Vizcaya is one of the classiest bed-and-breakfasts you'll encounter. Calico and teddy bears would definitely be out of place here. Stately antiques, thick carpeting, and fine art set the theme.

Pink, white, and red roses flank the pillared porch of the big house, which is set on a slope above a busy street where you may park; there are a few more parking spaces in back. Traditional furniture faces a white brick fireplace in the parlor, where beverages are available, by request, in the afternoons.

Breakfast is served at glass-topped tables in the dining room (or in your room, for a $15 fee). Fresh fruit, juice, and excellent coffee are prepared along with Belgian waffles, French toast, quiche, or other main dishes.

The six guest rooms in the main house all have antiques or reproductions, desks, private phones, TV, and shirred white curtains at wide, leaded glass windows. The baths are in modern white tile with glass and brass showers; most have Jacuzzis. The Garden Suite has a large living room and an iron and brass bed in the bedroom. Room 2 has a four-poster bed, a sofa, and an oversized rolltop desk with a brass lamp fit for an executive. Room 4 is smaller and has a sleigh bed, but it also has a large marble bath with a two-person Jacuzzi and rose-colored stained glass windows.

The spacious third-floor Penthouse Suite has a contemporary look, with a black marble dining table that seats eight, a black marble coffee table, two comfortable sofas covered in salmon sateen, a writing desk, and a bed in a dormer window alcove in the living room. The bedroom has an iron and brass bed, a walk-in closet, and a small balcony. The suite also features a giant whirlpool tub surrounded by black marble.

The Carriage House, in a garden of brick walks edged with impatiens and shaded by oak, persimmon, and crape myrtle trees, has three rooms. One is furnished in white wicker and has a woodburning stove; another has an Oriental feel.

The *Sacramento Bee* is supplied, and the innkeeper will recommend restaurants and suggest sightseeing attractions if requested. With intuitive tact, she knows when to leave people alone. "I try to be available but not hover," she says. "We offer hotel-type accommodations, but with a warmer, more personal atmosphere."

Vizcaya now offers space in an attractive adjacent pavilion fronted by gardens and a fountain for banquets and receptions for up to 400 people.

South Lake Tahoe

Lakeland Village Resort

3535 Lake Tahoe Boulevard
South Lake Tahoe, CA 96156
530-544-1685
800-822-5969
Fax: 530-541-6278
lakeland@sierra.net
www.lakeland-village.com

> **A lakeside resort for year-round recreation**

General manager: Jerry Bindel. **Accommodations:** 210 units. **Rates:** $90–$220 for lodge rooms, $145–$750 for townhouses. **Added:** 10% tax. **Minimum stay:** 2–4 nights in some rooms. **Payment:** Major credit cards. **Children:** Welcome. **Pets:** Not allowed. **Smoking:** Allowed.

➤ **With up to 500 inches of snow and 300 days of sunshine yearly, Tahoe's slopes are famous for magnificent scenery and challenging skiing. Heavenly Valley has a network of lifts to Tahoe's highest skiing, with a top elevation of 10,100 feet and a vertical drop of 3,600 feet. About half the ski area is devoted to intermediate slopes, with the other half divided between beginner and advanced runs.**

The resort complex of Lakeland Village is on the southern shore of Lake Tahoe, facing 1,000 feet of private sandy beach. Under tall pine trees, its 19 acres contain two heated swimming pools, two tennis courts, saunas, a spa, a lakeside clubhouse, a children's playground and wading pool, and a boat dock.

Despite its proximity to Highway 50, location is the resort's major attraction. It borders the sapphire blue lake, Heavenly Valley ski area is a mile and a half away (a free shuttle is available), and the casinos of Nevada are 1 mile to the northeast.

More than twenty other ski areas surround the lake, many of them offering shuttle service. You can also ferry to the north shore on the *Tahoe Queen* paddlewheeler. Lakeland Village rents skis and equipment but does not offer ski storage; several rooms have porches that may be used for storage.

During the summer you can rent paddleboats, canoes, or kayaks, play golf at five courses in the area, or throw a private party at the clubhouse. Tennis lessons are available and other recreation includes bicycling, hiking the back country, fishing, windsurfing, rafting, and horseback riding.

The rooms in the three-story lodge range from studios with Murphy beds to one-bedroom suites; there are also privately owned three-story townhouses, which go up to four bedrooms and three baths. All the rooms have cable TV with HBO, equipped kitchens, fireplaces, and phones.

The townhouses, especially those on the waterfront, are recommended over the lodge rooms. Not only do they have enviable views and easy access to the beach, they're larger and better maintained. They are also farther from the highway. The furnishings in the lodge rooms are comfortable and functional, but they fall short of top resort standards.

A typical four-bedroom lakefront townhouse will have a bedroom with two beds and a vaulted ceiling that soars above two lofts, one with two bedrooms and the highest with windows overlooking the lake. Glass doors slide open to a deck on the beach. Plenty of closet space, an entryway where wet clothing can be hung to dry, and personal touches in books and artwork make this a homelike, all-purpose family choice.

There's a coin-operated laundry on the property, and parking is free.

Sutter Creek

The Foxes Bed and Breakfast Inn

P.O. Box 159
77 Main Street
Sutter Creek, CA 95685
209-267-5882
800-987-3344
Fax: 209-267-0712
foxes@cdepot.net
www.foxesinn.com

A luxurious bed-and-breakfast in the gold country

Innkeepers: Pete and Min Fox. **Accommodations:** 7 rooms (all with private bath). **Rates:** $120–$195. **Included:** Full breakfast. **Added:** 7.25% tax. **Minimum stay:** 2 nights on weekends when Saturday is included. **Payment:** Discover,

MasterCard, and Visa. **Children:** Maximum of 2 persons per room. **Pets:** Not allowed. **Smoking:** Not allowed indoors.

➤ **The innkeepers will direct you on sightseeing expeditions and make restaurant recommendations. Pick up a walking tour map of Sutter Creek and you'll learn some history and discover more of the town's charm as you stroll.**

Since the day the Foxes opened their gold country bed-and-breakfast in 1980 with a single guest room, the inn has been praised as one of the best in California. Gracious hosts with a sure sense of visitors' needs, the innkeepers go out of their way to provide every comfort. And they make it seem easy, a rare skill in this demanding business.

Their 1857 home is in the center of Sutter Creek, a pretty little town surrounded by hills studded with oak and pine trees. The town and the stream that runs through it were named for John Sutter, whose sawmill on the American River caught the sparkle of gold in 1848 and set off the great gold rush. Several mines operated in Sutter Creek, but all have long since closed.

Pete and Min Fox moved to Sutter Creek from southern California. They became antiques dealers, then opened their home as a B&B, and later expanded into the Carriage House in back. Now their inn is so well known for its consistent high quality, early reservations are a must.

Traffic noise from Highway 49 recedes when you enter the house, as the melodic strains of Chopin flood the foyer and parlor. Doors with etched glass panes lead to a parlor furnished with antiques. The windows overlook the front porch, its columns entwined with wisteria, and a yard filled with flowers and ferns.

You can have breakfast in the garden, but it's usually brought to your room on a silver tray, with items you selected the night before: fresh juice, eggs as you like them or the house specialty of cream-poached eggs on an English muffin, fruit, and muffins and jam.

The guest rooms are air conditioned. The Honeymoon Suite, on the ground floor in the main house, is spacious and has a private entrance. Blue velvet wingback chairs face a brick fireplace, the bed has a partial canopy, the armoire has an ornate door, and there's an unusual corner cupboard. A clawfoot tub and pull chain toilet add a nostalgic touch to the bath. The Hideaway has a separate living room with a small dining table for two and a fireplace. In the bedroom there's a half-canopy bed topped with a floral coverlet and draped in matching curtains.

The Victorian Suite, upstairs, was the Foxes' first bed-and-breakfast room. It has a handsome, nine-foot-long headboard on the bed and a matching dresser. The large bathroom has an old-fashioned tub with a separate shower. The Anniversary Room features a carved headboard and a ten-foot mirrored armoire under a cathedral ceiling.

All three rooms in the Carriage House have private entrances and cable TV hidden behind armoire doors. The Blue Room, decorated in powder blue, naturally, has an extra-large bath and a carved bedstead with a partial canopy. The bay window in the Garden Room overlooks the garden, while Fox Den is cozy with a library, wood-burning fireplace, and foxes everywhere. There are foxes dressed in red coats, foxes dressed in plaid, foxes on the wall, and even the wallpaper has a fox motif trim.

Among the amenities the Foxes provide are clock radios, tape decks and tapes of restful music, the *Sacramento Bee* at your doorstep in the morning, plenty of storage space for clothes, a safe for valuables, covered parking, and elegant breakfast settings with wineglasses and linen napkins. There's only one drawback here: Highway 49 runs through the middle of town, its cars and rumbling trucks more than a mild annoyance. The Foxes have installed storm windows, and some residents are hoping for a bypass, which would rescue Sutter Creek's serenity.

The Grey Gables Inn

P.O. Box 1687
161 Hanford Street
Sutter Creek, CA 95685
209-267-1039
800-GREY-GABLES
Fax: 209-267-0998
reservations@greygables.com
www.greygables.com

> A taste of English country
> in the heart of California's
> gold country

Innkeepers: Roger and Sue Garlick. **Accommodations:** 8 rooms. **Rates:** $95–$155. **Included:** Full breakfast, afternoon tea, and evening refreshments. **Added:** 7.25% tax. **Minimum stay:** 2 nights if Saturday is included. **Payment:** MasterCard, Visa. **Children:** $20 additional; not appropriate for children under 12. **Pets:** Not allowed. **Smoking:** Not allowed.

> ➤ **In keeping with the hosts' background, cakes and scones are served in the afternoon as part of a traditional English tea.**

It is easy to spot this attractive, many-gabled home while passing through the 19th-century mining town of Sutter Creek. If the inn — with a rose trellis, fountain, and benches sitting amid a glorious cottage garden abloom with columbine, foxgloves, pansies, California poppies, and coral bells — looks more like an English country manor than the Catholic school it once was, it is due to the innkeepers' heritage and vision.

Originally from Gloucestershire, England, Sue and Roger Garlick came to this country when Roger's work in computers brought him to California. Sue had always dreamed of opening an inn, and in 1992 the Garlicks purchased this property on the edge of Sutter Creek. It had originally been built as a school back in the 1870s by Bishop Patrick Manogue. The Garlicks then spent nearly two years extensively renovating and remodeling, resulting in the lovely Victorian-style structure guests see today.

Guests are welcomed in a formal parlor decorated with plush velvet furniture, English floral drapes, and an antique map of Gloucestershire.

A full breakfast, including chicken-mushroom or blackberry crêpes, poached pears, or a quiche, is served on fine china and crisp linens in the adjacent dining room, or in your guest room if you prefer.

The immaculate guest rooms were designed for comfort and have been decorated with polish and taste. Bearing the names of famous English poets, each has a private bath, gas fireplace, ceiling fan, clock radio, air conditioning, and an armoire for hanging clothes. In lavenders, mints, and creams, Browning has a country feel, with pine furnishings, lace curtains, and a clawfoot tub. Byron has a French bed, rich wood armoire, and a marble fireplace. In Wordsworth, floral wreaths adorn the walls and bay windows bring in lots of light. There's also an antique hand-painted Singer sewing machine, and a wedding dress hangs on a dressmaker's dummy in the corner.

Shelley, in blacks, tans, and plums, is more masculine than the others and is wheelchair accessible. Keats, a personal favorite, is a pretty room overlooking a portion of the garden; it has an eye-catching English dogwood print comforter and matching pillow shams. Brontë has a king-size bed and a full sofa, and Tennyson is decorated in Laura Ashley fabrics. With a dragon motif armoire, a collection of Oriental plates, and fringed satin lamps, the Victorian Suite has an Eastern feel. Alone on the top floor, it is also the most secluded room.

Sutter Creek Inn

P.O. Box 385
75 Main Street
Sutter Creek, CA 95685
209-267-5606
Fax: 209-267-9287
www.suttercreekinn.com

A gold-country bed-and-breakfast of character and charm

Innkeeper: Jane Way. **Accommodations:** 15 rooms and 2 suites (all with private bath). **Rates:** $65–$135 single or double; suites $155–$175. **Included:** Full breakfast and afternoon refreshments. **Minimum stay:** 2 nights on weekends.

Payment: MasterCard, Visa. **Children:** Over age 10 welcome, under age 15 not encouraged on weekends. **Pets:** Not allowed. **Smoking:** Allowed outdoors only.

➤ **The Amador County Museum, Chaw Se Indian Grinding Rock State Historic Park, and the Kennedy Tailing Wheels are among the historic sights. You'll find more active recreation at Mace Meadows Golf Course, Kirkwood ski area, and on Mokelumne River and Amador and Camanche lakes.**

This historic home with a breezy, friendly atmosphere was one of the first bed-and-breakfasts in California. Jane Way fell in love with the place while touring the gold country with her children in the mid-1960s. Since then she has continued to expand the inn; it's now a sizable complex that has retained its homey character.

The Greek Revival structure, built in 1859, stands on Sutter Creek's main street, Highway 49 (often heavy with traffic), behind attractive lawns and gardens. Some guest rooms are in the main house; others are tucked away in outbuildings by the grape arbor and terrace.

Visitors are drawn irresistibly to the large living room, for Jane has filled it with comfortable couches and chairs, a spinet, games, magazines, a chess table set up for play, and many of her hundreds of books. A corner cabinet holds antique china and a grandfather clock stands in dignity against one wall, faithfully sounding the Westminster chimes.

All the guest rooms have electric blankets and air conditioners. Nine rooms contain fireplaces, and some have swinging beds (which can be stabilized if you don't like the notion of gently swaying all night long). There are three rooms in the main house.

The Library Room has lots of books in addition to two beds (one queen and one single), and a small deck. The East Room is cheerful in sunny yellow with a cozy alcove painted in stenciled designs. (Traffic noise can be a problem in this room. Fortunately a sound conditioner emits the soothing murmur of rain and surf to help block any less welcome sounds.) The West Room has windows under the eaves. Its yellow bath, bright with flowers and stripes, is original. This was the first house in Sutter Creek to have an indoor bathroom.

The Garden Cottage, behind the grape arbor, is fronted by a porch with wicker furniture; its interior is dark in natural woods. The Patio has a swinging bed, window seat, and fully stocked bookshelves. The Lower Wash House has lots of windows and a fireplace; and Lindsay's Room, with twin beds, a fireplace, and a high, pitched roof, feels like a private cottage. The Miner's Cabin, Toolshed, and Cellar Room each have a fireplace.

The Carriage House is the most expensive accommodation. An old Chinese rug with all of the spiritual leaders of China represented hangs over the brick fireplace, and there's a queen-size bed with a view of the tub for two. One of the most romantic choices is the Loft, reached by climbing outside stairs past green clematis vines winding up the branches of a tall Chinese elm. It has a four-poster bed, a vaulted beamed ceiling, and high windows above the gardens.

The menu for the country breakfast varies, but typical of Jane's morning choices are corned beef hash with poached eggs, English muffins topped with eggs, cheese sauce, and capers; and fresh fruit picked from the inn's own trees. Hot cider or cold lemonade is set out for guests along with homemade cookies each afternoon.

The personable innkeeper has a wide range of interests, most of them reflected in the book titles and items displayed in her inn. Handwriting analysis, reflexology, and therapeutic massage are available by appointment. Psychic experiences are often topics of conversation, for Jane also enjoys visiting with guests as time allows. She and her assistants are happy to give visitors suggestions for day trips and points of interest. Sutter Creek's shops and restaurants are just steps from the inn's front door.

Truckee

Northstar at Tahoe

P.O. Box 2499
Truckee, CA 95734
916-562-1010
800-GO-NORTH
Fax: 916-562-2215

A family resort near Lake Tahoe

General manager: Tim Silva. **Accommodations:** Approximately 260 units. **Rates:** $99–$609 for 1–10 people (rates cover a range of accommodations from standard hotel rooms to up to 5-bedroom homes and are priced by unit rather than level of occupancy). **Minimum stay:** 2 nights. **Payment:** Major credit cards. **Children:** Welcome. **Pets:** Not allowed. **Smoking:** Nonsmoking rooms available.

➤ **While the kids are busy, their parents are skiing on Mount Pluto and Lookout Mountain, which have 2,200 vertical feet of ski slopes. Lifts include a high-speed gondola, four express quad chairs, three triple chairs, and two double chairs.**

Skiing and snow play draw crowds to Northstar in winter, while summer's pleasures on the 2,500-acre resort six miles from Lake Tahoe include hiking, mountain biking, fishing, swimming in the pool, working out in the gym, horseback riding, tennis, and golf; or just relaxing with a massage, sauna, or in one of three hot tubs.

The resort is ideal for family vacations because there's such a wide variety of recreation. Those who are too young for the ski slopes or tennis courts are happily ensconced in the Minors' Camp, a childcare program that accepts children ages 2 to 6. Every day they learn songs, listen to stories, paint, take walks, and are given snacks and a hot lunch. If they're in the Ski Cubs program (age 3 and older), they receive a skiing lesson, too. In the summer, an experienced staff gives children ages 2 to 10 tennis and swimming lessons and takes them horseback riding. There's also arts and crafts, a climbing wall, and a junior rope course.

With the expansion of downhill skiing facilities, Northstar has opened the Summit Deck & Grille at the top of Mount Pluto. The restaurant offers Mexican food, barbeque, and microbrewery beers.

Cross-country and telemark skiing lessons are available in the winter. There are 65 kilometers of groomed trails near the lodge. Golf is the big draw in summer, and golf packages offer a good value. The 18-hole, par-72 course has water hazards on 14 holes, a driving range, a resident pro, and a well-equipped pro shop. Tennis players appreciate the 2- and 5-day tennis camps. There are 10 courts.

Northstar Village has several restaurants, bars, and shops. Timbercreek serves dinner in summer and three meals a day in winter. The first floor of the Village Building holds a sport shop in winter that is a conference room in summer; its second and third floors have hotel rooms and loft suites.

The rest of Northstar's lodgings are in five clusters of privately owned condominiums scattered across the wooded hills. Each has a fireplace (firewood is provided), cable television, VCR, covered deck, and a kitchen with microwave oven. A typical two-bedroom, two-bath condo is a split-level unit with a living room, kitchen, and bath on the upper level and two bedrooms and a laundry room downstairs.

The condos in the Indian Hills cluster are farthest from the village, high on a hill with a view of the surrounding mountains and the valley below. A free shuttle bus takes guests back and forth in winter; in summer, buses come upon request.

Winter is busier than summer at Northstar, but that is likely to change as the resort continues to entice visitors with special packages and a wide array of activities and events.

The Truckee Hotel

10007 Bridge Street
P.O. Box 884
Truckee, CA 96161
530-587-4444
800-659-6921
Fax: 530-587-1599
thetruckeehotel@sierra.net
www.thetruckeehotel.com

A restored historic hotel

Owners: Jeffrey and Karen Winter. **Accommodations:** 37 rooms. **Rates:** $85–$125 for rooms with shared baths, $115–$125 for rooms with private baths. **Included:** Continental breakfast. **Added:** 10% tax. **Payment:** Major credit cards. **Children:** Age 5 and under are free. **Pets:** Not allowed. **Smoking:** Not allowed.

➤ **One of Truckee's most famous visitors was Charlie Chaplin, who came to the area to film his movie *The Gold Rush*.**

The town of Truckee, named for a Paiute Indian chief, began as a stagecoach stop in the 1860s. Yet, unlike many towns in Sierra country, Truckee's early growth was due more to the expansion of the transcontinental railroad than to prospecting. Truckee became a lumber town, providing materials for the railroad's construction.

Nearby lakes and cold winters also made Truckee a center for ice production in the days before refrigeration, while the town's proximity to beautiful Lake Tahoe and surrounding mountain terrain brought tourists as early as the turn of the century.

The Truckee Hotel's history mirrors that of the town itself. Built in 1868, the hotel, then known as the American Hotel, offered accommodations to lodgers traveling along the stagecoach route. Then it became home to laborers working on the railroad and in the ice and timber industries. Today the hotel is frequented mainly by tourists who come to the area for outdoor recreation such as skiing, boating, fishing, hiking, or bicycling.

The current owners bought the Truckee Hotel in the early 1990s and immediately began restoring it. Their efforts won them an award for historic preservation and resulted in a comfortable lodging that retains its historic flavor. Although the 37 guest rooms are not overly luxurious, they are pleasantly furnished. Each is individually decorated and most have a Victorian theme, with lace curtains, floral comforters, and furniture original to the hotel. Eight rooms have private baths with clawfoot tubs; the rest share hall baths. Some rooms have television and all have coffeemakers. The Whitney Room on the second floor has a television and stereo that all guests are welcome to use.

In the afternoons guests relax over tea that is set out in the cozy common living room in front of a gas fireplace and green marble tile hearth. A Continental breakfast of muffins, bagels, hot cereal, fresh fruit, teas, and juices is served in the adjoining dining area. The Passage Restaurant adjacent to the hotel lobby serves more substantial meals, including grilled swordfish with mango salsa and black bean chili and a focaccia sandwich with grilled eggplant, roasted red peppers, and mozzarella cheese in a tomato-garlic sauce. The restaurant also boasts a fine wine list and home-baked desserts such as mixed berry cobbler and triple chocolate mousse cake. For day-trippers, picnic lunches and fresh pastries can be purchased from the Passage Way.

To recapture some of the spirit of the Old West, many guests follow Truckee's walking tour and visit sites along the Emigrant Trail. Others prefer to window-shop or head to the ski slopes; there are multiple ski areas within a half hour of Truckee. The hotel provides a locker room for ski equipment.

Wawona

Wawona Hotel

Yosemite National Park, CA 95389
Reservations: Yosemite Reservations
5410 East Home Street
Fresno, CA 93727
559-252-4848
Fax: 559-456-0542
www.yosemitepark.com

A gracious, traditional lodge in south Yosemite

Manager: A. Gonzalez. **Accommodations:** 104 rooms (48 with private bath). **Rates:** $94 for shared bath, $120.75 for private bath in high season. **Added:** 7.25% tax. **Payment:** MasterCard, Visa. **Children:** Under 12 free in room with parents. **Pets:** Not allowed. **Smoking:** Allowed in some rooms. Nonsmoking rooms available. **Open:** Year-round.

➤ **The famed Mariposa Grove is south of Wawona, just inside the southernmost park entrance. Yosemite's largest tree grows here, soaring skyward in a community of giant sequoias. Trams operate daily, and a trail winds through the awesome grove.**

Wawona, in the southwestern corner of a park that is one of the world's great natural wonders, resembles a fine plantation home in the South. The main hotel has a big verandah with white columns and wicker furniture overlooking an expanse of lawn and a waterlily pond. The pace is slower here, compared to the midsummer rush in Yosemite Valley.

Some wilderness lodges feature rough logs and antler trophies, but not this one. Here the lobby is white and pink, with a flowered ceiling border and carpeting in teal and burgundy. Vintage furniture provides seating near the two stone fireplaces.

On one side of the lobby is a restaurant, a large white room with two walls of high windows framing views of the trees. Dinners and buffet lunches feature American fare — steak, chicken, and roast beef. At the opposite end of the lobby is a small lounge with high ceilings, round marble tables, and a grand piano. The tall windows still have the original wavy glass put in more than a century ago, when Henry Washburn and John Bruce opened the hotel. It was owned by the Washburn family until 1932. Now Wawona, like the rest of Yosemite's lodgings, is run by the Yosemite Concession Services Corporation.

All the rooms at Wawona are reserved early, often as far as a year in advance. Upstairs in the main building are 26 guest rooms; a few have private baths but most share four men's and four women's baths. Modern and well maintained, they have showers and are tiled in white with tan, green, and pink accents. Typical of the small, comfortable accommodations is Room 202, a tidy space with a white iron bed, flowered wallpaper, pegs (but no closet), and a stack of towels on the dresser. The largest rooms are 213 and 220, good choices for a family.

Other rooms are in five side buildings with one or two stories. The oldest is Clark Cottage, which dates from 1876. Cool and green under a cloak of vines, it has eight boxy rooms with windows to the wraparound porch.

The Annex is ideal for golfers. Encircled by porches, it stands on the edge of a 9-hole golf course and has a golf shop on the lower level. There's a large lounge, appropriately called the Sun Room for the light that floods through glass doors on three sides of the room.

On the property there are tennis courts, a pool, a putting green, and riding stables. Near the stables is the Pioneer Yosemite History Center, a collection of historic buildings and horse-drawn wagons. A self-guided trail and tours led by a ranger describe the people and events that led to the establishment of the park.

You can relive the days of stage travel in Yosemite with a 10-minute stage ride and hear legends and stories at evening campfire talks given regularly by park rangers.

Yosemite

The Ahwahnee

Yosemite National Park, CA 95389
Reservations: Yosemite Reservations
5410 East Home Street
Fresno, CA 93727
209-252-4848
Fax: 209-372-1463
www.yosemitepark.com

| **A grand lodge in a glorious natural setting** |

Manager: Val B. Hardcastle. **Accommodations:** 123 rooms, 4 suites. **Rates:** $265.50–$280 single or double; suites $500–$800. **Added:** 10% tax. **Payment:** Major credit cards. **Children:** Under 12 free in room with parents. **Pets:** Not allowed. **Smoking:** Not allowed in restaurants or public areas; nonsmoking guest rooms are available.

➤   **Everything in the six-story hotel is on a grand scale. Fireplaces are big enough to stand in, windows are 24 feet high, the restaurant is 130 feet long and has a 34-foot ceiling supported by pillars of sugar pine. Yet despite the size, it's not intimidating — just impressive.**

The Ahwahnee, faced with granite and concrete stained to resemble redwood, fits comfortably into its magnificent surroundings — the great granite cliffs, roaring waterfalls, and majestic forests of Yosemite Valley. The hotel stands among pine and cedar trees on the valley floor, with the Royal Arches soaring 2,000 feet behind it.

Since it opened in 1927, celebrities and unknowns alike have adored the Ahwahnee. Winston Churchill, John F. Kennedy, Will Rogers, Greta Garbo, Walt Disney, and Lucille Ball slept under its imposing roof, as have hosts of others, including Queen Elizabeth and the Duke of Edinburgh.

Dinner at the Ahwahnee is an unforgettable experience. Two walls of floor-to-ceiling windows look over the grassy meadows to Glacier Point and the long ribbon of Yosemite Falls. Tables extend the length of the immense room and each holds a single tall candle. Overhead, dozens of candles are suspended from pine beams in wrought-iron holders. The atmosphere is at once festive and formal, contrasting wilderness and urbanity in a single setting. Jackets and ties are requested, but no longer required. A pianist performs during dinner.

Several special events are offered during the year. The oldest is the Bracebridge Dinner, a celebration based on Washington Irving's story of a Yorkshire Christmas. The feast and theatrical production are now so in demand that five dinners are held, so that 1,800 of the 60,000 applicants can attend. They're chosen by lottery.

A Native American motif enlivens the hotel's heavy beams and sturdy furniture. Some of the most interesting designs are on the ceiling of the Great Lounge.

The Indian theme continues in the geometric fabric patterns in the guest rooms. The rooms are more elegant than rustic, with amenities such as clock radios, phones, robes, and hairdryers. Many have king-size beds and all have private baths. Most suites have their own fireplace. The highlight of the Presidential Suite is its open balcony, from which you have a spectacular view up and down the valley. Other rooms are in cottages in the woods, reached via lighted paths. Each has a slate front porch, chunky furniture, dark woodwork, and deep windows.

Amenities at the Ahwahnee include afternoon tea and cookies, evening demitasse, nightly turndown, and morning coffee with daily newspapers. There's also a gift shop selling Indian baskets, weavings, and books on Yosemite. There is a swimming pool, bicycles can be rented, and guided tours arranged. A 26-mile, 2-hour tour by bus or tram car across the valley floor will introduce you to the history, geology, and plant and animal life that abounds here.

There are times when the most abundant life appears to be human, as three million visitors a year stream through the park. That's when you may want to explore the 750 miles of trails in Yosemite's backcountry. But whether you're alone at the top of a waterfall or basking in the sun in the Ahwahnee's solarium, you're sure to feel the power of this magnificent natural wonder.

Southern California

Beverly Hills
Hollywood
Pasadena
Lake Arrowhead
Big Bear Lake

Santa Monica
Los Angeles
10

Anaheim
15
Idyllwild

Seal Beach
Long Beach
Balboa
Newport Beach
Laguna Beach
Temecula

Dana Point
Avalon

Carlsbad
Vista

Rancho Santa Fe
Del Mar
Rancho Bernardo
Julian

La Jolla
8

Coronado
San Diego

Bahme '99

Anaheim
Disneyland Hotel, 388
Avalon
Zane Grey Pueblo Hotel, 389
Balboa
Balboa Inn, 391
Beverly Hills
The Peninsula Beverly Hills, 392
The Regent Beverly Wilshire, 394
Big Bear Lake
Windy Point Inn on Big Bear Lake, 396
Carlsbad
La Costa Resort and Spa, 398
Pelican Cove Inn, 399
Coronado
Coronado Victorian House, 401
Hotel Del Coronado, 403
Loews Coronado Bay Resort, 405
Dana Point
Blue Lantern Inn, 407
Laguna Cliffs Marriott Resort, 409
The Ritz-Carlton Laguna Niguel, 410
Del Mar
L'Auberge Del Mar, 412
Hollywood
Sunset Marquis Hotel and Villas, 414
Idyllwild
Strawberry Creek Inn, 415
Julian
Julian Hotel, 417
Shadow Mountain Ranch, 419
La Jolla
La Jolla Beach & Tennis Club, 421
La Valencia Hotel, 422
Prospect Park Inn, 424
Laguna Beach
Surf & Sand Hotel, 425
Lake Arrowhead
Château du Lac, 426

Long Beach
Hotel Queen Mary, 428
Los Angeles
The Argyle, 430
Hotel Bel-Air, 432
Hotel Sofitel, 434
The New Otani Hotel & Garden, 435
The Regal Biltmore Hotel, 437
Wyndham Checkers Hotel, 438
Newport Beach
Doryman's Inn, 440
Pasadena
The Ritz-Carlton Huntington Hotel
and Spa, 441
Rancho Bernardo
Rancho Bernardo Inn, 443
Rancho Santa Fe
The Inn at Rancho Santa Fe, 445
Rancho Valencia, 447
San Diego
The Cottage, 448
Horton Grand Hotel, 450
U.S. Grant Hotel, 452
The Westgate Hotel, 453
The Wyndham Emerald Plaza, 454
Santa Monica
Hotel Shangri-La, 456
Loews Santa Monica Beach Hotel, 457
Miramar Sheraton Hotel, 459
Shutters on the Beach, 460
Seal Beach
The Seal Beach Inn and Gardens, 462
Temecula
Loma Vista Bed & Breakfast, 464
Vista
Cal-a-Vie, 465

Best Bed-and-Breakfasts

Avalon
Zane Grey Pueblo Hotel, 389
Idyllwild
Strawberry Creek Inn, 415
Julian
Julian Hotel, 417
Shadow Mountain Ranch, 419
Temecula
Loma Vista Bed & Breakfast, 464

Best Intimate City Stops

Beverly Hills
The Peninsula Beverly Hills, 392
Hollywood
Sunset Marquis Hotel and Villas, 414
Los Angeles
The Argyle, 430
Hotel Bel-Air, 432
Wyndham Checkers Hotel, 438
San Diego
Horton Grand Hotel, 450
The Westgate Hotel, 453

Best Family Favorites

Anaheim
Disneyland Hotel, 388

Best Grand City Hotels

Beverly Hills
The Regent Beverly Wilshire, 394
Los Angeles
Hotel Sofitel, 434
The New Otani Hotel & Garden, 435
The Regal Biltmore Hotel, 437

San Diego
U.S. Grant Hotel, 452
The Wyndham Emerald Plaza, 454

Inns by the Sea

Balboa
Balboa Inn, 391
Carlsbad
Pelican Cove Inn, 399
Coronado
Hotel Del Coronado, 403
Dana Point
Blue Lantern Inn, 407
Laguna Cliffs Marriott Resort, 409
Del Mar
L'Auberge Del Mar, 412
La Jolla
La Jolla Beach & Tennis Club, 421
La Valencia Hotel, 422
Prospect Park Inn, 424
Laguna Beach
Surf & Sand Hotel, 425
Long Beach
Hotel Queen Mary, 428
Santa Monica
Hotel Shangri-La, 456
Loews Santa Monica Beach Hotel, 457
Miramar Sheraton Hotel, 459
Shutters on the Beach, 460
Seal Beach
The Seal Beach Inn and Gardens, 462

Best on a Budget

San Diego
The Cottage, 448

Best Resorts

Carlsbad
  La Costa Resort and Spa, 398
Coronado
  Loews Coronado Bay Resort, 405
Dana Point
  The Ritz-Carlton Laguna Niguel, 410
Pasadena
  The Ritz-Carlton Huntington Hotel and Spa, 441
Rancho Bernardo
  Rancho Bernardo Inn, 443
Rancho Santa Fe
  The Inn at Rancho Santa Fe, 445
  Rancho Valencia, 447

Best Romantic Hideaways

Coronado
  Coronado Victorian House, 401
Lake Arrowhead
  Château du Lac, 426
Newport Beach
  Doryman's Inn, 440

Best Spas

Vista
  Cal-a-Vie, 465

Best Wilderness Retreats

Big Bear Lake
  Windy Point Inn on Big Bear Lake, 396

Southern California, from Malibu to San Diego, is richly diverse
and full of contrast. There are gorgeous white beaches and palatial
homes, mountain lakes and simple cottages. In the metropolitan
sprawl of greater **Los Angeles,** you'll find movie studios, freeways,
smog, great museums, surfers, chic shops, and nine million people,

all spread over 4,083 square miles. Los Angeles, founded by eleven families from Mexico in 1781, was a sleepy village until the railroad arrived in the late 1860s and a land boom began. Lured by images of a subtropical paradise, immigrants sought their fortunes in oranges. By 1889, 13,000 acres were producing oranges for shipment. Then the discovery of oil brought enormous wealth.

But it was the film industry, begun in 1910, that established the town as the glamour capital of the world. The Los Angeles area offers nonstop entertainment and numerous sporting and cultural events. Shopping is important recreation, especially in the designer boutiques of Rodeo Drive in **Beverly Hills** and the dozens of clothing and antiques shops on Melrose Avenue.

Symphony, ballet, and opera companies are active, and the museums are outstanding. The downtown Los Angeles County Museum of Art (LACMA) holds an important collection of pre-Columbian works, American paintings spanning two centuries, Indian and Southeast Asian art, and European and Japanese masterworks. In the Museum of Contemporary Art (MOCA), works of the postwar period are displayed under natural light in open galleries.

The Huntington is noted for its British art collection, botanical gardens, and library of rare books and manuscripts. The J. Paul Getty Museum, on a seaside hilltop in Malibu, may be the richest museum in the world. Ancient Greek and Roman sculptures and European masterpieces are displayed in a perfect replica of a Pompeiian villa.

North of Los Angeles loom the San Gabriel and San Bernardino mountains, high enough to be capped with snow in winter. Traveling south along the coast, each community has individual character, from arty **Laguna Beach** to a touch of New England in **Dana Point,** from the thoroughbred racing in **Del Mar** to **La Jolla's** exclusive shops and stunning setting.

San Diego, the seventh largest city in the country, is best known for its ideal climate and extraordinary visitor attractions. The beach at **Coronado** and Balboa Park's marvelous zoo are not to be missed. Young and old alike are thrilled by Sea World; the killer whale show is nothing less than astonishing. The city has a major waterfront convention center, a restored Old Town with walkthrough exhibitions on life in early San Diego, and a Gaslamp District of restored 19th-century buildings. In the heart of downtown is Horton Plaza, an innovative, multilevel shopping center that offers entertainment and restaurants as well as dozens of intriguing shops.

Inland from the beach and the bay, in the hills north of San Diego, are the wealthy communities of **Rancho Santa Fe** and **Rancho Bernardo.** A few miles away, tucked against the hot, dry hills, lie the peaceful enclaves of **Vista**, an avocado- and citrus-growing center, and Escondido, the heart of San Diego County's wine industry. Farther east there's a quaint old gold-mining town, **Julian,** now known for its apple orchards and relaxed atmosphere.

Anaheim

Disneyland Hotel

1150 West Cerritos Avenue
Anaheim, CA 92802
714-778-6600
Fax: 714-956-6597
www.disneyland.com

A jolly hotel complex near Disneyland

Manager: Rod Schinnerer. **Accommodations:** 990 rooms and suites. **Rates:** $190–$290 single or double; suites $425–$2,000. **Added:** 15% tax. **Payment:** Major credit cards. **Children:** Under age 18 free in room with parents. **Pets:** Not allowed, but hotel will recommend nearby kennel. **Smoking:** Nonsmoking rooms available.

➤ **The landscaping at Disneyland Hotel is extraordinary. A team of gardeners works continually to keep the floral color blazing, and the property is kept as immaculate as the clean streets of Disneyland.**

Here's a resort to thrill the young at heart. Not only does it have all kinds of entertainment, recreation, and restaurants, it's just a short tram ride from the Magic Kingdom itself — a fantasy playground for kids of all ages.

The hotel was built in 1955 by Jack Wrather, a Texas oilman who agreed with Walt Disney that the new theme park would draw enough visitors to merit a new hotel. So he acquired 60 acres adjoining Disneyland and built the Official Hotel of the Magic Kingdom. Now it's a major attraction in its own right and an award-winning convention hotel. The accommodations are in three towers, two with eleven stories and the other with fourteen, surrounding the Never Land pool area.

Despite the hotel's size it is easy to find your way around, helped by signs and paths that cross the villagelike grounds. There are three swimming pools, a sandy beach, a workout room, and an arcade. Free entertainment adds to the hotel's considerable vacation value. Regular features are Fantasy Waters — a twice-nightly display of fountains, lights, and music — and there's live musical entertainment at the Lost Bar overlooking the Never Land pool.

There's also a variety of restaurants to choose from. Granville's Steak House features steak, prime rib, and lobster in a casually elegant setting. The children's favorite is Goofy's Kitchen, with an all-you-can-eat buffet taking second place to the Disney characters that visit with kids as they dine. Others include Hook's Pointe and Wine Cellar serving mesquite-grilled specialties, and the Wharf Gallery, where burgers are the main bill of fare. Special children's menus are available at all the hotel's restaurants.

With all this, guest rooms seem almost secondary. On the other hand, they're crucial to the hotel's appeal. A standard room is clean and comfortable and has a TV with a closed-circuit channel and of course the Disney channel, as well as a narrow balcony overlooking the pool area. (From one of the towers you can see the ocean on a clear day.) Each room has reproduction Disney artwork, while the originals hang in the public spaces.

Avalon

Zane Grey Pueblo Hotel

P.O. Box 216
199 Chimes Tower Road
Avalon, CA 90704
310-510-0966
800-378-3256

A western adobe inn overlooking Santa Catalina harbor

Owner: Karen Baker. **General manager:** Laurie Carter. **Accommodations:** 16 rooms (all with private bath). **Rates:** $59–$175 single or double, $35 additional person; rates vary seasonally. **Included:** Continental breakfast. **Added:** 9% tax. **Minimum stay:** 2 or 3 nights on weekends. **Payment:** Major credit cards. **Children:** Charged as an additional person if more than 2 people in room. **Pets:** Not allowed. **Smoking:** Outdoors only.

➤ **By the time you've spent a few days on lovely Catalina, enjoying the dreamlike quiet and casual ambience of the Zane Grey Hotel, you may find yourself in agreement with Grey's own words about the island: "It is an environment that means enchantment to me. Sea and Mountain! Breeze and roar of Surf! Music of Birds! Solitude and Tranquility! A place for rest, dream, peace, sleep."**

Zane Grey, the famous author of Westerns and adventure stories, was born in Ohio in 1872 but moved west after his first novel was published. His robust, romantic tales reflected his love of the outdoors and made him the foremost writer on the American West for two generations of readers.

In 1926 he and his family decided that Santa Catalina Island, 26 miles from the southern California coast, was the ideal location for a home. So they built the Pueblo on a hillside above the village of Avalon, facing east to the harbor, the sea, and the mainland. There Grey lived and worked until his death in 1939. Now the adobe home is a hotel with modern plumbing and queen-size beds; otherwise, it is much as it was when Zane Grey made it his haven.

A courtesy taxi will pick you up at the boat landing and wind up the hill to the hotel. Before you enter, you'll notice unusual artwork that deceives the eye: John Bailey's realistic wall paintings of cacti and geraniums.

Most of the guest rooms, named for Zane Grey novels, are divided by a long hall. Half overlook the ocean; half view the hills. The rooms are simply but comfortably furnished in a southwestern theme, with Hopi designs in rugs and weavings. Some can accommodate up to four people. None has television or phones.

At the end of the hall is Zane Grey's living room with the original fireplace and log mantel, mosaic art, beam ceiling, hewn plank door, and oak dining table. Grey himself brought the teak beams from one of his fishing trips to Tahiti. Guests are welcome to play the grand piano, or you may prefer to curl up by the fire with one of Grey's books from the hotel's collection. Better yet, step from the rustic living room onto the terrace to drink in one of the island's most beautiful views — the yacht-filled harbor, rolling hills, and blue sea.

An arrowhead-shaped swimming pool lies beside gardens of jade and pepper trees. Morning coffee and toast are served here, on the outer terrace, or in the living room.

Balboa

Balboa Inn

105 Main Street
Balboa, CA 92661
949-675-3412
877-BALBOA-9
Fax: 949-673-4587

A 1920s villa-style hotel near the ocean

General manager: Lalith James. **Accommodations:** 34 rooms and suites. **Rates:** $109–$300. **Included:** Continental breakfast. **Added:** 10% tax. **Payment:** Major credit cards. **Children:** Free in room with parents. **Pets:** Not allowed. **Smoking:** Nonsmoking rooms available.

➤ **Sun worshippers on the sand, T-shirt shops, boutiques, sidewalks crowded with tourists and roller skaters, a ferris wheel, a carousel — they're all here, creating an atmosphere of fun and perpetual summer.**

Balboa, at Newport Beach, south of Los Angeles, is the image of a southern California beach scene. In the heart of the hubbub is the Balboa Inn, a historic landmark that resembles a European villa.

Built in 1928, the restored hotel has retained hints of the period. The tiled lobby is cool and usually quiet. Beyond it is a shady courtyard for outdoor dining next to the Green Leaf restaurant, which serves Italian food. An outdoor staircase leads to the guest rooms on the second and third floors. There are sixteen types of rooms and eight small suites, each with slight differences in decor. Typical is Room 217, with pine furniture and a view of the ocean and pier. If you're tall, Room 220 is ideal. Designed for the basketball player Kareem Abdul Jabbar, who once owned the hotel, it has high doors and an extra-long king-size bed.

There's a large pool surrounded by a sun deck. Room service is available. Activities in the area include concerts at the Balboa Pavilion a few blocks away, ferry rides to Balboa Island, and rides on the Catalina Flyer to Catalina Island, 26 miles away. Balboa and Newport have numerous restaurants, several specializing in fresh seafood.

Beverly Hills

The Peninsula Beverly Hills

9882 Little Santa Monica Blvd.
Beverly Hills, CA 90212
310-551-2888
800-462-7899
Fax: 310-788-2319
www.peninsula.com

> An elegant, luxurious villa in the city

General manager: Ali Kasikci. **Accommodations:** 196 rooms, including 32 suites. **Rates:** Start at $330, suites $550–$3,000. **Added:** 15.2% tax. **Payment:** Major credit cards. **Children:** Free in room with parents. **Pets:** Not allowed. **Smoking:** Nonsmoking rooms available.

➤ **A member of the exclusive Peninsula Group, this hotel opened in 1991 and caters mostly to a moneyed clientele of individual travelers and small groups — you'll never find convention crowds here. It's 12 miles from downtown Los Angeles and the L.A. airport.**

Like a carefully tended residential estate, the Peninsula Beverly Hills is surrounded by lush gardens and foliage. Tiles, planters, trellises, and fountains add to the European character of this outstanding hotels landscape. In the heart of Beverly Hills, it's an oasis of elegance and beauty, with a quality attained by very few hotels.

Only four stories high, this French Renaissance-style hotel resembles a grand private villa. The narrow, cool white lobby opens to the Living Room, a salon with a fireplace and windows overlooking sculpture and greenery. Light lunches and high tea are served here while a harpist plays.

Pale apricot walls, fine fabrics, peach marble, and detailed woodwork are some of the design touches that create the atmosphere of a luxurious home. When you arrive in your room, you are greeted with Chinese tea or lemonade and homemade cookies — another gracious, personal touch. There are night-lights by the bedside console, baskets filled with a traveler's needs such as a toothbrush and razor, and orchids and deep soaking tubs in the bathrooms. Each room has a stocked bar and refrigerator, three phones, computer and fax hookups, and a safe.

Suites feature full sound systems, art objects from around the world, and, as a final reminder that you are staying in out-of-the-ordinary lodgings, personal stationery that says you are in residence at the Peninsula.

Separated from the main hotel, five two-story villas contain sixteen lavishly furnished rooms and suites. They range in size from 580 to 2,250 square feet. Some have kitchens, individual security systems, spas, terraces, and fireplaces.

One of the hotel's best features is its rooftop garden with spa and 60-foot heated outdoor pool overlooking Beverly Hills and Century City. White poolside cabanas may be reserved for a fee, which includes a phone, fruit basket, and other amenities. The rooftop café serves light meals and cocktails.

The hotel's main restaurant is the Belvedere, with garden views and a classic Continental cuisine. By contrast, the Club Bar is a handsome lounge in maple and brass, with a collection of museum-quality California landscapes.

The Regent Beverly Wilshire

9500 Wilshire Blvd.
Beverly Hills, CA 90212
310-275-5200
800-421-4354
Fax: 310-274-2851
reservations-RBW@fourseasons.com
www.fourseasons.com

A glamorous landmark hotel

Manager: Peter O'Colmain. **Accommodations:** 395 rooms, including 120 suites. **Rates:** Rooms start at $325, suites range up to $7,500. **Added:** 15.368% tax. **Payment:** Major credit cards. **Children:** Under 16, free in room with parents when occupying existing bedding; cribs available free of charge; rollaway additional $30. **Pets:** Allowed. **Smoking:** Nonsmoking rooms available.

➤ **The Beverly Wilshire's Hollywood ties run deep. Elvis Presley often stayed in the hotel when shooting films, Warren Beatty lived in the hotel for a number of years, and motion picture deals are often struck over a meal in one of the hotel's restaurants. In recent years the hotel has become something of a celebrity in its own right as the backdrop for some of the scenes in the popular movie *Pretty Woman*.**

The rococo facade of the Beverly Wilshire Hotel has been a famous landmark since 1928. It was glamorous then, but now, after a $100-million renovation in 1989 and another $35 million in 1998, the word has new meaning. As the Regent Beverly Wilshire, it's one of the world's grand hotels.

The lobby, with its marble columns, inlaid woods, massive bouquets, and tall palms, whispers of elegance and good taste and is the first evidence that you're checking into a first-rate establishment. (The hotel spends thousands of dollars a month on flowers alone and employs six florists.) The brass elevators with pressed motifs from the '20s, mahogany paneling, and an elegant bench in case you want to rest on the way to your floor, add to the sense of luxury and comfort.

Through the years the hotel has hosted many famous figures, including former presidents Carter, Reagan, and Ford; Emperor Hirohito of Japan; the Dalai Lama; the Aga Kahn; Elton John; Ringo Starr; Mick Jagger; Andrew Lloyd Webber; and the royal families of Monaco and Great Britain. Many of them stayed in the five-room, three-bath Wilshire Presidential Suite. There's a long entrance hallway, a formal dining room, and a regal master bedroom with a high half-canopy bed. The guest bedroom has an Oriental look, and each bedroom has its own sumptuous bath and formal parlor. While the suite retains the hotel's period flavor, even down to the skylights and original pegwood floors, modern amenities such as a shower/steam room in the master bath have been incorporated for maximum guest comfort. Other special suites are the Cabana and Verandah suites.

Guest rooms are in two buildings, the Beverly and the Wilshire, which are divided by a domed entrance road lit by gas lanterns that once held court at Edinburgh Castle.

Rooms in the Wilshire building are spacious and are well furnished in sunny pastels. Rooms in the Beverly wing, which was constructed in 1971, are also pleasant, in yellows and deep greens with bleached wood pieces and windows that offer fine views and lots of light. All rooms have the expected amenities of a modern luxury hotel, including three phones and a mini-TV in the bathroom. There are hair dryers, scales, robes, shaving mirrors, high-quality toiletries, wonderfully fluffy pillows, and lots of pink marble. On each floor there's a room attendant who can be summoned with the push of a button. The attendant will mend a hem, pack your bags, produce an iron and ironing board, or bring in a basket of baby needs and a crib.

The Regent Beverly Wilshire takes justifiable pride in all its eating spots, but the award-winning Dining Room is in a class by itself. The decor is highlighted by lush French art, Regency furnishings, and parquet floors; the menu features California-influenced Continental cuisine. The lengthy wine list offers a wide range of labels and prices. Sunday brunch, with a lavish appetizer buffet, and Saturday fashion luncheons are also popular meals served in the Dining Room. The Lobby Lounge is the place to go for tea and lighter fare. The Bar, with its mahogany bar and French marquetry panels, is an elegant and intimate spot to enjoy a cocktail and perhaps spot a celebrity or two.

On the second floor of the Beverly Wing is a fitness center with weight machines, saunas, hot tubs, a snack bar, and an outdoor pool (a replica of Sophia Loren's pool in Italy) surrounded by jardinières of bougainvillea and creeping fig. Massages, facials, manicures, and pedicures are available. Business travelers appreciate the secretarial, Internet, copying, computer, and delivery services. Shoppers revel in the hotel's location — it's directly across the street from Rodeo Drive, the famous street of designer shops. Other nearby streets have appealing boutiques, cafés, and art galleries, while major department stores are represented on Wilshire Boulevard.

Big Bear Lake

Windy Point Inn on Big Bear Lake

Mailing address: P.O. Box 375
Physical address:
39015 North Shore Drive
Fawnskin, CA 92333
909-866-2746
Fax: 909-866-1593
www.windypointinn.com

> A secluded, contemporary
> home on the lake

Innkeepers: Val and Kent Kessler. **Accommodations:** 2 rooms and 3 suites (all with private bath). **Rates:** $105–$145 single, $125–$265 double, $205–$245 suites. **Included:** Full breakfast and afternoon refreshments. **Added:** 10% tax. **Minimum stay:** 2 nights on most weekends. **Payment:** Major credit cards. **Children:** Not appropriate; maximum 2 guests per room. **Pets:** Not allowed. **Smoking:** Not allowed.

➤   **At the Windy Point Inn you can rent a boat from a nearby marina and explore the lake (the inn has a private dock), or make the 12-minute drive to Big Bear's ski slopes.**

On the north shore of Big Bear Lake, in the San Bernardino Mountains east of Los Angeles, this contemporary home stands on a tiny private peninsula bordered by secluded sandy beaches. Through every window you see a different aspect of the lake, forest, and mountains.

Windy Point offers both serenity and stimulation. You can go for quiet walks, watch the sunset, play the grand piano, or snuggle up by the blazing hearth in the sunken living room. Or you can admire artwork from around the world and visit with the interesting guests who come to the inn.

The guest rooms are on three levels. In the Pines, on the first floor, you step down to a queen-size bed with a feather bed. The Pines has a corner fireplace in the cozy sitting area, a separate entrance, a refrigerator, and a skylighted Jacuzzi. Least expensive, but intimate and romantic, is the Sands, which has a wet bar, a private deck, and a sunrise view.

The most spectacular room is the Peaks, which has glass on three sides revealing wide views through the tops of the pine trees to the lake and often snow-capped mountains. Vaulted ceilings give the suite a grand and open feel, and even the wall above the walk-through galley wet bar is cut out to take advantage of the views. An oversize sofa offers a prime viewing spot, while interesting objets d'art and weathered driftwood pieces add a timeless style to the modern decor. Sliding glass doors open onto a large deck from which you could almost dive right into the lake, the water seems so close. In the suite's sleeping area there's a king-size platform bed, and the tiled bath has a bidet, a whirlpool tub, and a separate steam shower.

Amenities abound: thick towels, individually controlled heat, stereos, VCRs, barbecues. But it's style and personality that make the inn outstanding. Its whimsical sculptures, paintings, and exotic artifacts combine with a sophisticated decorating sense to create a memorable retreat.

Breakfast includes out-of-the-ordinary treats such as bananas Foster crêpes and cinnamon French toast with sautéed fruit. The innkeepers offer afternoon appetizers in the living room or on the deck. They're happy to provide suggestions on restaurants and give driving directions.

Carlsbad

La Costa Resort and Spa

Costa del Mar Road
Carlsbad, CA 92009
760-438-9111
800-854-5000
Fax: 760-438-3758
info@lacosta.com
www.lacosta.com

A large luxury resort in the country

Managing director: John Peto. **Accommodations:** 400 rooms, 77 suites, and 6 executive homes. **Rates:** $340–$515 single or double, $35 each additional adult, suites $550 and up, executive homes $1,300 and up. **Payment:** Major credit cards. **Children:** Under age 18 free in room with parents. **Pets:** Not allowed. **Smoking:** Nonsmoking rooms available.

➤ **In the Clubhouse you can see the paintings of golf greats who have won the Tournament of Champions on La Costa's greens. In the evening, live entertainment is presented in the Tournament of Champions Lounge.**

La Costa combines a concern for health and fitness with luxury, fine dining, outdoor recreation, and lavish entertainment — all in a resort complex that sprawls over 400 acres of hills in the southern California sun. It's just off I-5, 90 minutes south of Los Angeles, and 30 minutes north of San Diego. Opened in 1965, La Costa underwent a $100 million remodeling in 1987 that gave it a softer, more romantic appearance, with rose-colored buildings, red tile roofs, and arched walkways and windows.

The guest rooms are decorated in teal, peach, and tan. The best rooms in the main building are those inside, overlooking tall ferns and eucalyptus trees. The outside rooms, which view the road and parking lots, are more susceptible to noise. The other rooms are near the spa center, golf courses, and tennis courts. Suites are twice the size of standard rooms, but all are spacious and have terrycloth robes, large mirrors, lighted vanity tables, television and phones, and baskets of individual toiletries — La Costa's brand of course. Most of La Costa's suites have one or two bedrooms; the executive homes have two to five bedrooms and up to three and a half baths. Valet parking and transportation to your rooms are provided.

The spa facilities are extensive, featuring rock steam baths, bracing Swiss showers, facials, massages, herbal wraps, and loofah scrubs. There's a complete fitness program of exercise and nutrition classes. However, La Costa is more a worldly resort than a sequestered spa. It bustles with activity and caters to groups looking for a variety of pleasures.

The resort's conference center can hold up to 1,000 people for a reception. The complex, which includes a grand ballroom and 14 meeting rooms, boasts advanced audiovisual systems and simultaneous translation capability.

La Costa's restaurants offer a range of dining choices. The Brasserie is casual and serves health-conscious spa cuisine in addition to more traditional fare. Classical music plays in the background in Ristorante Figaro, where tapas, pastas, and meats are served with a Mediterranean slant. Pisces, with appropriate fish-patterned fabric wall coverings and shell-shaped lighting fixtures, serves seafood. There's also a snack bar adjacent to center court at the racquet club.

The resort has 21 tennis courts, swimming pools, and two 18-hole championship golf courses where major golf events take place. Bicycles are available to rent. A special program, Camp La Costa, is devoted to children ages 5 to 12. Arts and crafts, golf and tennis lessons, and nature walks are some of the activities pursued at the day camp.

Pelican Cove Inn

320 Walnut Avenue
Carlsbad, CA 92008
760-434-5995
888-PELCOVE
Fax: 760-434-7649
pelicancoveinn@sandcastleweb.com
www.Pelican-Cove.com

A B&B in a beach resort town

Innkeepers: Kris and Nancy Nayudu. **Accommodations:** 8 rooms (all with private bath). **Rates:** $90–$180 single or double, $15 additional person. **Included:** Full breakfast. **Added:** 10% tax. **Minimum stay:** 2 nights on weekends. **Payment:** Major credit cards. **Children:** Age 12 and older welcome; charged as an additional person if third person in room. **Pets:** Not allowed. **Smoking:** Not allowed.

➤ **Pelican Cove is just 200 yards from the beach. Two walkways along the beachfront are popular strolling, bicycling, and jogging paths. The friendly and accommodating innkeepers will lend you beach chairs, towels, and picnic baskets for jaunts around the area.**

Carlsbad, once known for its mineral waters, is a comparatively little-known resort town 30 miles north of San Diego. The Nayudus are happy to tell their guests about its attractions, and their charming inn is certainly one of them.

The gray exterior with burgundy trim and white-railinged walkways that lead to rooms and decks on several levels give the inn a boatlike appearance — appropriate for this lodging that is just two blocks from the beach. Colorful plants at the entrance are cheerful and inviting.

All the guest rooms in this comfortable bed-and-breakfast are light and airy and have private entrances, fireplaces, and ceiling fans. Each has a feather bed with a down comforter, a television, and antique furnishings. Thoughtful details include clock radios, good reading lamps, handmade herbal soaps, and candy.

Coronado, in light peaches and greens, has a draped canopy pole bed and an oversize Jacuzzi tub. Laguna, with a colorful lavender and floral decor, has white wicker furniture. La Jolla, sunny in cream-colored tones, has a fainting couch. Newport, facing the street, features an unusual lofty conical ceiling of green beams beneath the inn's distinctive cupola. Carlsbad has a high bed, an antique reproduction complete with step-stool and mirrored headboard. Carlsbad adjoins Balboa, the smallest room.

Breakfast — ham and asparagus strata, cottage cheese pancakes, artichoke quiche, and Scotch eggs — is set on a table in a corner of the front parlor. This small room serves as the lobby, phone room, and visiting area, so it can be cramped. Better to take a tray back to your room, to the gazebo in the garden, or up to the sun deck or rooftop deck.

The inn is close to tennis, golf, fishing, sailing, and shopping. It's within walking distance of several restaurants, such as Chin's, where Szechuan fare is served. Try Dini's for its ocean view, Neiman's for a Victorian atmosphere, and Dominic's for tasty Italian food and good service.

Coronado

Coronado Victorian House

1000 Eighth Street
Coronado, CA 92118
619-435-2200
888-299-2822
Fax: 619-435-4760

> A unique bed-and-breakfast
> in the heart of Coronado

Innkeeper: Bonni Marie Kinosian. **Accommodations:** 7 rooms (all with private bath). **Rates:** Start at $200; each package is individually designed and priced accordingly. **Included:** Gourmet breakfast. **Added:** 10% tax. **Payment:** Major credit cards. **Children:** $25–$50 additional, depending on age. **Pets:** Not allowed. **Smoking:** Allowed outdoors only.

➤ **Holidays get special attention at the inn. The innkeeper cooks an elaborate Valentine's Day dinner, and the house is festively decorated during the holiday season. Murder mystery weekends are also offered.**

At this far from ordinary bed-and-breakfast you can brush up on your tap, ballet, or ballroom dancing; take an exercise class; solve a murder mystery; dine on ethnic cuisine, then learn how to cook it; or walk to the beach with a gourmet picnic basket in tow — all thanks to the efforts of the energetic innkeeper. Bonni Marie Kinosian is a woman of many talents. A long-time dance teacher, Bonni Marie's dance studio adjoins the inn, and guests often take a private dance lesson at some point during their stay.

Bonni Marie is also an excellent cook. Of Armenian descent, she incorporates ethnic dishes in the meals she prepares, with many recipes coming from a simple old Armenian cookbook with family recipes tucked between the pages. At breakfast there's homemade yogurt alongside fruit and more traditional breakfast items. In the afternoons zucchini salsa and sarma (rolled grape leaves) are served with home-baked Armenian bread. If you're intrigued as to how these delicacies are made, Bonni Marie can give you a cooking lesson and supply you with the recipes so you can try your hand at replicating them at home. Since the beach is just under four blocks from the inn, she'll also make up a picnic basket for you, including ethnic foods if you'd like them.

Bonni Marie put the same time and enthusiasm in creating the inn as she does in welcoming her guests. The Victorian that houses the inn was built in 1894. Bonni Marie spent four years restoring the home before opening it as a bed-and-breakfast in 1993, and she won an award for its preservation in the process. The inn is furnished with antiques and stunning Persian rugs, some of which were brought over by her father when he immigrated to the United States.

Rooms, named for famous dancers or ballets, are individually decorated. Although all of the beds are antiques, they have modern mattresses and feather beds, and all of the rooms have small televisions and refrigerators. In burgundies and blues, Baryshnikov is handsome with twin sleigh beds that date back to 1810. Footstools are provided because the beds are high in order to accommodate trundles underneath. Nutcracker is a small room, but it has its own private entrance and porch with a wicker settee. The room, in plums and silvers, has a white spool bed and a clawfoot tub.

As one might expect, a beautiful door leads out to a balcony in the romantic Romeo and Juliet suite. The high brass bed is topped with a cross-stitched quilt, and the large bath has a Jacuzzi tub, double shower, and a vanity made from a Victorian dresser. Pavlova, with pretty floral wallpaper, also has a brass bed.

On the top floor a Persian-rug-lined hallway leads to guest rooms named after the legendary dancing pair Fred Astaire and Ginger Rogers. Fred, a cheerful room, has a daybed, as well as a double, covered in chintz. Its bath, which is located down a flight of stairs, has a pull-chain toilet original to the home. In Ginger, cozy beds tucked under the eaves are perfect for children, and the two rooms combined might make a good choice for families. All guests are welcome to use the living room on the second floor, where seven-foot windows can be opened from either the top or the bottom to bring in the ocean breeze. Here the decor includes everything from a bronze angel chandelier and a fainting couch to a table laid with a checkers set. Breakfast is served in the adjoining dining room on a table elegantly set with lace, gold leaf china, and silverware with mother-of-pearl handles. When not taking a dance class or a cooking lesson, guests can enjoy the bilevel terrace off the dining room, head to the beach, explore charming Coronado, or visit San Diego's many attractions just across the bridge.

Hotel Del Coronado

1500 Orange Avenue
Coronado, CA 92118
619-435-6611
800-HOTEL-DEL
Fax: 619-522-8238
www.hoteldel.com

> **A historic landmark resort on the beach**

General manager: Michael Hardisty. **Accommodations:** 691 rooms. **Rates:** $255 and up, single or double, $25 additional person; suites $655 and up. **Added:** 8% tax. **Minimum stay:** 2 nights on weekends. **Payment:** Major credit cards. **Children:** Under age 15 free in room with parents. **Pets:** Not allowed. **Smoking:** Not allowed.

➤   **Numerous films and television shows have been made on the grounds of the Del Coronado. The most famous and enduring was *Some Like It Hot*, filmed in 1958 with Marilyn Monroe, Jack Lemmon, and Tony Curtis.**

The Del, as it's affectionately called by frequent guests, is a living legend, a significant piece of southern California's history. Here modern comforts have been added to the rich patina of past glories.

The Del Coronado opened in 1888, the result of the grand dreams of Elisha Babcock, a railroad tycoon who wanted to build a resort that would be the talk of the Western World. The hotel he and his partner, H. L. Story, built on a peninsula in San Diego Bay was the largest structure outside New York City to have electric lights. It's said that Thomas Edison supervised the installation of the incandescent lamps and that he pulled the switch for the hotel's first electrically lighted Christmas tree. Quickly established as a cultural oasis in the sparsely settled West, the resplendent Del drew celebrities, dignitaries, and royalty. Twelve U.S. presidents stayed at the hotel during its first hundred years. Charles Lindbergh had a reception here following his solo flight over the Atlantic. L. Frank Baum wrote part of *The Wizard of Oz* on the premises and based the Emerald City on the towered Victorian structure. The Prince of Wales — later King Edward VIII and then the Duke of Windsor — was honored at a dinner here in 1920, when he reportedly met Wallis Simpson for the first time.

All this history is on display in the hotel's lower level corridors, providing glimpses of change from 1888 to the present. Today, most people arrive at the Del by car and catch their first glimpse of the red and white Victorian extravaganza while driving across a high bridge that connects San Diego and Coronado. There's a quaintness to the village of Coronado, with its winding, tree-lined streets and shops tucked away in courtyards, yet the city of San Diego is just minutes across the bay. Coronado also has a municipal golf course, several small hotels, and a Navy presence.

The original five-story, amply curved structure of the Del Coronado is still in use today, along with two newer sections closer to the beach. The lobby is a throwback to an earlier era with its oak ceiling and muted lighting, and guest rooms in the main building are grouped around a lush garden courtyard. Lawns, palm trees, and a latticed gazebo make this a favorite spot for weddings and relaxation away from the hubbub of the lobby and arcades of shops. Between the courtyard and the lobby is Palm Court, where you may purchase a Continental breakfast in the morning and order coffee all day.

In the lobby, an old-fashioned birdcage elevator still operates in a corner near the door to the Crown Room, the Del's majestic dining room. Here crown-shaped chandeliers hang from one of the largest support-free structures in the country. The lofty, redwood-paneled room has a 30-foot-high elliptical ceiling made of sugar pine that was crafted without a single nail. Banquets and formal state dinners are held here, though the food is less spectacular than the atmosphere.

Downstairs, the Prince of Wales restaurant, named for the Duke of Windsor, is elegant. In soft beiges and creams, the restaurant is art deco in decor and intimate in ambience. Pictures of the Duke of Windsor and Wallis Simpson hang on one wall, and the table below is considered the most romantic, in honor of their relationship. (The Duke's uniform is on display just outside the restaurant.) For dinner, traditional American favorites such as broiled salmon and lamb chops are given modern treatments. The broiled salmon comes with artichokes and Port Salut ravioli in a tomato tarragon sauce, and the lamb chop is topped with mustard marmalade and served with baby beans and oven-roasted potatoes. A private dining room, seating up to 16, adjoins the restaurant and can be reserved for small functions.

The more casual Ocean Terrace is open for breakfast on weekends and lunch and cocktails daily. It overlooks the gazebo bar, the Olympic-size swimming pool, two miles of sandy beach, and tennis courts where you half expect the women to be wearing 1920s-style tennis dresses. On the terrace, glass panels shield diners from the wind while maintaining the marvelous ocean view. For quick meals, you can buy snacks in the Basement Deli, which was carved from the hotel's original stone cistern.

Guest rooms retain their period decor while meeting the expectations of today's travelers. The large rooms with private verandahs facing the sea are preferred; they have tall windows, comfortable couches, king- or queen-size beds with wicker headboards and floral spreads, and roomy baths with showers. All have ceiling fans, alarm-clock radios, televisions, phones, safes, and stocked minibars. Some rooms are even rumored to be haunted. Movies filmed at the hotel are shown nightly on one of the TV channels.

In Ocean Towers, the newer annex, seven floors contain more than 300 rooms, all redecorated. The guest rooms lack the Victorian flavor that gives the original Del its charm, but they're softer and lighter in decor and provide a retreat from the bustle across the way. The annex has its own swimming pool, and most of the rooms have balconies. All have air conditioning and king-size beds.

The service at the Del Coronado is outstanding. The award-winning staff is enthusiastic and eager to please, from the youngest valets to those who've been loyal to the Del for 40 years and more. The hotel has meeting and conference rooms and a convention center that accommodates up to 1,500. Services at the hotel's spa include facials, massages, body masks, fitness instruction, steam baths, and whirlpool baths.

Loews Coronado Bay Resort

4000 Coronado Bay Road
Coronado, CA 92118
619-424-4000
800-81-LOEWS
Fax: 619-424-4400

A waterside resort across the bay from San Diego

Manager: Kathleen Cochran. **Accommodations:** 406 rooms and 32 suites. **Rates:** $245–$295 single or double, $20 additional person; Bayside units start at $625 and can accommodate up to 6 people. **Added:** 8% tax. **Payment:** Major credit cards. **Children:** Welcome. **Pets:** Small pets allowed. **Smoking:** Non-smoking rooms available.

➤ **The resort's major appeal lies in its recreational facilities. There are five tennis courts, three pools, a small putting green, and easy access to**

miles of beach. Classes in surfing, aerobics, yoga, and tai chi are all given at the resort, and Wave Runners, paddleboats, sailboats, and kayaks are available for rent.

San Diego's downtown skyline is across the bay from this lovely waterside resort. The city is only a water taxi ride away, while the marina and beach are just out the door — so visitors here get the best of both worlds. Often conventioneers meeting in San Diego stay here for a change of scene. Boaters like the fully secured 80-slip anchorage, directly in front of the hotel, which can accommodate both small cruisers and mega-yachts.

The curving, three-story buildings of the main hotel are fully connected by a hallway and stand on a 14-acre private peninsula between Crown Isle Marina and San Diego Bay. Inside there's a broad lobby with crystal chandeliers and a double staircase rising to a mezzanine. From here, wide, arching windows frame views of the bay and city.

The restaurants are like the rest of the hotel — informal but impeccably tasteful. Critically acclaimed Azzura Point is the resort's fine-dining restaurant, romantic and candlelit in the evenings. On the second floor on the bay side, it features fresh seafood dishes such as black sea bass with caramelized kumquats and lobster risotto with porcini and white truffles. For more casual meals there's the Market Café, overlooking the boats of the marina, and a wonderful market and deli off the lobby where you can buy box lunches as well as gourmet foods, cookbooks, and various gifts and sundries. Musicians play nightly in Cays Lounge.

Newly redecorated guest rooms are attractive and inviting, and every room has a balcony and a view of the bay, pool, or marina. Big windows, sand-colored walls, and splashy floral fabrics in sea green and blues emphasize the sunny resort atmosphere, while spacious baths with marble vanities, deep soaking tubs, separate showers, scales, hair dryers, and makeup mirrors add a note of luxury and comfort. The hotel also appeals to business travelers who need desks, phones, a business center, and lots of meeting space; and for executives who need to stay in touch with their offices — each suite has its own fax machine. Loews also has one of the largest ballrooms in San Diego, as well as several breakout rooms and audiovisual equipment.

The Bayside units are an excellent lodging choice for small groups or families traveling together because they have private entrances, kitchen areas, and separate living rooms. Stretched along the bay, these units with peach-stuccoed exteriors and red tile roofs are nicely landscaped on the outside and furnished in soothing pastel tones on the inside. Large bay windows accentuate the view, and San Diego Bay laps the shore beneath each unit's balcony. The most deluxe accommodations at the resort, their baths have double Jacuzzi tubs.

For families, the resort's Loews Loves Kids program has a roster of entertainment activities for children, and daycare is provided by licensed caregivers at the Clubhouse. For area sightseeing, a shuttle service runs every day to Coronado and San Diego, and to Mexico on weekends.

Dana Point

Blue Lantern Inn

34343 Street of the Blue Lantern
Dana Point, CA 92629
949-661-1304
800-950-1236
Fax: 949-496-1483
www.foursisters.com

> **A stylish clifftop inn
> overlooking the harbor**

General manager: Lin McMahon. **Accommodations:** 29 rooms (all with private bath). **Rates:** $150–$220 single or double, suites $275–$500, $15 additional person. **Included:** Breakfast buffet and afternoon refreshments. **Added:** 10% tax. **Payment:** Major credit cards. **Children:** Under age 2, free in room with parents. **Pets:** Not allowed. **Smoking:** Not allowed.

➤ **Near the inn is the Cannon restaurant, where you can enjoy candlelight dining with a stunning view. For a livelier spot with festive crowds, good mesquite-broiled seafood, and fast service, go to the Harbor Grill in Mariners' Village at the water's edge.**

High on a bluff above the Dana Point Yacht Harbor, the Blue Lantern presents panoramic views as well as comfortable accommodations and fine service. Its gabled gray frame trimmed in white reflects the Cape Cod theme of Dana Point.

The Blue Lantern is similar to the other Four Sisters inns in its commitment to high quality, capable staff, and attention to detail. Everything here is done well. The reception area, sitting room, library, and dining room are peaceful, welcoming places where you can enjoy complimentary wine and hors d'oeuvres in the afternoon, talk to the concierge about Dana Point's attractions, relax in front of a fire, and pick up a cookie on the way to your room.

The guest rooms, done in coastal colors, have traditional and antique furniture, televisions, coffeemakers, phones, terry bathrobes, shuttered windows, and attractive molding detail. All rooms have whirlpool tubs, gas fireplaces, irons, ironing boards, and hair dryers. Pacific Edge rooms have a balcony or flower-lined terrace that overlooks the harbor, where waves crash against a long stone breakwater. Although Point rooms don't overlook the ocean, they are still delightful; and Harbor View rooms have bay windows. Room 309, with its harbor view, has a writing desk, wicker furnishings, bay windows, and a skylight in the bath. The Tower rooms are worth the splurge. The second floor Tower room (#201), decorated in mints, creams, and lavenders, has multiple windows that bring in lots of light, a large terrace, a four-poster bed topped with plenty of pillows, and an oval Jacuzzi tub. In the first floor Tower room you step down to the living room.

In the morning, the *Los Angeles Times* is delivered to your door. An ample buffet breakfast of juice, granola, muffins, and a hot dish such as baked French toast is served in the sun room, off the lobby. Downstairs is a small exercise room with a stairclimber, treadmill, lifecycle, and weight machine. Bicycles are available as well.

Stuffed-animal lovers will be certain to notice the inn's teddy bears. The fluffy creatures climb the central staircase and rest on each guest bed. For guests who happen to fall in love with a particular bear, adoption papers are available at the front desk.

Laguna Cliffs Marriott Resort

25135 Park Lantern
Dana Point, CA 92629
949-661-5000
800-533-9748
Fax: 949-661-5358

A stylish, casual resort on a hill above the sea

Manager: Gordon Luster. **Accommodations:** 329 rooms, 17 suites. **Rates:** $179–$259 single or double, suites start at $350. **Added:** 10% tax. **Payment:** Major credit cards. **Children:** Free in room with parents. **Pets:** Allowed. **Smoking:** Nonsmoking rooms available

➤ **The mood at the Laguna Cliffs Marriott Resort is that of a casual country club where guests come for outdoor recreation. You can play tennis, golf at the Links course, take a fishing or whale-watching cruise, or exercise in the health center, which has stationary bicycles, weights, a rowing machine, and a sauna. Massages are available by appointment.**

South of Laguna Beach is a point of land named for Richard Henry Dana, Jr., who wrote *Two Years Before the Mast*. Dana Point has a yacht harbor, a lighthouse filled with nautical lore, a marine institute, and a complex of shops and restaurants designed to recreate the flavor of the port's 19th-century trading days. And it has, on a grassy hill above the harbor, Laguna Cliffs Marriott Resort.

The gabled four-story resort, painted gray with white trim, stands on landscaped grounds overlooking the 2,500-slip harbor. All the rooms have either a full or partial sea view; some have balconies, others their own terraces. They occupy four wings: Laguna, Capistrano, San Clemente, and Del Mar.

The rooms are spacious and comfortably furnished, but it's not the decor that draws the eye in these rooms; it's the gorgeous view. Guests will immediately open the sliding glass doors and admire the panorama of blue sea and sky. Kimonos with a nautical design hang in the closets. Baths in warm gold marble have a tub and shower, hair dryers, and makeup mirrors.

Commodore's Bar and Deck is beyond the light and open lobby on the first floor. A pianist plays mellow jazz here during the day, and it's a pleasant spot for lunch, as local businessfolk will attest. It's a high-ceilinged, bright space with many windows that have a good view of the resort's lawns and flowers. Outside on the deck, the view is even better. Regatta Bar and Grill, with its nautical theme, is on the lower level, near the lawn that slopes to the road and marina. It serves three meals a day and a Sunday blue-jean brunch. Lighter fare is emphasized.

At the marina, you can rent sailboards and kayaks, go rowing or parasailing, or take the five-mile walk around the harbor's edge. Jet skis and sailboats may be rented. In the summer months the resort offers a special day program for children called Club Cowabunga. Supervised activities include flying kites in the park, playing games, and visiting the Marine Institute to explore tide pools and see the whale exhibition. In the evenings, movies and videos are shown.

The Ritz-Carlton Laguna Niguel

One Ritz Carlton Drive
Dana Point, CA 92629
949-240-2000
800-241-3333
Fax: 949-240-0829
www.ritzcarlton.com

An opulent resort on the coast

General manager: John Dravinski. **Accommodations:** 362 rooms, 31 suites. **Rates:** $235–$435 single or double, suites start at $420. **Added:** 10% tax and $9 resort fee per room per night. **Payment:** Major credit cards. **Children:** Under age 17 free in room with parents. **Pets:** Not allowed. **Smoking:** Nonsmoking rooms available.

➤   **This hotel, like the others in the Ritz-Carlton collection, is an example of first-class opulence with a formality unusual in casual California. Those who prefer subdued, classic elegance and strict dress codes to more laid-back lifestyles find it a perfect retreat.**

On a 150-foot shoreline bluff, five miles south of the resort and arts community of Laguna Beach, the Ritz-Carlton stands like a Mediterranean aristocrat transplanted to southern California. Outside the surf crashes and the beach beckons, while four tennis courts, an 18-hole golf course, and two swimming pools sprawl enticingly over the landscaped grounds. Indoors, Old World tradition takes over.

With crystal chandeliers, marble fireplaces, beveled mirrors, richly paneled walls, and custom-made furniture, the hotel is the epitome of the Ritz tradition begun in 1898 by the legendary French hotelier Caesar Ritz. Since 1927, when the first Ritz-Carlton opened in Boston, the hotels have been noted for their high standards.

The guest services include same-day valet service, airport transportation, secretarial and babysitting services, valet parking, golf bag and luggage storage, twice-daily maid service, a shuttle to and from the golf course and beach, and a multilingual staff. In addition to golf, tennis, and swimming, there is a fitness center with exercise and weight-training equipment, a sauna, and exercise classes. Individual fitness assessment programs and massages are also available.

Many of these facilities are offered by other luxury resorts. What makes this one different is its standard of consistent quality and service — and its art collection. Museum-quality European paintings, prints, and tapestries hang throughout the hotel, each cataloged and photographed by an art conservator.

The artwork starts at the porte-cochere with a fountain full of bronze dolphins sculpted by California artist John Edward Svenson. It continues through the long lobby, with its Italian marble and hand-loomed carpets, and into the maritime-themed library. In the library are portraits of early American naval officers. A model sailing ship encased in glass stands on a mahogany table before a window that frames a magnificent view of the sea. Shelves of leatherbound books stand beside the black marble fireplace, completing the atmosphere of a peaceful refuge. The seagoing motif continues with paintings of clipper ships and steamers in the bar. Opposite the bar is the formal Dining Room, where French art complements the decor. Mediterranean cuisine is featured. The Club Grill is livelier, with a menu dominated by à la carte seafood, steak, and pasta. The food is well sauced and the mode is hunt-club sporty. Music from the up-tempo combo will entice you to whirl on the dance floor. Have breakfast or Sunday brunch in the Terrace restaurant above the south side swimming pool and terrace; in warm months, enjoy light lunches and cocktails at the pool bar. High tea, a Ritz tradition, is served in the library.

Each guest room has its own balcony overlooking the curving beach or the gardens and courtyards. Rare ferns, sycamore trees, weeping willows, palms, and native plants surround fountains and lawns. When you can tear yourself away from the view, you'll see that your room has a classical look and antique reproduction furniture. Stocked honor bars, TVs with complimentary movies, armoires, safes, terrycloth robes, and marble bathrooms are standard in all guest rooms. Suites are extra spacious, with separate living rooms and wet bars; some even have fireplaces.

There is enough at the resort to keep any vacationer occupied, but if you wish to explore, Laguna Beach is a short drive away. The charming village, long known for its devotion to the arts, would be idyllic if a highway didn't slice through the center. The shops are delightful, and there are several good restaurants.

Del Mar

L'Auberge Del Mar

P.O. Box 2889
1540 Camino Del Mar
Del Mar, CA 92014
858-259-1515
800-553-1336
Fax: 858-793-6433
www.destinationtravel.com

> A modern, open resort in a
> coastal town

General manager: Gordon MacMitchell. **Accommodations:** 112 rooms and 8 suites. **Rates:** $205–$320 in low season, $235–$385 in high season, suites $650–$2,000. **Added:** 10% tax. **Payment:** Major credit cards. **Children:** Under age 18 free in room with parents (cribs available). **Pets:** Not allowed. **Smoking:** Non-smoking rooms available.

➤ **Many guests enjoy continuing the tradition begun when Del Mar was famous for its glamorous visitors. Old photos throughout L'Auberge pay tribute to those earlier times.**

On a hill overlooking the ocean, 20 minutes north of San Diego and 90 miles south of Los Angeles, L'Auberge is a stylish resort with a reputation for excellent quality. It's on the site of the old

Hotel Del Mar, which was frequented by Hollywood celebrities during the '20s, '30s, and '40s. Rudolph Valentino, Bing Crosby, Jimmy Durante, Rita Hayworth, and others have suites and meeting rooms named in their honor in the hotel. The atmosphere is light and open, typical of southern California lodgings. In the marble lobby, which has a double-sided fireplace, skylights allow the sun to stream through to the potted palms and lavish bouquets. This is the heart of the resort, where guests gather for afternoon tea and weekend dinner dances. A buffet brunch is set out on Sunday. Beyond is the terrace, with a fountain and flowers and, on a level above, a swimming pool.

You can eat on the terrace, by the pool, or inside in the sunny dining room, which serves regional California cuisine. Durante's Pub has microbrewery beer and wine by the glass. For recreation, L'Auberge offers two tennis courts (private lessons with a tennis pro can be arranged), two pools, a full-service spa (single- and multiday packages are available), and the attractions of Del Mar: golf (Torrey Pines, Aviara, and Whispering Palms golf courses are all nearby), shopping, bicycling, surfing, strolling to the beach, visiting the Torrey Pines Reserve, and attending the horse races at the famous Del Mar Race Track. The inn, with nine meeting rooms and a spacious terrace, has facilities for groups of up to 250 people; for children ages 4 to 15 there's the VIK (Very Important Kids) program.

The guest rooms, tastefully decorated in appealing colors with lush floral bedspreads and checked fabric sofas in complementing tones, all have a private balcony or terrace; some have panoramic ocean views while others look out on the garden, village, or pool. There are full-length mirrors, telephones with voice mail, large marble baths, stocked mini-bars, and amenities such as hair dryers, Neutrogena toiletries, robes, coffeemakers, irons, and ironing boards. Many rooms have gas fireplaces, and third-floor rooms have elevated domed ceilings with fans.

Hollywood

Sunset Marquis Hotel and Villas

1200 N. Alta Loma Road
West Hollywood, CA 90069
310-657-1333
800-858-9758
Fax: 310-652-5300
smhsales@aol.com

A secluded group of villas set in landscaped gardens

General manager: Rod Gruendyke. **Accommodations:** 102 suites, 12 villas. **Rates:** Suites $280–$360, villas $600–$1,200. **Payment:** Major credit cards. **Children:** Under age 12 free in room with parents; $25 for rollaways. **Pets:** Not allowed. **Smoking:** Nonsmoking rooms available.

➤ **A fountain trickles on a patio, parakeets chirp in the trees, and rabbits can be seen hopping among the calla lilies and azaleas. White lounge chairs sit by the pool, each with a monogrammed pink towel. There's also an exercise room, a spa, and a sauna.**

This lovely retreat is ideal if you're looking for quiet luxury in the heart of Hollywood's bustle. The hotel is close to production studios, tourist attractions, and businesses, just a half-block south of Sunset Boulevard, but these seem a world away once you step into the lobby. A few diners may be seated in the romantic little restaurant on your right, where soft music plays. A cordial staff member will show you to your room.

The three-story stucco hotel and its individual villas stand on two acres of cloistered gardens and hills.

You may lunch among the tropical plants at the poolside café or, if your villa is near the secluded second pool, have your order delivered there by the butler.

In the hotel building, rooms are grouped around the main swimming pool. Decorated in green, brown, and beige tones, bedrooms are separated from living rooms by French doors. Each suite has two televisions, a safe, and two-line telephones. Some rooms have VCRs and wet bars. Baths come with makeup mirrors and hair dryers and, in addition to the usual shampoos and soaps, sunscreen lotion is provided.

If the rooms are attractive, the villas, with one or two bedrooms and baths, are grand. All are light and spacious, with hanging plants, kitchens, and well-proportioned furniture. Some have private terraces overlooking the gardens and herringbone brick walkways; villas on the street have their own parking spaces. Chocolates and wine await your arrival, and the butler will light your fireplace and bring in kitchen equipment if you need it.

The attentive service at Sunset Marquis equals the setting. Valet parking and shoeshines are available 24 hours a day. (Self-parking is available in the garage under the hotel). At evening turndown you're given a weather report, and if you place your breakfast order on the door, it will be delivered to your room in the morning. Limousine service is also available. The concierge can arrange for theater tickets, tours, flowers, and appointments with hairdressers — all with a smile.

The Sunset Marquis is where many well-known names and faces go for privacy and relaxation, so you may spot a familiar face or two in the hotel's Whiskey Bar, which is open only to guests and VIPs — many of them in the music business. The hotel's restaurant across the hall has only eight tables. With La Cienega's restaurant row within easy walking distance, the hotel decided to keep its own eatery small and intimate.

Idyllwild

Strawberry Creek Inn

P.O. Box 1818
26370 Highway 243
Idyllwild, CA 92549
909-659-3202
800-262-8969
Fax: 909-659-4707
www.strawberrycreekinn.com

A traditional home in the mountains

Innkeepers: Diana Dugan and Jim Goff. **Accommodations:** 9 rooms and 1 cottage (all with private bath). **Rates:** $85–$105 single or double; cottage $150, $20 additional person. **Included:** Full breakfast, except in cottage. **Added:** 10% tax. **Minimum stay:** 2 nights on weekends, longer on holidays. **Payment:** Major credit cards. **Children:** Welcome in cottage. **Pets:** Not allowed. **Smoking:** Not allowed.

> ➤ **The savvy innkeepers have combined old-fashioned furnishings with modern comforts in this 1941 house that lies on wooded grounds above Strawberry Creek. From every window there are views of tall pines and oaks.**

In the rustic mountain village of Idyllwild, high above the desert near Palm Springs, stands Strawberry Creek Inn, a rambling, shingled home with a sense of nostalgia.

In the big, open living room, guests like to sit by the fire or browse among the ceiling-high shelves of books (including *How to Open a Country Inn*) in the cozy reading nook. Country antiques, an old-fashioned pie chest, and heirloom quilts furnish the room. On one side, next to a wall of windows, is the breakfast area.

Most of the guest rooms are fairly small. In the main house, the Evergreen Room, on the ground floor, has a queen-size canopy bed and a fireplace. The upstairs rooms are comfortably and individually furnished with patchwork quilts, ruffled cushions, fresh flowers, and good reading lamps.

Behind the main house is a separate building with rooms that face a courtyard. These are cabinlike retreats with fireplaces, refrigerators, and skylights. Santa Fe has a southwestern decor; Helen's Room is Victorian, with a carved walnut bed; Autumn has a four-poster bed and the rich colors of fall and is handicapped accessible. San Jacinto is a favorite for its stone fireplace, rag rugs, and rustic atmosphere.

The cedar-shake cottage down by the creek is a quaint spot, nice for honeymooners. (It can also hold four people, using the Murphy bed.) The cottage, decorated in blue, has a stone fireplace, two bathrooms, and a glassed-in dining porch, as well as a kitchen with a microwave oven, a gas stove, dishes, and staples for cooking. The bedroom is upstairs under the eaves and has a deep whirlpool tub.

Most visitors have high praise for Strawberry Creek. In the guest books they write, "Beautiful memories," "Friendly atmosphere," and "All you need for a romantic weekend."

Julian

Julian Hotel

P.O. Box 1856
2032 Main Street
Julian, CA 92036
760-765-0201
800-734-5854 in California
Fax: 760-765-0327
www.julianhotel.com

> **A historic hotel in a former mining town**

Innkeepers: Steve and Gig Ballinger. **Accommodations:** 14 rooms, 1 suite (all with private bath). **Rates:** $49 single, $72–$105 double, suites $135–$175. **Included:** Full breakfast and afternoon tea. **Added:** 9% tax. **Minimum stay:** 2 nights on weekends. **Payment:** Major credit cards. **Children:** Welcome. **Pets:** Not allowed. **Smoking:** Allowed outdoors only.

➤ **You're in another century as soon as you step into the Julian's large lobby. A woodstove stands in the center of the room, red velvet curtains hang at the tall windows, and a couple of cats may amble through. You'll be invited to join the other guests for tea and cakes at five o'clock.**

A hundred years ago, the mining town of Julian was a two-day stage ride from San Diego and had fifteen hotels lodging prospectors with gold fever. Now the trip takes less than two hours and only one hotel is left. The town still draws visitors, but these days they're tourists looking for reminders of the Old West.

The Julian Hotel is the oldest continuously operating hotel in southern California. It was built by freed slaves, Albert and Margaret Robinson, who started with a restaurant and bakery and, as their reputation for hospitality grew, put up the two-story wood frame hotel. Albert planted the cedar and locust trees that circle the hotel today. The Robinsons' venture was a success, and so it remains. It's on the National Register of Historic Places; a landmark with a frontier flavor.

In the large parlor classical music plays in the evenings while guests read, browse through turn-of-the-century Sears catalogs, or play Parcheesi. An ample breakfast of eggs Florentine, date nut raisin bread, fresh fruit, oats, coffee, tea, and juice is served here at tables for four.

The upstairs rooms are small but pleasant, and each has enough space for an antique bed with a modern mattress topped by a patchwork quilt, a dresser with a mirror (some are original to the hotel), a closet, a window covered in lace curtains, and a table and chair. All beds have electric blankets — nights are chilly at Julian's misty 4,000-foot elevation.

There are three rooms off the hotel's porch, and there are two cottages in back. The one-room cottage off the patio is cozy, with white muslin curtains, a white wicker chair, and a black iron bed under a flowered quilt. In the Honeymoon House you'll have a wood-burning Franklin stove on a brick hearth, a queen-size bed with a satin spread, and a dressing alcove with a clawfoot tub.

The Ballingers, who have owned the Julian Hotel since the late 1970s, have been careful to retain and restore the hotel's original decor. They have put together a walking tour that points out historic landmarks and will direct you to Julian's several antiques stores, gift shops, and a couple of good restaurants. Try Romano's, the Julian Grill, and, for lunch, Mom's Apple Pies. Julian apples are famous in the region; harvest season brings crowds of tourists and apple buyers.

To add to the memories of the time warp you're visiting, take the half-hour horse and carriage ride and then stop at the Bad Blood Studio Saloon and have your photograph taken in frontier costume. An excellent way to see more of the area is by following one of the Ballingers' detailed itineraries to nearby Cuyamaca Ranch State Park, the Anza-Borrego Desert, and Palomar Mountain.

Shadow Mountain Ranch

P.O. Box 791
2771 Frisius Road
Julian, CA 92036
760-765-0323
Fax: 760-765-0323
www.bnbcily.clerer.net/inns

**A homey bed-and-breakfast
in the country**

Innkeepers: Jim and Loretta Ketcherside. **Accommodations:** 6 rooms (all with private bath). **Rates:** $100–$130 single or double, $200 cottage for 4. **Included:** Full breakfast and refreshments. **Added:** 9% tax. **Minimum stay:** 2 nights on weekends. **Payment:** Personal checks or cash. **Children:** Age 1 and under welcome; additional $20. **Pets:** Not allowed. **Smoking:** Not allowed indoors.

➤ **This unique lodging has much to offer the visitor — a lovely rural setting, plentiful activities, down-home hospitality, and creative accommodations that will help restore the most cherished memories of childhood.**

This peaceful retreat lies in the rolling, wooded hills outside Julian, a historic mining town east of San Diego. Once an apple orchard and cattle ranch, it is now a bed-and-breakfast and the Ketchersides' home. Visitors can join in feeding their cows and horse.

Loretta, a former nurse, and Jim, a retired superintendent of schools, enjoy meeting people and sharing their country hideaway. If you arrive in the afternoon, you'll be in time for tea and snacks, served on the deck under the trees or by the fire in their large, homey living room. There are games, magazines, and books, and the musically inclined hosts have a piano, violin, and guitars for guests to use.

In the Apple Pantry underneath Grandma's Attic or on an outdoor patio called the Cocina, Loretta and Jim serve a ranch-style breakfast: steak or sausage, eggs with steamed vegetables, hot cereal, orange juice, and an endless supply of coffee that will prepare you for an active day. On Sundays, the cook adds strawberry pancakes topped with whipped cream to the array of food. After a few laps in the indoor pool, fishing in the Ketchersides' catch and release pond, a game of horseshoes, croquet, or badminton, and a hike in the Pine Hills forest, you may feel like eating again. The Apple Pantry's kitchen, which has a toaster oven, refrigerator, and two burners, can be used by guests and comes in handy if you'd like to stay put rather than drive in to Julian for dinner.

Each guest room is different and often decorated with an imaginative flair. Victorian Rose, in the main house, is the most traditional and has a brick sitting area, wood-burning stove, country antiques, and a wonderfully shaped clawfoot tub. Grandma's Attic, across a wooden bridge from the main deck, is named for Loretta, who is now a grandmother. Spacious and sunny, the room has a white iron bed with brass accents that's topped with a pink damask and white lace comforter, wicker furnishings, and a cozy sitting area in a bay window. Loretta's wedding dress is also on display. Outside, next to the path by the wall, is an elaborate miniature village, complete with bridges, trees, and churches. It was made by Loretta's father years ago.

The Enchanted Cottage, on a grassy knoll, is quaint and cozy. It has a wood-burning stove and a cushioned seat by a mullioned window that looks into the pine trees; rabbit motifs appear on a throw and a footstool. Manzanita is a two-bedroom, two-bathroom cottage perfect for couples traveling together. On chilly mornings the woodstove on the brick hearth warms the living room, with its cowhide rug, coffee table, and gameboard. One bedroom is decorated in peach tones, the other is paneled and opens onto a porch. The full kitchen has a breakfast nook and window seat overlooking a pasture. Each bedroom has a private entrance and a private bathroom.

If you've always wanted to sleep in a tree or have nostalgic memories of a tree house, reserve the Tree House. In the branches of an ancient oak tree, the rustic room is reached by a stairway from the lower deck that surrounds the tree. The room contains a queen-size bed, a sitting area, and toilet facilities — the shower is located downstairs. Its windows view the treetops of the Cleveland National Forest and fields below. What could be more satisfying than falling asleep to the sighs of mountain breezes, sheltered in the arms of a great oak?

For a true return to the fairy tales of childhood, request the Gnome Home — the most unusual and enchanting accommodation at Shadow Mountain Ranch. The charming cottage is made from cement sculpted to look like the bark of a tree. Gnome footprints are embedded in the cement at the doorstep. Inside the circular structure, the whimsical carved furnishings were handmade by a local artist, and playful touches are everywhere. A carved tree stump doubles as a footstool, a hand-forged wrought-iron chandelier designed to resemble tree branches hangs from the central skylight, carved swinging doors of gnomes kissing shield the toilet area, the rock shower has the appearance of a forest waterfall, and even the sink has a face of its own. There is no telling what fantastic dreams may visit you in the night while sleeping in this bewitching chamber.

La Jolla

La Jolla Beach & Tennis Club

2000 Spindrift Drive
La Jolla, CA 92037
619-454-7126
800-624-2582
Fax: 619-456-3805
www.ljbtc.com

A beach resort for tennis, golf, and swimming

General manager: John Campbell. **Accommodations:** 90 rooms and apartments. **Rates:** $129–$629 double occupancy. **Added:** 10.5% tax. **Payment:** Major credit cards. **Children:** Over age 2, $20 additional per night. **Pets:** Not allowed. **Smoking:** Nonsmoking rooms available.

➤   **The Marine Room is a restaurant so close to the water that cresting waves, illuminated at night, sometimes splash against the windows. Seahorses swim in the aquarium and skylights open to the sun or stars. In the evening, live entertainment provides background music for dancing.**

The guest apartments at this private tennis club stretch along a quarter-mile of beautiful beach 15 miles north of San Diego. About a thousand families in the well-heeled La Jolla area belong to the club, which is located in a palm grove in a residential district, but visitors have full membership privileges during their stay.

With 12 championship tennis courts (eight of them lighted) and a pro instructor, and pro shop, the club is a favorite with tennis players. Around the 10-acre property's tropical lagoon there's a 9-hole pitch-and-putt golf course that guests may use for a nominal fee. A heated junior Olympic–size swimming pool lies next to the patio where lunch is served daily. You may also eat in the club dining room, facing the esplanade by the private beach.

The guest rooms and apartments are in low stucco buildings with red tile roofs. Most face the water, and some are just a step

from the smooth sand. A typical room, decorated in a seaside motif, will have two double beds with rattan headboards, comfortable
seating, and an equipped kitchenette. All the rooms are supplied
with bottled water or piped purified water.

The club's seahorse logo is everywhere: at the bottom of a pool
on a seaside terrace, in a tiled fountain in the central courtyard,
and on the bright blue boards supplied as wind protection on the
beach. The club also provides beach towels, chairs, and multi-
colored umbrellas for protection from the sun. You may rent scuba
and snorkeling gear, wetsuits, and surfboards from a nearby surf
shop. Snorkeling in La Jolla Cove will allow you to see coral and
undersea marine life among the wavy strands of kelp.

With apartment sizes up to three bedrooms, this lodging appeals
to families. It provides daily maid service, cable television, and
self-service Laundromats.

La Valencia Hotel

1132 Prospect Street
La Jolla, CA 92037
619-454-0771
800-451-0772
Fax: 619-456-3921
reservations@lavalencia.com
www.lavalencia.com

> **A vintage hotel with a
> Mediterranean atmosphere**

Manager: Michael J. Ullman. **Accommodations:** 117 rooms and suites. **Rates:**
$235–$1,500. **Added:** 10.5% tax. **Payment:** Major credit cards. **Children:** Under
18 free in room with parents. **Pets:** Not allowed. **Smoking:** Nonsmoking rooms
available.

➤ **From the parlor you look down on tall palm trees, a green park flash-
ing with Frisbees, a sandy shore, and the blue Pacific. Double glass doors**

open to a balcony above a curved swimming pool and terraced gardens that descend to the road.

In the heart of La Jolla, ten miles north of San Diego, this pink stucco hotel has been welcoming travelers and holding social events since 1926. The hotel and the town grew up together on the California Riviera, where palms sway in gentle breezes and the sun shines beneficently on sheltered La Jolla Cove.

On the street level (which is also the fourth floor; three more stories descend a hillside toward the water and several others rise above), you pass through a colonnade beside a palm-shaded patio to the lobby. Beyond the small, usually crowded registration area and down a few tiled stairs is a long parlor with colorful Spanish mosaics, a hand-painted ceiling, and, at the far end, a floor-to-ceiling window with a compelling view of the sea.

La Valencia boasts three restaurants. Mediterranean Room, with its vibrant colors, fresh flowers, superb view, and acclaimed menu is a popular spot for breakfast, lunch, or dinner. The Tropical Patio, the outdoor section of the Mediterranean Room, is ideal for a leisurely lunch on a sunny day. The Whaling Bar and Grill has a New England nautical decor. The bar contains New Bedford harpoons and lanterns, ivory scrimshaw, and pewter candle holders. There's a model of a full-rigged sailing ship behind the leather booths and a mural depicting the old whaling days. The romantic tenth-floor Sky Room, an elegant, intimate space, overlooks the ocean. The imaginative dinner menu features French cuisine for fish and meat eaters alike.

The hotel has one elevator — the original, still with a human operator. It's swift but is likely to be crowded at peak times. The attractively furnished guest rooms have a traditional European look that combines stately lines with the softness of floral fabrics and clear colors. Each has its own climate control, television, queen- or king-size beds, coffeemaker, VCR, and mini-bar.

A deluxe oceanfront room offers a panoramic view beyond double-glazed windows. A brass chandelier in the living room, mint-green carpeting, soft gold walls, potted plants, and a stocked mini-bar are among the room's furnishings. In keeping with the European flavor, some suites have bidets and others have whirlpool tubs.

The hotel has a small fitness room with sauna. You can lounge by the pool or on the beach, or join the vacationers shopping along Prospect Street. The La Jolla Museum of Contemporary Art is a few blocks from the hotel.

Prospect Park Inn

1110 Prospect Street
La Jolla, CA 92037
619-454-0133
800-433-1609
Fax: 619-454-2056
www.Tales.com/Ca/ProspectParkInn/

A small inn in downtown La Jolla

Innkeeper: John Heichman. **Accommodations:** 20 rooms, 2 suites. **Rates:** $120–$185 single, $120–$200 double; suites $275–$375. **Included:** Continental breakfast and afternoon refreshments. **Added:** 10.5% tax. **Payment:** Major credit cards. **Children:** Free in room with parents. **Pets:** Not allowed. **Smoking:** Not allowed.

➤ **For bird's-eye views of the coastline from Oceanside to Mexico, take the scenic drive up Mount Soledad to the top. To get a close look at some of California's most exciting surfing action, go to Windansea Beach. Boomer Beach is also a favorite of experienced surfers.**

Like La Jolla (The Jewel) itself, Prospect Park Inn is a jewel of a place. The small hotel has a perfect resort location, between chic, busy Prospect Street and the green parks, palm trees, and sandy beaches of La Jolla Cove.

It's easy to overlook the brick hotel, for its entrance is sandwiched between a corner shop and the showy pink La Valencia Hotel. But behind the teal awnings and small, light lobby are three floors of charming rooms, all of them furnished in Mediterranean pastels, California style.

There's a minuscule library on the ground floor, with just enough room for a couch, two chairs, and a sideboard where you may help yourself to tea, coffee, chocolate, and cookies any time of day. There are a few shelves of books and magazines and a phone for guests' use. Coke and ice machines are down the hall.

All the rooms have television. Studios and penthouses have kitchenettes with microwave and toaster ovens; the mini-suite has a full kitchen. Since the front door is locked and there's no desk clerk on duty after 2:00 A.M., your room key also opens a wrought-iron gate to a side entrance. Underground parking is available.

The Cove Suite is a penthouse that opens to a sun deck overlooking the shops and cafés on the corner of Jenner and Prospect and the park and lovely cove to the west. Continental breakfast and afternoon tea are served on the deck. The suite has a spacious bedroom, a living area with a fold-down queen-size bed, and a self-contained kitchenette. The Village Suite has similar features. The two penthouses share an entry foyer that may be closed off if a family or couples traveling together wish to share the hotel's upper story.

A few steps away from the inn are the famed attractions of La Jolla: beaches, art galleries, boutiques, and restaurants. Highly recommended for dinner is George's at the Cove.

Laguna Beach

Surf & Sand Hotel

1555 South Coast Highway
Laguna Beach, CA 92651
949-497-4477
800-524-8621
Fax: 949-494-7653
www.jcresorts.com

A sophisticated beachside hotel

General manager: Blaise Bartell. **Accommodations:** 164 rooms and suites. **Rates:** $220–$410 single or double, $10 additional person; suites $400–$1,050; winter discounts available. **Added:** 10% tax. **Minimum stay:** 2 nights in July, 3 nights in August. **Payment:** Major credit cards. **Children:** $10 additional if third person in room. **Pets:** Not allowed. **Smoking:** Nonsmoking rooms available.

➤ **Surf & Sand has facilities for groups of up to 250 people, but individuals also receive attentive care. Attendants will set up umbrellas on the beach and serve cocktails and lunch by the pool.**

A $25 million renovation, which took place in the early 1990s, turned the Surf & Sand from quaint to elegant. Now it occupies four buildings of varying heights and all but three guest rooms have ocean views from private balconies. Directly above the sandy beach, south of the shops and restaurants and crowds of Laguna Beach, this hotel has one of southern California's prime locations.

The rooms vary in size but have the same Mediterranean decor and the same amenities: phones, radios, televisions, cotton and silk fabrics, original art, and hair dryers and robes in bathrooms of beige marble. They were refurbished in a contemporary style by the noted designer James Northcutt. Guests find a split of champagne when they arrive, and returning guests receive Godiva chocolates as well. The most luxurious rooms are the two-bedroom penthouses, both with stunning panoramic views.

In the center of the complex is a terrace with a pool; below it, overlooking the surf, is Splashes, the hotel's attempt to prove that fine food and a beachfront location can go together. The Mediterranean-influenced menu changes daily. Examples of the provocative dishes are seared scallops with potato risotto and caramelized onion sauce, and lamb osso bucco with basil fettucine.

Lake Arrowhead

Château du Lac

P.O. Box 1098
911 Hospital Road
Lake Arrowhead, CA 92352
909-337-6488
800-601-8722
Fax: 909-337-6746
Chateau@JS-Net.com
www.LakeArrowhead.com

> A gracious modern home
> above the lake

Innkeepers: Jody and Oscar Wilson. **Accommodations:** 5 rooms (all with private bath). **Rates:** $125–$235. **Included:** Full breakfast and afternoon tea. **Added:** 9% tax. **Minimum stay:** 2 nights on weekends. **Payment:** Major credit cards. **Children:** Over age 14 welcome; additional $10 per child. **Pets:** Not allowed. **Smoking:** Not allowed

➤ **Jody, who serves breakfast by the dining room windows, is an expert cook who once had a catering company. She prepares eggs Benedict, potato casserole, quiche, pancakes, sausages in cider, and other entrées that are accompanied by fruit, juice, and hot breads.**

On a bluff overlooking Lake Arrowhead, in the San Bernardino mountains, the Wilsons welcome guests who want to enjoy the tranquillity of the area and their large, attractive home. Château du Lac is a place to sleep late, enjoy an excellent breakfast, relax during the day, and be back in time for afternoon tea and hors d'oeuvres. "This is a do-nothing area," Oscar Wilson says. Formerly in the television industry in Los Angeles, he makes birdhouses, helps run the B&B, and plays the role of gracious host to perfection.

There's a touch of Queen Anne style in the contemporary cedar house that Oscar and his wife, Jody, completed in 1988. Built around an atrium with oak trees, it has more than 100 windows that flood each room with light. You enter to a living room with a brick fireplace and high ceilings. Beyond is the dining area, with doors to a deck and spectacular view of the lake and mountains. The deck curves around to a gazebo and stairs that lead to a balcony upstairs. From every angle there's another panoramic vista to admire.

Upstairs, the spacious Lakeview Room is often reserved months in advance by honeymooning couples. The room has high, vaulted ceilings, a brick fireplace, and a mirrored antique armoire — the only antique in the house; other furnishings are reproductions. A dried floral swag hangs over the bed, which is topped with a white eyelet lace comforter, teddy bear, and lots of pillows. The private balcony offers fine views of the lake and the San Gabriel Mountains in the distance, as does the Jacuzzi tub in the bath set beneath a bay window. Downstairs there's a suite with a bedroom and a separate living room with a sleeper sofa.

The Loft Suite is another good choice for those seeking privacy as it is set off from the other rooms and has its own entrance. Decorated in blue and rose tones, it has a four-poster bed and a loveseat in front of a gas fireplace. A dressing table is set in a dormer window, and a rolltop writing desk is in another dormer. The large bath has a Jacuzzi and a separate shower. Room 4 has a romantic iron and brass bed, floral wallpaper, a cushioned window seat, and a sofa tucked away in an alcove. Room 3 is the least expensive room because it has a shower only. All rooms have TVs and VCRs, and guests can borrow movies from the Wilsons' video library.

Hotel Queen Mary

1126 Queens Highway
Long Beach, CA 90802
562-435-3511
800-437-2934
Fax: 562-437-4531
www.queenmary.com

> A historic cruise ship
> docked in Long Beach
> harbor

President: Joseph F. Prevratil. **Accommodations:** 365 staterooms and suites. **Rates:** $75–$400. **Added:** 12% tax. **Payment:** Major credit cards. **Children:** Under age 18 free in room with adult. **Pets:** Not allowed. **Smoking:** Nonsmoking rooms available.

➤ **Despite knowing that you can walk off anytime, and despite the fact that the portholes (2,000 of them) view the lights and oil refineries of Long Beach, there's a distinct sense of being in an enclosed world, far out at sea, that lends a festive atmosphere to the Queen Mary.**

The last and most luxurious of the great ocean liners, the *Queen Mary* is now permanently docked at Long Beach. Her first voyage was in 1936, her last in 1967, when first-class passengers paid a top rate of $1,282 to travel from Southampton around Cape Horn to Long Beach Harbor. Now owned by the City of Long Beach, the ship is open for tours and to overnight guests who want a cruise experience without leaving the wharf. Called "the ship of beautiful woods," its paneling and inlaid decoration of rare woods create a warm and beautiful interior.

The *Queen Mary* is immense. Taller than Niagara Falls, longer than the Eiffel Tower is high, weighing 81,000 tons, she's a majestic sight, even anchored next to a parking lot. Thousands of visitors troop aboard all year round — some to spend a night, others to dine in one of the three restaurants or dance in the art deco lounge, and many who want simply to tour the historic curiosity.

It's like visiting a theme park. There are marching jazz bands, lifeboat demonstrations, weddings (hundreds each year), and shops selling English imports. Exhibits show the history of the *Queen Mary*. From royal cruises to World War II transport, the story is fascinating.

The staterooms, in what was once the first-class section, are the largest ever built on a ship. They are on three of the vessel's twelve decks and have the authentic decor of a stylish, if somewhat worn, '30s ship — paneled walls, portholes, and the original bathtub spigots for fresh or salt water. The most preferred staterooms are the Duke of Edinburgh, King George, and Queen Mary suites, and the Churchill Suite where Sir Winston himself stayed.

Sir Winston's, dimly lit, with a view of Long Beach Harbor, is the ship's top restaurant, serving California and Continental cuisine with dishes such as venison, portobello, and beef phyllo, and Sir Winston's beef tenderloin foie gras wrapped in phyllo. The Promenade Café, also with a view of the harbor, is more casual. The Chelsea features a buffet breakfast and lunch and a seafood menu for dinner. On Sunday mornings, the Grand Salon is open for champagne brunch. You can help yourself to 50 or so entrées — just as you're likely to find on a real cruise. The Observation Bar is a stunning art deco cocktail lounge. Live entertainment is offered here nightly.

Los Angeles

The Argyle

8358 Sunset Boulevard
Los Angeles, CA 90069
323-654-7100
800-225-2637
Fax: 323-654-9287
www.argylehotel.com

An elegant city hotel with
art deco ambience

General manager: Lesley Carey. **Accommodations:** 64 rooms and suites. **Rates:** $240–$950. **Added:** 13% tax. **Payment:** Major credit cards. **Children:** Free in room with parents, but only a limited number of rooms can accommodate families. **Pets:** With prior approval only and a $500 security deposit. **Smoking:** Nonsmoking rooms available.

➤   **Close to the hotel are such landmark restaurants as Hollywood's oldest, Musso & Frank's, which opened in 1919; Engine Co. No. 28, a restored firehouse; and the oldest eatery in Los Angeles, Philippe, known for its French dip sandwiches and pickled eggs.**

In the 1930s this opulent hotel was the Sunset Towers, the first all-electric apartment building in California and the tallest (14 stories) building on Sunset Boulevard. Charlie Chaplin, Errol Flynn, Clark Gable, Jean Harlow, and other screen stars called it home. Now extensively restored and a member of the Lancaster Hotel Group, it's an art deco landmark on the National Registry of Historic Places and a stunning example of its period.

The Argyle's fanciful white exterior is easy to spot as you travel along Hollywood's famed Sunset Boulevard. Inside the front door the '30s theme continues with white marble, frosted glass light fixtures, and metal railings with art deco motifs.

In silvers, blacks, and golds, guest rooms are delightful throwbacks to Hollywood's heyday. Deco originals and reproductions grace every room, showcasing furniture with walnut burl veneer and replicas of Emile Ruhlmann's classic gondola beds. Marble baths have European fixtures and individual heaters and some have Jacuzzi tubs.

Although the rooms have the distinctive flavor of an earlier era, modern conveniences have not been forgotten. In fact, cutting edge technology can be found next to the bed, where a computer keypad lets you control your lights, room temperature, music, and TV without ever having to get up. All rooms have mini-bars, VCRs, two-line speaker phones, safes, and CD players. For a homey touch, freshly baked cookies are left at bedside during nightly turndown.

Single rooms are the smallest, with only a twin bed, but they still have ample living space for one. Some tower suites have two baths, but for a real treat rent one of the penthouses. The two Penthouse Suites share the entire 15th floor, and each has a terrace that wraps around half the building affording some of the best views of Los Angeles and the Hollywood Hills you'll find. The spacious suites have a separate living room with dining area, a large bedroom, and a bath fit for even the most finicky Hollywood idol, with marbled black tile, an oversize steam shower, deep whirlpool tub, double sinks, and a bidet.

The fenix restaurant has Los Angeles talking about chef Ken Frank's French/Californian cuisine. He incorporates French-inspired sauces — many of them vegetable-based with fresh California produce. Signature dishes include spinach soup with Maine Lobster, rosti potato with caviar, and filet mignon with red wine, shallots, marrow, and cèpes. In fenix you can enjoy fine cuisine and a city view, then you can move on to the Argyle's lounge, where there's live entertainment.

The hotel has a well-equipped health club and a heated outdoor swimming pool. (You may recognize the pool area with its city views and wrought-iron palm tree sculptures from the movie *The Player.*) If you're looking for more celebrity-oriented entertainment, Thunder Roadhouse, owned by Peter Fonda, Dennis Hopper, and Dwight Yoakum, is just across the street; the Comedy Store in on the same block; and Dan Ackroyd's House of Blues, one block from the hotel, is always jammed.

Hotel Bel-Air

701 Stone Canyon Road
Los Angeles, CA 90077
310-472-1211
800-648-4097
Fax: 310-476-5890

| A luxurious inn of charm and style |

General manager: Frank Bowling. **Accommodations:** 92 rooms and suites. **Rates:** $350–$500 single or double, suites $600–$2,500. **Added:** 14% tax. **Payment:** Major credit cards. **Children:** Welcome. **Pets:** Not allowed. **Smoking:** Nonsmoking rooms available.

➤ **To enter the hotel you cross an arched bridge and walk past a waterfall and Swan Lake. The main building is crowned by a tower that is partly obscured by the brilliant red of flowering trumpet vines.**

In 1922 the oil millionaire Alonzo E. Bell created a subdivision of estates in the foothills and canyons north of Sunset Boulevard, where today palatial homes lie off winding, tree-shaded roads. Named Bel-Air, it became one of the most prestigious residential areas in Los Angeles.

Bell's planning and sales offices were in a Mission-style building that was later converted to hotel accommodations — the centerpiece of the present Hotel Bel-Air. Now considerably expanded, it is renowned for its luxury and its sequestered location. It is also close to city shopping, restaurants, and offices.

The one- and two-story pink buildings are set on 11-1/2 acres of towering ferns, palms, California sycamores, and native live oaks that shade fountained courtyards, a tumbling stream, and a tranquil pond. In the pond, beautiful (but cranky) swans float regally.

In season the gardens glow with color. Jasmine and gardenia scent the balmy air; red bougainvillea climbs to terra cotta tiled roofs. The lush grounds are tended by a team of ten gardeners. One of the plantings in their expert care is a 50-foot pink-flowering silk floss tree, the largest of its kind in California. It was planted by Alonzo Bell.

When you arrive in the parlorlike lobby, you are asked which newspaper you'd like to have delivered to your door in the morning and then are escorted through the gardens to your room. Classical music plays softly on your radio when you arrive, and the lamps are lit.

Most of the rooms and suites are on the ground level, with glimpses of gardens through their rose-draped windows. They vary widely in size and decor; most have a patio or fireplace or both. Some are furnished in a French country style that is light, simple, and classic. Others are traditional American or have a California mission theme. The white tiled baths have brass fixtures.

The best choices in the old section are the suites. For consistency in size and style, request a room in the newer section. Each is elegant in peach tones with needlepoint rugs on terra cotta floors. Selected suites have their own fountain and whirlpool in a private patio. A few have small kitchens. All guests receive tea service upon arrival and nightly turndown service. Some of the amenities available are same-day laundry and dry cleaning, 24-hour room service, a video library, and a complimentary shoeshine.

The restaurant, at the end of a graceful arcade, has banquettes and romantic tables for two by the windows, which face tropical plantings and a terrace that is set for outdoor dining. Contemporary California cuisine is served, using fresh regional ingredients and herbs from the hotel's gardens. Breakfasts are outstanding, and the presentation is stylish. You may have breakfast, lunch, dinner, and afternoon tea in the restaurant or, for a change, eat lightly in the bar next door. With a pianist and vocalist performing nightly, the cozy bar is a favorite evening gathering place for Bel-Air residents as well as hotel guests.

Although the Bel-Air is mostly a place to retreat and relax and maybe take a stroll through the quiet, sun-dappled gardens before dinner, there is a heated swimming pool and fitness center with cardiovascular equipment on the property, and tennis and golf are easily accessible. And don't forget the shopping opportunities — you're close to Beverly Hills and Rodeo Drive, where glamorous boutiques and designer displays draw shoppers who can afford the best.

Hotel Sofitel

8555 Beverly Blvd.
Los Angeles, CA 90048
310-278-5444
800-221-4542
Fax: 310-657-2816
www.sofitel.com

> **A contemporary hotel with a convenient location**

Manager: Cindy Johnson. **Accommodations:** 311 rooms and suites. **Rates:** $290–$325 single or double, $25 each additional person, suites $400–$500. **Added:** 14% tax. **Payment:** Major credit cards. **Children:** Under age 15 free in room with parent. **Pets:** Allowed by prior arrangement. **Smoking:** Nonsmoking rooms available

➤ **La Cajole Brasserie is a copy of a popular French restaurant in Paris. Wooden cutouts of people reading *Le Monde* add to the eatery's genial atmosphere, while French favorites such as crêpes and escargot can be found on the menu.**

This sleek ten-story hotel occupies a choice spot in West Los Angeles. It's close to the Pacific Design Center and Cedars Sinai Hospital and across the street from the famed shops of Beverly Center. It's also convenient to Beverly Hills, westside offices, and Melrose Avenue boutiques. Part of a French chain, the hotel is functional and attractive, with a Mediterranean ambience. The lobby has stone floors, a sweeping staircase, and textured walls and columns. Colors are muted throughout.

The rooms, too, reflect a southern European style, with French country fabrics and decor. They include flowered bedspreads and drapes and walls of soft brick or green with matching carpeting. Upper-floor rooms have French doors leading to outside terraces where one can sit and sip a drink or watch the world pass by below. The hotel was designed primarily to serve business travelers with conveniences such as 24-hour room service, three phones per room with fax/modern capability and voice-activated message centers, mini-bars, and morning newspapers. Hair dryers and Nina Ricci toiletries are amenities that women travelers will especially appreciate.

Since some rooms are quite small and lack workable desk space, an Executive King room is a good choice if you plan to work during your visit. It has separate areas for sitting, sleeping, and dressing and includes a desk. These partial suites can be used as one large space or the areas can be separated by drapes for privacy. The closets are ample, but drawer space is very limited. The best rooms are on the north side, facing what residents call the Blue Whale (the Pacific Design Center) and the Hollywood Hills beyond. The nighttime view — when it's clear — is spectacular.

The hotel's conference facilities consist of 7 rooms that vary in capacity from 12 to 240. There's a health club for guests' use with Nautilus machines and a sauna, and an outdoor pool surrounded by decking, lounge chairs, and umbrella tables.

Setting Hotel Sofitel above many city hotels are its constant room service, babysitting, and same-day valet service. Also worth noting, if you're bored with airline food, is the box lunch prepared for air travelers; it's available upon request. Rushed travelers appreciate the Three-Minute Breakfast, a selection of beverages, croissants, pastries, and seasonal fruit set up buffet style in the lobby. All guests receive a freshly baked French baguette upon check-out.

The New Otani Hotel & Garden

120 South Los Angeles Street
Los Angeles, CA 90012
213-629-1200
800-273-2294 in California
800-421-8795 in U.S. and Canada
Fax: 213-622-0980
www.newotani.com

A Western city hotel with Japanese character

General manager: Kenji Yoshimoto. **Accommodations:** 434 rooms, including 20 suites. **Rates:** Singles start at $185, doubles start at $210, suites $475–$1,800. **Added:** 14% tax. **Payment:** Major credit cards. **Children:** Under age 12 free in room with parents. **Pets:** Not allowed. **Smoking:** Nonsmoking rooms available

➤ **East meets West in this 21-story hotel, where you may dine on New York steaks or yakitori, sleep on an American bed or a futon, and listen to cocktail piano music or a Koto player.**

When the New Otani opened in 1977, the management did not stress its Japanese heritage and connections. "We didn't want Americans to feel we were simply a Japanese hotel where they could not get by in English or find their eggs and bacon," says Kenji Yoshimoto, the hotel's general manager. But it soon became clear that the touch of Japan was one of the hotel's main attractions. Now it's strongly emphasized, though all employees speak English; in fact, front desk personnel collectively speak nineteen languages.

When you leave your car with the valet and enter the three-story lobby, you'll see a dramatic glass sculpture and behind it the Rendezvous Lounge. In this raised, open area a pianist plays on weekdays. To the left is a shopping arcade; on the right a sweeping staircase winds up to a mezzanine and guest rooms above it.

The Azalea Restaurant and Bar, on the lobby level, offers appetizers and American cuisine with a California slant. Upstairs, A Thousand Cranes features Japanese meals at standard tables or in private tatami rooms. This is the place to try sushi, uni (fresh sea urchin), awabi (abalone cooked with sake wine), and tempura in a traditional setting. The restaurant overlooks the "garden in the sky," a tranquil half-acre roof garden of pathways, ponds, and waterfalls bordered with azaleas. Also with a view of the garden is the contemporary Garden Grill, open for Teppan Yaki dining.

In keeping with the hotel's Japanese ownership, guest rooms are contemporary with an oriental flavor in their artwork and decor. The bathrooms have phones, hand-held showers, and thick white towels with the hotel's name handsomely embroidered in red. Yukatas (Japanese kimonos) are available, as well as standard robes.

For the most interesting experience the New Otani offers, reserve one of the Japanese suites. The parlor is Western, with modern couches and soft chairs, while the sleeping area behind sliding shoji screens is a large, elevated tatami room with a futon. The bath has a sunken tub, traditional in Japan. At the Sanwa Health Spa, you may relax in a sauna or herb-scented Jacuzzi and enjoy a shiatsu massage. Other features are room service, same-day cleaning, a beauty salon, and concierge services.

Special events and cultural programs exploring Japanese culture take place throughout the year. You can learn about the tea ceremony, take a calligraphy lesson, or study one of the many forms of ikebana (flower arranging). Traditional celebrations include Setsubun (the end of winter), the Hina Doll Festival, and Temari (a demonstration of a 1,400-year-old folk art in which colorful silk balls are created).

The New Otani, in Little Tokyo, is close to Los Angeles City Hall, the Music Center, city and county courthouses, and the Los Angeles *Times* building. Across the street is St. Vibiana Cathedral, one of L.A.'s oldest.

The Regal Biltmore Hotel

506 South Grand Avenue
Los Angeles, CA 90071
213-624-1011
800-245-8673
Fax: 213-612-1545

> **A grand hotel of traditional grace and elegance**

Manager: Armel Santenes. **Accommodations:** 640 rooms and 43 suites. **Rates:** $210–$390 single, $240–$395 double, $30 additional person, suites $375–$2,000. **Added:** 14% tax. **Payment:** Major credit cards. **Children:** Under age 16 free in room with parents. **Pets:** Not allowed. **Smoking:** Nonsmoking rooms available.

➤ **It's worth visiting the Biltmore just to see the wonderfully ornate Rendezvous Court, where you may take afternoon tea, cocktails, or dessert as you listen to the melodic strains of a piano.**

When the Biltmore opened in 1923, it was the largest and most elaborate hotel west of Chicago. Constructed in Spanish-Italian Renaissance style, with lavish interior ceilings and wall paintings by Italian artist Giovanni Smeraldi, the hotel was — and is — splendid. It has hosted presidents, kings, and Hollywood stars as well as more mundane travelers, and along the way it has become a historic landmark.

It's been refurbished several times, most recently with a $40 million restoration that spruced up all the public spaces and guest rooms. Furnishings and bathrooms now reflect contemporary luxury, but the artistry that made the Biltmore famous in the '20s may still be seen in the hand-oiled paneling, fine moldings and millwork, carvings, vivid frescoes, and stately columns and pilasters.

Next to the beautiful Rendezvous Court lounge is a steakhouse. Ristorante Smereldi's serves northern Italian and California cuisine. It's open for three meals a day. The Grand Avenue Sports Bar, off the main lobby, is noted for its weekday lunch buffet, wines, and jazz, while the European-style Gallery Bar and Cognac Room features beer and liquors. Yet another restaurant is Sai Sai, with a menu of Japanese dishes. The hotel also has sixteen grand banquet and meeting rooms.

The Biltmore's concierge desk will handle almost any request: theater tickets, reservations, tours, laundry, and clothes pressing are a few. Room service is available all day. Several languages are spoken by the staff; in this worldwide crossroads, they're all needed.

The guest rooms are spacious and comfortable, if somewhat bland in their furnishings. They have modern or traditional French furniture, including writing tables, armoires that house television sets, and extender reading lamps. You can choose a king- or queen-size or two double beds. There are 26 room configurations, with varying color schemes. Each room has a mini-bar stocked with pricey snacks and drinks. Toiletries in the baths are beautifully packaged with scenes of the hotel. All guests have the use of the Biltmore's art deco spa, equipped with a Roman-style indoor swimming pool, steam room, sauna, whirlpool, Keiser equipment, and massage service.

To attract the affluent business traveler, the Biltmore offers corporate packages that include an array of special services and amenities. The Regal Club Floor features the hotel's most luxurious accommodations, express check-in and check-out, daily newspaper, shoeshine, and twice-daily maid service. On the Club Floor you have access to the Club Lounge, where a concierge, copy machines, translators, and a small library are available. Complimentary tea, cocktails, and a Continental breakfast are served in the Lounge. Business travelers who need fewer amenities like the Regal Class floor, which has no concierge or lounge but does offer such services as computer hookups.

The Biltmore represents opulence on the grand scale. It's a fine old hotel that has fortunately been revived with style and a genuine sense of tradition.

Wyndham Checkers Hotel

535 South Grand Avenue
Los Angeles, CA 90071
213-624-0000
800-WYNDHAM
Fax: 213-626-9906
checkerla@aol.com

A classic, small hotel of urban elegance

General manager: Joseph Mottershead. **Accommodations:** 171 rooms, 17 suites. **Rates:** $209–$322 single, $219–$344 double, suites $450–$1,000. **Added:** 14% tax. **Payment:** Major credit cards. **Children:** Free in room with parents. **Pets:** Not allowed. **Smoking:** Nonsmoking rooms available.

➤ **Near the rooftop lap pool there's an equipped weight room and Jacuzzi. Some guests like to work out in the mornings, read the paper, and order a light breakfast here. Robes are provided.**

In the heart of downtown Los Angeles, near Pershing Square, the Museum of Contemporary Art, and the remodeled public library, this posh little hotel offers a tranquil and elegant retreat. Built as the Mayflower Hotel in 1927, the 14-story building underwent a $50 million restoration to be reborn as Checkers, which opened in 1989 with the finest in residential furnishings, antiques, artwork, accommodations, and service. The building's creamy stone exterior with intricate ornamentation is as lovely as it was when the hotel first opened.

The lobby is divided into three sections, each displaying beautiful pieces of contemporary and antique art. Among them are rare old Japanese vases, a Chinese red lacquer screen, and a German armoire of ebony and rosewood that dates from 1725. On the mezzanine above are meeting rooms and a library/sitting room in soft gray with more Oriental antiques, including two 19th-century mother-of-pearl elephants. It's a favored gathering place for small groups, ideal when the lobby is too public and a guest room too private.

All the guest rooms, furnished alike, are decorated in light woods and soothing, soft colors. They have clock radios, TVs with movie and sports channels, mini-bars, writing tables, and phones with voice mail and international signs on the buttons in deference to the hotel's many foreign visitors. Suites have separate living rooms and two baths. Marble bathrooms, tub thermometers, makeup mirrors, coffeemakers, robes, and closets that light when the door opens are a few of the special touches common to all rooms.

Attention to detail in appointments and service makes Checkers exceptional. The well-trained staff can respond to almost any need: valet assistance, same-day laundry service, secretarial help, and 24-hour room service are routine. Guests receive complimentary limousine service to any downtown business area.

Checkers' restaurant, serene and elegant, fits in well with the hotel's overall intimate tone. Dinner is served on lovely Wedgwood china bearing an Oriental motif, and the glassware is crystal. Mahimahi and grilled New Zealand scampi with honey and pink peppercorn sauce, and roasted chili and sugar-cured beef tenderloin are examples of chef Tony Hodge's inventive cuisine.

Newport Beach

Doryman's Inn

2102 West Ocean Front
Newport Beach, CA 92663
949-675-7300
800-634-3303
Fax: 949-675-7300

> **A small, romantic hotel by the beach**

General manager: Jeannie Lawrence. **Accommodations:** 10 rooms. **Rates:** $180–$340 single or double, $25 additional person. **Included:** Expanded Continental breakfast. **Added:** 10% tax. **Payment:** Major credit cards. **Children:** Over age 10, $25 additional. **Pets:** Not allowed. **Smoking:** Allowed on patio only.

➤ **Other than the beach, points of interest in the area are the 1904 Balboa Pavilion, which has been restored as a restaurant and boat terminal for Catalina Island; the Balboa Island ferry; and Lido Isle, or "Fashion Isle," as it's called for its many shops.**

This spot on the Pacific shore is unabashedly romantic; the guest rooms have been designed for lovers. Canopy beds piled with ruffled pillows are topped with silk rosettes, lush tropical plants stand in the corners, and fireplaces light at the touch of a switch (these are gas fireplaces, of course, lacking the crackle and character of the real thing, but as a substitute they're not bad.) Most of the beds are backed by wide mirrors. All the bathrooms have marble sunken tubs.

The rooms are lavishly furnished with antiques that recall the 1890s period when the brick hotel was built. The small lobby and rooms are on the second floor, off paneled halls with skylights and hanging ferns. Room 1 is a corner room with a three-door armoire and a down comforter on a brass and white iron bed. Lighter and larger is Room 2, which has an ocean view. Four others also have ocean views. The largest, most expensive, and probably the most romantic is the Master Suite, which has an ocean view, a bed with a draped canopy, and a sunken whirlpool tub.

Coffee is always available in the little breakfast room, where morning pastries, boiled eggs, sliced fruits, and yogurt are set out. You may have breakfast here, in your room, or on the rooftop terrace, with its view of Santa Catalina Island.

Parking and a morning paper are provided at Doryman's. The manager is glad to help with any other needs, from an aspirin to a boat reservation to Catalina.

The inn is a seaside retreat for holidays and romance, not a place to do business. The rooms have antique reproduction phones, but they're not convenient, and the hall telephone is squeezed into a tiny booth.

The only real flaw here is not in the inn itself. Since this is beach resort town, summer brings noisy crowds and traffic.

Pasadena

The Ritz-Carlton Huntington Hotel and Spa

1401 South Oak Knoll Avenue
Pasadena, CA 91106
626-568-3900
800-241-3333
Fax: 626-585-6420
www.ritzcarlton.com

> **A luxurious hotel of classic elegance and style**

General manager: Ralph Grippo. **Accommodations:** 383 rooms and suites. **Rates:** $185–$295 single or double, suites start at $345. **Added:** 11.49% tax. **Payment:** Major credit cards. **Children:** Under age 18 free in room with parents. **Pets:** Not allowed. **Smoking:** Nonsmoking rooms available.

> ➤ **Tasteful art objects are displayed and 18th- and 19th-century oil paintings hang on the walls. Overstuffed sofas, fresh flowers, and Oriental carpets add to the atmosphere of comfort and graciousness.**

Combining resort and hotel amenities, the Ritz-Carlton Huntington has tennis courts and a tennis pro, a swimming pool, and a spa offering beauty and body treatments, fitness equipment, saunas, and steam rooms. The complex is set on 23 acres at the base of the San Gabriel Mountains, a 15-minute drive from downtown Los Angeles.

The hotel opened in 1991, a reconstructed version of the Huntington, a grand and famous hotel built in 1906. The rebuilt version closely follows the original architecture, with its tiled roof and imposing design. Two rooms were kept intact: the elegant Viennese Ballroom and the lovely Georgian Room. The genteel ambience was also retained. Guests at the Ritz-Carlton recognize, appreciate, and can afford the finest.

A typical room has a king-size or two double beds, yellow damask walls, three telephones, and an honor bar. The distinctive black and white marble bathroom has gray walls of shot silk and assorted toiletries. Guests receive twice-daily maid service, robes, evening turndown, and devoted attention from the staff. Those who want even more amenities stay on the Ritz-Carlton club floors and enjoy a private lounge and complimentary breakfast, afternoon tea, hors d'oeuvres, and cocktails. The hotel also has six cottages.

A major draw for business groups are the eight handsomely appointed meeting rooms, large ballroom, and computer and secretarial facilities.

You can dine in style in the Grill and, for casual fare, the Terrace restaurant. Cocktails are available both indoors and out at the Bar, and traditional afternoon tea is served in the Lobby Lounge.

The swimming pool is a restoration of California's first Olympic-size pool. A whirlpool has been added, and a pool lounge offering tropical drinks and light fare. To reach the Health Club, you cross the Picture Bridge, a part of the original hotel. Under its peaked roof are carefully restored triangular panels, each painted with a California scene.

Such reminders of its origins give the Ritz-Carlton a timeless atmosphere. Fostering this sense of continuity, the hotel participates in the annual Rose Parade with a float, as it has for 75 years.

Rancho Bernardo

Rancho Bernardo Inn

17550 Bernardo Oaks Drive
San Diego, CA 92128
619-675-8500
800-542-6096
Fax: 619-675-8437
ranchobernardoinn@jcresorts.com
www.jcresorts.com

A Spanish-style resort in the hills

General manager: Rick Mansur. **Accommodations:** 285 rooms and suites. **Rates:** Start at $249. **Added:** 10.7% tax. **Payment:** Major credit cards. **Children:** Under age 12 free in room with parents. **Pets:** Not allowed. **Smoking:** Nonsmoking rooms available.

➤ **The original lobby is now the Fireside Room, where you may relax by a fire with board games or cards. On Friday nights, meet the staff over complimentary cocktails at the general manager's reception.**

Balmy days and cool nights; tennis, golf, and fine dining; broad loggias and pathways that wind through courtyards with gardens and antique fountains — these are a few of the pleasures at Rancho Bernardo Inn, one of California's outstanding resorts. The setting is lovely — a green valley in the sepia-toned San Pasqual Mountains 30 miles from San Diego.

The hotel was built in 1962 as part of a development of Spanish-style homes for commuters and retirees. The main building, stucco with a red tile roof, shelters a warm, quiet lobby with low beamed ceilings of limed wood and adobe walls etched with straw. To the left of the entrance is the Music Room, where antique musical instruments are displayed. Twice weekly, piano music begins at four o'clock, announcing tea time. Complimentary tea, sandwiches, port, and sherry are brought in on silver trays. For casual meals, guests dine in the Veranda. El Bizcocho — "El Biz" for short — with its classic French cuisine and extensive wine list, is the inn's gourmet dinner spot.

The guest rooms and suites are in eight low haciendas, each by a courtyard of palm trees and flowers. The rooms are furnished similarly in muted tones and have stocked honor bars, televisions, and patios overlooking the golf course or a courtyard. In the white tile bathrooms are phones, magnifying makeup mirrors, and hair dryers. Robes hang in the closets, and there are safes for your valuables.

Original artwork graces the guest room walls, while artifacts from Mexico and early California are displayed throughout the inn. The museum-quality works begin at the entrance, near the porte-cochere, where a Zuniga bronze statue stands on a manicured lawn.

The swimming pools have adjoining hydrospas, and there are five other whirlpools on the property. A sports fitness center offers training equipment, steam rooms, and spa services such as massage, aromatherapy, and facials. The inn's twelve tennis courts are a major recreational draw, as are the special tennis packages. The Tennis College, begun in 1971, has a team of five pros who offer courses in improving your stroke, strategy, and game. Also available are video critiques, tournament arrangements, partner match-ups, tennis movies, and demonstrations.

If you prefer golf, you have a number of choices, including the 72-par West Course, which unrolls down the valley for 6,400 yards of tricky play. Under the olive and eucalyptus trees are two lakes, a stream, doglegs, and numerous bunkers. Five pros are on hand to help with instruction or arrange tournaments. Other courses open to guests include the Temecula Creek Inn course, the 27-hole Oaks North, and the Twin Oaks and Encinitas Ranch courses with 18 holes each.

Rancho Santa Fe

The Inn at Rancho Santa Fe

P.O. Box 869
5951 Linea del Cielo
Rancho Santa Fe, CA 92067
619-756-1131
800-843-4661
Fax: 619-759-1604
www.theinnatranchosantafe.com

A resort of quiet charm and luxury

General manager: Duncan Royce Hadden. **Accommodations:** 90 rooms, suites, and cottages. **Rates:** $100–$210 rooms and suites, single or double; cottages $340–$600. **Added:** 9% tax. **Minimum stay:** 2–5 nights on some holidays and weekends. **Payment:** Major credit cards. **Children:** Under age 17 free; cot or crib $20 per night. **Pets:** Allowed in certain cottages. **Smoking:** Allowed.

➤   One of the inn's special features is not in Rancho Santa Fe: it's a beach cottage seven miles away on the coast at Del Mar. If you want to spend an afternoon by the sea, you'll have a place to shower, dress, and borrow beach equipment.

The scent of money, old and new, is an integral part of Rancho Santa Fe, a quietly wealthy community set in the eucalyptus-covered hills 27 miles north of San Diego. The Spanish-style village, known for its attractive shops, restaurants, and two golf courses, began in 1923 with a guest house for prospective land-owners. The Santa Fe Railroad had imported three million eucalyptus trees from Australia and planted them on 10,000 acres, planning to use them as railroad ties. It didn't work out — the gum trees just weren't suitable — so the railroad turned the land over to residential development. Eventually the adobe guest house became the Inn at Rancho Santa Fe, and cottages and gardens were added. Steve Royce bought the place in 1958, and it's been a family operation ever since, with daughters and sons, nephews and cousins involved.

The low cottages, containing from two to ten guest rooms, were placed on twenty acres of landscaped grounds and terraced gardens. The main building, the original guest house, has eight guest rooms, a suite, a restaurant, a communal library, and a comfortable living room. Guests dine in the Vintage Room (actually comprising several rooms, including a cheerful sun room), where American and Continental dishes are served at lunch and dinner, and cocktails are available in the evening. Lunches and beverages are also served near the long outdoor pool.

Jackets are suggested for dinner but the atmosphere at the inn is unpretentious and casual. The service, however, is not at all casual, though it may be unhurried. The staff seems genuinely interested in meeting the guests' needs promptly and with a smile. The inn is the type of place where couples and families return year after year, and the staff knows many of the guests by name. Evidence that it's a well-loved place is obvious in everything from the attentive service to the inn's rose garden.

Croquet, tennis, and golf are major diversions. The Rancho Santa Fe Croquet Club plays regularly at the inn, while golfers may choose between two private 18-hole courses. The inn has three tennis courts and lessons may be arranged. For indoor relaxation there are hundreds of books in the library, as well as backgammon, and chess.

Guest rooms are traditionally furnished and have air conditioning, television, and writing desks; most have patios with views of the gardens. Some rooms have fireplaces and kitchens or wet bars. The baths are roomy, with dressing areas and separate showers. There are several private cottages with one, two, and three bedrooms and baths. The largest has its own patio and swimming pool.

Airport limousine service is available for a fee.

Rancho Valencia

P.O. Box 9126
5921 Valencia Circle
Rancho Santa Fe, CA 92067
619-756-1123
800-548-3664
Fax: 619-756-0165
reservations@ranchovalencia.com
www.ranchovalencia.com

**A luxurious tennis resort
near San Diego**

General manager: Michael Ullman. **Accommodations:** 43 suites. **Rates:** $425–
$510 Del Mar suites, $580–$650 Rancho Sante Fe suites, 3-suite Hacienda
$4,000. **Added:** 9% tax. **Payment:** Major credit cards. **Children:** Under 16 free in
room with parents. **Pets:** Allowed for an additional $75 per night. **Smoking:**
Nonsmoking rooms available.

➤ **The resort's widely acclaimed, elegant restaurant overlooks the hills
and serves California cuisine. The Sunrise Room has brilliant blue and
yellow painted tiles and a patio for outdoor dining. A terrace runs the
length of the building, overlooking the tennis courts.**

Like a grand private estate, this tranquil resort lies on a hill among
terraced gardens and citrus orchards. Twenty miles from the San
Diego airport, it's one of the loveliest places in southern California.
The resort opened in 1989, but it has the atmosphere of a long-
established hacienda, with red tile roofs, scuffed Mexican pavers in
the lobby, wicker furniture, a tile fireplace, and bleached beams.
Fountains splash in the courtyards and arches over cool walkways
are smothered in bougainvillea. The courtyard by the lobby is open
for dining.

The suites, housed in twenty casitas, are gems of comfort and
country luxury. The Rancho Santa Fe suites are the largest. Each
has a fireplace, a tiled bath, a walk-in closet and dressing room,
shuttered windows, hand-painted tiles on the walls, and a garden
terrace. Smaller, but with similar amenities and southwestern decor, are the Del Mar Suites. In the morning, fresh orange juice from
the trees on the grounds is brought to your door on a tray with a
newspaper and a single red rose.

The stone Hacienda Suite is a former private home with three
bedrooms, four baths, a central living room, a large kitchen with a
fireside sitting area, and outdoor private pool and Jacuzzi sur-

rounded by gardens, palms, and fruit trees. Each of the three bedrooms has its own bath and patio, and one has its own sitting room. Exposed adobe walls and Mexican tiles, pottery, and decor throughout gives the Hacienda a distinct south-of-the-border flavor. Used mainly for VIPs and hospitality events, it would also be a lovely spot to hold a family reunion or small wedding.

The focus of activity at the resort is tennis; about 25 percent of the resort's guests come for the 18 courts, lessons, clinics, and tennis packages. But many other activities are offered. You can swim in the 25-meter pool, relax in two Jacuzzis, jog on the trails, golf, go deep-sea fishing or hot air ballooning, play polo and croquet, or head for the horse races in nearby Del Mar (a limited number of Turf Club passes are available for resort guests).

San Diego

The Cottage

3829 Albatross Street
San Diego, CA 92103
619-299-1564
Fax: 619-299-6213

> A secluded cottage in a
> residential neighborhood

Innkeepers: Carol and Bob Emerick. **Accommodations:** 1 room and 1 cottage (both with private bath). **Rates:** $65–$110 single or double, $10 additional person. **Included:** Continental breakfast. **Added:** 10.5% tax. **Minimum stay:** 2 nights. **Payment:** MasterCard, Visa. **Children:** $10 additional per night. **Pets:** Not allowed. **Smoking:** Allowed outside only.

➤ **Carol brings a hot breakfast from her kitchen in the mornings. Fresh bread, blueberry muffins, and apple cake are a few of the specialties that accompany coffee and juice or fresh fruit.**

The old homes and undeveloped canyons in the Hillcrest section of San Diego make it a quiet part of the city, with an unhurried atmosphere. The Cottage, built in 1913 behind the Emericks' homestead-style residence, fits well with the peaceful mood and the sense of a bygone day. When you arrive, Carol greets you at the front door of the main house and guides you past the herb garden and hibiscus hedge, under the rose-covered trellis, to the cozy cottage in back.

In the cottage, a woodstove (wood is supplied), a sofa bed, and an oak pump organ stand in the living room. An Austrian carved breakfront holds books, along with menus of San Diego restaurants, in a rack by the rocker. There's a small gas stove in the kitchen and fresh coffee beans in the refrigerator. With the sofa bed, three people will fit nicely in the cottage; any more would be crowding it. A king-size bed almost fills the snug bedroom with fabric-covered walls. Corner windows view a tiny, fenced garden. A television is hidden in a wall niche; the room also has reading lamps, a phone, and a clock radio. Travelers appreciate the padded hangers and the iron and ironing board in the closet. The immaculate blue and white bathroom, with vibrant touches of red, has both a tub and a shower.

The Emericks have also opened a room in the main house to guests. The Garden Room has a private entrance, TV, and a refrigerator. If you stay in the Garden Room you'll have breakfast in the Emericks' pleasant, homey dining room. You're welcome to relax in the parlor, too, listening to the stereo and tape deck or looking through the books on opera. Other interesting items from the couple's collection include old bottles, a stereopticon, and a working player organ that dates from 1875. Bob is an expert on piano and organ restoration; the pump organ in the Cottage is an example of his work.

Most of the furnishings here come from the owners' previous business as antiques dealers. Now Bob teaches sociology at San Diego State College and, with their two daughters grown and gone, Carol manages the guest house.

Horton Grand Hotel

311 Island Avenue
San Diego, CA 92101
619-544-1886
800-542-1886
Fax: 619-544-0058
horton@connect.net
www.hortongrand.com

> **An updated historic
> landmark of old San Diego**

Owners: John and Dori Rose. **Accommodations:** 110 rooms and 24 suites. **Rates:** $139–$169 single or double, suites $209. **Added:** 10.5% tax. **Payment:** Major credit cards. **Children:** Free in room with parents. **Pets:** Under 25 pounds allowed in first-floor rooms only with a $45 nonrefundable fee. **Smoking:** Nonsmoking rooms available.

➤ **The brick courtyard is one of the hotel's most charming features. Four floors of guest rooms surround it, their balconies overlooking white garden furniture, birds that dart among the potted ficus, and vines climbing over lattices.**

The Horton Grand is in San Diego's historic Gaslamp District, once a downtown core gone to seed but now prime urban property. The ornate hotel, two Victorian buildings joined by a courtyard and atrium, stands as a well-restored tribute to comforts past and present. The district is not yet the showcase planners envision, but restaurants and nightspots have sprouted, there's a convention center, and Horton Plaza, an open-air, multilevel complex of shops and theaters, draws hordes of curious visitors. It's lively and interesting, a cultural as well as a shopping experience.

When the site for Horton Plaza was announced in the 1970s, the Horton Grand — built in 1886 as a replica of the Innsbruck Hotel in Vienna and the oldest hotel in San Diego — was in danger of being razed. So in 1980 it was purchased from the city by a group of historical preservationists for $1, dismantled, and rebuilt on its present location, two blocks from the Plaza. The Horton Grand was connected by an atrium to another historic hotel, the Kahle Saddlery Hotel, which was reconstructed next door. In 1986, 100 years after the two hotels originally opened their doors, they reopened in style under one name — the Horton Grand Hotel. Now, when you drive up to the front door, energetic young valets whisk your car and luggage away and you step into a conservatory that turns out to be the lobby. Skylights, white wicker furniture, and a cage of chirping finches create a bright and cheerful atmosphere. The clerks at the front desk, dressed in period costume, add to the turn-of-the-century ambience. Despite its monumental-sounding name, the hotel is more an example of intimate Victorian charm than of imposing grandeur.

On one side of the lobby there's a tea room where high tea is served on Friday and Saturday. On the other is a beautifully carved staircase and the Palace Bar, a combination parlor and saloon. Next to the bar is Ida Bailey's Restaurant, serving American food.

The rather small rooms are decorated individually, though they all have gas fireplaces and antique furniture. The best and quietest are the rooms overlooking the courtyard. The Bridal Suite has a canopied antique bed. All have small sitting areas, rich Victorian draperies, lace curtains, and television sets hidden in wall niches behind mirrors.

One room, 309, is supposedly haunted. Guests and chambermaids have felt an unusual presence there, and some speculate that it's the ghost of Roger Whitaker, who was killed in the hotel a hundred years ago by a gambling associate. The room has been booked solid since the phenomena was investigated by psychics. "The ghost is harmless," they said. "He's really very nice."

As the hotel now stands in the section of the city that was once San Diego's Chinatown, it has a suite dedicated to Ah Quin — Chinatown's unofficial mayor. The most Asian of all the rooms, it has an ornately carved Chinese bed with hand-painted murals, and Ah Quin's photograph hangs on the wall.

There's also a third building, which provides large, deluxe suites geared to corporate travelers on extended stays. The Horton Grand offers several special packages, such as a Jazz Special, the Victorian Grand Tradition (including afternoon tea, breakfast in bed, and a sightseeing tour on San Diego's quaint trolley), and one "For Hopeless Romantics."

U.S. Grant Hotel

326 Broadway
San Diego, CA 92101
619-232-3121
800-HERITAGE
Fax: 619-232-3626
www.grandheritage.com

> A classic historic hotel in
> downtown San Diego

Manager: Joe Duncalfe. **Accommodations:** 220 rooms, 60 suites. **Rates:** $195 single, $215 double, suites start at $275. **Added:** 10.5% tax. **Payment:** Major credit cards. **Children:** Under age 18 free in room with parents. **Pets:** Allowed by prior arrangement. **Smoking:** Nonsmoking rooms available.

➤ **In the large lobby, a concierge is on duty, prepared to obtain tickets for any cultural, theatrical, or recreational event or to arrange for secretarial and other business services. A wide marble staircase leads to the meeting rooms on the mezzanine.**

In 1985 the historic U.S. Grant Hotel underwent a four-year, $80-million restoration. The hotel had become rundown and had been closed for nine years, a far cry from its illustrious beginnings in 1910, when it was built by Ulysses S. Grant, Jr., in honor of his father. It had been a San Diego landmark for decades before it fell into disrepair. A striking building on the outside, the expensive restoration returned the hotel's interior to classic grandeur, with a palatial lobby marked by Palladian columns, a series of crystal chandeliers, 18th-century reproduction furnishings, Dutch and Venetian oil paintings, and Chinese porcelains.

The U.S. Grant takes up a full block in the heart of San Diego's renewed downtown district, across from Horton Plaza, a multilevel shopping center. However, when you drive up to the hotel, you don't enter at this front door but at the parking lot entrance to the lobby, where a valet will take your car to the hotel garage.

The guest rooms, though small, are well furnished with Queen Anne mahogany two-poster beds, armoires, and wingback chairs. Each has television with cable, and movies are available. Baths of travertine marble and ceramic tile have hand-milled soaps and terrycloth robes. The suites feature decorative fireplaces and built-in bars; their decor is comfortably traditional and their large casement windows open to views of the city and downtown redevelopment. There are few complaints about the service at U.S. Grant; not only is it prompt and courteous, but it is given with genuine warmth.

The cocktail lounge is a congenial room with polished paneling, high ceilings, and a fireplace. Next door is the Grant Grill, where grilled steaks, chops, and seafood are served in a men's club atmosphere of rich wood and brass, with fresh flowers on crisp linens and cozy booth seating. The hotel's sidewalk café is busy during the noon hour, serving gourmet pizzas, pastas, and sandwiches. As their names suggest, Bruegger's Bagel Bakery and The Coffee People specialize in bagels and coffee, respectively, and are open for breakfast and lunch. Afternoon tea is served in the lobby to the strains of harp or violin music.

The Westgate Hotel

1055 Second Avenue
San Diego, CA 92101
619-238-1818
800-221-3802
Fax: 619-557-3737
www.littleamerica.com

A touch of Versailles in downtown San Diego

General manager: George Hochfilzer. **Accommodations:** 223 rooms. **Rates:** $169–$249 single, $219–$269 double; $10 each additional person; suites $440–$1,600. **Added:** 10.5% tax. **Payment:** Major credit cards. **Children:** Under age 18 free in room with parents. **Pets:** Not allowed. **Smoking:** Nonsmoking rooms available.

➤ **In the heart of downtown, the Westgate is within easy walking distance of the convention center, Horton Plaza, and the Gaslamp District. The hotel provides complimentary limousine service to the airport as well as to a number of tourist and downtown business locations.**

From the outside, there isn't much to set the Westgate Hotel apart from its neighbors. Construction on the hotel began in 1969, and the 20-story structure blends in easily with the surrounding office buildings of downtown San Diego. Yet any resemblance to a typical city office building fades as soon as you step inside the Westgate's front door.

In the lobby, Baccarat crystal chandeliers, 18th-century furnishings trimmed in gold, one of the first Steinway pianos ever built, Aubusson tapestries, paintings by Utrillo and Velazquez, polished parquet floors topped with expansive Persian rugs, creamy paneled walls with fanciful moldings, and chairs crafted by Marie Antoinette's personal furniture maker create an opulent ambience. The ornate decor is deliberate, as the room was designed to be a re-creation of the anteroom at Versailles.

Guest rooms, each individually decorated in the Louis XV, Louis XVI, and Regency periods with reproduction furniture and fine fabrics, are also elegant. Standard rooms have either a king-size bed or two oversize doubles, two-line speaker phones with computer capabilities, and an Italian marble bath with brass fixtures. The most regal accommodations are the Governor's and Presidential suites, with antique furnishings, a large living room, two bedrooms, two baths, and a full kitchen.

White glove service, crystal chandeliers, and French cuisine are all part of the experience when dining in the Westgate's Fountainebleau restaurant. The Westgate Room, cheerful in lime greens, is more casual and serves both American and Continental cuisine. In the afternoons, high tea is served in the lobby.

The Wyndham Emerald Plaza

400 West Broadway
San Diego, CA 92101
619-239-4500
800-626-3988
Fax: 619-239-4527
pcipkins@wyndham.com
www.wyndham.com

A contemporary downtown hotel

General manager: Jim Hollister. **Accommodations:** 436 rooms and suites. **Rates:** $179–$229 single, $199–$249 double; suites $550–$2,500. **Added:** 10.5% tax. **Payment:** Major credit cards. **Children:** Under age 18 free in room with parent. **Pets:** Not allowed. **Smoking:** Nonsmoking rooms available.

➤ **The hotel is close to San Diego's splashy convention center, the performing arts center, Horton Plaza's shopping complex, and the Paladion fashion center. The Museum of Contemporary Art is just a few blocks away.**

The Wyndham Emerald Plaza, which opened in 1991 as the Pan Pacific, is an example of the redevelopment that has sparked San Diego's urban renaissance, creating a busy district of office towers, restaurants, hotels, nightclubs, and stores. Part of the Emerald-Shapery Center (a complex that includes offices and shops), the glittery hotel with its hexagonal glass towers is one of the most highly visible and distinctive buildings in downtown San Diego. A 100-foot atrium rises from the lobby and lounge, and glass elevators soar 25 stories. The centerpiece of the atrium is *Flying Emeralds*, an immense sculpture of hanging green glass. Beneath this canopy is a lounge featuring cocktails, appetizers, and piano music.

The restaurant, called the Grill, serves California cuisine that includes heart-healthy entrées. Inside you can watch the cooking action — the Grill has an open-display kitchen — or take a table on the outdoor patio. When you want a quick, light breakfast, stop in at Creative Croissants on the corner for coffee and rolls.

The hotel occupies three towers (called *pods*) of the complex's eight. It has a health club on the third level, adjacent to the lap pool, Jacuzzi, and sun deck. Sauna, aerobics classes, and massage are on the fitness program. Business and corporate travelers are well served at the hotel. They have the use of the most extensive business support system of any hotel in the region. Secretarial and courier services, telephone, fax, telex, word processing, office supplies, meeting rooms, computers, a notary public, and desktop publishing are available. There's even a law library. Ballrooms and conference facilities total 22,000 square feet.

The guest rooms start at the fourth floor and go up to the Presidential Suite on the twenty-fifth floor. Because of each pod's hexagonal shape, rooms have interesting configurations. They're furnished comfortably in beige tones, in modern hotel style, and have atrium, city, and some bay views. They all have multiline phones, TV, mini-bars, desks, and express check-out. Standard rooms have two doubles or one queen-size bed, parlor suites have a sleeper sofa in the sitting room and a queen-size bed in the bedroom, and executive suites have separate bed and living rooms and marble baths with whirlpools and Neutrogena toiletries.

Part of the Wyndham hotel chain, the Emerald Plaza has numerous features that appeal to travelers in the city — the best one is the service. The staff is outstanding. Virtually everyone is courteous, knowledgeable, and eager to help. They're glad to recommend and provide directions to nightspots, visitor attractions, and restaurants. If you like to arrive in style, there's a helipad on top of the hotel. For in-town transportation, a courtesy van will take you to close destinations, and buses and bright red trolley cars provide service to a wider area.

Santa Monica

Hotel Shangri-La

1301 Ocean Avenue
Santa Monica, CA 90401
310-394-2791
800-345-STAY
Fax: 310-451-3351
www.shangrila-hotel.com

A deco hotel facing the
beach

General manager: Dino Nanni. **Accommodations:** 55 rooms and suites. **Rates:** $145–$505, 1–4 people, $15 each additional person. **Included:** Continental breakfast and afternoon refreshments. **Added:** 12% tax. **Payment:** Major credit cards. **Children:** Under age 16 free in room with parents. **Pets:** Not allowed. **Smoking:** Nonsmoking rooms available.

➤ **For updated comfort with a touch of vintage L.A. in a light, bright setting by the beach, the Shangri-La is an excellent choice for those traveling on a budget.**

Like the setting for a Hollywood movie of the 1930s, the Shangri-La has an art deco motif that is skillfully accomplished. It's rare to find a theme carried through so well while keeping guests' comfort a priority. The small lobby contains soft green couches, torch lamps, and a large version of the hotel's signature design — stylized palm trees and a vast blue ocean — viewed from behind a pink balcony railing.

The rooms on the first six floors range from studios to two-bedroom, two-bath suites. The seventh floor is reserved for two penthouse suites with sun decks. All the rooms have televisions, phones, and movie posters that are reminders of the period the decor evokes. Most rooms, except for those on the fifth and sixth floors, come with equipped kitchens. The open gallery design of the building, with exterior hallways, provides cross-ventilation and ocean views.

One typical studio room contains curved chrome chairs and a painting of pink flamingos. There's a dressing area near the white tile bath and a kitchen with a gas stove. For this location, $120 is not a bad price. And you get breakfast and afternoon tea, served in a pretty little breakfast room off the courtyard.

A one-bedroom suite on the sixth floor will have its own wrap-around deck and sleek gray furniture striped with burgundy in the spacious living room and bedroom. All rooms on the sixth floor have private sun decks facing west. The Shangri-La has no restaurant and no recreational facilities. There's a tiled terrace with lounge chairs in back in the large courtyard, which has the only thing out of scale with the art deco flavor of the hotel — a chunky, oversize gazebo.

The artfully curved seven-story hotel stands on a busy corner in Santa Monica, directly across the street from Palisades Park and the beach. Several fine restaurants and Santa Monica's Third Street Promenade are within walking distance, and a major shopping mall is close by.

Loews Santa Monica Beach Hotel

1700 Ocean Avenue
Santa Monica, CA 90401
310-458-6700
800-23-LOEWS
Fax: 310-458-6761

One of L.A.'s only luxury hotels near the beach

General manager: Richard Caselli. **Accommodations:** 350 rooms, including 31 suites. **Rates:** $275–$390 single, $295–$410 double, $20 additional person, suites $590–$2,500. **Added:** 12% tax. **Payment:** Major credit cards. **Children:** Under age 18 free in room with adult. **Pets:** Not allowed. **Smoking:** Nonsmoking rooms available.

➤ **There are several restaurants and cafés on Third Street Promenade, a tree-lined plaza closed to traffic. Busy and festive, it has three blocks of shops, eateries, nightclubs, and theaters.**

Facing a broad stretch of Santa Monica sand, but not directly on the beach, this eight-story hotel has a light, open atmosphere befitting its oceanfront location. Sunshine streams through Palladian windows and the skylight over an extensive five-story atrium lobby. Couches and chairs are grouped in conversation areas in the lobby, which has a cheerful array of fountains, palms, orchids, and even a koi pond.

Off the lobby are United Airlines and Hertz car rental counters. The hotel offers valet and self-parking, multilingual concierge service, a business center, dry cleaning, laundry, and shoeshines. Guests can rent bicycles, skates, and rollerblades.

You're likely to see people in the film and television industries here; Santa Monica has become a popular site for production companies. Once the area was a getaway for movie stars. Charlie Chaplin and Mary Pickford built homes that still stand on the beach directly below the hotel. Two blocks away is the historic Santa Monica pier, with its famous restored carousel and other rides.

Location makes the difference in rates; all rooms are spacious and have the same decor. Most guest rooms have partial ocean views. They have narrow balconies, mini-bars, hair dryers, robes, irons and ironing boards, and small TVs in marble baths in addition to large televisions with all channels in the room. Most suites are corner rooms, so they enjoy both a pool view and full ocean view. The pool, 30 feet above the beach, is designed for both indoor and outdoor use. Near it is the Pritikin Longevity Center and Spa. This excellent fitness center provides state-of-the-art equipment, classrooms, Jacuzzi, sauna and steam, massage, beauty treatments, and personal training sessions.

The bewildering array of restaurants in Santa Monica — some 400 within eight square miles — makes choosing where to dine a pleasant dilemma. In the hotel you have your choice of two restaurants, plus 24-hour room service and a lobby bar that serves snacks. Both restaurants are relaxing spots with ocean views.

Miramar Sheraton Hotel

101 Wilshire Boulevard
Santa Monica, CA 90401
310-576-7777
800-325-3535
Fax: 310-458-7912
www.sheraton.com

> Ocean views, comfort, and
> elegance are all features of
> this Santa Monica hotel

General manager: William T. Worcester. **Accommodations:** 302 rooms and
suites. **Rates:** $315–$800. **Added:** 12% tax. **Payment:** Major credit cards. **Children:** Under 17 free in room with parents; $20 additional if rollaway is required.
Pets: Not Allowed. **Smoking:** Nonsmoking rooms available.

➤ **The Miramar is well situated. The Pacific is just across the street, and
the Santa Monica Pier and Third Street Promenade are both within walking distance.**

The lobby's polished marble floors, bamboo furniture, and potted
palms are the first clues that the Miramar Sheraton offers sophisticated lodging in a relaxed atmosphere. A friendly staff member will
lead you from the lobby to your room or suite in either the Palisades Building, Ocean Tower, or a 1930s bungalow — each represents a different stage of the hotel's development.

The present day hotel stands on what was once John P. Jones's
private estate. Jones, who made his fortune in silver, was the founder of Santa Monica. His mansion was constructed on the site in
1889 and for a short while the home belonged to King C. Gillette of
razor fame; it was also a military academy before becoming a hotel
in 1921. In the late 1930s the mansion was torn down to make way
for guest bungalows and a hotel. The ten-story Ocean Tower was
added in 1959.

The guest rooms in the Ocean Tower are the least formal. Decorated in California style with light wood furnishings, they have
mini-bars, clock radios, hair dryers, coffeemakers, makeup mirrors,
and irons and ironing boards. Angled to take advantage of the
ocean views on the upper floors, the rooms also have balconies.
The Palisades Building has a more classic look, with paneled hallways, antique replica furniture in rich woods, and larger rooms
with roomier baths.

The cream-colored stuccoed bungalows provide the most private
and deluxe accommodations at the hotel. Each with its own en-

trance, they are sunny with large windows, hardwood floors, and high ceilings. In addition to the standard amenities, they have scales, heat lamps, Swiss toiletries, and marble vanities in the baths, as well as in-room safes, extra feather pillows, three telephones, and an entertainment center complete with a VCR, stereo, and built-in bath speaker. The list of celebrities who have stayed at the Miramar over the years is a long one (it includes Garbo, JFK, Eleanor Roosevelt, Marilyn Monroe, and Charles Lindbergh), and bungalows bear the names of former famous guests.

The buildings all surround a garden courtyard with palms, a lush lawn, fountain, and swimming pool. The Miramar also has a good fitness center with a covered outdoor Jacuzzi, sun deck, locker rooms with sauna and steam rooms, and a pleasant workout room where you can see the ocean while you exercise.

The Miramar Grille and the Miramar Café are the hotel's restaurants. A Pacific-style eatery, the Grille has a demonstration kitchen that serves up meals such as seared boneless trout over spaghettied vegetables and rice noodles spiced with shiitaki broth, and shrimp and lobster tail over fennel and spinach risotto. A good wine selection, tapas, and tasty desserts round out the menu. The cuisine is Continental and the mood is casual at the Café, which serves all three meals. As Santa Monica boasts some 400 restaurants, additional dining choices are close at hand.

Shutters on the Beach

One Pico Boulevard
Santa Monica, CA 90405
310-458-0030
800-334-9000
Fax: 310-458-4589
www.shuttersonthebeach.com

| A classy beachfront hotel

General manager: Armella Stepan. **Accommodations:** 198 rooms including 12 suites. **Rates:** $335–$550 single or double, suites $750–$2,000. **Added:** 12% tax. **Payment:** Major credit cards. **Children:** Under age 12 free in room with parents. **Pets:** Not allowed. **Smoking:** Nonsmoking rooms available.

➤ **Attentive service, fine dining, and comfortably elegant decor all add to the appeal of this attractive seaside lodging.**

Although the gray and white hotel looks as though it could have been built in the 1920s, Shutters on the Beach, which opened in 1993, is one of Santa Monica's newest lodgings. Shutters is also one of the closest oceanside hotels to Los Angeles, making it ideal for a quick weekend escape from the city.

Urban cares and pressures seem to dissipate as soon as you step into the understated elegance of the lobby — a long room with a light, stenciled ceiling and beautiful parquet floors set with comfortable sitting areas, plants, and fresh flowers. Artwork on the walls bear the names of artists such as David Hockney, William Wegman, Jasper Johns, Roy Lichtenstein, and Robert Motherwell. At the far end of the room, glass doors open onto a white-railinged terrace overlooking the sandy beach dotted with palms and the ocean beyond.

The best seats in the house can be found in One Pico, the hotel's fine dining restaurant, which adjoins the lobby. Every table has an ocean view, and seafood and fresh California cuisine are emphasized in dishes such as applewood-smoked salmon with creamed spinach, and wide ribbon pasta with shredded duck and snap peas. You can watch the roller bladers and bicyclists zip by downstairs in the aptly named Pedals, a casual bistro serving Italian-influenced pizza, pasta, salads, and sandwiches from an exhibition kitchen.

The preferred guest rooms and suites are those located in this main three-story building that skirts the beach. With balconies that practically open out to the edge of the sand, they are priced accordingly. The rooms on the upper two floors are better, as first-floor balconies are a little too close to the bike path for comfort.) Bright sunlight and the blue of the ocean fill these spacious rooms, and white shutters — hence the hotel's name — can be drawn closed to keep the sun's rays from disturbing late sleepers.

Rooms have a crisp, clean look with color schemes and decor appropriate for the oceanside location — blue-trimmed white linens on two-poster beds, fish prints on the walls, and comfortable sofas and easy chairs covered in cool mint, blue, and white stripes. Televisions are hidden behind latticework doors in armoires, and baths are luxurious with whirlpool tubs, white marble floors, and handsome green marble vanities. Other comforts include terry robes, three two-line telephones with computer capabilities, CD players, VCRs, complimentary in-room movies with additional videos available for rental, mini-bars, safes, makeup mirrors, and natural soaps. Some suites have extras such as large oceanview Jacuzzis, separate living rooms, and fireplaces. Guest rooms in the rear five-story building without views, or with partial ocean views, are less expensive.

A brick pool deck and lower terrace that extends toward the beach connect the two lodging buildings. Chaise longues topped with blue and white cushions for soaking up the rays are plentiful, and there's a heated whirlpool and an outdoor fireplace to warm chillier days. Poolside service means you needn't interrupt your siesta to dine if you don't wish to. If you crave more active recreation, you can work out in the hotel's fitness center or rent a bike and cycle to nearby Santa Monica Pier or down the shore to offbeat Venice Beach.

Seal Beach

The Seal Beach Inn and Gardens

212 5th Street
Seal Beach, CA 90740-6115
562-493-2416
800-HIDEAWAY
Fax: 562-799-0483
hideaway@sealbeachinn.com
www.sealbeachinn.com

A colorful inn surrounded
by flowers

Innkeeper: Marjorie Bettenhausen-Schmaehl. **Accommodations:** 24 rooms (all with private bath). **Rates:** $125–$225 single or double, $10 additional person. **Included:** Full breakfast and afternoon refreshments. **Added:** 9% tax. **Payment:** Major credit cards. **Children:** Discouraged, $10 additional per night. **Pets:** Not allowed. **Smoking:** Not allowed.

➤ **Marjorie wants contented guests, and she goes out of her way to make sure they're happy. You'll find homemade chocolate chip cookies in your room at night and a list of local points of interest. You can order a**

picnic basket or get a restaurant recommendation from the innkeeper or her staff.

Seal Beach is a pleasant, friendly, quiet town on Highway 1, south of Long Beach. Busy in summer, it's a popular place for surfing, sailboarding, and strolling on the beach, though it doesn't have the glamour of some southern California resort areas. Go to Seal Beach to enjoy the fresh ocean breezes, some good casual restaurants, the shops of Old Town and Seaport Village, fishing off the pier, bicycle riding, and maybe a gondola ride through the canals. And when you're here, stay at the charming Seal Beach Inn, a block from the sea.

The first thing you notice about the inn is color. The brick terrace is overflowing with bright flowers. Bougainvillea cascades over wrought-iron railings; Boston ivy climbs the walls. Blue canopies and old-fashioned red street lamps add further touches of color.

Built in the 1920s, the long-neglected inn has been restored by innkeeper Marjorie Bettenhausen-Schmaehl. She has created a showplace reminiscent of the inns along the Mediterranean coast of France. Antiques from her travels are in all the rooms and gardens. They include a 300-year-old French fountain, an oak fireplace mantel and altar from a historic Chicago church, a Persian tile mural four centuries old, and numerous frescoes and marble pieces. The bed from John Barrymore's estate is here, along with a French armoire that was part of a trousseau in 1839.

The rooms, named for flowers, have TVs and phones. Fourteen have kitchens and six have fireplaces. The suites have sitting areas with antiques, lacy curtains, and lots of chintz and ruffles that are almost — but not quite — too fussy for comfort. Most expensive and largest are the interior King Suites, all eight of them considered honeymoon suites. Some rooms have paneled walls and ceilings. They can be quite dark, so if you prefer a lighter atmosphere, you may want to request it. Vienna Woods is a favorite for its elaborately carved bed from pre–Civil War Virginia. Mexican pavers form the floor and German lace curtains hang at the windows. Black and white glass tiles from France give the bathroom a dramatic look.

A buffet breakfast is provided in the cozy tearoom; if you're like most guests, you'll want to enjoy it by the pool or on the terrace. The fare includes Belgian waffles, homemade breads, granola, quiches or a casserole, juice, and coffee or gourmet teas. Afternoon wine and cheese are served near the fire in the tearoom.

Temecula

Loma Vista Bed & Breakfast

33350 La Serena Way
Temecula, CA 92390-5049
909-676-7047
Fax: 909-676-0077

A Mission-style hilltop home overlooking vineyards

Innkeepers: Sheila and Walt Kurczynski. **Accommodations:** 6 rooms (private baths). **Rates:** $105–$165. **Included:** Full champagne breakfast and afternoon refreshments. **Added:** 10% tax. **Minimum stay:** 2 nights on weekends, 3 nights on holidays. **Payment:** MasterCard, Visa. **Children:** $25 additional for rollaway. **Pets:** Not allowed. **Smoking:** Not allowed.

➤ **You'll find sherry and a basket of fruit in your room and evening wine and cheese on the patio. Afterward there's an outdoor hot tub to soak in.**

With its curved archways, red tile roofs, and cool courtyards, Loma Vista was designed in Spanish mission style when it was built in 1987. The interior of the imposing hilltop home is light and spacious, but the decor is more American traditional than early California, with a carpeted living room and white and flower-patterned couches by a brick fireplace. The windows overlook the vineyards of Temecula Valley, a wine producing region north of San Diego.

Loma Vista's guest rooms, named after wine grapes, are air conditioned and have queen- or king-size beds and clock radios. Each is decorated distinctively. Fume Blanc is light and airy, with white wicker and plants; Sauvignon Blanc features the desert hues and white pine of the Southwest. Zinfandel has gracious Queen Anne furnishings and a balcony with a view of Palomar Observatory. With oak furnishings, Chardonnay has a country feel. Its balcony looks out over the hills.

The most striking room is Champagne. Though it has no balcony or view, it's a glamorous retreat with curved black lacquer furniture, a satin quilt, and framed photos of Fred Astaire and Marilyn Monroe lending a Hollywood/art deco flavor.

In the morning a champagne breakfast is served family-style in the dining room. It includes hot entrées such as chicken mushroom crepes or Huevos Loma Vista (half an avocado is topped with poached eggs and nestled in refried beans), as well as sundaes made from fresh fruit, muffins, yogurt, and granola.

The innkeepers will urge you to explore the historic Temecula area. The village was a stagecoach stop 150 years ago, on the Butterfield State Line between St. Louis and San Francisco, and has retained some of its Old West atmosphere. You can shop for antiques, tour the wineries, go hot air ballooning, play golf, fish at Lake Skinner, and try the local restaurants the innkeepers recommend.

Vista

Cal-a-Vie

2249 Somerset Road
Vista, CA 92084
760-945-2055
Fax: 760-630-0074
www.cal-a-vie.com

| **A luxury spa in the hills** |

General manager: Deborah Zie. **Accommodations:** 24 cottages. **Rates:** $4,850 per person per week, European plan; $4,550 per week California plan. **Included:** All meals. **Added:** Tax. **Minimum stay:** 7 days. **Payment:** Major credit cards. **Children:** Age 18 and older welcome. **Pets:** Not allowed. **Smoking:** Allowed in designated smoking rooms only. **Open:** Year-round except Christmas and New Year weeks.

➤ Throughout the year, Cal-a-Vie offers women's sessions, men's sessions, and coed sessions; they begin on Sunday afternoon and end the following Sunday morning. Transportation to and from the San Diego International Airport is provided at no charge.

Forty miles north of San Diego, this exclusive spa nestles against a rural hillside like a Mediterranean village. From the tile-roofed stucco cottages, the view is of citrus and avocado orchards, mountains, and blue sky. The air is clean, the climate balmy. It's an ideal setting for a retreat into self-improvement.

At Cal-a-Vie you'll find an emphasis on balance, combining the American approach to fitness with a European focus on skin and body care. Heavy exercise takes place in the mornings; the afternoons are devoted to rest, relaxation, and therapeutic treatments. The day begins with a brisk walk in the adjacent hills; then it's breakfast and a series of warm-ups, aerobics, and exercise classes. Since the spa never has more than 24 people at a time, each guest receives attention and instruction.

Afternoon skin and body treatments include facials, Swedish and shiatsu massage, seaweed wraps, hydrotherapy, and aromatherapy – all of which leave you feeling rejuvenated.

In this busy schedule, time is allotted for lounging by the pool and relaxing in the gardens of roses, lavender, and agapanthus. There's no television and no piped-in music, just the rustle of vines, the sound of a trickling waterfall, and a few bird songs. The spicy scent of eucalyptus mingles with the inviting smells of good foods baking, and you begin to think of dinner.

Three meals and two snacks a day add up to just 1,200 calories, but they don't leave you hungry. The Cal-a-Vie cuisine features fresh ingredients and a variety of spices and herbs. Examples of the light and elegant fare are grilled swordfish with papaya salsa, mango sorbet with raspberries, Italian pear cake, and even strawberry cheesecake and a few chocolate desserts.

The spa provides the gear and clothing you'll need and launders it daily; all you need to pack are your swimsuit, underwear, shoes, and toothbrush. Your room, in one of the four buildings around the swimming pool, will have a clock radio, phone, armoire, a duvet on the bed, and a closet with an umbrella for the occasional rain sprinkle. All the units are the same size, with slightly different decorating schemes, and have private patios.

Wine Country

Boyes Hot Springs
Sonoma Mission Inn, Spa, & Country Club, 473
Calistoga
Brannan Cottage Inn, 475
Cottage Grove Inn, 476
Foothill House, 478
Meadowlark Country House, 480
Mount View Hotel, 482
Scott Courtyard, 484
Silver Rose Inn and Spa, 485
Geyserville
The Hope-Merrill House, 488
Glen Ellen
Beltane Ranch, 490
Gaige House Inn, 492
Guerneville
Applewood, 494
Healdsburg
Belle de Jour Inn, 496
The George Alexander House, 498
Madrona Manor, 500
Kenwood
The Kenwood Inn, 502
Napa
Churchill Manor, 504
La Residence Country Inn, 506
The Old World Inn, 507
Silverado Country Club & Resort, 508

Occidental
The Inn at Occidental, 510
Rutherford
Auberge du Soleil, 512
St. Helena
Bartels Ranch and Country Inn, 514
Deer Run, 516
The Inn at Southbridge, 517
Meadowood, 519
Vineyard Country Inn, 521
The Wine Country Inn, 522
Zinfandel Inn, 523
Santa Rosa
The Gables, 525
Vintners Inn, 527
Sonoma
El Dorado Hotel, 528
Sonoma Hotel, 530
Victorian Garden Inn, 531
Yountville
Burgundy House, 532
Maison Fleurie, 533
Napa Valley Lodge, 535

Best Bed-and-Breakfasts

Calistoga
  Brannan Cottage Inn, 475
  Foothill House, 478
  Meadowlark Country House, 480
  Scott Courtyard, 484
Geyserville
  The Hope-Merrill House, 488
Glen Ellen
  Beltane Ranch, 490
  Gaige House Inn, 492
Healdsburg
  Belle de Jour Inn, 496
  The George Alexander House, 498
Napa
  Churchill Manor, 504
  The Old World Inn, 507
Occidental
  The Inn at Occidental, 510
St. Helena
  Bartels Ranch and Country Inn, 514
  Deer Run, 516
  Zinfandel Inn, 523
Santa Rosa
  The Gables, 525
Sonoma
  Victorian Garden Inn, 531
Yountville
  Burgundy House, 532
  Maison Fleurie, 533

Best Country Inns

Guerneville
  Applewood, 494
Healdsburg
  Madrona Manor, 500
Kenwood
  The Kenwood Inn, 502
Napa
  La Residence Country Inn, 506

Rutherford
Auberge du Soleil, 512
St. Helena
Vineyard Country Inn, 521
The Wine Country Inn, 522

Best Intimate City Stops

Calistoga
Cottage Grove Inn, 476
Mount View Hotel, 482
St. Helena
The Inn at Southbridge, 517
Santa Rosa
Vintners Inn, 527
Sonoma
El Dorado Hotel, 528
Sonoma Hotel, 530
Yountville
Napa Valley Lodge, 535

Best Resorts

Napa
Silverado Country Club & Resort, 508
St. Helena
Meadowood, 519

Best Romantic Hideaways

Calistoga
Silver Rose Inn and Spa, 485

Best Spas

Boyes Hot Springs
Sonoma Mission Inn, Spa, & Country Club, 473

Although there are small pockets of wine-growing regions in other parts of the state, the Napa and Sonoma valleys north of San Francisco are the areas that people generally refer to as the California wine country. Between the towns of **Napa** and **Healdsburg** some of the state's finest and best-known wines are produced. Vineyards cover the valley floor, border the Russian River, climb almost every hillside, and grow between farmlands and towns near historic **Sonoma,** where wineries have been producing wines for over a hundred years. The lesser-known Alexander Valley near **Geyserville** is also worth exploring and adds even greater depth to the famed wine-growing region.

The highest concentration of wineries, including some of California's largest, face Highway 29, which runs right through the heart of the Napa Valley. For this reason the route is often crammed with traffic and weekend wine tasters. Hence Sonoma tends to be somewhat less crowded with tourists than the Napa Valley, while Napa has a slight edge when it comes to acclaimed eateries that incorporate the region's natural bounty in their creative cuisine. Both valleys have charming towns, such as Sonoma, with its central town plaza surrounded by historic buildings, **St. Helena** and **Yountville,** with their smart shops and first-rate restaurants, and **Boyes Hot Springs** and **Calistoga,** where visitors have been coming for decades to soak in health-giving mineral waters. In recent years, hot air balloon companies have sprung up to offer travelers the chance to soar over the region and witness its abundant beauty.

Ultimately, whether you decide to focus your attention on either Napa or Sonoma, both are lovely and have a wide selection of good wineries, excellent restaurants, and fine inns. Best of all, each valley is easily accessible from the other, no matter where you stay in the area.

Boyes Hot Springs

Sonoma Mission Inn, Spa, & Country Club

18140 Sonoma Highway 12
Boyes Hot Springs, CA
Mailing Address: P.O. Box 1447
Sonoma, CA 95476
707-938-9000
800-862-4945
Fax: 707-996-5358
www.sonomamissioninn.com

> **A mission-style hotel with spa facilities and a golf course**

General manager: Charles Henning. **Accommodations:** 228 rooms, including 63 suites. **Rates:** $175–$770 single or double, $30 for additional person. **Added:** 9% tax. **Minimum stay:** 2 nights on weekends. **Payment:** Major credit cards. **Children:** Under age 12 free in room with parents. **Pets:** Not allowed. **Smoking:** Allowed outdoors only.

➤ **Since the mid-1800s, San Franciscans have been traveling 40 miles north to the Boyes Hot Springs site for the curative mineral waters of its underground springs. The area was long considered a sacred healing ground by Native Americans.**

In 1895 an enterprising young Englishman, Captain H. E. Boyes, built a bathhouse and hotel that later burned to the ground. In 1927 the present Sonoma Mission Inn was constructed. Typifying the romantic revivalism of the era, the new building was designed as a California mission, complete with arcade and bell tower.

The inn's fortunes waxed and waned over the years, until in the 1980s it was restored and brought to its present state of luxury as a top resort. The rambling beige hotel stands on seven acres of grounds shaded by big maple and eucalyptus trees in the thriving little town of Boyes Hot Springs, two miles north of Sonoma.

The mission motif stops at the front door. Inside, the big open lobby has white walls, a beamed ceiling, tile floors, and comfy sofas and chairs situated in front of a large fireplace topped by a wreath of dried flowers.

Adjacent to the lobby are a bar and The Grille, a restaurant in pinks and greens with soft linens and fresh orchids on the tables, all glowing in candlelight. The Grille features California cookery. Entrées include a mesquite-grilled veal chop with sun-dried tomato butter and grilled lamb chops with hazelnut-mint pesto. Fresh local ingredients are emphasized. The menu also has imaginative and tasty spa cuisine for those who are watching calories, and its wine list features over 200 area wines. Another restaurant, the Café, is located on a corner at the north end of the property. It has a wine bar and an adjoining market selling a variety of wines, gifts, kitchenware, and T-shirts.

The guest rooms are in the three-story main hotel and in newer, separate buildings. The older rooms are smaller but have the most charm and character, with half-canopy beds, pretty floral fabrics, and walk-in closets. Stocked bars hold complimentary wine. The air-conditioned rooms have similar furnishings and contain writing tables, TV sets, digital clocks, and phones. In the Wine Country section of the resort, some rooms have fireplaces and overlook the inner courtyard and landscaped grounds. In 1997, 30 suites were added ranging from one-room junior suites to deluxe one-bedroom suites. These suites feature limestone and marble baths with Jacuzzi tubs and separate showers, and they have amenities such as terry robes, in-room safes, irons and ironing boards, CD players, and two-line telephones with data ports. The deluxe one-bedroom suites have two fireplaces and dining tables that seat eight people. Rates are based on room size.

The resort's much-touted spa and fitness facility was expanded to 27,000 square feet in 1999 and the services seem unending. You can get at least four kinds of massage, a seaweed body wrap, a grape seed body polish, a salt scrub, clay packs, facials, waxings, and numerous hair, nail, and skin treatments. There are herbal steam rooms, watsu treatment pools, private whirlpools, and mineral baths, as well as treatment rooms especially designed for couples. There's an extra charge for use of the spa.

The inn offers aerobics classes, a weight room, and an Olympic-size swimming pool — heated in winter — that is open to guests and supervised children. Another, smaller exercise pool is for adults only. There are also two tennis courts on the property, and the inn's 18-hole championship golf course is about a mile away.

Calistoga

Brannan Cottage Inn

P.O Box 81
109 Wapoo Avenue
Calistoga, CA 94515
707-942-4200
www.bbinternet.com/brannan

**A small, historic inn close
to Calistoga's attractions**

Innkeepers: Dieter and Ruth Back. **Accommodations:** 6 rooms (all with private bath). **Rates:** $135 single, $175 double, $200 suite. **Included:** Full breakfast. **Added:** 12% tax. **Payment:** MasterCard, Visa. **Children:** Over 10 welcome; additional $25. **Pets:** Not allowed. **Smoking:** Not allowed.

➤   **A breakfast that varies daily is served in the dining room, though with the Napa Valley's benign weather, guests can often eat outdoors in an enclosed, lemon-fragrant courtyard.**

Sam Brannan was one of the first people to recognize the commercial potential in the hot springs at the northern end of the Napa Valley. In 1859, he purchased 2,000 acres surrounding the hot springs and named the area Calistoga (a combination of California and Saratoga, New York's famous mineral water spa).

The elaborate resort he built included 25 guest cottages. The only one remaining is now a bed-and-breakfast inn. Its Greek Revival architecture, with an intricate gingerbread gableboard and scalloped ridge-cresting, was intended to bring a sense of civilization to Calistoga in the rugged 1860s. The building has been completely restored and is on the National Register of Historic Places.

In 1985 it received the prestigious Napa Landmarks award for its contribution to historic preservation in Napa County.

The charming white cottage with green trim stands behind a white picket fence, roses, and a palm tree that was planted by Sam Brannan. Robert Louis Stevenson referred to it as a "weedy palm" in *Silverado Squatters*. Now the tree is tall and stately.

The rooms are light and simple, with oak floors, cozy loveseats, primitive pine antiques, and white wicker furnishings. Fresh flowers and stenciled borders on the walls provide touches of color in the cheerful and uncluttered surroundings. Each room is named for the wildflower stencil that decorates its walls: sweet pea, poppy, morning glory, wild rose, wood violet, and iris. Poppy is a favorite and has a clawfoot tub in the bath. The carriage house can accommodate up to four people. All rooms have private entrances, ceiling fans, and air conditioning. They do not have telephones, but there is one centrally located phone for guest use. Several rooms have televisions.

In the parlor, furnished with pink velvet loveseats near a brick fireplace, stenciled clusters of grapes and leaves decorate the walls, and bunches of flowers from the surrounding garden brighten every corner. Sherry and tea are available all day in the parlor.

Cottage Grove Inn

1711 Lincoln Avenue
Calistoga, CA 94515
707-942-8400
800-799-2284
Fax: 707-942-2653
cottage@sonic.net
www.cottagegrove.com

> **Private luxury cottages with downtown convenience**

Innkeeper: Valerie Beck. **Accommodations:** 16 cottages. **Rates:** $195–$245 single or double, $50 per additional person. **Included:** Continental breakfast and afternoon wine and cheese. **Added:** 12% tax. **Minimum stay:** 2 nights on weekends. **Payment:** Major credit cards. **Children:** Age 12 and over welcome, $50 additional if third person in room. **Pets:** Not allowed. **Smoking:** Not allowed.

➤ **Just off Calistoga's main street, the Cottage Grove is in easy walking distance of the town's spas, shops, and restaurants. Wineries are a short drive away.**

It's hard to believe that a few short years ago the lot the Cottage Grove Inn stands on was a trailer park. Today the lot has been transformed into an inn that offers its guests both privacy and modern amenities in sixteen luxury cottages in a shady grove of stately elm trees on the edge of downtown Calistoga.

From the outside, the cottages, which were built in 1996, look similar. Each has its own driveway (covers are provided to protect cars from leaves and sap) and a front porch set with white wicker rocking chairs. Inside, the cottages have high ceilings and over-stuffed chairs with ottomans or sofas in front of wood-burning fireplaces. Each is attractively decorated and named for a specific theme, such as Equestrian, Rose Floral, Audubon, Nautical, Victorian, Vintners, and Fly Fishing. In Music, a drum doubles as a coffee table. In Library, lamp bases are made from faux leather volumes and the sofa is covered with a book motif fabric.

Baths, with hand-painted details, are almost as big as the cottage's main rooms. Skylights illuminate Jacuzzi tubs for two, and vanities have two sinks. About half of the cottages can accommodate three people as they have sleeper sofas. All rooms have remote-controlled TV/VCRs, wet bars, refrigerators, CD stereo systems, hair dryers, robes, irons and ironing boards — and of course, bottled Calistoga water.

A Continental breakfast is served in a small main dining room where a fire blazes on cool days, and bright oil paintings of wine country scenes adorn the walls. In the afternoons, wine and cheese is set out for guests.

Foothill House

3037 Foothill Boulevard
Calistoga, CA 94515
707-942-6933
800-942-6933
Fax: 707-942-5692
www.foothillhouse.com

**A well-run B&B near
wineries and mineral baths**

Innkeepers: Doris and Gus Beckert. **Accommodations:** 3 suites plus cottage (all with private bath, 3 with Jacuzzi tubs). **Rates:** $165–$325 single or double, $50 additional person. **Included:** Full breakfast and evening hors d'oeuvres and wine. **Minimum stay:** 2 nights on weekends, 3 nights on holiday weekends. **Payment:** Major credit cards. **Children:** Not appropriate. **Pets:** Not allowed. **Smoking:** Not allowed indoors.

➤ **The innkeepers will arrange for winery and sightseeing tours and will make dinner reservations for you. Recommended nearby restaurants include Catahoula's in the Mount View Hotel and Terra in nearby St. Helena.**

Everything is done well at this fine inn, but when guests leave Foothill House, they always rave about the food. Doris Beckert, a long-time culinary student, loves to prepare breakfast specialties and afternoon appetizers, artistically presented, for her guests. Appetizers such as chunky marinara sauce topped with brie cheese and toasted pine nuts accompanied by French bread and roasted garlic, or feta cheese in a garlic cream base with fresh basil, pine nuts, and roasted red peppers are tied in to the wine selection for the day. Breakfast could be a frittata or soufflé served in individual ramekins and adorned with edible flowers from the inn's front garden. The morning meal is served in the sun room or on a terrace, in the shade of an immense redwood tree, or can be delivered to your room. Some guests like to take their coffee up the grassy slope to the pretty white gazebo.

The small inn also offers well-furnished, attractive, spacious rooms with good reading lamps and stacks of books and magazines. Bottles of Calistoga mineral water chill in each refrigerator. Sherry is provided at bedtime, and a teddy bear or other stuffed animal holds freshly made cookies. Most rooms have a telephone, but if yours doesn't, it does have a phone jack so that the house phone may be borrowed. Wood is laid in the fireplace and the fire is ready to light. Other amenities include coffeemakers, irons, ironing boards, terry robes, televisions, CD players with CDs, radio, extra pillows, hair dryers, makeup mirrors, Q-tips, cotton balls, and soaps wrapped in calico in the baths. Three suites have Jacuzzi tubs.

The Evergreen Suite, in burgundy and creams, has over 450 square feet of space to relax in. A blanket chest stands at the foot of the king-size four-poster canopy bed. Other features include a loveseat, a wingback chair, a fireplace, a bay window with a view of Mount St. Helena, a deck with a fountain, and a twin bed in an alcove with drapes surrounding it that can be closed to shield light from a sleeping traveling companion if one decides to stay up late reading a book. The bath has an extra-deep Jacuzzi tub.

The Lupine, in blues and greens, is also pleasant. A small dining table divides the bedroom from the living room, and there's a cozy sitting area in front of a fireplace. The Redwood Room is the smallest, but it's particularly attractive and mirrors have been used to make the space appear larger. It's decorated with red velvet sofas, grape print wallpaper, and Laura Ashley's fruit-patterned fabric in rich burgundies, golds, dark greens, and olives.

Quail's Roost is the inn's largest suite. In a separate hillside cottage, it offers a full kitchen, wet bar, four-poster bed, and a smaller bed by a bay window. A quail made of driftwood stands on a dresser, and even the china in the kitchen has a quail motif. There's a large entertainment center housing a TV and VCR with many videos to choose from, and the fireplace is visible from the living room, bedroom, and bath. A two-person whirlpool tub and double-headed shower are in a very private glass-walled bathroom that faces a waterfall flowing down a rocky slope. The roost makes a great retreat for those seeking both space and privacy.

Meadowlark Country House

601 Petrified Forest Road
Calistoga, CA 94515
707-942-5651
800-942-5651
Fax: 707-942-5023
www.meadowlarkinn.com

| **A quiet country home in the Napa Valley** |

Innkeeper: Kurt Stevens. **Accommodations:** 7 rooms (all with private bath). **Rates:** $125–$195 single or double. **Included:** Breakfast. **Added:** 10.5% tax. **Minimum stay:** 2 nights on weekends. **Payment:** Major credit cards. **Children:** Not appropriate. **Pets:** Well-behaved dogs allowed by prior arrangement. **Smoking:** Not allowed.

➤ **After a day spent exploring, sightseeing, and wine tasting, you can relax on the peaceful verandah, or enjoy a picnic poolside or in the meadow.**

This stylish house in the country sits on 20 acres of rolling hills and meadows one mile outside Calistoga, at the northern end of the Napa Valley. Here Kurt Stevens has created an inn that is a pleasure to visit. A white covered bridge leads you across a creek onto the estate, which features oak groves, a lovely meadow, an arena where Kurt's show horses are trained, walking paths, a large flower garden, and a secluded swimming pool with an adjoining sauna and hot tub. The country house is set well back from the road, making it a quiet refuge from the world beyond. Kurt welcomes guests hospitably and turns the house over to them. "I treat them as my friends," he says. "I hope they feel that this is their own home in the country."

Each morning guests are served a substantial "California-style" breakfast in an elegant, antique-filled dining room. The adjoining living room has overstuffed chairs perfect for relaxing in, as well as a large library where guests can browse and read before the fire. French doors lead from the sitting room to a large verandah — a pleasant spot for enjoying a cup of coffee and the tranquil surroundings.

The guest rooms offer views of the forest, garden, or meadow. They're furnished in a mixture of antique and contemporary styles done with fine taste, and an awareness of travelers' needs for space and amenities. Each is decorated with objects from Kurt's personal collections. The well-traveled host, who came to California from Germany in the early 1970s, has collected beautiful pieces of art, many of which have an equestrian motif. Some rooms feature four-poster beds with French doors opening onto flagstone terraces or decks. All of the rooms have private baths, queen beds, TVs, VCRs, telephones, and answering machines. A fax machine can be provided upon request, and in-house massages can also be arranged.

Meadowlark is just a short distance from Calistoga's mineral baths, the town center, and the valley's numerous wineries and restaurants. Yet it's truly a retreat from the crowds and traffic that can clog Highway 29.

Mount View Hotel

1457 Lincoln Avenue
Calistoga, CA 94515
707-942-6877
800-816-6877
Fax: 707-942-6904
www.mountviewhotel.com

> A wine country hotel with
> art deco style

General manager: Laurie Jordan. **Accommodations:** 32 rooms. **Rates:** $130–$240. **Included:** Continental breakfast. **Added:** 12% tax. **Minimum stay:** 2 nights on weekends; 3 nights on holiday weekends. **Payment:** Major credit cards. **Children:** Discouraged; older children $25 additional. **Pets:** Not allowed. **Smoking:** Not allowed. **Open:** January 15-December 31.

➤   **In back of the hotel is a terrace and a swimming pool bordered by fan palms, daisies, aloe in terra cotta pots, and a row of deer fountains.**

The first owner of the Mount View was Johnny Ghisolfo, an Italian immigrant with little education but a keen business sense. He became the first mayor of Calistoga, a village at the north end of the Napa Valley known then and now for its mineral waters. In 1917 Ghisolfo built the hotel on the town's main street. Additional wings were added in 1939, and a complete restoration of the Mount View to its original art deco style was completed in 1980. Two years later it was placed on the National Register of Historic Places.

Some of the original furnishings are still in place in the two-story stucco building. Graceful palms stand in the corners of the busy lobby, designed to capture a 1930s European flavor. Over-stuffed sofas, a fireplace, and bouquets of flowers make it a pleasant gathering place for conversation.

On one side of the lobby is Catahoula's, serving California cuisine spiced with a touch of Louisiana. The chef is Jan Birnbaum, formerly of San Francisco's famed Campton Place. Rock shrimp cakes with yellow pepper coulis, oven roasted squid salad with honey caramelized endive, and grilled salmon with white beans and maple cap mushrooms are just a few of the dishes Birnbaum's open kitchen turns out.

Continental breakfast is delivered to guest rooms each morning. The rooms are located in two parallel wings that extend back toward the pool area. In a typical corner room in back you'll have a glimpse of palm trees and the pool and terrace from one casement window. All rooms are air conditioned and have phones, cable TV, fresh flowers, in-room coffee service, hair dryers, irons and ironing boards, complimentary Calistoga water, feather beds, and duvets. Patterns painted on guest room walls complement the colors and designs of other furnishings in the room, which include contemporary pieces and a blend of antiques.

Balcony suites are at the front of the building overlooking Calistoga's main street. The Hoover Suite, named after the president who stayed there, has a clawfoot tub in its bath and a separate bedroom. In the living room there's a velvet sofa and a beautiful coffee table inlaid with mother-of-pearl. The Jacob Schram Suite, named for the founder of Schramsberg winery, is a handsome suite with an ornate carved bed and matching armoire. Flamboyant Sam Brannan, the San Franciscan who founded Calistoga, would likely be pleased with his namesake suite, which is richly furnished in Victorian style.

Most in keeping with the hotel's theme is the Carole Lombard Suite. The actress never stayed at the Mount View but she would have been comfortable in the large and airy rooms with their French art deco furniture. Framed photographs of the Lombard era hang on pink walls. The bed has a stunning mirrored headboard of smoked, beveled glass. Matching end tables hold French porcelain lamps. The tile bath has a shower only.

Across the driveway in back of the hotel are three deluxe cottages. Clematis vines and private patios shield hot tubs outside each cottage, and inside, high ceilings and skylights only add to the cheerful decor. Comforters have cut-out patterns reminiscent of Matisse's playful designs, and sun motifs are stenciled on the walls in gold. Cottages have wet bars, televisions, clock radios, and refrigerators stocked with a split of champagne. Their blue and white checkerboard tiled baths have hair dryers, brass fixtures, and Aveda toiletries.

There's a spa located on hotel property. Its services, such as mud baths, facials, massages, and body wraps, are available to hotel guests for an additional fee.

Scott Courtyard

1443 Second Street
Calistoga, CA 94515
707-942-0948
800-942-1515
Fax: 707-942-5102
www.scottcourtyard.com

> **A secluded inn of suites in a historic town**

Innkeepers: Derek and Robin Werrett. **Accommodations:** 6 suites (all with private bath). **Rates:** $180–$200 single or double. **Included:** Full breakfast and afternoon wine and refreshments. **Added:** 12% tax. **Payment:** MasterCard, Visa. **Minimum stay:** 2 nights on weekends. **Children:** Over age 12 welcome in bungalows; $25 additional. **Pets:** Not allowed. **Smoking:** Not allowed.

➤ **At Scott Courtyard you can be as sociable or secluded as you wish. There's plenty to do, from Calistoga's nearby pleasures to art studio seminars. Or you can relax in the sauna or in your spacious room.**

Courtyard is an apt name for this complex of four pale yellow buildings; they surround a latticed courtyard and garden that gives guests a sense of privacy and seclusion, though the inn is within walking distance of most of Calistoga's attractions — restaurants, shops, spas, the glider port, and the Sharpsteen Museum. The inn is a relaxing haven, with an aviary, garden, pool, art studio, exercise room, three suites in the main house, and three separate bungalows with kitchens suitable for light cooking.

Each of the 1930s-era bungalows has its own entrance and a theme such as Tropical, Philadelphia, and Hollywood. Two have fireplaces. Furnishings are eclectic, with vintage chenille bedspreads and tropical-style art deco antiques selected from curio and antiques shops in the Bay area. Burgundy Suite is the smallest, but still quite comfortable, with a separate sitting room and an iron and brass bed in the bedroom. Philadelphia Suite has light terra cotta walls and a sleigh daybed in the living room bursting with pillows. Rose Suite, on the ground floor of the main house, is like a residential apartment, with a private entrance, rattan furniture, and peach walls. If you take the Palisades Suite upstairs, you have exclusive use of the upper floor. All the rooms have queen-size beds and air conditioning.

In the Social Room, the innkeepers serve evening refreshments, and invite guests to enjoy their books and CD player, or play chess with an elaborate chess set. This high-ceilinged, airy room has a gorgeous Oriental rug on the floor before a brick fireplace and French doors that open to the courtyard and swimming pool.

Eggs pesto, dijon dill quiche, freshly baked banana bread, lemon-poppyseed French toast, and chicken-apple sausage are some of the items that might appear in the morning breakfast buffet. The menu changes every day, and the innkeepers try to concentrate on healthy ingredients. The meal is served at umbrella tables by the pool or in a dining area with bistro-style tables for two.

Silver Rose Inn and Spa

351 Rosedale Road
Calistoga, CA 94515
707-942-9581
800-995-9381
Fax: 707-942-0841
silvrose@napanet.net
www.silverrose.com

A top-quality romantic country inn amidst vineyards

Innkeepers: Sally, J. Paul, and Derrick Dumont. **Accommodations:** 20 rooms (all with private bath). **Rates:** $160–$275. **Included:** Breakfast and afternoon refreshments. **Added:** 12% tax. **Minimum stay:** 2 nights on weekends. **Payment:** Major credit cards. **Children:** Not appropriate. **Pets:** Not allowed. **Smoking:** Not allowed.

➤ **If you decide to venture beyond this lovely enclave, the Dumonts can provide suggestions on places to go. They will make restaurant or wine**

tour reservations for you, or arrange for a hot air balloon trip over nearby vineyards.

If you want more from the Napa Valley than winery tours, the Silver Rose offers appealing options. Once you're settled in this outstanding bed-and-breakfast inn, you may be reluctant to leave for anything but dinner. It's tempting to sit by the pool all day, sharpen your chipping and putting skills on the inn's putting green, play a game of tennis on one of the two tennis courts, or relax on your private balcony and watch the grapes grow.

Silver Rose's original Inn on the Knoll was built as a B&B, with the owners' quarters separate from the side used by guests. The Dumonts' favorite flower, the rose, pervades the inn, from the etched glass rose on the oak front door to the private Silver Rose wine label and the masses of roses in the garden.

Guests enjoy complimentary wine and cheese in the large living room, which has a stone fireplace, dark beams, and tile flooring. Breakfast — a rose-garnished fruit plate and freshly made breads — is served here or can be taken to your room or out on the terrace.

Each guest room has a theme. Turn of the Century is romantic in old rose and lace, with a half-canopy bed topped with a floral swag, antique dolls atop a mirrored armoire, and a clawfoot tub. Peach Delight, which gets morning sun, has a four-poster bed and calico wallpaper. Cat-lovers will appreciate the collection of stuffed cats in this room.

Country Blue has a country motif, and Bears in Burgundy features some thirty teddy bears. There are bears in a hot air balloon basket, bears of brass, stuffed bears, a Beefeater bear, a "Bogie" bear, and bears in formal dress. The Oriental Suite is the largest and has shoji screens, hardwood floors, Oriental rugs, rattan furniture, and Japanese lacquered wood. The good-size bath has two sinks, a Jacuzzi tub, and a bidet.

Western, fittingly furnished with cowboy wrought-iron lamps, horseshoes, a saddle, and southwestern prints, has high ceilings, a gas fireplace, and a patio overlooking the pool. Safari is Sally's personal favorite. Cuddly stuffed animals are perched above the closet, African masks hang above the fireplace, and a papier mâché zebra and giraffe stand on the mantel. Leopard-print wallpaper, a zebra-striped comforter on the half-canopy bed, and rattan furnishings complete the exotic look.

In 1996 the Dumonts opened Inn the Vineyard, with eleven additional individually decorated suites in a separate building with its own wine-bottle-shaped swimming pool. Theme rooms here include the Vineyard Suite, with a whirlpool tub by the fireplace;

Mardi Gras, with its metal four-poster bed draped in gold lame; the Grapevine, with a grape motif; the Library, with its own supply of reading material; Cleopatra's Room, with a Jacuzzi tub for two; and Hello Hollywood, with art deco furnishings.

At Silver Rose, the hospitality is generous, and thought and care went into every aspect of the inn's design. Soft music makes the perfect accompaniment to a soothing moonlit soak in the inn's mineral-water-fed hot tub and adjoining swimming pool. Throughout the lovely grounds there are plenty of nooks and corners that make ideal spots to relax in a chaise and admire the surrounding vineyards and the riot of color in the flowerbeds.

For a relatively small inn, the Silver Rose offers many services one would only expect to find at a much larger resort — such as the inn's Heavenly Spa, where angels adorn walls and attractive shoji screens separate the treatment rooms from one another. Spa treatments include massages, facials, body wraps, and hydrotherapy. The inn has a conference center that can handle groups of up to 50 and also provides fax, laundry, and wine shipping services.

The Dumonts originally settled in Calistoga with the idea of becoming vintners, and they hoped to have producing vineyards on the twenty acres that surround the inn within the next few years. At press time, plans were in the works to open a winery and restaurant; if their professionalism in running the Silver Rose is any indication, their new ventures will most likely be terrific successes as well.

Geyserville

The Hope-Merrill House

P.O. Box 42
21253 Geyserville Avenue
Geyserville, CA 95441
707-857-3356
800-825-4233
Fax: 707-857-4673
moreinfo@hope-inns.com
www.hope-inns.com

> A superbly restored
> example of Eastlake Stick
> architecture

Innkeepers: Cosette and Ron Scheiber. **Accommodations:** 8 rooms (all with private bath). **Rates:** $111–$187 single or double, $30 additional person. **Included:** Full breakfast. **Added:** 10% tax. **Minimum stay:** 2 nights on weekends April–November; 3 nights on holiday weekends. **Payment:** Major credit cards. **Children:** Not appropriate. **Pets:** Not allowed. **Smoking:** Not allowed indoors.

➤ **Geyserville lies in the fertile Alexander Valley, where the vineyards produce some of California's finest wines. Several wineries along the Russian River Wine Trail are open for tours and tastings. From the inn you have a view of Geyser Peak and the steam clouds rising from a geothermal field.**

More than a hundred years ago, J. P. and Martha Merrill settled in Geyserville, a small town 74 miles north of San Francisco. The grand redwood home they built, a striking example of Eastlake Stick architecture, is now an inn. The Hope-Merrill House opened to guests in 1981. Since then, hundreds of visitors have come to see the stunning restoration and to enjoy the inn's informal hospitality.

The inn is furnished with treasures throughout. Most outstanding are the wallpapers, silk-screened by the designer Bruce Bradbury as replicas of the bold Victorian papers used a hundred years ago. Intricate and fanciful, they cover the walls with exotic designs. Other appealing architectural features include hand-tooled linoleum walls in the hallway and a stained glass window over the stairs.

The guest rooms have ceiling fans and all are individually decorated. The Victorian Room has an antique double bed as well as a chaise longue in the bay alcove window and a clawfoot tub. The Peacock Room, in burgundy and rose, features a fireplace and a whirlpool tub for two set in old marble below a 100-year-old etched glass window. Briar Rose has a wicker fainting couch in a bay window with a matching wicker loveseat and chair. Bachelor Button is the smallest room. Its bath, which is across the hall, has a clawfoot tub. Carpenter Gothic takes its name from its motif.

Bradbury and Vineyard View both have fireplaces and double showers. Bradbury displays an astonishing array of wallpapers — nine separate designs swirling around the room in brilliant color. Vineyard View, in colors of plum and wine, has long narrow windows overlooking the vineyard and grape arbor. Sterling Suite is the largest room and has a fireplace, a sitting area, a queen-size four-poster bed, and a patio.

Downstairs in the front parlor is a collection of Victoriana — baskets, eggs, ceramics, plates, and tureens. The sun room, by contrast, is casual and light, with wide windows and tables strewn with magazines. Here guests look over restaurant menus and discuss their sightseeing plans.

Continuing the Victorian theme, the backyard is fenced with a stone wall and a wrought-iron fence. There are raised flowerbeds, a kiwi arbor, rhododendrons, and persimmon and fig trees on the grounds, as well as a deck and a nice-size swimming pool.

Cosette serves a country breakfast of juice, French roast coffee, fruit, homemade breads and pastries, and egg dishes. Popovers, blueberry sour cream cake, fruit tarts (maybe made with figs from the inn's own trees), and tomato frittatas are specialties. Later in the day, if you want soft drinks or local wine, they're available for purchase.

The innkeepers also offer less formal lodging in the Hope-Bosworth House, a historic landmark across the street. Furnished in a sophisticated country style, it is quite different from its impressive Victorian sister, with a cozy atmosphere. The Hope-Bosworth has four rooms and is slightly less expensive. It stands behind tall palm trees and a picket fence covered with old roses. Concord grapes grow over the arbor in the backyard; from them, Cosette makes and sells spicy grape jelly.

Several weekends a year the innkeepers offer "pick and press" weekends where guests come to try their hands at picking and pressing grapes. Gourmet meals, private vineyard tours and tastings, and lodgings are included in the package.

Glen Ellen

Beltane Ranch

P.O. Box 395
11775 Highway 12
Glen Ellen, CA 95442
707-996-6501
Fax: 707-833-4233

> A country inn overlooking vineyards

Owner: Rosemary Wood. **Innkeeper:** Anne Soulier. **Accommodations:** 5 rooms, 1 garden cottage (all with private bath). **Rates:** $130–$180 in main house, garden cottage $220. **Included:** Full breakfast. **Added:** 9% tax. **Payment:** No credit cards; personal checks accepted. **Children:** Welcome by arrangement; additional $20 if third person in room. **Pets:** Not allowed. **Smoking:** Not allowed indoors.

> ➤ **Built in the 1890s as a bunkhouse when this was a working ranch, the ranch house was purchased in the 1930s by the present owner's aunt and uncle. They raised turkeys, sheep, and cattle on acreage where Rosemary now grows chardonnay and cabernet grapes for local wineries and olives for her own label olive oil.**

This century-old sunny yellow ranch house with white gingerbread trim and wraparound verandah and balcony stands on a hill above Highway 12 in the Sonoma Valley wine country north of San Francisco. Rosemary Wood restored the old place in the 1970s and opened it as a bed-and-breakfast for wine country travelers in 1981. In this peaceful country setting she has created a quiet retreat, complete with tennis court, under the oak trees. Behind a low white picket fence are the two-story house where fragrant jasmine vines grow on porch railings and the well-tended gardens bursting with California poppies, irises, and roses. Ever-bearing raspberry bushes supply breakfast fruit.

Indoors, there's a dining area by the front door where breakfast is served in cool weather. On sunny days breakfast is brought to your own table on the balcony or, if you're traveling with a group, to a table under the trees. Breakfasts are made with fresh vegetables and fruits from the inn's garden whenever possible. Pancakes and waffles are topped with homemade raspberry syrup, and frittatas and omelettes use ingredients such as leeks and fennel.

The guest room on the ground floor is the smallest but it's pleasant, with a cozy wicker rocking chair and ceiling fan. The upstairs rooms, off the long balcony, are larger and airier. One suite, which extends the width of the house, has a fireplace and daybed in the sitting area and, in the bedroom, a queen bed of black iron and gracefully curved brass. Fresh flowers are on the dresser. Books by the noted Glen Ellen author M.F.K. Fisher mingle with travel guidebooks on the table. Works by Jack London, another author who lived in Glen Ellen, are in the opposite corner suite, which also has a daybed and a settee.

Out on the balcony a hammock swings in the gentle breeze, inviting you to relax while the ranch's cat snoozes on the railing beside you. Or you can head for the swing on the verandah below, a restful perch for viewing the garden and valley, vineyards, fields, and the shadowed hills against the horizon.

Gaige House Inn

13540 Arnold Drive
Glen Ellen, CA 95442
707-935-0237
800-935-0237
Fax: 707-935-6411
gaige@sprynet.com
www.gaige.com

> **A bed-and-breakfast in a historic home**

Innkeepers: Ken Burnet, Jr., and Greg Nemrow. **Accommodations:** 13 rooms (all with private bath). **Rates:** $225–$375 single or double. **Included:** Full breakfast. **Added:** 9% tax. **Minimum stay:** 2 nights on weekends. **Payment:** Major credit cards. **Children:** Over 12 welcome; additional $25 if third person in room. **Pets:** Not allowed. **Smoking:** Not allowed.

➤ **Gaige House is a comfortable place to relax after touring the Valley of the Moon. A major attraction is Jack London State Historic Park, about a mile from the inn. The author's former home is now a museum of his life and work. Also in the park are the ruins of London's fabulous Wolf House and walking and horse trails.**

Glen Ellen is a tree-shaded village in the Sonoma Valley north of San Francisco. The Gaige House is one of its historic homes, set on 1.5 acres near Calabasas Creek and surrounded by the wooded hills of the California Coast Range. The Italianate Queen Anne home on Glen Ellen's main street was built around 1890 for A. E. Gaige, the town's butcher. As the years passed, the large Victorian was used as a boarding house and school and finally, after falling into disrepair, was restored as a small inn in 1980.

At the front of the house two parlors offer seating on hot summer days. Beyond the parlors is the kitchen and a large dining room where guests eat breakfast at several tables. The meal is prepared by a professional chef. While the menu changes daily, Gaige House sunrise scrambled eggs served with smoked salmon and balsamic tomato slices, or creole eggs in a spicy tomato sauce with turkey andouille sausage are examples of the tempting fare.

The guest rooms are furnished with a combination of antiques and art. They all have air conditioning, television, telephones, and CD players, and several have fireplaces. One first-floor room is spacious, with a fireplace, a clawfoot tub, and a king bed topped with fluffy comforters. On the second floor, the Gaige Suite is popular for its fireplace, immense blue tile bath with a whirlpool tub, and a private wraparound balcony that overlooks the pool and backyard lawn. The suite is equally well done and includes a king canopy bed with carved posters and a daybed covered in creamy canvas and plump pillows. Also on the second floor are two rooms with seating by bay windows. Room One has a desk in its bay window and a walk-in closet. Up two stairs from the second floor is cozy Room Four, with a fireplace and floors of polished oak.

Five rooms on the lower level have individual entrances. Room Seven is popular in the summer because its location off the shaded, vine-covered porch is cool and dark, but ivory tones lighten up the room's interior. Room Eight is the quietest room, and Room Nine has its own Japanese garden. In Room Ten you can relax on the large window seat set beneath a bay window, in the whirlpool tub, or on the private deck.

Glen Ellen is a few miles from Sonoma, where you may see several restored buildings from California's Spanish and Mexican history. The Sonoma area has wineries that are open for touring and tastings, and there are several excellent restaurants.

Guerneville

Applewood

13555 Highway 116, Pocket Canyon
Guerneville, CA 95446
707-869-9093
800-555-8509
Fax: 707-869-9170
stay@applewoodinn.com
www.applewoodinn.com

A luxurious mansion near the Russian River

Owner: Jim Caron. **Accommodations:** 16 rooms and suites (all with private bath). **Rates:** $135–$325 single or double. **Included:** Full breakfast and evening refreshments. **Added:** 9% tax. **Minimum stay:** 2 nights on weekends, 3 nights on some holidays. **Payment:** Major credit cards. **Children:** Not appropriate. **Pets:** Not allowed. **Smoking:** Not allowed.

➤ **In the 1920s, San Franciscans would ferry across the bay and take the train north to Guerneville to fish, swim, ride horses through the redwoods, and dance to swing bands.**

The Russian River between Highway 101 and the coast has long been a scenic playground for vacationers. One of the grand homes built during the 1920s was the Belden Mansion, intended to be a "centerpiece of elegant living." Today it's an inn of great quality and charm. Jim Caron brought his experience in business and interior decorating to the venture when he purchased the home in 1985. His goal was to achieve the ideal country inn, which he has done with style and warm hospitality.

When you enter the peach-colored stucco and tile-roofed main home, which sits on a knoll outside Guerneville, you're in a large common room with a stone fireplace, dark woodwork, and comfortable couches. Around the corner is the solarium. Curved walls, lots of glass and views of the trees, leaf patterns against green walls, and tall palms in terra cotta pots give this room an outdoor atmosphere. The stone fireplace makes it cozy. Coffee and tea with the newspaper are served here in the morning.

All the guest rooms in the original home, which are on various levels, have phones, television, fresh flowers, down comforters, and a harmonious blend of family heirlooms, antique botanical prints, books, and art. One room has a covered porch, another a walled patio where roses and camellias grow. One room on the ground level has a secretary desk against apple green walls and a sitting area overlooking the trees.

Seven larger suites occupy three floors of the Mediterranean style "piccola casa" which is adjacent to the main house. The airy suites have amenities such as fireplaces, double showers, individually controlled heat and air conditioning, and have garden courtyard or orchard views. Two have Jacuzzi tubs, and the honeymoon suite has its own rooftop sundeck.

In Room 14 there's a loveseat in creams and salmons, and fringed pillows sit atop the high queen-size bed. A window seat looks out to towering redwoods in Room 13, and there's a needlepoint bench at the foot of the sleigh bed. Room 12, in tans and greens, is masculine with bark canoes, a stone hearth, four-poster bed, Jacuzzi, and enclosed patio with a fountain.

The inn's three most luxurious suites are in the Gatehouse where guests register upon checking in. The suites have Jacuzzis, fireplaces, and air conditioning.

Applewood's fifty-seat restaurant, which is open to the public, is located in a batten board and river rock structure on one side of the inn's central courtyard. Dinners, prepared by Executive Chef David Frakes, who was formerly with the Ritz Carlton in San Francisco, are served Tuesday through Saturday. Billed as "wine country rustic," a typical meal on the changing menu might include prawns with habanero aioli and cucumber peach relish for starters, Chilean sea bass with mustard greens, tomato, and garlic fondue, tarragon beurre blanc and sesame basmati for the main course, and a dessert of chocolate cheesecake with raspberry coulis and fudge sauce or lemon roulade with brandied cherries and crème Anglaise. There are more than 120 selections to choose from on the wine list, or if you prefer, you can bring your own bottle of wine that you purchased from one of the area's many wineries (a corkage fee is charged). Dinner reservations are recommended.

When you return to your room after dinner, you'll find chocolates, the bedclothes turned down, and your clothing neatly folded or hung in the closet. In the morning, another outstanding meal is served.

The inn has a swimming pool behind a wrought-iron gate; beyond is a small vineyard, the garden, and the wooded hills. You can tour nearby wineries, buy the region's famous apples, fish for steelhead, taste fresh jam at Koslowski's, or take a Japanese enzyme bath at Osmosis Company. In Armstrong Park, walk among majestic giants — some of the redwood trees are more than 300 feet high and 1,000 years old.

Healdsburg

Belle de Jour Inn

16276 Healdsburg Avenue
Healdsburg, CA 95448
707-431-9777
Fax: 707-431-7412
www.belledejourinn.com

> A romantic bed-and-breakfast near wineries

Innkeepers: Tom and Brenda Hearn. **Accommodations:** 4 cottages and 1 carriage house. **Rates:** $165–$275 single or double. **Included:** Full breakfast. **Added:** 10% tax. **Minimum stay:** 2 nights on weekends, 3 nights on some holidays. **Payment:** Major credit cards. **Children:** Not appropriate. **Pets:** Not allowed. **Smoking:** Not allowed.

> ➤ **The little town of Healdsburg lies in the Alexander Valley wine country 70 miles north of San Francisco. On its outskirts, directly across the road from Simi Winery, is this romantic country getaway.**

At Belle de Jour an Italianate farmhouse built around 1873 stands on a hill surrounded by six acres of gardens and fields. This is the owners' residence; a few yards up the slope are the white, rough-hewn guest cottages and a carriage house.

Rooms are decorated in a light, French country theme and have refrigerators, air conditioning, hair dryers, robes, and gas fireplaces. Atelier, once used as a studio, has rattan furnishings and a bed with a Battenburg lace canopy. Posters of France hang on the walls. There's a streamlined pedestal sink and a whirlpool tub in the white tile bath. More sophisticated is the Terrace Room, with a fireplace, a king-size brass bed, colors of mauve, deep green, and rose, and a terrace with views of an expansive lawn and the Alexander Valley beyond. The rosy-hued bath has a shower and a whirlpool tub for two with valley views. A whirlpool tub and views are also highlights of the Carriage House — a deluxe suite with a king-size bed and sitting areas.

The Caretaker's Suite, which was the caretaker's quarters for many years (the other cottages were built in the 1970s), is a large, barnlike room in buff, white, and tan. It boasts a bed with a lacy canopy and crisp white linens and a sitting area with a fireplace. This suite also has an oversize whirlpool tub. Double doors lead to a trellised deck that overlooks rolling hills. A favorite among repeat guests for its lovely view is Morning Hill. Green pine walls, dark green shutters, and throw rugs on wood floors add rustic atmosphere to the comfortable room. Floral watercolors above the bed echo the gardens outside.

The breakfast menu changes daily. "Guests are at my mercy," Brenda says with a laugh. She may prepare mushroom-chive omelettes, eggs Benedict, or parmesan eggs and bacon to accompany her sour cream cinnamon swirl bread or blueberry muffins, orange juice, fresh fruit and coffee. Breakfast is served in the farmhouse.

Brenda and Tom came to Healdsburg and Belle de Jour in 1986 from Los Angeles. "We had the house, the exotic cars, the toys," says Brenda. "Then one day we were in freeway traffic, talking to each other on our car phones, and decided we didn't want to live that way anymore." Now they happily tend vegetable and herb gardens, hang linens to dry in the sun, and welcome travelers looking for a secluded wine country retreat.

The George Alexander House

423 Matheson Street
Healdsburg, CA 95448
707-433-1358
800-310-1358
Fax: 707-433-1367

A well-run bed-and-breakfast in a wine country town

Innkeeper: Don Krohn. **Accommodations:** 4 rooms (all with private bath). **Rates:** $159–$259. **Included:** Full breakfast and tax. **Minimum stay:** Two nights on weekends April through October. **Payment:** MasterCard, Visa. **Children:** Welcome; rooms only accommodate two people; rollaways are not available. **Pets:** Not allowed. **Smoking:** Not allowed indoors.

➤ **Like other towns in the wine country, Healdsburg has no shortage of tempting eateries. The Kendall-Jackson tasting room is also here. Only four blocks from Healdsburg's plaza, the George Alexander House is convenient to all.**

The George Alexander House is a solid turn-of-the-century house with quatrefoil windows. Shaker blue and maroon trim adds cheer to its deep taupe exterior. Birch trees and lively gardens provide even more color and appeal to this handsome inn. The house was built in 1905 by George Alexander — son of Cyrus Alexander, founder of the Alexander Valley. The house was turned into a bed-and-breakfast in 1991.

Two of the inn's guest rooms are named for the Alexanders. The Mr. and Mrs. George Alexander room is Italian in theme, and has a bay window, fireplace, a carved four-poster queen bed, and a steam shower in the bath. The Lucille Alexander room is named for the Alexanders' daughter. A bright, cheerful room, it has a fluffy white comforter on its queen bed, and there's a clawfoot tub in the bath. The Butler's Room has hardwood floors, and a lovely antique bed.

With its own entrance, the Savannah room is the most expensive and private of all of the guest rooms. Earthen tones, a decorative screen adorned with majestic cranes in front of the wood-burning stove, and leopard print pillows on the wicker sofas give the room an African flavor. There's a two-person Jacuzzi tub in the bath, and the Savannah is also the most accessible room to the back courtyard and sauna.

Guests gather in the two front parlors. The first is illuminated by stained glass windows original to the home, and has a sunny corner window seat. Both parlors have Victorian furnishings and striking Oriental rugs.

A full hot breakfast is served in the formal dining room. Smoked salmon quiche and home-baked French bread are typical breakfast fare. On weekends a tray of coffee and juice is delivered to your door first thing in the morning, and breakfast is served a little later so that guests can sleep in.

The innkeeper emphasizes service and guest comfort. He provides extra towels along with robes in the rooms for trips to the sauna. On weekend evenings he serves homemade desserts such as blackberry liqueur cheesecake with a roasted pistachio chocolate cookie crust. Guests staying two nights or more are given a complimentary bottle of local wine upon check-in. When the temperature climbs in the summertime, guests are happy to find that the inn is fully air-conditioned.

Madrona Manor

1001 Westside Road
Healdsburg, CA 95448
707-433-4231
800-258-4003
Fax: 707-433-0703
www.madronamanor.com

> **A historic mansion on a wine-country estate**

Innkeepers: Joe and Maria Hadley. **Accommodations:** 21 rooms. **Rates:** $175–$330 single or double, $30 additional person. **Included:** Full breakfast. **Added:** 9% tax. **Payment:** Major credit cards. **Children:** Welcome in some rooms; $20 for rollaway. **Pets:** Not allowed. **Smoking:** Not allowed.

➤ **A morning newspaper and coffee are set out before breakfast. Then it's an assortment of fresh fruits and juices, a fine meat-and-cheese plate, and vegetable frittata with fresh salsa. Finish it all off with bread pudding or a spoonful of the inn's prize-winning kiwi or dwarf mandarin orange marmalade on homemade toast.**

West of the Napa Valley lies Sonoma County, a less touristed wine region with a rural ambience and calm that many visitors prefer. In Dry Creek Valley, near the village of Healdsburg, an elaborate three-story, seventeen-room mansion was built in 1881 by John Paxton, a wealthy businessman, state legislator, and promoter of Sonoma County's wine industry. The house remained in the Paxton family until 1913.

Restored and opened as an inn and restaurant in the 1980s, Madrona Manor has been receiving acclaim since it opened. The inn is set on a hillside on eight landscaped acres, under eucalyptus and oak trees and the tall madrones that give the place its name. There's a large garden of vegetables, herbs, roses, and dozens of other flowers that are used to create the bouquets that are placed throughout the homelike hotel. If you arrive at dinnertime you may see a member of the kitchen staff picking fresh herbs from the garden for use in that evening's meal.

Staying at Madrona Manor is like visiting a friend with a country estate — a friend from another century. Victorian antiques fill the spacious rooms. The music room, with a square rosewood grand piano, an ongoing jigsaw puzzle, and books and scrapbooks, is a genteel gathering place to sip wine before dinner.

Next to it is the restaurant, noted for its California cuisine with a Mediterranean flair. Todd Muir, whose family owned the inn for more than fifteen years, oversees the menu. A graduate of the California Culinary Academy, he worked at renowned Chez Panisse before opening the restaurant at the manor. The menu features such delicacies as veal ravioli with gorgonzola cream and rack of lamb stuffed with chicken basil farce. For dessert you can treat yourself to chocolate cherry mousse cake or orange almond crepes with caramel ice cream. The menu changes seasonally to reflect Sonoma County's fresh products.

Nine guest rooms are in the main house. Their fireplaces, antiques, and decor create the atmosphere of an earlier day, while private baths and individual climate control provide modern comforts. The furnishings are impressive: intricately carved four-poster beds, dressing tables with beveled glass mirrors, paintings, and tall armoires. The most popular is Paxton's Room, with a tile fireplace, a curtained alcove with bay windows, and a fine view of Mount St. Helena and Fitch Mountain from the balcony. This is one of two rooms with French doors opening to private balconies.

The third floor, formerly the servants' quarters, features ornate beds and Victorian wallpapers. The other rooms are in separate cottages: nine in the Carriage House, two in Meadow Wood, and one in Garden Cottage. These are less formal and more "countrified" than those in the main house. The Carriage House was built for the Paxton family's carriages; it now houses visitors in luxury with a Far Eastern touch. The front door and filigreed rosewood interior trim were brought from Nepal. One room in the Carriage House is furnished with reproduction antiques, while the rest are contemporary.

Farther up the hill, near the terraced garden and under oak trees, is the Garden Cottage. It has its own deck and yard, a marble fireplace, and a tub for two. There are phones in all the rooms, but there aren't any television sets at Madrona Manor. All guests are welcome to use the swimming pool on the hill behind the manor.

Kenwood

The Kenwood Inn

10400 Sonoma Highway
Kenwood, CA 95452
707-833-1293
800-353-6966
Fax: 707-833-1247
www.kenwoodinn.com

> **A luxurious inn offering spa services**

Proprietor: Terry Grimm. **Accommodations:** 12 suites (all with private bath). **Rates:** $255–$395. **Included:** Gourmet breakfast. **Added:** 9% tax. **Payment:** Major credit cards. **Children:** Not appropriate. **Pets:** Not allowed. **Smoking:** Not allowed.

➤ **Only fifteen minutes from Sonoma, the Kenwood Inn makes a good base for exploring wineries. The Kunde Estate vineyard is just across the street from the inn.**

This charming inn and spa is located on Highway 12 just north of Glen Ellen. A wall shields the inn compound from the busy road, and once inside the enclosure you'll quickly recognize a lodging of comfort and taste. For an inn of its size, the Kenwood offers a surprising number of amenities.

The lobby is adjacent to the spa treatment rooms, where guests can indulge themselves in seaweed masks and herbal wraps. From the reception area, a shady ramada leads to the heart of the complex, where gardens, fountains, a swimming pool, and a hot tub are surrounded by the four remaining buildings that compose the inn. On one side there are two stucco duplexes housing two guest rooms each, and across the garden there's a similarly constructed "fourplex." Although they were built in 1995, care went into their design in order to give them an ageless, European look.

From the duplexes, flower-lined stone walkways lead to the main house, which was built in the 1930s. Covered in ivy, it too looks as though it could be centuries old. Here there's a wonderful country farmhouse kitchen with colorful pottery, slate floors, and baskets, herbs, and chiles hanging from the ceiling. In the adjoining dining room guests dine on three-course breakfasts such as crostini with prosciutto, poached eggs in a basil cream sauce, croissants, and a fruit parfait at tables for two. There's also a central living room that serves as a gathering spot if you're feeling social, or you want to peruse menus from the area's many fine restaurants.

There are four guest suites in the main house. Suite Seven, which is smaller than most, is furnished in golds and greens and has a grape motif bedspread and pillow shams. Suite Eight, with its ivy-framed windows, leaf wreath, and slate hearth, has an autumnal feel. Another suite in the main house has a separate living room. Dark and masculine, it has rich velvet sofas and a model ship.

Plaster walls in the newer buildings have been stained to give the look of age. Outside the fourplex a pyramid of wooden wine barrels stand as a reminder of the inn's locale, and a fountain trickles at the base of the stairs. Upstairs rooms have balconies. In Suite Three, fringed gold velvet chairs offer seating in front of the fireplace, while a gargoyle-carved tapestry-upholstered chair stands in a corner. The bed is covered with a fluffy striped duvet and matching pillows, and the bath has an antique washstand.

No matter which room you choose, it will be elegantly furnished with antiques, coordinating armoire and bed sets, a fireplace, and a queen-size bed topped by a feather bed and down comforter. Rooms also have stereos with CD players and baths with marble-topped wooden washstands and brass fixtures. Just to make sure you feel welcome, fresh flowers and a bottle of wine are placed in your room before your arrival.

Napa

Churchill Manor

485 Brown Street
Napa, CA 94559
707-253-7733
Fax: 707-253-8836

> **A grand wine country mansion**

Innkeepers: Joanna Guidotti and Brian Jensen. **Accommodations:** 10 rooms (all with private bath). **Rates:** $105–$215 single or double, $25 additional person. **Included:** Full breakfast, freshly baked cookies, and wine and cheese reception. **Added:** 12% tax. **Minimum stay:** 2 nights on weekends. **Payment:** Major credit cards. **Children:** Over age 12 welcome, $25 if third person in room. **Pets:** Not allowed. **Smoking:** Not allowed indoors.

➤ **Thousands of daffodils and tulips bloom in spring. There are rose beds, boxwood hedges, and an herb garden. Guests enjoy playing croquet in the side garden, exploring the area on a tandem bicycle borrowed from the innkeepers, and relaxing on the wide verandah.**

One of the grand old mansions of the wine country has been turned into a bed-and-breakfast that is a wonderful romantic retreat. The stately three-story house, a National Historic Landmark, was built in 1889 and restored with loving care a hundred years later.

Innkeeper Brian Jensen is a builder who has recreated the original style of the mansion even while modernizing it. The original gas light fixtures have been rewired and hang in the front parlor. Leaded glass, Oriental carpets, intricately carved woodwork, and Victorian furnishings add period atmosphere to the large (10,000 square feet) B&B. "This is our hobby," Joanna says. Once a tax lawyer in San Francisco, Guidotti moved to Napa to restore and run the inn with her husband, Brian.

There are fireplaces in all four parlors and in three of the guest rooms. Each room is decorated individually, from cheery Amy's Room on the third floor to the Edward Churchill Room, the original master bedroom. It has a matching antique seven-piece bedroom set from France, the original fireplace with gold leaf tiles, an oversize soaking tub mounted on a mahogany pedestal, and a two-person shower. The Mary Wilder Room is romantic with a fireplace, double shower, and an antique cast iron clawfoot tub for two.

A breakfast of fresh muffins, croissants, fruit, and hot dishes such as omelets or French toast is served in the enclosed sun room or outside on the veranda, overlooking the colorful gardens and croquet lawn.

Churchill Manor is in a historic residential district of Napa, but it still stands head and shoulders above all of its neighbors. Because of its large, elegant, public rooms, wide porches, and expansive lawns, it's a popular spot for weddings, and the entire inn is often booked well in advance by wedding parties. The manor is also convenient to Napa's restaurants, wineries, and the Napa Valley wine train.

La Residence Country Inn

4066 St. Helena Highway North
Napa, CA 94558
707-253-0337
Fax: 707-253-0382
www.laresidence.com

> **A country inn with
> luxurious amenities**

Innkeepers: David Jackson and Craig Claussen. **Accommodations:** 20 rooms
(all with private bath). **Rates:** $175–$300 single or double, $20 additional per-
son. **Included:** Full breakfast and afternoon wine and hors d'oeuvres. **Minimum stay:** 2 nights when a Saturday is included. **Payment:** Major credit cards.
Children: Older children charged as an additional person if third person in
room. **Pets:** Not allowed. **Smoking:** Not allowed indoors.

> ➤ **Outside the back door, pear trees shade a brick patio. Across the way,
> on the patio by Cabernet Hall, wine is served in the late afternoon under a
> 200-year-old oak tree.**

This sophisticated country inn is one of a growing number of small
inns that combine the personal touch of a bed-and-breakfast with
the luxuries of a larger hotel.

La Residence, north of the city of Napa, is set back from the rush
of Highway 29. Its two buildings stand on two acres of parklike
grounds with lawns, gardens, ponds, vineyards, and oak and acacia
trees. One is the Mansion, an 1870 Gothic Revival home. The
other is Cabernet Hall, built in 1987 in the style of a French barn.
Between them are the parking lot and a heated swimming pool
surrounded by gazebos, trellises, brick patios, and pots of flowers.

There are nine rooms in the Mansion, all furnished with American antiques. On the main floor, left of the entrance, is a suite with
a marble fireplace and a Victrola, ready to be wound up for playing

old Decca records. Fruit garlands border the walls, and louvered shutters cover the windows. There's a white iron bed, an armoire, and a bath of white and green tile. Across the hall is a similar room, this one in plum and peach.

All the suites in Cabernet Hall have working fireplaces and access to a balcony or the ground-floor verandah. Comforters, wicker chairs, flowered wallpapers, and painted tiles are in most rooms. Pine antiques from France and England were imported for the inn.

The dining room by the patio is a cheery breakfast spot where David Jackson, who handles the inn's cooking, sees that guests receive their fill of fresh fruit, pastries, and an egg dish, as well as hot coffee or tea and the morning newspaper.

The Old World Inn

1301 Jefferson Street
Napa, CA 94559
707-257-0112
800-966-6624
Fax: 707-257-0118
www.oldworldinn.com

A wine country bed-and-breakfast with distinctive style

Innkeeper: Sam Van Hoeve. **Accommodations:** 10 rooms (all with private bath). **Rates:** $135–$225 single or double. **Included:** Full breakfast, afternoon tea, wine and cheese, and evening dessert buffet. **Added:** 12% tax. **Payment:** Major credit cards. **Minimum stay:** 2 nights on weekends, April through November. **Children:** Not appropriate. **Pets:** Not allowed. **Smoking:** Not allowed.

➤ **To showcase his skills, the builder combined several architectural styles — shingle style in the sweeping roof line, Craftsman in the use of rough cinder brick, Colonial Revival in the porch columns, and Queen Anne in the two-story corner tower. The curly redwood he used in the living and dining rooms glows with the patina of finely crafted woodwork.**

The room rate for the Old World Inn includes much more than a breakfast of crêpes or frittatas, fruits, and freshly baked breads. Guests are treated to a lavish afternoon tea, a wine and cheese hour with scrumptious hors d'oeuvres, and a late evening dessert buffet of homemade treats such as chocolate amaretto cake. This inn is a food-lover's delight.

The innkeeper pampers his guests in other ways, with fresh flowers, soft music, restaurant reservations, a bubbling outdoor hot tub in a fenced courtyard, and rooms furnished in fresh Scandinavian style. The Swedish artist Carl Larsson inspired the decor, which is bright with color and unusual designs. Homilies and fanciful bows are painted on the walls above the moldings, and linens and fabrics are all in coordinated colors.

Most of the antique-furnished rooms have Victorian clawfoot tubs, and one has a private Jacuzzi. Anne, eye-catching in periwinkle blue and peach tones, has a fireplace and a bed draped in pretty Laura Ashley fabric. Mint, in cool mints, is a sunny room with an iron stove and a white iron and brass bed. Birch has a tiny balcony.

The historic inn was built in 1906 by Napa's foremost builder, E. W. Doughty, as his own residence. You can see other examples of Doughty's work on a walking tour through Old Town Napa, where vintage buildings have been restored. Sam will direct you to nearby antiques shops, restaurants, and wineries.

Silverado Country Club & Resort

1600 Atlas Peak Road
Napa, CA 94558
707-257-0200
800-532-0500
Fax: 707-257-2867
resv@silveradoresort.com
www.silveradoresort.com

| **A gracious golf resort in the wine country** |

General manager: Kirk Candland. **Accommodations:** 290 condominium units. **Rates:** $160 single or double, junior suites $240, 1-bedroom condo for 2 people $320, 2-bedroom condo for up to 4 people $460, and 3-bedroom condo for up to 6 people $535, presidential suite $1,400. **Added:** 10.5% tax. **Payment:** Major credit cards. **Children:** $15 for rollaway. **Pets:** Not allowed. **Smoking:** Nonsmoking rooms available.

➤ **Immense old eucalyptus trees line the road to the entrance, perfuming the air with their pungent oil. Passing a circle of lawn with tall palm trees, you reach a curving driveway where a valet relieves you of your car and smiling bellmen help with your luggage. It's a busy place, as the resort is frequently used for meetings and conferences.**

In an idyllic grove of trees above Milliken Creek, Silverado began as a classic 14-room mansion. Built in the 1870s, it was the estate of John F. Miller, a Civil War general who moved to California and became influential in state politics. He and his wife wanted their house to reflect the Italian and French architecture they had admired on their travels abroad.

Now their home, with its Palladian windows, two-story columns, white railings, and flower-filled urns, is the main lodge of a 1,200-acre luxury resort. It's 45 minutes north of San Francisco, just outside Napa in the Napa Valley wine country.

Beyond the small lobby is a lounge with a sunken bar of polished granite. Windows overlook a sun room and terrace. An 18-hole golf course, one of two on the property, lies across the creek from the terrace. The 250-foot-long stone wall bordering the terrace is a remarkable example of the masonry skills common when the house was built. Today, trimmed ivy grows over the low wall and roses bloom beside it. This is a choice spot for lingering over cocktails while you watch the golfers and listen to the birds warbling in the great oak trees that arch over the fairways.

Silverado has 20 tennis courts, three of them with lights, as well as pro shops and instructors. There are eight swimming pools, one of them a lap pool. The resort also has a 16,000-square-foot spa with a full-service salon, cardiovascular and strength-training equipment, fitness classes, steam rooms, saunas, and Swiss showers.

Three restaurants offer varying degrees of formality. The casual Bar & Grill, overlooking the North Course, serves breakfast and lunch. Royal Oak is a pseudo-rustic steak house with a mesquite grill, open beams, and copper pans on the walls. California cuisine with Mediterranean influences is presented in Vintner's Court, a pretty salon with white and pink linens, pink roses on a white grand piano, and candlelight on the tables. On Sundays, elaborate ice sculptures decorate brunch buffet tables. A seafood buffet is served on Fridays.

The guest rooms, most of them private condominiums furnished and decorated by their owners, are in clusters called Mansion Cottages, Silverado Cottages, and Oak Creek East. They range from standard rooms with no kitchens to three-bedroom units. Studio rooms combine sitting and sleeping areas and have kitchenettes. A typical one-bedroom lodging has contemporary rattan furnishings, mirrored sliding doors on a roomy closet, television, phone, and a corner fireplace. The kitchen is fully equipped and the bath has both a tub and shower. The two- and three-bedroom apartments are in Oak Creek East, the most secluded cluster. They border quiet culs-de-sac and have private patios and balconies overlooking the fairways.

Special holiday packages are available at Silverado. Most include a round of golf and unlimited tennis, along with seasonal festivities.

Occidental

The Inn at Occidental

3657 Church Street
P.O. Box 857
Occidental, CA 95465
707-874-1047
800-522-6324
Fax: 707-874-1078
innkeeper@innatoccidental.com
www.innatoccidentalcom

A well-run inn that is convenient to both wineries and the Sonoma coast

Innkeeper: Jack, Bill, and Jean Bullard. **Accommodations:** 16 rooms (all with private bath). **Rates:** $175–$255 single or double; suites $245–$270. **Included:** Full breakfast, afternoon refreshments, and evening wine and cheese. **Added:** 9% tax. **Payment:** Major credit cards. **Children:** Over age 10 welcome. **Pets:** Not allowed. **Smoking:** Allowed outdoors only.

➤ **The Occidental area is home to some of the county's most respected nurseries: one emphasizes plants from the Mediterranean; another features more than two thousand varieties of antique roses.**

The Inn at Occidental is one of those special places where everything runs the way it should. The rooms are spotless and filled with fine antiques, and the hospitality provided by the gracious innkeepers is genuine.

The inn is set on a hill overlooking Occidental — a small town founded in 1876 which grew up around a narrow-gauge railway that connected San Francisco with the Russian River. A cheerful Victorian that dates to Occidental's early days, the inn has a pleasant verandah that wraps around the front of the home. Guests are often seen relaxing here in the plentiful wicker chairs and sofas, or on cushioned bent-willow chaises in a side yard with a fountain.

Hand-painted wisteria vines crown the entrance hallway, and there's a small chest adorned with painted bunnies as well as a corner cupboard decorated with cats. Beyond is the main living room where Oriental rugs grace hardwood floors, and sofas face a brick fireplace topped by a rocking horse. Soft music plays in the background and a fire blazes in the hearth. Jack's collection of green majolica plates — there are sixty-five in all and no two are alike — hangs on the sitting room's wall.

Guest rooms are equally charming and have amenities such as featherbeds, down comforters, and fine Italian linens. Cut glass pickling jars are on display in the Cut Glass Room on the first floor. There's also a king-size sleigh bed and a rocking chair in the window. Sliding glass doors, which let in a nice breeze when open, lead out to a patio with Adirondack chairs and a private hot tub.

Tiffany silver is framed upstairs in the Tiffany Room, and light lavender walls reflect the sunlight streaming in through the windows from a private deck. Attractive, with a four-poster canopy bed dressed in white battenburg lace, the room has a tapestry print loveseat facing its wood-burning fireplace.

Down the hall, the Quilt Suite is a personal favorite for its whimsical decor set off by sunny yellow walls. A large oil painting of a giraffe by artist Woodward Payne, framed by hand stenciling, is the focal point of the wall above the fireplace. On another wall there's a primitive painting of a cat on cloth. A striking star-patterned quilt hangs on the wall above the pine queen-size bed, a stuffed lion stands guard atop the comforter, and a bright yellow and red hand-sewn quilt is folded at the foot of the bed. Playful animal print curtains at the windows, a bean bag calico cat on the dresser, giant scissors on one wall, a drummer-boy wastebasket, a needlepoint doorstop with animals, antique bowling pins on the hearth, and wooden pedestal lamps with hand-painted faces on either side of the fireplace, make this room a happy delight for children of all ages. A deep Jacuzzi tub for two (with a rubber duckie of course) adds a touch of luxury to the merry milieu.

Other rooms in the main house include the Marbles Suite with its collection of antique marbles, two-person spa tub, and separate sitting room with fireplace; the Ivory Room with antique ivory carvings; the Sugar Suite, which is handicapped accessible, and the Sandwich Glass Suite.

In 1999 eight additional rooms were constructed in a separate building behind the original Victorian home. Each of the new rooms has a gas fireplace, whirlpool tub for two, and a private deck. With furnishings to complement their names, each room — with names such as the Safari Room, the Kitchen Cupboard Room, and the Wild West Room — is individually decorated. In the Wine Country Room, the king bed is made from antique doors and covered with a grape-bordered quilt. The Summer Room has wicker furniture and a wonderful watercolor of aspens (again by Woodward Payne).

A breakfast of homemade granola, fresh fruit, pastries, juice, tea, coffee and a hot entrée such as orange thyme pancakes, Belgian waffles, and eggs Florentine is served in the Victorian inn's wine cellar or on an adjacent patio. On a regular basis, winemaker dinners are held in this basement function room. With a massive stone fireplace, wine racks, a marvelous Victorian dollhouse, a piano, and game tables set for chess or backgammon, it is a comfortable place to linger even when there isn't a meal in progress.

Occidental feels far removed from the world at large, but it actually makes a good base for Russian River and Sonoma coast sightseeing. There are enzyme baths five minutes away, and the local arts council sponsors a chamber music series. The innkeepers can direct you to area restaurants. One of their favorites is the Willowside Cafe.

Rutherford

Auberge du Soleil

180 Rutherford Hill Road
Rutherford, CA 94573
707-963-1211
800-348-5406
Fax: 707-963-8764

A sophisticated country inn with a valley view

General manager: George Goeggel. **Accommodations:** 52 units. **Rates:** $300–$575 single or double, suites $600–$950, cottages $1,500–$2,000, depending on season. **Added:** Tax. **Minimum stay:** 2 nights on weekends. **Payment:** Major credit cards. **Children:** Not appropriate. **Pets:** Not allowed. **Smoking:** Allowed; nonsmoking rooms available.

➤ **The restaurant, lounge, and terrace all face a panorama of valley and hills that sprawls to the horizon. Terraced against the hillside, reached by winding paths dotted with sculptures and bordered by sweet-scented flowering shrubs, are the guest villas, named for French wine-growing regions.**

First the inn was a restaurant, set against a steep hillside above Napa Valley's grape-growing heartland. The venture of a renowned San Francisco restaurateur, Claude Rouas, Auberge du Soleil opened in 1981 to great acclaim. It wasn't long before its visitors, impressed by the stunning location and cuisine, yearned for lodgings as well. So, in the mid-1980s some of the valley's most exclusive lodgings joined one of its most fashionable eateries. The views are spectacular from the inn's 33 acres of olive and oak groves, similar to inland country vistas of the French Riviera.

The one- and two-bedroom suites are roomy and comfortable. Each has a fireplace, television, and wet bar stocked with a complimentary bottle of wine. The floors are polished terra cotta tile, the furniture of natural wood and leather. The beds, sofas, and oversized chairs with ottomans are outfitted with giant pillows in bright pinks and yellows. Upstairs suites have high, vaulted ceilings, and some suites have kitchenettes with a coffeemaker and full-size refrigerator. Baths have separate tubs and showers and two-sink vanities.

Near the villas and below the restaurant terrace is a large swimming pool with lounge chairs. There are three tennis courts, and a workout room has aerobics equipment and free weights. Room service is available, and the restaurant is open for breakfast.

The Auberge du Soleil menu, showcasing locally grown ingredients, is labeled "wine country cuisine." Lunch may be taken inside or out, on the sun-dappled terrace at umbrella tables. Dinners include pistachio-crusted salmon, honey-sage roasted pheasant, and grilled sea bass with red pepper risotto and roast squash romesco sauce. A pianist plays on weekends in the bar and lounge across the lobby from the restaurant. The round room has a southwestern flavor, with a single pole in the center reaching to a cone ceiling. A high circular shelf holds firewood for the adobe fireplace. Windows look out on a curving deck and over the treetops to the countryside.

Auberge du Soleil retains the chic cachet it has had since it opened. This is not the place to go for cozy warmth. A cool professionalism best characterizes the approach of most of the staff, and the well-dressed clientele is here to see and be seen as well as to dine and enjoy the beautiful setting.

St. Helena

Bartels Ranch and Country Inn

1200 Conn Valley Road
St. Helena, CA 94574
707-963-4001
Fax: 707-963-5100
bartelsranch@webtv.net
bartelsranch.com

> **A friendly home in the wine country hills**

Innkeeper: Jami Bartels. **Accommodations:** 4 rooms (all with private bath). **Rates:** $175–$245 single, $175–$285 double, $315–$395 suites. **Included:** Full breakfast and evening refreshments. **Added:** 10.5% tax. **Minimum stay:** 2 nights on weekends. **Payment:** Major credit cards. **Children:** Allowed by prior arrangement, $50 additional. **Pets:** Not allowed. **Smoking:** Allowed outside only.

➤ **If you want a complete itinerary for your wine country tour, Jami will plan it. She'll make arrangements for hot air ballooning, glider flights, and limousine and helicopter service. You may borrow her bicycles for a ride to Lake Hennessey, play bocce ball or croquet (a tennis court is in the works), or just relax by the pool.**

Conn Valley lies 4 miles east of St. Helena, in the Napa Valley wine country about 60 miles north of San Francisco. Vineyards line the road that winds through oak-covered hills leading to Jami Bartels's 60-acre estate. The sprawling stone ranch house stands on a hilltop that overlooks pastures and sloping fields of grapevines. Its landscaped grounds include fig trees, flowering plums, cypress, and magnificent old oaks.

Jami Bartels is the energetic force who created this unusual inn. She designed all 7,000 square feet of her home, from the formal dining room, where she serves catered dinners, to the thirteen-sided game room with a brick fireplace and redwood walls. The huge room holds an amazing array of entertainment possibilities, including table tennis, a pool table, CD sound system, and shelves crammed with books and magazines. There are also games, puzzles, an organ, exercise equipment, and even a Wurlitzer jukebox. Throughout the house are examples of Jami's collections and artwork: butterflies, Chinese perfume bottles, glassware, baskets, and watercolors.

The Blue Valley guest room, with a private terrace overlooking the croquet lawn and valley beyond, has a queen-size canopy bed, Queen Anne wingback chairs, and a Victorian table for two, while the Brass Monarch Room features an Empire brass bed dating from the 1850s. Glass doors open to a terrace by the pool. The Sunset Hillside Room, in burgundy and ivory, has a willow bed, alcohol fireplace, and an etagere with a TV/VCR.

The Heart of the Valley Suite is lavishly appointed. It has a king-size bed, ivory silk linens, a sofa in white damask, a mahogany desk, an English walnut armoire, whirlpool, TV/VCR, CD player, and a private deck. Cherubs kiss over the huge stone fireplace, and Venus de Milo stands watch over the sunken, heart-shaped whirlpool tub for two.

The innkeeper's hospitality adds the crowning touch that makes her B&B exceptional. She's an expert at pampering, yet you will never feel stifled by all the attention. In the laundry room, an ironing board is always set up. "You know the fancy French restaurants around here; you can't show up wrinkled," Jami says. Fresh flowers abound, bubble bath awaits in the bathrooms, and refreshments are served every evening, as well as a late-evening dessert.

Breakfast, which is served in one of several locations at the time of your choice, changes everyday. The meal generally includes a heaping plate of fresh fruit, croissants (sometimes flavored with almond, apricot, or chocolate — sometimes plain), banana bread, granola, and yogurt. An egg entrée such as Bartels Benedict or Sunrise Surprise (an egg and potato dish) is also served, but Jami's specialty is Iowa raisin bread pudding ("I'm from Iowa, can you tell?" she asks with a laugh).

Bartels Ranch is well known as a superb place to stay in the valley, away from the mainstream of tourism; but everyone who comes here considers it a private find. The inn has attracted the orchestra conductor at La Scala, concert violinists, movie stars and producers, chefs, artists, and the cast of *A Chorus Line,* among others.

Deer Run

3995 Spring Mountain Road
P.O. Box 311
St. Helena, CA 94574
707-963-3794
800-843-3408
Fax: 707-963-9026
www.virtualcities.com

> A quiet, woodsy retreat
> above the Napa Valley

Innkeepers: Tom and Carol Wilson. **Accommodations:** 4 rooms (all with private bath). **Rates:** $150–$195 single or double. **Included:** Full breakfast. **Added:** 10.5% tax. **Minimum stay:** 2 nights on weekends, April 1-November 1. **Payment:** Major credit cards. **Children:** Age 6 months and under welcome. **Pets:** Not allowed. **Smoking:** Not allowed.

➤   **It's quiet here on Spring Mountain. You can hike a one-mile trail, walk to a winery, or swim in the pool. In every nook and corner, strawberry pots overflow with blue lobelia, marigolds flame yellow, and orange and lemon trees glow in sun or shade.**

Imagine a sixty-year-old cedar bungalow with a stone chimney and a wash porch back in the hills among tall pine trees. Picture it with rough paneling, a fireplace, and a king-size bed with a down quilt, and you've visualized the master bedroom in this woodsy bed-and-breakfast on Spring Mountain in the Napa Valley.

The original cabin is only part of this delightful B&B, however. For the most seclusion, reserve the Cottage. A good honeymooners' choice, it has whitewashed pine, an open beam ceiling in the living room, and Laura Ashley decor. Breakfast is brought to the cottage in the morning.

Another private spot is the Carriage Room, with a large guest room decorated in forest green and burgundy. A vaulted ceiling of bleached pine with charcoal-stained beams covers part of the room. On the other side, sliding glass doors open to a porch under the trees. It's a quiet place; all you hear are crickets. There's also a separate studio with a large bedroom and bath, beamed ceilings, and Ralph Lauren fabrics.

But all is not as rustic as you might expect. A lot of expansion has taken place since the home was built in the 1930s. There are large living and dining areas and a wraparound deck that looks right into the treetops. Guests in the main house have breakfast at an antique French table near a buffet set with coffee, fresh fruit, nut breads, quiche or frittata, granola, and berries from the garden.

In the comfortable, casual living/dining room, collections on display reveal the Wilsons' interests: antiques, silver, German helmets, insulators, spoons, and salt cellars. They like the whimsical, too. A cabbage-shaped teapot with a rabbit handle perches on the sideboard, and a ceramic rabbit tureen stands on an antique sewing machine table.

Tom is extremely creative. A watercolorist, his paintings hang in the residence as well as the guest rooms. On the deck, along with barrels of flowers and a picnic table, are examples of his work with twigs. He makes baskets and tiny chairs as holders for pots and dried flowers or for ornamentation. The wood comes from hazelnut trees on the 4-acre property, which also has walnut and maple trees. Yet another interest of Tom's — and his pride and joy — is a shiny yellow and black Model A automobile. It's kept under shelter, but he's happy to show it off if you ask.

The Wilsons opened Deer Run in 1981. Since then a good many venturesome travelers have followed the winding, 4-1/2-mile road in search of the romantic inn, and most are not disappointed with what they find.

The Inn at Southbridge

1020 Main Street
St. Helena, CA 94574
707-967-9400
800-520-6800
Fax: 707-967-9486

> **California chic in the heart of St. Helena**

General manager: Jeff Niezgoda. **Accommodations:** 20 rooms, 1 suite. **Rates:** $260–$490. **Included:** Continental breakfast. **Added:** 12% tax. **Minimum stay:** 2 nights on weekends. **Payment:** Major credit cards. **Children:** Welcome. **Pets:** Not allowed. **Smoking:** Nonsmoking rooms available.

➤ **Although the Inn at Southbridge is a village inn, guests have access to resort amenities at Meadowood, the inn's sister property, located five minutes from downtown. In addition, guests have complimentary use of the lap pool, Jacuzzi, workout room, and sauna at a health spa next door to the inn. Spa services such as massages and facials are extra.**

The stylish Inn at Southbridge opened its doors late in 1995 and quickly garnered rave reviews for its simple elegance and up-to-the-minute decor. The inn is part of a complex designed by architect William Turnbull, Jr., to resemble a European town square. St. Helena's main street, with its charming boutiques and acclaimed restaurants, is a few hundred yards from the inn.

A fountain bubbles near the inn's front entrance. Inside, smooth and shiny cement floors stained slate green give the lobby a modern look, while a large floral arrangement at the far end of the room adds a splash of color. In an adjacent sitting room a Continental breakfast with pastries from a local bakery is served, and wine tastings are held on Friday nights.

A hallway from the lobby leads to a meeting room (which can hold up to 60 people for dinner), and then to Tomatina, a casual eatery run by restaurateur Michael Chiarello of Tra Vigne fame. Gourmet pizzas cooked in a stone oven are the specialty at Tomatina, but pastas and salads are also available from the demonstration kitchen. Seating is either in the large, open dining room or outside on the patio.

The inn's guest rooms are on the second floor of the building. With clean lines, tasteful decor, and walls the color of butter, the rooms are comfortably elegant. French doors that open out onto mini-balconies, handsome stained cherry furniture in provincial Shaker style, iron lamps with twisted bases, black and white photographs of vineyards, vaulted ceilings, fireplaces, and king-size beds with matelasse spreads and feather duvets only add to each room's appeal. Other amenities include terry robes, in-room safes, coffeemakers, TVs with VCRs (videos are available at the front desk), honor bars, and dual-line phones with voice mail and fax/modem ports. The white tile baths have hair dryers, Neutrogena toiletries, and a second telephone.

Meadowood

900 Meadowood Lane
St. Helena, CA 94574
707-963-3646
800-458-8080
Fax: 707-963-3532
www.meadowood.com

> **An exclusive resort in the country**

General manager: Seamus McManus. **Accommodations:** 85 rooms and suites. **Rates:** $295–$650 single or double, $25 additional person; $1,520–$2,915 for a 4-bedroom suite. **Added:** 10.5% tax. **Minimum stay:** 2 nights on weekends. **Payment:** Major credit cards. **Children:** Under age 12 free in room with parents. **Pets:** Not allowed. **Smoking:** Allowed.

➤ **Other than winery tours, area activities include bicycling on country roads, fishing at Conn Dam and Lake Berryessa, shopping in the boutiques of St. Helena and Yountville, floating above the valley in a hot-air balloon, and soaking in the mud baths of Calistoga.**

On 250 acres of oak groves and green meadows in the Napa Valley, outside the village of St. Helena, this luxurious resort welcomes discriminating travelers. Formerly an exclusive private club, it opened to the public in 1985. Driving up the quiet, shady entrance road is like approaching a country estate, with vineyards on one side and walnut orchards on the other. After the guarded entry, you wind past madrone and oak trees sheltering guest houses, tennis courts, and a swimming pool and up to the main lodge. The three-story, white and gray gabled building and the clubhouse on a hill above the golf course resemble the grand New England resorts of the early 20th century.

Inside is a large, bright room with a registration desk and couches by a stone fireplace. Pillows are piled on the window seat of one curving alcove, a comfortable spot to retreat with an apple from the basket on the table and a book from the array of classic novels in the glass-covered bookshelves.

Up in the clubhouse are two restaurants and an executive conference center with 4,000 square feet of meeting space. The formal restaurant serves California cuisine with a Provençal influence and has a wine list that reads like a catalog of the finest vineyards in the valley. More casual is The Grill, serving light meals indoors and on the terrace.

The guest rooms are in the Croquet Lodge as well as in cottages tucked away in the woods above the pool, near the tennis courts, and by the golf course. The Croquet Lodge directly faces a carpet of perfectly manicured grass — English regulation croquet courts. From your balcony or patio you can watch the white-clad players intent on a game or instruction from the resident pro. Beyond the croquet courts, among the cedar, oak, and tall pine trees, are the sweeping fairways of the 9-hole golf course. Seven championship tennis courts lie on the other side of the property, between the main lodge and the entrance, not far from the swimming pool. Light meals and bar service are available by the pool during the summer months.

The cottages' porches face woodlands so they feel nice and private. Each cottage room has its own separate entrance, a king-size bed, wicker chairs, a television, ample closet space, and skylights — some of which will open with the press of a button. Cool luxury combined with great comfort is the rule. Walls are gray with white woodwork, the vaulted ceilings have rough white beams, and the artwork is minimal (winery maps and wine labels).

Most suites have stone fireplaces with a fire already laid and ready to go at the strike of a match. Other amenities include stocked refrigerators, coffeemakers, terrycloth robes, baskets of fresh fruit, down comforters with floral covers, lots of pillows, room service, and a daily newspaper at your door. Baths, which also have vaulted ceilings, have a fresh look.

Wine tastings and classes are an important part of the activities at Meadowood. John Thoreen, a winemaker, writer, and educator, teaches regular courses in wine appreciation. If you wish to go farther afield to explore regional wines, the concierge will arrange tours.

Active guests will want to take advantage of the full-service spa at Meadowood. It has Cybex weight machines, treadmills, Lifecycles, stair climbers, lockers, aerobics classes, saunas, steam rooms, and an outdoor whirlpool and lap pool. For an additional charge you can treat yourself to a salt glow, massage, or aloe wrap. Families will appreciate the children's swimming pool and playground on the property. Nature lovers should enjoy walking in the woods around Meadowood — it's an experience in serenity and dreamlike natural beauty. Just be sure to stick to the paths to avoid contact with poison oak.

Vineyard Country Inn

201 Main Street
St. Helena, CA 94574
707-963-1000
Fax: 707-963-1794

> **Comfortable suites are the main attraction at this Napa Valley inn**

General manager: Gene Lubberstadt. **Accommodations:** 21 suites. **Rates:** $150–$220 single or double, $15 additional person. **Included:** Buffet breakfast. **Added:** 12% tax. **Minimum stay:** Two nights on weekends, three nights on holiday weekends. **Payment:** Major credit cards. **Children:** Over age 5, $15 additional if third person in room. **Pets:** Not allowed. **Smoking:** Nonsmoking rooms available.

➤ **Because of its location on Highway 29, the Vineyard Country Inn, which opened in 1992, is convenient to wineries and restaurants throughout Napa Valley.**

The grapevines grow so high around the sign for the Vineyard Country Inn that it's easy to miss even though it's right on busy Route 29, just outside of St. Helena. The inn consists of twenty-one suites, an outdoor swimming pool and spa, and a cheerful breakfast room with bay windows that look out to the vineyards beyond. A buffet breakfast of homemade granola, breads, and seasonal fruits is included in the room rate.

Brick walkways bordered by flowers lead to the suites housed in a number of one-story cottages and one long two-story building. With stucco exteriors, slate tile roofs, and brick chimneys that are decorative as well as functional, the cottages look as if they've been transplanted from the European countryside.

The suites themselves are attractive, with tapestry-covered sofas, beamed ceilings, wood-burning brick fireplaces, refrigerators, TVs, and wet bars in their living rooms, and four-poster beds with iron headboards and soft peach comforters in the separate bedrooms.

Most have patios overlooking the vineyards. Floral linen ruffles atop the tub/shower combinations add appeal to the baths, which also have two separate vanities, each with its own sink.

The Wine Country Inn

1152 Lodi Lane
St. Helena, CA 94574
707-963-7077
Fax: 707-963-9018
romance@winecountryinn.com
www.winecountryinn.com

| An inn with a vineyard view |

Innkeeper: Jim Smith. **Accommodations:** 24 rooms (all with private bath). **Rates:** $140–$270 single, $160–$300 double, $220–$300 suite, $20 additional person; winter and midweek rates available. **Included:** Full breakfast and afternoon wine and appetizers. **Added:** 10.5% tax. **Minimum stay:** 2 nights on weekends in some rooms. **Payment:** MasterCard, Visa. **Children:** Not appropriate; over 6 charged as an additional person. **Pets:** Not allowed. **Smoking:** Not allowed.

➤ **In the 1970s, when the Napa Valley was rapidly becoming the major tourist destination it is today, this inn was built on three acres above a country lane. Its landscaped grounds are bright with roses and other seasonal flowers, and a sweep of lawn descends to a swimming pool and spa.**

The Wine Country Inn's gray-brown siding has a weathered look, and the mansard roof above the central stone section creates the Old World impression the builders, Ned and Marge Smith, wanted. Now the inn is run by Marge and her son, Jim.

The guest rooms are divided among three buildings. Most of them are in the main lodge; six are behind it in Brandy Barn, and four are in Hastings House. Each room is furnished distinctively, with country antiques, handmade quilts, and color schemes reflecting the valley's seasonal changes. Most have patios or balconies; fifteen have fireplaces. All the rooms are comfortable, but those upstairs are preferred if you're bothered by the sounds of drainpipes and footsteps overhead. There are phones but no TVs in the rooms.

A breakfast buffet is presented in the large common room in the main house. You can sit at one of several tables here or in a smaller neighboring room by a deck overlooking lawns and vineyards. Coffee, tea, fruit, granola, a choice of juices, a hot egg dish, and a variety of fresh breads such as pecan rolls, poppyseed bread, and strawberry bread constitute a typical breakfast, enough to start you on a tour of the countryside. The inn has a refrigerator for chilling your wine purchases and a stock of wineglasses.

In addition to tasting wine at the dozens of wineries nearby, the inn offers a private wine tasting for guests each afternoon. Appetizers are provided, and a different local winery is featured each day. For additional activities, you can visit Bale Grist Mill Historic Park, climb Mt. St. Helena, and see Robert Louis Stevenson memorabilia at the Silverado Museum. You may also go shopping in the many boutiques and galleries and, at the top of everyone's list, eat at wonderful area restaurants. Some outstanding valley favorites are Tra Vigne, Mustard's Grill, Showley's, Brava Terrace, and Terra.

Zinfandel Inn

800 Zinfandel Lane
St. Helena, CA 94574
707-963-3512
Fax: 707-963-5310
www.zinfandelinn.com

A wine country bed-and-breakfast

Innkeeper: Diane Payton. **Accommodations:** 3 rooms (all with private bath). **Rates:** $175–$330 single or double, $50 additional person. **Included:** Full breakfast. **Added:** 10.5% tax. **Minimum stay:** 2 nights on weekends. **Payment:** MasterCard, Visa. **Children:** Discouraged. **Pets:** Not allowed. **Smoking:** Not allowed indoors.

➤ **Diane will book balloon flights, make restaurant reservations, and arrange for mud baths at Calistoga's spas. If you request flowers or champagne for a special occasion, she'll see that they are in your room when you arrive.**

On the outside, this bed-and-breakfast inn in the heart of the Napa Valley wine country resembles a European manor house, with a stone facade, towers, and a curving driveway with a fountain in the center. Inside, it's a comfortable, casual family home.

The inn is on a quiet road off Highway 29, south of St. Helena and a 90-minute drive from San Francisco. It was built in the early 1980s on two acres and has been open to guests since 1988. "I want visitors to feel at home here," says Diane. She encourages guests to relax during their visit.

The Chardonnay Room, on the main floor, has a brass and white iron bed facing an immense stone fireplace. A small TV rests on the corner of the hearth. In shades of hunter green and burgundy, Chardonnay has a vaulted beamed ceiling, a curving bay window, and double doors leading to the back deck. Romantic touches include candles on the ledge of the oversize bathtub and a basket with champagne and truffles.

Upstairs, past a landing where guests enjoy perching on the curved window seat to watch hot air balloons floating over nearby vineyards, are the other two rooms. Petite Sirah is the smallest. It has a 19th-century French feather bed and a view of the vineyards. The romantic Zinfandel Suite has a king-size four-poster bed, a fireplace, and a private balcony. As you relax on the balcony, you can enjoy the view of Mount St. Helena and the surrounding hills. The tile bath has a whirlpool tub and double-headed shower.

The balcony is a pleasant place to enjoy a breakfast of fresh fruits and a hot dish such as Belgian waffles, gringo ranchero eggs, pesto eggs, eggs Benedict, or banana pancakes; or you may eat at the formal dining table downstairs.

In the back garden, pepper trees grow by a curving lawn, a bubbling hot tub, and a lagoon with a fish pond and waterfall. There's also a natural looking free-form swimming pool, and a gazebo.

Santa Rosa

The Gables

4257 Petaluma Hill Road
Santa Rosa, CA 95404
707-585-7777
800-GABLES-N
Fax: 707-584-5634
innkeeper@thegablesinn.com
www.thegablesinn.com

A Victorian country mansion

Innkeepers: Michael and Judy Ogne. **Accommodations:** 8 rooms and cottage (all with private bath). **Rates:** $145–$225. **Included:** Full breakfast and afternoon tea. **Added:** 9% tax. **Minimum stay:** 2 nights on weekends. **Payment:** Major credit cards. **Children:** Discouraged. **Pets:** Not allowed. **Smoking:** Not allowed.

➤ **A fire burns in the dining room on cool mornings while guests enjoy a breakfast that varies daily — it might include apricot cobbler with cream or a frittata, as well as coffee cake, muffins, and fruit.**

In 1877 William and Mary Jane Roberts built one of the most interesting homes in Sonoma County — a Gothic Revival mansion with 15 gables above keyhole-shaped windows. Inside there are 12-foot ceilings, marble fireplaces, and a spiral staircase of mahogany.

The Roberts's home is now a bed-and-breakfast, a graceful combination of formal elegance and country comforts. It's only 3-1/2 miles from downtown Santa Rosa, but with wooded acreage, a 150-year-old barn, a creek, and chickens providing breakfast eggs, its atmosphere is one of rural tranquillity.

Soft music plays in the parlor where tea is served in the afternoon. You climb the curved staircase to reach the spacious guest rooms. They have antique furnishings, brass beds with down comforters, and literary classics to read in bed or by the windows that overlook the countryside. No two rooms are alike, and there's a gable at every angle. Sunrise is filled with light from bay windows; Sunset has a view of the hills and lights of Sebastopol in the distance, and on the south overlooks the pasture.

Meadow, crisp in blue and white, is furnished in bird's-eye maple. Garden View is a favorite for its flowery decor, clawfoot tub in an arched alcove, and sunset view. The Parlor Suite is luxurious, with a king-size four-poster, an Italian marble fireplace, and a clawfoot tub. Brookside, in creams and pale greens, has a gas stove. (As both the Parlor Suite and Brookside face the busy highway that passes in front of the inn, they can be subject to traffic noise at certain times of the day.)

Behind the main house is a separate, romantic cottage with a roomy living room, a woodstove, wet bar, kitchenette, and a Jacuzzi for two. In this trim little home, built in the 1850s, the Robertses raised seven children and worked to build their estate. Now completely restored, it's a cozy spot for honeymooners. It has a loft with just enough space for a queen-size bed and a trunk. The loft has a pitched ceiling, so the only place you can stand upright is in the center of the room.

Michael and Judy are gracious innkeepers, happy to make suggestions for dining and sightseeing. They'll direct you to award-winning wineries, antiques shops, the Luther Burbank gardens, and the coast. Recommended restaurants in Santa Rosa include La Gare for French, Fabiano's for Italian, and John Ash & Co. for wine country cuisine.

If you'd like to take a cup of coffee to the inn's back deck and join the snoozing cats, you're welcome to do so. You'll have a view of the rose garden, lilacs, grapevines, the weathered barn, and the old outhouse, now covered with roses.

Vintners Inn

4350 Barnes Road
Santa Rosa, CA 95403
707-575-7350
800-421-2584
Fax: 707-575-1426
www.vintnersinn.com

> **A Mediterranean village in California wine country**

General manager: Cindy Duffy. **Accommodations:** 44 rooms. **Rates:** $168–$228 single or double, $20 additional person; suites $208–$258. **Included:** Expanded Continental breakfast. **Added:** 9% tax. **Minimum stay:** 2 nights on weekends. **Payment:** Major credit cards. **Children:** Age 6 and over additional $20. **Pets:** Not allowed. **Smoking:** Not allowed.

➤ **Jeffrey Madura is a talented, award-winning chef who works culinary magic with fresh local produce, the bounty of regional ranches and vineyards, and herbs grown just outside the window.**

Santa Rosa is a sprawling town 60 miles from San Francisco, between the vineyards of Sonoma on the south and Alexander Valley on the north. Just north of town and adjacent to Highway 101, Vintners Inn stands in the center of 45 acres of chardonnay and sauvignon blanc grapes. Some of the grapes are sold to local wineries, while some are bottled under the inn's own label.

Like a luxury complex transplanted from the south of France, the country inn is composed of stucco buildings centered around lawns and a fountain courtyard. Red tile roofs, arched doorways and windows, and wrought-iron railings add to the Mediterranean theme. Because the owners want an authentic village atmosphere, there are no swimming pools or tennis courts. However, nearby country clubs and health clubs are accessible to guests.

The rooms, divided among three two-story buildings, are furnished with European antiques. They all have air conditioning as well as French doors that open to a patio or balcony. In a typical mid-range room, you will find wingback chairs by tall windows overlooking the landscaped grounds, an armoire concealing a television set, phones, matching pine nightstands, a desk, and a refrigerator. The well-lighted bath has an oversize tub and shower. Five junior suites are larger and have wet bars, refrigerators, and fireplaces. Beer and wine will be delivered to your room upon request.

The library off the lobby in the main building is a comfortable place to relax by the fire. Across the lobby is the breakfast room, where croissants, waffles, homemade breakfast breads, fruits, and cereals are served. In the lobby itself, sun streams through high, curving windows to light walls and tiled floors, creating a welcoming entrance. For the area's few rainy days, a basket of umbrellas stands by the door.

Next to the inn is John Ash & Co., a restaurant that is one of the best reasons for lodging at Vintners Inn. The restaurant has three dining areas separated by graceful arches and furnished with Spanish antiques.

An after-dinner stroll among the vineyards, a soak in the whirlpool tub by the sun deck, and you may be ready for a book or movie from the library — or the bed that has been turned down while you were out. VCRs are available for $10, which includes the rental fee for your first videotape.

Sonoma

El Dorado Hotel

405 First Street West
Sonoma, CA 95476
707-996-3030
800-289-3031
Fax: 707-996-3148

| A historic hotel in a historic wine country town |

General manager: Bonnie Reynolds. **Accommodations:** 26 rooms. **Rates:** $150–$225. **Included:** Continental breakfast. **Added:** 10% tax. **Minimum stay:** 2 nights on weekends. **Children:** Under age 7 free. **Pets:** Not allowed. **Smoking:** Not allowed.

➤ **The restaurant has a latticed courtyard with an old fig tree in the center. Here you can sit at umbrella tables, swim in the heated lap pool, or have a party for 100 people.**

Old Mexico meets contemporary California — with a colorful dash of Italy — at the El Dorado in historic Sonoma. The two-story Mission revival hotel, overlooking the town's shady plaza, has an interesting past. Built in 1843 as a home for Don Salvador Vallejo (brother of the Mexican commandante), it was a refuge during the Bear Flag uprising of 1846 and became a hotel in 1851. Later it was a literary college, a winemaking shop, a home, and finally a hotel again.

Grape leaves are hand-painted on guest room doors, and each pale taupe room is simply furnished with a steel four-poster bed, a peach duvet, and a dresser. Bedside tables are covered with floral tablecloths and there's a wicker chair in the corner. There are no curtains, and the walls are plain except for one mirror, artfully framed with twigs. A woven throw rug lies on the tile floor; a TV is on the dresser. White louvered doors slide open to reveal a narrow balcony overlooking the courtyard or the town plaza. Baths have Mexican tile floors and oversized showers.

A breakfast of orange juice, fruit, and fresh breads and muffins is served in a lounge off the white, open lobby. Each guest also receives a split of Sonoma Valley wine. The hotel's acclaimed restaurant, Ristorante Piatti, is noted for its innovative Italian cookery. Artichokes, asparagus, and other foods are painted on the walls in this casual setting.

The obliging staff at the El Dorado will advise you on winery tours and nearby attractions.

Sonoma Hotel

110 West Spain Street
Sonoma, CA 95476
707-996-2996
707-996-7014
www.sonomahotel.com

A historic Old West hotel by a shady plaza

Innkeepers: Tim Farfan and Craig Miller. **Accommodations:** 16 rooms (all with private bath). **Rates:** $95–$235 single or double. **Included:** Continental breakfast; late-afternoon wine in the lobby. Added: 10% tax. **Payment:** Major credit cards. **Children:** Not appropriate. **Pets:** Not allowed. **Smoking:** Not allowed.

➤ **Mexican-era adobes surround the grassy, shaded plaza, which was laid out by General Vallejo in 1835 and is now the largest in California. It has flower gardens, picnic tables, a playground, a duck pond, and an outdoor theater.**

More than a century ago, a bar and dance hall were built across the street from the plaza in Sonoma, a town of significance in California history. This was where the state's wine industry was founded, where the short-lived Bear Flag Revolt took place, and where the northernmost (and last) of the twenty-one missions was built in 1823. Part of the adobe mission still stands.

In the early 1900s, the two-story dance hall gained a third floor and was converted to a hotel. The Sonoma Hotel has been providing rooms to travelers since then, in an atmosphere that is still turn-of-the-century.

If the hotel is not yet full when you check in, you can go upstairs and pick the room you like the best. Each is individually decorated in a French country style. While the historic charm has been maintained, all rooms have modern amenities such as telephones, air conditioning, televisions, and private baths.

Adjoining the lobby is a saloon with genuine Old West flavor. It has wooden floors, a gleaming old oak and mahogany bar, and even a bullet hole in the mirrored back bar to add authenticity. Ask the friendly bartender to tell you about the hotel's ghost. Some guests and staff members swear they've seen a Chinese spirit — perhaps from the days when there was a Chinese laundry on the back patio. Heirloom, the hotel's restaurant, serves French-influenced cuisine at lunch and dinner daily.

Victorian Garden Inn

316 East Napa Street
Sonoma, CA 95476
707-996-5339
800-543-5339
Fax: 707-996-1689
vgardeninn@aol.com
www.victoriangardeninn.com

A stylish Victorian home in town

Innkeeper: Donna Lewis. **Accommodations:** 4 rooms (3 with private bath). **Rates:** $99–$195 single or double, $20 additional person. **Included:** California breakfast. **Added:** 10% tax. **Minimum stay:** 2 nights on weekends, 3 nights on holiday weekends. **Payment:** Major credit cards. **Children:** Discouraged. **Pets:** Not allowed. **Smoking:** Allowed outside only.

➤ **Donna will recommend winery tours, pack a picnic basket, and recommend Sonoma's best restaurants. Breakfast is served on the patio, in the dining room, or can be brought on a wicker tray to your room.**

Follow the path past lavish flower gardens and you'll come to this charming Victorian home built in the 1870s. It's on a comparatively busy street in Sonoma, but because it is set back, the atmosphere is one of seclusion. Guests will find lots of cozy sitting areas amidst the well-established gardens as well as a hot tub and swimming pool.

Donna Lewis, an interior designer, has furnished and decorated the rooms with flair. The most popular is Top o' the Tower, with its own entrance. Done in blue and white and wicker, it has the country charm of painted floors and braided rugs. The tower overlooks the maze of gardens and the swimming pool. Below it, with a door to the garden, is the Garden Room, which has a high bed with crisp white linens, a wicker rocker in front of the fireplace, and a clawfoot tub draped in Battenburg lace.

Woodcutter's Cottage, next to the pool and brick patio, is cool and dark in green with peach accents. It has a fireplace, window seat, country antiques, a brass bed piled with pillows, a ceiling fan and skylight in the pitched roof, and a clawfoot tub and stained glass window in the bath. The least expensive accommodations are two antiques-furnished rooms in the main house; together they are called the Classic. You have a choice of a room with twin beds or one with a queen-size iron bed. A basket of towels is provided to use in the adjacent bathroom.

Laundry facilities and a refrigerator are available.

Yountville

Burgundy House

P.O. Box 3156
6711 Washington Street
Yountville, CA 94599
707-944-0889
www.bbinternet.com/burgundy

| **A picturesque stone inn with a country flavor**

Innkeeper: Deanna Roque. **Accommodations:** 6 rooms (all with private bath). **Rates:** $135 single, $165 double, $25 additional person. **Included:** Breakfast. **Added:** 10% tax. **Minimum stay:** 2 nights on weekends. **Payment:** MasterCard, Visa; personal checks required to secure room reservation. **Children:** Over age 10 welcome; $25 additional. **Pets:** Not allowed. **Smoking:** Not allowed indoors.

➤ **When you arrive, perhaps after a day of touring the wineries that make the valley famous, you'll find fresh flowers and a decanter of wine in your room.**

Like an old stone house in the French countryside, this Napa Valley inn built in 1891 has 22-inch thick walls, hand-hewn posts and lintels, and rustic masonry. Originally a brandy distillery, it also housed a winery, a hotel, and a warehouse before becoming the bed-and-breakfast it is today.

The guest rooms are named for cities in Burgundy such as Beaune, Autun, Dijon, Pommard, and Cluny. Although they've been remodeled, you can see traces of the old stone walls in each. The rooms are quiet, as the inn is off the main highway. Beaune and Autun occupy the front corners of the inn. Dijon, in a back corner, has a cozy window seat with a view of the lovely rose garden. Pommard, with its own entrance off the garden, has a fireplace, a white iron bed, and white walls and rustic beams. Outside the door is a patio under a sweet-scented orange tree.

The innkeeper serves breakfast in the comfortable little parlor or on the patio. She'll assist you in planning winery tours, balloon and glider rides, and selecting one of the many highly rated restaurants in the area.

Maison Fleurie

6529 Yount Street
Yountville, CA 94599
707-944-2056
800-788-0369
Fax: 707-944-9342
www.foursisters.com

A French-style inn in wine country

Owners: Roger and Sally Post. **Innkeeper:** Virginia Marzan. **Accommodations:** 13 rooms. **Rates:** $110–$260. **Included:** Full breakfast and afternoon hors d'oeuvres. **Added:** 10% tax. **Payment:** Major credit cards. **Children:** Additional $15 if third person in room. **Pets:** Not allowed. **Smoking:** Not allowed.

➤ **The vineyards and grapevine-covered hills of the Napa Valley are often best explored at a leisurely pace. Maison Fleurie has bicycles available to help facilitate such a tour of the lovely surrounding countryside.**

If traveling through the California wine country puts you in the mood for a European sojourn, then a night or two at Maison Fleurie may be just what you need. The charming inn, consisting of three ivy-covered buildings, feels as if belongs in the countryside of Provence. The main building was built as a small hotel and saloon back in 1872. The two adjacent buildings are the old carriage house and the bakery building, which housed a bakery called the Court of Three Sisters until the mid-1970s. In 1994 the Four Sisters Inns, a small group known for their high-quality lodgings, opened Maison Fleurie as a bed-and-breakfast.

In the lobby of the main building there's a cozy sitting area with a fruit-patterned sofa and comfortable chairs in front of a fireplace guarded by the Four Sisters Inns' signature teddy bears. The breakfast room, with its exposed brick walls, terra cotta floor tiles, and antique French thatch-backed chairs, was added onto the original structure around 1901. Here a full breakfast of bagels, English muffins, muesli, coffee cake, and a hot dish such as Spanish eggs is served each morning. Vegetarians will be pleased to know that meat is not a breakfast staple at this inn.

There are seven guest rooms in the main building — one on the first floor, four on the second floor, and two rooms on the top floor. Rooms are attractively decorated with floral carpeting and a mixture of original antiques and French country furniture. Hand-painted designs by a Monterey artist in each of the guest rooms is an appealing personal touch. All rooms have terry robes and private baths.

The bakery building has four guest rooms, each with a fireplace and king-size bed. Room 10, upstairs, opens onto a terrace overlooking the backyard gardens and swimming pool. A floral bouquet painted above the fabric headboard is the crowning stroke to the bed with its floral comforter, red checked pillows, and cuddly teddy bear.

The two remaining guest rooms are in the carriage house. One has a queen-size bed with vineyard views and the other has a king-size bed and a fireplace. All rooms have extra-large beach towels for lounging by the pool or soaking in the outdoor spa that's surrounded by teak furniture and pots of blooming flowers.

Wine and hors d'oeuvres are set out each evening between 5:00 and 7:00. There is always a cheese board along with another appetizer such as pumpkin surprise or a chocolatey Texas sheet cake. For other meals, the fine restaurants of Yountville are within easy walking distance.

At press time the Four Sisters Inns group was planning to open another inn in Yountville called Lavender. If Maison Fleurie is full during your planned visit, you may wish to inquire if there are any rooms available at Lavender.

Napa Valley Lodge

2230 Madison Street
Yountville, CA 95499
707-944-2468
800-368-2468
Fax: 707-944-9362
jwolf@napavalleylodge.com
www.woodsidehotels.com

An amiable hostelry on the edge of Yountville

General manager: Bella Cimpher. **Accommodations:** 55 rooms. **Rates:** $182–$385. **Included:** Champagne breakfast buffet. **Added:** 10% tax. **Payment:** Major credit cards. **Children:** Additional $25 if third person in room. **Pets:** Not allowed. **Smoking:** Not allowed.

➤ **When guests reserve their room they are sent a brochure highlighting 101 things to do in the Napa Valley — which could come in handy should you decide to tear yourself away from the pool.**

You'll be greeted by a friendly staff member when you walk into the lobby of the Napa Valley Lodge. You can sit by the fire under vaulted ceilings in the adjoining library while nibbling on the cookies that have been set out along with coffee and tea. Or you can play the piano (which will also play electronically if you don't know how), browse through the lending library for a novel to read during your stay, or pick that evening's restaurant selection from the menu book. On Friday evenings, guests gather in the library for the weekly wine tastings.

Guest rooms are in several long, two-story wings that radiate out from the lobby. Pleasant and spacious, the rooms have floral fabrics, wicker furniture, ceiling fans, refrigerators, hair dryers, coffeemakers, bathrobes, and telephones with data ports. They have patios with pool or vineyard views and more than half have fireplaces. Rooms have either one king-size bed, two queens, or one queen and a sofa bed. Wet bars and sinks are surrounded by Mexican tile. Four luxury suites have additional amenities.

A champagne breakfast is served poolside each morning. In poor weather the buffet is moved indoors, near a massive Italian stone fireplace in an adjacent function room. In the same building there's a small exercise room and a redwood sauna. Both the outdoor swimming pool and spa are heated year round.

What's What

Bicycling

American River Inn, 333
Bartels Ranch and Country Inn, 514
Blue Lantern Inn, 407
Carmel Valley Ranch, 152
Cobblestone Inn, 139
La Costa Resort and Spa, 398
Four Seasons Biltmore, 195
The Gingerbread Mansion, 265
La Mancha, 232
Maison Fleurie, 533
Ojai Valley Inn and Spa, 180
The Old Yacht Club Inn, 198
The Ritz-Carlton Huntington Hotel and Spa, 441
Secret Garden Inn and Cottages, 200
Simpson House Inn, 202
The Stanford Inn by the Sea, 299

Boating

The Alisal Guest Ranch, 209
Dockside Boat & Bed
Disneyland Hotel, 388
Edelweiss Lodge, 345
Laguna Cliffs Marriott Resort, 409
Lakeland Village Resort, 366
The Regal Biltmore, 437
The Stanford Inn by the Sea, 299

Business Services

The Alisal Guest Ranch, 209
Campton Place, 45
Carmel Valley Ranch, 152
The Clift, 48
La Costa Resort and Spa, 398
Disneyland Hotel, 388
The Fairmont Hotel, 50
Four Seasons Biltmore, 195
Hartley House, 361
Hotel De Anza, 100
Hotel Del Coronado, 403
The Inn at Spanish Bay, 191
The Inn at the Tides, 249
The Maxwell Hotel, 79
Meadowood, 519
The New Otani Hotel & Garden, 435
Ojai Valley Inn and Spa, 180
The Pan Pacific Hotel, 80
Rancho Bernardo Inn, 443
The Regent Beverly Wilshire, 394
San Ysidro Ranch, 170
Sheraton Palace Hotel, 89
Surf & Sand Hotel, 425
U.S. Grant Hotel, 452
Westin St. Francis, 96
The White Swan Inn, 98
Wyndham Emerald Plaza, 454

Croquet

The Alisal Guest Ranch, 209
American River Inn, 333
Abigail's Elegant Victorian Mansion, 260
Churchill Manor, 504
Circle Bar B Guest Ranch, 163
Four Seasons Biltmore, 195
Furnace Creek Inn, 220
The Inn at Rancho Santa Fe, 445
Joshua Grindle Inn, 291
La Jolla Beach & Tennis Club, 421

La Mancha, 232
Meadowood, 519
Olallieberry Inn, 133
The Old Milano Hotel, 270
Rancho Valencia, 447
Simpson House Inn, 202
Stonepine, 157
Union Hotel (Los Alamos), 165
The Wedgewood Inn, 341

Fine Dining

The Argyle, 430
Applewood, 494
Auberge du Soleil, 512
Campton Place, 45
Casa Madrona Hotel, 103
Hotel Vintage Court, 66
La Mancha, 232
Madrona Manor, 500
The Majestic, 71
Mandarin Oriental, 73
Meadowood, 519
Mount View Hotel, 482
The Old Yacht Club Inn, 198
Prescott Hotel, 83
Post Ranch Inn, 130
The Regal Biltmore, 437
The Regent Beverly Wilshire, 394
The Sterling Hotel, 363
Timberhill Ranch, 251
Ventana Inn and Spa, 131
Villa Florence Hotel, 95
Vintners Inn, 527
Westin St. Francis, 96

Golf

The Alisal Guest Ranch, 209
Carmel Valley Ranch, 152
La Costa Resort and Spa, 398
Furnace Creek Inn, 220

The Inn at Spanish Bay, 191
The Lodge at Pebble Beach, 193
Meadowood, 519
Ojai Valley Inn and Spa, 180
Quail Lodge, 156
La Quinta Resort and Club, 225
Rancho Bernardo Inn, 443
Resort at Squaw Creek, 354
The Ritz-Carlton Laguna Niguel, 410
The Ritz-Carlton Rancho Mirage, 236
The Sea Ranch, 309
Silverado Country Club & Resort, 508
Sonoma Mission Inn, Spa, & Country Club, 473
Wawona Hotel, 377
Westin Mission Hills Resort, 238

Historic Hotels

City Hotel, 327
Fallon Hotel, 329
Horton Grand Hotel, 450
The Hotel Jeffery, 330
Imperial Hotel, 321
Julian Hotel, 417
Mount View Hotel, 482
The National Hotel, 343
Sheraton Palace Hotel, 89
Sonoma Hotel, 530
The Union Hotel (Benicia), 10
U.S. Grant Hotel, 452
Westin St. Francis, 96

Horseback Riding

The Alisal Guest Ranch, 209
Circle Bar B Guest Ranch, 163
Furnace Creek Inn, 220
The Lodge at Pebble Beach, 193
San Ysidro Ranch, 170
Stonepine, 157
Trinity Alps Resort, 276
Wawona Hotel, 377

Kitchen/Cooking Facilities

Carriage House Bed and Breakfast, 36
Casa Madrona Hotel, 103
The Cottage, 448
Edelweiss Lodge, 345
Gray's Retreat, 38
Holly Tree Inn, 19
Hotel Bel-Air, 432
Hotel Shangri-La, 456
The Inn at Rancho Santa Fe, 445
La Jolla Beach & Tennis Club, 421
La Mancha, 232
Pigeon Point Lighthouse Hostel, 34
Prospect Park Inn, 424
Railroad Park Resort, 253
Scott Courtyard, 484
Silverado Country Club & Resort, 508
Sorensen's, 337
Squaw Valley Lodge, 355
Stillwater Cove Ranch, 275
Tamarack Lodge Resort, 348
Trinity Alps Resort, 276
Vagabond's House, 151

Pets Allowed with Permission

American River Inn, 333
The Clift, 48
Cypress Inn (Carmel), 141
Edelweiss Lodge, 345
Four Seasons Biltmore, 195
Greenwood Pier Inn, 256
Hotel Monaco, 59
The Inn at Rancho Santa Fe, 445
Laguna Cliffs Marriott Resort, 409
The Lodge at Pebble Beach, 193
Meadowlark, 480
Quail Lodge, 156
The Regent Beverly Wilshire, 394
San Ysidro Ranch, 170
Sorensen's, 337

The Stanford Inn by the Sea, 299
Stillwater Cove Ranch, 275
Trinity Alps Resort, 276
Vagabond's House, 151

Restaurant Open to Public

The Ahwahnee, 379
Applewood, 494
Auberge du Soleil, 512
Campton Place, 45
Carmel Valley Ranch, 152
Carter House Victorians, 263
Casa Madrona Hotel, 103
La Casa del Zorro, 218
Circle Bar B Guest Ranch, 163
The Claremont Resort, Spa and Tennis Club, 26
The Cliffs at Shell Beach, 208
The Clift, 48
La Costa Resort and Spa, 398
Crystal Rose Inn, 124
The Delta King Hotel, 359
Disneyland Hotel, 388
El Dorado Hotel, 528
The Fairmont Hotel, 50
Four Seasons Biltmore, 195
Furnace Creek Inn, 220
Galleria Park Hotel, 52
Garden Court Hotel, 33
Harbor Court Hotel, 55
Harbor House, 258
Hill House Inn, 289
Hotel Bel-Air, 432
Hotel De Anza, 100
Hotel Del Coronado, 403
Hotel Nikko (San Francisco), 61
Hotel Queen Mary, 428
Hotel Sofitel, 434
Hotel Triton, 64
Hotel Vintage Court, 66
Ingleside Inn, 228
Inn at the Opera, 69
The Inn at Rancho Santa Fe, 445

The Inn at Spanish Bay, 191
The Inn at the Tides, 249
Julian Hotel, 417
Laguna Cliffs Marriott Resort, 409
Little River Inn, 282
The Lodge at Pebble Beach, 193
The Majestic, 71
La Mancha, 232
Mandarin Oriental, 73
The Mark Hopkins Intercontinental, 77
McCloud Guest House, 284
Meadowood, 519
Mount View Hotel, 482
The National Hotel, 343
The New Otani Hotel & Garden, 435
Ojai Valley Inn and Spa, 180
The Old Milano Hotel, 270
Pan Pacific Hotel, 80
Pelican Inn, 25
Peninsula Beverly Hills, 392
Post Ranch Inn, 130
Prescott Hotel, 83
Quail Lodge, 156
Railroad Park Resort, 253
Rancho Bernardo Inn, 443
Rancho Valencia, 447
The Regal Biltmore Hotel, 437
The Regent Beverly Wilshire, 394
Renaissance Esmeralda Resort, 223
Resort at Squaw Creek, 354
The Ritz-Carlton Laguna Niguel, 410
The Ritz-Carlton Rancho Mirage, 236
The Ritz-Carlton San Francisco, 86
San Ysidro Ranch, 170
Sheraton Palace Hotel, 89
Shutters on the Beach, 460
Silverado Country Club & Resort, 508
Sonoma Mission Inn, Spa, & Country Club, 473
Sorensen's, 337
Squaw Valley Lodge, 355
The Stanford Inn by the Sea, 299
The Sterling Hotel, 363
Surf & Sand Hotel, 425
Tamarack Lodge Resort, 348

U.S. Grant Hotel, 452
The Union Hotel (Benicia), 10
The Villa Florence Hotel, 95
Villa Royale, 235
Vintners Inn, 527
Wawona Hotel, 377
Westin St. Francis, 96
Westin Mission Hills Resort, 238
Wyndham Emerald Plaza, 454

Tennis

The Ahwahnee, 379
The Alisal Guest Ranch, 209
Auberge du Soleil, 512
Carmel Valley Ranch, 152
La Casa del Zorro Desert Resort, 218
Circle Bar B Guest Ranch, 163
The Claremont Resort, Spa and Tennis Club, 26
La Costa Resort and Spa, 398
Disneyland Hotel, 388
Four Seasons Biltmore, 195
Furnace Creek Inn, 220
Hotel Del Coronado, 403
The Inn at Rancho Santa Fe, 445
The Inn at Spanish Bay, 191
La Jolla Beach & Tennis Club, 421
Lakeland Village Resort, 366
La Mancha, 232
Little River Inn, 282
The Lodge at Pebble Beach, 193
Meadowood, 519
Ojai Valley Inn and Spa, 180
Quail Lodge, 156
La Quinta Resort and Club, 225
Rancho Bernardo Inn, 443
Rancho Valencia, 447
Renaissance Esmeralda Resort, 223
Resort at Squaw Creek, 354
The Ritz-Carlton Huntington Hotel and Spa, 441
The Ritz-Carlton Laguna Niguel, 410
The Ritz-Carlton Rancho Mirage, 236
San Ysidro Ranch, 170

Silverado Country Club & Resort, 508
Silver Rose Inn, 485
Sonoma Mission Inn, Spa, & Country Club, 473
Squaw Valley Lodge, 355
Stonepine, 157
Timberhill Ranch, 251
Wawona Hotel, 377
Westin Mission Hills Resort, 238

Wheelchair Access

The Ahwahnee, 379
The Babbling Brook Inn, 206
Blue Lantern Inn, 407
The Clift, 48
Delta King Hotel, 359
Disneyland Hotel, 388
El Dorado Hotel, 528
The Fairmont Hotel, 50
Four Seasons Biltmore, 195
Galleria Park Hotel, 52
Grey Gables Inn, 370
Holly Tree Inn, 19
Hotel Bel-Air, 432
Hotel De Anza, 100
Hotel Del Coronado, 403
Hotel Juliana, 58
Hotel Nikko, 61
The Inn at Occidental, 510
Inn at the Opera, 69
The Inn at Spanish Bay, 191
The Inn at the Tides, 249
Laguna Cliffs Marriott Resort, 409
The Lodge at Pebble Beach, 193
Olallieberry Inn, 133
Pan Pacific Hotel, 80
Peninsula Beverly Hills, 392
Point Reyes Seashore Lodge, 29
La Quinta Resort and Club, 225
Rancho Bernardo Inn, 443
Rancho Valencia, 447
The Regal Biltmore Hotel, 437
Resort at Squaw Creek, 354

The Ritz-Carlton Laguna Niguel, 410
The Ritz-Carlton Rancho Mirage, 236
The Ritz-Carlton San Francisco, 86
Sheraton Palace Hotel, 89
Sonoma Mission Inn, Spa, & Country Club, 473
Spindrift Inn, 178
Squaw Valley Lodge, 355
Surf & Sand Hotel, 425
Timberhill Ranch, 251
U.S. Grant Hotel, 452
The Union Hotel (Benicia), 10
Wyndham Emerald Plaza, 454

Recommended Reading

Adventuring in the California Desert, Lynne Foster (Sierra Club Books), $15.00. Part of the Sierra Club series focusing on outdoor activities, camping facilities, natural history. How to best enjoy the Great Basin, Mojave, and Colorado Desert regions. A few drawings and maps. Carefully crafted, lots of information.

California: The Ultimate Guidebook, by Ray Riegert (Ulysses Press), $13.95. Riegert knows California well and is a trustworthy guide. His book divides the state by area and includes restaurants, lodging, nightlife, shopping, beaches and parks, and offbeat attractions. It covers so much ground the information is limited. Contains simple maps.

The Family Guide to Point Reyes, Karen Gray (Chardon Press), $12.95. Comprehensive guide to the nature trails, state parks, and beaches of the Point Reyes Penninsula, Tomales Bay, and Stinson Beach. Geared to families exploring with children, the book has a naturalist slant and includes driving directions, information on facilities, and naturalist illustrations and stories.

Fielding's California: The Mission Trail, San Diego to San Francisco, Lynn Foster, $10.95. For the history buff. Contains practical tips and suggestions for activities and explains historical events along the mission trail.

Fishing in Northern California and Fishing in Southern California, Ken Albert (Marketscope Books), $14.95 each. Everything you need to know about fishing California's 5,000 lakes and 30,000 miles of streams. Clear format.

Inside San Francisco, Don and Betty Martin (Pine Cone Press), $8.95. Detailed, witty, opinionated city guide. Convenient size.

Insight Guide: California (Houghton Mifflin Co.), $19.95. Grand overview of the state, with essays on its history, social fabric, ethnic cultures, and geography. Includes maps and superb color photographs.

Los Angeles Access, Richard S. Wurman (Access Press), $12.95. Divides the L.A. area by neighborhood and reviews the hotels, restaurants, and attractions in each. Color-coded and mapped. Intriguing, workable system, once you figure it out. Strong architectural focus.

Northern California Handbook, Kim Weir (Moon Publications), $19.95. Crammed with information but well organized. Contains thoughtful commentaries, maps, and some color photographs.

Northern California Travel-Smart Trip Planner, Paul Otteson (John Muir Publications), $15.95. Recommends the most worthwhile sights in the region. Includes lodging and dining information as well as suggested itineraries and planning maps.

San Francisco Access, Richard S. Wurman (Access Press), $12.95. Divides the San Francisco area by neighborhood; color-coded (see Los Angeles Access.)

Southern California Travel-Smart Trip Planner, Paul Otteson (John Muir Publications), $14.95. Recommends the most worthwhile sights in the region. Includes lodging and dining information as well as suggested itineraries and planning maps.

Index

Abigail's Elegant Victorian
  Mansion Lodging
  Accommodations, 260
Agate Cove Inn, 286
The Ahwahnee, 379
The Alisal Guest Ranch, 209
Amber House, 357
American River Inn, 333
Apple Lane Inn, 118
Applewood, 494
The Archbishop's Mansion, 43
The Argyle, 430
Auberge du Soleil, 512

The Babbling Brook Inn, 206
Balboa Inn, 391
The Ballard Inn, 126
Bartels Ranch and Country Inn,
  514
Bayview Hotel, 120
Belle de Jour Inn, 496
Beltane Ranch, 490
Benbow Inn, 268
Blackthorne Inn, 17
Blue Lantern Inn, 407
The Blue Spruce Inn, 211
Brannan Cottage Inn, 475
Burgundy House, 532

Cal-a-Vie, 465
Campton Place, 45
Carmel Valley Ranch, 152
Carriage House Bed and
  Breakfast, 36
Carter House Victorians, 263
Casa Arguello, 47

Casa del Mar, 108
Casa Madrona Hotel, 103
The Centrella, 182
Chalfant House, 323
Château du Lac, 426
Churchill Manor, 504
Circle Bar B Guest Ranch, 163
City Hotel, 327
The Claremont Resort, Spa and
  Tennis Club, 26
The Cliffs at Shell Beach, 208
The Clift, 48
Cobblestone Inn, 139
The Coloma Country Inn, 325
Coronado Victorian House, 401
The Cottage, 448
Cottage Grove Inn, 476
Country Rose Inn Bed and
  Breakfast, 162
Crystal Rose Inn, 124
Cypress Inn on Miramar Beach,
  12
Cypress Inn, 141

Davenport Bed & Breakfast Inn,
  159
Deer Run, 516
Deetjen's Big Sur Inn, 128
The Delta King Hotel, 359
Disneyland Hotel, 388
Dockside Boat & Bed, 28
Doryman's Inn, 440
Dunbar House, 1880, 350

East Brother Light Station, 40
Edelweiss Lodge, 345

El Dorado Hotel, 528
Elk Cove Inn, 254

The Fairmont Hotel, 50
Fallon Hotel, 329
Featherbed Railroad Company
    Bed & Breakfast Resort, 303
Foothill House, 478
Four Seasons Biltmore, 195
The Foxes Bed and Breakfast
    Inn, 367
Furnace Creek Inn, 220

The Gables, 525
Gaige House Inn, 492
Galleria Park Hotel, 52
Garden Court Hotel, 33
Gate House Inn, 339
Gatehouse Inn, 184
The George Alexander House,
    498
The Gingerbread Mansion, 265
The Glenborough Inn, 197
Glendeven, 278
Golden Gate Hotel, 53
Gray's Retreat, 38
The Green Gables Inn, 185
Greenwood Pier Inn, 256
The Grey Gables Inn, 370

Half Moon Bay Lodge, 13
Happy Landing Inn, 143
Harbor Court Hotel, 55
Harbor House, 258
Hartley House, 361
The Headlands Inn, 288
Heritage House, 280
Highlands Inn, 144
Hill House Inn, 289
Holiday Harbor, 305
Holly Tree Inn, 19
The Hope-Merrill House, 488
Horton Grand Hotel, 450
Hotel Bel-Air, 432

Hotel De Anza, 100
Hotel Del Coronado, 403
Hotel Griffon, 56
The Hotel Jeffery, 330
Hotel Juliana, 58
Hotel Monaco, 59
Hotel Nikko, 61
Hotel Queen Mary, 428
Hotel Rex, 63
Hotel Sausalito, 105
Hotel Shangri-La, 456
Hotel Sofitel, 434
Hotel Triton, 64
Hotel Vintage Court, 66
The Huntington Hotel, 67

Imperial Hotel, 321
Ingleside Inn, 228
The Inn Above Tide, 106
Inn at Depot Hill, 137
The Inn at Occidental, 510
The Inn at Rancho Santa Fe,
    445
The Inn at Saratoga, 101
The Inn at Shallow Creek Farm,
    307
The Inn at Southbridge, 517
The Inn at Spanish Bay, 191
Inn at the Opera, 69
The Inn at the Tides, 249
The Inn at Union Square, 70

The Jabberwock, 172
Jasmine Cottage, 39
John Gardiner's Tennis Ranch,
    154
Joshua Grindle Inn, 291
Julian Hotel, 417

The Kenwood Inn, 502
Korakia Pensione, 230

L'Auberge Del Mar, 412
L'Horizon, 234

La Casa del Zorro Desert
Resort, 218
La Costa Resort and Spa, 398
La Jolla Beach & Tennis Club,
421
La Mancha Resort Village, 232
La Playa Hotel, 146
La Quinta Resort and Club, 225
La Residence Country Inn, 506
La Valencia Hotel, 422
Laguna Cliffs Marriott Resort,
409
Lakeland Village Resort, 366
Little River Inn, 282
The Lodge at Pebble Beach, 193
Loews Coronado Bay Resort,
405
Loews Santa Monica Beach
Hotel, 457
Loma Vista Bed & Breakfast,
464
The Lost Whale Inn, 311

MacCallum House, 293
Madrona Manor, 500
Maison Fleurie, 533
The Majestic, 71
Mammoth Mountain Inn, 346
Mandarin Oriental, 73
Mangels House, 122
The Mansions, 75
The Mark Hopkins
Intercontinental, 77
The Martine Inn, 187
The Maxwell Hotel, 79
McCloud Guest House, 284
Meadowlark Country House,
480
Meadowood, 519
Mendocino Hotel, 295
Miramar Sheraton Hotel, 459
Mission Ranch, 148
Montecito Inn, 169
Monterey Plaza Hotel, 174

Mount View Hotel, 482

Napa Valley Lodge, 535
The National Hotel, 343
The New Otani Hotel &
Garden, 435
Northstar at Tahoe, 373

Ojai Valley Inn and Spa, 180
Olallieberry Inn, 133
The Old Milano Hotel, 270
Old Monterey Inn, 176
Old Thyme Inn, 15
The Old World Inn, 507
The Old Yacht Club Inn, 198

The Pan Pacific Hotel, 80
Pelican Cove Inn, 399
The Pelican Inn, 25
The Peninsula Beverly Hills,
392
Petite Auberge, 82
Pigeon Point Lighthouse
Hostel, 34
The Pillar Point Inn, 41
Point Reyes Seashore Lodge,
29
Post Ranch Inn, 130
Prescott Hotel, 83
Prospect Park Inn, 424

Quail Lodge Resort and Golf
Club, 156
The Queen Anne Hotel, 85

Railroad Park Resort, 253
Rainbow Tarns Bed &
Breakfast, 332
Rancho Bernardo Inn, 443
Rancho Valencia, 447
Red Castle Historic Lodgings,
352
Reed Manor, 297
The Regal Biltmore Hotel, 437

The Regent Beverly Wilshire, 394

Renaissance Esmeralda Resort, 223

Resort at Squaw Creek, 354

The Ritz-Carlton Huntington Hotel and Spa, 441

The Ritz-Carlton Laguna Niguel, 410

The Ritz-Carlton Rancho Mirage, 236

The Ritz-Carlton San Francisco, 86

Rockwood Lodge, 335

Roundstone Farm, 31

San Ysidro Ranch, 170

Scott Courtyard, 484

The Sea Ranch, 309

The Seal Beach Inn and Gardens, 462

Seal Cove Inn, 23

Secret Garden Inn and Cottages, 200

Seven Gables Inn, 189

Shadow Mountain Ranch, 419

Sheehan Hotel, 88

Sheraton Palace Hotel, 89

The Sherman House, 91

Shutters on the Beach, 460

Silver Rose Inn and Spa, 485

Silverado Country Club & Resort, 508

Simpson House Inn, 202

Sonoma Coast Villa, 247

Sonoma Hotel, 530

Sonoma Mission Inn, Spa, & Country Club, 473

Sorensen's, 337

Spindrift Inn, 178

Squaw Valley Lodge, 355

The Squibb House, 135

St. Orres, 272

The Stanford Inn by the Sea, 299

The Sterling Hotel, 363

Stillwater Cove Ranch, 275

Stonepine, 157

Strawberry Creek Inn, 415

Sundial Lodge, 149

Sunset Marquis Hotel and Villas, 414

Surf & Sand Hotel, 425

Sutter Creek Inn, 371

Tamarack Lodge Resort, 348

Ten Inverness Way Bed and Breakfast, 21

Timberhill Ranch, 251

Travellers Repose, 222

Trinidad Bay Bed & Breakfast, 312

Trinity Alps Resort, 276

The Truckee Hotel, 375

U.S. Grant Hotel, 452

The Union Hotel, 10

Union Hotel, 165

Vagabond's House Inn, 151

Ventana Inn and Spa, 131

Victorian Garden Inn, 531

Victorian Inn on the Park, 93

Victorian Mansion, 167

The Villa Florence Hotel, 95

Villa Rosa, 204

Villa Royale, 235

Vineyard Country Inn, 521

Vintners Inn, 527

Vizcaya, 364

Wawona Hotel, 377

The Wedgewood Inn, 341

The Westgate Hotel, 453

The Westin Mission Hills Resort, 238

The Westin St. Francis, 96

The Whale Watch Inn, 273
The White Swan Inn, 98
The Whitegate Inn, 301
Windy Point Inn on Big Bear
   Lake, 396
The Wine Country Inn, 522
Wyndham Checkers Hotel, 438
The Wyndham Emerald Plaza,
   454

Zane Grey Pueblo Hotel, 389
Zinfandel Inn, 523

Best Places Report

Authors of the Best Places to Stay series travel extensively in their research to find the best places for all budgets, styles, and interests. However, if we've missed an establishment that you find worthy, please write to us with your suggestion. Detailed information about the service, food, setting, and nearby activities or sights is most important. Finally, let us know how you heard about the place and how long you've been going there.

Send suggestions to:

> The Harvard Common Press
> Best Places to Stay Suggestions
> 535 Albany Street
> Boston, Massachusetts 02118

NAME OF HOTEL_____

TELEPHONE_____

ADDRESS_____

_____ ZIP _____

DESCRIPTION_____

_____

_____

_____

_____

_____

_____

YOUR NAME_____

TELEPHONE_____

ADDRESS_____

_____ ZIP _____

The Whale Watch Inn, 273
The White Swan Inn, 98
The Whitegate Inn, 301
Windy Point Inn on Big Bear
    Lake, 396
The Wine Country Inn, 522
Wyndham Checkers Hotel, 438
The Wyndham Emerald Plaza,
    454

Zane Grey Pueblo Hotel, 389
Zinfandel Inn, 523

Best Places Report

Authors of the Best Places to Stay series travel extensively in their research to find the best places for all budgets, styles, and interests. However, if we've missed an establishment that you find worthy, please write to us with your suggestion. Detailed information about the service, food, setting, and nearby activities or sights is most important. Finally, let us know how you heard about the place and how long you've been going there.

Send suggestions to:

The Harvard Common Press
Best Places to Stay Suggestions
535 Albany Street
Boston, Massachusetts 02118

NAME OF HOTEL_____

TELEPHONE_____

ADDRESS_____

_____ ZIP _____

DESCRIPTION_____

_____

_____

_____

_____

_____

_____

YOUR NAME_____

TELEPHONE_____

ADDRESS_____

_____ ZIP _____

Best Places Report

Authors of the Best Places to Stay series travel extensively in their research to find the best places for all budgets, styles, and interests. However, if we've missed an establishment that you find worthy, please write to us with your suggestion. Detailed information about the service, food, setting, and nearby activities or sights is most important. Finally, let us know how you heard about the place and how long you've been going there.

Send suggestions to:

The Harvard Common Press
Best Places to Stay Suggestions
535 Albany Street
Boston, Massachusetts 02118

NAME OF HOTEL_____

TELEPHONE_____

ADDRESS_____

_____ ZIP _____

DESCRIPTION_____

_____

_____

_____

_____

_____

_____

YOUR NAME_____

TELEPHONE_____

ADDRESS_____

_____ ZIP _____

Best Places Report

Authors of the Best Places to Stay series travel extensively in their research to find the best places for all budgets, styles, and interests. However, if we've missed an establishment that you find worthy, please write to us with your suggestion. Detailed information about the service, food, setting, and nearby activities or sights is most important. Finally, let us know how you heard about the place and how long you've been going there.

Send suggestions to:

> The Harvard Common Press
> Best Places to Stay Suggestions
> 535 Albany Street
> Boston, Massachusetts 02118

NAME OF HOTEL_____

TELEPHONE_____

ADDRESS_____

_____ ZIP _____

DESCRIPTION_____

_____

_____

_____

_____

_____

_____

YOUR NAME_____

TELEPHONE_____

ADDRESS_____

_____ ZIP _____

Best Places Report

Authors of the Best Places to Stay series travel extensively in their research to find the best places for all budgets, styles, and interests. However, if we've missed an establishment that you find worthy, please write to us with your suggestion. Detailed information about the service, food, setting, and nearby activities or sights is most important. Finally, let us know how you heard about the place and how long you've been going there.

Send suggestions to:

The Harvard Common Press
Best Places to Stay Suggestions
535 Albany Street
Boston, Massachusetts 02118

NAME OF HOTEL _____

TELEPHONE _____

ADDRESS _____

_____ ZIP _____

DESCRIPTION _____

_____

_____

_____

_____

_____

_____

YOUR NAME _____

TELEPHONE _____

ADDRESS _____

_____ ZIP _____

Best Places Report

Authors of the Best Places to Stay series travel extensively in their research to find the best places for all budgets, styles, and interests. However, if we've missed an establishment that you find worthy, please write to us with your suggestion. Detailed information about the service, food, setting, and nearby activities or sights is most important. Finally, let us know how you heard about the place and how long you've been going there.

Send suggestions to:

The Harvard Common Press
Best Places to Stay Suggestions
535 Albany Street
Boston, Massachusetts 02118

NAME OF HOTEL _____

TELEPHONE _____

ADDRESS _____

_____ ZIP _____

DESCRIPTION _____

_____

_____

_____

_____

_____

_____

YOUR NAME _____

TELEPHONE _____

ADDRESS _____

_____ ZIP _____